ETHICS

*Classical Western Texts in Feminist
and Multicultural Perspectives*

Edited by

JAMES P. STERBA

New York   Oxford
OXFORD UNIVERSITY PRESS
2000

Oxford University Press

Oxford   New York
Athens   Auckland   Bangkok   Bogotá   Buenos Aires   Calcutta
Cape Town   Chennai   Dar es Salaam   Delhi   Florence   Hong Kong   Istanbul
Karachi   Kuala Lumpur   Madrid   Melbourne   Mexico City   Mumbai
Nairobi   Paris   São Paulo   Singapore   Taipei   Tokyo   Toronto   Warsaw

and associated companies in
Berlin   Ibadan

Copyright © 2000 by Oxford University Press, Inc.

Published by Oxford University Press, Inc.,
198 Madison Avenue, New York, New York 10016
http://www.oup-usa.org

Library of Congress Cataloging-in-Publication Data

Ethics : classical Western texts in feminist and multicultural
   perspectives / edited by James P. Sterba.
       p.   cm.
   Includes bibliographical references.
   ISBN-13 978-0-19-512726-3
   ISBN 0-19-512726-9 (pbk. : alk. paper)
   1. Ethics.   2. Feminist ethics.   3. Ethics, Comparative.
I. Sterba, James P.
BJ1012.E8937   1999
170—dc21   99-22801
                                                CIP

CONTENTS

PREFACE

There are a growing number of philosophy anthologies that either attempt to survey non-Western philosophies or to introduce a multicultural perspective. There are also a growing number of feminist anthologies on the market. *Ethics: Classical Western Texts in Feminist and Multicultural Perspectives* attempts to take advantage of both of these growing trends in the teaching of philosophy to provide an anthology that will enable philosophy teachers to integrate the historical development of Western moral philosophy with both feminist and multicultural perspectives.

The aim of this anthology is twofold: (1) to provide an introductory sampling of some of the classical works of the Western tradition in moral philosophy, and (2) to situate these readings within feminist and multicultural perspectives so that they can be better understood and evaluated. As far as I know, there is no other anthology on the market that attempts to achieve this twofold aim.

As one would expect, I benefited from many different people in putting together this anthology. In particular, I would like to thank my partner and colleague Janet Kourany, Paul Weithman of the University of Notre Dame, Christina Korsgaard of Harvard University, Rae Langton of the University of Sheffield, Maria Morales of Florida State University, Thomas Wren of Loyola University of Chicago, and the following reviewers: Hugh LaFollette of East Tennessee State University, T. K. Seung of University of Texas at Austin, Rosemarie Tong of Davidson College, Anthony Weston of Elon College, Laurence M. Thomas of Syracuse University, and Naomi Zack of University at Albany, SUNY. I would also like to thank Robert Miller, Senior Editor at Oxford University Press under whose encouragement the very idea for this anthology was both conceived and developed, and Patrick Frierson for help with the proofreading.

J. P. S.

General Introduction

Many people think that morality is a matter of opinion and that what is right for you may be wrong for me even if we are similarly situated. Such people are moral relativists, and they take their view to be amply supported by the diverse moral views held in different societies, as well as by the level of moral disagreement that exists within any one society, such as my own, where there is presently radical disagreement over abortion, welfare, homosexuality, and humanitarian intervention, to name but a few issues. Yet these disagreements seem to pall when my society is compared with other societies that presently condone infanticide, polygamy, and even cannibalism.

Nevertheless, for moral relativists to draw support for their view from this moral diversity, they must be able to show that the same act could be both right and wrong, right for one society, group, or individual, and wrong for some other society, group, or individual.[1] Frequently, however, the act that is condemned by one society, group, or individual is not the same act that is sanctioned by another society, group, or individual. For example, the voluntary euthanasia that is sanctioned by Eskimos as a transition to what they take to be a happier existence for their aged members is significantly different from the euthanasia that the AMA opposes, which does not assume a happier afterlife.[2] Likewise, when the Nuer gently lay their deformed infants in the river because they believe that such infants are baby hippos accidentally born to humans, their action is significantly different from the infanticide that most people condemn.[3] Even in the case of abortion, what some people judge to be right (permissible) and what other people judge to be wrong (impermissible) would not appear to be the same act because of the different views that people hold with respect to the moral status of the fetus. Those opposing abortion usually claim that the fetus is a full-fledged human person with the same right to life as you or me, while those favoring abortion usually deny that the fetus has this status.[4]

Yet even when the same act is being compared, for that act to be right for a person to perform, it must be possible for that person, following her best deliberation, to come to judge the act as right. Acts that are inaccessible to people's best judgment (like avoiding carcinogens in the Middle Ages) are not acts that could be morally right for them to do, because morality requires a certain accessibility.[5] Accordingly, when we evaluate people's moral judgments in the context in which they formed them, it will sometimes be the case that we will recognize that they couldn't have arrived at the judgments that we think are morally right. If so, their judgments would not relevantly conflict with our own, even if what they think is right is not what we think is right, for example, as in the need for cleanliness in medical operations.

Of course, this is not to suggest that what we *think* is right for us to do necessarily *is* right for us to do. After all, we could be mistaken. It is only to suggest that if we are moral agents capable of moral deliberation, any discrepancy between what we think is right for us to do, and what is right for us to do must be explained in terms of some kind of past or present failure on our part to follow our best deliberation with regard to the opportunities available to us. If it is going to make any sense to say that something is right for us to do, knowledge of that fact must somehow be accessible to us, so that any discrepancy between what we think is right for us to do and what is right for us to do must somehow be traceable to a failure on our part to deliberate wisely.[6] Consequently, for moral relativism to draw support from the existing moral diversity, there must be acts that are sufficiently accessible to people's moral deliberation such that the same act is judged right by some people using their best moral judgment and judged wrong by other people using their best moral judgment.

But even this is not enough. Moral relativism must also tell us what morality is supposed to be relative to.[7] Is it to be relative to the common beliefs of a society, to those of a smaller group, to those of just any individual, or could it be relative to any of these? If it could be relative to any of these, any act (e.g., contract killing) could be wrong from the point of view of some particular society, right from the point of view of some subgroup of that society (e.g., the Mafia), and wrong again from the point of view of some particular member of that society or subgroup. But if this is the case, individuals would not have any reasonable grounds for deciding what they ought to do, all things considered.

Yet even supposing that some particular reference group could be shown to be preferable (e.g., the reference group of one's own society), problems remain. First, in deciding what to do, should we simply ask what the members of our appropriate reference group think ought to be done? But if everyone in our reference group did that, we would all be waiting for everyone else to decide, so no one would decide what ought to be done. Or we might construe moral relativism to be a second-order theory requiring that the members of our appropriate reference group first decide on some other grounds what is right and then take a vote. If a majority or a consensus emerges from such a vote, then that is what is right, all things considered. So interpreted, "moral relativism" would have some merit as a theory of collective decision making, but it clearly would require some yet-to-be-deter-mined nonrelativist grounds for first-order moral judgments, and so it would not essentially be a relativist theory at all.

Second, the very claim that morality should be specified relativistically is not itself a relativistic claim. Rather, it claims to be a truth for all times and places. But how could this be possible? Shouldn't the truth of relativism itself be assertible as a relativistic claim? One might maintain that while moral judgments are relativistic, the thesis of moral relativism is not itself a moral claim and hence need not be relativistic. But if truth is not relativistic, why should we think that the good is relativistic?

In sum, moral relativism as an account of moral judgments faces a number of difficulties. First, it is difficult for moral relativists to show that amid the existing moral diversity there are acts that are sufficiently accessible to people's moral deliberation such that the same act is judged right by some and wrong by others when all are following their best moral deliberation. Second, it is difficult for moral relativists to specify the appropriate reference group from which morality is to be determined. Third, even assuming the appropriate reference group can be determined, it is difficult for moral relativists to explain why their theory is not committed to some nonrelativist account of at least first-order moral judgments. Last, it is difficult for moral relativists to explain why they are committed to a nonrelativist account of truth.

Yet while these difficulties obviously render moral relativism an implausible theory, they do not completely defeat it in the absence of a better, nonrelativistic account of morality. The history of ethics is, for the most part, the history of attempts to provide such an account of morality. In each attempt, one or another moral ideal is set forth and defended. Putting it all too briefly, we can say that Plato appeals to the an ideal of justice in the state and in the person, Aristotle to an ideal of happiness or human fulfillment, Augustine to the ideal of eternal life, Thomas Aquinas to an ideal of natural law, David Hume to an ideal of sympathy, Immanuel Kant to an ideal of the categorical imperative, John Stuart Mill and Harriet Taylor to an ideal of the maximization of utility, Friedrich Nietzsche to a ideal of moral revolution, Jean-Paul Sartre to an ideal of absolute freedom and then later, along with Simone de Beauvoir, to an ideal of situated freedom, John Rawls to an ideal of fairness, R. M. Hare to an ideal of universal prescriptivism, Alasdair MacIntyre and Martha Nussbaum to an ideal of a virtuous society, Alan Gewirth to an ideal of an equal right to freedom and well-being, Christina Korsgaard to an ideal of reflective endorsement, Martin Luther King Jr, to an ideal of racial equality, and Carol Gilligan to an ideal of a caring ethic. The degree to which these different ideals, insofar as they are morally defensible, can be reconciled with each other is an important theoretical question and an even more important practical question.

Obviously, the distinctive feature of this anthology is its inclusion of feminist and multicultural perspectives. As it turns out, the inclusion of these two perspectives is actually required for the defensibility of any moral ideal. This is because to defend any moral ideal, it must be shown that that ideal can survive in a comparative evaluation with other moral ideals, including feminist and multicultural social and political ideals. Feminist moral ideals demand that we no longer support the subordination of women, which is surely a reasonable requirement. Multicultural moral ideals place a variety of different demands on us, some of which are justified while others are not.

What then would a curriculum that appropriately combines traditional works with feminist and multicultural works in moral philosophy look like? Obviously, this text attempts to answer this question. In this text, a survey of some of the greatest works of Western moral philosophy is combined with some of the greatest related works of non-Western moral philos-

ophy. Some of these non-Western works are chosen because they parallel the views defended in the Western works (e.g., Confucius's work parallels that of Plato or Aristotle). But other non-Western works are chosen because they challenge the views defended in the Western works (e.g., American Indian works provide an interesting challenge to the Western moral philosophy). Obviously, these challenges to Western moral philosophy could lead to reinterpretations of the Western moral ideals in a variety of ways. For example, an examination of American Indian works might lead some of us brought up in Western culture to favor greater reparations to existing Indian tribes. In any case, what is clear is that the task of determining a defensible moral ideal will be satisfied with nothing less than a consideration of feminist and multicultural perspectives. The only question that remains is: Why has it taken moral philosophers so long to recognize the need to do so?

NOTES

1. See Richard B. Brandt, *Ethical Theory* (Englewood Cliffs: Prentice Hall, 1959) Chapter 1.
2. See Knud Rasmussen, *The People of the Polar North* (London: Kegan Paul, Trench, Trubner & Co. Ltd, 1908), pp. 106 ff.; and Peter Freuchen, *Book of the Eskimos* (New York: World Publishing Company, 1961, pp. 193–206. And cf. Hans Reusch, *Top of the World* (New York: Pocket Books, 1951), pp. 123–126.
3. See Mary Douglas, *Purity and Danger,* (London: Praeger, 1966) p. 39.
4. It may be possible, however, to show that even those who deny that the fetus is a person should still oppose abortion in a wide range of cases. See my "Abortion and the Rights of Distant Peoples and Future Generations" *The Journal of Philosophy* Vol. 77 (1980) pp. 424–440; *How To Make People Just* (Totowa: Rowman and Littlefield, 1988) and "Response to Nine Commentators" *The Journal of Social Philosophy* Vol. 22 (1991), pp. 100–118.

5. This is not to deny that it would have been a good thing to avoid carcinogens in the Middle Ages; it is just that without the concept of a carcinogen, there couldn't have been any moral requirement to do so.

6. For more on this requirement, see my *Contemporary Social and Political Philosophy* (Belmont: Wadsworth Publishing Co, 1995), pp. 2–5. It should also be pointed out that this requirement necessitates interpreting the Kantian notion of acts that accord with duty in particular circumstances as acts that certain moral agents, but not necessarily all moral agents, would have a duty to do in those circumstances.

7. See W. T. Stace, *The Concept of Morals* (New York: Macmillian, 1937) Chapters 1 and 2.

PART I

❦

PLATO

INTRODUCTION

Plato was born in 427 B.C. and died at the age of eighty in 347 B.C. Both his parents came from distinguished families. On his father's side, his ancestry can be traced to the last king of Athens and, on his mother's side, to the family of Solon, the founder of Athenian law. His birth coincided closely with the death of Pericles, the greatest leader of Athenian democracy, and with the beginning of the Peloponnesian War. As a child of twelve, he had seen the Athenian fleet set sail on the disastrous expedition against Syracuse, and he was twenty-three when Athens capitulated and lost its empire to Sparta at the end of the Peloponnesian War. A few years after his death, Athens was conquered by the Macedonians. As far as we can tell, he never married.

His family's position and wealth enabled Plato to receive the best education possible for an Athenian youth. In his twenties, along with his two older brothers Glaucon and Adeimantus, he came under the influence of Socrates. By skillful exchanges of questions and answers, Socrates was able to expose people's unexamined beliefs and lead them in the direction of more defensible views. Plato became Socrates's devoted student and faithful defender. However, his genius resided in his ability to construct a philosophical system in which he integrated his own insights with those of Socrates.

The teachings of Socrates were as disturbing to the Athenian populace as they were attractive to his followers. In 399 B.C., Socrates was condemned to death on the charge of impiety and corrupting the youth. The trial and death of Socrates is described in Plato's *Apology, Crito,* and *Phaedo.* Disillusioned with political life in Athens, Plato left the city and traveled for twelve years, spending time in Egypt, Greece, Italy, and Sicily. In his fortieth year, he returned to Athens and founded the first of the great schools of antiquity, the Academy, where he taught with outstanding success and increasing fame. The Academy was to last for over 900 years, until the Christian Emperor Justinian had it closed in 529 A.D. because it was a pagan institution. No other school has existed for so long.

The writings of Plato are in dialogue form, which is well suited to show the strength of the Socrates's question and answer way of doing philosophy. Plato himself does not appear as a character in the dialogues, but he does speak through Socrates in almost all of them. As a result, it is not always possible to distinguish with historical accuracy between Socrates's and Plato's views in the dialogues. However, it is generally thought that in the earlier dialogues Plato does not to go beyond the teachings of Socrates, whereas in the later ones, such as the *Republic,* he does go on to develop his own positive doctrine.

The *Republic* is an extended discussion of a wide range of moral, social, and metaphysical issues framed as a search for the nature of justice. Our selection opens after Socrates has seemingly demolished Thrasymachus's definition of justice as what serves the interests of the strongest and has further argued that justice is superior to injustice. Glaucon and Adeimantus, both dissatisfied with Socrates's arguments, challenge him to show that justice in itself (stripped of its normal consequences) is superior in itself to injustice.

Socrates responds by suggesting that the nature of justice is more easily discovered in the macrocosm, the state, than in the microcosm, the individual. Socrates offers an account of a just state and then by analogy an account of a just individual, and he tries to show that, in each case, justice in itself is superior in itself to injustice. A just state, he says, will contain three classes—guardians, soldiers, and artisans. After characterizing the selection and education of the guardians, and arguing that both women and men could be guardians, Socrates concludes that a state is just when each class performs well the work for which it is suited. Socrates further claims that a perfectly just state is not possible unless wisdom and power are united in the person of a philosopher-king.

In "Plato's *Republic* and Feminism," Julia Annas argues that it is quite wrong to think of Plato as "the first feminist," despite the opening up of his guardian class to women because his reason for doing so was neither to end women's subordination to men nor to establish equality between the sexes, but rather simply to benefit the state by securing the best people for his guardian class. He was not interested, as contemporary feminists are, in securing equal opportunity for women generally. It might also be questioned whether any political ideal, like Plato's, that is committed to radical inequalities between different classes of people can be appropriately termed feminist. To be consistent, doesn't equality for women require equality for other discriminated groups as well? Nevertheless, whatever its limitation from a feminist perspective, what Plato's work shows is that even in classical times the idea of equality for women was there to be considered.

Kung Fu-Tzu or Confucius, his Latinized name, lived from 551 B.C. to 479 B.C. about 150 years before Plato. He was not known to the Western world until the late sixteenth century when Jesuit missionaries, in an effort to convert Chinese rulers, steeped themselves in ancient Confucian literature, and were overwhelmed by what they found.[1]

Soon reports made their way back to Europe. Leibniz wrote that the Chinese surpass Europeans in practical philosophy, and he recommended that Chinese missionaries be sent to Europe; Voltaire declared that in morality Europeans "ought to become disciples" of the Chinese.[2] Christian Wolff said of the Chinese that "in the Art of Governing, this Nation has ever surpassed all others without exception."[3] Confucius became known as the patron saint of the Enlightenment.[4]

Confucius was born in the small state of Lu (in modern Shanrung). He traveled to Ch'i and later to Chou, serving in minor government posts. When he was fifty-six, he fell out of favor and spent the next thirteen years traveling and teaching. At sixty-eight, Confucius returned to Lu and taught there until his death eight years later.

The *Analects* is a collection of the sayings of Confucius, probably compiled by his students. Confucius was remarkably successful as a teacher. Of the twenty-two students mentioned in the *Analects,* nine attained important government posts and a tenth turned one down. Moreover, his impact was far-reaching. For 2,500 years, he was "the Master" to all of China; his influence continued even after the communist revolution and is more in evidence today.

Like Plato and later Aristotle, Confucius advocates a virtue ethics, but the list of virtues that he advocates is longer than the list of virtues advocated by Plato and different in certain respects from the list advocated by Aristotle. One distinctive feature of Confucius's ethics is his stress on filial obligation. For Plato, the just individual is modeled on the just state, but for Confucius, the state should be thought of as the family writ large. Confucius also advocates meritocracy, various forms of which were incorporated into Chinese society. The British civil service system was actually modeled on the system found in China, and the civil service system in the United States was in turn modeled after the British system, and so ultimately on the Chinese system as well. One also finds in Confucius negative versions of the Golden Rule: "What you do not want done to yourself, do not do to others." No wonder then that one of the Jesuit missionaries, impressed by Confucius's views, affirmed that if Confucius had lived in the seventeenth century, "he would have been the first to become a Christian."

NOTES

1. H. G. Creel, *Confucius: The Man and the Myth* (Westport, CT: Greenwood Press, 1972)
2. Ibid.
3. Ibid.
4. Ibid.

1. THE REPUBLIC

PLATO

BOOK II

With these words I was thinking that I had made an end of the discussion; but the end, in truth, proved to be only a beginning. For Glaucon, who is always the most pugnacious of men, was dissatisfied at Thrasymachus' retirement; he wanted to have the battle out. So he said to me: Socrates, do you wish really to persuade us, or only to seem to have persuaded us, that to be just is always better than to be unjust?

I should wish really to persuade you, I replied, if I could.

Then you certainly have not succeeded. Let me ask you now:—How would you arrange goods—are there not some which we welcome for their own sakes, and independently of their consequences, as, for example, harmless pleasures and enjoyments, which delight us at the time, although nothing follows from them?

I agree in thinking that there is such a class, I replied.

Is there not also a second class of goods, such as knowledge, sight, health, which are desirable not only in themselves, but also for their results?

Certainly, I said.

And would you not recognize a third class, such as gymnastic, and the care of the sick, and the physician's art; also the various ways of money-making—these do us good but we regard them as disagreeable; and no one would choose them for their own sakes, but only for the sake of some reward or result which flows from them?

There is, I said, this third class also. But why do you ask?

Because I want to know in which of the three classes you would place justice?

In the highest class, I replied,—among those goods which he who would be happy desires both for their own sake and for the sake of their results.

Then the many are of another mind; they think that justice is to be reckoned in the troublesome class, among goods which are to be pursued for the sake of rewards and of reputation, but in themselves are disagreeable and rather to be avoided.

I know, I said, that this is their manner of thinking, and that this was the thesis which Thrasymachus was maintaining just now, when he censured justice and praised injustice. But I am too stupid to be convinced by him.

I wish, he said, that you would hear me as well as him, and then I shall see whether you and I agree. For Thrasymachus seems to me, like a snake, to have been charmed by your voice sooner than he ought to have been; but to my mind the nature of justice and injustice have not yet been made clear. Setting aside their rewards and results, I want to know what they are in themselves, and how they inwardly work in the soul. If you please, then, I will revive the argument of Thrasymachus. And first I will speak of the nature and origin of justice according to the common view of them. Secondly, I will show that all men who practise justice do so against their will, of necessity, but not as a good. And thirdly, I will argue that there is reason in this view, for the life of the unjust is after all far better than the life of the just—if what they say is

Reprinted from *The Republic*, Bks. II, IV–V Translated by B. Jowett (London: Macmillan, 1892).

true, Socrates, since I myself am not of their opinion. But still I acknowledge that I am perplexed when I hear the voices of Thrasymachus and myriads of others dinning in my ears; and, on the other hand, I have never yet heard the superiority of justice to injustice maintained by anyone in a satisfactory way. I want to hear justice praised in respect of itself; then I shall be satisfied, and you are the person from whom I think that I am most likely to hear this; and therefore I will praise the unjust life to the utmost of my power, and my manner of speaking will indicate the manner in which I desire to hear you too praising justice and censuring injustice. Will you say whether you approve of my proposal?

Indeed I do; nor can I imagine any theme about which a man of sense would oftener wish to converse.

I am delighted, he replied, to hear you say so, and shall begin by speaking, as I proposed, of the nature and origin of justice.

They say that to do injustice is, by nature, good; to suffer injustice, evil; but that the evil is greater than the good. And so when men have both done and suffered injustice and have had experience of both, not being able to avoid the one and obtain the other, they think that they had better agree among themselves to have neither; hence there arise laws and mutual covenants; and that which is ordained by law is termed by them lawful and just. This they affirm to be the origin and nature of justice;—it is a mean or compromise, between the best of all, which is to do injustice and not be punished, and the worst of all, which is to suffer injustice without the power of retaliation; and justice, being at a middle point between the two, is tolerated not as a good, but as the lesser evil, and honoured by reason of the inability of men to do injustice. For no man who is worthy to be called a man would ever submit to such an agreement if he were able to resist; he would be mad if he did. Such is the received account, Socrates, of the nature and origin of justice.

Now that those who practice justice do so involuntarily and because they have not the power to be unjust will best appear if we imagine something of this kind: having given both to the just and the unjust power to do what they will, let us watch and see whither desire will lead them; then we shall discover in the very act the just and unjust man to be proceeding along the same road, following their interest, which all natures deem to be their good, and are only diverted into the path of justice by the force of law. The liberty which we are supposing may be most completely given to them in the form of such a power as is said to have been possessed by Gyges, the ancestor of Croesus the Lydian. According to the tradition, Gyges was a shepherd in the service of the king of Lydia; there was a great storm, and an earthquake made an opening in the earth at the place where he was feeding his flock. Amazed at the sight, he descended into the opening, where, among other marvels, he beheld a hollow brazen horse, having doors, at which he stooping and looking in saw a dead body of stature, as appeared to him, more than human, and having nothing on but a gold ring; this he took from the finger of the dead and reascended. Now the shepherds met together, according to custom, that they might send their monthly report about the flocks to the king; into their assembly he came having the ring on his finger, and as he was sitting among them he chanced to turn the collet of the ring inside his hand, when instantly he became invisible to the rest of the company and they began to speak of him as if he were no longer present. He was astonished at this, and again touching the ring he turned the collet outwards and reappeared; he made several trials of the ring, and always with the same result—when he turned the collet inwards he became invisible, when outwards he reappeared. Whereupon he contrived to be chosen one of the messengers who were sent to the court; where as soon as he arrived he seduced the queen, and with her help conspired against the king and slew him, and took the kingdom. Suppose now that there were two such magic rings, and the just put on one of them and the unjust the other; no man can be imagined to be of such an iron nature that he would stand fast in justice. No man would keep his hands off what was not his own when he could safely take what he liked out of the market, or go into houses and lie with anyone of his pleasure, or kill or release from prison whom he would, and in all respects be like a God among men. Then the actions of the just would be as the actions of the unjust; they would both come at last to the same point. And this we may truly affirm to be a great proof that a man is just, not willingly or because he thinks that justice is any good to him individually, but of necessity, for wherever anyone thinks that he can safely be unjust, there he is unjust. For all men believe in their hearts that injustice is far more profitable to the individual than justice, and he who argues as I have been supposing, will say that they are right. If you could imagine anyone obtaining this power of becoming invisible, and never doing any wrong or touching what was another's, he would be thought by the lookers-on to be a most wretched idiot, although they would praise him to one another's faces, and keep up appearances with one another from a fear that they too might suffer injustice. Enough of this.

Now, if we are to form a real judgment of the life of the just and unjust, we must isolate them; there is no other way; and how is the isolation to be effected? I answer: Let the unjust man be entirely unjust, and the just man entirely just; nothing is to be taken away from either of them, and both are to be perfectly furnished for the work of the respective lives. First, let the unjust be like other distinguished masters of craft; like the skilful pilot or physician, who knows intuitively his own powers and keeps within their limits, and who, if he fails at any point, is able to recover himself. So let the unjust make his unjust attempts in the right way, and lie hidden if he means to be great in his injustice: (he who is

found out is nobody:) for the highest reach of injustice is, to be deemed just when you are not. Therefore I say that in the perfectly unjust man we must assume the most perfect injustice; there is to be no deduction, but we must allow him, while doing the most unjust acts, to have acquired the greatest reputation for justice. If he has taken a false step he must be able to recover himself; he must be one who can speak with effect, if any of his deeds come to light, and who can force his way where force is required by his courage and strength, and command of money and friends. And at his side let us place the just man in his nobleness and simplicity, wishing, as Aeschylus says, to be and not to seem good. There must be no seeming, for if he seems to be just he will be honoured and rewarded, and then we shall not know whether he is just for the sake of justice or for the sake of honours and rewards; therefore, let him be clothed in justice only, and have no other covering; and he must be imagined in a state of life the opposite of the former. Let him be the best of men, and let him be thought the worst; then he will have been put to the proof; and we shall see whether he will be affected by the fear of infamy and its consequences. And let him continue thus to the hour of death; being just and seeming to be unjust. When both have reached the uttermost extreme, the one of justice and the other of injustice, let judgment be given which of them is the happier of the two.

Heavens! my dear Glaucon, I said, how energetically you polish them up for the decision, first one and then the other, as if they were two statues.

I do my best, he said. And now that we know what they are like there is no difficulty in tracing out the sort of life which awaits either of them. This I will proceed to describe; but as you may think the description a little too coarse, I ask you to suppose, Socrates, that the words which follow are not mine.—Let me put them into the mouths of the eulogists of injustice: They will tell you that the just man who is thought unjust

will be scourged, racked, bound—will have his
eyes burnt out; and, at last, after suffering every
kind of evil, he will be impaled: Then he will
understand that he ought to seem only, and not
to be, just; the words of Aeschylus may be more
truly spoken of the unjust than of the just. For
the unjust is pursuing a reality; he does not live
with a view to appearances—he wants to be
really unjust and not to seem only:—

> His mind has a soil deep and fertile,
> Out of which spring his prudent counsels.[1]

In the first place, he is thought just, and therefore bears rule in the city; he can marry whom he
will, and give in marriage to whom he will; also
he can trade and deal where he likes, and always
to his own advantage, because he has no misgiv-
ings about injustice; and at every contest,
whether in public or private, he gets the better of
his antagonists, and gains at their expense, and is
rich, and out of his gains he can benefit his
friends, and harm his enemies; moreover, he can
offer sacrifices, and dedicated gifts to the gods
abundantly and magnificently, and can honour
the gods or any man whom he wants to honour
in a far better style than the just, and therefore he
is likely to be dearer than they are to the gods.
And thus, Socrates, gods and men are said to
unite in making the life of the unjust better than
the life of the just.

I was going to say something in answer to
Glaucon, when Adeimantus, his brother, inter-
posed: Socrates, he said, you do not suppose that
there is nothing more to be urged?

Why, what else is there? I answered.

The strongest point of all has not been even
mentioned, he replied.

Well, then, according to the proverb, "Let
brother help brother"—if he fails in any part do
you assist him; although I must confess that
Glaucon has already said quite enough to lay me
in the dust, and take from me the power of helping justice.

Nonsense, he replied. But let me add something more: There is another side to Glaucon's

argument about the praise and censure of justice
and injustice, which is equally required in order
to bring out what I believe to be his meaning.
Parents and tutors are always telling their sons
and their wards that they are to be just; but why?
Not for the sake of justice, but for the sake of
character and reputation; in the hope of obtaining for him who is reputed just some of those
offices, marriages, and the like which Glaucon
has enumerated among the advantages accruing
to the unjust from the reputation of justice.
More, however, is made of appearances by this
class of persons than by the others; for they
throw in the good opinion of the gods, and will
tell you of a shower of benefits which the heavens, as they say, rain upon the pious; and this
accords with the testimony of the noble Hesiod
and Homer, the first of whom says, that the gods
make the oaks of the just—

> To bear acorns at their summit, and bees in
> the middle;
> And the sheep are bowed down with the
> weight of their fleeces,[2]

And many other blessings of a like kind are provided for them. And Homer has a very similar
strain; for he speaks of one whose fame is—

> As the fame of some blameless king who, like
> a god,
> Maintains justice; to whom the black earth
> brings forth
> Wheat and barley, whose trees are bowed
> with fruit,
> And his sheep never fail to bear, and the
> sea gives him fish.[3]

Still grander are the gifts of heaven which
Musaeus and his son[4] vouchsafe to the just; they
take them down into the world below, where
they have the saints lying on couches at a feast,
everlastingly drunk, crowned with garlands;
their idea seems to be that an immortality of
drunkenness is the [finest wage] of virtue. Some
extend their rewards yet further; the posterity, as
they say, of the faithful and just shall survive to

the third and fourth generation. This is the style in which they praise justice. But about the wicked there is another strain; they bury them in a slough in Hades, and make them carry water in a sieve; also while they are yet living they bring them to infamy, and inflict upon them the punishments which Glaucon described as the portion of the just who are reputed to be unjust; nothing else does their invention supply. Such is their manner of praising the one and censuring the other.

Once more, Socrates, I will ask you to consider another way of speaking about justice and injustice, which is not confined to the poets, but is found in prose writers. The universal voice of mankind is always declaring that justice and virtue are honourable, but grievous and toilsome; and that the pleasures of vice and injustice are easy of attainment, and are only censured by law and opinion. They say also that honesty is for the most part less profitable than dishonesty; and they are quite ready to call wicked men happy, and to honour them both in public and private when they are rich or in any other way influential, while they despise and overlook those who may be weak and poor, even though acknowledging them to be better than the others. But most extraordinary of all is their mode of speaking about virtue and the gods: they say that the gods apportion calamity and misery to many good men, and good and happiness to the wicked. And mendicant prophets go to rich men's doors and persuade them that they have a power committed to them by the gods of making an atonement for a man's own or his ancestor's sins by sacrifices or charms, with rejoicings and feasts; and they promise to harm an enemy, whether just or unjust, at a small cost; with magic arts and incantations binding heaven, as they say, to execute their will. And the poets are the authorities to whom they appeal, now smoothing the path of vice with the words of Hesiod:—

Vice may be had in abundance without trouble; the way is smooth and her dwelling-place is near. But before virtue the gods have set toil,[5]

and a tedious and uphill road: then citing Homer as a witness that the gods may be influenced by men; for he also says:—

The gods, too, may be turned from their purpose; and men pray to them and avert their wrath by sacrifices and soothing entreaties, and by libations and the odour of fat, when they have sinned and transgressed.[6]

And they produce a host of books written by Musaeus and Orpheus, who were children of the Moon and the Muses—that is what they say—according to which they perform their ritual, and persuade not only individuals, but whole cities, that expiations and atonements for sin may be made by sacrifices and amusements which fill a vacant hour, and are equally at the service of the living and the dead; the latter sort they call mysteries, and they redeem us from the pains of hell, but if we neglect them no one knows what awaits us.

He proceeded: And now when the young hear all this said about virtue and vice, and the way in which gods and men regard them, how are their minds likely to be affected, my dear Socrates,—those of them, I mean, who are quickwitted and, like bees on the wing, light on every flower, and from all that they hear are prone to draw conclusions as to what manner of persons they should be and in what way they should walk if they would make the best of life? Probably the youth will say to himself in the words of Pindar—

Can I by justice or by crooked ways of deceit ascend a loftier tower which may be a fortress to me all my days?

For what men say is that, if I am really just and am not also thought just, profit there is none, but the pain and loss on the other hand are unmistakable. But if, though unjust, I acquire the reputation of justice, a heavenly life is promised to me. Since then, as philosophers prove, appearance tyrannizes over truth and is lord of happiness, to appearance I must devote myself. I will describe around me a picture and shadow of virtue to be the vestibule and exterior of my house; behind I will trail the subtle and crafty fox, as Archilochus, greatest of sages, recommends. But I hear someone exclaiming that the concealment of wickedness is often difficult; to which I answer, Nothing great is easy. Nevertheless, the argument indicates this, if we would be happy, to be the path along which we should proceed. With a view to concealment we will establish secret brotherhoods and political clubs. And there are professors of rhetoric who teach the art of persuading courts and assemblies; and so, partly by persuasion and partly by force, I shall make unlawful gains and not be punished. Still I hear a voice saying that the gods cannot be deceived, neither can they be compelled. But what if there are no gods? or, suppose them to have no care of human things—why in either case should we mind about concealment? And even if there are gods, and they do care about us, yet we know of them only from tradition and the genealogies of the poets; and these are the very persons who say that they may be influenced and turned by "sacrifices and soothing entreaties and by offerings." Let us be consistent then, and believe both or neither. If the poets speak truly, why then we had better be unjust, and offer of the fruits of injustice; for if we are just, although we may escape the vengeance of heaven, we shall lose the gains of injustice; but, if we are unjust, we shall keep the gains, and by our sinning and praying, and praying and sinning, the gods will be propitiated, and we shall not be punished. "But there is a world below in which either we or our posterity will suffer for our unjust deeds." Yes, my friend, will be the [reply], but there are mysteries and atoning deities, and these have great power. That is what mighty cities declare; and the children of the gods, who were their poets and prophets, bear a like testimony. On what principle, then, shall we any longer choose justice rather than the worst injustice? When, if we only unite the latter with a deceitful regard to appearances, we shall fare to our mind both with gods and men, in life and after death, as the most numerous and the highest authorities tell us. Knowing all this, Socrates, how can a man who has any superiority of mind or person or rank or wealth, be willing to honour justice; or indeed to refrain from laughing when he hears justice praised? And even if there should be someone who is able to disprove the truth of my words, and who is satisfied that justice is best, still he is not angry with the unjust, but is very ready to forgive them, because he also knows that men are not just of their own free will; unless, peradventure, there be someone whom the divinity within him may have inspired with a hatred of injustice, or who has attained knowledge of the truth—but no other man. He only blames injustice who, owing to cowardice or age or some weakness, has not the power of being unjust. And this is proved by the fact that when he obtains the power, he immediately becomes unjust as far as he can be.

The cause of all this, Socrates, was indicated by us at the beginning of the argument, when my brother and I told you how astonished we were to find that of all the professing panegyrists of justice—beginning with the ancient heroes of whom any memorial has been preserved to us, and ending with the men of our own time—no one has ever blamed injustice or praised justice except with a view to the glories, honours, and benefits which flow from them. No one has ever adequately described either in verse or prose the true essential nature of either of them abiding in the soul, and invisible to any human or divine eye; or shown that of all the things of a man's soul which he has within him, justice is the greatest good, and injustice the greatest evil. Had this been the universal strain, had you sought to persuade us of this from our youth upwards, we should not have been on the watch to keep one another from doing wrong, but everyone would have been his own watchman, because afraid, if he did wrong, of harbouring in himself the greatest of evils. I dare say that Thrasymachus and others would seriously hold the language which I have been merely repeating, and words even stronger than these about justice and injustice, grossly, as I conceive, perverting their true nature. But I speak in this vehement manner, as I must frankly confess to you, because I want to hear from you the opposite side; and I would ask you to show not only the superiority which justice has over injustice, but what effect they have on the possessor of them which makes the one to be a good and the other an evil to him. And please, as Glaucon requested of you, to exclude reputations; for unless you take away from each of them his true reputation and add on the false, we shall say that you do not praise justice, but the appearance of it; we shall think that you are only exhorting us to keep injustice dark, and that you really agree with Thrasymachus in thinking that justice is another's good and the interest of the stronger, and that injustice is a man's own profit and interest, though injurious to the weaker. Now as you have admitted that justice is one of that highest class of goods which are desired indeed for their results, but in a far greater degree for their own sakes—like sight or hearing or knowledge or health, or any other real and natural and not merely conventional good—I would ask you in your praise of justice to regard one point only: I mean the essential good and evil which justice and injustice work in the possessors of them. Let others praise justice and censure injustice, magnifying the rewards and honours of the one and abusing the other; that is a manner of arguing which, coming from them, I am ready to tolerate, but from you who have spent your whole life in the consideration of this question, unless I hear the contrary from your own lips, I expect something better. And therefore, I say, not only prove to us that justice is better than injustice, but show what they either of them do to the possessor of them, which makes the one to be a good and the other an evil, whether seen or unseen by gods and men.

I had always admired the genius of Glaucon and Adeimantus, but on hearing these words I was quite delighted, and said: Sons of an illustrious father, that was not a bad beginning of the Elegiac verses which the admirer of Glaucon made in honour of you after you had distinguished yourselves at the battle of Megara:—

"Sons of Ariston," he sang, "divine offspring of an illustrious hero."

The epithet is very appropriate, for there is something truly divine in being able to argue as you have done for the superiority of injustice, and remaining unconvinced by your own arguments. And I do believe that you are not convinced—this I infer from your general character, for had I judged only from your speeches I should have mistrusted you. But now, the greater my confidence in you, the greater is my difficulty in knowing what to say. For I am in a strait between two; on the one hand I feel that I am unequal to the task; and my inability is brought home to me by the fact that you were not satisfied with the answer which I made to Thrasymachus, proving, as I thought, the superiority which justice has over injustice. And yet I cannot refuse to help, while breath and speech remain to me; I am afraid that there would be an impiety in being present when justice is evil spoken of and not lifting up a hand in her defence. And therefore I had best give such help as I can.

Glaucon and the rest entreated me by all means not to let the question drop, but to proceed in the investigation. They wanted to arrive at the truth, first, about the nature of justice and injustice, and secondly, about their relative advantages. I told them, what I really thought, that the enquiry would be of a serious nature, and would require very good eyes. Seeing then, I said, that we are no great wits, I think that we had better adopt a method which I may illustrate thus; suppose that a short-sighted person had been asked by someone to read small letters from a distance; and it occurred to someone else that they might be found in another place which was larger and in which the letters were larger—if they were the same and he could read the larger letters first, and then proceed to the lesser—this would have been thought a rare piece of good fortune.

Very true, said Adeimantus; but how does the illustration apply to our enquiry?

I will tell you, I replied; justice, which is the subject of our enquiry, is, as you know, sometimes spoken of as the virtue of an individual, and sometimes as the virtue of a State.

True, he replied.

And is not a State larger than an individual?

It is.

Then in the larger the quantity of justice is likely to be larger and more easily discernible. I propose therefore that we enquire into the nature of justice and injustice, first as they appear in the State, and secondly in the individual, proceeding from the greater to the lesser and comparing them.

That, he said, is an excellent proposal.

And if we imagine the State in process of creation, we shall see the justice and injustice of the State in process of creation also.

I dare say.

When the State is completed there may be a hope that the object of our search may be more easily discovered.

Yes, far more easily.

But ought we to attempt to construct one? I said; for to do so, as I am inclined to think, will be a very serious task. Reflect therefore.

I have reflected, said Adeimantus, and am anxious that you should proceed.

A State, I said, arises, as I conceive, out of the needs of mankind; no one is self-sufficing, but all of us have many wants. Can any other origin of a State be imagined?

There can be no other.

Then, as we have many wants, and many persons are needed to supply them, one takes a helper for one purpose and another for another; and when these partners and helpers are gathered together in one habitation the body of inhabitants is termed a State.

True, he said.

And they exchange with one another, and one gives, and another receives, under the idea that the exchange will be for their good.

Very true.

Then, I said, let us begin and create in idea a State; and yet the true creator is necessity, who is the mother of our invention.

Of course, he replied.

Now the first and greatest of necessities is food, which is the condition of life and existence.

Certainly.

The second is a dwelling, and the third clothing and the like.

True.

And now let us see how our city will be able to supply this great demand: We may suppose that one man is a [farmer], another a builder, someone else a weaver—shall we add to them a shoemaker, or perhaps some other purveyor to our bodily wants?

Quite right.

The barest notion of a State must include four or five men.

Clearly.

And how will they proceed? Will each bring the result of his labours into a common stock?—the individual [farmer], for example, producing for four, and labouring four times as long and as much as he needs in the provision of food with which he supplies others as well as himself; or will he have nothing to do with others and not be at the trouble of producing for them, but provide for himself alone a fourth of the food in a fourth of the time, and in the remaining three fourths of his time be employed in making a house or a coat or a pair of shoes, having no partnership with others, but supplying himself all his own wants?

Adeimantus thought that he should aim at producing food only and not at producing everything.

Probably, I replied, that would be the better way; and when I hear you say this, I am myself reminded that we are not all alike; there are diversities of natures among us which are adapted to different occupations.

Very true.

And will you have a work better done when the worker has many occupations, or when he has only one?

When he has only one.

Further, there can be no doubt that a work is spoilt when not done at the right time?

No doubt.

For business is not disposed to wait until the doer of the business is at leisure; but the doer must follow up what he is doing, and make the business his first object.

He must.

And if so, we must infer that all things are produced more plentifully and easily and of a better quality when [each person] does one thing which is natural to him and does it at the right time, and leaves other things.

Undoubtedly.

Then more than four citizens will be required; for the [farmer] will not make his own plough or mattock, or other implements of agriculture, if they are to be good for anything. Neither will the builder make his tools—and he too needs many; and in like manner the weaver and shoemaker.

True.

Then carpenters, and smiths, and many other artisans, will be sharers in our little State, which is already beginning to grow?

True.

Yet even if we add [cowherds], shepherds, and other herders, in order that our [farmers] may have oxen to plough with, and builders as well as [farmers] may have draught cattle, and curriers and weavers fleeces and hides,—still our State will not be very large.

That is true; yet neither will it be a very small State which contains all these.

Then, again, there is the situation of the city—to find a place where nothing need be imported is wellnigh impossible.

Impossible.

Then there must be another class of citizens who will bring the required supply from another city?

There must.

But if the trader goes empty-handed, having nothing which they require who would supply his need, he will come back empty-handed.

That is certain.

And therefore what they produce at home must be not only enough for themselves, but such both in quantity and quality as to accommodate those from whom their wants are supplied.

Very true.

Then more [farmers] and more artisans will be required?

They will.

Not to mention the importers and exporters, who are called merchants?

Yes.

Then we shall want merchants?

We shall.

And if merchandise is to be carried over the sea, skilful sailors will also be needed, and in considerable numbers?

Yes, in considerable numbers.

Then, again, within the city, how will they exchange their productions? To secure such an exchange was, as you will remember, one of our principal objects when we formed them into a society and constituted a State.

Clearly they will buy and sell.

Then they will need a market-place, and a money-token for purpose of exchange.

Certainly.

Suppose now that a [farmer], or an artisan, brings some production to market, and he comes at a time when there is no one to exchange with him,—is he to leave his calling and sit idle in the market-place?

Not at all; he will find people there who, seeing the want, undertake the office of salesmen. In well-ordered states they are commonly those who are the weakest in bodily strength, and therefore of little use for any other purpose; their duty is to be in the market, and to give money in exchange for goods to those who desire to sell and to take money from those who desire to buy.

This want, then, creates a class of retail-traders in our State. Is not "retailer" the term which is applied to those who sit in the market-place engaged in buying and selling, while those who wander from one city to another are called merchants?

Yes, he said.

And there is another class of servants, who are intellectually hardly on the level of companionship; still they have plenty of bodily strength for labour, which accordingly they sell, and are called, if I do not mistake, hirelings, hire being the name which is given to the price of their labour.

True.

Then hirelings will help to make up our population?

Yes.

And now, Adeimantus, is our State matured and perfected?

I think so.

Where, then, is justice, and where is injustice, and in what part of the State did they spring up?

Probably in the dealings of these citizens with one another. I cannot imagine that they are more likely to be found any where else.

I dare say that you are right in your suggestion, I said; we had better think the matter out, and not shrink from the enquiry.

Let us then consider, first of all, what will be their way of life, now that we have thus established them. Will they not produce corn, and wine, and clothes, and shoes, and build houses for themselves? And when they are housed, they will work, in summer, commonly, stripped and barefoot, but in winter substantially clothed and shod. They will feed on barley-meal and flour of wheat, baking and kneading them, making noble cakes and loaves; these they will serve up on a mat of reeds or on clean leaves, themselves reclining the while upon beds strewn with yew or myrtle. And they and their children will feast,

drinking of the wine which they have made, wearing garlands on their heads, and hymning the praises of the gods, in happy converse with one another. And they will take care that their families do not exceed their means; having an eye to poverty or war.

But, said Glaucon, interposing, you have not given them a relish to their meal.

True, I replied, I had forgotten; of course they must have a relish—salt and olives, and cheese, and they will boil roots and herbs such as country people prepare; for a dessert we shall give them figs, and peas, and beans; and they will roast myrtle-berries and acorns at the fire, drinking in moderation. And with such a diet they may be expected to live in peace and health to a good old age, and bequeath a similar life to their children after them.

Yes, Socrates, he said, and if you were providing for a city of pigs, how else would you feed the beasts?

But what would you have, Glaucon? I replied.

Why, he said, you should give them the ordinary conveniences of life. People who are to be comfortable are accustomed to lie on sofas, and dine off tables, and they should have sauces and sweets in the modern style.

Yes, I said, now I understand: the question which you would have me consider is, not only how a State, but how a luxurious State is created; and possibly there is no harm in this, for in such a State we shall be more likely to see how justice and injustice originate. In my opinion the true and healthy constitution of the State is the one which I have described. But if you wish also to see a State at fever-heat, I have no objection. For I suspect that many will not be satisfied with the simpler way of life. They will be for adding sofas, and tables, and other furniture; also dainties, and perfumes, and incense, and courtesans, and cakes, all these not of one sort only, but in every variety; we must go beyond the necessaries of which I was at first speaking, such as houses, and clothes, and shoes: the arts of the painter and the embroiderer will have to be set in motion, and gold and ivory and all sorts of materials must be procured.

True, he said.

Then we must enlarge our borders; for the original healthy State is no longer sufficient. Now will the city have to fill and swell with a multitude of callings which are not required by any natural want; such as the whole tribe of hunters and actors, of whom one large class has to do with forms and colours; another will be the votaries of music—poets and their attendant train of rhapsodists, players, dancers, contractors; also makers of divers kinds of articles, including women's dresses. And we shall want more servants. Will not tutors be also in request, and nurses wet and dry, tirewomen and barbers, as well as confectioners and cooks; and swineherds, too, who were not needed and therefore had no place in the former edition of our State, but are needed now? They must not be forgotten: and there will be animals of many other kinds, if people eat them.

Certainly.

And living in this way we shall have much greater need of physicians than before?

Much greater.

And the country which was enough to support the original inhabitants will be too small now, and not enough?

Quite true.

Then a slice of our neighbours' land will be wanted by us for pasture and tillage, and they will want a slice of ours, if, like ourselves, they exceed the limit of necessity, and give themselves up to the unlimited accumulation of wealth?

That, Socrates, will be inevitable.

And so we shall go to war, Glaucon. Shall we not?

Most certainly, he replied.

Then, without determining as yet whether war does good or harm, this much we may affirm, that now we have discovered war to be derived from causes which are also the causes of almost all the evils in States, private as well as public.

Undoubtedly.

And our State must once more enlarge; and this time the enlargement will be nothing short of a whole army, which will have to go out and fight with the invaders for all that we have, as well as for the things and persons whom we were describing above.

Why? he said; are they not capable of defending themselves?

No, I said; not if we were right in the principle which was acknowledged by all of us when we were framing the State: the principle, as you will remember, was that one [person] cannot practice many arts with success.

Very true, he said.

But is not war an art?

Certainly.

And an art requiring as much attention as shoemaking?

Quite true.

And the shoemaker was not allowed by us to be a [farmer], or a weaver, or a builder—in order that we might have our shoes well made; but to him and to every other worker was assigned one work for which he was by nature fitted, and at that he was to continue working all his life long and at no other; he was not to let opportunities slip, and then he would become a good workman. Now nothing can be more important then that the work of a soldier should be well done. But is war an art so easily acquired that a man may be a warrior who is also a [farmer], or shoemaker, or other artisan; although no one in the world would be a good dice or draught player who merely took up the game as a recreation, and had not from his earliest years devoted himself to this and nothing else? No tools will make a man a skilled workman, or master of defence, nor be of any use to him who has not learned how to handle them, and has never bestowed any attention upon them. How then will he who takes up a shield or other implement of war become a good fighter all in a day, whether with heavy-armed or any other kind of troops?

Yes, he said, the tools which would teach men their own use would be beyond price.

And the higher the duties of the guardian, I said, the more time, and skill, and art, and application will be needed by him?

No doubt, he replied.

Will he not also require natural aptitude for his calling?

Certainly.

Then it will be our duty to select, if we can, natures which are fitted for the task of guarding the city?

It will. . . .

BOOK IV

But where, amid all this, is justice? son of Ariston, tell me where. Now that our city has been made habitable, light a candle and search, and get your brother and Polemarchus and the rest of our friends to help, and let us see where in it we can discover justice and where injustice, and in what they differ from one another, and which of them the man who would be happy should have for his portion, whether seen or unseen by gods and men.

Nonsense, said Glaucon: did you not promise to search yourself, saying that for you not to help justice in her need would be an impiety?

I do not deny that I said so; and as you remind me, I will be as good as my word; but you must join.

We will, he replied.

Well, then, I hope to make the discovery in this way: I mean to begin with the assumption that our State, if rightly ordered, is perfect.

That is most certain.

And being perfect, is therefore wise and valiant and temperate and just.

That is likewise clear.

And whichever of these qualities we find in the State, the one which is not found will be the residue?

Very good.

If there were four things, and we were searching for one of them, wherever it might be, the one sought for might be known to us from the first, and there would be no further trouble; or we might know the other three first, and then the fourth would clearly be the one left.

Very true, he said.

And is not a similar method to be pursued about the virtues, which are also four in number?

Clearly.

First among the virtues found in the State, wisdom comes into view, and in this I detect a certain peculiarity.

What is that?

The State which we have been describing is said to be wise as being good in counsel?

Very true.

And good counsel is clearly a kind of knowledge, for not by ignorance, but by knowledge, do men counsel well?

Clearly.

And the kinds of knowledge in a State are many and diverse?

Of course.

There is the knowledge of the carpenter; but is that the sort of knowledge which gives a city the title of wise and good in counsel?

Certainly not; that would only give a city the reputation of skill in carpentering.

Then a city is not to be called wise because possessing a knowledge which counsels for the best about wooden implements?

Certainly not.

Nor by reason of a knowledge which advises about brazen pots, he said, nor as possessing any other similar knowledge?

Not by reason of any of them, he said.

Nor yet by reason of a knowledge which cultivates the earth; that would give the city the name of agricultural?

Yes.

Well, I said, and is there any knowledge in our recently-founded State among any of the citizens which advises, not about any particular thing in the State, but about the whole, and considers how a State can best deal with itself and with other States?

There certainly is.

And what is this knowledge, and among whom is it found? I asked.

It is the knowledge of the guardians, he replied, and is found among those whom we were just now describing as perfect guardians.

And what is the name which the city derives from the possession of this sort of knowledge?

The name of good in counsel and truly wise.

And will there be in our city more of these true guardians or more smiths?

The smiths, he replied, will be far more numerous.

Will not the guardians be the smallest of all the classes who receive a name from the profession of some kind of knowledge?

Much the smallest.

And so by reason of the smallest part or class, and of the knowledge which resides in this presiding and ruling part of itself, the whole State, being thus constituted according to nature, will be wise; and this, which has the only knowledge worthy to be called wisdom, has been ordained by nature to be of all classes the least.

Most true.

Thus, then, I said, the nature and place in the State of one of the four virtues has somehow or other been discovered.

And, in my humble opinion, very satisfactorily discovered, he replied.

Again, I said, there is no difficulty in seeing the nature of courage, and in what part that quality resides which gives the name of courageous to the State.

How do you mean?

Why, I said, everyone who calls my State courageous or cowardly, will be thinking of the part which fights and goes out to war on the State's behalf.

No one, he replied, would ever think of any other.

The rest of the citizens may be courageous or may be cowardly, but their courage or cowardice will not, as I conceive, have the effect of making the city either the one or the other.

Certainly not.

The city will be courageous in virtue of a portion of herself which preserves under all circumstances that opinion about the nature of things to be feared and not to be feared in which our legislator educated them; and this is what you term courage.

I should like to hear what you are saying once more, for I do not think that I perfectly understand you.

I mean that courage is a kind of [preservation].

[Preservation] of what?

Of the opinion respecting things to be feared, what they are and of what nature, which the law implants through education; and I mean by the words "under all circumstances" to intimate that in pleasure or in pain, or under the influence of desire or fear, a man preserves, and does not lose this opinion. Shall I give you an illustration?

If you please.

You know, I said, that dyers, when they want to dye wool for making the true sea-purple, begin by selecting their white colour first; this they prepare and dress with much care and pains, in order that the white ground may take the purple hue in full perfection. The dyeing then proceeds; and whatever is dyed in this manner becomes a fast colour, and no washing either with lyes or without them can take away the bloom. But, when the ground has not been duly prepared, you will have noticed how poor is the look wither of purple or of any other colour.

Yes, he said; I know that they have a washed-out and ridiculous appearance.

Then now, I said, you will understand what our object was in selecting our soldiers, and educating them in music and gymnastic; we were contriving influences which would prepare them to take the dye of the laws in perfection, and the colour of their opinion about dangers and of every other opinion was to be indelibly fixed by their nurture and training, not to be washed away by such potent lyes as pleasure—a far mightier agent in washing the soul than any soda or lye; or by sorrow, fear, and desire, the mightiest of all other solvents. And this sort of universal saving power of true opinion in conformity with law about real and false dangers I call and maintain to be courage, unless you disagree.

But I agree, he replied; for I suppose that you mean to exclude mere uninstructed courage, such as that of a wild beast or of a slave—this, in your opinion, is not the courage which the law ordains, and ought to have another name.

Most certainly.

Then I may infer courage to be such as you describe?

Why, yes, said I, you may, and if you add the words "of a citizen," you will not be far wrong;—hereafter, if you like, we will carry the examination further, but at present we are seeking not for courage but justice; and for the purpose of our enquiry we have said enough.

You are right, he replied.

Two virtues remain to be discovered in the State—first, temperance, and then justice which is the end of our search.

Very true.

Now, can we find justice without troubling ourselves about temperance?

I do not know how that can be accomplished, he said, nor do I desire that justice should be brought to light and temperance lost sight of; and therefore I wish that you would do me the favour of considering temperance first.

Certainly, I replied, I should not be justified in refusing your request.

Then consider, he said.

Yes, I replied; I will; and as far as I can at present see, the virtue of temperance has more of the nature of harmony and symphony than the preceding.

How so? he asked.

Temperance, I replied, is the ordering or controlling of certain pleasures and desires; this is

curiously enough implied in the saying of "a man being his own master;" and other traces of the same notion may be found in language.

No doubt, he said.

There is something ridiculous in the expression "master of himself;" for the master is also the servant and the servant the master; and in all these modes of speaking the same person is denoted.

Certainly.

The meaning is, I believe, that in the human soul there is a better and also a worse principle; and when the better has the worse under control, then a man is said to be master of himself; and this is a term of praise; but when, owing to evil education or association, the better principle, which is also the smaller, is overwhelmed by the greater mass of the worse—in this case he is blamed and is called the slave of self and unprincipled.

Yes, there is reason in that.

And now, I said, look at our newly-created State, and there you will find one of these two conditions realized; for the State, as you will acknowledge, may be justly called master of itself, if the words "temperance" and "self-mastery" truly express the rule of the better part over the worse.

Yes, he said, I see that what you say is true.

Let me further note that the manifold and complex pleasures and desires and pains are generally found in children and women and servants, and in the freemen so called who are of the lowest and more numerous class.

Certainly, he said.

Whereas the simple and moderate desires which follow reason, and are under the guidance of mind and true opinion, are to be found only in a few, and those the best born and best educated.

Very true.

These two, as you may perceive, have a place in our State; and the meaner desires of the many are held down by the virtuous desires and wisdom of the few.

That I perceive, he said.

Then if there be any city which may be described as master of its own pleasures and desires, and master of itself, ours may claim such a designation?

Certainly, he replied.

It may also be called temperate, and for the same reasons?

Yes.

And if there be any State in which rulers and subjects will be agreed as to the question who are to rule, that again will be our State?

Undoubtedly.

And the citizens being thus agreed among themselves, in which class will temperance be found—in the rulers or in the subjects?

In both, as I should imagine, he replied.

Do you observe that we were not far wrong in our guess that temperance was a sort of harmony?

Why so?

Why, because temperance is unlike courage and wisdom, each of which resides in a part only, the one making the State wise and the other valiant; not so temperance, which extends to the whole, and runs through all the notes of the scale, and produces a harmony of the weaker and the stronger and the middle class, whether you suppose them to be stronger or weaker in wisdom or power or numbers or wealth, or anything else. Most truly then may we deem temperance to be the agreement of the naturally superior and inferior, as to the right to rule of either, both in states and individuals.

I entirely agree with you.

And so, I said, we may consider three out of the four virtues to have been discovered in our State. The last of those qualities which make a state virtuous must be justice, if we only knew what that was.

The inference is obvious.

The time then has arrived, Glaucon, when, like huntsmen, we should surround the cover, and look sharp that justice does not steal away, and pass out of sight and escape us; for beyond a doubt she is somewhere in this country: watch therefore and strive to catch a sight of her, and if you see her first, let me know.

Would that I could! but you should regard me rather as a follower who has just eyes enough to see what you show him—that is about as much as I am good for.

Offer up a prayer with me and follow.

I will, but you must show me the way.

Here is no path, I said, and the wood is dark and perplexing; still we must push on.

Let us push on.

Here I saw something: Halloo! I said, I begin to perceive a track, and I believe that the quarry will not escape.

Good news, he said.

Truly, I said, we are stupid fellows.

Why so?

Why, my good sir, at the beginning of our enquiry, ages ago, there was justice tumbling out at our feet, and we never saw her; nothing could be more ridiculous. Like people who go about looking for what they have in their hands—that was the way with us—we looked not at what we were seeking, but at what was far off in the distance; and therefore, I suppose, we missed her.

What do you mean?

I mean to say that in reality for a long time past we have been talking of justice, and have failed to recognise her.

I grow impatient at the length of your exordium.

Well then, tell me, I said, whether I am right or not: You remember the original principle which we were always laying down at the foundation of the State, that one man should practise one thing only, the thing to which his nature was best adapted;—now justice is this principle or a part of it.

Yes, we often said that one man should do one thing only.

Further, we affirmed that justice was doing one's own business, and not being a busybody; we said so again and again, and many others have said the same to us.

Yes, we said so.

Then to do one's own business in a certain way may be assumed to be justice. Can you tell me whence I derive this inference?

I cannot, but I should like to be told.

Because I think that this is the only virtue which remains in the State when the other virtues of temperance and courage and wisdom are abstracted; and, that this is the ultimate cause and condition of the existence of all of them, and while remaining in them is also their preservative; and we were saying that if the three were discovered by us, justice would be the fourth or remaining one.

That follows of necessity.

If we are asked to determine which of these four qualities by its presence contributes most to the excellence of the State, whether the agreement of rulers and subjects, or the preservation in the soldiers of the opinion which the law ordains about the true nature of dangers, or wisdom and watchfulness in the rulers, or whether this other which I am mentioning, and which is found in children and women, slave and freeman, artisan, ruler, subject,—the quality, I mean, of everyone doing his own work, and not being a busybody, would claim the palm—the question is not so easily answered.

Certainly, he replied, there would be a difficulty in saying which.

Then the power of each individual in the State to do his own work appears to compete with the other political virtues, wisdom, temperance, courage.

Yes, he said.

And the virtue which enters into this competition is justice?

Exactly.

Let us look at the question from another point of view: Are not the rulers in a State those to whom you would entrust the office of determining suits at law?

Certainly.

And are suits decided on any other ground but that a man may neither take what is another's, nor be deprived of what is his own?

Yes, that is their principle.

Which is a just principle?

Yes.

Then on this view also justice will be admitted to be the having and doing what is a man's own, and belongs to him?

Very true. . . .

Very good; and if we were to affirm that we had discovered the just man and the just State, and the nature of justice in each of them, we should not be telling a falsehood?

Most certainly not.

May we say so, then?

Let us say so.

And now, I said, injustice has to be considered.

Clearly.

Must not injustice be a strife which arises among the three principles—a meddlesomeness, and interference, and rising up of a part of the soul against the whole, an assertion of unlawful authority, which is made by a rebellious subject against a true prince, of whom he is the natural vassal,—what is all this confusion and delusion but injustice, and intemperance and cowardice and ignorance, and every form of vice?

Exactly so.

And if the nature of justice and injustice be known, then the meaning of acting unjustly and being unjust, or, again, of acting justly, will also be perfectly clear?

What do you mean? he said.

Why, I said, they are like disease and health; being in the soul just what disease and health are in the body.

How so? he said.

Why, I said, that which is healthy causes health, and that which is unhealthy causes disease.

Yes.

And just actions cause justice, and unjust actions cause injustice?

That is certain.

And the creation of health is the institution of a natural order and government of one by another in the parts of the body; and the creation of disease is the production of a state of things at variance with this natural order?

True.

And is not the creation of justice the institution of a natural order and government of one by another in the parts of the soul, and the creation of injustice the production of a state of things at variance with the natural order?

Exactly so, he said.

Then virtue is the health and beauty and well-being of the soul, and vice the disease and weakness and deformity of the same?

True.

And do not good practices lead to virtue, and evil practices to vice?

Assuredly.

Still our old question of the comparative advantage of justice and injustice has not been answered: Which is the more profitable, to be just and act justly and practise virtue, whether seen or unseen of gods and men, or to be unjust and act unjustly, if only unpunished and unreformed?

In my judgment, Socrates, the question has now become ridiculous. We know that, when the bodily constitution is gone, life is no longer endurable, though pampered with all kinds of meats and drinks, and having all wealth and all power; and shall we be told . . . life is still worth having to a man, if only he be allowed to do whatever he likes with the single exception that he is not to acquire justice and virtue, or to escape from injustice and vice; assuming them both to be such as we have described?

Yes, this is ridiculous. . . .

BOOK V

Well, I replied, I suppose that I must retrace my steps and say what I perhaps ought to have said before in the proper place. The part of the men has been played out, and now properly enough comes the turn of the women. Of them I will proceed to speak, and the more readily since I am invited by you.

For men born and educated like our citizens, the only way, in my opinion, of arriving at a right conclusion about the possession and use of women and children is to follow the path on which we originally started, when we said that the men were to be the guardians and watchdogs of the herd.

True.

Let us further suppose the birth and education of our women to be subject to similar or nearly similar regulations; then we shall see whether the result accords with our design.

What do you mean?

What I mean may be put into the form of a question, I said: Are dogs divided into hes and shes, or do they both share equally in hunting and in keeping watch and in the other duties of dogs? or do we entrust to the males the entire and exclusive care of the flocks, while we leave the females at home, under the idea that the bearing and suckling [of] their puppies is labour enough for them?

No, he said, they share alike; the only difference between them is that the males are stronger and the females weaker.

But can you use different animals for the same purpose, unless they are bred and fed in the same way?

You cannot.

Then, if women are to have the same duties as men, they must have the same nurture and education?

Yes.

The education which was assigned to the men was music and gymnastic.

Yes.

Then women must be taught music and gymnastic and also the art of war, which they must practise like the men?

That is the inference, I suppose.

I should rather expect, I said, that several of our proposals, if they are carried out, being unusual, may appear ridiculous.

No doubt of it.

Yes, and the most ridiculous thing of all will be the sight of women naked in the palaestra, exercising with the men, especially when they are no longer young; they certainly will not be a vision of beauty, any more than the enthusiastic old men who in spite of wrinkles and ugliness continue to frequent the gymnasia.

Yes, indeed, he said: according to present notions the proposal would be thought ridiculous.

But then, I said, as we have determined to speak our minds, we must not fear the jests of the wits which will be directed against this sort of innovation; how they will talk of women's attainments both in music and gymnastic, and above all about their wearing armour and riding upon horseback!

Very true, he replied.

Yet having begun we must go forward to the rough places of the law; at the same time begging of these gentlemen for once in their life to be serious. Not long ago, as we shall remind them, the Hellenes were of the opinion, which is still generally received among the barbarians, that the sight of a naked man was ridiculous and improper; and when first the Cretans and then the Lacedaemonians introduced the custom, the wits of that day might equally have ridiculed the innovation.

No doubt.

But when experience showed that to let all things be uncovered was far better than to cover them up, and the ludicrous effect to the outward eye vanished before the better principle which reason asserted, then the man was perceived to be a fool who directs the shafts of his ridicule to any other sight but that of folly and vice, or seriously inclines to weigh the beautiful by any other standard but that of the good.

Very true, he replied.

First, then, whether the question is to be put in jest or in earnest, let us come to an understanding about the nature of woman: Is she capable of sharing either wholly or partially in the actions of men, or not at all? And is the art of war one of those arts in which she can or can not share? That will be the best way of commencing the enquiry, and will probably lead to the fairest conclusion.

That will be much the best way.

Shall we take the other side first and begin by arguing against ourselves; in this manner the adversary's position will not be undefended.

Why not? he said.

Then let us put a speech into the mouths of our opponents. They will say: "Socrates and Glaucon, no adversary need convict you, for you yourselves, at the first foundation of the State, admitted the principle that everybody was to do the one work suited to his own nature." And certainly, if I am not mistaken, such an admission was made by us. "And do not the natures of men and women differ very much indeed?" And we shall reply: Of course they do. Then we shall be asked, "Whether the tasks assigned to men and to women should not be different, and such as are agreeable to their different natures?" Certainly they should. "But if so, have you not fallen into a serious inconsistency in saying that men and women, whose natures are so entirely different, ought to perform the same actions?"— What defence will you make for us, my good Sir, against anyone who offers these objections?

That is not an easy question to answer when asked suddenly; and I shall and I do beg of you to draw out the case on our side.

These are the objections, Glaucon, and there are many others of a like kind, which I foresaw long ago; they made me afraid and reluctant to take in hand any law about the possession and nurture of women and children.

By Zeus, he said, the problem to be solved is anything but easy.

Why yes, I said, but the fact is that when a man is out of his depth, whether he has fallen into a little swimming bath or into mid ocean, he has to swim all the same.

Very true.

And must not we swim and try to reach the shore: we will hope that Arion's dolphin or some other miraculous help may save us?

I suppose so, he said.

Well then, let us see if any way of escape can be found. We acknowledged—did we not?—that different natures ought to have different pursuits, and that men's and women's natures are different. And now what are we saying?—that different natures ought to have the same pursuits,—this is the inconsistency which is charged upon us.

Precisely.

Verily, Glaucon, I said, glorious is the power of the art of contradiction!

Why do you say so!

Because I think that many a man falls into the practice against his will. When he thinks that he is reasoning he is really disputing, just because he cannot define and divide, and so know that of which he is speaking; and he will pursue a merely verbal opposition in the spirit of contention and not a fair discussion.

Yes, he replied, such is very often the case; but what has that to do with us and our argument?

A great deal; for there is certainly a danger of our getting unintentionally into a verbal opposition.

In what way?

Why we valiantly and pugnaciously insist upon the verbal truth, that different natures ought to have different pursuits, but we never considered at all what was the meaning of sameness or difference of nature, or why we distinguished them when we assigned different pursuits to different natures and the same to the same natures.

Why, no, he said, that was never considered by us.

I said: Suppose that by way of illustration we were to ask the question whether there is not an opposition in nature between bald men and hairy men; and if this is admitted by us, then, if bald men are cobblers, we should forbid the hairy men to be cobblers, and conversely?

That would be a jest, he said.

Yes, I said, a jest; and why? because we never meant when we constructed the State, that the opposition of natures should extend to every dif-

ference, but only to those differences which affected the pursuit in which the individual is engaged; we should have argued, for example, that a physician and one who is in mind a physician may be said to have the same nature.

True.

Whereas the physician and the carpenter have different natures?

Certainly.

And if, I said, the male and female sex appear to differ in their fitness for any art or pursuit, we should say that such pursuit or art ought to be assigned to one or the other of them; but if the difference consists only in women bearing and men begetting children, this does not amount to a proof that a woman differs from a man in respect to the sort of education she should receive; and we shall therefore continue to maintain that our guardians and their wives ought to have the same pursuits.

Very true, he said.

Next, we shall ask our opponent how, in reference to any of the pursuits or arts of civic life, the nature of a woman differs from that of a man?

That will be quite fair.

And perhaps he, like yourself, will reply that to give a sufficient answer on the instant is not easy; but after a little reflection there is no difficulty.

Yes, perhaps.

Suppose then that we invite him to accompany us in the argument, and then we may hope to show him that there is nothing peculiar in the constitution of women which would affect them in the administration of the State.

By all means.

Let us say to him: Come now, and we will ask you a question:—when you spoke of a nature gifted or not gifted in any respect, did you mean to say that one man will acquire a thing easily, another with difficulty; a little learning will lead the one to discover a great deal; whereas the other, after much study and application, no sooner learns than he forgets; or again, did you mean, that the one has a body which is a good servant to his mind, while the body of the other is a hindrance to him?—would not these be the sort of differences which distinguish the man gifted by nature from the one who is ungifted?

No one will deny that.

And can you mention any pursuit of mankind in which the male sex has not all these gifts and qualities in a higher degree than the female? Need I waste time in speaking of the art of weaving, and the management of pancakes and preserves, in which womankind does really appear to be great, and in which for her to be beaten by a man is of all things the most absurd?

You are quite right, he replied, in maintaining the general inferiority of the female sex: although many women are in many things superior to many men, yet on the whole what you say is true.

And if so, my friend, I said, there is no special faculty of administration in a state which a woman has because she is a woman, or which a man has by virtue of his sex, but the gifts of nature are alike diffused in both; all the pursuits of men are the pursuits of women also, but in all of them a woman is inferior to a man.

Very true.

Then are we to impose all our enactments on men and none of them on women?

That will never do.

One woman has a gift of healing, another not; one is a musician, and another has no music in her nature?

Very true.

And one woman has a turn for gymnastic and military exercises, and another is unwarlike and hates gymnastics?

Certainly.

And one woman is a philosopher, and another is an enemy of philosophy; one has spirit, and another is without spirit?

That is also true.

Then one woman will have the temper of a guardian, and another not. Was not the selection of the male guardians determined by differences of this sort?

Yes.

Men and women alike possess the qualities which make a guardian; they differ only in their comparative strength or weakness.

Obviously.

And those women who have such qualities are to be selected as the companions and colleagues of men who have similar qualities and whom they resemble in capacity and in character?

Very true.

And ought not the same natures to have the same pursuits?

They ought.

Then, as we were saying before, there is nothing unnatural in assigning music and gymnastic to the wives of the guardians—to that point we come round again.

Certainly not.

The law which we then enacted was agreeable to nature, and therefore not an impossibility or mere aspiration; and the contrary practice, which prevails at present, is in reality a violation of nature.

That appears to be true.

We had to consider, first, whether our proposals were possible, and secondly whether they were the most beneficial?

Yes.

And the possibility has been acknowledged?

Yes.

The very great benefit has next to be established?

Quite so.

You will admit that the same education which makes a man a good guardian will make a woman a good guardian; for their original nature is the same?

Yes.

I should like to ask you a question.

What is it?

Would you say that all men are equal in excellence, or is one man better than another?

The latter.

And in the commonwealth which we were founding do you conceive the guardians who have been brought up on our model system to be more perfect men, or the cobblers whose education has been cobbling?

What a ridiculous question!

You have answered me, I replied: Well, and may we not further say that our guardians are the best of our citizens?

By far the best.

And will not their wives be the best women?

Yes, by far the best.

And can there be anything better for the interests of the State than that the men and women of a State should be as good as possible?

There can be nothing better.

And this is what the arts of music and gymnastic, when present in such manner as we have described, will accomplish?

Certainly.

Then we have made an enactment not only possible but in the highest degree beneficial to the State?

True.

Then let the wives of our guardians strip, for their virtue will be their robe, and let them share in the toils of war and the defence of their country; only in the distribution of labours the lighter are to be assigned to the women, who are the weaker natures, but in other respects their duties are to be the same. And as for the man who laughs at naked women exercising their bodies from the best of motives, in his laughter he is plucking

A fruit of unripe wisdom,

and he himself is ignorant of what he is laughing at, or what he is about;—for that is, and ever will be, the best of sayings, *That the useful is the noble and the hurtful is the base.*

Very true.

Here, then, is one difficulty in our law about women, which we may say that we have now escaped; the wave has not swallowed us up alive for enacting that the guardians of either sex should have all their pursuits in common; to the utility and also to the possibility of this arrange-

ment the consistency of the argument with itself bears witness.

Yes, that was a mighty wave which you have escaped.

Yes, I said, but a greater is coming; you will not think much of this when you see the next.

Go on; let me see.

The law, I said, which is the sequel of this and of all that has preceded, is to the following effect,—"that the wives of our guardians are to be common, and their children are to be common, and no parent is to know his own child, nor any child his parent."

Yes, he said, that is a much greater wave than the other; and the possibility as well as the utility of such a law are far more questionable.

I do not think, I said, that there can be any dispute about the very great utility of having wives and children in common; the possibility is quite another matter, and will be very much disputed.

I think that a good many doubts may be raised about both.

You imply that the two questions must be combined, I replied. Now I meant that you should admit the utility; and in this way, as I thought, I should escape from one of them, and then there would remain only the possibility.

But that little attempt is detected, and therefore you will please to give a defence of both.

Well, I said, I submit to my fate. Yet grant me a little favour: let me feast my mind with the dream as day dreamers are in the habit of feasting themselves when they are walking alone; for before they have discovered any means of effecting their wishes—that is a matter which never troubles them—they would rather not tire themselves of thinking about possibilities; but assuming that what they desire is already granted to them, they proceed with their plan, and delight in detailing what they mean to do when their wish has come true—that is a way which they have of not doing much good to a capacity which was never good for much. Now I myself am beginning to lose heart, and I should like, with your permission, to pass over the question of possibility at present. Assuming therefore the possibility of the proposal, I shall now proceed to enquire how the rulers will carry out these arrangements, and I shall demonstrate that our plan, if executed, will be of the greatest benefit to the State and to the guardians. First of all, then, if you have no objection, I will endeavour with your help to consider the advantages of the measure; and hereafter the question of possibility.

I have no objection; proceed.

First, I think that if our rulers and their auxiliaries are to be worthy of the name which they bear, there must be willingness to obey in the one and the power of command in the other; the guardians must themselves obey the laws, and they must also imitate the spirit of them in any details which are entrusted to their care.

That is right, he said.

You, I said, who are their legislator, having selected the men, will now select the women and give them to them;—they must be as far as possible of like natures with them; and they must live in common houses and meet at common meals. None of them will have anything specially his or her own; they will be together, and will be brought up together, and will associate at gymnastic exercises. And so they will be drawn by a necessity of their natures to have intercourse with each other—necessity is not too strong a word, I think?

Yes, he said;—necessity, not geometrical, but another sort of necessity which lovers know, and which is far more convincing and constraining to the mass of mankind.

True, I said; and this, Glaucon, like all the rest, must proceed after an orderly fashion; in a city of the blessed, licentiousness is an unholy thing which the rulers will forbid.

Yes, he said, and it ought not to be permitted.

Then clearly the next thing will be to make matrimony sacred in the highest degree, and what is most beneficial will be deemed sacred?

Exactly.

And how can marriages be made most beneficial?—that is a question which I put to you,

because I see in your house dogs for hunting, and of the nobler sort of birds not a few. Now, I beseech you, do tell me, have you ever attended to their pairing and breeding?

In what particulars?

Why, in the first place, although they are all of a good sort, are not some better than others?

True.

And do you breed from them all indifferently, or do you take care to breed from the best only?

From the best.

And do you take the oldest or the youngest, or only those of ripe age?

I choose only those of ripe age.

And if care was not taken in the breeding, your dogs and birds would greatly deteriorate?

Certainly.

And the same of horses and of animals in general?

Undoubtedly.

Good heavens! my dear friend, I said, what consummate skill will our rulers need if the same principle holds of the human species!

Certainly, the same principle holds; but why does this involve any particular skill?

Because, I said, our rulers will often have to practise upon the body corporate with medicines. Now you know that when patients do not require medicines, but have only to be put under a regimen, the inferior sort of practitioner is deemed to be good enough; but when medicine has to be given, then the doctor should be more of a man.

That is quite true, he said; but to what are you alluding?

I mean, I replied, that our rulers will find a considerable dose of falsehood and deceit necessary for the good of their subjects: we were saying that the use of all these things regarded as medicines might be of advantage.

And we were very right.

And this lawful use of them seems likely to be often needed in the regulations of marriages and births.

How so?

Why, I said, the principle has been already laid down that the best of either sex should be united with the best as often, and the inferior with the inferior, as seldom as possible; and that they should rear the offspring of the one sort of union, but not of the other, if the flock is to be maintained in first-rate condition. Now these goings on must be a secret which the rulers only know, or there will be a further danger of our herd, as the guardians may be termed, breaking out into rebellion.

Very true.

Had we not better appoint certain festivals at which we will bring together the brides and bridegrooms, and sacrifices will be offered and suitable [hymns] composed by our poets: the number of weddings is a matter which must be left to the discretion of the rulers, whose aim will be to preserve the average of population? There are many other things which they will have to consider, such as the effects of wars and diseases and any similar agencies, in order as far as this is possible to prevent the State from becoming either too large or too small.

Certainly, he replied.

We shall have to invent some ingenious kind of lots which the less worthy may draw on each occasion of our bringing them together, and then they will accuse their own ill-luck and not the rulers.

To be sure, he said.

And I think that our braver and better youth, besides their other honours and rewards, might have greater facilities of intercourse with women given them; their bravery will be a reason, and such fathers ought to have as many sons as possible.

True.

And the proper officers, whether male or female or both, for offices are to be held by women as well as by men—

Yes—

The proper officers will take the offspring of the good parents to the pen or fold, and there they will deposit them with certain nurses who dwell in a separate quarter; but the offspring of the inferior, or of the better when they chance to be deformed, will be put away in some mysterious, unknown place, as they should be.

Yes, he said, that must be done if the breed of the guardians is to be kept pure.

They will provide for their nurture, and will bring the mothers to the fold when they are full of milk, taking the greatest possible care that no mother recognises her own child; and other wet-nurses may be engaged if more are required. Care will also be taken that the process of suckling shall not be protracted too long; and the mothers will have no getting up at night or other trouble, but will hand over all this sort of thing to the nurses and attendants.

You suppose the wives of our guardians to have a fine easy time of it when they are having children.

Why, said I, and so they ought. Let us, however, proceed with our scheme. We were saying that the parents should be in the prime of life?

Very true.

And what is the prime of life? May it not be defined as a period of about twenty years in a woman's life, and thirty in a man's?

Which years do you mean to include?

A woman, I said, at twenty years of age may begin to bear children to the State, and continue to bear them until forty; a man may begin at five-and-twenty, then he has passed the point at which the pulse of life beats quickest, and continue to beget children until he be fifty-five.

Certainly, he said, both in men and women those years are the prime of physical as well as of intellectual vigour.

Anyone above or below the prescribed ages who [engages in reproduction] shall be said to have done an unholy and unrighteous thing; the child of which he is the father, if it steals into life, will have been conceived under auspices very unlike the sacrifices and prayers, which at each [wedding] priestesses and priests and the whole city will offer, that the new generation may be better and more useful than their good and useful parents, whereas his child will be the offspring of darkness and strange lust.

Very true, he replied.

And the same law will apply to anyone of those within the prescribed age who forms a connection with any woman in the prime of life without the sanction of the rulers; for we shall say that he is raising up a bastard to the State, uncertified and unconsecrated.

Very true, he replied.

This applies, however, only to those who are within the specified age: after that we allow them to range at will, except that a man may not marry his daughter or his daughter's daughter, or his mother or his mother's mother; and women, on the other hand, are prohibited from marrying their sons or fathers, or son's son or father's father, and so on in either direction. And we grant all this, accompanying the permission with strict orders to prevent any embryo which may come into being from seeing the light; and if any force a way to the birth, the parents must understand that the offspring of such a union cannot be maintained, and arrange accordingly.

That also, he said, is a reasonable proposition. But how will they know who are fathers and daughters, and so on?

They will never know. The way will be this:—dating from the day [a man becomes a] bridegroom, . . . [he] will call all the male children who are born in the seventh and the tenth month afterwards his sons, and the female children his daughters, and they will call him father, and he will call their children his grandchildren, and they will call the elder generation grandfathers and grandmothers. All who were begotten at the time when their fathers and mothers came together will be called their brothers and sisters, and these, as I was saying, will be forbidden to intermarry. This, however, is not to be understood as an absolute prohibition of the marriage of brothers and sisters; if the lot favours them, and they receive the sanction of the Pythian oracle, the law will allow them.

Quite right, he replied.

Such is the scheme, Glaucon, according to which the guardians of our State are to have their wives and families in common. And now you would have the argument show that this community is consistent with the rest of our polity, and also that nothing can be better—would you not?

Yes, certainly.

Shall we try to find a common basis by asking of ourselves what ought to be the chief aim of the legislator in making laws and in the organization of a State—what is the greatest good, and what is the greatest evil, and then consider whether our previous description has the stamp of the good or of the evil?

By all means.

Can there be any greater evil than discord and distraction and plurality where unity ought to reign? or any greater good than the bond of unity?

There cannot.

And there is unity where there is community of pleasures and pains—where all the citizens are glad or grieved on the same occasions of joy and sorrow?

No doubt.

Yes; and where there is no common but only private feeling a State is disorganized—when you have one half of the world triumphing and the other plunged in grief at the same events happening to the city or the citizens?

Certainly.

Such differences commonly originate in a disagreement about the use of the terms "mine" and "not mine," "his" and "not his."

Exactly so.

And is not that the best-ordered State in which the greatest number of persons apply the terms "mine" and "not mine" in the same way to the same thing?

Quite true.

Or that again which most nearly approaches to the condition of the individual—as in the body, when but a finger of one of us is hurt, the whole frame, down towards the soul as a centre and forming one kingdom under the ruling power therein, feels the hurt and sympathizes all together with the part affected, and we say that the man has a pain in his finger; and the same expression is used about any other part of the body, which has a sensation of pain at suffering or of pleasure at the alleviation of suffering.

Very true, he replied; and I agree with you that in the best-ordered State there is the nearest approach to this common feeling which you describe.

Then when anyone of the citizens experience any good or evil, the whole State will make his case their own, and will either rejoice or sorrow with him?

Yes, he said, that is what will happen in a well-ordered State.

It will now be time, I said, for us to return to our State and see whether this or some other form is most in accordance with these fundamental principles.

Very good.

Our State like every other has rulers and subjects?

True.

All of whom will call one another citizens?

Of course.

But is there not another name which people give to their rulers in other States?

Generally they call them masters, but in democratic States they simply call them rulers.

And in our State what other name besides that of citizens do the people give the rulers?

They are called saviours and helpers, he replied.

And what do the rulers call the people?

Their maintainers and foster-fathers.

And what do they call them in other States?

Slaves.

And what do the rulers call one another in other States?

Fellow-rulers.

And what in ours?

Fellow-guardians.

Did you ever know an example in any other State of a ruler who would speak of one of his colleagues as his friend and of another as not being his friend?

Yes, very often.

And the friend he regards and describes as one in whom he has an interest, and the other as a stranger in whom he has no interest?

Exactly.

But would any of your guardians think or speak of any other guardian as a stranger?

Certainly he would not; for everyone whom they meet will be regarded by them either as a brother or sister, or father or mother, or son or daughter, or as the child or parent of those who are thus connected with him.

Capital, I said; but let me ask you once more: Shall they be a family in name only; or shall they in all their actions be true to the name? For example, in the use of the word "father," would the care of a father be implied and the filial reverence and duty and obedience to him which the law commands; and is the violator of these duties to be regarded as an impious and unrighteous person who is not likely to receive much good either at the hands of god or of man? Are these to be or not to be the strains which the children will hear repeated in their ears by all the citizens about those who are intimated to them to be their parents and the rest of their kinsfolk?

These, he said, and none other; for what can be more ridiculous than for them to utter the names of family ties with the lips only and not to act in the spirit of them?

Then in our city the language of harmony and concord will be more often heard than in any other. As I was describing before, when anyone is well or ill, the universal word will be "with me it is well" or "it is ill."

Most true.

And agreeably to this mode of thinking and speaking, were we not saying that they will have their pleasures and pains in common?

Yes, and so they will.

And they will have a common interest in the same thing which they will alike call "my own," and having this common interest they will have a common feeling of pleasure and pain?

Yes, far more so than in other States.

And the reason of this, over and above the general constitution of the State, will be that the guardians will have a community of women and children?

That will be the chief reason.

And this unity of feeling we admitted to be the greatest good, as was implied in our own comparison of a well-ordered State to the relation of the body and the members, when affected by pleasure or pain?

That we acknowledged, and very rightly.

Then the community of wives and children among our citizens is clearly the source of the greatest good to the State?

Certainly.

And this agrees with the other principle which we were affirming,—that the guardians were not to have houses or lands or any other property; their pay was to be their food, which they were to receive from the other citizens, and they were to have no private expenses; for we intended them to preserve their true character of guardians.

Right, he replied.

Both the community of property and the community of families, as I am saying, tend to make them more truly guardians; they will not tear the city in pieces by differing about "mine" and "not mine;" each man dragging any acquisition which he has made into a separate house of his own, where he has a separate wife and children and private pleasures and pains; but all will be affected as far as may be by the same pleasures and pains because they are all of one opinion about what is near and dear to them, and therefore they all tend towards a common end.

Certainly, he replies.

And as they have nothing but their persons which they can call their own, suits and complaints will have no existence among them; they will be delivered from all those quarrels of which money or children or relations are the occasion.

Of course they will.

Neither will trials for assault or insult ever be likely to occur among them. For that equals should defend themselves against equals we shall maintain to be honourable and right; we shall make the protection of the person a matter of necessity.

That is good, he said.

Yes; and there is a further good in the law; viz. that if a man has a quarrel with another he will satisfy his resentment then and there, and not proceed to more dangerous lengths.

Certainly.

To the elder shall be assigned the duty of ruling and chastising the younger.

Clearly.

Nor can there be a doubt that the younger will not strike or do any other violence to an elder, unless the magistrates command him; nor will he slight him in any way. For there are two guardians, shame and fear, mighty to prevent him: shame, which makes men refrain from laying hands on those who are to them in the relation of parents; fear, that the injured one will be succoured by the others who are his brothers, sons, fathers.

That is true, he replied.

Then in every way the laws will help the citizens to keep the peace with one another?

Yes, there will be no want of peace.

And as the guardians will never quarrel among themselves there will be no danger of the rest of the city being divided either against them or against one another.

None whatever.

I hardly like even to mention the little meannesses of which they will be rid, for they are beneath notice: such, for example, as the flattery of the rich by the poor, and all the pains and pangs which men experience in bringing up a family, and in finding money to buy necessaries for their household, borrowing and then repudiating, getting how they can, and giving the money into the hands of women and slaves to keep—the many evils of so many kinds which people suffer in this way are mean enough and obvious enough, and not worth speaking of.

Yes, he said, a man has no need of eyes in order to perceive that.

And from all these evils they will be delivered, and their life will be blessed as the life of Olympic victors and yet more blessed.

How so?

The Olympic victor, I said, is deemed happy in receiving a part only of the blessedness which is secured to our citizens, who have won a more glorious victory and have a more complete maintenance at the public cost. For the victory which they have won is the salvation of the whole State; and the crown with which they and their children are crowned is the fulness of all that life needs; they receive rewards from the hands of their country while living, and after death have an honourable burial.

Yes, he said, and glorious rewards they are.

Do you remember, I said, how in the course of the previous discussion someone who shall be nameless accused us of making our guardians unhappy—they had nothing and might have possessed all things—to whom we replied that, if an occasion offered, we might perhaps hereafter consider this question, but that, as at present advised, we would make our guardians truly guardians, and that we were fashioning the State with a view to the greatest happiness, not for any particular class, but of the whole?

Yes, I remember.

And what do you say, now that the life of our protectors is made out to be far better and nobler than that of Olympic victors—is the life of shoemakers, or any other artisans, or of [farmers], to be compared with it?

Certainly not.

At the same time I ought here to repeat what I have said elsewhere, that if any of our guardians shall try to be happy in such a manner that he will cease to be a guardian, and is not content with this safe and harmonious life, which, in our judgment, is of all lives the best, but infatuated by some youthful conceit of happiness which gets up into his head shall seek to appropriate the whole state to himself, then he will have to learn how wisely Hesiod spoke, when he said, "half is more than the whole."

If he were to consult me, I should say to him: Stay where you are, when you have the offer of such a life.

You agree then, I said, that men and women are to have a common way of life such as we have described—common education, common children; and they are to watch over the citizens in common whether abiding in the city or going out to war; they are to keep watch together, and to hunt together like dogs; and always and in all things, as far as they are able, women are to share with the men? And in so doing they will do what is best, and will not violate, but preserve the natural relation of the sexes.

I agree with you, he replied. . . .

Let me begin by reminding you that we found our way hither in the search after justice and injustice.

True, he replied; but what of that?

I was only going to ask whether, if we have discovered them, we are to require that the just man should in nothing fail of absolute justice; or may we be satisfied with an approximation, and the attainment in him of a higher degree of justice than is to be found in other men?

The approximation will be enough.

We were enquiring into the nature of absolute justice and into the character of the perfectly just, and into injustice and the perfectly unjust, that we might have an ideal. We were to look at these in order that we might judge of our own happiness and unhappiness according to the standard which they exhibited and the degree in which we resembled them, but not with any view of showing that they could exist in fact.

True, he said.

Would a painter be any the worse because, after having delineated with consummate art an ideal of a perfectly beautiful man, he was unable to show that any such man could ever have existed?

He would be none the worse.

Well, and were we not creating an ideal of a perfect State?

To be sure.

And is our theory a worse theory because we are unable to prove the possibility of a city being ordered in the manner described?

Surely not, he replied.

That is the truth, I said. But if, at your request, I am to try and show how and under what conditions the possibility is highest, I must ask you, having this in view, to repeat your former admissions.

What admissions?

I want to know whether ideals are ever fully realized in language? Does not the word express more than the fact, and must not the actual, whatever a man may think, always, in the nature of things, fall short of the truth? What do you say?

I agree.

Then you must not insist on my proving that the actual State will in every respect coincide with the ideal: if we are only able to discover how a city may be governed nearly as we proposed, you will admit that we have discovered the possibility which you demand; and will be contented. I am sure that I should be contented—will not you?

Yes, I will.

Let me next endeavour to show what is that fault in States which is the cause of their present maladministration, and what is the least change which will enable a State to pass into the truer form; and let the change, if possible, be of one thing only, or, if not, of two; at any rate, let the changes be as few and slight as possible.

Certainly, he replied.

I think, I said, that there might be a reform of the State if only one change were made, which is not a slight or easy though still a possible one.

What is it? he said.

Now then, I said, I go to meet that which I liken to the greatest of the waves; yet shall the word be spoken, even though the wave break and drown me in laughter and dishonour; and do you mark my words.

Proceed.

I said: *Until philosophers are kings, or the kings and princes of this world have the spirit and power of philosophy, and political greatness and wisdom meet in one, and those commoner natures who pursue either to the exclusion of the other are compelled to stand aside, cities will never have rest from their evils,—no, nor the human race, as I believe,—and then only will this our State have a possibility of life and behold the light of day.* Such was the thought, my dear Glaucon, which I would fain have uttered if it had not seemed too extravagant; for to be convinced that in no other State can there be happiness private or public is indeed a hard thing.

NOTES

1. Aeschylus, *Seven against Thebes*, 574.
2. Hesiod, *Works and Days*, 230.
3. Homer, *Odyssey*, xix. 109.
4. Eumolpus.
5. Hesiod, *Works and Days*, 287.
6. Homer, *Iliad*, ix. 493.

2. PLATO'S REPUBLIC AND FEMINISM

JULIA ANNAS

Not many philosophers have dealt seriously with the problems of women's rights and status, and those that have, have unfortunately often been on the wrong side.[1] In fact Plato and Mill are the only great philosophers who can plausibly be called feminists. But there has been surprisingly little serious effort made to analyze their arguments, perhaps because it has seemed like going over ground already won.

This paper is concerned only with Plato. I shall maintain what may surprise some: It is quite wrong to think of Plato as "the first feminist."[2] His arguments are unacceptable to a feminist, and the proposals made in *Republic* V are irrelevant to the contemporary debate.

The idea that Plato is a forerunner of Women's Liberation has gained support from the fact that in *Republic* V Plato proposes not only that women should share men's tasks but also that the nuclear family should be abolished.[3] This idea is put forward by some radical feminists today as an essential part of any program for the liberation of women. But I shall argue that Plato's grounds for the proposal are so different from the modern ones that he is in no sense a forerunner of them. Furthermore, where they differ, empirical evidence suggests that it is Plato who is wrong.

Plato's proposals about women[4] come at the beginning of Book V, where Socrates is represented as having to surmount three waves of opposition. The first wave concerns the admission of women as Guardians; the second concerns the communal life of the Guardians; the third concerns the practicability of the ideal state, and this leads into the discussion which occupies the rest of Books V–VII. The figure of separate "waves" is constantly brought before us; for Plato the capacity of women to be Guardians is a separate question from the replacement of nuclear family life.[5]

Plato begins his treatment of the first problem (*Rep.* 451) by extending the metaphor he has used already. Female watchdogs do just what the male ones do, except that they are weaker, and their lives are interrupted by giving birth. By analogy, the same is true of women; though they are weaker than men and their lives are interrupted by childbirth, they are otherwise the same, and so should be given the same upbringing and tasks as men, however distasteful the sight of ugly old women exercising in the gymnasium may be.

Now this is only metaphor—and in fact it does not pretend to be serious argument. Plato wants to give us a picture first, perhaps so that we have a vivid idea of what the arguments are about before they are presented, perhaps also so that he can meet and deflect mere ridicule right at the start, before the serious discussion. Still, the initial metaphor is important, for it continues to influence Plato in the actual argument.

Plato now (*Rep.* 453b–c) puts forward what he regards as a serious objection to the idea of women being Guardians. The opponent is made to say that it contradicts the principle on which the ideal state is constructed—namely, that each person is to do his own work, according to his nature (*Rep.* 453b5). As women differ greatly in nature from men, they should surely have different functions in the city (*Rep.* 453b10–11).

Reprinted from *Plato's Republic and Feminism* with the permission of Cambridge University Press.

Plato dismisses this objection as merely captious. Of course it is true that different natures should do different things, but it does not follow that men and women should do different things unless it can be shown that they have natures that are different in the important respect of affecting their capacity for the same pursuit. Otherwise it would be like letting bald men, but not hairy men, be cobblers. Plato now claims that men and women differ only in their sexual roles: men impregnate, women give birth (*Rep.* 454d–e). The objector fails to show that there is any capacity that is peculiar to women, and Plato claims to show that there are no civic pursuits which belong to a woman as such or to a man as such (this is the part of the argument we shall come back to). Since there are no specific male or female competencies, men and women should follow the same pursuits, and women who have natures suitable to be Guardians should therefore be appropriately trained.

This is how Plato deals with the first "wave." There are three important points to be made about his argument.

1. Firstly, there is something very odd about the actual course of the argument from 455a–d. Plato has established the undeniable point that while women are different from men in some ways and similar in others, discussion at that level is sterile; the interesting question is whether the undisputed differences matter when we decide whether women should be able to hold certain jobs. This is the crucial point not only for Plato but for any sensible discussion of the topic. But Plato's argument is seriously incomplete.

At 455a9–b2 he poses the question, "Are there any occupations which contribute towards the running of the state which only a woman can do?" Very swiftly he claims to show that there are none. Men are better equipped both mentally and physically (455b4–c6). So in every pursuit men can do better than women, though it is not true that all men do better than all women (455d3–5). Women, he says, are ridiculed when men do such traditional feminine tasks as cooking and weaving better than they do; still, it follows from what has been said that if men bothered to turn their attention to these tasks they would do them better. "The one sex is, so to speak, far and away beaten in every field by the other" (455d2–3).

Now it is hardly a feminist argument to claim that women do not have a special sphere because men can outdo them at absolutely everything. What is more important in the present context, however, is that Plato sums up his argument at 455d6–e1 by saying that there is no civic pursuit which belongs to a woman as such or to a man as such. But while he has argued that there are no pursuits appropriate for a woman as such, because men could do them all better, where is the argument that there are no specifically male competencies? There is not a trace of any such argument in the text, nor of any materials which could be used for one.

This is a serious gap, both because it is the point that the objector, if he were not being shepherded by Socrates (cf. 455a5–b2), would in fact press and because what Plato says about male and female capacities actually provides material for such an objector.

Anyone acquainted with the modern literature will realize at once that someone objecting to the idea that men and women should share all roles is not very worried about whether there are some jobs that only women are suited for. The reason for this is obvious enough: jobs that women usually do are badly paid or unpaid and lack status, and men are generally not interested in doing them. What really interests the objector is the claim that there are some occupations in society which only men are suited for: being doctors, lawyers, judges, taking part in politics by voting or holding office, owning and managing property. In the Athens of Plato's day women were not allowed to do any of these things, and the average Athenian would no doubt have simply assumed that they could not do them (as we can see from Aristophanes' *Ecclesiazusae*). Any feminist must take this objection seriously and meet it, simply because it has been historically the main objection to attempts by women to enter hitherto male professions or obtain hitherto male rights like the vote.[6] Yet Plato not only does nothing to meet this overwhelmingly obvious objection, he even provides materials for the objector. At 455b4–c6 he distinguishes three ways in which a gifted nature differs from an ungifted one. The gifted learn quickly, the ungifted only with difficulty. The gifted do not have to be taught very long before they can go on to make discoveries of their own; the ungifted need long instruction and are hard put to it to retain what they have learn. The gifted can put their thoughts into action; the ungifted are clumsy. Plato then asks rhetorically, "Do you know of any human pursuit in which men do not greatly excel women in all these qualities?" Clearly the answer is "No." But if men always excel women in these very important respects, the objector has all he wants: surely there are some pursuits (e.g., generalship) where these qualities are needed in a high degree and which it is therefore not reasonable to open to women. It is no good saying, as Plato at once does, that, "many women are better than many men at many things" (455d3–4). The objector does not need to claim that all men are always better than all women in a specific respect. If only men excel in a quality, then if efficiency is our aim[7] surely that makes it reasonable to regard a pursuit that requires a high degree of that quality as suited specially to men. The fact that women will not invariably come out on bottom is neither here nor there. In Plato's fiercely specialized state, the aim will be the maximum number of alpha performances.

This is an important argument. Scientific research into sex differences is an area of great controversy precisely because its results do have important social consequences; if men and women did have different types of intelligence, for example, then different types of education would surely be appropriate. But why does Plato not even notice the gap in his argument or the ammunition he is handing to the opposition? Of course he does not want to make the opponent's case seem strong. But it is possible that he genuinely does not see the disastrous relevance of his claims about men's superior intellectual gifts to his point about distinct fields of activity. He may be doing here what Aristotle often criticizes him for—taking metaphor for argument.

The metaphor of male and female watchdogs with which the subject was introduced would naturally lead Plato to think predominantly of human tasks which are analogous. And this is what we find. At 455e1, after the argument just discussed, he mentions that women are weaker than men at all pursuits. This suits his use of the analogy with the dogs, for there the difference in strength between male and female was not succinct reason to give them different tasks. And in the whole discussion that follows he simply shelves the question of intellectual differences between men and women. He never seriously discusses activities where these differences would matter and which are nevertheless to be open to women in the ideal state. There is only one reference to women officials (460b9–10) and even then they have a traditionally "feminine" role (inspecting newborn children). There is possibly a reference to women doctors at 454d1–3 (but the text is very uncertain), and some women are said to be capable of being doctors at 455e6–7. Against these two (or possibly three) meager and offhand references to women doing jobs requiring some intellectual capacity, there are at least nine references[8] to women fighting, serving in the army, and doing gymnastics. On this topic Plato's discussion is full and emphatic. He is taking seriously the idea that the life of the human female is like that of any other female animal, with reproduction making only short breaks in physical activity otherwise like the male's. No doubt this is because he is mainly interested in the eugenic possibilities for his "herd."[9] The picture of the female watchdog diverts him from the problems he faces given his beliefs about female intellectual capacities.

So Plato's argument here is not one which a feminist would find useful or even acceptable. In any case, it has a serious gap, and it is not clear that Plato could repair it except by abandoning his beliefs about the intellectual inferiority of women.[10]

2. Secondly, the argument is not based on, and makes no reference to, women's desires or needs. Nothing at all is said about whether women's present roles frustrate them or whether they will lead more satisfying lives as Guardians than as house-bound drudges.

This is rather striking, since women in fourth-century Athens led lives that compare rather closely to the lives of women in present-day Saudi Arabia. The place of women in Athenian life is summed up forcibly in the notorious statement, "We have courtesans for our pleasure, concubines for the requirements of the body, and wives to bear us lawful children and look after the home faithfully" (Pseudo-Demosthenes, *Against Neaera,* 122). The contrast between this and the life of the Guardians is so striking that one would have thought some comparison inevitable. Yet Plato shows no interest in this side of the picture. Later on in Book V (456b12–c7) he talks about the liberating effect of communal life in freeing people from the struggle to make ends meet and the need to hand one's money over to women and slaves to take care of it. Here the woman's position in the household is presented as something that the *man* is to be liberated from. There is nothing about the effect on *her* of communal living.

Of course Plato is not bound to be interested in the psychology of women, but his complete lack of interest underlines the fact that his argument does not recommend changing the present state of affairs on the ground that women suffer from being denied opportunities that are open to men.

His argument has quite different grounds, in fact. The state benefits from having the best possible citizens, and if half the citizens sit at home doing trivial jobs then usable talent is being wasted. Here Mrs. Huby gets the point exactly right: "There was nothing worth while for a woman to do at home; she should therefore share in man's work outside the home" (Huby, 1972, 23). Plato's sole ground for his proposals is their usefulness to the state; the point is repeated several times.[11]

Of course there is nothing non-feminist about this argument.[12] But Plato's argument gains rather different significance from the fact that this is his *only* ground. His argument is authoritarian in spirit rather than liberal; if a woman did not want to be a Guardian, Plato would surely be committed to compelling her to serve the state. Though this question never arises in the *Republic,* at *Laws* 780a–c the Athenian says openly that women are to be compelled to attend the communal meals (all that is left of the communal life of the *Republic*), because most women will be shy and used to seclusion and so will not want to take part. This is rather far from modern liberal arguments that women should have equal opportunities with men because otherwise they lead stunted and unhappy lives and lack the means for self-development.

This point may have been missed because at 456c1–2 Plato says that the present set-up of society is "contrary to nature" (*para phusin*). We are not, however, entitled to claim that for Plato confinement to the home thwarts the nature of women. What is "contrary to nature" surely has to be understood as the opposite of what has just been said to be "according to nature" (*kata phusin,* 456c1), and this is the principle that similar natures should follow similar pursuits. The present set-up is contrary to nature only in the sense that women do not in fact do jobs that they are capable of doing. There is no suggestion in the present passage that by "contrary to nature" Plato means anything stronger, such as for example that women's present roles are imposed on them in a way which deforms their lives. (This is not a point peculiar to the discussion of women. The arguments in Book II that each person should have one occupation make no appeal to people's happiness or satisfaction in doing only one thing. Cf. 370b–c, 374b–d.)

In the *Laws* also (805a–b) Plato says that it is stupid not to train and bring up boys and girls in the same way to have the same pursuits and purposes, and adds that nearly every state is half a state as things are, whereas it could double its resources (cf. 806c). For Plato the reason why housewifery is not a real occupation is that it makes no irreplaceable contribution to the state, and absorbs time and energy that could be put to publicly beneficial use. He is completely unconcerned with the sort of objection which is nowadays familiar, namely that housewifery is incapable of providing an intelligent woman with a satisfying life, and leads to boredom, neurosis, and misery.[13]

3. The third point leads on naturally from the second, since it is also a consequence of the fact that Plato justifies his proposals solely in terms of benefit to the state. The proposals for women are not a matter of their rights. There is nothing in *Republic* V that one could apply to the question of women's rights; the matter is simply not raised.

Of course Plato nowhere discusses men's rights either, and notoriously has no word for "rights," any more than he has for "duty" or "obligation." But the point is not lost if we abandon talk of rights and merely notice instead that Plato nowhere says that his proposals for women are *just*. It is remarkable in a work which makes proposals about women as radical as the *Republic's*, and which has as much to say about justice as the *Republic* has, that inequality of the sexes is not presented as an injustice, and that the proposals to treat the sexes equally are not presented as measures which will make the state more just than its rivals. Yet the ideal state is just for reasons, explained in Books II–IV, which have nothing to do with the position of women in it. Nothing is said about any connection between the decline to the various forms of unjust state and the position of women in them.[14]

In fact it is rather unclear how the proposals of Book V relate to justice at all, whether in the

state or in the soul. If women are to be Guardians, they must have just souls. We know from Book IV that the just soul has rightly organized parts—the *logistikon* or rational element, *epithumetikon* or desiring element, and *thumoeides,* the part usually called "spirit" or the like. If the Guardian women are just, presumably they have these parts of soul. But do women's souls have a *thumoeidic* part? As it is introduced in Book IV, *thumoeides* appears to be a capacity for aggressive and violent behavior, visible even in animals, but, one would have thought, notably lacking in fourth-century Athenian women. It is true that *thumoeides* is not limited to unthinking aggression, but even the more developed forms of behaviors that Plato regards as typically thumoeidic display, what Gosling[15] calls "admiration for manliness," are what we might call *machismo.* Unless the account of the just soul is to be done all over again for women Guardians to take account of female psychology, Plato must assume that women have the same aggressive tendencies as men. And in Book V he does make this assumption, and says that some women at any rate will be of the predominantly thumoeidic type (456a1–5). But this seems to conflict with his statements elsewhere which say or imply that women's psychology differs from men's precisely in that they lack the thumoeidic qualities of courage and "guts"; by contrast with men they are weak, devious, and cowardly.[16]

I have argued so far that for Plato his proposals about women are justified entirely by the resulting benefit to the state and not at all by women's needs or rights. It is important that the state in question is the ideal state. As far as I can see, there is nothing in *Republic* V which would commit Plato to the view that it was unjust for fourth-century Athenian women to be treated as they were. The proposals for women arise when the just constitution of the ideal state has been determined. There seems no reason why analogous proposals should be made in an unreformed state. Why should women be able to do men's jobs where this will merely have the result that instead of operating in a private sphere in the home, they will be operating in a private sphere at work? Plato would have no grounds for arguing that it would be best and useful for the state for this to happen.

Is this an ungenerous way to take the spirit of Plato's proposals? We should notice that even in the ideal state Plato limits his proposals for women to the Guardian class. There is nothing to suggest that the worker class do not live like fourth-century Greeks, with the women at home doing the cooking and weaving. This seems to show that whether women should do men's jobs depends, for Plato, on the nature of the jobs. The ideal state might contain many discontented potters' wives wanting to be potters; but presumably the Guardians (male and female) would only tell them to stay at home and learn *sôphrosunê* in carrying out their appointed tasks.

If Plato's argument applies only to the performance of tasks which contribute towards the public good in the direct way that the Guardians' tasks do, it is clearly irrelevant to modern arguments for equality of opportunity. No modern feminist would argue that women should be able to do men's jobs when this will result in greater direct benefit to the state, and otherwise stay at home. The moment it could be shown that the state did not need the extra women public servants, there would be no grounds for letting them have the jobs.

It would in fact be surprising if Plato's argument were relevant to women's rights, because it is a purely utilitarian argument. This is, however, precarious ground for a feminist, for once more efficient means to the desired end are found, women can at once be thrust back into the home. Mill begins *On the Subjection of Women* with the statement that "the legal subordination of one sex to the other is wrong in itself." Plato is not committed to this by the *Republic*, and I see no reason whatsoever to believe that he thought that it was true. He

thinks only that the present situation is wasteful and inefficient, and, under ideal conditions, should be changed.

This makes it easier to understand what seemed puzzling earlier, namely that Plato should combine a belief that the jobs of (Guardian) men should be open to women with a belief that women are physically and mentally inferior to men. It has always been difficult for those who see Plato as a feminist to understand why he stresses so much the comparative feebleness of women's contribution, for it is not usual to combine proposals like Plato's with extreme contempt for women. But on a purely utilitarian argument, since women represent a huge pool of untapped resources, it does not matter in the least if their contribution is not as good as that of men; and that is just what Plato seems to think.

Throughout Plato's works there are scattered examples of conventional contempt for women. At *Cratylus* 392b1–d10, for example, we are told that the Trojan men called Hector's son Astyanax and the Trojan women called him Scamandrius, and that this means that the former is the right name, as men are more intelligent than women. Of course nothing can be built on this kind of remark, and it would be unprofitable as well as depressing to comb Plato's works for such passages. Nevertheless they are significant in that taken together they build up a consistent tone which is hard to reconcile with an attitude that could be called feminist. Even in Book V itself Plato remarks that the practice of despoiling the dead shows a "small and womanish mind" (469d7)—this in a context where half of the army doing the killing and despoiling are women. This might be put down to carelessness were it not for the *Timaeus,* where Plato not only says (42e), "Human nature being twofold, the better sort was that which should thereafter be called man," but says twice (42b3–c4, 90e6–91a4) that evil and cowardly men are reborn as women, that being the first step downwards to rebirth as animals. There could hardly be a more open declaration that women are inferior to men. If the

Timaeus was written at roughly the same time as the *Republic,* this embarrasses those who want to see Plato in the *Republic* as a feminist. But if what I have argued is right, then the *Timaeus* is quite compatible with the *Republic.* Even if women are inferior to men, it will still be of advantage to the state to have women do what men do if it is of public benefit. The argument in the *Republic* does not need, or claim, more than this.

There is one striking and revealing passage which shows that even in the *Republic* Plato holds the view of women's inferiority which has its uglier expression in the *Timaeus.* At 563b7–9, equality (*isonomia*) and freedom between men and women turns up as one of the deplorable corruptions of the democratic state. Now what is wrong with the democratic state, in Plato's view, is that unequals are treated equally—young and old, for example, and slave and free. The only possible inference is that Plato himself holds that women are naturally inferior to men[17] and that any actual state where they are on terms of equality has corrupted the natural hierarchy. It is true that in his hostile portrait of the democratic state Plato carries over some details from contemporary Athens (for example, the fact that slaves cannot be distinguished at sight from free men by their clothes) and so not all features of his description embody serious theses. But even at his most careless Plato could hardly have thought of fourth-century Athens as an example of a place where men and women were on terms of freedom and equality. The passage must, then, be taken as a deliberate and important statement of what Plato believes, and it shows conclusively that the *Republic* does not differ on this point from the *Timaeus.* Even in the *Republic,* Plato never advocates the view that men and women are equal.

It comes as no surprise, then, that when Plato stops believing that the ideal state can be realized, he also stops thinking that women should do the same jobs as men, even in a greatly improved state. In the *Laws* he has abandoned the idea that men and women might be totally devoted to the state as the Guardians were. And the *Republic's* radical proposals about women lapse. Although women are still educated and forced into public to some extent, this is merely so that they can be controlled, since their potential for virtue is less than man's and they would get up to mischief (780d9–781b6). They are still to learn how to fight, but only so as to defend their homes and children in the last resort (804–806, 813e–814c). The only office they hold seems to be that of organizing a kind of women's moral vigilante group. Otherwise they are left in the position of fourth-century Greek women. They take no part in any political process, they are unable to own or inherit property in their own right, and they are perpetual legal minors always under the authority of male relatives or guardians. Women are married off by their fathers or brothers, and an heiress passes with the property to the nearest male relative,[18] as was the normal Greek practice of the time.[19]

Plato's argument that women should be Guardians thus has three crucial defects: it is not valid against an anti-feminist, it is irrelevant to facts about women's desires, and it is irrelevant to the injustice of sexual inequality.

NOTES

1. Rousseau (1911, ch. 5) and Schopenhauer (1974) are the most striking examples.
2. (R. Lucas, 1973). The claim that Plato was a feminist is very common in discussions of *Republic* V, and also in recent feminist discussions. (Cf. A. Rosenthal 1973): "The feminism of Plato is exemplary and unparalleled in philosophy or political theory."
3. The term "nuclear family" may be found dislikable, but it is useful in avoiding the suggestion that Plato wants to abolish the family in favor of impersonal institutions of a *1984* type. He stresses that family affection will remain, though spread over a wider class of people (463d–e).
4. And children, though I shall not be considering them in this paper. In modern discussions the question of children's rights is often raised along

with that of women's rights, but significantly no one has ever tried to see Plato as a precursor of these ideas.

5. Plato justifies the abolition of the nuclear family solely on grounds of eugenics and of the unity of the state (see below) and there seems no reason why these grounds should not hold even if women were not full Guardians and had a subordinate status; Plato's second proposal is thus in principle independent of his first.

6. Mill in *On the Subjection of Women* deals with this type of argument as an objection to women having political rights. Nowadays the idea that women differ intellectually from men is directed rather against women having serious careers comparable to men's; cf. C. Hutt (1973, ch. 5).

7. As it certainly is Plato's aim. He does not use the patronizing argument that on grounds of "respect for persons" women should have equal pay and status with men even if their contribution is recognized to be inferior.

8. 452a4–5, a10–b3, b8–c2, 453a3–4, 457a6–9, 458d1–2, 466c6–d1, 467a1–2, 468d7–e1.

9. The word is used literally at 459e1, e3, and (possibly) as a metaphor at 451c7–8.

10. It is, however, true that Plato's argument breaks some ground at least, in making it possible to consider women as individuals and not as a class with mixed capacities, at 455e–456a, after the argument just considered, women are compared with other women in various ways, not with men. Hence Plato has removed objections to considering his proposals at all on the ground that women as a class are incompetent.

11. 456c4–9: the question is, are the proposals best, *beltista*. Jowett (1871) translates this and similar phrases by "most beneficial." At 457a3–4 the proposals are "best for the city," *ariston polei*. At 457b1–2 women's nakedness in the gymnasium will be "for the sake of what is best," *tou beltistou heneka*, and people who find it ludicrous will be foolish, because "what is useful (*ophelimon*) is fair and what is harmful (*blaberon*) is ugly," and the proposals are useful as well as possible (c1–2). Cf. 452d3–e2, where the supposed analogy of men exercising naked is justified in terms of benefit.

12. It *is* found even in Firestone (1970, 206–210), though her main argument is not utilitarian.

Interestingly, it is not the main argument in the utilitarian Mill, for whom the main objection to sexual inequality is the curtailment of the freedom, and hence the happiness, of women. Mill causes confusion, however, by also including utilitarian arguments.

13. Of course there are other objections to housewifery as an occupation for women, e.g. that it is hard, unpleasant and unpaid, and these may well be more important from the viewpoint of practical reforms, but the charge that it does not satisfy a woman's capacities is the most relevant to discussion of Plato's argument.

14. However, the equal and free association of men and women appears as one of the bad effects of the completely democratic state (563b7–9). This is discussed below.

15. Gosling (1973, ch. 3 "Admiration for Manliness."). As the title suggests. Gosling conducts the discussion wholly in terms of male ideals, and does not remark on any difficulty arising from the fact that half the Guardians will be women.

16. *Laws* 802e declares that pride and courage are characteristic of men (and should be expressed in their music) whereas what is characteristic of women is restraint and modesty. Plato seems to endorse in the *Meno* the idea that the scope of men's and women's virtue is different—that of a man is to manage his own and the city's affairs capably, that of a woman is to be a good and thrifty housewife and to obey her husband (71e, 73a). This makes it hard to see how women can possess the thumoeidic part of the soul necessary for the complete justice of a Guardian. The *Laws* concludes, consistently, that a woman has less potentiality for virtue than a man (781b2–4): Plato says that it is women's weakness and timidity that makes them sly and devious.

17. Cf. *Laws* 917a4–6, where this is clearly brought out.

18. A woman can choose her own husband, if she is an heiress, only in the extremely unlikely situation of there being absolutely no suitable male relative available; and even then her choice is to be in consultation with her guardians.

19. Even so, a limited amount of gymnastic activity and fighting is left open for women in the *Laws;* this shows how little this has to do with real liberation of women.

3. THE ANALECTS

CONFUCIUS

1:2. The philosopher Yu said, "They are few who, being filial and fraternal, are fond of offending against their superiors. There have been none who, not liking to offend against their superiors, have been fond of stirring up confusion.

"The superior man bends his attention to what is radical. That being established, all practical courses naturally grow up. Filial piety and fraternal submission!—are they not the root of all benevolent actions?"

1:4. The philosopher Tsang said, "I daily examine myself on three points:—whether, in transacting business for others, I may have been not faithful;—whether, in intercourse with friends, I may have been not sincere;—whether I may have not mastered and practiced the instructions of my teacher."

1:6. The master said, "A youth, when at home, should be filial, and, abroad, respectful to his elders. He should be earnest and truthful. He should overflow in love to all, and cultivate the friendship of the good. When he has time and opportunity, after the performance of these things, he should employ them in polite studies."

1:7. Tsze-hsia said, "If a man withdraws his mind from the love of beauty, and applies it as sincerely to the love of the virtuous; if, in serving his parents, he can exert his utmost strength; if, in serving his prince, he can devote his life; if, in his intercourse with his friends, his words are sincere:—although men say that he has not learned, I will certainly say that he has."

1:11. The Master said, "While a man's father is alive, look at the bent of his will; when his father is dead, look at his conduct. If for three years he does not alter from the way of his father, he may be called filial."

2:4. The Master said, "At fifteen, I had my mind bent on learning.

"At thirty, I stood firm.

"At forty, I had no doubts.

"At fifty, I knew the decrees of Heaven.

"At sixty, my ear was an obedient organ *for the reception of truth.*

"At seventy, I could follow what my heart desired, without transgressing what was right."

4:15. The Master said, "Shan, my doctrine is that of an all-pervading unity."

The disciple Tsang replied, "Yes."

The Master went out, and the other disciples asked, saying, "What do his words mean?" Tsang said, "The doctrine of our master is to be true to the principles of our nature and the benevolent exercise of them to others,—this and nothing more."

4:16. The Master said, "The mind of the superior man is conversant with righteousness; the mind of the mean man is conversant with gain."

4:17. The Master said, "When we see men of worth, we should think of equaling them; when we see men of a contrary character, we should turn inwards and examine ourselves."

4:18. The Master said, "In serving his parents, a son may remonstrate with them, but gently; when he sees that they do not incline to follow his advice, he shows an increased degree of reverence, but does not abandon his purpose; and should they punish him, he does not allow himself to murmur."

4:23. The Master said, "The cautious seldom err."

4:24. The Master said, "The superior man wishes to be slow in his speech and earnest in his conduct."

Reprinted from *The Four Books*, edited and translated by James Legge. Originally published in *The Chinese Classics*, Volume I (Oxford: Clarendon, 1893).

4:25. The Master said, "Virtue is not left to stand alone. He who practices it will have neighbors."

5:11. Tsze-kung said, "What I do not wish men to do to me, I also wish not to do to men." The Master said, "Tsze, you have not attained that."

5:12. Tsze-kung said, "The Master's personal displays of his principles and ordinary descriptions of them may be heard. His discourses about man's nature, and the way of Heaven, cannot be heard."

6:18. The Master said, "They who know the truth are not equal to those who love it, and they who love it are not equal to those who delight in it."

6:20. Fan Ch'ih asked what constituted wisdom. The Master said, "To give one's self earnestly to the duties due to men, and, while respecting spiritual beings, to keep aloof from them, may be called wisdom." He asked about perfect virtue. The Master said, "The man of virtue makes the difficulty to be overcome his first business, and success only a subsequent consideration;—this may be called perfect virtue."

6:25. The Master said, "The superior man, extensively studying all learning, and keeping himself under the restraint of the rules of propriety may thus likewise not overstep what is right."

6:27. The Master said, "Perfect is the virtue which is according to the Constant Mean! Rare for a long time has been its practice among the people."

6:28. Tsze-kung said, "Suppose the case of a man extensively conferring benefits on the people, and able to assist all, what would you say of him? Might he be called perfectly virtuous?" The Master said, "Why speak only of virtue in connection with him? Must he not have the qualities of a sage? Even Yao and Shun were still solicitous about this.[1]

"Now the man of perfect virtue, wishing to be established himself, seeks also to establish others; wishing to be enlarged himself, he seeks also to enlarge others.

"To be able to judge of others by what is nigh in ourselves;—this may be called the art of virtue."

7:27. The Master said, "There may be those who act without knowing why. I do not do so. Hearing much and selecting what is good and following it; seeing much and keeping it in memory—this is the second style of knowledge."

7:36. The Master said, "The superior man is satisfied and composed; the mean man is always full of distress."

7:37. The Master was mild, and yet dignified; majestic, and yet not fierce; respectful, and yet easy.

8:2. The Master said, "Respectfulness, without the rules of propriety, becomes laborious bustle; carefulness, without the rules of propriety, becomes timidity; boldness, without the rules of propriety, becomes insubordination; straightforwardness, without the rules of propriety, becomes rudeness.

"When those who are in high stations perform well all their duties to their relations, the people are aroused to virtue. When old friends are not neglected by them, the people are preserved from meanness."

8:8. The Master said, "It is by Odes that the mind is aroused.

"It is by the Rules of Propriety that the character is established.

"It is from Music that the finish is received."

8:13. The Master said, "With sincere faith he unites the love of learning; holding firm to death, he is perfecting the excellence of his course.

"Such a one will not enter a tottering state, nor dwell in a disorganized one. When right principles of government prevail in the kingdom, he will show himself; when they are prostrated, he will keep concealed.

"When a country is well governed, poverty and a mean condition are things to be ashamed of. When a country is ill governed, riches and honor are things to be ashamed of."

9:4. There were four things from which the Master was entirely free. He had no foregone conclusions, no arbitrary predetermination, no obstinacy and no egoism.

9:24. The Master said, "Hold faithfulness and sincerity as first principles. Have no friends not equal to yourself. When you have faults, do not fear to abandon them."

11:11. Chi Lu asked about serving the spirits of the dead. The Master said, "While you are not able to serve men, how can you serve their spirits?" Chi Lu added, "I venture to ask about death?" He was answered, "While you do not know life, how can you know about death?"

12:1. Yen Yüan asked about perfect virtue. The Master said, "To subdue one's self and return to propriety, is perfect virtue. If a man can for one day subdue himself and return to propriety, all under heaven will ascribe perfect virtue to him. Is the practice of perfect virtue from a man himself, or is it from others?"

Yen Yüan said, "I beg to ask the steps of that process." The Master replied, "Look not at what is contrary to propriety; listen not to what is contrary to propriety; speak not what is contrary to propriety; make no movement which is contrary to propriety." Yen Yüan then said, "Though I am deficient in intelligence and vigor, I will make it my business to practice this lesson."

12:2. Chung-kung asked about perfect virtue. The Master said, "It is, when you go abroad, to behave to everyone as if you were receiving a great guest; to employ the people as if you were assisting at a great sacrifice; not to do to others as you would not wish done to yourself; to have no murmuring against you in the country, and none in the family." Chung-kung said, "Though I am deficient in intelligence and vigor, I will make it my business to practice this lesson."

12:9. The duke Ai inquired of Yu Zo, saying, "The year is one of scarcity, and the returns for expenditure are not sufficient;—what is to be done?"

Yu Zo replied to him, "Why not simply tithe the people?"

"With two tenths," said the duke, "I find them not enough;—how could I do with that system of one tenth?"

Yu Zo answered, "If the people have plenty, their prince will not be left to want alone. If the people are in want, their prince cannot enjoy plenty alone."

12:15. The Master said, "By extensively studying all learning, and keeping himself under the restraint of the rules of propriety, *one* may thus likewise not err from what is right."

12:17. Chi K'ang asked Confucius about government.

Confucius replied, "To govern means to rectify. If you lead on the people with correctness, who will dare not to be correct?"

12:22. Fan Ch'ih asked about benevolence. The Master said, "It is to love all men." He asked about knowledge. The Master said, "It is to know all men."

Fan Ch'ih did not immediately understand these answers.

The Master said, "Employ the upright and put aside all the crooked; in this way the crooked can be made to be upright."

Fan Ch'ih retired, and, seeing Tsze-hsia, he said to him, "A little while ago, I had an interview with our Master, and asked him about knowledge. He said, 'Employ the upright and put aside all the crooked;—in this way, the crooked will be made to be upright.' What did he mean?"

13:6. The Master said, "When a prince's personal conduct is correct, his government is effective without the issuing of orders. If his personal conduct is not correct, he may issue orders, but they will not be followed."

13:9. When the Master went to Wei, Zan Yu acted as driver of his carriage.

The Master observed, "How numerous are the people!"

Yu said, "Since they are thus numerous, what more shall be done for them?" "Enrich them," was the reply.

"And when they have been enriched, what more shall be done?"

The Master said, "Teach them."

13:11. The Master said, "'If good men were to govern a country in succession for a hundred years, they would be able to transform the violently bad, and dispense with capital punishments.' True indeed is this saying!"

13:13. The Master said, "If a minister make his own conduct correct, what difficulty will he have in assisting in government? If he cannot rectify himself, what has he to do with rectifying others?"

13:16. The duke of Sheh asked about government.

The Master said, "Good government obtains

when those who are near are made happy, and those who are far off are attracted."

13:18. The duke of Sheh informed Confucius, saying, "Among us here are those who may be styled upright in their conduct. If their fathers have stolen a sheep, they will bear witness to the fact."

Confucius said, "Among us, in our part of the country, those who are upright are different from this. The father conceals the misconduct of the son, and the son conceals the misconduct of the father. Uprightness is to be found in this."

13:19. Fan Ch'ih asked about perfect virtue. The Master said, "It is, in retirement, to be sedately grave; in the management of business, to be reverently attentive; in intercourse with others, to be strictly sincere. Though a man go among rude, uncultivated tribes, these qualities may not be neglected."

14:30. The Master said, "The way of the superior man is threefold, but I am not equal to it. Virtuous, he is free from anxieties; wise, he is free from perplexities; bold, he is free from fear."

Tsze-kung said, "Master, that is what you yourself say."

14:36. Someone said, "What do you say concerning the principle that injury should be recompensed with kindness?"

The Master said, "With what then will you recompense kindness?"

"Recompense injury with justice, and recompense kindness with kindness."

15:17. The Master said, "The superior man in everything considers righteousness to be essential. He performs it according to the rules of propriety. He brings it forth in humility. He completes it with sincerity. This is indeed a superior man."

15:18. The Master said, "The superior man is distressed by his want of ability. He is not distressed by men's not knowing him."

15:19. The Master said, "The superior man dislikes the thought of his name not being mentioned after his death."

15:20. The Master said, "What the superior man seeks, is in himself. What the mean man seeks, is in others."

15:21. The Master said, "The superior man is dignified, but does not wrangle. He is sociable, but not a partisan."

15:22. The Master said, "The superior man does not promote a man simply on account of his words, nor does he put aside good words because of the man."

15:23. Tsze-kung asked, saying, "Is there one word which may serve as a rule of practice for all one's life?" The Master said, "Is not RECIPROCITY such a word?" What you do not want done to yourself, do not do to others."

15:38. The Master said, "In teaching there should be no distinction of classes."

16:10. Confucius said, "The superior man has nine things which are subjects with him of thoughtful consideration. In regard to the use of his eyes, he is anxious to see clearly. In regard to his ears, he is anxious to hear distinctly. In regard to his countenance, he is anxious that it should be benign. In regard to his demeanor, he is anxious that it should be respectful. In regard to his speech, he is anxious that it should be sincere. In regard to his doing business, he is anxious that it should be reverently careful. In regard to what he doubts about, he is anxious to question others. When he is angry, he thinks of the difficulties [his anger may involve him in]. When he sees gain to be got, he thinks of righteousness."

17:2. The Master said, "By nature, men are nearly alike; by practice, they get to be wide apart."

17:6. Tsze-chang asked Confucius about perfect virtue. Confucius said, "To be able to practice five things everywhere under heaven constitutes perfect virtue." He begged to ask what they were, and was told, "Gravity, generosity of soul, sincerity, earnestness, and kindness. If you are grave, you will not be treated with disrespect. If you are generous, you will win all. If you are sincere, people will repose trust in you. If you are earnest, you will accomplish much. If you are kind, this will enable you to employ the services of others."

NOTES

1. Confucius, Mencius, and other Chinese philosophers refer to Yao, Shun, and Duke Chou as ideal rulers and sages. Yao and Shun were legendary, successive rulers of the third millenium B.C.E. Duke Chou helped to establish the Chou dynasty in 1111 B.C.E.

RECOMMENDED READINGS

Texts

Annas, Julia. *An Introduction to Plato's Republic.* Oxford: Oxford University Press, 1981.
Cropsey, Joseph. *Plato's World.* Chicago: University of Chicago Press, 1995.
Cross, R. C., and A. D. Woozley. *Plato's Republic: A Philosophical Commentary.* London: Macmillan, 1964.
Irwin, T. H. *Plato's Ethics.* Oxford: Oxford University Press, 1995.
Kraut, Richard. *Socrates and the State.* Princeton: Princeton University Press, 1984.
White, N. P. *A Companion to Plato's Republic.* Indianapolis: Hacket, 1979.

Feminist Perspective

Canto, Monique. "The Politics of Women's Bodies: Reflections on Plato." In *The Female Body in Western Culture: Contemporary Perspectives,* edited by Susan Rubin Suleiman, 339–353. Cambridge, MA: Harvard University Press, 1986.
Dickason, Anna. "Anatomy and Destiny: The Role of Biology in Plato's View of Women." In *Women and Philosophy,* edited by C. Gould and M. Wartofsky, 45–53. New York: Putnam, 1976.
Saxonhouse, Arlene. "The Philosopher and the Female in the Political Thought of Plato." *Political Theory* 4, no. 2 (1976).

Multicultural Perspective

Dawson, Raymond. *Confucius.* New York: Hill and Wang, 1981.
Hsu, Leanard. *The Political Philosophy of Confucius.* London: Routledge and Sons, 1932.

PART II

❦

ARISTOTLE AND MUSONIUS RUFUS

INTRODUCTION

Aristotle was born in 384 B.C. in the northern Greek city of Stagira in Macedonia. His father, Nicomachus, held the post of physician to Amnytas II, King of Macedonia and father of Philip the Great. When he was eighteen, he entered Plato's Academy, where he studied and taught for approximately twenty years. Plato is said to have considered him "the mind" of the Academy. Nevertheless, in his will, Plato named his nephew Speusippus head of the Academy rather than his gifted student Aristotle. So Aristotle left Athens and went to Assos in Asia Minor, where he established a branch campus of the Academy and married Pythias, the niece and adopted daughter of Hermias, another former student of Plato's who had become King of Assos. Aristotle and Pythias had a daughter. Ten years later, Pythias died, and Aristotle married Herpyllis. They had a son, Nicomachus. In 343 B.C., Philip of Macedon invited Aristotle to tutor his thirteen-year-old son, Alexander, who was to become Alexander the Great.

Soon after the death of Philip, Aristotle returned to Athens and began his own school, the Lyceum. In adjacent buildings, Aristotle assembled a large library and a museum of natural history with the help of a grant of money from Alexander and specimens that Alexander had sent in from around his empire. Aristotle worked at the Lyceum for twelve or thirteen years, producing most of the works that survive to this day in the form of lecture notes. As a consequence of anti-Macedonian feeling that swept through Greece after the death of Alexander, Aristotle was accused of impiety (one of the two charges that had been brought against Socrates). Aristotle left Athens lest, as he is said to have put it, the Athenians sin a second time against philosophy. He died, at age sixty-two, in Chalis one year later in 322 B.C. of a stomach ailment. He left

51

behind a will in which he generously provided for Herpyllis and their son, and his daughter by Pythias, and for the emancipation of his four slaves and their children. He also requested to be buried beside his first wife, Pythias.

The first selection is from Aristotle's *Nicomachean Ethics* (named after his son who is supposed to have edited these notes). In this selection, Aristotle tries to provide ethics with a firm foundation. He begins by noting that all human activity aims at some good. He then argues that for humans, happiness is the ultimate good, but that happiness is wrongly thought to consist simply in pleasure, wealth, and honor. Rightly understood, Aristotle argues, happiness is the activity of the soul exhibiting the best and most complete excellence of virtue. He further argues that happiness also requires certain external goods like friends, wealth, political power, good birth, children, and beauty. Aristotle goes on to define virtue as a state of character that is a mean between two vices, one of defect, the other of excess. For example, liberality is a virtue that is a mean between meanness, a vice of defect, and extravagance, a vice of excess; courage is a mean between cowardliness, a vice of defect, and rashness, a vice of excess. However, Aristotle allows that not every action or passion admits of a mean. For example, he thinks that the actions of adultery, theft, and murder are always wrong, whatever their consequences.

While Aristotle identifies happiness with virtuous activity, it is not clear how these two things can or should be identified. Thus, imagine that you are engaged in the following dialogue with Aristotle:

YOU: Why should I be virtuous?

A: Well, we agree, don't we, that it is a good thing to be happy?

YOU: Suppose we do.

A: It turns out that being virtuous will make you happy. So that is why you should be virtuous.

YOU: But according to the ordinary notion of happiness, it seems possible to be happy without always being virtuous.

A: But as I define happiness, being happy is the same as being virtuous.

YOU: But then doesn't my original question return in a different form? Why should I seek happiness in your sense and thereby always be virtuous rather than seek happiness in the ordinary sense and only sometimes be virtuous?

A: That is an interesting objection.

YOU: Things are even more complicated than I have indicated so far. With respect to the ordinary notion of happiness, what makes you happy can make other people unhappy, and so the question arises: Whose happiness should you pursue, yours or theirs?

A: But as I define happiness this can never happen. When happiness and virtue are interdefined, there are no conflicts between one person's happiness and the happiness of others.

YOU: But given your definition of happiness, we can still ask the question: Why should I strive to be happy/virtuous in your sense of the term, when it may not make me happy or may not make others happy in the ordinary sense of the term?

A: That is another interesting objection.

Does Aristotle have adequate responses to these objections? What do you think?

The second selection is from Aristotle's *Politics*. Here Aristotle argues that in nature, it is proper for one's soul to rule over one's body, for humans to rule over other animals, and for males to rule over females. In all these cases, the ruler/ruled relationship is for the common good, claims Aristotle. It follows for Aristotle that since natural slaves participate in reason only insofar as they recognize it but do not possess it, they can be properly ruled. Here too the ruler/ruled relationship is supposedly for the common good. The justification for ruling, then, is that the deliberative faculty is not present at all in slaves, in females it is present but ineffective, and in children present but undeveloped.

Aristotle's views about women and slaves were very widely held in the classical world; still there were well-known exceptions, and one of these was Musonius Rufus. Musonius was born of an Etruscan family in the town of Volsinii, probably sometime before 30 A.D. He is considered to be one of the founders of Stoic philosophy. In his time, he was compared to Socrates, both in his life and work; modern scholars sometimes refer to him as "the Roman Socrates."[1] As a prominent Stoic philosopher, he fell out of favor with Nero and was executed sometime before 101 A.D. One of the stories that has come down to us about him is that when he was lying chained in the prison of Nero, a friend communicated with him, inquiring what he might do to secure his release. Musonius acknowledged his friend's thoughtfulness, yet politely but firmly refused assistance. When his friend replied, "Socrates the Athenian refused to be released by his friends, and consequently went to trial and was put to death," Musonius answered, "Socrates was put to death because he did not take the trouble to defend himself, but I intend to make my defense."[2]

Like Socrates, Musonius left no writings of his own. His views, as we have them, come only from reports of his discussions written down many years later by his students. A distinctive feature of Musonius's views is his argument for equality between women and men found in the selection exerpted here. Obviously, from a feminist perspective, there is much to appreciate in Musonius's views.

In "Women, Slaves, and 'Love of Toil' in Aristotle's Moral Philosophy," Eve Browning Cole argues that for Aristotle the virtuous woman is industrious and hardworking, whereas the virtuous (free) man strives to avoid productive labor as much as possible. Cole also argues that in Aristotle's own theory, the inability to deliberate, which he takes to be characteristic of slaves, and the inability to have one's deliberations carry authority into action, which he takes to be characteristic of women, are actually failures of education. This is because in Aristotle's own theory, phronesis or practical wisdom, which is the authority imparted to our practical reasoning power, emerges only through a process of education. So why then didn't Aristotle propose an educational program for slaves and women to overcome their deficiencies? Cole speculates that it was the economic importance of the labor of women and slaves to (free) men that kept Aristotle and others from exploring this possibility.

All we know about the identity of Chaung Tzu, who lived from 369 to 288 B.C., is that his personal name was Chou and that he was a native of a place in China called Meng, probably near present day Honan, and that he once served as "an official in a lacquer garden." *The Book of Chaung* from which our selection is drawn is the second most famous text of classical Taoism after the *Tao Te Ching* of Lao Tsu, but it is unclear exactly what parts of the book Chaung actually wrote. What is clear is that the book seeks to provide an alternative to the Confucian and other schools of philosophy that were dominant at the time. A central idea of the book, brought out in the selection, is the need to free oneself from the baggage of conventional values to follow the way (Tao) of nature. In this respect, *The Book of Chaung Tzu* contrasts sharply with Aristotle's work, given that Aristotle was seeking, for the most part, to articulate and provide a justification for the conventional values of his time.

NOTES

1. Cora E. Lutz, Musonius Rufus: 'The Roman Socrates,'" *Yale Classical Studies* (1947) pp. 3–117; R. Hirzel, *Der Dialog,* (Leipzig, 1985) II, p. 239.
2. Lutz, p. 3.

4. NICOMACHEAN ETHICS

ARISTOTLE

BOOK I, CHAPTER 1

Every science and every investigation, and likewise every practical pursuit and undertaking, appears to aim at some good: and consequently the good has been well defined as the object at which all things aim. It is true that a certain variety can be observed among the ends aimed at; sometimes the mere activity of practising the pursuit is the object of pursuing it, whereas in other cases the end aimed at is some product over and above the pursuit itself; and in the pursuits that aim at certain objects besides their mere practice, those products are essentially superior in value to the activities that produce them. But as there are numerous pursuits and sciences and branches of knowledge, it follows that the ends at which they aim are correspondingly numerous. Medicine aims at producing health, naval architecture at building ships, strategic science at winning victories, economics at acquiring wealth. And many pursuits of this sort are subordinate to some single faculty—for instance bitmaking and the other departments of the harness trade are subordinate to the art of horsemanship, and the latter together with every other military activity to the science of strategies, and similarly other arts to different arts again. Now in all these cases the ends of the master sciences are of higher value than the objects of the subordinate ones, the latter being only pursued for the sake of the former. Nor does it make any difference whether the end aimed at by the pursuit is the mere activity of pursuing it or something else besides this, as in the case of the sciences mentioned.

If, therefore, among the ends at which our conduct aims there is one which we will for its own sake, whereas we will the other ends only for the sake of this one, and if we do not choose everything for the sake of some other thing—that would clearly be an endless process, making all desire futile and idle—it is clear that this one ultimate end will be the good, and the greatest good. Then will not a knowledge of this ultimate end be of more than theoretic interest? Will it not also have great practical importance for the conduct of life? Shall we not be more likely to attain our needs if like archers we have a target before us to aim at? If this be so, an attempt must be made to ascertain at all events in outline what precisely this supreme good is, and under which of the theoretical or practical sciences it falls.

Now it would be agreed that it must be the subject of the most authoritative of the sciences—the one that is in the fullest sense of the term a master-craft. This term clearly describes the science of politics, since it is that which ordains which of the sciences ought to exist in states and what branches of knowledge the various classes of citizens must study and up to what point; we observe that even the most highly esteemed faculties, such as strategies and domestic economy and oratory, are subordinate to political science. As then this science employs the rest of the sciences, and as it moreover lays down laws prescribing what people are to do and what things they are to abstain from, the end of political science must comprise the ends, of the other sciences. Consequently the good of man must be

Reprinted from *Nicomachean Ethics*, Bk. I–II, by permission of Blackwell Publishers (1989).

the subject pursued by the science of politics. No doubt it is true that the good is the same for the individual and for the state; but still the good of the state is manifestly a greater and more perfect object both to ascertain and to secure. To procure the good of only a single individual is better than nothing; but to effect the good of a nation or a state is a nobler and more divine achievement.

This then being the object of our present investigation, it is in a sense the science of politics.

The present investigation therefore, as directed to these objects, may be termed Political Science.

Our treatment of this science will be adequate if it achieves the degree of accuracy that is appropriate to the subject. The same amount of precision is not requisite in every department of philosophy, any more than in every product of the arts and crafts. Questions of right and of justice, which are the matters investigated by Political Science, involve much difference of opinion and much uncertainty; indeed this has given rise to the view that such things are mere conventions, and not realities in the order of nature. There is a similar uncertainty as to the meaning of the term 'good', owing to the fact that good things may often lead to harmful consequences; before now people have been ruined by wealth, and courage has been the undoing of others. Therefore in dealing with subjects and starting from conceptions so indefinite we must be content to obtain no more than a rough outline of the truth, and to reach conclusions which, like the matters dealt with and the principles postulated, have merely general validity. And accordingly the reader likewise must accept the various views propounded in the same spirit. It is the mark of an educated mind to expect that degree of precision in each department which the nature of the subject allows: to demand rigorous demonstration from a political orator is on a par with accepting plausible probabilities from a mathematician. Also a man judges correctly about matters that are within his personal knowledge, and of these he is a competent student. Conse-

quently while a specialist can make judgements as to his own particular subject it requires a person of all-round education to form competent judgements about things in general. That is why a young man is not a competent student of political science,[1] because he has had no practical experience of the affairs of life, which supply the premises and form the subjects of political theory. Moreover, as he is liable to be guided by his emotions it will be waste of time for him to attend lectures on Ethics. He will get no profit from them, inasmuch as the real object of ethical instruction is not to impart knowledge but to influence conduct. Nor does it make any difference whether the student is young in years or immature in character; his deficiency is not a matter of age but is due to his living his life and pursuing his various aims under the guidance of emotion. For the immature, ethical study is of no value, any more than it is for persons deficient in self-control; but those who regulate their aims and guide their conduct by principle may derive great benefit from the science.

So much by way of preface in regard to the student and to the manner in which our discourse is to be received and the object which we have in view.

To resume: inasmuch as all study and all deliberate action is aimed at some good object, let us state what is the good which is in our view the aim of political science, and what is the highest of the goods obtainable by action.

Now as far as the name goes there is virtual agreement about this among the vast majority of mankind. Both ordinary people and persons of trained mind define the good as happiness. But as to what constitutes happiness opinions differ; the answer given by ordinary people is not the same as the verdict of the philosopher. Ordinary men identify happiness with something obvious and visible, such as pleasure or wealth or honour—everybody gives a different definition, and sometimes the same person's own definition alters: when a man has fallen ill he thinks that happiness is health, if he is poor he thinks it is wealth. And when people realize their own ignorance they regard with admiration those who propound some grand theory that is above their heads. The view has been held by some thinkers[2] that besides the many good things alluded to above there also exists something that is good in itself, which is the fundamental cause of the goodness of all the others.

Now to review the whole of these opinions would perhaps be a rather thankless task. It may be enough to examine those that are most widely held, or that appear to have some considerable argument in their favour.

But it is important for us to realize that there is a difference between lines of argument which proceed *from* first principles and those that lead *to* first principles. This was a point properly raised by Plato, who used to ask the question whether the right method is to work down from, or work up to, first principles—just as on a racecourse the runners are either going out from the start to the turning-point at the end of the track or coming back to the finish. A line of argument necessarily starts from something known; but the term 'known' has two meanings: some things are known to us, other things are known absolutely. Now presumably we for our part are bound to start from things known to us. Consequently in order to be a competent student of questions of right and justice and of political matters in general, the pupil must himself have been trained in good habits of conduct; for one has to start from facts; and if these be sufficiently clear there will be no need for reasons in addition. The student trained in right conduct knows the principles already, or can easily acquire them. As for one who has neither qualification, let him listen to the verses of Hesiod:

Best is the man who can himself advise;
He too is good who hearkeneth to the wise.
But whoso, being witless, cannot heed
Another's wisdom, is a dolt indeed![3]

But to resume. To judge by men's mode of living, the mass of mankind think that good and happiness consist in pleasure, and consequently are content with a life of mere enjoyment. There are in fact three principal modes of life—the one just mentioned, the life of active citizenship, and the life of contemplation. The masses, being utterly servile, obviously prefer the life of mere cattle; and indeed they have some reason for this, inasmuch as many men of high station share the tastes of Sardanapallus.[4] The better people, on the other hand, and men of action, give the highest value to honour, since honour may be said to be the object aimed at in a public career. Nevertheless, it would seem that honour is a more superficial thing than the good which we are in search of, because honour seems to depend more on the people who render it than on the person who receives it, whereas we dimly feel that good must be something inherent in oneself and inalienable. Moreover men's object in pursuing honour appears to be to convince themselves of their own worth; at all events they seek to be honoured by persons of insight and by people who are well acquainted with them, and to be honoured for their merit. It therefore seems that at all events in the opinions of these men goodness is more valuable than honour, and probably one may suppose that it has a better claim than honour to be deemed the end at which the life of politics aims. But even virtue appears to lack completeness as an end, inasmuch as it seems to be possible to possess it while one is asleep or living a life of perpetual inactivity, and moreover one can be virtuous and yet suffer extreme sorrow and misfortune; but nobody except for the sake of maintaining a paradox would call a man happy in those circumstances.

However, enough has been said on this topic which has indeed been sufficiently discussed in popular treatises.[5]

The third life is the life of contemplation, which we shall consider later.

The life of money-making is a cramped way of living, and clearly wealth is not the good we are in search of, as it is only valuable as a means to something else. Consequently a stronger case might be made for the objects previously specified, because they are valued for their own sake; but even they appear to be inadequate, although a great deal of discussion has been devoted to them.

What then is the precise nature of the practicable good which we are investigating? It appears to be one thing in one occupation or profession and another in another: the object pursued in medicine is different from that of military science, and similarly in regard to the other activities. What definition of the term 'good' then is applicable to all of them? Perhaps 'the object for the sake of attaining which all the subsidiary activities are undertaken'. The object pursued in the practice of medicine is health, in a military career victory, in architecture a building—one thing in one pursuit and another in another, but in every occupation and every pursuit it is the end aimed at, since it is for the sake of this that the subsidiary activities in all these pursuits are undertaken. Consequently if there is some one thing which is the end and aim of all practical activities whatsoever, that thing, or if there are several, those things, will constitute the practicable good.

Our argument has therefore come round again by a different route to the point reached before. We must endeavour to render it yet clearer.

Now the objects at which our actions aim are manifestly several, and some of these objects, for instance, money, and instruments in general, we adopt as means to the attainment of something else. This shows that not all the objects we pursue are final ends. But the greatest good manifestly is a final end. Consequently if there is only one thing which is final, that will be the object for which we are now seeking, or if there are several, it will be that one among them which possesses the most complete finality.

Now a thing that is pursued for its own sake we pronounce to be more final than one pursued as a means to some other things, and a thing that is never desired for the sake of something else we call more final than those which are desired for the sake of something else as well as for their own sake. In fact the absolutely final is something that is always desired on its own account and never as a means for obtaining something else. Now this description appears to apply in the highest degree to happiness, since we always desire happiness for its own sake and never on account of something else; whereas honour and pleasure and intelligence and each of the virtues, though we do indeed desire them on their own account as well, for we should desire each of them even if it produced no external result, we also desire for the sake of happiness, because we believe that they will bring it to us, whereas nobody desires happiness for the sake of those things, nor for anything else but itself.

The same result seems to follow from a consideration of the subject of self-sufficiency, which is felt to be a necessary attribute of the final good. The term self-sufficient denotes not merely being sufficient for oneself alone, as if one lived the life of a hermit, but also being sufficient for the needs of one's parents and children and wife, and one's friends and fellow-countrymen in general, inasmuch as man is by nature a social being.

Yet we are bound to assume some limit in these relationships, since if one extends the connection to include one's children's children and friends' friends, it will go on *ad infinitum*. But that is a matter which must be deferred for later consideration. Let us define self-sufficiency as the quality which makes life to be desirable and lacking in nothing even when considered by itself; and this quality we assume to belong to happiness. Moreover when we pronounce happiness to be the most desirable of all things, we do not mean that it stands as one in a list of good things—were it so, it would obviously be more desirable in combination with even the smallest of the other goods, inasmuch as that addition would increase the total of good, and of two good things the larger must always be the more desirable.

Thus it appears that happiness is something

final and complete in itself, as being the aim and end of all practical activities whatever.

Possibly, however, the student may feel that the statement that happiness is the greatest good is a mere truism, and he may want a clearer explanation of what the precise nature of happiness is. This may perhaps be achieved by ascertaining what is the proper function of man. In the case of flute-players or sculptors or other artists, and generally of all persons who have a particular work to perform, it is felt that their good and their well-being are found in that work. It may be supposed that this similarly holds good in the case of a human being, if we may assume that there is some work which constitutes the proper function of a human being as such. Can it then be the case that whereas a carpenter and a shoemaker have definite functions or businesses to perform, a man as such has none, and is not designed by nature to perform any function? Should we not rather assume that, just as the eye and hand and foot and every part of the body manifestly have functions assigned to them, so also there is a function that belongs to a man, over and above all the special functions that belong to his members? If so, what precisely will that function be? It is clear that the mere activity of living is shared by man even with the vegetable kingdom, whereas we are looking for some function that belongs specially to man. We must therefore set aside the vital activity of nutrition and growth. Next perhaps comes the life of the senses; but this also is manifestly shared by the horse and the ox and all the animals. There remains therefore what may be designated the practical life of the rational faculty.

But the term 'rational' life has two meanings: it denotes both the mere possession of reason, and its active exercise. Let us take it that we here mean the latter, as that appears to be the more proper signification of the term. Granted then that the special function of man is the active exercise of the mind's faculties in accordance with rational principle, or at all events not in

detachment from rational principle, and that the function of anything, for example, a harper, is generally the same as the function of a good specimen of that thing, for example a good harper (the specification of the function merely being augmented in the latter case with the statement of excellence—a harper is a man who plays the harp, a good harper one who plays the harp well)—granted, I say, the truth of these assumptions, it follows that the good of man consists in the active exercise of the faculties in conformity with excellence or virtue, or if there are several virtues, in conformity with the best and most perfect among them.

Moreover, happiness requires an entire lifetime. One swallow does not make a summer, nor does a single fine day; and similarly one day or a brief period of prosperity does not make a man supremely fortunate and happy.

Let this then stand as a first sketch of the good, since perhaps our right procedure is to begin by drawing a preliminary outline, and then to fill in the details later on. Given a good outline to start with, it would seem to be within anybody's capacity to carry on, and to put in all the details. In discovering these time is a good collaborator; and that is in fact the way in which advances in the arts and crafts have actually been achieved, as anybody is capable of filling in the gaps.

It is also important to bear in mind the warning already given, that we must not expect the same degree of accuracy in every department of study, but only so much precision as corresponds with the nature of the particular subject and is proper to the enquiry in hand. A carpenter and a mathematician employ different methods of finding a right angle; the carpenter only aims at such degree of accuracy as is necessary for his work, but the mathematician must arrive at the essential nature and qualities of a right angle, inasmuch as he is a student of truth. In other matters also therefore one must follow the same method, in order that the main task in hand may not be outbalanced by side issues. Nor should we in the case of everything alike expect a statement of the cause *why* the thing is so; in some cases it is enough if we achieve a satisfactory demonstration of the fact *that* it is so. This holds good in regard to first principles: the fact *is* a first principle, a point to start from.

Moreover, first principles are apprehended in various ways, some by the method of induction, some by direct intuition and some by a sort of familiarization: different methods are used in different cases, and we must endeavour to arrive at each first principle by the method appropriate to its particular nature. Also extreme care must be taken to define the first principles correctly, as they have a most important influence on the subsequent course of the argument. To make a right beginning is more than half the battle, and to start from the right first principle throws light straight away on many of the problems under investigation.

Accordingly, we must examine our first principle[6] not only as a logical conclusion deduced from given premises but also in the light of the opinions currently put forward with regard to it, inasmuch as if a theory is correct, all the data of experience will be in harmony with it, but if it is false they are quickly found to clash with it.

Goods then have been classified in three groups—external goods, goods of the body and goods of the mind; and of these we pronounce the goods of the mind to be good in the most important sense and in the highest degree. But our definition of happiness identifies it with goods of the mind, and so is at all events supported by the classification of good referred to, which has held the field for a long time and is accepted by philosophers.

Our theory is also correct in speaking of the aim and end as consisting in particular modes of conduct or activities, since this classes happiness among the goods of the mind and not among external goods. And it is in agreement with the popular phrase describing the happy man as a man who 'lives well' or 'does well', since our for-mula virtually defines happiness as a form of good living and good conduct.

Indeed the happy man as we describe him appears to possess all the qualifications that are deemed requisite for happiness. Some people identify happiness with virtue, others with prudence or wisdom of some kind, and others with these things or one of them accompanied by pleasure, or not devoid of pleasure; others also include material prosperity. Some of these definitions are widely held and have been current for a long time; others are put forward by a few eminent thinkers. It is not reasonable to suppose that either can be entirely mistaken, but it is probable that the accepted definitions are at least partly, or indeed mainly, correct.

Now our formula agrees with the view that identifies happiness with excellence, or with some particular virtue, inasmuch as activity conforming with excellence presupposes excellence in the agent. Perhaps however it makes an important difference whether the greatest good is judged to consist in possessing excellence or in employing it—whether it is classed as a quality of character or as the exercise of a quality in action. A man may possess a good quality without its producing any good effect, for instance when he is asleep or has in some other way ceased to function; but active virtue cannot be inoperative, since if present it will necessarily be exercised in action, and in good action. The garlands at the Olympic games are not awarded to the handsomest and strongest men present but to the handsomest and strongest who enter for the competitions, as it is among these that the winners are found. Similarly it is people who act rightly that win distinction and credit in life.

Moreover the life of active virtue is intrinsically pleasant. To feel pleasure is a psychological, not a physical experience; and when a man is described as being a 'lover' of so and so, it means that the thing in question gives him pleasure: for instance a lover of horses derives pleasure from a horse, and a lover of the theatre from a play; and similarly a lover of justice derives pleasure from just actions, and a lover of virtue from good actions in general. In most cases people's pleasures conflict with one another, because they are not natural pleasures; but lovers of what is noble take pleasure in things that are by nature pleasant, and such is virtuous conduct, so that it is intrinsically pleasant as well as pleasant to them.

In consequence of this their life has no need of pleasure as an external appendage; it contains pleasures within itself. For in addition to what has been said, if a man does not enjoy performing noble actions he is not a good man at all. Nobody would call a man just who did not enjoy acting justly, nor liberal if he did not enjoy acting liberally, and similarly with the other virtues. But if this is so, actions in conformity with virtue will be intrinsically pleasant. Moreover, they are also good and noble; and good and noble in the highest degree, inasmuch as the virtuous man must be a good judge of these matters, and his judgement is as we have said.

Consequently happiness is at once the best and the noblest and the pleasantest thing there is, and these qualities do not exist in separate compartments, as is implied by the inscription at Delos:

The noblest thing is justice, health the best,
But getting your desire the pleasantest.

For all these qualities are combined in the highest activities, and it is these activities or the best one among them which according to our definition constitutes happiness. All the same it is manifest that happiness requires external goods in addition, since it is impossible, or at all events difficult, to perform noble actions without resources. Many of them require the aid of friends and of wealth and power in the state. Also a lack of such advantages as good birth or a fine family of children or good looks is a blot on a man's supreme felicity. A very ugly man or one of low birth or without children cannot be classed as completely happy; and still less perhaps can a man whose children or friends are utterly base, or though worthy have died.

As we said then, happiness seems to require prosperity of this kind in addition; and this has led some people to identify happiness with good fortune.

This leads to the question whether happiness is something that can be acquired by study or by a course of training, or whether it comes to us by divine dispensation, or merely by chance.

Now if there is any other thing that comes to men as a gift of providence, it is reasonable to hold that happiness is given us by the gods, and more so than any other of man's possessions inasmuch as it is the best of them all. This however is perhaps a matter that belongs more properly to another line of enquiry. But even if happiness is not sent by the gods but acquired by virtue or by some process of study or training, it is nevertheless among the most divine things that exist; for it would seem that the prize of virtue must be the highest aim and end, and something divine and supremely felicitous.

It would also be something that is widely distributed, since everybody not incapable of virtue could acquire it by means of study and by effort. And if happiness thus acquired is a better thing than prosperity due to fortune, it is reasonable to assume that it can be won in this way, inasmuch as nature's order is planned on the best lines possible, as likewise are works of art and the various products of design, and especially those of the highest form of design. For the greatest and noblest of all matters to be attributable to mere chance would seem too great a violation of the harmony of things.

This definition of happiness also throws light on our question how happiness may be attained. We pronounced it to be the active exercise of the faculties on certain lines; whereas goods of the other kinds are only requisite as a foundation, or else serviceable as auxiliaries and for their utility as instruments.

Moreover this would be in agreement with what we said at the outset, when we laid it down that the end at which statesmanship aims is the highest good, and that the statesman's chief concern is to produce a certain type of character in the citizens, namely to make them good men and capable of noble action. This justifies our refusal to apply the term 'happy' to an ox, or a horse or any other animal, inasmuch as no animal is capable of taking part in activity of the kind indicated. For this reason a child also cannot be happy in the proper sense, as he is not old enough to engage in conduct of this nature. When we speak of children as happy we are merely congratulating them on their promise for the future. For happiness, as we said, complete excellence is requisite; and also a life prolonged to its full limit, inasmuch as in the course of a lifetime a great many reverses and accidents of all sorts may occur, and it is possible that the most prosperous man may encounter severe misfortunes in old age, as legend tells us was the case with Priam in the tale of Troy. No one applies the term happy to one who encounters such disasters and comes to such a miserable end as Priam.

Must we then pronounce no other human being either to be happy as long as he is alive? Must we, as Solon[7] puts it, 'first see the end'? And if we are indeed to make that rule, is it really true that a man can be happy when he is dead? Is not that a very curious thing to assert, especially for us who define happiness as a form of activity? If on the other hand we refuse to speak of a dead man as happy, and if Solon does not mean this, but that only when a man is dead, and not before, is it safe to congratulate him as finally beyond the reach of evils and misfortunes, yet even this is open to question. It is generally believed that both good and evil can befall a man when he is dead, just as they can happen to one who is still alive without his being aware of them—for instance, the bestowal of honour and of dishonour, and the successes and misfortunes of his children and descendants. In regard to these moreover a difficulty arises; it is possible that a man may have lived in complete happiness till

old age and have made an equally happy end, but that then a number of reverses may befall his descendants, some of whom may be good men and may enjoy a life in accordance with their deserts, but others the contrary; and these descendants may obviously stand in any degree of proximity to the ancestor in question. Now it would be strange if a dead man's condition altered together with that of his descendants, and if he became happy and miserable in turn; but it would also be strange if no cognizance at all of people's fortunes reached their forebears, even over a limited period.

However, we must return to the previous question raised, whether it is possible to pronounce a man happy before his death, as that may perhaps throw light on the problem before us now. It may be essential to see how a man's life ends, and perhaps even then he cannot be congratulated as being happy but only as having been happy previously. Yet surely it is paradoxical to say that happiness does not really belong to him at the time when he is in fact happy, and to refuse to call people happy while they are alive, on the ground that fortune may change, but we think of happiness as something stable and not easily liable to change, whereas the wheel of fortune often turns full circle in the same person's experience. It is clear that if we are to wait attendance on the changes of fortune we shall frequently apply the terms happy and miserable to the same person by turns, and so make out our happy man to be

Chameleon—hued, built on no firm foundation.

Or is it a complete mistake merely to wait in attendance on fortune? Good and evil do not consist in fortune's vicissitudes, although these do form a part of life, as we said. Happiness is controlled by activities in conformity with virtue and unhappiness by their opposite.

Moreover the difficulty now raised affords further support to our definition. No human actions possess such a degree of permanence as the active exercise of virtue. This appears to be more permanent than our possession of the various branches of knowledge; and even of these the most permanent are the more honourable, because men blest by fortune find their life in them most fully and most continuously. This indeed seems to be the reason why knowledge of this kind when once acquired is not easily forgotten. . . .

May we not then confidently define the happy man as 'the man who is engaged in virtuous activities and who is adequately equipped with external goods'? Or ought we to add, 'and who is destined to continue to live thus not for some chance period but throughout his whole lifetime, and to end his life correspondingly'? We must add this proviso because the future is hidden from us, and happiness as we define it is an aim and end, something possessing complete finality of every sort and kind. If this is so, it will be possible to ascribe felicity to persons still living who possess and are destined to continue to possess the blessings specified above—though of course we mean felicity on the human level. . . .

Happiness then we define as the active exercise of the mind in conformity with perfect goodness or virtue. It will therefore be necessary to investigate the nature of virtue, as to do so will contribute to our understanding the nature of happiness. Moreover it appears that the true statesman must have made a special study of virtue, because it is his aim to make the citizens good and law-abiding men. As an example of this we have the law-givers of Crete and of Sparta, and the other founders of constitutions recorded in history. But if the investigation of the nature of virtue is a duty of statesmanship, that investigation will clearly fit in with the original plan of this treatise.

Now obviously the virtue which we have to investigate is human virtue, inasmuch as the good and the happiness which we set out to discover were human good and human happiness.

And by human virtue we mean not bodily excellence but goodness of the mind; and happiness also we define as an activity of the mind. This being so, it is clearly necessary for the statesman to have some acquaintance with psychology—just as the doctor in order to cure an affection of the eye or any other part of the body must know their anatomical structure. This background of science is even more essential for the statesman, inasmuch as statesmanship is a higher and more honourable profession than medicine; and even physicians of a high standard give a great deal of time to studying anatomy and physiology. Consequently the student of politics must study psychology, though he must study it for its bearing on politics, and only so far as is sufficient to throw light on the matters which fall to him to consider. To pursue it to a greater degree of precision would be a more laborious task than his purpose requires.

BOOK I, CHAPTER 2

Virtue, then, falls into two divisions, intellectual excellence and goodness of character. A good intellect is chiefly produced and fostered by education, and consequently requires experience and time, but moral goodness is formed mainly by training in habit. This shows that none of the moral virtues are implanted in us by nature, because natural characteristics can never be altered by training: for instance, a stone, which naturally moves downward, could not be trained to move upward even if one tried to accustom it to do so by throwing it up into the air ten thousand times; nor can a flame be trained to move downward, nor anything else that naturally acts in one way be educated to act in another way. Consequently the virtues are not formed in us by nature, but they result from our natural capacity to acquire them when that capacity has been developed by training.

Moreover in the case of the endowments given us by nature, we first receive the power of using them and exercise these powers in action subsequently. This is clear in the case of the sense faculties: we did not acquire our sight and hearing by repeatedly seeing and hearing things, but the other way round: we started in possession of those senses and then began to use them, we did not acquire them by using them. But we acquire the virtues by first acting virtuously, just as in the case of the arts and crafts: we learn these by actually doing the things that we shall have to do when we have learnt them—for instance men become builders by building houses and harpers by playing the harp. Similarly by acting justly we become just, by acting temperately we become self-controlled, and by acting bravely we become courageous.

This is confirmed by what occurs in the state. Lawgivers make the citizens good by training them in good habits—at least that is every legislator's intention; and those who fail as legislators are those who do not establish a good system of education. In this lies the difference between a good constitution and a bad one.

Moreover all excellence is both produced and destroyed by the same means. This is the case with the arts and crafts; both good harpers and bad harpers are made by playing on the harp, and the same with building and all the other trades—a man will become a good builder by building well and a bad one by building badly. Were this not so, there would be no need of a period of apprenticeship, but people would all be born either good tradesmen or else bad ones.

Similarly with the virtues: it is by actually transacting business with our fellow-citizens that some of us become honest and others dishonest; it is by encountering danger and forming a habit of being frightened or else of keeping up our courage that some of us become brave men and others cowards; and the same is the case in regard to indulging the appetites and giving way to anger—people become self-controlled and gentle, or self-indulgent and passionate, from behaving in the one way or in the other in the fields of conduct concerned. To sum up, habits of character are formed as the result of conduct of the same kind. Consequently it is essential for us to give a certain quality to our actions, since differences of conduct produce differences of character. Hence the formation of habits, good or bad, from early childhood up is not a matter of small moment; on the contrary it is something of very great or more truly speaking of the supremest importance.

The present investigation then, unlike our other studies, is not undertaken for the purpose of attaining knowledge in the abstract—we are not pursuing it in order to learn what virtue is but in order to become virtuous; otherwise it would be of no value. We are therefore bound to carry the enquiry further, and to ascertain the rules that govern right conduct, since, as we have said, our conduct determines our characters.

The rule of acting in conformity with right principle is generally accepted, and may be taken for granted. Let us also take it as agreed that ethics is not an exact science, any more than are medicine and the art of navigation; and consequently the rules of conduct that it lays down are only of general validity, and their application must vary with the circumstances of the particular occasion, and be modified by the discretion of the agent.

The first point to have in view then is that in matters of conduct both excess and deficiency are essentially detrimental. It is the same here as in the case of bodily health and strength. Our strength is impaired by taking too much exercise, and also by taking too little; and similarly too much and too little food and drink injure our health, while the right amount produces health and increases it and preserves it. This also applies to self-control and courage and the other virtues. The man who runs away from every danger and never stands his ground becomes a coward, and the man who is afraid of nothing whatever and walks into everything becomes foolhardy; and similarly one who partakes of every pleasure and refrains from no gratification becomes self-indulgent, while one who shuns all pleasures becomes a boor and a dullard. It follows that self-control and courage are impaired by excess and by deficiency and are preserved by moderation. . . .

. . . In the case of every whole that is divisible into parts, it is possible to take a larger or a smaller share of it, or an equal share; and those amounts may be measured either in relation to the thing itself or in relation to us. I mean that whereas the middle of an object is the point equally distant from each of its extremities, which is one and the same for everybody, the medium quantity in its relation to us is the amount that is not excessive and not deficient, and this is not the same for everybody. For instance, if ten is many and two is few, to take the actual middle amount between them gives six (because 6 is the arithmetical mean between 2 and 10: 6 − 2 = 10 − 6); but a medium quantity relative to us cannot be arrived at in this way. For instance, supposing that for an athlete in training ten pounds of food is too large a ration and two pounds too small, the trainer will not necessarily advise six pounds, as possibly that will be too large or too small an allowance for the particular person—a small ration for a Milo[1] but a large one for a novice in athletics; and the same applies to the amount of running or wrestling prescribed in training. This is how every expert avoids excess and deficiency and adopts the middle amount—not the exact half of the object he is dealing with, but a medium quantity in relation to the person concerned.

Such then is the manner in which every kind of skill operates successfully, by looking to the middle point and making its products conform with it. This accounts for the remark commonly made about successful productions, that you cannot take anything away from them or add anything to them. The implication is that excess and deficiency impair excellence, and a middle quantity secures it. If then we are right in saying that good craftsmen when at work keep their eyes fixed on a middle point, and if virtue, no less

than nature herself, surpasses all the arts and crafts in accuracy and excellence, it follows that excellence will be the faculty of hitting a middle point. I refer to moral excellence or virtue; and this is concerned with emotions and actions, in which it is possible to have excess, or deficiency, or a medium amount. For instance you can feel either more or less than a moderate amount of fear and boldness, and of desire and anger and pity, and of pleasant or painful emotions generally; and in both cases the feelings will be wrong. But to feel these emotions at the right time and on the right occasion and towards the right people and for the right motives and in the right manner is a middle course, and the best course; and this is the mark of goodness. And similarly there is excess and deficiency or a middle amount in the case of actions. Now it is with emotions and actions that virtue is concerned; excess and deficiency in them are wrong, and a middle amount receives praise and achieves success, both of which are marks of virtue. It follows that virtue is a sort of middle state, in the sense that it aims at the middle.

Moreover, though it is possible to go wrong in many ways (according to the conjecture of the Pythagorean school evil is a property of the infinite and good of the finite), it is only possible to go right in one way:

Goodness is one, but badness manifold.[2]

This is why to go wrong is easy but to go right difficult; it is easy to miss the target but difficult to hit it. Here then is another reason why vice is a matter of excess and deficiency and virtue a middle state.

It follows that virtue is a fixed quality of the will, consisting essentially in a middle state—middle in relation to ourselves, and as determined by principle, by the standard that a man of practical wisdom would apply. And it is a middle state between two vices, one of excess and one of deficiency: and this in view of the fact that vices either exceed or fall short of the right amount in emotions or actions, whereas virtue ascertains the mean and chooses that. Consequently while in its essence and by the principle defining its fundamental nature virtue is a middle state, in point of excellence and rightness it is an extreme.

But not every action or every emotion admits of a middle state: the very names of some of them suggest wickedness—for instance spite,[3] shamelessness, envy, and among actions, adultery, theft, murder; all of these and similar emotions and actions are blamed as being wicked intrinsically and not merely when practised to excess or insufficiently. Consequently it is not possible ever to feel or commit them rightly: they are always wrong, nor are the qualifications 'well' or 'ill' applicable to them—for instance, you cannot commit adultery with the right woman and at the right time and in the right place: the mere commission of adultery with any woman anywhere at any time is an offence. Similarly it is equally erroneous to think that there can be a middle amount and an excess and a deficiency of injustice or cowardice or self-indulgence, as that would mean that you can have a medium quantity of excess and deficiency or too much excess or too little deficiency. So just as there is no such thing as an excess or a deficiency of self-control and courage, because in these the middle is in a sense the top point, so there can be no middle amount or excess or deficiency of self-indulgence or cowardice, but actions of that sort however committed are an offence. There is no such thing as a medium amount of excess or deficiency, nor an excessive or insufficient amount of observance of a mean.

It is not enough, however, merely to give a general definition of moral goodness; it is necessary to show how our definition applies to particular virtues. In theories of conduct although general principles have a wider application, particular rules are more accurate, inasmuch as actual conduct deals with particular cases, and theory must be in agreement with these. Let us then take the particular virtues and vices from the diagram.[4]

The middle state as regards fear and boldness is courage. Excessive fearlessness has no name (as is the case with many types of character); excessive boldness is called rashness, and excessive fear and insufficient boldness cowardice.

In regard to pleasure, and in a less degree to pain, the middle state is self-control,[5] and the excess self-indulgence.[6] Persons deficient in sensibility to pleasure are scarcely to be found, so that this class has no recognized name; they may however be called insensitive.

The middle disposition in respect of giving and getting money is liberality; the excess and the deficiency are extravagance and meanness, both of these vices in opposite ways displaying both excess and deficiency—the extravagant man exceeds in spending money and is deficient in acquiring it, and the mean man exceeds in acquiring money but is deficient in spending it.

We are for the present giving a description of these characters in outline only, as that is sufficient for our present purpose. A more detailed account of them will be given later.

There are also other dispositions in regard to money—the middle state called munificence (which is not the same as liberality, as munificence is concerned with large sums of money whereas liberality is displayed in dealing with minor amounts), the excess which is tasteless vulgarity and the deficiency shabbiness in the use of money; the differences between the two latter will be stated later, and also two extremes corresponding with liberality.

The middle state in regard to honour and dishonour is pride;[7] the excess is called conceit and the deficiency lack of spirit. There is another middle state which stands in the same relation to pride as that which was described as existing between generosity and munificence: pride being concerned with high honours, the state indicated is similarly concerned with minor honours. These also may be desired in a proper manner, or more than is proper, or less. The man who covets them to excess is called ambitious and the man who is too little desirous of them unambitious; but there is no name for the person in between, who has a proper desire for such honours. Consequently the two extremes both lay claim to the middle place; and in fact in our ordinary use of the words we sometimes call a man of middle character in this respect ambitious and sometimes unambitious: both words are occasionally employed as terms of approval.

The reason for this ambiguity will be stated later. For the present let me speak about the remaining characters, in pursuance of our plan.

There are also excess and deficiency and a middle disposition in regard to anger, but there are virtually no accepted names to denote them. However, we speak of the person of intermediate character in regard to anger as good-tempered, so let us call the middle state good temper; while of the two extremes the man who exceeds may be called irascible and his vice irascibility, and for the man who is deficient perhaps we may use the term spiritless, and call his deficiency lack of spirit.

There are also three other middle dispositions which somewhat resemble one another and yet are really distinct, as although they all are concerned with our daily intercourse with our fellows in conversation and in conduct, they differ in that one is a matter of sincerity in social intercourse and the others denote agreeableness, displayed either in hours of relaxation or in the business of life. These dispositions must also be dealt with, to bring it home to us that in all affairs the middle course is to be commended and the extremes are neither commendable nor right, but reprehensible.

These dispositions also for the most part have no names attached to them, but for the sake of clearness and to enable the reader to follow us more easily we must attempt to invent terms of our own to denote them, as we have done for the other dispositions.

In regard to sincerity, the middle person may be called frank and the middle disposition frankness. To exaggerate one's own merits is boastfulness and the person possessing that quality a boaster; to deprecate oneself is mock-modesty and the man who does so is mock-modest. In respect of being pleasant in giving amusement the middle person is witty and his characteristic wit; the excess is buffoonery and its possessor a boor. In regard to pleasantness in the affairs of life in general, one who is agreeable in the proper way is kindly and the middle state of character kindliness; one who is agreeable to excess is obsequious if it is for no interested motive and a toady if he hopes to get something out of it; one who is deficient in kindliness and always disagreeable in intercourse may be called churlish or surly.

There are also middle dispositions in respect of the emotions. In these also one man is said to be of a middle character, another excessive. There is the bashful man who is ashamed of everything, whereas another is deficient or entirely devoid of the emotion in question, who is impudent; while the middle character is called modest; though modesty is not a virtue, 'modest' is a term of commendation.

Righteous indignation is the middle state between envy and malice in regard to pain or pleasure at what happens to one's neighbours. The righteously indignant man is distressed when they prosper undeservedly; the jealous man goes further, and feels aggrieved at any prosperity of others; the malicious man is so far from feeling distress at other people's misfortunes that they give him actual pleasure.

There are then three kinds of dispositions, two of them vices, one a vice of excess and the other a vice of deficiency, and one a virtue, which is a middle state, and each of the three dispositions is in a manner opposed to both of the others: the extremes are the opposites of each other and the middle one is the opposite of each of the extremes—because just as in mathematics a is greater than $a - b$ and less than $a + \beta$, similarly middle dispositions of character are excessive as compared with the deficiencies and deficient as compared with the excesses. This holds good both of emotions and of actions. A brave man appears rash when compared with a coward and cowardly when compared with a rash man; and similarly a self-controlled man seems self-indulgent in comparison with a man insensitive to pleasure and pain but insensitive in comparison with a self-indulgent one, and a generous man extravagant in comparison with a mean man and mean in comparison with a spendthrift. Because of this people at either extreme push the man in the middle over to the other extreme—cowards call brave men rash and rash men call them cowardly, and similarly with the other types of character. But although the two extreme dispositions are opposed in this way to the middle one, it is the two extremes that are most widely opposed, as these are further away from each other than they are from the middle—just as in mathematics, if x, y and z are in descending order of magnitude, $x - z$ is greater than $x - y$ or $y - z$; and the things farthest apart from each other are defined as absolute opposites, so that the farther apart things are the more contrary they are.

Moreover in some cases there appears to be some resemblance between one of the extremes and the middle point—for instance, rashness is somewhat like courage and extravagance like liberality; whereas the extremes are most unlike each other. But it is things that are furthest apart from each other that are defined as contraries, so that things that are farther apart are more contrary.

In some cases there is more opposition between the deficiency and the middle point, in other cases between the excess and the middle—for example, the special opposite of courage is not rashness, which is the excess, but cowardice, which is the deficiency, and the special opposite of self-control is not insensitiveness, the deficiency, but extravagance, the excess. Of this there are two causes, one arising out of the facts of the case. If one of the two extremes appears to be closer than the other to the middle and to resemble it more, we do not consider it but rather the other one as the opposite of the mid-

dle. For instance, rashness seems to be more like courage and nearer to it and cowardice seems more unlike it; consequently we consider cowardice rather than rashness to be the opposite of courage, for the qualities that are farther away from the middle seem more contrary to it. The other cause is due to ourselves. The things to which we are more prone by our own nature seem more opposite to the middle: for instance, we are disposed by nature to enjoy pleasure, and consequently we are more liable to self-indulgence than we are to insensitiveness. So we speak of the things we are disposed by our nature to lapse into as more contrary to what is right: and consequently self-indulgence, which is a vice of excess, seems more contrary than insensitiveness to self-control.

It has now been shown that moral goodness is a middle state, and in what sense this is so—namely, that it is intermediate between two vices, one a vice of excess and the other a vice of deficiency; and that it holds this position in virtue of its quality of aiming to hit the middle point in emotions and in actions.

A consequence of this is that to be virtuous is no easy task. It is difficult to hit the middle point in anything—for instance, it takes a mathematician to find the centre of a circle. And similarly anybody can get angry—that is easy enough; and so is giving and spending money, but to bestow our money on the proper person and in the proper amount and at the proper time and for the proper motive and in the proper manner—all this is not within everybody's capacity, nor is it easy. Consequently right conduct is rare and praiseworthy and noble. The first rule in aiming at a middle course is to keep well away from that extreme which is the more opposite to it, as Calypso advises:[8]

Steer the ship wide of yonder spray and surge.

For of two extreme courses one is a greater mistake than the other. Inasmuch then as to hit the mean is extremely difficult, we must sail the second best way,[9] as they say, and the best method of doing this will be the one that we describe.

The second rule is to notice what are the errors to which we are ourselves most prone. Some of us have a natural tendency to one fault and others to another, and we can discover what our tendencies are from the pleasure or pain that different things give us. Then we must drag ourselves away in the opposite direction: to steer clear of our besetting error will bring us into the middle course. This is how carpenters straighten out timber that is warped.

And thirdly we must in everything keep a most careful watch on pleasant things and pleasant feelings. When mistress Pleasure is on her trial, we the jury have been tampered with. Our attitude towards her must be that of the Elders of Troy towards Helen;[10] on all occasions we must apply to Pleasure their remarks about Helen. We shall be less liable to go wrong if we just send her about her business.

These then, to sum up the matter, are the measures that will best enable us to hit the middle point. No doubt it is a difficult thing to do, especially in particular cases—for instance, it is difficult to define the conditions that justify getting angry: how we ought to show anger, and against whom, and on what occasion, and for how long. In fact we do sometimes praise those who are deficient in anger and call them good-tempered, and sometimes we applaud the hot-tempered for what we call their manliness.

A small departure from the right amount, either in the direction of excess or of deficiency, is not censured, though a wider divergence is bound to be noticed. Still it is not easy to give a formula defining the limit—*how wide* a divergence is reprehensible. No more indeed is any other matter of direct observation easy to define; such questions of degree depend on the particular circumstances, and can only be judged by intuition.

This much then is clear, that the middle course in everything is commendable, but that we should diverge sometimes towards excess and sometimes towards deficiency, as that is the easiest way of hitting the middle course, which is the right one.

NOTES TO BOOK I, CHAPTER 1

1. This dictum floated down to Shakespeare, *Troilus and Cressida* II, ii 165:

   Most like young men, whom Aristotle thought unfit to hear moral philosophy.

2. Plato and the Academy.
3. From *Works and Days,* an early agricultural epic.
4. A mythical Assyrian king; two versions of his epitaph are recorded, one containing the words 'Eat, drink, play, since all else is not worth that snap of the fingers,' the other ending 'I have what I ate, and the delightful deeds of wantonness and love in which I shared; but all my wealth is vanished.'
5. There follows a technical refutation, omitted in this version, of Plato's Theory of Ideas as a basis for ethics.
6. I.e., the definition of happiness given above.
7. Herodotus I, 30-3. The famous sage visited Croesus, king of Sardis, and was shown his treasures, but refused to call him the happiest of mankind while he was still alive and therefore still liable to misfortune. 'It is necessary to see the end of every matter, and to discover how it is going to turn out; for to many men God has given a glimpse of prosperity and then has destroyed them root and branch.'

NOTES TO BOOK I, CHAPTER 2

1. A famous wrestler.
2. A quotation from an unknown poem.
3. *Schadenfreude,* delight in the misfortunes of other people.
4. It appears that the lecturer here exhibited a table in which the virtues in the various fields of emotion and action were displayed as lying halfway between the two extremes of excess and deficiency in each. This is developed in detail in the latter part of chapter III and in chapter IV.
5. The Greek term, literally 'soundmindedness', was represented in Latin by *temperantia,* and is commonly rendered 'temperance'.

6. The usual translation 'profligacy' is too strong. The adjective means literally 'unchastized', and it was applied to naughty children.

7. The Greek term means literally 'greatness of soul', but that expression bears a different shade of meaning in English from what it suggests in Greek. It was rendered in Latin by *magnanimitas,* but our 'magnanimity' again is different. As is seen in Book VI, the Greek word means lofty and dignified pride, justified by real distinction of character and position.

8. I.e., advises the helmsman of Odysseus sailing through the Straits of Messina between Scylla and Charybdis, *Odyssey* XII, 219: but as a matter of fact it was Circe who had warned Odysseus, and the line quoted is Odysseus's order to his crew.

9. I.e. when the wind drops or is contrary, lower sail and take to the oars. Compare our phrase 'Shanks's mare', meaning having to walk.

10. *Iliad* III, 156ff. 'No one can quarrel with the Trojans and the well-greaved Achaeans for enduring sorrow so long with such a woman as the prize. Truly she is fair of face as the immortal goddesses. But albeit she is so fair, nevertheless, let her depart on shipboard, and not remain to plague us and our children hereafter.'

5. POLITICS

ARISTOTLE

BOOK I

He who thus considers things in their first growth and origin, whether a state or anything else, will obtain the clearest view of them. In the first place there must be a union of those who cannot exist without each other; namely, of male and female, that the race may continue (and this is a union which is formed, not of choice, but because, in common with other animals and with plants, [humankind] have a natural desire to leave behind them an image of themselves), and of natural ruler and subject, that both may be preserved. For that which can foresee by the exercise of mind is by nature lord and master, and that which can with its body give effect to such foresight is a subject, and by nature a slave; hence master and slave have the same interest.

Now nature has distinguished between the female and the slave. For she is not . . . like the smith who fashions the Delphian knife for many uses; she makes each thing for a single use, and every instrument is best made when intended for one and not for many uses. But among barbarians no distinction is made between women and slaves, because there is no natural ruler among them: they are a community of slaves, male and female. That is why the poets say,—

It is meet that Hellenes should rule over barbarians;

as if they thought that the barbarian and the slave were by nature one.

Out of these two relationships the first thing to arise is the family, and Hesiod is right when he says,—

First house and wife and an ox for the plough,

for the ox is the poor man's slave. The family is

Reprinted from *The Politics,* Bk. I, B. Jowett (Oxford: Clarendon Press, 1905).

the association established by nature for the supply of men's everyday wants, and the members of it are called by Charondas, "companions of the cupboard," and by Epimenides the Cretan, "companions of the manger.". . .

For that some should rule and others be ruled is a thing not only necessary, but expedient; from the hour of their birth, some are marked out for subjection, others for rule. And there are many kinds both of rulers and subjects (and that rule is the better which is exercised over better subjects—for example, to rule over men is better than to rule over wild beasts; for the work is better which is executed by better workmen, and where one man rules and another is ruled, they may be said to have a work); for in all things which form a composite whole and which are made up of parts, whether continuous or discrete, a distinction between the ruling and the subject element comes to light. Such a duality exists in living creatures, originating from nature as a whole; even in things which have no life there is a ruling principle, as in a musical mode. But perhaps this is matter for a more popular investigation. A living creature consists in the first place of soul and body, and of these two, the one is by nature the ruler and the other the subject. But then we must look for the intentions of nature in things which retain their nature, and not in things which are corrupted. And therefore we must study the man who is in the most perfect state both of body and soul, for in him we shall see the true relation of the two; although in bad or corrupted natures the body will often appear to rule over the soul, because they are in an evil and unnatural condition. At all events we may firstly observe in living creatures both a despotical and a constitutional rule; for the soul rules the body with a despotical rule, whereas the intellect rules the appetites with a constitutional and royal rule. And it is clear that the rule of the soul over the body, and of the mind and the rational element over the passionate, is natural and expedient; whereas the equality of the two or the rule of the inferior is always hurtful. The same holds good of animals in relation to men; for tame animals have a better nature than wild and all tame animals are better off when they are ruled by man; for then they are preserved. Again the male is by nature superior, and the female inferior; and the one rules, and the other is ruled; this principle, of necessity, extends to all mankind. Where then there is such a difference as that between soul and body, or between men and animals (as in the case of those whose business is to use their body, and who can do nothing better), the lower sort are by nature slaves, and it is better for them as for all inferiors that they should be under the rule of a master. . . .

Of household management we have seen that there are three parts—one is the rule of a master over slaves, which has been discussed already, another of a father, and the third of a husband. A husband and father rules over wife and children, both free, but the rule differs, the rule over his children being a royal, over his wife a constitutional rule. For although there may be exceptions to the order of nature, the male is by nature fitter for command than the female, just as the elder and full-grown is superior to the younger and more immature. But in most constitutional states the citizens rule and are ruled by turns, for the idea of a constitutional state implies that the natures of the citizens are equal, and do not differ at all. Nevertheless, when one rules and the other is ruled we endeavour to create a difference of outward forms and names and titles of respect, which may be illustrated by the saying of Amasis about his foot-pan. The relation of the male to the female is of this kind, but there the inequality is permanent. The rule of a father over his children is royal, for he receives both love and the respect due to age, exercising a kind of royal power. And therefore Homer has appropriately called Zeus "father of Gods and men," because he is the king of them all. For a king is the natural superior of his subjects, but he should be of the same kin or kind with them, and such is the relation of elder and younger, of father and son.

Thus it is clear that household management attends more to men than to the acquisition of inanimate things, and to human excellence more than to the excellence of property which we call wealth, and to the virtue of freemen more than to the virtue of slaves. A question may indeed be raised, whether there is any excellence at all in a slave beyond merely instrumental and ministerial qualities—whether he can have the virtues of temperance, courage, justice, and the like; or whether slaves possess only bodily and ministerial qualities. And, whichever way we answer the question, a difficulty arises; for, if they have virtue, in what will they differ from freemen? On the other hand, since they are men and share in reason, it seems absurd to say that they have no virtue. A similar question may be raised about women and children, whether they too have virtues: ought a woman to be temperate and brave and just, and is a child to be called temperate, and intemperate, or not? So in general we may ask about the natural ruler, and the natural subject, whether they have the same or different virtues. For a noble nature is equally required in both, but if so, why should one of them always rule, and the other always be ruled? Nor can we say that this is a question of degree, for the difference between ruler and subject is a difference of kind, and therefore not of degree; yet how strange is the supposition that the one ought, and that the other ought not, to have virtue! For if the ruler is intemperate and unjust, how can he rule well? if the subject, how can he obey well? If he be licentious and cowardly, he will certainly not do his duty. It is evident, therefore, that both of them must have a share of virtue, but varying according to their various natures. And this is at once indicated by the soul, in which one part naturally rules, and the other is subject, and the virtue of the ruler we maintain to be different from that of the subject;—the one being the virtue of the rational, and the other of the irrational part. Now, it is obvious that the same principle applies generally, and

therefore almost all things rule and are ruled according to nature. But the kind of rule differs;—the freeman rules over the slave after another manner from that in which the male rules over the female, or the man over the child; although the parts of the soul are present in all of them, they are present in different degrees. For the slave has no deliberative faculty at all; the woman has, but it is without authority,[1] and the child has, but it is immature. So it must necessarily be with the moral virtues also; all may be supposed to partake of them, but only in such manner and degree as is required by each for the fulfilment of his duty. Hence the ruler ought to have moral virtue in perfection, for his duty is entirely that of a master artificer, and the master artificer is reason; the subjects, on the other hand, require only that measure of virtue which is proper to each of them. Clearly, then, moral virtue belongs to all of them; but the temperance of a man and of a woman, or the courage and justice of a man and of a woman, are not, as Socrates maintained, the same; the courage of a man is shown in commanding, of a woman in obeying. And this holds of all other virtues, as will be more clearly seen if we look at them in detail, for those who say generally that virtue consists in a good disposition of the soul, or in doing rightly, or the like, only deceive themselves. Far better than such definitions is their mode of speaking, who, like Gorgias, enumerate the virtues. All classes must be deemed to have their special attributes; as the poet says of women,

Silence is a woman's glory,

but this is not equally the glory of man. The child is imperfect, and therefore obviously his virtue is not relative to himself alone, but to the perfect man and to his teacher,[2] and in like manner the virtue of the slave is relative to a master. Now we determined that a slave is useful for the wants of life, and therefore he will obviously require only so much virtue as will prevent him from failing in his duty through cowardice and intemperance. Someone will ask whether, if what we are saying is true, virtue will not be required also in the artisans, for they often fail in their work through misconduct? But is there not a great difference in the two cases? For the slave shares in his master's life; the artisan is less closely connected with him, and only attains excellence in proportion as he becomes a slave, [i.e., is under the direction of a master]. The meaner sort of mechanic has a special and separate slavery; and whereas the slave exists by nature, not so the shoemaker or other artisan. It is manifest, then, that the master ought to be the source of excellence in the slave; but not merely because he possesses the art which trains him in his duties. Wherefore they are mistaken who forbid us to converse with slaves and say that we should employ command only,[3] for slaves stand even more in need of admonition than children.

The relations of husband and wife, parent and child, their several virtues, what in their intercourse with one another is good, and what is evil, and how we may pursue the good and escape the evil, will have to be discussed when we speak of the different forms of government. For, inasmuch as every family is a part of a state, and these relationships are the parts of a family, the virtue of the part must have regard to the virtue of the whole. And therefore women and children must be trained by education with an eye to the state, if the virtues of either of them are supposed to make any difference in the virtues of the state. And they must make a difference: for the children grow up to be citizens, and half the free persons in a state are women.[4]

NOTES

1. Or, ineffective.
2. "His father who guides him" (Bernays).
3. Plato Laws, vi. 777.
4. Plato Laws, vi. 781 B.

6. DISCOURSES

MUSONIUS RUFUS

THAT MAN IS BORN WITH AN INCLINATION TOWARD VIRTUE

All of us, he used to say, are so fashioned by nature that we can live our lives free from error

Reprinted from *Discourses* II–IV, by permission of the Department of Classics, Yale University.

and nobly; not that one can and another cannot, but all. The clearest evidence of this is the fact that lawgivers lay down for all alike what may be done and forbid what may not be done, exempting from punishment no one who disobeys or does wrong, not the young nor the old, not the strong nor the weak, not anyone whomsoever. And yet if the whole notion of virtue were something that came to us from without, and we shared no part of it by birth, just as in activities pertaining to the other arts no one who has not learned the art is expected to be free from error, so in like manner in things pertaining to the conduct of life it would not be reasonable to expect anyone to be free from error who had not learned virtue, seeing that virtue is the only thing that saves us from error in daily living. Now in the care of the sick we demand no one but the physician to be free from error, and in handling the lyre no one but the musician, and in managing the helm no one but the pilot, but in the conduct of life it is no longer only the philosopher whom we expect to be free from error, though he alone would seem to be the only one concerned with the study of virtue, but all men alike, including those who have never given any attention to virtue. Clearly, then, there is no explanation for this other than that the human being is born with an inclination toward virtue. And this indeed is strong evidence of the presence of goodness in our nature, that all speak of themselves as having virtue and being good. For take the common man; when asked whether he is stupid or intelligent, not one will confess to being stupid; or again, when asked whether he is just or unjust, not one will say that he is unjust. In the same way, if one asks him whether he is temperate or intemperate, he replies at once that he is temperate; and finally, if one asks whether he is good or bad, he would say that he is good, even though he can name no teacher of virtue or mention any study or practice of virtue he has ever made. Of what, then, is this evidence if not of the existence of an innate inclination of the human soul toward goodness and nobleness, and of the presence of the seeds of virtue in each one of us? Moreover, because it is entirely to our advantage to be good, some of us deceive ourselves into thinking that we are really good, while others of use are ashamed to admit that we are not. Why then pray, when one who has not learned letters or music or gymnastics never claims to have knowledge of these arts nor makes any pretence of knowing them, and is quite unable even to name a teacher to whom he went, why, I say, does everyone profess that he has virtue? It is because none of those other skills is natural to man, and no human being is born with a natural facility for them, whereas an inclination toward virtue is inborn in each one of us.

THAT WOMEN TOO SHOULD STUDY PHILOSOPHY

When someone asked him if women too should study philosophy, he began to discourse on the theme that they should, in somewhat the following manner. Women as well as men, he said, have received from the gods the gift of reason, which we use in our dealings with one another and by which we judge whether a thing is good or bad, right or wrong. Likewise the female has the same senses as the male; namely sight, hearing, smell, and the others. Also both have the same parts of the body, and one has nothing more than the other. Moreover, not men alone, but women too, have a natural inclination toward virtue and the capacity for acquiring it, and it is the nature of women no less than men to be pleased by good and just acts and to reject the opposite of these. If this is true, by what reasoning would it ever be appropriate for men to search out and consider how they may lead good lives, which is exactly the study of philosophy, but inappropriate for women? Could it be that it is fitting for men to be good, but not for women? Let us examine in detail the qualities which are suitable for a woman who would lead a good life, for it will appear that each one of them would accrue to her most readily from the study of philosophy. In the first place, a woman must be a good housekeeper; that is a careful accountant of all that pertains to the welfare of her house and capable of directing the household slaves. It is my contention that these are the very qualities which would be present particularly in the woman who studies philosophy, since obviously each of them is a part of life, and philosophy is nothing other than knowledge about life, and the philosopher, as Socrates said, quoting

Homer, is constantly engaged in investigating precisely this: "Whatsoever of good and of evil is wrought in thy halls." But above all a woman must be chaste and self-controlled; she must, I mean, be pure in respect of unlawful love, exercise restraint in other pleasures, not be a slave to desire, not be contentious, not lavish in expense, nor extravagant in dress. Such are the works of a virtuous woman, and to them I would add yet these: to control her temper, not to be overcome by grief, and to be superior to uncontrolled emotion of every kind. Now these are the things which the teachings of philosophy transmit, and the person who has learned them and practices them would seem to me to have become a well-ordered and seemly character, whether man or woman. Well then, so much for self-control. As for justice, would not the woman who studies philosophy be just, would she not be a blameless life-partner, would she not be a sympathetic helpmate, would she not be an untiring defender of husband and children, and would she not be entirely free of greed and arrogance? And who better than the woman trained in philosophy—and she certainly of necessity if she has really acquired philosophy—would be disposed to look upon doing a wrong as worse than suffering one (as much worse as it is the baser), and to regard being worsted as better than gaining an unjust advantage? Moreover, who better than she would love her children more than life itself? What women would be more just than such a one? Now as for courage, certainly it is to be expected that the educated woman will be more courageous than the uneducated, and one who has studied philosophy than one who has not; and she will not therefore submit to anything shameful because of fear of death or unwillingness to face hardship, and she will not be intimidated by anyone because he is of noble birth, or powerful, or wealthy, no, not even if he be the tyrant of her city. For in fact she has schooled herself to be high-minded and to think of death not as an evil and life not as a good, and likewise not to shun hardship and never for a moment to seek ease and indolence. So it is that

such a woman is likely to be energetic, strong to endure pain, prepared to nourish her children at her own breast, and to serve her husband with her own hands, and willing to do things which some would consider no better than slaves' work. Would not such a woman be a great help to the man who married her, an ornament to her relatives, and a good example for all who know her? Yes, but I assure you, some will say, that women who associate with philosophers are bound to be arrogant for the most part and presumptuous, in that abandoning their own households and turning to the company of men they practice speeches, talk like sophists, and analyze syllogisms, when they ought to be sitting at home spinning. I should not expect the women who study philosophy to shirk their appointed tasks for mere talk any more than men, but I maintain that their discussions should be conducted for the sake of their practical application. For as there is no merit in the science of medicine unless it conduces to the healing of man's body, so if a philosopher has or teaches reason, it is of no use if it does not contribute to the virtue of man's soul. Above all, we ought to examine the doctrine which we think women who study philosophy ought to follow; we ought to see if the study which presents modesty as the greatest good can make them presumptuous, if the study which is a guide to the greatest self-restraint accustoms them to live heedlessly, if what sets forth intemperance as the greatest evil does not teach self-control, if what represents the management of a household as a virtue does not impel them to manage well their homes. Finally, the teachings of philosophy exhort the woman to be content with her lot and to work with her own hands.

SHOULD DAUGHTERS RECEIVE THE SAME EDUCATION AS SONS?

Once when the question arose as to whether or not sons and daughters ought to be given the same education, he remarked that trainers of horses and dogs make no distinction in the training of the male and the female; for female dogs are taught to hunt just as the males are, and one can see no difference in the training of mares, if they are expected to do a horse's work, and the training of stallions. In the case of man, however, it would seem to be felt necessary to employ some special and exceptional training and education for males over females, as if it were not essential that the same virtues should be present in both alike, in man and woman, or as if it were possible to arrive at the same virtues, not through the same, but through different instruction. And yet that there is not one set of virtues for a man and another for a woman is easy to perceive. In the first place, a man must have understanding and so must a woman, or what pray would be the use of a foolish man or woman? Then it is essential for one no less than the other to live justly, since the man who is not just would not be a good citizen, and the woman would not manage her household well if she did not do it justly; but if she is unjust she will wrong her husband like Eriphyle in the story. Again, it is recognized as right for a woman in wedlock to be chaste, and so it is likewise for a man; the law, at all events, decrees the same punishment for committing adultery as for being taken in adultery. Gluttony, drunkenness, and other related vices, which are vices of excess and bring disgrace upon those guilty of them, show that self-control is most necessary for every human being, male and female alike; for the only way of escape from wantonness is through self-control; there is no other. Perhaps someone may say that courage is a virtue appropriate to men only. That is not so. For a woman too of the right sort must have courage and be wholly free of cowardice, so that she will neither be swayed by hardships nor by fear; otherwise, how will she be said to have self-control, if by threat or force she can be constrained to yield to shame? Nay more, it is necessary for women to be able to repel attack, unless indeed they are willing to appear more cowardly than hens and other female birds which fight with creatures much larger than themselves to defend their young. How then should women not need courage? That women have some prowess in arms the race of the Amazons demonstrated when they defeated many tribes in war. If, therefore, something of this courage is lacking in other women, it is due to lack of use and practice rather than because they were not endowed with it. If then men and women are born with the same virtues, the same type of training and education must, of necessity, befit both men and women. For with every animal and plant whatsoever, proper care must be bestowed upon it to produce the excellence appropriate to it. Is it not true that, if it were necessary under like circumstances for a man and a woman to be able to play the flute, and if, furthermore, both had to do so in order to earn a living, we should give them both exactly the same thorough training in flute playing; and similarly if it were necessary for either to play the harp? Well then, if it is necessary for both to be proficient in the virtue which is appropriate to a human being, that is for both to be able to have understanding, and self-control, and courage, and justice, the one no less than the other, shall we not teach them both alike the art by which a human being becomes good? Yes, certainly we must do that and nothing else. "Come now," I suppose someone will say "do you expect that men should learn spinning the same as women, and that women should take part in gymnastic exercises the same as men?" No, that I should not demand. But I do say that, since in the human race man's constitution is stronger and woman's weaker, tasks should be assigned which are suited to the nature of each; that is the heavier tasks should be given to the stronger and lighter ones to the weaker. Thus spinning and indoor work would be more fitting for women than for men, while gymnastics and outdoor work would be more suitable for men. Occasionally, however, some men might more fittingly handle certain of the lighter tasks and what is generally considered women's work, and again, women might do heavier tasks which seem more appropriate for men whenever conditions of strength, need, or circumstance warranted. For all human tasks, I am inclined to believe, are a common obligation and are common for men and women, and none is necessarily appointed for either one exclusively, but some pursuits are more suited to the nature of one, some to the other, and for this reason some are called men's work and some women's. But whatever things have reference to virtue, these one would properly say are equally appropriate to the nature of both, inasmuch as we agree that virtues are in no respect more fitting for the one than the other. Hence I hold it reasonable that the things which have reference to virtue ought to be taught to male and female alike; and furthermore that straight from infancy they ought to be taught that this is right and that is wrong, and that it is the same for both alike; that this is helpful, that is harmful, that one must do this, one must not do that. From this training understanding is developed in those who learn, boys and girls alike, with no difference. Then they must be inspired with a feeling of shame toward all that is base. When these two qualities have been created within them, man and woman are of necessity self-controlled. And most of all the child who is trained properly, whether boy or girl, must be accustomed to endure hardship, not to fear death, not to be disheartened in the face of any misfortune; he must in short be accustomed to every situation which calls for courage. Now courage, it was demonstrated above, should be present in women too. Furthermore to shun selfishness and to have high regard for fairness and, being a human being, to wish to help and to be unwilling to harm one's fellow men is the noblest lesson, and it makes those who learn it just. What reason is there why it is more appropriate for a man to learn this? Certainly if it is fitting for women to be just, it is necessary for both to learn the same lessons which are in the highest degree appropriate to the character of each and supremely important. If it happens that a man knows a little something about a certain skill and a woman not, or again she knows something and he not, that suggests no difference in the education of either. But about the all-important things let not one know and the other not, but let them know the same things. If you ask me what doctrine produces such an education, I shall reply that as without philosophy no man would be properly educated, so no woman would be. I do not mean that women should possess technical skill and acuteness in argument. It would be quite superfluous, since they will use philosophy for the ends of their life as women. Even in men I do not prize this accomplishment too highly. I only urge that they should acquire from philosophy goodness in conduct and nobility of character. Now in very truth philosophy is training in nobility of character and nothing else.

7. WOMEN, SLAVES, AND "LOVE OF TOIL" IN ARISTOTLE'S MORAL PHILOSOPHY

EVE BROWNING COLE

In Plato's *Meno,* Socrates asks his conversation-partner to say what virtue is. Meno responds eagerly as follows:[1]

> It is not hard to tell you, Socrates. First, if you want the virtue of a man, it is easy to say that a man's virtue consists of being able to manage public affairs and in so doing to benefit his friends and harm his enemies and to be careful that no harm comes to himself; if you want the virtue of a woman, it is not difficult to describe: she must manage the home well, preserve its possessions, and be submissive to her husband ... And there are many other virtues, so that one is not at a loss to say what virtue is. There is a virtue for every action and every age, for every task of ours and every one of us—and, Socrates, the same is true for wickedness.

The variation of virtue which occurs to Meno first of all is that between male and female virtues. It is unsurprising, given what is known of Greek culture (and alas of most cultural history since this period), that the sphere of male virtue is not restricted to the home and the marital relationship, but ranges throughout the political universe. Women's virtues, however, can be exercised only within a special "indoors" provided by the male head of the household, which is dependent upon his favor for its maintenance. There is no balanced situation of separate spheres, each of which counts equally, but

rather a circle inscribed within a much larger circle. The interior circle represents women's moral domain, and the exterior embracing circle represents the male moral domain defining and including that of the female.

But this tidy duality of political and domestic virtue-spheres quickly gets muddled in Meno's response; for he steps off from it to embrace a radical pluralism about virtue: there are separate types of virtue not only for males and females, but also for "every action and every age, for every task of ours and every one of us", in short for every conceivable variant context.

In the ensuing pages of the dialogue, Socrates points out the multiple problems he finds inherent in this view. For Socrates and Plato held that if virtue is realizable, it must be knowable; if knowable, it must be definable; and if definable, it must be some *one thing*. Its essence must be specifiable without reference to any particular facts about its possessor, and must remain the same throughout various different instantiations and contexts.

This view of the nature of virtue, perhaps traceable to the historical Socrates but developed by Plato in other dialogues, is a minority view in classical Greek culture. Far more common is the ethical pluralism of which Meno provides an extreme example. On this view, forms of virtue correspond to gender, social class, and political function. The main philosophical proponent of this widespread ethical pluralism is Aristotle.

In this chapter I will explore the virtues which, in Aristotle's moral system, are said to be appropriate to free women and to slaves, and

---

will locate a theoretical instability or contradiction pertaining to the theory's placement of them in the scheme of human life as a whole. And since Aristotle remains much closer to the traditionally dominant values of the culture he inhabits than, for example, Plato, he is in some ways the spokesperson for the ideology of the classical Greek polis. So in examining his views I am more broadly surveying some central values of that peculiar social and political institution.

Exploring the moral typology of free women and male and female slaves in classical antiquity will be illuminating in two ways. First, it will shed light on the general issue of gender and class in ethics by providing one clear example of an ethical outlook which considers gender and class to be variables in moral philosophy. Secondly, it will enrich the understanding of the ancient Greek views of human nature, especially insofar as these views tend toward polarization of traits along gender and class lines. I will try to show that the gender- and class-differentiated ethics of Aristotle, and of the dominant culture of which he is the philosophical spokesperson, both presuppose and validate a conception of the natures of women and slaves which ranks them as borderline creatures, lacking full humanity in ways importantly analogous to the ways non-human animals lack humanity.[2] For slaves, beasts, and (non-slave) women all are essentially *marginal beings* in the Greek male outlook.[3] I am thus dealing with a powerful ideology defining an onto-logical-status stratification of gender, race, class, and species. It is important to understand how such an ideology works, how it hangs together, what its motivating assumptions are, and thus how it can most effectively be deconstructed.

SECTION I: ARISTOTLE ON GENDER AND CLASS IN ETHICS

It is Aristotle's view that male and female human beings differ from one another morally in crucial ways. One key text pinpointing a difference appears in the first book of his *Politics,* which presents a three-level moral typology corresponding to men, women, and slaves (the latter being treated as genderless in the context). The topic under discussion is the question whether slaves can be said to possess virtue.

> ... (T)he freeman rules over the slave after another manner from that in which the male rules over the female, or the man over the child; although the parts of the soul are present in all of them, they are present in different degrees. For the slave has no deliberative ability at all; the woman has, but it is without authority (akyron); and the child has, but it is immature. So it must necessarily be supposed to be with the excellences of character also; all should partake of them, but only in such manner and degree as is required by each for the fulfillment of his function.[4]

By contrast to slaves, women, and children, the free man has a deliberative ability (*to bouleutikon*) which possesses the authority requisite to permit his rational choices to govern his behavior. From this critical advantage in practical reasoning-power, it follows that the free man has also the privilege and responsibility of directing the lives of the others: women, children, and slaves. They benefit from his management, because he is doing something for them which they cannot do for themselves.

Aristotle is emphatic in maintaining that this responsibility on the free male's shoulders is a seriously *moral* responsibility. It is not merely everyday how-to advice which he must issue to his charges, but moral guidance as well; for insofar as they are to display virtue, they must do so in relation to the male—their virtue is essentially relative to him.

> The child is imperfect, and therefore obviously his excellence is not relative to himself alone, but to the perfect man and to his teacher, and in like manner the excellence of a slave is relative to a master ... It is manifest, then, that the master ought to be the source of such excel-

lence in the slave, and not a mere possessor of the art of mastership which trains the slave in his functions. That is why they are mistaken who forbid us to converse with slaves and say that we should employ command only, for slaves stand even more in need of admonition than children.[5]

And it is urgently important that the women, children, and slaves be trained for virtue.

> For inasmuch as every family is a part of a state . . ., and the excellence of the part must have regard to the excellence of the whole, women and children must be trained by education with an eye to the constitution, if the excellences of either of them are supposed to make any difference in the excellences of the state. And they must make a difference: for the children grow up to be citizens, and half the free persons in a state are women.[6]

Thus, free women, children, and slaves share a certain moral relatively in Aristotle's view. The well-being of the state depends on their achieving their own specific excellence, but that excellence or virtue is defined in relation to the male who directs them and whose interests they serve. For children (at least male children) this relativity is only temporary; for with the passage of time, they will take over the direction and non-relative moral status at present enjoyed by their male parents. The status of free women and slaves will be the focus of the remainder of this chapter. It is more interesting, because it carries with it a static marginality, an ontologically fixed residence on the fringes of (male) human concerns.[7]

SECTION II: WOMEN'S VIRTUES

In this section I will argue that Aristotle conceives of women's virtues as being essentially relative and subservient to the larger domain of male-defined human existence. The specific content of women's virtues is supplied by traditional Greek popular morality, and lays heavy emphasis on work. This emphasis pulls in the exact opposite direction from the emphasis in men's ethical lives on freedom from toil, on leisure, on *distancing oneself from slaves as far as possible.* And Aristotle's own interest in leisure as a condition of the good life, an interest shared by many of his articulate predecessors and contemporaries, rules women out of its achievement. Aristotle's great ethical works, the *Nichomachean* and *Eudemian Ethics,* are directed to the free male, whose practical reasoning can be presumed to be at least capable of authoritative conclusions; they therefore have little to say about the virtues of women. The deliberative capacity of the female is not thus authoritative; and moreover, the virtues taken up in these works, and the context in which they are to be actualized, are primarily public and political. The public and the political do not define the context of women's lives in the classical period. Aristotle is not, however, totally silent on the subject of women's virtue.

In the *Rhetoric,* Aristotle describes women's virtues as being two-fold: ". . . in body, beauty and stature; in soul, self-command and an industry that is not sordid".[8] "Philergia", translated "industry" above, really means "love of toil" or "delight in hard work"; it is to be dissociated from sordidness (aneleutherias; literally "unfreedom" or perhaps "servility").

"Sophrosyne" (translated "self-command") is an unsurprising virtue to find here, since it is a basic virtue in much of Greek moral thinking. In the immediately preceding passage, it is also ascribed to men (along with courage). So male and female alike must have this critical virtue which entails moderation, self-control, a certain sober and balanced view of what is important in life, an avoidance of excesses. In addition, females must delight in hard work and males must display courage.

The association of women with work, both in actuality and in ideology, is very old and very deep in the Greek cultural tradition, though it has attracted surprisingly little attention.[9]

Herodotus tells the story of a prodigiously hard-working woman of Paeonia, whose brothers parade her before Darius in order to catch his admiration. Her brothers, Pigres and Mantyes,

> came to Sardis and brought with them their sister, who was tall and beautiful. They waited until Darius had established himself in the outskirts of the Lydian city, and this is what they did: they dressed up their sister as well as ever they could and sent her out to bring water, with a vessel on her head, leading a horse behind her with a bridle on her arm, and spinning flax. As she passed the king, Darius noticed her, for what was done by this woman was not done like the women of the Persians, Lydians, or any of the people of Asia. . . . (W)hen she came to the river, she watered the horse; and after watering him she filled the vessel with water and went back the way she had come, bearing the water on her head and drawing the horse after her . . . , while she constantly turned the spindle. (Darius) asked them if all the women in that country were as diligent workers (ergatides) as this girl. To which they readily answered "Yes" . . .[10]

There is a note of unmistakable Greek chauvinism in the contrast between this wonder-woman and "the women of the Persians, Lydians, or any of the people of Asia". "Ergatis" is a term frequently used of work-animals, and can connote grinding labor. Herodotus takes a nationalistic pride in this symbol of industrious Greek womanhood, capable of performing three useful jobs simultaneously.

In the Homeric poetry, women are almost invariably presented at work, and this is true from the top to the bottom of the social scale. In the *Odyssey*, Nausicaa does laundry, though she is a royal princess;[11] her mother, a queen, weaves from morning until late at night.[12] Penelope, also a queen, weaves tirelessly alongside her domestic slaves.[13] The goddesses Calypso and Circe weave, cook, and garden.[14] By contrast, Odysseus' father Laertes' willingness to tend his vineyard himself is taken as evidence of mental derangement.[15] In the *Iliad*, even Helen is at work on a large tapestry in which (of course) she

herself figures prominently. Cassandra lives the exhausting life of a prophetess/priestess, serving at the shrine of Apollo day and night.

Laziness is a widely deplored female vice. In Semonides' "Catalogue of Women", a lyric poem of the mid-seventh century B.C., four of the nine undesirable female types are characterized by laziness. . . .

The signal desirable female type, the bee-woman, is (like her animal namesake) a regular workaholic.

> The man who gets her is fortunate, for on her alone blame does not settle. She causes his property to grow and increase, and she grows old with a husband whom she loves and who loves her, the mother of a handsome and reputable family . . . She takes no pleasure in sitting among women in places where they tell stories about love. Women like her are the best and most sensible whom Zeus bestows on men.[16]

Hardworking and productive of a large number of children, she deprives herself of female companionship in order to more efficiently serve "his property".

Here is what could properly be called a *gender-specific work ethic*. For it would not be at all virtuous for a free male to display "philergia". In the classical period, it is perfectly acceptable and even expected for a free male to express contempt for persons who work, precisely because they are workers. There are abundant sources expressing this attitude.

Demosthenes' speech "On the Crown" contains a class-based diatribe against a litigant of humble origins. Damaging evidence of those humble origins consists in the work which the litigant has done, all his life.

> As a child you were brought up in great poverty, helping your father in a school, grinding the ink, wiping the benches, sweeping the waiting-room, doing the duty of a slave and not a free-born boy . . . (In adulthood) you hired your services to actors, you played the

third roles ... Then ask these gentlemen here whose fate each of them would choose. You taught writing, I went to school; you initiated, I was being initiated; you were a scribe, I took part in the assembly; you played third roles, I was a spectator; you fell down, I booed.[17]

The employment history of the unfortunate litigant is a deep strike against him; he has spent his life laboring to provide the services which truly free Athenian men enjoy without labor. Demosthenes stresses the passivity of his client's role in relation to the activities of his opponent; with the exception of taking part in the assembly and booing, both rational exercises and therefore permissible to free males, the concluding passage is a study in the passive voice.

Plutarch's life of Pericles also contains some choice meditations on work.

> We take pleasure in perfumes and purple garments, but we regard dyers and perfumers as men unworthy to be free and as mean artisans. Antisthenes was therefore quite right in saying, when he was told that Ismenias was an excellent flute-player, "He is good for nothing, for he would not otherwise be such a good flute-player." Similarly Philip, when his son was playing the cithara at a banquet with much charm and skill, asked him, "Are you not ashamed to play so well?" ... No young man of good birth having seen the Zeus of Pisa or the Hera of Argos desired to become Pheidias or Polycleitus, nor Anacreon, Philemon, or Archilochus for having been delighted with their poems. A work may delight us with its charm, but there is no need to regard its creator with admiration.[18]

Well-born Athenian males will take all the pleasure they like in the productions of others, but will shrink from producing anything themselves.

Aristotle shares Demosthenes' high disdain for labor. In Aristotle's ideal state, the citizens (male) will do *no work whatsoever.*

> ... (A) state with an ideal constitution—a state which has for its members men who are

absolutely just, and not men who are merely just in relation to some particular standard,—cannot have its citizens living the life of mechanics or shopkeepers, which is ignoble and inimical to goodness. Nor can it have them engaged in farming: leisure is a necessity both for growth in goodness and for the pursuit of political activity.[19]

It can be readily seen that if women are typified morally by a fondness for labor, and if labor is inimical to the good life, then women are excluded from the good life by a well-ordered syllogism. I turn now to the women's near neighbors on the margins of polis life: slaves.

SECTION III: THE VIRTUES OF SLAVES

Aristotle is notorious among philosophers for having provided one of the most extended arguments in favor of slavery in the history of western culture. He maintains that some humans are naturally suited for slavery, though not all slaves are natural slaves and not all free people are naturally free. The decisive difference is the aforementioned capacity for rational deliberation, which slaves are said to lack altogether. However, Aristotle says little that is explicit about the virtues of slaves. Apart from the claim that they lack the deliberative capacity, there are only scattered comments and implications concerning the slave's potential for achieving a form of goodness. And even that one claim, clear though it seems, is a vexing one to interpret. What can Aristotle mean by denying to slaves the ability to conduct rational deliberations within themselves? Any answer one supplies must also accommodate the fact that Aristotle *does* allow that slaves should be given reasoned explanations for the commands they are to follow. He maintains, with explicit reference to others who have argued otherwise, that a slave is not merely to be commanded, or spoken to in the imperative mood, but must also be a party to some sort of discussion about the project in hand.

That is why they are mistaken who forbid us to converse with slaves and say that we should employ command only, for slaves stand even more in need of admonition (noutheteteon) than children.[20]

Though hardly the expression of a liberal sentiment, this passage does complicate Aristotle's case for natural slavery. For the "admonition", or reasoned guidance, if it is to have any point at all, must be intended to form the basis for future decisions, to shape future behavior. 'Nouthetesis' is not punishment but rational reproof, as in "Don't do that because it makes the vines wilt", or the like. It is instructive that, in the passage just quoted, Aristotle compares slaves to *children* in this regard. For the reproofs people offer to children are intended precisely as part of the children's education and development into rational choosers on their own. In what spirit are they to be offered to slaves?

The problem deepens when one reads Aristotle denying than slaves can life a life "based on choice". The context is the assertion that political society has a larger and more comprehensive end than mere survival. It is not for life alone that states are formed, but for the sake of the good life.

> (I)f life only were the object, slaves and brute animals might form a state, but they cannot, for they have no share in happiness or in a life based on choice.[21]

It may be that there are many serious contradictions in Aristotle's views on natural slaves, as some have argued.[22] But there is a contradiction here and it will prove fatal to the entire project of gender and class ideology-construction in which Aristotle is here engaged, and which was broadly based within his culture. Before I turn to that contradiction, however, I would like to try to deepen the description of the virtues of slaves by appealing, as I did in the case of the association of women and work in an earlier section, to the views of the average upper-class free Greek citizen—how were slaves regarded by the dominant culture, as concerned their moral attributes?

Here, too, one comes up against a problem of evidence. Unlike the later Romans, whose bureaucratic proclivities bequeathed a wealth of legal doctrine and jurisprudential speculation about the statues of slaves, the classical Greeks did not devote a large amount of discussion to the issues here involved.[23]

It is known that Athenian law during the classical period decreed mandatory torture for any slave (male or female) who was to testify in court.[24] This obviously presupposes in the slave a deep constitutional disposition toward dishonesty, even an incapacity to be honest without the coercion of considerable pain. It is also known that there were set amounts of restitution which could be recovered by the owners of such slaves as were damaged (i.e., injured or killed) during this process of torture. It was possible to withhold one's slave from torture, but only at risk of appearing to have something to hide.

Another thing that known is that slaves worked alongside the free women of the household in many cases. This co-worker relationship must have been extremely interesting. First of all, it would establish in one obvious sense a parity between slave and free woman; as Aristotle himself remarks repeatedly, shared projects are the very firmest basis for solidarity. One can only speculate whether it would also instill a sense of shared status, with slave-mothers nursing their babies alongside free mothers doing likewise, slaves working wool beside free wool-workers, etc. In middle-to-lower income households, there can have been little outward distinction of dress or ornament to mark the status of freedom. Herodotus writes that, before the institution of slavery took root in Athenian society, the work which slaves would later do was done by women.[25] With respect to political involvement, the free woman and the slave were equally distant (at least if one refuses to accept the theory that free women would have had political influence through their husbands, a theory which I find most implausible). In other words, there are several important ways in which slaves and free women resemble one another, both politically and morally.

And finally, it seems perfectly safe to infer that the slave, like the woman, is essentially typified by work as a continuing activity which represents his/her function. Even more clearly in the slave's case than in that of the (free) woman, work is life. Naturally enough, then, the paramount virtue of a slave is willingness to work long and hard.

In Roman times, the prejudice against taking the subject of slave-management seriously (which Aristotle enunciates in *Politics*) begins to fade, and there are texts such as that of Columella, the *Res Rusticae,* which treats the main vices and virtues of slaves, and how most efficiently to encourage the latter while discouraging the former. Paramount among the vices is a kind of stubborn laziness (*desidia, pigritia*).[26] It is plausible to suppose that this would be the most significant slave "vice" in any society. Also continuous into Roman times is the association of women's virtue with industriousness. The common epitaph for a dead Roman woman of even the upper classes is "Lanam fecit, domum servavit"—"She made wool, she served the household."[27]

I would like to conclude this section by suggesting, somewhat speculatively, that western culture presents, at its classical base, a gender- and class-differentiated *work-ethic,* which set itself the difficult task of ennobling labor only as done by certain sectors of the population (slaves and free women), and maintaining a distaste for work as done by the dominant class (free men).

SECTION IV: DELIBERATION, EDUCATION, AND EMANCIPATION

There is a deep contradiction in Aristotle's moral outlook on women and slaves, however, and it concerns the very skill or capacity which women and slaves lack fully or partially: deliberation. For Aristotle is willing to maintain that the capacity to deliberate successfully is *the kind of capacity which is wholly the result of education.*

In the *Nichomachean Ethics,* one is told that ". . . intellectual virtue in the main owes both its birth and its growth to teaching (for which reason it requires experience and time)".[28] And practical wisdom, and the deliberation which it makes possible, are parts of intellectual virtue, and therefore also the products of education. What slaves and women fail to achieve is entirely within the province of education to train into them. The inability to deliberate, evinced by slaves, and the inability to have one's deliberations carry authority into action, evinced by women, are alike failures of education, on Aristotle's own grounds.[29]

Given that this is so, and it seems undeniable, it is difficult to see how we can explain Aristotle's failure to draw the conclusion of a practical syllogism as follows:

1. Women and slaves suffer from a deficiency in respect of practical reason:

2. Practical reasoning is the result of education; Therefore

3. Women and slaves should be educated.

It would be easy, perhaps too easy, to refer here to the common charge that Aristotle shares unreflectively the prejudices of his day.[30] For there are a number of important prejudices which Aristotle conspicuously does *not* hold. For example, he is willing to inveigh with all his considerable logical resources against contemporary Athenian squeamishness about biological and botanical research.[31] In fact, in carrying out his own research agenda, Aristotle must have come perilously close to offending his principles regarding the indignity of manual labor. The collection of specimens, observation of animal behavior, and dissections can all be fairly arduous activities.

It has been argued that Aristotle denies the deliberative capacity to women and slaves in a biological sense, meaning that women and slaves are intellectually defective in the way they are because of a kind of natural lobotomizing which occurs early in their fetal development.[32] This way of understanding Aristotle comes out of texts such as the following, from his *Generation of Animals*:

> Just as the young of mutilated parents are sometimes born mutilated and sometimes not, so also the young born a female are sometimes female and sometimes male instead. For the female is, as it were, a mutilated male . . .[33]

It is also argued that Aristotle's biological outlook encourages him to analyze gender difference in terms of innate physiological capacities and deficiencies.[34] All this might lead one to suppose that what women and slaves lack in deliberative skill cannot be supplied by education in any quantity; the defect is part of the normal functioning of the biological organism, as it were.

It is undeniably true that Aristotle finds real physiological differences between male and female animals of many species including the human, and that many of these differences are described in language which privileges the male animal and derogates the female. But the question at issue concerns the nature and origin of one very specific human capacity: *phronesis* or practical wisdom, the exercise of which in moral and political deliberation is the mark of complete humanity. A person whose practical reasonings carry authority over his or her decisions and the actions they entail is a potentially valuable contributor to the life of the city-state. And authority is imparted to practical reasoning-power *through education and training*.

It may well be that Aristotle would never have granted that women and slaves could deliberate as authoritatively and skillfully as free men, and that he would have explained this by reference to biological causes. Thus he might have maintained an innate in-principle limitation on their educability. But this leaves open an indeterminately large area for potential improvement, within which women and slaves if properly educated and trained could expand their *phronesis* and thereby increase their participation in the goods which constitute human fulfillment.[35] Given that Aristotle has all of the ingredients for a radical proposal for education and emancipation, why does he not combine them?

I would like to suggest that Aristotle does not conclude his syllogism for a deeper reason, having to do with the virtues of women and slaves in themselves. Women and slaves are marginal to Greek society, politically and morally, because they are untrained in practical reasoning; and they remain untrained in practical reasoning because they are marginal. What stabilizes this vicious circle of exclusionary thinking is the fact that neither women nor slaves are the slightest bit marginal from the economic standpoint. It is their virtuous labor which provides the work-free open space in which democratic political life is lived by citizen males, and free women even provide those citizen males themselves through their reproductive labor.

In Euripides' *Bacchae,* one of the eerier elements of Dionysus' onslaught on Thebes consists in the fact that he has caused the Theban women to abandon their work. The chorus sings,

> Soon all the land will dance . . .
> Dance off to the mountains, to the mountains,
> Where the throng of women await,
> Driven from loom and shuttle
> By the frenzy of Dionysus.

And at the gruesome conclusion of this play, as Agave holds the head of her dismembered son, she cries:

> I have left my shuttle by the loom; I have gone to greater things, to hunting animals with my hands. I bring in my arms, as you see, this prize of my courage, to hang on your walls . . .[36]

Significantly, Agave has appropriated the male virtue of courage, the gender-symmetric partner of the emblem-virtue of "philergia", which she has abandoned.

I submit that it is this economic obstacle which blocks the classical Greek mind from promulgating education for women and slaves which would enable them to develop the reasoning skills and strength so crucial to political participation. Aristotle and his contemporaries construct a moral ideology which ratifies what is in essence an economic need—for willing laborers to construct and reproduce the material basis of the culture. Aristotle can do this, in spite of his own views on how practical reasoning comes about in human beings, and in spite of his commitment to state-supported general education for citizen males precisely so that they will be able to function as political deliberators.

> . . . (F)or the exercise of any faculty or art a previous training and habituation are required: clearly therefore for the practice of excellence. And since the whole city has one end, it is manifest that education should be one and the same for all, and that it should be public, not private . . .[37]

From one standpoint, one can applaud Aristotle for bringing together the raw materials for an education proposal which would be deeply radical and emancipatory. From another standpoint, though, the mysteriously missing conclusion of that syllogism provides sad and sober testimony to the limits of the human imagination. One lesson one can learn from this particular failure concerns the deep pull of economic factors on the belief-structures which they nurture and ground. The relegation of women and slaves to the margins of moral life in classical antiquity in as much a function of the importance of their physical labor as it is a function of beliefs about their incapacity for meaningful moral labor. As a recognition of their importance, it is a bitter accolade. Here as elsewhere, ethics and economics are deeply intertwined, and mutually supportive.

NOTES

1. *Meno* 71e–72. The translation is that of G.M.A. Grube, in *Plato: Five Dialogues;* Hackett, 1981.

2. The expression "women and slaves" will sometimes be used for its brevity, though it will be remembered that the category "slaves" includes women and men, along with children of both sexes.

3. For an illuminating study of this marginality with special attention to the iconography of monuments, see Page duBois, *Centaurs and Amazons: Women and the Prehistory of the Great Chain of Being* (Ann Arbor: University of Michigan Press, 1982).

4. *Politics* 1260a9–16.

5. *Politics* 1260a31–33; 1260b2–8.

6. *Politics* 1260b14–20.

7. But for a very interesting discussion of the importance of the theoretical treatment of children in the formation of the western moral-philosophical tradition, see Judith Hughes, "The Philosopher's Child", in *Feminist Perspectives in Philosophy* edited by Morwenna Griffiths and Margaret Whitford (Indiana University Press, 1988), pp. 72–89.

8. *Rhetoric* 1361a8–9.

9. An interesting and controversial study of the iconography of women's work in vase-painting is Eva Keuls, *The Reign of the Phallus: Sexual Politics in Ancient Athens* (Harper & Row, 1985), ch. 9, "The Sex Appeal of Female Toil"; pp. 229–267.

10. Herodotus, *The History* V.12–13, tr. David Grene (University of Chicago Press, 1987).

11. *Odyssey,* book VI; lines 90–95.

12. *Odyssey,* book VI; lines 51–3 (morning), 305–7 (night).

13. *Odyssey,* book I; lines 355–7.

14. Calypso's weaving: *Odyssey* book V, lines 61–2; her gardening: the same book, lines 68–9; her cooking, the same book, lines 92–3. Circe weaving: *Odyssey* book X, lines 221–3; her rather sinister cooking: the same book, lines 234–6.

15. *Odyssey* book XVI, lines 140–141.

16. In Euripides' *Trojan Women,* Andromache also mentions her avoidance of female companionship as something that contributed to her reputation as the ideal wife. "I did not admit inside my doors the smart talk of women" (lines 651–2).

17. Demosthenes, "On the Crown," 257–65. In *Economic and Social History of Ancient Greece,* M. M. Austin and P. Vidal-Naquet (University of California Press, 1977), pp. 344–5.

18. Austin and Vidal-Naquet op. cit., p. 178.

19. *Politics* 1328b37–1329a2.
20. *Politics* 1260b5–7.
21. *Politics* 1280a31–34.
22. See Nicholas Smith, "Aristotle's Theory of Natural Slavery" (*Phoenix* 37, 1983, pp. 109–122), especially pp. 110–111 which list the apparent contradictions.
23. On Roman slavery, see K. R. Bradley, *Slaves and Masters in the Roman Empire:* A Study in Social Control (Oxford University Press 1987); and Jane F. Gardner, *Women in Roman Law and Society* (Indiana University Press, 1986), chapter 10, "Slaves and Freedwomen" (pp. 205–233).
24. See Yvon Garlan, *Slavery in Ancient Greece* (tr. Janet Lloyd; Cornell University Press, 1988), pp. 42–45, for a discussion of the mandatory torture of slaves, and the value of testimony extracted under such conditions.
25. Herodotus VI 137; quoted in Austin and Vidal-Naquet op.cit., pp. 184–185. See also the quote from Pherecrates on p. 185: "In those days no one had any slaves ... but the women had to do themselves all the housework. What is more, they had to grind the corn at dawn, so that the village rang with the noise of their mills."
26. On Columella's treatise, see K. R. Bradley op.cit., chapter 1, "Loyalty and Obedience".
27. See Eva Cantarella, *Pandora's Daughters: The Role and Status of Women in Greek and Roman Antiquity* (Johns Hopkins University Press, 1987), ch.9.
28. Aristotle, *Nichomachean Ethics* 1130a14–15; tr. W. D. Ross, *The Complete Works of Aristotle,* ed. Jonathan Barnes (Princeton, 1985), volume 2.
29. Here it might be objected that there is a qualification in the *NE* passage; intellectual virtue is only said to originate and grow by means of education *for the most part (to pleion)*. This could be read, and indeed has most commonly been read, as limiting the scope of such virtue to free men. But the subsequent line actually emphasizes the fact that intellectual virtue *comes to be in the first place* because of education; it owes both its *genesis* and its *auxesis* to education (the *kai..kai* construction makes this precise). Aristotle here insists, perhaps polemically, on the essential importance of education in moral development.
30. The prejudice explanation of Aristotle's general outlook on women and slaves is offered by Jean Bethke Elshtain, *Public Man, Private Woman* (Princeton University Press, 1981), p. 51.
31. *Parts of Animals* I.5.
32. See, for example, W. W. Fortenbaugh, "Aristotle on Slaves and Women", in *Articles on Aristotle* vol. II, Ethics & Politics; St. Martin's Press, 1977, pp. 135–139. Fortenbaugh argues that women and "natural slaves" (of whom he believes there are none) are deprived of a portion of the mind, specifically that portion which F. designates "the logical part of the reasoning half" of the soul. But the texts he cites in support of this convey only Aristotle's denial of certain intellectual operations, not of a section of mind which could perform their operations.
33. Aristotle, *Generation of Animals* 2.3 737a26–7. Oxford translation. An illuminating discussion of this passage and other similar ones is given by Gareth Matthews, "Gender and Essence in Aristotle"; *Australasian Journal of Philosophy* (Supplement to Vol. 64; June 1986), pp. 16–25.
34. Dorothea Wender, in "Plato: Misogynist, Paedophile, and Feminist", *Arethusa* 6 (1973) pp. 75–91, links Aristotle with other biologically-oriented thinkers, among them Freud and Dr. Spock, who track the construction of gender dimorphic human behavior to biological difference. She maintains that it is Plato's *non*-biological outlook which enables him to advance arguments for equal-opportunity guardianship in his *Republic,* while still holding views about women which are deeply sexist.

More recently Diana H. Coole, in *Women in Political Theory* (Wheatsheaf/Lynne Rienner, 1988), tracks Aristotle's views of the status of women to his theories about the relative contributions of male and female animals to reproduction, designating the latter theories "symptomatic of his whole approach."
35. Aristotle comes perilously close to admitting that slaves *can* in fact be educated to a degree that would enable them to direct their own lives, thus removing the rationale for their enslavement, when he argues that slaves must be given "reasoned admonition" rather than simple commands (*Politics* 1260b5–7). "Reasoned admonition" is a key ingredient in moral education.
36. Euripides, *The Bacchants;* in *Euripides: Ten Plays,* ed. Moses Hadas (Bantam Classics, 1960).
37. *Politics* 1337a20–23.

8. THE BOOK OF CHUANG TZU

CHUANG TZU

A horse's hooves can tread upon frost and snow, its hair can withstand the wind and the cold. It eats grass and drinks water; it prances about briskly. This is a horse's true nature. Though one might provide a horse with magnificent terraces and splendid bedrooms, they are of no use to it. But then came Poleh, who said, "I am skilled at training horses." And men began to singe them, clip their hair, trim their hooves, and brand them. They led them with bridles and hobbles, lined them up in stable and stall, resulting in the deaths of two or three out of ten. They made the horses go hungry and thirsty, raced them, and galloped them, arrayed them in rows and columns. In front were the tribulations of the bit and the ornamental halter, behind were the threats of the whip and the crop, resulting in the deaths of over half the horses.

The potter said, "I am skilled at working clay. My round pieces fit the compass and my square pieces fit the L-square." The carpenter said, "I am skilled at working wood. My angular pieces fit the bevel and my straight pieces match the ruler." Yet is it in the nature of clay and wood that they should fit the compass, the L-square, the bevel, and the ruler? Nonetheless, generation after generation extol them, saying, "Poleh was skilled at training horses; the carpenter and the potter are skilled at working clay and wood." This is also the error made by those who govern all under heaven.

I suspect, however, that those who are skilled at governing all under heaven would not do so. Their people, having a constant nature, would weave cloth to wear and plow the land in order to eat. This is called "common integrity." They would remain unified and not split into factions; this condition we may style "natural freedom." Therefore, in an age of ultimate integrity, they would walk with quiet confidence, look ahead with focused composure. In such an age, there would be no paths and tunnels through the mountains, no boats or bridges to cross the swamps. The myriad things would live in groups, their settlements lined up next to each other. Birds and beasts would form groups, the grasses and trees would thrive. Thus birds and beasts could be tamed but still wander about; one could climb up to the nests of magpies and peep in without disturbing them.

In a world of ultimate integrity, men would dwell together with the birds and the beasts. They would come together in tribes with the myriad things. What would they know of superior men and petty men? Equally without knowledge, they would not stray from their integrity. Equally without desire, this is called "the simplicity of the unhewn log." With the simplicity of the unhewn log, the people would attain their nature. Then along comes the sage, assiduous in his exercise of humaneness, plodding in his exercise of righteousness, and all under heaven begin to doubt. Music begins to multiply, rites begin to proliferate, and all under heaven begin to divide. Therefore, if the simple, unhewn log remained intact, who would carve a sacrificial vessel from it? If the white jade remained unimpaired, who would make scepters and tallies from it? If the Way and integrity were

Victor H. Mair, tr., *Wandering on the Way: Early Taoist Tales and Parables of Chuang Tzu.* Honolulu: University of Hawaii Press, 1998. Originally published by Bantam Press, 1994.

not discarded, who would choose humaneness and righteousness? If the attributes of our individual natures were not set aside, what use would there be for rites and music? If the five colors were not confused, who would make colorful patterns? If the five sounds were not confused, who would conform to the six pitch-pipes? The carving of the unhewn log into instruments is the fault of the craftsman; the impairment of the Way and integrity with humaneness and righteousness is the error of the sage.

Returning to the subject of horses, if they are allowed to live on the open land, they eat the grass and drink the water. When they are happy, they cross necks and rub against each other. When they are angry, they turn back to back and kick each other. The knowledge of horses amounts to this and no more. But if you put a yoke upon them and array them evenly with little moon-mirrors on their foreheads, all they know is to try to break the cross-bar, twist out of the yoke, smash the chariot cover, expel the bit, and bite through the reins. Therefore, to take the knowledge of a horse and make it behave like a brigand is the crime of Poleh.

In the time of the clansman Hohsü, when people stayed at home, they did not know what they were doing, and when they went outside, they did not know where they were going. They filled their mouths with food and were happy, strolling about with their bellies stuffed tight as a drum. The abilities of the people were this and no more. Then along came the sages to rectify the form of all under heaven with their bowing and scraping to the rites and music. They unveiled their humaneness and righteousness from on high to soothe the hearts of all under heaven, but the people began to be plodding in their fondness for knowledge. They ended up contending for profit and then they could not be stopped. This, too, is the error of the sages. . . .

When Confucius met Old Longears, he told him about humaneness and righteousness.

"In winnowing," said Old Longears, "the chaff can get in your eyes and blind you so that heaven, earth, and the four directions will all change their places. If mosquitoes and snipeflies pierce your skin, you won't be able to sleep the whole night long. But there is no greater confusion than that caused by humaneness and righteousness which maliciously muddle one's mind. If, sir, you were to cause all under heaven not to lose the simplicity of the unhewn log, you too could move with the abandon of the wind and stand forth in the wholeness of integrity. Instead, why must you overexert yourself as though you were carrying a bass drum and looking for a lost son? The swan does not bathe every day, yet it is white; the crow does not smudge itself every day, yet it is black. The natural simplicity of black and white is not worth disputing over; the spectacle of fame and praise is not worth bragging about."

Confucius did not speak for three days after returning from this meeting with Old Longears. . . .

Confucius said to Old Longears, "I have been studying the six classics—the *Odes, Documents, Ritual, Music, Changes,* and *Spring and Autumn Annals*—for what I myself would consider a long time and I know their contents thoroughly. I have discussed the ways of the former kings with seventy-two villainous rulers and have explained the achievements of dukes Chou and Shao, but not a single ruler has employed me. How very difficult it is to convince men and to explain the Way!"

"It's fortunate, sir, that you didn't encounter a ruler who could govern the world!" said the Old Master. "The six classics are the stale traces of the former kings, but they do not tell what created the traces! Now, sir, what you talk about are traces. Traces, however, are produced by shoes; they're not the shoes themselves!

"A pair of white egrets look at each other with motionless pupils and fertilization takes place. A male insect chirps from an air current above, a female answers from below, and fertilization takes place. The hermaphrodite is both male and female, hence fertilization takes place by itself. One's nature cannot be changed; destiny cannot be altered; time cannot be stopped; the Way cannot be blocked. If one attains the Way, there's nothing one cannot achieve. If one loses the Way, there's nothing one can achieve."

Confucius did not go outside for three months after this until he went to see Old Longears again and said, "I've finally got it! Birds brood, fish milt, the solitary wasp trans- mutes, and when a new baby boy is born the older brother cries because he can no longer share the teat. I have long been a man who has not shared in evolution. But how can a man who does not share in evolution help other men to evolve?"

"All right, Hillock," said the Old Master. "You've finally got it!"

RECOMMENDED READINGS

Texts

Broadie, Sarah. *Ethics with Aristotle*. Oxford: Oxford University Press, 1991.
Cooper, John. *Reason and Human Good in Aristotle*. Cambridge, MA: Harvard University Press, 1975; Indanapolis: Hackett, 1986.
Irwin, T. H. *Aristotle's First Principles*. Oxford: Oxford University Press, 1988.
Keyt, David, and Fred Miller, eds. *Essays on Aristotle's Politics*. Oxford: Blackwell's, 1991.
Kraut, Richard. *Aristotle on the Human Good*. Princeton: Princeton University Press, 1989.
Lutz, Cora. "Musonius Rufus: The Roman Socrates." *Yale Classical Studies* (1947): 3–117.
Miller, Fred. *Nature, Justice, and Rights in Aristotle's Politics*. Oxford: Oxford University Press, 1997.
Nussbaum, Martha C. *The Fragility of Goodness*. Cambridge: Cambridge University Press, 1986.
von Leyden, W. *Aristotle on Equality and Justice*. London: Macmillan, 1985.

Feminist Perspective

Allen, Prudence. *The Concept of Woman: The Aristotelian Revolution 750 B.C.–A.D. 1250*. Montreal: Eden Press, 1985.
Fortenbaugh, W. W. "Aristotle on Slaves and Women." In *Articles on Aristotle,* edited by Jonathan Barnes, Malcolm Schofield, and Richard Sorabji, 2:135–139. New York: St. Martin's Press, 1977.
Matthews, Gareth B. "Gender and Essence in Aristotle." In *Women and Philosophy,* edited by Janna L. Thompson. Bundoora, Australia: Australian Association of Philosophy, 1986.

Multicultural Perspective

Allinson, Robert. *Chuang Tzu for Spiritual Transformation*. Albany: SUNY, 1989.
Wu, Kuang-ming, *Chuang Tzu: World Philosopher at Play*. New York: Crossroad, 1982.

PART III

❧❧

AUGUSTINE

INTRODUCTION

Augustine (Aurelius Augustinas) was born in 353 in the north African town of Thagaste (located in what is now Algeria). His mother, Monica, was a Christian, but his father Patricius remained a pagan until shortly before his death. Augustine and his brother and sister were brought up as Christians, but Augustine, as he describes in his *Confessions,* soon strayed from the fold. Sent to school in Carthage—"a hissing cauldron of lust," as he subsequently described it, his boyhood faith gave way to worldly impulses and non-Christian ideas. He lived with a mistress and fathered a son by her whom they named Adeodatus (literally meaning "given by God").

Inspired by reading Cicero to search for wisdom, Augustine joined the sect of Manichaeans, who believed that the world is a scene of perpetual conflict between two forces—one of light and goodness, the other of darkness and evil. But Augustine soon become dissatisfied with their answers to the questions that troubled him, and he turned to neoplatonism. Later in rereading St. Paul, he discovered that "whatever truth I had found in the Platonists was set down here as well." Having come to Milan to take up a chair as professor of rhetoric, he happened to hear Bishop Ambrose preach and was impressed by the style and content of his sermons. Monica had also followed Augustine to Milan and urged him to give up his mistress and marry someone respectable. Marriage plans were made, and his mistress was sent back to Africa, leaving Adeodatus with Augustine. But Augustine could not wait for the marriage and took another mistress.

The turning point of Augustine's life came in his thirty-second year. Intellectually reconciled to Christianity, yet lacking the strength of will to break with his lustful habits, one summer day in the garden of the house where he was staying, he flung himself beneath a tree and wept. Then from a neighboring house came the voice of a child chanting the words, "Take and read: take and read." He understood this to mean the *New Testament,* and opening it at random he read the first passage on which his eyes fell (Romans 13:13–14): "Not in reveling or drunkenness, not in debauchery or vice, not in quarreling or jealousy, but put on the Lord Jesus Christ, and make no provision for the flesh, to gratify its desires." Suddenly, Augustine's conversion was complete: "In an instant, as I came to the end of the sentence, it was as though the light of confidence flooded into my heart . . ." Augustine now believed that God had given him the strength to subdue his wayward inclinations: "O Lord . . . it was your power that drained dry the well of corruption in the depths of my heart." So, in 387, Augustine and his son were baptized by Ambrose.

In 388, Augustine, Monica, and Adeodatus left Milan to return to Africa, but Monica contracted a fever and died along the way. Augustine established a small monastic community in Tagaste, planning to devote himself to writing. But in 391, his bishop, Valerius, prevailed upon him to accept ordination and move to Hippo. When Valerius died in 396, Augustine succeeded him as Bishop of Hippo and remained in that post for the rest of his life. Augustine was a prolific writer, and he left us an enormous body of books and pamphlets. His *Confessions* and *The City of God* still rank as classics of Western civilization.

In 430, Hippo was besieged by the Vandals. Choosing to remain in the city to carry out his duties, Augustine died at the age of seventy-six just before the Vandals broke through the city's defenses. When the Vandals burned the city, out of respect for Augustine, they left his Cathedral and library unscathed.

Augustine wrote *The City of God* against those who blamed Christianity for the sacking of Rome by the Goths in 410, and for the general crumpling of the Roman Empire. *The City of God* records the careers of two "cities"—the earthly city, which is composed of the nonsaved whose eternal destiny is damnation in hell, and the city of God, which is composed of the saved whose eternal destiny is the beatific vision of God in heaven.

In our selection, Augustine contrasts the perspectives of the two cities regarding the supreme good and evil. Those of the city of God contend that life eternal is the supreme good and death eternal the supreme evil, and those of the earthly city contend that the supreme good and the supreme evil are found in this world. Augustine, however, argues that the occupants of both cities commonly desire peace, and that conflict only arises between them when those of the earthly city seek to impose laws of religion that conflict with the divine teachings of the city of God. Yet while Augustine objects to imposing laws of religion on those of the city of God that conflict with Christian teachings, would he similarly object to imposing laws based on Christian teachings on those of the earthly city when they have no grounds for accepting those laws?

In the selection from his *Confessions,* Augustine argues for the subordination of women to men. The most relevant passage from the Bible is *Genesis* 1:27–28: "God made man in the image of God. God made him; male and female He made them, and blessed them." This passage strongly implies that woman as well as man reflects the divine image. But Paul implies the contrary, calling man the glory of God, woman the glory of man, and prescribing on that basis different rules of conduct for the two sexes: "For man indeed ought not to cover his head, forasmuch as he is the image and glory of God; but the woman is the glory of man." (I Corinthians 11:7).

In her "Misogynism and Virginal Feminism in the Fathers of the Church," Rosemary Radford Ruether shows how Augustine tried to reconcile the apparent conflict between the two passages by arguing that while man alone reflects the divine image and woman alone does not, man and woman considered together also reflect the divine image. In his reconciliation, Augustine takes woman to stand in her relationship to man as body to soul. Thus, women are associated with bodiliness in a way that men are not. Still, Augustine, along with the other Church Fathers, allowed that there was one way that women could escape their lesser status; they could embrace virginity and live the monastic, angelic life. Not surprisingly, Ruether hopes some way will be found to introduce a full-bodied equality into this Augustinian perspective on the relationship between men and women.

Of course, a more egalitarian interpretation of the relationship between men and women would surely have been easier to come by if the religious texts themselves had portrayed the Godhead in feminine as well as masculine terms. As Jorge Valadez points out in his "Pre-Columbian Perspectives," that is exactly how the Aztecs conceived of their supreme deity Ometeotl. Ometeotl was referred to as "the lord and lady of our maintenance" and "our mother, our father." Valadez also points out that the Mayans saw themselves as not standing against nature but rather as an integral part of it, which led them to be more respectful of nature than Eurocentric societies have been. Is it possible, then, that these Pre-Columbian societies possessed a wisdom that has yet to take hold in Eurocentric societies like our own?

9. THE CITY OF GOD

AUGUSTINE

What the Christians believe regarding the supreme good and evil, in opposition to the philosophers, who have maintained that the supreme good is in themselves.

If, then, we be asked what the city of God has to say upon these points, and, in the first place, what its opinion regarding the supreme good and evil is, it will reply that life eternal is the supreme good, death eternal the supreme evil, and that to obtain the one and escape the other we must live rightly. And thus it is written, "The just lives by faith,"[1] for we do not as yet see our good, and must therefore live by faith; neither have we in ourselves power to live rightly, but can do so only if He who has given us faith to believe in His help do help us when we believe and pray. As for those who have supposed that the sovereign good and evil are to be found in this life, and have placed it either in the soul or the body, or in both, or, to speak more explicitly, either in pleasure or in virtue, or in both; in repose or in virtue, or in both; in pleasure and repose, or in virtue, or in all combined; in the primary objects of nature, or in virtue, or in both,—all these have, with a marvellous shallowness, sought to find their blessedness in this life and in themselves. Contempt has been poured upon such ideas by the Truth, saying by the prophet, "The Lord knoweth the thoughts of men" (or, as the Apostle Paul cites the passage, "The Lord knoweth the thoughts of the *wise*") "that they are vain."[2]

For what flood of eloquence can suffice to detail the miseries of this life? Cicero, in the *Con-solation* on the death of his daughter, has spent all his ability in lamentation; but how inadequate was even his ability here? For when, where, how, in this life can these primary objects of nature be possessed so that they may not be assailed by unforeseen accidents? Is the body of the wise man exempt from any pain which may dispel pleasure, from any disquietude which may banish repose? The amputation or decay of the members of the body puts an end to its integrity, deformity blights its beauty, weakness its health, lassitude its vigour, sleepiness or sluggishness its activity,—and which of these is it that may not assail the flesh of the wise man? Comely and fitting attitudes and movements of the body are numbered among the prime natural blessings; but what if some sickness makes the members tremble? what if a man suffers from curvature of the spine to such an extent that his hands reach the ground, and he goes upon all-fours like a quadruped? Does not this destroy all beauty and grace in the body, whether at rest or in motion? What shall I say of the fundamental blessings of the soul, sense and intellect, of which the one is given for the perception, and the other for the comprehension of truth? But what kind of sense is it that remains when a man becomes deaf and blind? Where are reason and intellect when disease makes a man delirious? We can scarcely, or not at all, refrain from tears, when we think of or see the actions and words of such frantic persons, and consider how different from and even opposed to their own sober judgment and ordinary conduct their present demeanour is. And what shall I say of those who suffer from demoniacal possession? Where is their own intelligence hidden and buried while the malignant spirit is using their body and soul according to his

Reprinted from *The Works of Aurelius Augustine* Vol. II. Translated by Marcus Dods (Ediburgh: T & T Clark, 1872).

own will? And who is quite sure that no such thing can happen to the wise man in this life? Then, as to the perception of truth, what can we hope for even in this way while in the body, as we read in the true book of Wisdom, "The corruptible body weigheth down the soul, and the earthly tabernacle presseth down the mind that museth upon many things?"[3] And eagerness, or desire of action, if this is the right meaning to put upon the Greek ὁρμή is also reckoned among the primary advantages of nature; and yet is it not this which produces those pitiable movements of the insane, and those actions which we shudder to see, when sense is deceived and reason deranged?

In fine, virtue itself, which is not among the primary objects of nature, but succeeds to them as the result of learning, though it holds the highest place among human good things, what is its occupation save to wage perpetual war with vices,—not those that are outside of us, but within; not other men's, but our own,—a war which is waged especially by that virtue which the Greeks call σωφροσύνη and we temperance,[4] and which bridles carnal lusts, and prevents them from winning the consent of the spirit to wicked deeds? For we must not fancy that there is no vice in us, when, as the apostle says, "The flesh lusteth against the spirit;"[5] for to this vice there is a contrary virtue, when, as the same writer says, "The spirit lusteth against the flesh." "For these two," he says, "are contrary one to the other, so that you cannot do the things which you would." But what is it we wish to do when we seek to attain the supreme good, unless that the flesh should cease to lust against the spirit, and that there be no vice in us against which the spirit may lust? And as we cannot attain to this in the present life, however ardently we desire it, let us by God's help accomplish at least this, to preserve the soul from succumbing and yielding to the flesh that lusts against it, and to refuse our consent to the perpetration of sin. Far be it from us, then, to fancy that while we are still engaged in this intestine

war, we have already found the happiness which we seek to reach by victory. And who is there so wise that he has no conflict at all to maintain against his vices?

What shall I say of that virtue which is called prudence. Is not all its vigilance spent in the discernment of good from evil things, so that no mistake may be admitted about what we should desire and what avoid? And thus it is itself a proof that we are in the midst of evils, or that evils are in us; for it teaches us that it is an evil to consent to sin, and a good to refuse this consent. And yet this evil, to which prudence teaches and temperance enables us not to consent, is removed from this life neither by prudence nor by temperance. And justice, whose office it is to render to every man his due, whereby there is in man himself a certain just order of nature, so that the soul is subjected to God, and the flesh to the soul, and consequently both soul and flesh to God,—does not this virtue demonstrate that it is as yet rather labouring towards its end than resting in its finished work? For the soul is so much the less subjected to God as it is less occupied with the thought of God; and the flesh is so much the less subjected to the spirit as it lusts more vehemently against the spirit. So long, therefore, as we are beset by this weakness, this plague, this disease, how shall we dare to say that we are safe? and if not safe, then how can we be already enjoying our final beatitude? Then that virtue which goes by the name of fortitude is the plainest proof of the ills of life, for it is these ills which it is compelled to bear patiently. And this holds good, no matter though the ripest wisdom co-exists with it. And I am at a loss to understand how the Stoic philosophers can presume to say that these are no ills, though at the same time they allow the wise man to commit suicide and pass out of this life if they become so grievous that he cannot or ought not to endure them. But such is the stupid pride of these men who fancy that the supreme good can be found in this life, and that they can become happy by their own resources, that their wise man, or at least the man whom they fancifully depict as such, is always happy, even though he become blind, deaf, dumb, mutilated, racked with pains, or suffer any conceivable calamity such as may compel him to make away with himself; and they are not ashamed to call the life that is beset with these evils happy. O happy life, which seeks the aid of death to end it! If it is happy, let the wise man remain in it; but if these ills drive him out of it, in what sense is it happy? Or how can they say that these are not evils which conquer the virtue of fortitude, and force it not only to yield, but so to rave that it in one breath calls life happy and recommends it to be given up? For who is so blind as not to see that if it were happy it would not be fled from? And if they say we should flee from it on account of the infirmities that beset it, why then do they not lower their pride and acknowledge that it is miserable? Was it, I would ask, fortitude or weakness which prompted Cato to kill himself? for he would not have done so had he not been too weak to endure Cæsar's victory. Where, then, is his fortitude? It has yielded, it has succumbed, it has been so thoroughly overcome as to abandon, forsake, flee this happy life. Or was it no longer happy? Then it was miserable. How, then, were these not evils which made life miserable, and a thing to be escaped from?

And therefore those who admit that these are evils, as the Peripatetics do, and the Old Academy, the sect which Varro advocates, express a more intelligible doctrine; but theirs also is a surprising mistake, for they contend that this is a happy life which is beset by these evils, even though they be so great that he who endures them should commit suicide to escape them. "Pains and anguish of body," says Varro, "are evils, and so much the worse in proportion to their severity; and to escape them you must quit this life." What life, I pray? This life, he says, which is oppressed by such evils. Then it is happy in the midst of these very evils on account of which you say we must quit it? Or do you call it happy because you are at liberty to escape these evils by death? What, then, if by some secret judgment of God you were held fast and not permitted to die, nor suffered to live without these evils? In that case, at least, you would say that such a life was miserable. It is soon relinquished, no doubt, but this does not make it not miserable; for were it eternal, you yourself would pronounce it miserable. Its brevity, therefore, does not clear it of misery; neither ought it to be called happiness because it is a brief misery. Certainly there is a mighty force in these evils which compel a man—according to them, even a wise man—to cease to be a man that he may escape them, though they say, and say truly, that it is as it were the first and strongest demand of nature that a man cherish himself, and naturally therefore avoid death, and should so stand his own friend as to wish and vehemently aim at continuing to exist as a living creature, and subsisting in this union of soul and body. There is a mighty force in these evils to overcome this natural instinct by which death is by every means and with all a man's efforts avoided, and to overcome it so completely that what was avoided is desired, sought after, and if it cannot in any other way be obtained, is inflicted by the man on himself. There is a mighty force in these evils which make fortitude a homicide—if, indeed, that is to be called fortitude which is so thoroughly overcome by these evils, that it not only cannot preserve by patience the man whom it undertook to govern and defend, but is itself obliged to kill him. The wise man, I admit, ought to bear death with patience, but when it is inflicted by another. If, then, as these men maintain, he is obliged to inflict it on himself, certainly it must be owned that the ills which compel him to this are not only evils, but intolerable evils. The life, then, which is either subject to accidents, or environed with evils so considerable and grievous, could never have been called happy, if the men who give it this name had condescended to yield to the truth, and to be conquered by valid arguments, when they inquired after the happy life, as they yield to unhappiness, and are overcome by overwhelming evils, when they put themselves to death, and if they had not fancied that the supreme good was to be found in this mortal life; for the very virtues of this life, which are certainly its best and most useful possessions, are all the more telling proofs of its miseries in proportion as they are helpful against the violence of its dangers, toils, and woes. For if these are true virtues,—and such cannot exist save in those who have true piety,—they do not profess to be able to deliver the men who possess them from all miseries; for true virtues tell no such lies, but they profess that by the hope of the future world this life, which is miserably involved in the many and great evils of this world, is happy as it is also safe. For if not yet safe, how could it be happy? And therefore the Apostle Paul, speaking not of men without prudence, temperance, fortitude, and justice, but of those whose lives were regulated by true piety, and whose virtues were therefore true, says, "For we are saved by hope: now hope which is seen is not hope; for what a man seeth, why doth he yet hope for? But if we hope for that we see not, then do we with patience wait for it."[6] As, therefore, we are saved, so we are made happy by hope. And as we do not as yet possess a present, but look for a future salvation, so is it with our happiness, and this "with patience;" for we are encompassed with evils, which we ought patiently to endure, until we come to the ineffable enjoyment of unmixed good; for there shall be no longer anything to endure. Salvation, such as it shall be in the world to come, shall itself be our final happiness. And this happiness these philosophers refuse to believe in, because they do not see it, and attempt to fabricate for themselves a happiness in this life, based upon a virtue which is as deceitful as it is proud. . . .

Of the happiness of the eternal peace, which constitutes the end or true perfection of the saints.

And thus we may say of peace, as we have said of eternal life, that it is the end of our good; and the rather because the Psalmist says of the city of God, the subject of this laborious work, "Praise the Lord, O Jerusalem; praise thy God, O Zion:

for He hath strengthened the bars of thy gates; He hath blessed thy children within thee; who hath made thy borders peace."[7] For when the bars of her gates shall be strengthened, none shall go in or come out from her; consequently we ought to understand the peace of her borders as that final peace we are wishing to declare. For even the mystical name of the city itself, that is, *Jerusalem,* means, as I have already said, "Vision of Peace." But as the word peace is employed in connection with things in this world in which certainly life eternal has no place, we have preferred to call the end or supreme good of this city life eternal rather than, peace. Of this end the apostle says, "But now, being freed from sin, and become servants to God, ye have your fruit unto holiness, and the end life eternal."[8] But, on the other hand, as those who are not familiar with Scripture may suppose that the life of the wicked is eternal life, either because of the immortality of the soul, which some of the philosophers even have recognised, or because of the endless punishment of the wicked, which forms a part of our faith, and which seems impossible unless the wicked live for ever, it may therefore be advisable, in order that every one may readily understand what we mean, to say that the end or supreme good of this city is either peace in eternal life, or eternal life in peace. For peace is a good so great, that even in this earthly and mortal life there is no word we hear with such pleasure, nothing we desire with such zest, or find to be more thoroughly gratifying. So that if we dwell for a little longer on this subject, we shall not, in my opinion, be wearisome to our readers, who will attend both for the sake of understanding what is the end of this city of which we speak, and for the sake of the sweetness of peace which is dear to all.

That even the fierceness of war and all the disquietude of men make towards this one end of peace, which every nature desires.

Whoever gives even moderate attention to human affairs and to our common nature, will recognise that if there is no man who does not wish to be joyful, neither is there any one who does not wish to have peace. For even they who make war desire nothing but victory,—desire, that is to say, to attain to peace with glory. For what else is victory than the conquest of those who resist us? and when this is done there is peace. It is therefore with the desire for peace that wars are waged, even by those who take pleasure in exercising their warlike nature in command and battle. And hence it is obvious that peace is the end sought for by war. For every man seeks peace by waging war, but no man seeks war by making peace. For even they who intentionally interrupt the peace in which they are living have no hatred of peace, but only wish it changed into a peace that suits them better. They do not, therefore, wish to have no peace, but only one more to their mind. And in the case of sedition, when men have separated themselves from the community, they yet do not effect what they wish, unless they maintain some kind of peace with their fellow-conspirators. And therefore even robbers take care to maintain peace with their comrades, that they may with greater effect and greater safety invade the peace of other men. And if an individual happen to be of such unrivalled strength, and to be so jealous of partnership, that he trusts himself with no comrades, but makes his own plots, and commits depredations and murders on his own account, yet he maintains some shadow of peace with such persons as he is unable to kill, and from whom he wishes to conceal his deeds. In his own home, too, he makes it his aim to be at peace with his wife and children, and any other members of his household; for unquestionably their prompt obedience to his every look is a source of pleasure to him. And if this be not rendered, he is angry, he chides and punishes; and even by this storm he secures the calm peace of his own home, as occasion demands. For he sees that peace cannot be maintained unless all the members of the same domestic circle be subject to one head, such as he himself is in his own house. And therefore if a city or nation offered to submit itself to him, to serve him in the same style as he had made his household serve him, he would no longer lurk in a brigand's hiding-places, but lift his head in open day as a king, though the same covetousness and wickedness should remain in him. And thus all men desire to have peace with their own circle whom they wish to govern as suits themselves. For even those whom they make war against they wish to make their own, and impose on them the laws of their own peace.

But let us suppose a man such as poetry and mythology speak of,—a man so insociable and savage as to be called rather a semi-man than a man.[9] Although, then, his kingdom was the solitude of a dreary cave, and he himself was so singularly bad-hearted that he was named Κακός, which is the Greek word for *bad;* though he had no wife to soothe him with endearing talk, no children to play with, no sons to do his bidding, no friend to enliven him with intercourse, not even his father Vulcan (though in one respect he was happier than his father, not having begotten a monster like himself); although he gave to no man, but took as he wished whatever he could, from whomsoever he could, when he could; yet in that solitary den, the floor of which, as VIRGIL[10] says, was always reeking with recent slaughter, there was nothing else than peace sought, a peace in which no one should molest him, or disquiet him with any assault or alarm. With his own body he desired to be at peace; and he was satisfied only in proportion as he had this peace. For he ruled his members, and they obeyed him; and for the sake of pacifying his mortal nature, which rebelled when it needed anything, and of allaying the sedition of hunger which threatened to banish the soul from the body, he made forays, slew, and devoured, but used the ferocity and savageness he displayed in these actions only for the preservation of his own life's peace. So that, had he been willing to make with other men the same peace which he made with himself in his own cave, he would neither have been called bad, nor a monster, nor a semi-man. Or if the appearance of his body and his vomiting smoky fires frightened men from having any dealings with him, perhaps his fierce ways arose not from a desire to do mischief, but from the necessity of finding a living. But he may have had no existence, or, at least, he was not such as the poets fancifully describe him, for they had to exalt Hercules, and did so at the expense of Cacus. It is better, then, to believe that such a man or semi-man never existed, and that this, in common with many other fancies of the poets, is mere fiction. For the most savage animals (and he is said to have been almost a wild beast) encompass their own species with a ring of protecting peace. They cohabit, beget, produce, suckle, and bring up their young, though very many of them are not gregarious, but solitary,—not like sheep, deer, pigeons, starlings, bees, but such as lions, foxes, eagles, bats. For what tigress does not gently purr over he cubs, and lay aside her ferocity to fondle them? What kite, solitary as he is when circling over his prey, does not seek a mate, build a nest, hatch the eggs, bring up the young birds, and maintain with the mother of his family as peaceful a domestic alliance as he can? How much more powerfully do the laws of man's nature move him to hold fellowship and maintain peace with all men so far as in him lies, since even wicked men wage war to maintain the peace of their own circle, and wish that, if possible, all men belonged to them, that all men and things might serve but one head, and might, either through love or fear, yield themselves to peace with him! It is thus that pride in its perversity apes God. It abhors equality with other men under Him; but, instead of His rule, it seeks to impose a rule of its own upon its equals. It abhors, that is to say, the just peace of God, and loves its own unjust peace; but it cannot help loving peace of one kind or other. For there is no vice so clean contrary to nature that it obliterates even the faintest traces of nature.

He, then, who prefers what is right to what is wrong, and what is well-ordered to what is perverted, sees that the peace of unjust men is not worthy to be called peace in comparison with the peace of the just. And yet even what is perverted must of necessity be in harmony with, and in dependence on, and in some part of the order of things, for otherwise it would have no existence at all. Suppose a man hangs with his head downwards, this is certainly a perverted attitude of body and arrangement of its members; for that which nature requires to be above is beneath, and *vice versâ*. This perversity disturbs the peace of the body, and is therefore painful. Nevertheless the spirit is at peace with its body, and labours for its preservation, and hence the suffering; but if it is banished from the body by its pains, then, so long as the bodily framework holds together, there is in the remains a kind of peace among the members, and hence the body remains suspended. And inasmuch as the earthy body tends towards the earth, and rests on the bond by which it is suspended, it tends thus to its natural peace, and the voice of its own weight demands a place for it to rest; and though now lifeless and without feeling, it does not fall from the peace that is natural to its place in creation, whether it already has it, or is tending towards it. For if you apply embalming preparations to prevent the bodily frame from mouldering and dissolving, a kind of peace still unites part to part, and keeps the whole body in a suitable place on the earth,—in other words, in a place that is at peace with the body. If, on the other hand, the body receive no such care, but be left to the natural course, it is disturbed by exhalations that do not harmonize with one another, and that offend our senses; for it is this which is perceived in putrefaction until it is assimilated to the elements of the world, and particle by particle enters into peace with them. Yet throughout this process the laws of the most high Creator and Governor are strictly observed, for it is by Him the peace of the universe is administered. For although minute animals are produced from the carcase of a larger animal, all these little atoms, by the law of the same Creator, serve the animals they belong to in peace. And although the flesh of dead animals be eaten by others, no matter where it be carried, nor what it be brought into contact with, nor what it be converted and changed into, it still is ruled by the same laws which pervade all things for the conservation of every mortal race, and which bring things that fit one another into harmony. . . .

What produces peace, and what discord, between the heavenly and earthly cities.

But the families which do not live by faith seek their peace in the earthly advantages of this life; while the families which live by faith look for those eternal blessings which are promised, and use as pilgrims such advantages of time and of earth as do not fascinate and divert them from God, but rather aid them to endure with greater ease, and to keep down the number of those burdens of the corruptible body which weigh upon the soul. Thus the things necessary for this mortal life are used by both kinds of men and families alike, but each has its own peculiar and widely different aim in using them. The earthly city, which does not live by faith, seeks an earthly peace, and the end it proposes, in the well-ordered concord of civic obedience and rule, is the combination of men's wills to attain the things which are helpful to this life. The heavenly city, or rather the part of it which sojourns on earth and lives by faith, makes use of this peace only because it must, until this mortal condition which necessitates it shall pass away. Consequently, so long as it lives like a captive and a stranger in the earthly city, though it has already received the promise of redemption, and the gift of the Spirit as the earnest of it, it makes no scruple to obey the laws of the earthly city, whereby the things necessary for the maintenance of this mortal life are administered; and thus, as this life is common to both cities, so there is a harmony between them in regard to what belongs to it. But, as the earthly city has had some philosophers whose doctrine is condemned by the divine teaching, and who, being deceived either by their own conjectures or by

demons, supposed that many gods must be invited to take an interest in human affairs, and assigned to each a separate function and a separate department,—to one the body, to another the soul; and in the body itself, to one the head, to another the neck, and each of the other members to one of the gods; and in like manner, in the soul, to one god the natural capacity was assigned, to another education, to another anger, to another lust; and so the various affairs of life were assigned,—cattle to one, corn to another, wine to another, oil to another, the woods to another, money to another, navigation to another, wars and victories to another, marriages to another, births and fecundity to another, and other things to other gods: and as the celestial city, on the other hand, knew that one God only was to be worshipped, and that to Him alone was due that service which the Greeks call λατρεία, and which can be given only to a god, it has come to pass that the two cities could not have common laws of religion, and that the heavenly city has been compelled in this matter to dissent, and to become obnoxious to those who think differently, and to stand the brunt of their anger and hatred and persecutions, except in so far as the minds of their enemies have been alarmed by the multitude of the Christians and quelled by the manifest protection of God accorded to them. This heavenly city, then, while it sojourns on earth, calls citizens out of all nations, and gathers together a society of pilgrims of all languages, not scrupling about diversities in the manners, laws, and institutions whereby earthly peace is secured and maintained, but recognising that, however various these are, they all tend to one and the same end of earthly peace. It therefore is so far from rescinding and abolishing these diversities, that it even preserves and adopts them, so long only as no hindrance to the worship of the one supreme and true God is thus introduced. Even the heavenly city, therefore, while in its state of pilgrimage, avails itself of the peace of earth, and, so far as it can without injuring faith and godliness, desires and maintains a common agreement among men regarding the acquisition of the necessaries of life, and makes this earthly peace bear upon the peace of heaven; for this alone can be truly called and esteemed the peace of the reasonable creatures, consisting as it does in the perfectly ordered and harmonious enjoyment of God and of one another in God. When we shall have reached that peace, this mortal life shall give place to one that is eternal, and our body shall be no more this animal body which by its corruption weighs down the soul, but a spiritual body feeling no want, and in all its members subjected to the will. In its pilgrim state the heavenly city possesses this peace by faith; and by this faith it lives righteously when it refers to the attainment of that peace every good action towards God and man; for the life of the city is a social life.

NOTES

1. Hab. ii. 4.
2. Ps. xciv. 11, and 1 Cor. iii. 20.
3. Wisdom ix. 15.
4. Cicero, *Tusc. Quæst.* iii. 8.
5. Gal. v. 17.
6. Rom. viii. 24.
7. Ps. cxlvii. 12–14.
8. Rom. vi. 22.
9. He refers to the giant Cacus.
10. *Æneid,* viii. 195.

10. CONFESSIONS

❧❧

AUGUSTINE

Thanks to Thee, O Lord. We behold the heaven and the earth, whether the corporeal part, superior and inferior, or the spiritual and corporeal creature; and in the embellishment of these parts, whereof the universal mass of the world or the universal creation consisteth, we see light made, and divided from the darkness. We see the firmament of heaven, whether the primary body of the world between the spiritual upper waters and the corporeal lower waters, or—because this also is called heaven—this expanse of air, through which wander the fowls of heaven, between the waters which are in vapours borne above them, and which in clear nights drop down in dew, and those which being heavy flow along the earth. We behold the waters gathered together through the plains of the sea; and the dry land both void and formed, so as to be visible and compact, and the matter of herbs and trees. We behold the lights shining from above—the sun to serve the day, the moon and the stars to cheer the night; and that by all these, times should be marked and noted. We behold on every side a humid element,

Reprinted from *A Select Library of the Nicene and Post-Nicene Fathers of the Christian Church*, translated by Philip Schaff, (Christian Literature Company, 1887).

fruitful with fishes, beasts, and birds; because the density of the air, which bears up the flights of birds, is increased by the exhalation of the waters. We behold the face of the earth furnished with terrestrial creatures, and man, created after Thy image and likeness, in that very image and likeness of Thee (that is, the power of reason and understanding) on account of which he was set over all irrational creatures. And as in his soul there is one power which rules by directing, another made subject that it might obey, so also for the man was corporeally made a woman, who, in the mind of her rational understanding should also have a like nature, in the sex, however, of her body should be in like manner subject to the sex of her husband, as the appetite of action is subjected by reason of the mind, to conceive the skill of acting rightly. These things we behold, and they are severally good, and all very good.

11. Misogynism and Virginal Feminism in the Fathers of the Church

ROSEMARY RADFORD RUETHER

The usual image of the Fathers of the Church, especially among those promoting women's liberation, is that of fanatical ascetics and woman haters. Hatred of sex and hatred of women are identified.[1] But this view tends to ignore the high praise of women, in their new role as "virgins," in patristic theology. It also fails to explain the rise of that veneration of Mary that is characteristic of patristic thought in the fourth century A.D. I wish to show that this ambivalence between misogynism and the praise of the virginal woman is not accidental. One view is not more "characteristic" than the other. Both stand together as two sides of a dualistic psychology that was the basis of the patristic doctrine of man.

. . . The crucial biblical text for the creation of man was Genesis 1:27: "God created man in His own image; in the image of God he created him; male and female He created them." If the Fathers could have had the first part of the text without the final phrase, they would have been happier. Indeed, they often quote only the first part of this text without alluding to the second.[2] About the character of the image of God in man they had no doubts. This referred to man's soul or reason. The Hellenistic Jew Philo had already established this interpretation by the first century A.D.[3] The problem came with reconciling this spiritual interpretation of the image of God with the subsequent reference to bisexuality,

Reprinted from "Misogynism and Virginal Feminism in Augustine" by permission of the author.

which they saw as a bodily characteristic. Since God was wholly spiritual and noncorporeal, this appeared to mix contraries and imply either a sexed spirituality or a bodily God. Since it was anathema to think of God as bodily, with male and female characteristics, the two parts of the text must be separated so that the "image" could be defined in a monistic, spiritual way, and bisexuality could refer to something other than the nature of God as reflected in man.

For Greek thought it was axiomatic that spiritual reality was unitary (*monistic,* from which the words "monk" and "monastic" derive). Duality appears only with matter. So God cannot be dual, nor can man's spiritual image be bisexual. This does not mean an "androgynous" view of God and the original humanity, as some recent commentators have thought. The guiding view of the Fathers was not an androgyny that preserved bisexuality on a psychic level, but rather that monism which, alone, is appropriate to spirit.[4] This could be stated by identifying maleness with monism, making femaleness secondary, or else by a nonsexual monism, but not by a true androgyny. Gregory Nyssa chose the latter course, and Augustine the former.

. . .

. . . For Augustine, man as the image of God was summed up in Adam, the unitary ancestor of humanity. But Adam is compound, containing both male spirit and female corporeality. When Eve is taken from Adam's side, she symbolizes this corporeal side of man, taken from him in order to be his helpmate. But she is a helpmate solely for the corporeal task of procreation, for which alone she is indispensable.[5] For any spiritual task another male would be more suitable than a female as a helpmate.

Inexplicably, Augustine must also affirm that Eve, too, has a rational nature, being likewise a compound of spirit and body. Yet in relation to man she stands for body *vis-à-vis* male spirit.[6] Moreover, Augustine persists in calling this latter her "nature," not only with a view to sin but in the order of nature as well. Augustine defines

the male as, alone, the full image of God. Woman, by herself, is not this image, but only when taken together with the male, who is her "head." Augustine justifies this view by fusing the Genesis text with I Corinthians 11:3–12.

How then did the apostle tell us that the man is the image of God and therefore he is forbidden to cover his head, but that the woman is not so, and therefore she is commanded to cover hers? Unless forsooth according to that which I have said already, when I was treating of the nature of the human mind, that the woman, together with her own husband, is the image of God, so that the whole substance may be one image, but when she is referred to separately in her quality as a helpmate, which regards the woman alone, then she is not the image of God, but, as regards the man alone, he is the image of God as fully and completely as when the woman too is joined with him in one.[7]

This assimilation of male–female dualism into soul–body dualism in patristic theology conditions basically the definition of woman, both in terms of her subordination to the male in the order of nature and her "carnality" in the disorder of sin. The result of this assimilation is that woman is not really seen as a self-sufficient, whole person with equal honor, as the image of God in her own right, but is seen, ethically, as dangerous to the male. Augustine works this out explicitly, but patristic theology makes use of the same assumptions of woman's subordination to man in the order of nature, and her special "carnality" in the disorder of sin, which imply the same attitudes, however unjustified by the contrary assumption of the equivalence of male and female in the original creation. This definition of femaleness as body decrees a natural subordination of female to male, *as flesh must be subject to spirit in the right ordering of nature.*[8] It also makes her peculiarly the symbol of the Fall and sin, since sin is defined as the disordering of the original justice wherein the bodily principle revolts against its ruling spirit and draws the reason down to its lower dictates.

This double definition of woman, as submissive body in the order of nature and "revolting" body in the disorder of sin, allows the Fathers to slide somewhat inconsistently from the second to the first and attribute woman's inferiority first to sin and then to nature. In Augustine the stress falls decidedly on the side of woman's natural inferiority as body in relation to mind in the right ordering of nature, and thus he is somewhat temperate in his polemics against Eve as the original cause of the Fall. For him, the Fall could only occur, not when the body tempts, but when the male ruling principle agrees to "go along." This, however, does not imply a milder view of sin, only a more contemptuous view of Eve's capacity to cause the Fall "by herself."[9] In other Fathers, . . . Eve is made to sound as though she bore the primary responsibility.

· · ·

This assimilation of woman into bodiliness allows Augustine to explain why woman's subjugation is "natural" within the order of creation, but it makes for some contradiction when it comes time to defend woman's redeemability and her ability, like that of the man, to become "virgin" and return to the monistic incorporeal nature. This conflict does not appear in Nyssa in the same way, because he makes bisexuality, rather than femaleness, the symbol of corporeality, and thus makes woman and man equivalent, both in their spiritual natures and in their sexed bodily natures. But, then, the Greeks had the corresponding conflict of an inexplicable use of language which suggested that woman was subordinate to man in nature and peculiarly identified with "carnality"—a language to which they, too, were addicted.

Augustine attempts to explain this contradiction by distinguishing between what woman is, as a rational spirit (in which she is equivalent to the male), and what she "symbolizes" in her bodily nature, where she stands for the subjection of body to spirit in nature and that debasing carnality that draws the male mind down from its heavenly heights. But he thinks that what she thus symbolizes, in the eye of male perception, is also what she "is" in her female nature! It never occurs to him that defining woman as something other than what she is, and placing her in subjugation in the order of nature *from the perspective of the male visual impression of her as a "body"* is nothing else than an expression, in the male himself, of that disorder of sin, and thus, in no way a stance for the definition of woman's nature! For Augustine, however, this androcentric perspective is never questioned, but presupposed. Yet he, too, must admit that woman has "another" possibility beyond this androcentrically conceived bodiliness. She, too, has a rational nature and can be saved by overcoming the body and living according to the spirit. Augustine cannot deny this since he, along with all the Church Fathers, believes that woman can become "virgin" and live the monistic, angelic life.

· · ·

In this twilight period of antiquity, we see . . . the image of the virginal woman appearing as a new cultural ideal, raising up the possibility of woman as capable of the highest spiritual development, which could lead to the *summum bonum* of communion with the divine, intellectual nature of the Divine itself. Such heights had previously been reserved for men in antiquity . . .

. . . Virginal woman was thus bound for heaven, and her male ascetic devotees would stop at nothing short of this prize for her. But they paid the price of despising all real physical women, sex and fecundity, and wholly etherealizing women into incorporeal phantasms in order to provide love objects for the sublimated libido and guard against turning back to any physical expression of love with the dangerous daughters of Eve.

Perhaps the task of Christians today, as they take stock of this tradition and its defects, is not merely to vilify its inhumanity but rather to cherish the hard-won fruits of transcendence and spiritual personhood, won at such a terrible price of the natural affections of men and the natural humanity of women. Without discarding these achievements, we must rather find out how to pour them back into a full-bodied Hebrew sense of creation and incarnation, as male and female, but who can now be fully personalized auton-omous selves and also persons in relation to each other, not against the body, but in and through the body.

NOTES

1. William Phipps, *Was Jesus Married?* (New York: Harper & Row, 1970), pp. 142–163.
2. For example, Athanasius' *De Incarnatione* and Origen's *De Principiis* develop an anthropology built on the doctrine of the "image" without any mention of bisexuality.
3. Philo, *Leg. All.* I, 31–32; *De Conf.* 62–63; also see *De Migr. Abr.* 174.
4. M. N. Maxey, "Beyond Eve and Mary," *Dialog.* X (Spring 1971), 112 ff.
5. Augustine, *De Grat. Ch. et de Pecc. Orig.* II, 40.; *De Genesi ad Lit.* 9.5.
6. Augustine, *Confessiones* 13.32; *De Opere Monach.* 40.
7. Augustine, *De Trinitate* 7.7, 10.
8. Augustine, *De Contin.* I.23; Augustine parallels the supra- and subordinations of Christ and the Church; man and woman and the soul and the body. On the ambivalence between an equivalent and a subordinate view of women in the Fathers, especially Augustine, see Kari Elizabeth Børresen, *Subordination et Équivalence; Nature et rôle de la femme d'après Augustin et Thomas d'Aquin* (Oslo: Universitets-forlaget, 1968).
9. Augustine, *De Civitate Dei* 14, 11; *De Genesi ad Lit.* 11, 42.

12. Pre-Columbian Philosophical Perspectives

JORGE VALADEZ

COMPLEMENTARY DUALITIES

Dualities such as life/death, celestial world/un-derworld, male/female, night/day, and so forth were of central importance in the Mesoamerican worldview. These dualities were not conceived as being oppositional in nature; instead, they were understood as being different and necessary aspects of reality. One of the clearest examples of this type of nonoppositional duality was the supreme dual god of the Aztecs, Ometeotl. This supreme deity, who was the ultimate originator of all that exists, had a dual male and female nature. Ometeotl was sometimes called Ton-acatecuhtli-Tonacacihuatl, which means "lord and lady of our maintenance," and often he/she was referred to as "our mother, our father." The dual nature of Ometeotl enabled him/her to

Reprinted from *From Africa to Zen* by permission of Row-man and Littlefield (1993).

beget other beings and the universe from his/her own essence. It is clear that the Aztecs wanted to incorporate both the male and the female principle within a single supreme entity and that they saw no contradiction in a deity who was simultaneously male and female.

It is interesting and instructive to compare the conception of a male/female dual god with the monotheistic God of the Judeo-Christian tradition. Traditionally, the Christian god has been characterized primarily as having male qualities and has been referred to in explicitly male terms. For example, the first two substantive terms in the expression "the father, the son, and the holy ghost" refer to God in terms that are unequivocally male, while the third substantive term, "the holy ghost," has traditionally never been spoken of in female terms. And historically, rarely if ever have we heard the Christian God referred to by the female pronoun "she" or by the phrase "holy mother." He is usually characterized by predominantly male qualities that emphasized his power and authority instead of, say, his nurturance and unconditional acceptance. Some contemporary theologians have argued that these gender-specific characterizations of the Christian God deny women full spiritual participation in the Christian religious tradition. In any case, we can see that the Aztec conceptualization of the supreme deity Ometeotl incorporates the two aspects of the male/female duality into a single divine entity. . . .

THE ECOLOGICAL CULTURE OF THE MAYA

The Mayans had what we might call an ecological culture, that is, a culture whose basic metaphysical perspective reflected the idea of the cyclical regeneration of the earth. Their agricultural orientation was manifested in several ways. First, they were an agriculturally advanced culture: They built canal systems for crop irrigation, practiced slope-field and raised-field farm-ing, and cultivated corn, squash, beans, cotton, cacao, chili peppers, and other crops. Second, they recognized that the cultivation of maize and other crops had made possible the development of the permanent communities where the temples and pyramids that were important to the evolution of their culture and religion were built. Third, their rituals and their dominant metaphors indicated that they were intimately in tune with the seasonal and agricultural cycles of their rich vegetative environment.

The predominance of the ecological orientation in the Mayan world can be seen in the rich symbolism of the "cosmic tree." The cosmic tree is a symbol, used by many cultures throughout the world, of the earth as a fertile, living totality. In the Mayan culture this tree represents the earth as a living entity capable of periodic regeneration. Thus, according to the traditions of the present-day Tzutujil Mayas, the earth (and all that it contains) is seen as a tree or a maize plant that periodically sprouts, blossoms, dies, and is regenerated. The significance of this metaphor in which the world is seen as a biological unit is twofold: First, there is recognition of the fact that just as there is an interconnection between the different parts of a plant, so there is an interconnection between the different biological units of the earth; second, there is the conviction that just as plants need nurturance from the sun, the soil, and water in order to live, so there is corresponding need for the world to be nurtured and renewed in order for it to continue to exist. This renewal was achieved by religious rituals performed at specific times as determined by the temporal cycles that were measured by Mayan calendars. It is interesting to note here that the Mayan view of the earth as a regenerating biological unit is remarkably similar to the modern-day "Gaia hypothesis," which states that the earth consists of many complex, interacting ecological systems. Some biologists and ecologists have argued that by adopting this view of the earth we will be more aware of the need to maintain and protect the earth's own ecological balance.

One of the implications of the Mayan view of the earth is that because nature does not belong to human beings, they do not have the right to do with it as they please. Nature is not something to be "mastered" and controlled for human purposes. In the Mayan perspective people do not stand against nature, but are rather an integral part of it. Humans should take care of nature and nurture it, because they depend on the earth for their nourishment and survival, and because, as biological entities that are born, reproduce, and die, humans are also part of the natural life cycles that permeate the earth. Even among the contemporary Maya of Guatemala there is still a deep sense of respect for the earth because of the belief that ultimately it belongs to the gods and not to mortal man. People are the caretakers, not the owners, of the earth. This accounts for the traditional belief among members of such communities that it is not correct to partition tracts of land and sell them. The earth should be nurtured and cultivated for the good of the whole community; it is not something to be bought and sold for profit. The ancient Maya believed that it was not possible to buy and sell the earth in that it did not belong to them in the first place. This belief is maintained, though perhaps to a lesser degree, by some contemporary Mayan communities.

By contrast, Western culture has elevated the individual's right to own private property into a fundamental human right. We see this "right" as so basic that we consider it more important than the right of an individual to have enough to eat or to have adequate shelter. Nevertheless, despite the importance in the Western tradition of the individual right to own private property, it seems plausible to say that, as far as basic individual human rights are concerned, the individual right to have adequate nourishment or shelter is more basic or primary than the individual right to own private property. But perhaps even more important, an analysis of the ecological orientation of the Maya reminds us that it is only recently that Western societies have realized that a fundamental change in our attitude toward nature is necessary to ensure our ecological survival. We have used and abused nature to such an extent—through air pollutants, the use of toxic chemicals, the production of nonbiodegradable materials, and so forth—that we have placed our own survival, and the survival of other people in the world, in jeopardy. Our view of our relationship to the earth is starting to change so that we are beginning to see the world as an integrated ecological system that may be deeply affected by our actions.

RECOMMENDED READINGS

Texts

Chadwick, Henry. *Augustine.* Oxford, England: Oxford University Press, 1986.
Clark, Mary T., trans. *Augustine of Hippo: Selected Writings.* New York: Paulist Press, 1984.
D'Arcy, M. C. *St. Augustine.* New York: Meridian Books, Inc., 1957.
Markus, R. A., ed. *Augustine: A Collection of Critical Essays.* Garden City, NY: Doubleday & Co., 1972.
Marron, Henri. *Saint Augustine.* Trans. Patrick Hepburne-Scott. London: Longmans, Green and Co., 1957.
Meagher, Robert. *Augustine: An Introduction.* New York: Harper & Row, 1979.
O'Meara, John J, ed. *An Augustine Reader.* Garden City, NY: Image Books, 1973.

Feminist Perspective

Alexander, William. "Sex and Philosophy in Augustine," *Augustinian Studies* (1974): 197–208.
Power, Eileen. *Medieval Women*. Ed. M. M. Postan. Cambridge: Cambridge University Press.

Multicultural Perspective

Polanco, Hector Diaz. *Indigenous Peoples of Latin America*. Trans. Lucia Rayas. Colorado: Westview, 1997.
Ross, John. *The Annexation of Mexico*. Monroe, ME. Common Courage Press, 1998.

PART IV

❧❧❧

AQUINAS AND CHRISTINE DE PIZAN

INTRODUCTION

Thomas Aquinas was born in 1224 or 1225 in the castle of Roccaecca near Aquino, close to Naples. His family belonged to the lesser nobility of the area. When Aquinas was five, he was placed in the Benedictine monastery of Monte Cassino, where his uncle was the abbot. At fourteen, he entered the University of Naples, which had been founded by Emperor Frederick II in 1224. There he became acquainted with a new monastic order, the Dominicans, and in 1244 he decided to join the order. His family objected to this decision. They had hoped that he would join the local Benedictine order and someday become abbot of Monte Cassino. To change his mind, Aquinas's brothers kidnapped and imprisoned him in one of the family castles. After a year, however, his mother relented and arranged his escape. Aquinas then went to Paris to begin his Dominican novitiate and study with Albert the Great, the greatest teacher of the day. In 1248, Aquinas followed Albert to Cologne and later, on Albert's recommendation, Aquinas returned to Paris to complete his master (i.e., professor) of theology degree in 1256.

Aquinas was a highly successful teacher and attracted many students. In addition to teaching and extensive traveling on ecclesiastical business, in the space of twenty years, he wrote seventeen volumes on philosophy and theology. It is reported that he could dictate simultaneously to four secretaries, each on a different topic.

In 1264, Aquinas completed his *Summae Contra Gentiles,* and in 1266, he began work on what was to be his most important work, his *Summae Theologica,* which was intended to be a systematic introduction to theology for Dominican novices.

In 1274, he was called to Lyons by Pope Gregory X to participate in a council. Along the way, he struck his head and died of complications. Fifty years later, he was canonized by the Church.

Aquinas's overall goal was to reconcile reason, particularly as reflected in the work of Aristotle, with Christian faith. In the selection from the *Summa Contra Gentiles,* Aquinas pursues that goal by initially following Aristotle, arguing that every agent acts for an end, that the end is a good. But Aquinas then quickly goes beyond Aristotle, arguing that God is the end of all things and that to know God is the end of every intelligent substance. Like Augustine, Aquinas also maintains that our ultimate happiness or supreme good in not in this life and that we need divine assistance to obtain that happiness in the next life.

In our first selection from the *Summae Theologica,* Aquinas distinguishes between eternal law and natural law on the basis of their origins. Eternal law is God's plan directing all things to their ends. Natural law is that part of the eternal law that is knowable by human beings through reason alone. Aquinas argues that the first precept of the natural law is that good is to be done and pursued and evil to be avoided and that from this precept all other precepts are derived. Aquinas then discusses the senses in which natural law is the same and not the same for all humans, the senses in which natural law can be changed and not changed, and the senses in which natural law can be abolished and not abolished from the human heart. As a component of his attempt to reconcile faith and reason, it is difficult to object to Aquinas's general accounts of law and natural law. It is much easier to object to what are taken to be particular requirements of natural law.

Aquinas's views about women, set out in the second selection from the *Summae Theologica,* are outrageous from a feminist standpoint. Aquinas accepts Aristotle's view that a woman is a misbegotten man. He also claims that a woman is a helpmate to man only with respect to procreation and the care of children. For all other things, Aquinas contends, men are better served by other men.

Christine de Pizan was born in 1365 in Venice. Shortly after her birth, her father Tommaso di Benvenuto de Pizzano found favor with Charles V and was invited to join his court in Paris. Encouraged by her father, Christine used her family's close ties to the court to obtain a good education. At the age of fifteen, she married Estienne de Castel, a court notary who also encouraged Christine's learning and literary activity. When her husband died, leaving her at the age of twenty-five with three small children to support, Christine turned to writing to earn her living. She became recognized as an accomplished lyric poet and served as the official biographer of Charles V. She was also the chief correspondent in the quarrel over the *Romance of the Rose,* attacking this central work of medieval literature for being immoral and for slandering women. She produced a vast corpus of works in verse and prose. She wrote *The Book of the Ladies* in 1405. Christine's title alludes to Augustine's *The City of God,* not to rival that work, but to indicate that she, like Augustine, was working within a Christian tradition of political philosophy. Her book portrays a walled city constructed for the protection of women from both physical and moral harm. In it, Reason, Justice, and Duty, personified as Ladies, offer guidance to women.

In our selection from *The City of the Ladies,* Christine asks Reason whether God has ever wished to ennoble the mind of woman with the loftiness of the sciences. Reason replies affirmatively, citing examples of such women. Reason further explains that if women happen to know less than men, it is because they lack the opportunities that men have to learn more. Similarly, men who live relatively isolated in the mountains might seem savage or simple-minded compared with men who have more cultural and educational advantages. When Christine asks Reason whether prudence is found in the natural sensibility of women, Reason again answers affirmatively, but then points out that sometimes husbands take offense when their wives demonstrate this virtue because it shows up their own deficiencies.

In "Equality of Souls, Inequality of Sexes," Eleanor McLaughlin details the ways in which Aquinas, borrowing both from Aristotle and Augustine, conceived the subordination of women. Even with respect to reproduction—the activity that is more essentially associated with women, Aquinas holds that men have the active, life-giving role, women the passive, receptive role. According to Aquinas, the only way that a woman can escape the subordination and inferiority to which she is ordained by her sex is by choosing the virginal life in a religious order. This life involved renouncing what it was to be a woman and virtually assuming the nature of a man. But even in religious orders, women were not the equal of men because they were not allowed to enter the priesthood.

Opposed to this androcentrism and misogyny, McLaughlin argues for a new Christian anthropology characterized by a positive role for human sexuality, a true equality between the sexes, and a recognition of the extent to which sexual differences are conventional.

Maimonides, in our selection from *The Guide for the Perplexed,* like Aquinas, yet writing before him, sought to reconcile reason, particularly as reflected in the work of Aristotle, with faith; but in his case, it is Judaism, not Christianity, that is to be reconciled with reason. Maimonides claims that it is possible to reconcile all 613 commandments of the Jewish Law with reason, on the grounds that they all serve the general welfare. However, most people today would have difficulty believing that putting a stubborn and rebellious son to death or renouncing sexual intercourse would serve the general welfare or in any other way be a requirement of reason.

13. SUMMA CONTRA GENTILES

❦

THOMAS AQUINAS

CHAPTER II

That Every Agent Acts for an End

We must first show that every agent, by its action, intends an end.

For in those things which clearly act for an end, we declare the end to be that towards which the movement of the agent tends: for when this is reached, the end is said to be reached, and to fail in this is to fail in the end intended; as may be seen in the physician who aims at health, and in a man who runs towards an appointed goal. Nor does it matter, as to this, whether that which tends to an end be cognitive or not: for just as the target is the end of the archer, so is it the end of the arrow's flight. Now the movement of every agent tends to something determinate: since it is not from any force that any action proceeds, but heating proceeds from heat, and cooling from cold; wherefore actions are differentiated by their active principles. Action sometimes terminates in something made, for instance building terminates in a house, healing ends in health: while sometimes it does not so terminate, for instance, understanding and sensation. And if action terminate in something made, the movement of the agent tends by that action towards that thing made: while if it does not terminate in something made, the movement of the agent tends to the action itself. It follows therefore that every agent intends an end while acting, which end is sometimes the action itself, sometimes a thing made by the action.

Again. In all things that act for an end, that is said to be the last end, beyond which the agent seeks nothing further: thus the physician's action goes as far as health, and this being attained, his efforts cease. But in the action of every agent, a point can be reached beyond which the agent does not desire to go; else actions would tend to infinity, which is impossible, for since *it is not possible to pass through an infinite medium,*[1] the agent would never begin to act, because nothing moves towards what it cannot reach. Therefore every agent acts for an end. . . .

Again. Every agent acts either by nature or by intelligence. Now there can be no doubt that those which act by intelligence act for an end; since they act with an intellectual preconception of what they attain by their action, and act through such preconception, for this is to act by intelligence. Now just as in the preconceiving intellect there exists the entire likeness of the effect that is attained by the action of the intellectual being, so in the natural agent there pre-exists the similitude of the natural effect, by virtue of which similitude its action is determined to the appointed effect: for fire begets fire, and an olive produces an olive. Wherefore even as that which acts by intelligence tends by its action to a definite end, so also does that which acts by nature. Therefore every agent acts for an end. . . .

There are, however, certain actions which would seem not to be for an end, such as playful and contemplative actions, and those which are done without attention, such as scratching one's beard, and the like: whence some might be led to think that there is an agent that acts not for an end.—But we must observe that contemplative actions are not for another end, but are them-

Reprinted from *Summa Contra Gentiles* (London: Burns Oates & Washbourne, 1928).

selve an end. Playful actions are sometimes an end, when one plays for the mere pleasure of play; and sometimes they are for an end, as when we play that afterwards we may study better. Actions done without attention do not proceed from the intellect, but from some sudden act of the imagination, or some natural principle: thus a disordered humour produces an itching sensation and is the cause of a man scratching his beard, which he does without his mind attending to it. Such actions do tend to an end, although outside the order of the intellect. Hereby is excluded the error of certain natural philosophers of old, who maintained that all things happen by natural necessity, thus utterly banishing the final cause from things.

CHAPTER III

That Every Agent Acts for a Good

Hence we must go on to prove that every agent acts for a good.

For that every agent acts for an end clearly follows from the fact that every agent tends to something definite. Now that to which an agent tends definitely must needs be befitting to that agent: since the latter would not tend to it save on account of some fittingness thereto. But that which is befitting to a thing is good for it. Therefore every agent acts for a good.

Further. The end is that wherein the appetite of the agent or mover is at rest, as also the appetite of that which is moved. Now it is the very notion of good to be the term of appetite, since *good is the object of every appetite*.[2] Therefore all action and movement is for a good.

Again. All action and movement would seem to be directed in some way to being: either for the preservation of being in the species or in the individual; or for the acquisition of being. Now this itself, being to wit, is a good: and for this reason all things desire being. Therefore all action and movement is for a good. . . .

Moreover. The intellectual agent acts for an end, as determining on its end: whereas the nat-

ural agent, though it acts for an end, as proved above,[1] does not determine on its end, since it knows not the ratio of end, but is moved to the end determined for it by another. Now an intellectual agent does not determine the end for itself except under the aspect of good; for the intelligible object does not move except it be considered as a good, which is the object of the will. Therefore also the natural agent is not moved, nor does it act for an end, except in so far as this end is a good: since the end is determined for the natural agent by an appetite. Therefore every agent acts for a good. . . .

CHAPTER XVIII

How God is the End of Things

It remains to ask how God is the end of all things: and this shall be made clear from what has been said.

For He is the end of all things, yet so as to precede all in being. Now there is an end which, though it holds the first place in causing forasmuch as it is in the intention, is nevertheless last in execution. This applies to any end which the agent sets up by his action: thus the physician by his action sets up health in the sick man, which is nevertheless his end. There is also an end which, just as it precedes in causing, so also does it precede in being: even so that which one intends to acquire by one's motion or action, is said to be one's end, for instance fire seeks to reach a higher place by its movement, and the king seeks to take a city by fighting. Accordingly God is the end of things as something to be obtained by each thing in its own way.

Again. God is at once the last end of things, and the first agent, as we have shown. Now the end effected by the agent's action, cannot be the first agent, but rather is it the agent's effect. God, therefore, cannot be the end of things, as though He were something effected, but only as something already existing and to be acquired.

Further. If a thing act for the sake of something already in existence, and if by its action some result ensue; something through the agent's action must accrue to the thing for the sake of which it acts: thus soldiers fight for the cause of their captain, to whom victory accrues, which the soldiers bring about by their actions. Now nothing can accrue to God from the action of anything whatever: since His goodness is perfect in every way, as we proved in the First Book. It follows, then, that God is the end of things, not as something made or effected by them, nor as though He obtained something from things, but in this way alone, that things obtain Him.

Moreover. The effect must tend to the end, in the same way as the agent acts for the end. Now God, who is the first agent of all things, does not act as though He gained something by His action, but as bestowing something thereby: since He is not in potentiality so that He can acquire something, but solely in perfect actuality, whereby He is able to bestow. Things therefore are not directed to God, as to an end that can gain something, but that they may obtain Himself from Him according to their measure, since He is their end. . . .

CHAPTER XXV

That to know God is the End of Every Intelligent Substance

Now, seeing that all creatures, even those that are devoid of reason, are directed to God as their last end: and that all reach this end in so far as they have some share of a likeness to him. the intellectual creature attains to him in a special way, namely through its proper operation, by understanding him. Consequently this must be the end of the intelligent creature, namely to understand God.

For, as we have shown above, God is the end of each thing: wherefore as far as it is possible to it each thing intends to be united to God as its last end. Now a thing is more closely united to God by reaching in a way to the very substance of God; which happens when it knows something of the divine substance,—than when it reaches to a divine likeness. Therefore the intellectual substance tends to the knowledge of God as its last end.

Again. The operation proper to a thing is the end thereof: for it is its second perfection; so that when a thing is well conditioned for its proper operation it is said to be efficient and good. Now understanding is the proper operation of the intellectual substance: and consequently it is its end. Therefore whatever is most perfect in this operation, is its last end; especially in those operations which are not directed to some product, such as understanding and sensation. And since operations of this kind take their species from their objects, by which also they are known, it follows that the more perfect the object of any such operation, the more perfect is the operation. Consequently to understand the most perfect intelligible, namely God, is the most perfect in the genus of this operation which is to understand. Therefore to know God by an act of intelligence is the last end of every intellectual substance.

Someone, however, might say that the last end of an intellectual substance consists indeed in understanding the best intelligible: but that what is the best intelligible for this or that intellectual substance, is not simply the best intelligible; and that the higher the intellectual substance, the higher is its best intelligible. So that possibly the supreme intellectual substance has for its best intelligible that which is best simply, and its happiness will consist in understanding God: whereas the happiness of any lower intellectual substance will consist in understanding some lower intelligible, which however will be the highest thing understood by that substance. Especially would it seem not to be in the power of the human intellect to understand that which is simply the best intelligible, on account of its weakness: for it is as much adapted for knowing the supreme intelligible, *as the owl's eye for seeing the sun.*[3]

Nevertheless it is evident that the end of any intellectual substance, even the lowest, is to understand God. For it has been shown above[2] that God is the last end towards which all things tend. And the human intellect, although the lowest in the order of intelligent substances, is superior to all that are devoid of understanding. Since then a more exalted substance has not a less exalted end, God will be the end also of the human intelligence. Now every intelligent being attains to its last end by understanding it, as we have proved. Therefore the human intellect attains to God as its end, by understanding Him. . . .

Further. Everything tends to a divine likeness as its own end. Therefore a thing's last end is that whereby it is most of all like unto God. Now the intellectual creature is especially likened to God in that it is intellectual: since this likeness belongs to it above other creatures, and includes all other likenesses. And in this particular kind of likeness it is more like God in understanding actually than in understanding habitually or potentially: because God is always actually understanding, as we proved in the First Book. And in understanding actually he is especially like God, in understanding God: because by understanding Himself God understands all other things, as we proved in the First Book. Therefore the last end of every intelligent substance is to understand God.

Again. That which is lovable only on account of another, is for the sake of that which is lovable for its own sake alone: because we cannot go on indefinitely in the appetite of nature, since then nature's desire would be in vain, for it is impossible to pass through an infinite number of things. Now all practical sciences, arts and powers are lovable only for the sake of something else, since their end is not knowledge, but work. But speculative sciences are lovable for their own sake, for their end is knowledge itself. Nor can we find any action in connexion with man, that is not directed to some other end, with the exception of speculative consideration. For even playful actions, which would seem to be done without any purpose, have some end due to them, namely that the mind may be relaxed, and that

thereby we may afterwards become more fit for studious occupations: else we should always have to be playing, if play were desirable for its own sake, and this is unreasonable. Accordingly practical art is directed to speculative art, and again every human operation, to intellectual speculation, as its end. Now, in all sciences and arts that are mutually subordinate, the last end apparently belongs to the one from which others take their rules and principles: thus the art of sailing, to which belongs the ship's end, namely its use, provides rules and principles to the art of ship-building. And such is the relation of metaphysics to other speculative sciences, for all others depend thereon, since they derive their principles from it, and are directed by it in defending those principles; moreover metaphysics is wholly directed to God as its last end, wherefore it is called the *divine science*.[4] Therefore the knowledge of God is the last end of all human knowledge and actions.

Furthermore. In all mutually subordinate agents and movers, the end of the first agent must be the end of all: even as the end of the commander in chief is the end of all who are soldiering under him. Now of all the parts of man, the intellect is the highest mover: for it moves the appetite, by proposing its object to it; and the intellective appetite or will, moves the sensitive appetites, namely the irascible and concupiscible, so that we do not obey the concupiscence, unless the will command; and the sensitive appetite, the will consenting, moves the body. Therefore the end of the intellect is the end of all human actions. *Now the intellect's end and good are the true,*[5] and its last end is the first truth. Therefore the last end of all man and of all his deeds and desires, is to know the first truth, namely God.

Moreover. Man has a natural desire to know the causes of whatever he sees: wherefore through wondering at what they saw, and ignoring its cause, men first began to philosophize, and when they had discovered the cause they were at rest.[6] Nor do they cease inquiring until they come to the first cause; and *then do we deem ourselves to know perfectly when we know the first cause.*[7] Therefore man naturally desires, as his last end, to know the first cause. But God is the first cause of all. Therefore man's last end is to know God.

Besides. Man naturally desires to know the cause of any known effect. Now the human intellect knows universal being. Therefore it naturally desires to know its cause, which is God alone, as we proved in the Second Book. Now one has not attained to one's last end until the natural desire is at rest. Therefore the knowledge of any intelligible object is not enough for man's happiness, which is his last end, unless he know God also, which knowledge terminates his natural desire, as his last end. Therefore this very knowledge of God is man's last end. . . .

Now the last end of man and of any intelligent substance is called *happiness* or *beatitude:* for it is this that every intelligent substance desires as its last end, and for its own sake alone. Therefore the last beatitude or happiness of any intelligent substance is to know God.

Hence it is said (Matth. v. 8): *Blessed are the clean of heart, for they shall see God:* and (Jo. xvii. 3): *This is eternal life: that they may know thee, the only true God.* Aristotle agrees with this statement (10 *Ethic.* vii.) when he says that man's ultimate happiness is *contemplative, in regard to his contemplating the highest object of contemplation.* . . .

CHAPTER XLVIII

That Man's Ultimate Happiness is not in this Life

Seeing then that man's ultimate happiness does not consist in that knowledge of God whereby he is known by all or many in a vague kind of opinion, nor again in that knowledge of God whereby he is known in science through demonstration; nor in that knowledge whereby he is known through faith, and seeing that it is not possible in this life to arrive at a higher knowledge of God in His essence, or at least so that we understand other separate substances, and thus know God through that which is nearest to Him, so to say, and since we must place our ultimate happiness in some kind of knowledge of God, it is impossible for man's happiness to be in this life.

Again. Man's last end is the term of his natural appetite, so that when he has obtained it, he desires nothing more: because if he still has a movement towards something, he has not yet reached an end wherein to be at rest. Now, this cannot happen in this life: since the more man understands, the more is the desire to understand increased in him,—this being natural to man,—unless perhaps someone there be who understands all things: and in this life this never did nor can happen to anyone that was a mere man; . . . Therefore man's ultimate happiness cannot possibly be in this life.

Besides. Whatever is in motion towards an end, has a natural desire to be established and at rest therein: hence a body does not move away from the place towards which it has a natural movement, except by a violent movement which is contrary to that appetite. Now happiness is the last end which man desires naturally. Therefore it is his natural desire to be established in happiness. Consequently unless together with happiness he acquires a state of immobility, he is not yet happy, since his natural desire is not yet at rest. When therefore a man acquires happiness, he also acquires stability and rest; so that all agree in conceiving stability as a necessary condition of happiness: hence the Philosopher says (I *Ethic.* x.): *We do not look upon the happy man as a kind of chameleon.* Now, in this life there is no sure stability; since, however happy a man may be, sickness and misfortune may come upon him, so that he is hindered in the operation, whatever it be, in which his happiness consists. Therefore man's ultimate happiness cannot be in this life.

Moreover. It would seem unfitting and unreasonable for a thing to take a long time in becoming, and to have but a short time in being: for it would follow that for a longer duration of time nature would be deprived of its end; hence we see that animals which live but a short time, are perfected in a short time. But, if happiness consists in a perfect operation according to perfect virtue,[8] whether intellectual or moral, it cannot possibly come to man except after a long time. This is most evident in speculative matters, wherein man's ultimate happiness consists, for hardly is man able to arrive at perfection in the speculations of science, even though he reach the last stage of life: and then in the majority of cases, but a short space of life remains to him. Therefore man's ultimate happiness cannot be in this life.

Further. All admit that happiness is a perfect good: else it would not bring rest to the appetite. Now perfect good is that which is wholly free from any admixture of evil: just as that which is perfectly white is that which is entirely free from any admixture of black. But man cannot be wholly free from evils in this state of life; not only from evils of the body, such as hunger, thirst, heat, cold and the like, but also from evils of the soul. For no one is there who at times is not disturbed by inordinate passions; who sometimes does not go beyond the mean, wherein virtue consists, either in excess or in deficiency; who is not deceived in some thing or another; or at least ignores what he would wish to know, or feels doubtful about an opinion of which he would like to be certain. Therefore no man is happy in this life.

Again. Man naturally shuns death, and is sad about it: not only shunning it now when he feels its presence, but also when he thinks about it. But man, in this life, cannot obtain not to die. Therefore it is not possible for man to be happy in this life. . . .

Further. The more a thing is desired and loved, the more does its loss bring sorrow and pain. Now happiness is most desired and loved. Therefore its loss brings the greatest sorrow. But if there be ultimate happiness in this life, it will certainly be lost, at least by death. Nor is it certain that it will last till death: since it is possible for every man in this life to encounter sickness, whereby he is wholly hindered from the operation of virtue; such as madness and the like which hinder the use of reason. Such happiness therefore always has sorrow naturally connected with it: and consequently it will not be perfect happiness. . . .

For although man is below the separate substances in the natural order, he is above irrational creatures: wherefore he attains his ultimate end in a more perfect way than they. Now these attain their last end so perfectly that they seek nothing further: thus a heavy body rests when it is in its own proper place; and when an animal enjoys sensible pleasure, its natural desire is at rest. Much more therefore when man has obtained his last end, must his natural desire be at rest. But this cannot happen in this life. Therefore in this life man does not obtain happiness considered as his proper end, as we have proved. Therefore he must obtain it after this life. . . .

Besides. As long as a thing is in motion towards perfection it has not reached its last end. Now in the knowledge of truth all men are ever in motion and tending towards perfection: because those who follow, make discoveries in addition to those made by their predecessors. Therefore in the knowledge of truth man is not situated as though he had arrived at his last end. Since then as Aristotle himself shows (10 *Ethic.* vii.) man's ultimate happiness in this life consists apparently in speculation, whereby he seeks the knowledge of truth, we cannot possibly allow that man obtains his last end in this life.

Moreover. Whatever is in potentiality tends to become actual: so that as long as it is not wholly actual, it has not reached its last end. Now our intellect is in potentiality to the knowledge of the forms of all things: and it becomes actual when it knows any one of them. Consequently it will not be wholly actual, nor in possession of its last end, except when it knows all, at least these material things. But man cannot obtain this through speculative sciences, by which in this life we know truth. Therefore man's ultimate happiness cannot be in this life. . . .

Therefore man's ultimate happiness will consist in that knowledge of God which he possesses after this life.

CHAPTER CXLVII

That Man needs the Divine Assistance in Order to Obtain Beatitude

A thing of inferior nature cannot attain to what is proper to a higher nature except by virtue of that higher nature: thus the moon, that shines not of itself, is made to shine by the power and action of the sun: and water that is not hot of itself, becomes hot by the power and action of fire. Now, to see the First Truth itself in itself, so far surpasses the faculty of human nature, that it belongs to God alone. Therefore man needs the divine assistance in order to reach that end.

Again. Everything obtains its last end by its own operation. Now, an operation derives its efficacy from the operating principle: wherefore by the action of the seed something is produced in a definite species, through the efficacy pre-existing in the seed. Therefore man cannot, by his own operation, attain to his last end, which surpasses the faculty of his natural powers, unless his operation be enabled by the divine power to bring him thereto.

Besides. No instrument can achieve ultimate perfection by virtue of its own form, but only by virtue of the principal agent: although by virtue of its own form it can cause some disposition to the ultimate perfection. Thus a saw, by reason of its own form, causes the cutting of the wood, but the form of the bench is produced by the art that employs the instrument: likewise in the body of an animal, resolution and consumption is the result of the animal heat, but the formation of flesh, and regulation of increase and other such things, come from the vegetative soul, which uses heat as its instrument. Now, to God the first agent by intellect and will, all intellects and wills are subordinate,[9] as instruments under the principal agent. Consequently their operations have no efficacy in respect of their ultimate perfection, which is the attainment of final beatitude, except by the power of God. Therefore the rational nature needs the divine assistance in order to obtain its last end.

Further. Many obstacles prevent man from reaching his end. For he is hindered by the weakness of his reason, which is easily drawn into error which bars him from the straight road that leads to his end. He is also hindered by the passions of the sensitive faculty, and by the affections whereby he is drawn to sensible and inferior things, since the more he adheres to them, the further is he removed from his last end: for such things are below man, whereas his end is above him. Again he is often hindered by weakness of the body from doing acts of virtue, whereby he tends to beatitude. Therefore he needs the help of God, lest by such obstacles he turn away utterly from his last end.

NOTES

1. Aristotle, 1 *Poster.* xxii. 2.
2. Aristotle, 1 *Ethic.* 1.
3. 1 *Metaph.* i.
4. 1 *Metaph.* ii.
5. 6 *Ethic.* ii.
6. 1 *Metaph.* ii.
7. *Ibid.* iii.
8. 10 *Ethic.* vii.
9. Ch. lxviii., lxx.

14. SUMMA THEOLOGICA

❦

THOMAS AQUINAS

QUESTION 91. OF THE VARIOUS KINDS OF LAW.

First Article.
Whether There Is an Eternal Law?

We proceed thus to the First Article:—

Objection 1. It seems that there is no eternal law. Because every law is imposed on someone. But there was not someone from eternity on whom a law could be imposed: since God alone was from eternity. Therefore no law is eternal.

Obj. 2. Further, promulgation is essential to law. But promulgation could not be from eternity: because there was no one to whom it could be promulgated from eternity. Therefore no law can be eternal.

Obj. 3. Further, a law implies order to an end. But nothing ordained to an end is eternal: for the last end alone is eternal. Therefore no law is eternal.

On the contrary, Augustine says (*De Lib. Arb.* i.): *That Law which is the Supreme Reason cannot be understood to be otherwise than unchangeable and eternal.*

I answer that, a law is nothing else but a dictate of practical reason emanating from the ruler who governs a perfect community. Now it is evident, granted that the world is ruled by Divine Providence, that the whole community of the universe is governed by Divine Reason. Wherefore the very Idea of the government of things in God the Ruler of the universe, has the nature of a law. And since the Divine Reason's conception

of things is not subject to time but is eternal, according to Prov. viii. 23, therefore it is that this kind of law must be called eternal.

Reply Obj. 1. Those things that are not in themselves, exist with God, inasmuch as they are foreknown and preordained by Him, according to Rom. iv. 17: *Who calls those things that are not, as those that are.* Accordingly the eternal concept of the Divine law bears the character of an eternal law, in so far as it is ordained by God to the government of things foreknown by Him.

Reply Obj. 2. Promulgation is made by word of mouth or in writing; and in both ways the eternal law is promulgated; because both the Divine Word and the writing of the Book of Life are eternal. But the promulgation cannot be from eternity on the part of the creature that hears or reads.

Reply Obj. 3. The law implies order to the end actively, in so far as it directs certain things to the end; but not passively,—that is to say, the law itself is not ordained to the end,—except accidentally, in a governor whose end is extrinsic to him, and to which end his law must needs be ordained. But the end of the Divine government is God Himself, and His law is not distinct from Himself. Wherefore the eternal law is not ordained to another end.

Second Article.
Whether There Is in Us a Natural Law?

We proceed thus to the Second Article:—

Objection 1. It seems that there is no natural law in us. Because man is governed sufficiently by the eternal law: for Augustine says (*De Lib. Arb.* i.) that *the eternal law is that by which it is*

Reprinted from *Summa Theologica* (London: Burns Oates & Washbourne, 1912).

right that all things should be most orderly. But nature does not abound in superfluities as neither does she fail in necessaries. Therefore no law is natural to man.

· *Obj.* 2. Further, by the law man is directed, in his acts, to the end. But the directing of human acts to their end is not a function of nature, as is the case in irrational creatures, which act for an end solely by their natural appetite; whereas man acts for an end by his reason and will. Therefore no law is natural to man.

Obj. 3. Further, the more a man is free, the less is he under the law. But man is freer than all the animals, on account of his free-will, with which he is endowed above all other animals. Since therefore other animals are not subject to a natural law, neither is man subject to a natural law.

On the contrary, The gloss on Rom. ii. 14: *When the Gentiles, who have not the law, do by nature those things that are of the law,* comments as follows: *Although they have no written law, yet they have the natural law, whereby each one knows, and is conscious of, what is good and what is evil.*

I answer that law, being a rule and measure, can be in a person in two ways: in one way, as in him that rules and measures: in another way, as in that which is ruled and measured, since a thing is ruled and measured, in so far as it partakes of the rule or measure. Wherefore, since all things subject to Divine providence are ruled and measured by the eternal law; it is evident that all things partake somewhat of the eternal law, in so far as, namely, from its being imprinted on them, they derive their respective inclinations to their proper acts and ends. Now among all others, the rational creature is subject to Divine providence in the most excellent way, in so far as it partakes of a share of providence, by being provident both for itself and for others. Wherefore it has a share of the Eternal reason, whereby it has a natural inclination to its proper act and end, and this participation of the eternal law in the rational creature is called the natural law. Hence the Psalmist after saying (Ps. iv. 6): *Offer up the sacrifice of justice,* as though someone

asked what the works of justice are, adds: *Many say, Who showeth us good things?* in answer to which question he says: *The light of Thy countenance, O Lord, is signed upon us:* thus implying that the light of natural reason, whereby we discern what is good and what is evil, which is the function of the natural law, is nothing else than an imprint on us of the Divine light. It is therefore evident that the natural law is nothing else than the rational creature's participation of the eternal law.

Reply Obj. 1. This argument would hold, if the natural law were something different from the eternal law: whereas it is nothing but a participation thereof, as stated above.

Reply Obj. 2. Every act of reason and will in us is based on that which is according to nature ... for every act of reasoning is based on principles that are known naturally, and every act of appetite in respect of the means is derived from the natural appetite in respect of the last end. Accordingly the first direction of our acts to their end must needs be in virtue of the natural law.

Reply Obj. 3. Even irrational animals partake in their own way of the Eternal Reason, just as the rational creature does. But because the rational creature partakes thereof in an intellectual and rational manner, therefore the participation of the eternal law in the rational creature is properly called a law, since a law is something pertaining to reason. Irrational creatures, however, do not partake thereof in a rational manner, wherefore there is no participation of the eternal law in them, except by way of similitude.

Third Article.
Whether There Is a Human Law?

We proceed thus to the Third Article:—

Objection 1. It seems that there is not a human law. For the natural law is a participation of the eternal law. Now through the eternal law *all things are most orderly,* as Augustine states (*De Lib. Arb.* i.). Therefore the natural law suffices for the ordering of all human affairs. Consequently there is no need for a human law.

Obj. 2. Further, a law bears the character of a measure. But human reason is not a measure of things, but vice versa (*cf. Metaph.* x.). Therefore no law can emanate from human reason.

Obj. 3. Further, a measure should be most certain, as stated in *Metaph.* x. But the dictates of human reason in matters of conduct are uncertain, according to Wis. ix. 14: *The thoughts of mortal man are fearful, and our counsels uncertain.* Therefore no law can emanate from human reason.

On the contrary, Augustine (*De Lib. Arb.* i.) distinguishes two kinds of law, the one eternal, the other temporal, which he calls human.

I answer that a law is a dictate of the practical reason. Now it is to be observed that the same procedure takes place in the practical and in the speculative reason: for each proceeds from principles to conclusions. Accordingly we conclude that just as, in the speculative reason, from naturally known indemonstrable principles, we draw the conclusions of the various sciences, the knowledge of which is not imparted to us by nature, but acquired by the efforts of reason, so too it is from the precepts of the natural law, as from general and indemonstrable principles, that the human reason needs to proceed to the more particular determination of certain matters. These particular determinations, devised by human reason, are called human laws, provided the other essential conditions of law be observed. Wherefore Tully says in his *Rhetoric (De Invent. Rhet.* ii.) that *justice has its source in nature: thence certain things came into custom by reason of their utility; afterwards these things which emanated from nature and were approved by custom, were sanctioned by fear and reverence for the law.*

Reply Obj. 1. The human reason cannot have a full participation of the dictate of the Divine Reason, but according to its own mode, and imperfectly. Consequently, as on the part of the speculative reason, by a natural participation of Divine Wisdom, there is in us the knowledge of

certain general principles, but not proper knowledge of each single truth, such as that contained in the Divine Wisdom; so too, on the part of the practical reason, man has a natural participation of the eternal law, according to certain general principles, but not as regards the particular determinations of individual cases, which are, however, contained in the eternal law. Hence the need for human reason to proceed further to sanction them by law.

Reply Obj. 2. Human reason is not, of itself, the rule of things: but the principles impressed on it by nature, are general rules and measures of all things relating to human conduct, whereof the natural reason is the rule and measure, although it is not the measure of things that are from nature.

Reply Obj. 3. The practical reason is concerned with practical matters, which are singular and contingent: but not with necessary things, with which the speculative reason is concerned. Wherefore human laws cannot have that inerrancy that belongs to the demonstrated conclusions of sciences. Nor is it necessary for every measure to be altogether unerring and certain, but according as it is possible in its own particular genus. . . .

QUESTION 94. OF THE NATURAL LAW.

First Article.
Whether the Natural Law Is a Habit?

We proceed thus to the First Articles:—

Objection 1. It seems that the natural law is a habit. Because, as the Philosopher says (*Ethic.* ii.), *there are three things in the soul, power, habit and passion.* But the natural law is not one of the soul's powers: nor is it one of the passions; as we may see by going through them one by one. Therefore the natural law is a habit.

Obj. 2. Further, Basil (Damascene, *De Fide Orthod.* iv.) says that the conscience or *synderesis is the law of our mind;* which can only apply to the natural law. But the *synderesis* is a habit ... Therefore the natural law is a habit.

Obj. 3. Further, the natural law abides in man always. But man's reason, which the law regards, does not always think about the natural law. Therefore the natural law is not an act, but a habit.

On the contrary, Augustine says (*De Bono Conjug.* xxi.) that *a habit is that whereby something is done when necessary.* But such is not the natural law: since it is in infants and in the damned who cannot act by it. Therefore the natural law is not a habit.

I answer that, A thing may be called a habit in two ways. First, properly and essentially: and thus the natural law is not a habit. For natural law is something appointed by reason, just as a proposition is a work of reason. Now that which a man does is not the same as that whereby he does it: for he makes a becoming speech by the habit of grammar. Since then a habit is that by which we act, a law cannot be a habit properly and essentially.

Secondly, the term habit may be applied to that which we hold by a habit: thus faith may mean that which we hold by faith. And accordingly, since the precepts of the natural law are sometimes considered by reason actually, while sometimes they are in the reason only habitually, in this way the natural law may be called a habit. Thus, in speculative matters, the indemonstrable principles are not the habit itself whereby we hold those principles, but are the principles the habit of which we possess.

Reply Obj. 1. The Philosopher proposes there to discover the genus of virtue; and since it is evident that virtue is a principle of action, he mentions only those things which are principles of human acts, viz., powers, habits and passions. But there are other things in the soul besides these three: there are acts; thus *to will* is in the one that wills; again, things known are in the knower; moreover its own natural properties are in the soul, such as immortality and the like.

Reply Obj. 2. *Synderesis* is said to be the law of our mind, because it is a habit containing the precepts of the natural law, which are the first principles of human actions.

Reply Obj. 3. This argument proves that the natural law is held habitually: and this is granted.

To the argument advanced in the contrary sense we reply that sometimes a man is unable to make use of that which is in him habitually, on account of some impediment: thus, on account of sleep, a man is unable to use the habit of science. In like manner, through the deficiency of his age, a child cannot use the habit of understanding of principles, or the natural law, which is in him habitually.

Second Article.
Whether the Natural Law Contains Several Precepts, or One Only?

We proceed thus to the Second Article:—

Objection 1. It seems that the natural law contains, not several precepts, but one only. For law is a kind of precept. If therefore there were many precepts of the natural law, it would follow that there are also many natural laws.

Obj. 2. Further, the natural law is consequent to human nature. But human nature, as a whole, is one; though, as to its parts, it is manifold. Therefore, either there is but one precept of the law of nature, on account of the unity of nature as a whole; or there are many, by reason of the number of parts of human nature. The result would be that even things relating to the inclination of the concupiscible faculty belong to the natural law.

Obj. 3. Further, law is something pertaining to reason. Now reason is but one in man. Therefore there is only one precept of the natural law.

On the contrary, The precepts of the natural law in man stand in relation to practical matters, as the first principles to matters of demonstration. But there are several first indemonstrable principles. Therefore there are also several precepts of the natural law.

I answer that, the precepts of the natural law are to the practical reason, what the first principles of demonstrations are to the speculative reason; because both are self-evident principles. Now a thing is said to be self-evident in two ways: first, in itself; secondly, in relation to us. Any proposition is said to be self-evident in itself, if its predicate is contained in the notion of the subject: although, to one who knows not the definition of the subject, it happens that such a proposition is not self-evident. For instance, this proposition, *Man is a rational being,* is, in its very nature, self-evident, since who says *man,* says a *rational being:* and yet to one who knows not what a man is, this proposition is not self-evident. Hence it is that, as Boethius says (*De Hebdom.*), certain axioms or propositions are universally self-evident to all; and such are those propositions whose terms are known to all, as, *Every whole is greater than its part,* and, *Things equal to one and the same are equal to one another.* But some propositions are self-evident only to the wise, who understand the meaning of the terms of such propositions: thus to one who understands that an angel is not a body, it is self-evident that an angel is not circumscriptively in a place: but this is not evident to the unlearned, for they cannot grasp it.

Now a certain order is to be found in those things that are apprehended universally. For that which, before aught else, falls under apprehension, is *being,* the notion of which is included in all things whatsoever a man apprehends. Wherefore the first indemonstrable principle is that *the same thing cannot be affirmed and denied at the same time,* which is based on the notion of *being* and *not-being:* and on this principle all others are based. Now as *being* is the first thing that falls under the apprehension simply, so *good* is the first thing that falls under the apprehension of the practical reason, which is directed to action: since every agent acts for an end under the aspect of good. Consequently the first principle in the practical reason is one founded on the notion of good, viz., that *good is that which all*

things seek after. Hence this is the first precept of law, that *good is to be done and ensued, and evil is to be avoided.* All other precepts of the natural law are based upon this: so that whatever the practical reason naturally apprehends as man's good (or evil) belongs to the precepts of the natural law as something to be done or avoided.

Since, however, good has the nature of an end, and evil, the nature of a contrary, hence it is that all those things to which man has a natural inclination, are naturally apprehended by reason as being good, and consequently as objects of pursuit, and their contraries as evil, and objects of avoidance. Wherefore according to the order of natural inclinations, is the order of the precepts of the natural law. Because in man there is first of all an inclination to good in accordance with the nature which he has in common with all substances: inasmuch as every substance seeks the preservation of its own being, according to its nature: and by reason of this inclination, whatever is a means of preserving human life, and of warding off its obstacles, belongs to the natural law. Secondly, there is in man an inclination of things that pertain to him more specially, according to that nature which he has in common with other animals: and in virtue of this inclination, those things are said to belong to the natural law, *which nature has taught to all animals,* such as sexual intercourse, education of offspring and so forth. Thirdly, there is in man an inclination to good, according to the nature of his reason, which nature is proper to him: thus man has a natural inclination to know the truth about God, and to live in society: and in this respect, whatever pertains to this inclination belongs to the natural law; for instance, to shun ignorance, to avoid offending those among whom one has to live, and other such things regarding the above inclination.

Reply Obj. 1. All these precepts of the law of nature have the character of one natural law, inasmuch as they flow from one first precept.

Reply Obj. 2. All the inclinations of any parts whatsoever of human nature, *e.g.,* of the concupiscible and irascible parts, in so far as they are ruled by reason, belong to the natural law, and are reduced to one first precept, as stated above: so that the precepts of the natural law are many in themselves, but are based on one common foundation.

Reply Obj. 3. Although reason is one in itself, yet it directs all things regarding man; so that whatever can be ruled by reason, is contained under the law of reason.

Third Article.
Whether All Acts of Virtue Are Prescribed by the Natural Law?

We proceed thus to the Third Article:—

Objection 1. It seems that not all acts of virtue are prescribed by the natural law. Because it is essential to a law that it be ordained to the common good. But some acts of virtue are ordained to the private good of the individual, as is evident especially in regard to acts of temperance. Therefore not all acts of virtue are the subject of natural law.

Obj. 2. Further, every sin is opposed to some virtuous act. If therefore all acts of virtue are prescribed by the natural law, it seems to follow that all sins are against nature: whereas this applies to certain special sins.

Obj. 3. Further, those things which are according to nature are common to all. But acts of virtue are not common to all: since a thing is virtuous in one, and vicious in another. Therefore not all acts of virtue are prescribed by the natural law.

On the contrary, Damascene says (*De Fide Orthod.* iii.) that *virtues are natural.* Therefore virtuous acts also are a subject of the natural law.

I answer that, We may speak of virtuous acts in two ways: first, under the aspect of virtuous; secondly, as such and such acts considered in their proper species. If then we speak of acts of virtue, considered as virtuous, thus all virtuous acts belong to the natural law. For to the natural law belongs everything to which a man is inclined according to his nature. Now each thing is inclined naturally to an operation that is suitable to it according to its form: thus fire is inclined to give heat. Wherefore, since the rational soul is the proper form of man, there is in every man a natural inclination to act according to reason: and this is to act according to virtue. Consequently, considered thus, all acts of virtue are prescribed by the natural law: since each one's reason naturally dictates to him to act virtuously. But if we speak of virtuous acts, considered in themselves, i.e., in their proper species, thus not all virtuous acts are prescribed by the natural law: for many things are done virtuously, to which nature does not incline at first; but which, through the inquiry of reason, have been found by men to be conducive to well-living.

Reply Obj. 1. Temperance is about the natural concupiscence of food, drink and sexual matters, which are indeed ordained to the natural common good, just as other matters of law are ordained to the moral common good.

Reply Obj. 2. By human nature we may mean either that which is proper to man—and in this sense all sins, as being against reason, are also against nature, as Damascene states (*De Fide Orthod.* ii.): or we may mean that nature which is common to man and other animals; and in this sense, certain special sins are said to be against nature; thus contrary to sexual intercourse, which is natural to all animals, is unisexual lust, which has received the special name of the unnatural crime.

Reply Obj. 3. This argument considers acts in themselves. For it is owing to the various conditions of men, that certain acts are virtuous for some, as being proportionate and becoming to them, while they are vicious for others, as being out of proportion to them.

Fourth Article.
Whether the Natural Law Is the Same in All Men?

We proceed thus to the Fourth Article.—

Objection 1. It seems that the natural law is

not the same in all. For it is stated in the Decretals (*Dist.* i.) that *the natural law is that which is contained in the Law and the Gospel.* But this is not common to all men; because, as it is written (Rom. x. 16), *all do not obey the gospel.* Therefore the natural law is not the same in all men.

Obj. 2. Further, *Things which are according to the law are said to be just.* But it is stated in the same book that nothing is so universally just as not to be subject to change in regard to some men. Therefore even the natural law is not the same in all men.

Obj. 3. Further, to the natural law belongs everything to which a man is inclined according to his nature. Now different men are naturally inclined to different things; some to the desire of pleasures, others to the desire of honours, and other men to other things. Therefore there is not one natural law for all.

On the contrary, Isidore says (*Etym.* v.); *The natural law is common to all nations.*

I answer that, to the natural law belongs those things to which a man is inclined naturally: and among these it is proper to man to be inclined to act according to reason. Now the process of reason is from the common to the proper. The speculative reason, however, is differently situated in this matter, from the practical reason. For, since the speculative reason is busied chiefly with necessary things, which cannot be otherwise than they are, its proper conclusions, like the universal principles, contain the truth without fail. The practical reason, on the other hand, is busied with contingent matters, about which human actions are concerned: and consequently, although there is necessity in the general principles, the more we descend to matters of detail, the more frequently we encounter defects. Accordingly then in speculative matters truth is the same in all men, both as to principles and as to conclusions: although the truth is not known to all as regards the conclusions, but only as regards the principles which are called common notions. But in matters of action, truth or practical rectitude is not the same for all, as to matters of detail, but only as to the general principles: and where there is the same rectitude in matters of detail, it is not equally known to all.

It is therefore evident that, as regards the general principles whether of speculative or of practical reason, truth or rectitude is the same for all, and is equally known by all. As to the proper conclusions of the speculative reason, the truth is the same for all, but is not equally known to all: thus it is true for all that the three angles of a triangle are together equal to two right angles, although it is not known to all. But as to the proper conclusions of the practical reason, neither is the truth or rectitude the same for all, nor, where it is the same, is it equally known by all. Thus it is right and true for all to act according to reason: and from this principle it follows as a proper conclusion, that goods entrusted to another should be restored to their owner. Now this is true for the majority of cases: but it may happen in a particular case that it would be injurious, and therefore unreasonable, to restore goods held in trust; for instance if they are claimed for the purpose of fighting against one's country. And this principle will be found to fail the more, according as we descend further into detail, *e.g.,* if one were to say that goods held in trust should be restored with such and such a guarantee, or in such and such a way; because the greater the number of conditions added, the greater the number of ways in which the principle may fail, so that it be not right to restore or not to restore.

Consequently we must say that the natural law, as to general principles, is the same for all, both as to rectitude and as to knowledge. But as to certain matters of detail, which are conclusions, as it were, of those general principles, it is the same for all in the majority of cases, both as to rectitude and as to knowledge; and yet in some few cases it may fail, both as to rectitude, by reason of certain obstacles (just as natures subject to generation and corruption fail in some few cases on account of some obstacle), and as to knowledge, since in some the reason is perverted by passion, or evil habit, or an evil disposition of nature; thus formerly, theft, although it is expressly contrary to the natural law, was not considered wrong among the Germans, as Julius Caesar relates (*De Bello Gall.* vi.).

Reply Obj. 1. The meaning of the sentence quoted is not that whatever is contained in the Law and the Gospel belongs to the natural law, since they contain many things that are above nature; but that whatever belongs to the natural law is fully contained in them. Wherefore Gratian, after saying that *the natural law is what is contained in the Law and the Gospel,* adds at once; by way of example, *by which everyone is commanded to do to others as he would be done by.*

Reply Obj. 2. The saying of the Philosopher is to be understood of things that are naturally just, not as general principles, but as conclusions drawn from them, having rectitude in the majority of cases, but failing in a few.

Reply Obj. 3. As, in man, reason rules and commands the other powers, so all the natural inclinations belonging to the other powers must needs be directed according to reason. Wherefore it is universally right for all men, that all their inclinations should be directed according to reason.

Fifth Article.
Whether the Natural Law Can Be Changed?

We proceed thus to the Fifth Article:—

Objection 1. It seems that the natural law can be changed. Because on Ecclus. vxii. 9, *He gave them instructions, and the law of life,* the gloss says: *He wished the law of the letter to be written, in order to correct the law of nature.* But that which is corrected is changed. Therefore the natural law can be changed.

Obj. 2. Further, the slaying of the innocent, adultery, and theft are against the natural law. But we find these things changed by God: as when God commanded Abraham to slay his innocent son (Gen. xxii. 2); and when He ordered the Jews to borrow and purloin the ves-

sels of the Egyptians (Exod. xii. 35); and when He commanded Osee to take to himself *a wife of fornications* (*Osee* i. 2). Therefore the natural law can be changed.

Obj. 3. Further, Isidore says (*Etym.* v.) that *the possession of all things in common, and universal freedom, are matters of natural law.* But these things are seen to be changed by human laws. Therefore it seems that the natural law is subject to change.

On the contrary, It is said in the Decretals (*Dist.* v.): *The natural law dates from the creation of the rational creature. It does not vary according to time, but remains unchangeable.*

I answer that, A change in the natural law may be understood in two ways. First, by way of addition. In this sense nothing hinders the natural law from being changed: since many things for the benefit of human life have been added over and above the natural law, both by the Divine law and by human laws.

Secondly, a change in the natural law may be understood by way of subtraction, so that what previously was according to the natural law, ceases to be so. In this sense, the natural law is altogether unchangeable in its first principles: but in its secondary principles, which are certain detailed proximate conclusions drawn from the first principles, the natural law is not changed so that what it prescribes be not right in most cases. But it may be changed in some particular cases of rare occurrence, through some special causes hindering the observance of such precepts.

Reply Obj. 1. The written law is said to be given for the correction of the natural law, either because it supplies what was wanting to the natural law; or because the natural law was perverted in the hearts of some men, as to certain matters, so that they esteemed those things good which are naturally evil; which perversion stood in need of correction.

Reply Obj. 2. All men alike, both guilty and innocent, die the death of nature: which death of nature is inflicted by the power of God on account of original sin, according to I Kings ii. 6:

The Lord killeth and maketh alive. Consequently, by the command of God, death can be inflicted on any man, guilty or innocent, without any injustice whatever.—In like manner adultery is intercourse with another's wife; who is allotted to him by the law emanating from God. Consequently intercourse with any woman, by the command of God, is neither adultery nor fornication.—The same applies to theft, which is the taking of another's property. For whatever is taken by the command of God, to Whom all things belong, is not taken against the will of its owner, whereas it is in this that theft consists.—Nor is it only in human things, that whatever is commanded by God is right; but also in natural things, whatever is done by God is, in some way, natural.

Reply Obj. 3. A thing is said to belong to the natural law in two ways. First, because nature inclines thereto: *e.g.,* that one should not do harm to another. Secondly, because nature did not bring in the contrary: thus we might say that for man to be naked is of the natural law, because nature did not give him clothes, but art invented them. In this sense, *the possession of all things in common and universal freedom* are said to be of the natural law, because, to wit, the distinction of possessions and slavery were not brought in by nature, but devised by human reason for the benefit of human life. Accordingly the law of nature was not changed in this respect, except by addition.

Sixth Article.
Whether the Law of Nature Can Be Abolished from the Heart of Man?

We proceed thus to the Sixth Article:—

Objection 1. It seems that the natural law can be abolished from the heart of man. Because on Rom. ii. 14, *When the Gentiles who have not the law,* etc., the gloss says that *the law of righteousness, which sin had blotted out, is graven on the heart of man when he is restored by grace.* But the law of righteousness is the law of nature. Therefore the law of nature can be blotted out.

Obj. 2. Further, the law of grace is more efficacious than the law of nature. But the law of grace is blotted out by sin. Much more therefore can the law of nature be blotted out.

Obj. 3. Further, that which is established by law is made just. But many things are enacted by men, which are contrary to the law of nature. Therefore the law of nature can be abolished from the heart of man.

On the contrary, Augustine says (*Conf.* ii.): *Thy law is written in the hearts of men, which iniquity itself effaces not.* But the law which is written in men's hearts is the natural law. Therefore the natural law cannot be blotted out.

I answer that, there belong to the natural law, first, certain most general precepts, that are known to all; and secondly, certain secondary and more detailed precepts, which are, as it were, conclusions following closely from first principles. As to those general principles, the natural law, in the abstract, can nowise be blotted out from men's hearts. But it is blotted out in the case of a particular action, in so far as reason is hindered from applying the general principle to a particular point of practice, on account of concupiscence or some other passion. But as to the other, *i. e.,* the secondary precepts, the natural law can be blotted out from the human heart, either by evil persuasions, just as in speculative matters errors occur in respect of necessary conclusions; or by vicious customs and corrupt habits, as among some men, theft, and even unnatural vices, as the Apostle states (Rom. i.), were not esteemed sinful.

Reply Obj. 1. Sin blots out the law of nature in particular cases, not universally, except perchance in regard to the secondary precepts of the natural law, in the way stated above.

Reply Obj. 2. Although grace is more efficacious than nature, yet nature is more essential to man, and therefore more enduring.

Reply Obj. 3. This argument is true of the secondary precepts of the natural law, against which some legislators have framed certain enactments which are unjust. . . .

QUESTION 92.
THE PRODUCTION OF THE WOMAN.

First Article.
Whether the Woman Should Have Been Made in the First Production of Things?

We proceed thus to the First Article:—

Objection 1. It would seem that the woman should not have been made in the first production of things. For the Philosopher says (*De Gener. Animal.* ii. 3), that the *female is a misbegotten male*. But nothing misbegotten or defective should have been in the first production of things. Therefore woman should not have been made at that first production.

Obj. 2. Further, subjection and limitation were a result of sin, for to the woman was it said after sin (Gen. iii. 16): *Thou shalt be under the man's power;* and Gregory says that, *Where there is no sin, there is no inequality.* But women is naturally of less strength and dignity than man; *for that agent is always more honourable than the patient,* as Augustine says (*Gen. ad lit.* xii. 16). Therefore woman should not have been made in the first production of things before sin.

Obj. 3. Further, occasions of sin should be cut off. But God foresaw that the women would be an occasion of sin to man. Therefore He should not have made woman.

On the contrary, It is written (Gen. ii, 18): *It is not good for man to be alone; let us make him a helper like to himself.*

I answer that, It was necessary for woman to be made, as the Scripture says, as *a helper* to man; not, indeed, as a helpmate in other works, as some say, since man can be more efficiently helped by another man in other works; but as a helper in the work of generation. This can be made clear if we observe the mode of generation carried out in various living things. Some living things do not possess in themselves the power of generation, but are generated by some other specific agent, such as some plants and animals by the influence of the heavenly bodies, from some fitting matter and not from seed: others possess

the active and passive generative power together; as we see in plants which are generated from seed; for the noblest vital function in plants is generation. Wherefore we observe that in these the active power of generation invariably accompanies the passive power. Among perfect animals the active power of generation belongs to the male sex, and the passive power to the female. And as among animals there is a vital operation nobler than generation, to which their life is principally directed; therefore the male sex is not found in continual union with the female in perfect animals, but only at the time of coition; so that we may consider that by this means the male and female are one, as in plants they are always united; although in some cases one of them preponderates, and in some the other. But man is yet further ordered to a still nobler vital action, and that is intellectual operation. Therefore there was greater reason for the distinction of these two forces in man; so that the female should be produced separately from the male; although they are carnally united for generation. Therefore directly after the formation of woman, it was said: *And they shall be two in one flesh* (Gen. ii. 24).

Reply Obj. 1. As regards the individual nature, woman is defective and misbegotten, for the active force in the male seed tends to the production of a perfect likeness in the masculine sex; while the production of woman comes from defect in the active force or from some material indisposition, or even from some external influence; such as that of a south wind, which is moist, as the Philosopher observes (*De Gener. Animal.* iv. 2). On the other hand, as regards human nature in general, woman is not misbegotten, but is included in nature's intention as directed to the work of generation. Now the general intention of nature depends on God, Who is the universal Author of nature. Therefore, in producing nature, God formed not only the male but also the female.

Reply Obj. 2. Subjection is twofold. One is servile, by virtue of which a superior makes use of a subject for his own benefit; and this kind of subjection began after sin. There is another kind of subjection, which is called economic or civil, whereby the superior makes use of his subjects for their own benefit and good; and this kind of subjection existed even before sin. For good order would have been wanting in the human family if some were not governed by others wiser than themselves. So by such a kind of subjection woman is naturally subject to man, because in man the discretion of reason predominates. Nor is inequality among men excluded by the state of innocence.

Reply Obj. 3. If God had deprived the world of all those things which proved an occasion of sin, the universe would have been imperfect. Nor was it fitting for the common good to be destroyed in order that individual evil might be avoided; especially as God is so powerful that He can direct any evil to a good end.

Second Article.
Whether Woman Should Have Been Made from Man?

We proceed thus to the Second Article:—

Objection 1. It would seem that woman should not have been made from man. For sex belongs both to man and animals. But in the other animals the female was not made from the male. Therefore neither should it have been so with man.

Obj. 2. Further, things of the same species are of the same matter. But male and female are of the same species. Therefore, as man was made of the slime of the earth, so woman should have been made of the same, and not from man.

Obj. 3. Further, woman was made to be a helpmate to man in the work of generation. But close relationship makes a person unfit for that office; hence near relations are debarred from intermarriage, as is written (Lev. xviii. 6). Therefore woman should not have been made from man.

On the contrary, It is written (Ecclus. xvii. 5): *He created of him,* that is, out of man, *a helpmate like himself,* that is, woman.

I answer that, When all things were first formed, it was more suitable for the woman to be made from the man than (for the female to be from the male) in other animals. First, in order thus to give the first man a certain dignity consisting in this, that as God is the principle of the whole universe, so the first man, in likeness to God, was the principle of the whole human race. Wherefore Paul says that *God made the whole human race from one* (Acts xvii. 26). Secondly, that man might love woman all the more, and cleave to her more closely, knowing her to be fashioned from himself. Hence it is written (Gen. ii. 23, 24): *She was taken out of man, wherefore a man shall leave father and mother, and shall cleave to his wife.* This was not necessary as regards the human race, in which the male and female live together for life, which is not the case with other animals. Thirdly, because, as the Philosopher says (*Ethic.* viii. 12), the human male and female are united, not only for generation, as with other animals, but also for the purpose of domestic life, in which each has his or her particular duty, and in which the man is the head of the woman. Wherefore it was suitable for the woman to be made out of man, as out of her principle. Fourthly, there is a sacramental reason for this. For by this is signified that the Church takes his origin from Christ. Wherefore the Apostle says (Eph. v. 32): *This is a great sacrament; but I speak in Christ and in the Church.*

Reply Obj. 1 is clear from the foregoing.

Reply Obj. 2. Matter is that from which something is made. Now created nature has a determinate principle; and since it is determined to one thing, it has also a determinate mode of proceeding. Wherefore from determinate matter it produces something in a determinate species. On the other hand, the Divine Power, being infinite, can produce things of the same species out of any matter, such as a man from the slime of the earth, and a woman from a man.

Reply Obj. 3. A certain affinity arises from natural generation, and this is an impediment to matrimony. Woman, however, was not produced from man by natural generation, but by the Divine Power alone. Wherefore Eve is not called the daughter of Adam; and so this argument does not prove.

Third Article.
Whether the Woman Was Fittingly Made from the Rib of Man?

We proceed thus to the Third Article:—

Objection 1. It would seem that the woman should not have been formed from the rib of man. For the rib was much smaller than the woman's body. Now from a smaller thing a larger thing can be made only—either by addition (and then the woman ought to have been described as made out of that which was added, rather than out of the rib itself);—or by rarefaction, because, as Augustine says (*Gen. ad lit.* x.): *A body cannot increase in bulk except by rarefaction.* But the woman's body is not more rarefied than man's—at least, not in the proportion of a rib to Eve's body. Therefore Eve was not formed from a rib of Adam.

Obj. 2. Further, in those things which were first created there was nothing superfluous. Therefore a rib of Adam belonged to the integrity of his body. So, if a rib was removed, his body remained imperfect; which is unreasonable to suppose.

Obj. 3. Further, a rib cannot be removed from man without pain. But there was no pain before sin. Therefore it was not right for a rib to be taken from the man, that Eve might be made from it.

On the contrary, It is written (Gen. ii. 22): *God built the rib, which He took from Adam, into a woman.*

I answer that, It was right for the woman to be made from a rib of man. First, to signify the social union of man and woman, for the woman should neither *use authority over man,* and so she was not made from his head; nor was it right for her to be subject to man's contempt as his slave, and so she was not made from his feet. Secondly, for the sacramental signification; for from the side of Christ sleeping on the Cross the Sacraments flowed—namely, blood and water—on which the Church was established.

Reply Obj. 1. Some say that the woman's body was formed by a material increase, without anything being added; in the same way as our Lord multiplied the five loaves. But this is quite impossible. For such an increase of matter would either be by a change of the very substance of the matter itself, or by a change of its dimensions. Not by change of the substance of the matter, both because matter, considered in itself, is quite unchangeable, since it has a potential existence, and has nothing but the nature of a subject, and because quantity and size are extraneous to the essence of matter itself. Wherefore multiplication of matter is quite unintelligible, as long as the matter itself remains the same without anything added to it; unless it receives greater dimensions. This implies rarefaction, which is for the same matter to receive greater dimensions, as the Philosopher says (*Phys.* iv.). To say, therefore, that the same matter is enlarged, without being rarefied, is to combine contradictories—viz., the definition with the absence of the thing defined.

Wherefore, as no rarefaction is apparent in such multiplication of matter, we must admit an addition of matter: either by creation or, which is more probable, by conversion. Hence Augustine says (*Tract.* xxiv., *in Joan*) that *Christ filled five thousand men with five loaves, in the same way as from a few seeds He produces the harvest of corn*—that is, by transformation of the nourishment. Nevertheless, we say that the crowds were fed with five loaves, or that woman was made from the rib, because an addition was made to the already existing matter of the loaves and of the rib.

Reply Obj. 2. The rib belonged to the integral perfection of Adam, not as an individual, but as the principle of the human race; just as the semen belongs to the perfection of the begetter,

and is released by a natural and pleasurable operation. Much more, therefore, was it possible that by the Divine power the body of the woman should be produced from the man's rib.

From this it is clear how to answer the third objection.

15. THE BOOK OF THE CITY OF LADIES

CHRISTINE DE PIZAN

27. CHRISTINE ASKS REASON WHETHER GOD HAS EVER WISHED TO ENNOBLE THE MIND OF WOMAN WITH THE LOFTINESS OF THE SCIENCES; AND REASON'S ANSWER.

I.27.1 After hearing these things, I replied to the lady who spoke infallibly: "My lady, truly has God revealed great wonders in the strength of these women whom you describe. But please enlighten me again, whether it has ever pleased this God, who has bestowed so many favors on women, to honor the feminine sex with the privilege of the virtue of high understanding and great learning, and whether women ever have a clever enough mind for this. I wish very much to know this because men maintain that the mind of women can learn only a little."

She answered, "My daughter, since I told you before, you know quite well that the opposite of their opinion is true, and to show you this even more clearly, I will give you proof through examples. I tell you again—and don't doubt the contrary—if it were customary to send daughters to school like sons, and if they were then taught the natural sciences, they would learn as thoroughly and understand the subtleties of all the arts and sciences as well as sons. And by chance there happen to be such women, for, as I touched on before, just as women have more delicate bodies than men, weaker and less able to perform many tasks, so do they have minds that are freer and sharper whenever they apply themselves."

"My lady, what are you saying? With all due respect, could you dwell longer on this point, please. Certainly men would never admit this answer is true, unless it is explained more plainly, for they believe that one normally sees that men know more than women do."

She answered, "Do you know why women know less?"

"Not unless you tell me, my lady."

"Without the slightest doubt, it is because they are not involved in many different things, but stay at home, where it is enough for them to run the household, and there is nothing which so instructs a reasonable creature as the exercise and experience of many different things."

"My lady, since they have minds skilled in conceptualizing and learning, just like men, why don't women learn more?"

She replied, "Because, my daughter, the public does not require them to get involved in the affairs which men are commissioned to execute, just as I told you before. It is enough for women to perform the usual duties to which they are ordained. As for judging from experience, since one sees that women usually know less than men, that therefore their capacity for understanding is less, look at men who farm the flatlands or who live in the mountains. You will find that in many countries they seem completely savage because they are so simple-minded. All the same, there is no doubt that Nature provided them with the qualities of body and mind found in the wisest and most learned men. All of this stems from a failure to learn, though, just as I told you, among men and women, some possess better minds than others. Let me tell you about women who have possessed great learning and profound understanding and treat the question of the similarity of women's minds to men's."

28. SHE BEGINS TO DISCUSS SEVERAL LADIES WHO WERE ENLIGHTENED WITH GREAT LEARNING, AND FIRST SPEAKS ABOUT THE NOBLE MAIDEN CORNIFICIA.

I.28.1 "Cornificia, the noble maiden, was sent to school by her parents along with her brother Cornificius when they were both children, thanks to deception and trickery. This little girl so devoted herself to study and with such marvelous intelligence that she began to savor the sweet taste of knowledge acquired through study. Nor was it easy to take her away from this joy to which she more and more applied herself, neglecting all other feminine activities. She occupied herself with this for such a long period of time that she became a consummate poet, and she was not only extremely brilliant and expert in the learnedness and craft of poetry but also seemed to have been nourished with the very milk and teaching of perfect philosophy, for she wanted to hear and know about every branch of learning, which she then mastered so thoroughly that she surpassed her brother, who was also a very great poet, and excelled in every field of learning. Knowledge was not enough for her unless she could put her mind to work and her pen to paper in the compilation of several very famous books. These works, as well as her poems, were much prized during the time of Saint Gregory and he himself mentions them. The Italian, Boccaccio, who was a great poet, discusses this fact in his work and at the same time praises this woman: 'O most great honor for a woman who abandoned all feminine activities and applied and devoted her mind to the study of the greatest scholars!' As further proof of what I am telling you, Boccaccio also talks about the attitude of women who despise themselves and their own minds, and who, as though they were born in the mountains totally ignorant of virtue and honor, turn disconsolate and say that they are good and useful only for embracing men and carrying and feeding children. God has given them such beautiful minds to apply themselves, if they want to, in any of the fields where glorious and excellent men are active, which are neither more nor less accessible to them as compared to men if they wished to study them, and they can thereby acquire a lasting name, whose possession is fitting for most excellent men. My dear daughter, you can see how this author Boccaccio testifies to what I have told you and how he praises and approves learning in women." ...

43. CHRISTINE ASKS REASON WHERE PRUDENCE IS FOUND IN THE NATURAL SENSIBILITY OF WOMEN; AND REASON'S ANSWER TO HER.

I.43.1 Then I, Christine, said to her, "My lady, I can truly and clearly see that God—may He be praised for it—has granted that the mind of an intelligent woman can conceive, know, and retain all perceptible things. Even though there are so many people who have such subtle minds that they understand and learn everything which they are shown and who are so ingenious and quick to conceptualize everything that every field of learning is open to them, with the result that they have acquired extraordinary knowledge through devotion to study, I am baffled when eminent scholars—including some of the most famous and learned—exhibit so little prudence in their morals and conduct in the world. Certainly scholarship teaches and provides an introduction to morals. If you please, my lady, I would gladly learn from you whether a woman's mind (which, as it seems to me from your proofs as well as from what I myself see, is quite understanding and retentive in subtle questions of scholarship and other subjects) is equally prompt and clever in those matters which prudence teaches, that is, whether women can reflect on what is best to do and what is better to be avoided, and whether they remember past events and become learned from the examples they have seen, and, as a result, are wise in managing current affairs, and whether they have foresight into the future. Prudence, it seems to me, teaches those lessons."

"You speak correctly, my daughter," she replied, "but this prudence of which you speak is bestowed by Nature upon men and women, and some possess more, others less. But Nature does not impart knowledge of everything, as much as it simultaneously perfects in those who are naturally prudent, for you realize that two forces together are stronger and more resistant than one force alone. For this reason I say that the person who, from Nature, possesses prudence (which is called 'natural sense'), as well as acquired knowledge along with this prudence, deserves special praise for remarkable excellence. Yet just as you yourself have said, some who possess the one do not possess the other, for the one is the gift of God thanks to the influence of Nature, and the other is acquired through long study, though both are good. But some people prefer natural sense without acquired knowledge rather than a great deal of acquired knowledge with little natural sense. All the same, many opinions can be based upon this proposition, from which many questions can arise. For one could say that one achieves more good by choosing what is more useful for the profit and the utility of the general public. Therefore, one person's knowing the different fields of learning is more profitable for everyone than all the natural sense which he might possess which he could demonstrate to all: for this natural sense can only last as long as the life-time of the person who has it, and when he dies, his sense dies with him. Acquired learning, on the other hand, lasts forever for those who have it, because of their fame, and it is useful for many people insofar as it can be taught to others and recorded in books for the sake of future generations. In this way their learning does not die with them, and therefore I can show you, using the example of Aristotle and others through whom learning has been transmitted to the world, that their acquired knowledge was more useful to the world than all the prudence without acquired knowledge possessed by all men, past and present, although thanks to the prudence of many, several kingdoms and empires have been well-governed and directed. All of these things are transitory, however, and disappear with time, while learning endures forever.

I.43.2 "Nevertheless, I will leave these questions unanswered and for others to solve, for they do not pertain to the problem of building our City, and I will come back to the question you raised, that is, whether women possess natural prudence. Of course they do. You know this already from what I have said to you before, just as, in general, you can see from women's conduct in those duties assigned to them to perform. But be careful if you find this good, for you will see that all women, or the vast majority, are so very attentive, careful, and diligent in governing their households and in providing everything for them, according to their capacities, that sometimes some of their negligent husbands are annoyed; they think their wives are pushing and pressuring them too much to do what they are supposed to and they say their wives want to run everything and be smarter than they are. In this way, what many women tell their husbands with good intentions turns out to their disadvantage.

16. EQUALITY OF SOULS, INEQUALITY OF SEXES: WOMAN IN MEDIEVAL THEOLOGY

ELEANOR McLAUGHLIN

Medievalists today are often sensitive to the issue of the "relevance" of their chosen field of study. When the topic is the theological definition of the female sex, there is apparently even more question as to the timeliness of the medieval perspective, for surely the years between the decline of antiquity and the Renaissance seem to have been a Dark Age for the woman. Because I suspect that this is a widely held view even among readers with some professional interest in the history of theology, I begin this paper with a note on the importance of the medieval period for the history of the woman....

The student of the woman in the Christian tradition needs to look to the medieval centuries to discover what transformations occur in the biblical and patristic traditions during the period that saw the emergence of Western Christian civilization. The classical, antique Christian and Germanic components of that civilization merged and reformed each other into a new spiritual, intellectual, and sociopolitical reality that in many respects created the limits and possibilities of our own twentieth-century world. It is, therefore, a medieval reinterpretation of the antique and Christian heritage that we have inherited ... By ["we"] I do not mean solely those who stand closer to a continuity with the medieval Christian tradition—Roman Catholics, Eastern Orthodox or Anglicans—but I refer also to our secularized society, which in its assumptions about the woman and all her works has deep and unconscious roots in medieval culture. True liberation from the androcentrism and misogyny of those assumptions can come only when that past is made explicit and clear in its implications....

Reprinted from *Religion and Sexism* by permission of the editor.

I

A representative theological framework for our study is appropriately drawn from the work of the Dominican Doctor of the Church Thomas Aquinas, not because he dominated the thirteenth-century theological scene (which he did not) but rather because of his mediation between the patristic and predominantly Augustinian inheritance, which had shaped theological speculation through the twelfth century, and the new naturalistic world view of Aristotelian metaphysics and natural science that became known to scholars in his lifetime. . . .

Thomas' discussion of the creation of the human being, focusing, as did the Fathers, on the Genesis 2 account, does depart from Augustine's in a way that has important implications for the nature of the female human being. In accord with Aristotelian hylomorphism, man (homo) is a composite of body and soul, in contrast to the Platonized patristic anthropology that defined the human being as a soul imprisoned in the materiality of the flesh.[1] This more integrated view of the relation of body and soul made possible for Thomas an escape from the patristic dualism that identified vir, the male, with spirit, and the female polarity with the earthward drag of the body. Thomas not only defines the human being (homo) as an integrity of body and soul, he gives a positive valuation to the body. The body has an excellence with respect to its end as long as it serves that end.[2] This view might have helped overcome the patristic pessimism about sex and the body, a pessimism that always fed a fear and denigration of women. However, Thomas followed Aristotle and his patristic authorities in their intellectualist definition of man, homo, so that the body-denying dualism and its associated androcentrism were reinvigorated. He did this by determining that the end for man, the final fulfillment of the human being, life with God, is achieved by the operation of the rational soul.[3] Ultimately, therefore, the body is again left out.

Furthermore, in his discussion of the bisexual creation of mankind, male and female, Thomas follows Aristotle in his view that the male is ordered to the more noble activity, intellectual knowledge, whereas the female, although possessing a rational soul, was created solely with respect to her sexuality, her body, as an aid in reproduction for the preservation of the species.[4] Thomas also follows Aristotelian biology in his assertion that the girl child represents a defective human being, the result of an accident to the male sperm, which was thought to contain the complete human being in potentia and to reproduce by nature the likeness of its origin, that is, another male.[5] This finality of the female as a mere instrumentality, an aid to reproduction, is the only explanation Thomas can offer for the existence of a "second sex," since for any other activity—work or play—man would have been better served by a male helpmate. Thomas asks reasonably why human beings were not created in pairs like the other animals, answering with the litany of female subordination familiar from our patristic sources: that it is appropriate to the dignity of the first man to be the principle of the totality of the species, as God is principle of the totality of the universe; that the monogamous marriage might be better preserved, for man will love the woman all the more if he knows her to have been made from his flesh; also, as man in society is the head of the family, "in which each has his or her particular duty," it is fitting that the woman be formed out of him.[6] Finally, as the Church takes her origin from Christ, so sacramentally it is proper that woman be formed of man. Her creation from his side rather than his head is a reminder that she is not to be despised.[7] The subordination and inferiority of Eve—and therefore of all womankind—to the male are thus established before the Fall in the order of God's original creation: first, by reason of the primacy of Adam's creation, who was not only first in time and the founder of the human race but also the material source of the first woman; and second, by reason of finality, for Adam displays the peculiar end and essence of human nature, intellectual activity, whereas Eve's finality is purely auxiliary and summed up in her bodily, generative function.

Despite this natural prelapsarian subordination, the male and female do share an essential equivalence in that God created the human race to know and love Him, and both sexes are thus marked by the *imago dei* (the image of God) and the possession of a rational soul.[8] As soon as this is said one must quickly add that Thomas follows Augustine in the view that the male possesses the image of God in a way different from and superior to the image found in the woman, using the analogy of the differences in degree between superior and inferior angles.[9] Ultimately this difference resides in the fact that the rational faculties appear more strongly in the male than in the female, a proposition that Thomas supports with the Aristotelian notion that the inferior quality and finality of the female body inevitably works a deleterious effect on woman's soul.[10] Her sexuality, which is identified with her essence as a woman, involves a weaker and more imperfect body, which in turn affects the intelligence upon which moral discernment is based.[11] The inequality between male and female relates thus to the moral as well as physical and intellectual realms, and it seems to be the woman's body that is the ultimate source of her inferiority and subordination to the male. In addition, even that which is peculiarly the woman's, the generative function, is inferior to the male equivalent, for the man is the active and fecund force, the woman but a passive and receptive instrument. On every level she is subordinate and auxiliary. It is significant that nowhere does Thomas discuss in an extended and complete fashion the inferior and subordinate nature of the female, simply because he assumes this state of affairs and therefore makes little effort to prove what all perceive as given.

The role of the prototypical woman Eve in the Fall of man worsens this natural subordination into the punishment of male domination.

Yet a careful examination of Eve's role in the Fall deprives her even of the dignity of clear responsibility for her own situation. The essential sin of the first parents, pride, the desire to be like God, is the same for both, but the motivation was different, and the course of events assigns differing responsibility. Eve, rather than Adam, was approached by the serpent, for she was recognized as more credulous, easier to seduce and, as his mate, more capable of seducing the male.[12] Eve's inferior reasoning ability accounts for her actual belief that she could equal God, whereas Adam never really believed the serpent's promise, but acceded to the temptation out of hope that he might attain the knowledge of good and evil, and out of love for and solidarity with his spouse.[13] Adam's loyalty to Eve diminishes the gravity of his sin; his superior intellectual powers, however, make him more responsible for his act than Eve. Furthermore, in Adam the species of the human race fell, for Thomas feels that if Eve had fallen to the snake's temptation and Adam had resisted, there would have been no expulsion from Paradise.[14] Eve's role was instrumental but not decisive. On the other hand, Thomas argues that Eve's pride was more serious, her sin more grave, for she actually believed the snake, and she sinned against her neighbor as well as God in occasioning Adam's fall.[15] It would seem that Eve's sin was more grave than that of Adam, but somehow less effectual. From our perspective, she is denied even the "dignity" of being successful and independent in evil.

The punishment for the Fall which relates to human bisexuality differs according to the proper function of each sex. The male of the species, who in the original creation was responsible as the head of the family for its material support, must now procure bread by the sweat of his brow. The woman, whose punishment Thomas considered the more grave, suffered an aggravation of her natural state of subordination.[16] After the Fall she became subject to male domination, under which she must obey her husband even against her own will. Also, her peculiar function as aid in generation becomes a painful burden, with the introduction of the fatigue of pregnancy and the pain of childbearing. Even the woman who by reason of sterility avoids that pain is punished by the opprobrium brought on the female who does not fulfill her natural purpose.[17]

II

Marriage always gave the Christian Church great difficulty insofar as it empirically involved physical sex. Despite Thomas' Aristotelian naturalism, the married state never quite escaped the Pauline/patristic brush of dualist pessimism, for coitus was associated with concupiscence and irrationality—a disorder from both Greek and Christian viewpoints. Thus Thomas felt it necessary to insist that marriage was not a result of the Fall, but existed as an institution at creation for the purpose of fecundity, the multiplication of souls to know and love God.[18] However, he agreed with Augustine that prelapsarian sexuality was rational, without passion, the man implanting his semen as the farmer sows his seed. But within this hypothetical prelapsarian marriage the female was still subordinate to the male, her end auxiliary, procreation. Only the extent and harshness of her submission was less; and as noted, the absence of lust in the procreative act was balanced by an absence of pain in childbirth. Significantly, Thomas follows Augustine in speculating that this paradisical copulation would occur without destroying the woman's hymen: her virginity would remain undisturbed. In this Thomas follows the patristic view that defloration is a corruption of the female body.[19]

It must first be noted that in this fallen world marriage was the least acceptable of the three states of life open to the woman, the first being the virginal religious life, the second continent widowhood, the third "if you must" marriage.[20]

After the Fall, marriage became a remedy for the sin of lust, in addition to being the natural institution for the procreation and education of children to love and honor God. . . .

It must be remembered that the woman, defined with reference to her ultimate reason for being as an aid in reproduction, is more essentially involved in marriage than is the male. Her position in the marriage relationship is, however, subordinate and auxiliary . . .

III

We turn now to that better life through which the woman can in theory escape the natural subordination and inferiority to which she is ordained by her sex. That option is the virginal life, to which both males and females may be called by God for the pursuit of religious perfection while on earth. The monastic life, which is the highest institutional expression of the call to virginity, is also the single institutional reflection of the religious equivalence of the sexes. . . .

. . . Ultimately the Fathers of the early Christian centuries agreed that both sexes are created with a rational soul in the image of God, and accordingly, that both are called to the same end, life with God. Despite subordination on the level of creation, the order of salvation offers equality between the sexes. This was a new ideal in the late Hellenistic world, in which religion and philosophy often limited the heights of spiritual perfection to males. The startlingly prominent public role taken by women in the New Testament Church is probably reflective of the impact of this revolutionary Christian attitude in the first century of the Church's life. However, it is important to see how that theoretical equivalence between the sexes on the religious level was from the first undercut by fundamentally androcentric conceptions. In the patristic world the very idealization of virginity, which made it possible for a woman to pursue a religious life equal to that of the male, free of male domination, contained within itself the heavy burden of fear of the female as the ever-present threat to continence that underlies much of patristic misogyny.[21] The association of the mind/flesh dualism with the male/female bipolarity . . . lays the groundwork for a different and unequal definition of virginity as it is applied to the female. Thus only the female, whose whole existence and finality are bound up in her auxiliary procreative function, must deny what the society defined as her nature in order to follow the religious life. . . . For the female, virginity is not an affirmation of her being as a woman but an assumption of the nature of the male, which is identified with the truly human: rationality, strength, courage, steadfastness, loyalty. . . . One might object that the ideal of virginity demanded of both men and women a denial of their sexuality, of fatherhood as well as motherhood. That is of course correct, but what I am saying is that the male, already defined in terms of a superior rationality, with its possibility of self-transcendence, was upon entering the religious life, in contrast to the woman, denying something quite literally external to his being. . . .

In another aspect of the theoretical realm the religious equivalence of male and female is fundamentally undermined by the Church's development of a rationale for the denial to the woman of Holy Orders. Here the maleness of God and the Incarnation provide the foundations for this aspect of female insufficiency, for as Christ's humanity was of necessity male, the instrument of his grace, the priest, corresponding to the instrumentality of His flesh, must also be male. Furthermore, ordination confers a superiority of rank that cannot be received by one who is by the order of creation in a state of subjection. Thus the woman, like the slave, may not validly receive Holy Orders.[22] As the Church lives in the world, it properly follows the laws of society with respect to the subordinate status of the female. These arguments reflect the fundamentally soci-ological character of much of Thomas' discussion of the prohibition of women in Holy Orders. They presuppose the patriarchal and hierarchical structures of a premodern society. Thomas never explicitly forbids the priesthood to women, nor does he say directly, as Bonaventura did, that because Christ was male, so also his priests must be men.[23] Indeed, in Thomas' discussion of baptism, in an emergency he allows a laywoman as well as a layman to baptize validly as Christ's minister, citing Galatians 3 that in Christ there is neither male nor female. However, a woman performs this office instrumentally, by virtue of Christ's power, not by virtue of her spiritual equivalence to a layman, and her subordinate status is symbolized by the fact that she can baptize without incurring sin only privately and in the absence of an available male.[24] Without doubt for many reasons, having perhaps most of all to do with ancient and subconscious cultic taboos, Thomas would have abhorred the idea of female priests, but given the overwhelmingly androcentric character of thirteenth-century society and theology, he was less insistent on the theological necessity of a male priesthood than he might have been.

V

. . . Medieval misogyny had many sources: for example the antifemale rationalist bias of classical antiquity, the strongly patriarchal traditions of a Germanic warrior society, sexual and cultic taboos common to many civilizations, and the sexual projections Freud has taught us to recognize. The deeply androcentric and misogynist character of the medieval concept of the woman cannot be wholly accounted for by reference to the realm of theological ideas, for society, psychology, and experience also played their roles. Comparative studies of medieval and other premodern societies reveal, despite important differences in religious ideology, extensive similarities in attitudes toward women, sex-role differentiation, and sexuality in general. Yet the evidence is overwhelming that the medieval Christian theological tradition and the symbols that it generated, many of which are still with us, did provide important stimuli and a convenient ideology for the dehumanization of the female sex. Despite the truly revolutionary implications of the biblical admonition, "There is neither male nor female, for ye are all one in Christ Jesus" (an equivalence graphically illustrated by the single initiation rite, baptism, alike for men and women), at every level, theological, legal, institutional, popular piety, that paradisical equivalence of souls was undermined by a deeply felt androcentrism and misogyny. . . .

What is to be done? The first task is to make explicit the assumptions received from this tradition about male/female difference and hierarchy, and to expose with the help of historical understanding the now patently invalid intellectual foundations of these typologies. For example, have not the insights of the social sciences already called into question the implicitly rationalist definition of human nature by which the feeling and responding side of our being is denigrated and perceived as specifically feminine? The twentieth-century person may well believe himself to be free of Adam and Eve mythologies and the monastic imperative to virginity, yet still think and feel in terms of an identification of the mind/body dualism with the male/female bipolarity which supports our stereotypes of the passive, emotional, and seductive woman and the rational, idealistic, and active male. Behind the recently popular discussion of male and female complementarity lie some very traditional symbolism and feelings about the "eternal feminine" which need to be brought into the open.[25] The woman and the man must be demythologized.

More difficult, and ultimately more important, will be the constructive work, the evolution of a new Christian anthropology that first takes seriously the biblical affirmation of the goodness of creation and affirms the positive role of human sexuality as a vehicle of human love and true mutuality. This anthropology for human liberation calls for the building of a new model of sex identity which permits individual personality to flourish without the constraints of sex stereotypes or hierarchical power relationships.

For this reconstruction it will be necessary to affirm the fundamental moral equivalence of the sexes, not simply within the sexual relationship, as did the medieval church, but also in the world beyond the family, in which world, with fewer children and longer life spans, modern men and women are destined to spend more than half of their lives. This means that a new anthropology will be grounded in a recognition of the role of work in human self-fulfillment and the right, therefore, of women as well as men to meaningful work. In the medieval tradition work was a punishment for the Fall, assigned particularly to the sons of Adam; in Protestant capitalist societies work has become an alienating exploitive mode for dominating nature, both human and inanimate. The women's movement could well encourage the basic reconstitution of both economic structures and attitudes toward work, which would make possible a new balance between familial nurturing and socially productive work in the lives of women and men who share these roles and are not limited by their sex to a life of the hearth or the hunt.

A third aspect of a new anthropology will reside in the recognition that the categories underlying the theologians' or the psychologists' accounts of sex difference and role can be as time-bound as the dogmas of Aristotelian biology. A Christian view of the nature of woman and man needs to be dynamic and prophetic, not antiscientific, but also not taken in by the faith systems of the Freudians or their successors.

The medieval theological tradition does have, as we have seen, a positive core that can contribute to a new anthropology for free people, female and male. The medieval Church insisted in theory on a true mutuality and moral equivalence between the sexes in the area of sexual fidelity within marriage. In this regard the

Church opposed the then newly emergent ethic of courtly love and condemned the romantic view of a sexual relationship based on "feelings" rather than on mutual commitment and self-giving. Some careful thought will reveal that the idea of the woman as sex object—idealized, even unattainable, but existing ultimately for the gratification of the male sense of well-being—has important origins in the medieval courtly love tradition.[26] That tradition was condemned by the Church out of the conviction that mutual fidelity, reflecting the ultimate value of each partner as a child of God, is the only basis for the relationship between man and woman in marriage. In some sense, a woman never belonged wholly to her husband, was never completely defined in terms of her sexuality, for there was always the prior bond of the soul to God, in the context of which all other commitments were judged, the practice of medieval canonists notwithstanding. This medieval condemnation of the romantic ethic is a strong instance within the tradition of the rejection of the concept of woman as a purely sexual being. Insofar as the "new morality" sanctions the abandonment of a relationship when it ceases to please, or feel good, the medieval tradition opposes that reduction of the human being to a sensual instrumentality with an insistence that neither partner, female or male, exists to be used for the gratification of the other.

The eschatological dimension of the medieval theology of the sexes could also be of interest to those who seek to formulate a new anthropology. In the simplest of terms Thomas tells us that in Paradise all the inequalities and subordination of the order of creation shall be overcome. There will still be hierarchy, but it will be an ordering by merit, rather than by sex or status. So much of Christian eschatology has been secularized and brought down to earth. If one must have superiors and subordinates, why not on the basis of merit?

But is this hierarchical universe, with its fixed and ranked functions and orders, a positive basis

for a new anthropology? Is it not rather of our inheritances from the past the most pervasive and difficult to bring into line with the needs of twentieth-century persons in their individuality and society? It is easy to find recent literature within the Christian theological tradition that insists on a nondualist anthropology and on an unambiguous moral equivalence of the sexes, but dwells at the same time upon the differences between women and men that imply not only separate function but also an unambiguous superordination and subordination, grounded paradigmatically in the relationship of God to his creatures. Thus Karl Barth has spoken of man and woman as an A and a B; in respect of order woman is B, ". . . and therefore behind and subordinate to man."[27] The problem here is not a medieval anthropology but a medieval doctrine of creation and sociology, by which a specific order of precedence was assigned by divine fiat to man and woman, which order we are yet bound to maintain. There is indeed implied an inadequate definition of human nature: static, ahistorical, hierarchical, Platonizing in its assumption of ontologically fixed relationships between the sexes. The reader will pardon me if under every bush of "complementarity" I espy this hierarchical cosmos, this Great Chain of Being, in which difference becomes rationalized subordination.

In conclusion, despite this ambiguous legacy, the medieval Christian tradition did not only speak of the woman's spiritual equivalence with her brother. The Church provided an institution, and a calling, the monastic life, which symbolized and often gave concrete opportunity to exercise that spiritual equivalence in which all persons, female and male, are called alike to Christian perfection. Only within those portions of Christendom which after the sixteenth century renounced the dual ethic of monasticism and celibacy was the woman wholly limited in her Christian vocation to the home, to her role as procreator and nurturer. However often the medieval commitment to spiritual equivalence

was undermined by androcentric and patriarchal assumptions, the institution of monasticism
was for the Christian woman a real and concrete
option, a little world occasionally run by and for
women. She had an alternative to the authority
of father and husband. She had a choice.

NOTES

1. Thomas Aquinas, *Summa Theologica*, ed.
English Dominican Province, 3 vols. (New York,
1947), I, 76, 1. For the summary of Thomas'
views that follows I am indebted to K. E. Børresen, *Subordination et équivalence*.
2. *ST* I, 91, 3; Børresen, p. 126.
3. *ST* I, 92, 1; Børresen, p. 129.
4. Ibid.
5. *ST* I, 92, 1, ad 1; "Woman is said to be a misbegotten male, as being a product outside the purpose of nature considered in the individual case:
but not against the purpose of universal nature"
(*ST* I, 99, 2, ad 1).
6. *ST* I, 92, 2.
7. *ST* I, 92, 3.
8. Børresen, p. 136.
9. Børresen, p. 137.
10. *ST* II-II, 70, 3, concl.; *ST* II-II, 156, 1, ad 1; Børresen, p. 143.
11. Børresen, p. 143; e.g., the woman, like a child or
a fool, may not take a valid judicial oath.
12. *ST* II-II, 165, 2, ad 1.
13. *ST* II-II, 163, 4, concl.
14. *ST* I-II, 81, 5, ad 2; Børresen, p. 174.
15. *ST* II-II, 163, 4, concl.
16. *ST* II-II, 163, 4, concl.
17. *ST* II-II, 164, 2; Børresen, pp. 169–170. This pun-

ishment appropriate to each sex is, in addition to
the general effect of the Fall, the loss of the gift of
original justice, which entails mortality and a
diminishing of the natural inclination to virtue.
18. *ST* I, 98, 1 and 2; Børresen, pp. 150–151.
19. *ST* I, 98, 2, ad 4; Børresen, p. 153.
20. Within the first two states the woman can escape
the special penalty laid on the daughters of
Eve—direct subordination to a male.
21. *Reallexikon für Antike und Christentum* (Stuttgart,
1941 ff.), Lfrg. 58 (1970), "Frau," p. 258. It would
be useful to explore comparatively instructions to
male and female religious ascetics to determine if
the female ascetic perceived the opposite sex with
the same fear and even horror that is found in
ascetic literature addressed to men.
22. *ST* Suppl., 39, 1, concl.; Børresen, pp. 183–184.
For a recent discussion of this position, see
Joseph A. Wahl, *The Exclusion of Women from
Holy Orders*, Studies in Sacred Theology, 2d Ser.,
No. 110. Catholic University of America (Washington, D.C., 1959).
23. Børresen, p. 188.
24. *ST* III, 67, 4.
25. See, for example, F. X. Arnold, *Woman and Man,
Their Nature and Mission* (Freiburg and London,
1963), p. 50: "The focal point of woman's nature
is her heart, her affections and emotions. Man's
focal point on the other hand is more in his intelligence."
26. John F. Benton, "Clio and Venus: An Historical
View of Medieval Love," *The Meaning of Courtly
Love*, ed. F. X. Newman (Albany, N.Y., 1968), p.
35: "Courtesy was created by men for their own
satisfaction, and it emphasized a woman's role as
an object, sexual or otherwise."
27. Karl Barth, *Church Dogmatics* (Edinburgh,
1961), III, Part 4, p. 171.

17. Guide for the Perplexed

Maimonides

Book III

Chapter XXVII

The general object of the Law is twofold: the well-being of the soul, and the well-being of the body. The well-being of the soul is promoted by correct opinions communicated to the people according to their capacity. Some of these opinions are therefore imparted in a plain form, others allegorically; because certain opinions are in their plain form too strong for the capacity of the common people. The well-being of the body is established by a proper management of the relations in which we live one to another. This we can attain in two ways: first by removing all violence from our midst; that is to say, that we do not do everyone as he pleases, desires, and is able to do; but everyone of us does that which contributes towards the common welfare. Secondly, by teaching everyone of us such good morals as must produce a good social state. Of these two objects, the one, the well-being of the soul, or the communication of correct opinions, comes undoubtedly first in rank, but the other, the well being of the body, the government of the state, and the establishment of the best possible relations among men, is anterior in nature and time. The latter object is required first; it is also treated [in the Law] most carefully and most minutely, because the well-being of the soul can only be obtained after that of the body has been secured. For it has already been found that man has a double perfection: the first perfection is

that of the body, and the second perfection is that of the soul. The first consists in the most healthy condition of his mental relations, and this is only possible when man has all his wants supplied, as they arise; if he has his food, and other things needful for his body, e.g., shelter, bath, and the like. But one man alone cannot procure all this; it is impossible for a single man to obtain this comfort; it is only possible in society, since man, as is well known, is by nature social.

The second perfection of man consists in his becoming an actually intelligent being; i.e., he knows about the things in existence all that a person perfectly developed is capable of knowing. This second perfection certainly does not include any action or good conduct, but only knowledge, which is arrived at by speculation, or established by research.

It is clear that the second and superior kind of perfection can only be attained when the first perfection has been acquired; for a person that is suffering from great hunger, thirst, heat, or cold, cannot grasp an idea even if communicated by others, much less can he arrive at it by his own reasoning. But when a person is in possession of the first perfection, then he may possibly acquire the second perfection, which is undoubtedly of a superior kind, and is alone the source of eternal life. The true Law, which as we said is one, and beside which there is no other Law, viz., the Law of our teacher Moses, has for its purpose to give us the twofold perfection. It aims first at the establishment of good mutual relations among men by removing injustice and creating the noblest feelings. In this way the people in every land are enabled to stay and continue in one condition, and everyone can acquire his first perfec-

Reprinted from *Guide of the Perplexed*, translated by M. Friedlander (London: Routledge and Sons, 1904).

tion. Secondly, it seeks to train us in faith, and to impart correct and true opinions when the intellect is sufficiently developed. . . .

Chapter XXVIII

. . . The result of all these preliminary remarks is this: The reason of a commandment, whether positive or negative, is clear, and its usefulness evident, if it directly tends to remove injustice, or to teach good conduct that furthers the well-being of society, or to impart a truth which ought to be believed either on its own merit or as being indispensable for facilitating the removal of injustice or the teaching of good morals. There is no occasion to ask for the object of such commandments; for no one can, e.g., be in doubt as to the reason why we have been commanded to believe that God is one; why we are forbidden to murder, to steal, and to take vengeance, or to retaliate, or why we are commanded to love one another. But there are precepts concerning which people are in doubt, and of divided opinions, some believing that they are mere commands, and serve no purpose whatever, whilst others believe that they serve a certain purpose, which, however, is unknown to man. Such are those precepts which in their literal meaning do not seem to further any of the three above-named results: to impart some truth, to teach some moral, or to remove injustice. They do not seem to have any influence upon the well-being of the soul by imparting any truth, or upon the well-being of the body by suggesting such ways and rules as are useful in the government of a state, or in the management of a household. Such are the prohibitions of wearing garments containing wool and linen; of sowing divers seeds, or of boiling meat and milk together; the commandment of covering the blood [of slaughtered beasts and birds], the ceremony of breaking the neck of a calf [in case of a person being found slain, and the murderer being unknown]; the law concerning the firstborn of an ass, and the like. I am prepared to tell you my explanation of all these commandments, and to assign

for them a true reason supported by proof, with the exception of some minor rules, and of a few commandments, as I have mentioned above. I will show that all these and similar laws must have some bearing upon one of the following three things, viz., the regulation of our opinions, or the improvement of our social relations, which implies two things, the removal of injustice, and the teaching of good morals. . . .

Chapter XXXI

There are persons who find it difficult to give a reason for any of the commandments, and consider it right to assume that the commandments and prohibitions have no rational basis whatever. They are led to adopt this theory by a certain disease in their soul, the existence of which they perceive, but which they are unable to discuss or to describe. For they imagine that these precepts, if they were useful in any respect, and were commanded because of their usefulness, would seem to originate in the thought and reason of some intelligent being. But as things which are not objects of reason and serve no purpose, they would undoubtedly be attributed to God, because no thought of man could have produced them. According to the theory of those weak-minded persons, man is more perfect than his Creator. For what man says or does has a certain object, whilst the actions of God are different; He commands us to do what is of no use to us, and forbids us to do what is harmless. Far be this! On the contrary, the sole object of the Law is to benefit us. . . . But if no reason could be found for these statutes, if they produced no advantage and removed no evil, why then should he who believes in them and follows them be wise, reasonable, and so excellent as to raise the admiration of all nations? But the truth is undoubtedly as we have said, that every one of the six hundred and thirteen precepts serves to inculcate some truth, to remove some erroneous opinion, to establish proper relations in society, to diminish evil, to train in good manners, or to warn against bad habits. All this depends on three things: opinions, morals, and social conduct.... Thus these three principles suffice for assigning a reason for everyone of the Divine commandments.

Chapter XXXIII

It is also the object of the perfect Law to make man reject, despise, and reduce his desires as much as is in his power. He should only give way to them when absolutely necessary. It is well known that it is intemperance in eating, drinking, and sexual intercourse that people mostly rave and indulge in; and these very things counteract the ulterior perfection of man, impede at the same time the development of his first perfection, and generally disturb the social order of the country and the economy of the family. For by following entirely the guidance of lust, in the manner of fools, man loses his intellectual energy, injures his body, and perishes before his natural time; sighs and cares multiply; there is an increase of envy, hatred, and warfare for the purpose of taking what another possesses. The cause of all this is the circumstance that the ignorant considers physical enjoyment as an object to be sought for its own sake. God in His wisdom has therefore given us such commandments as would counteract that object, and prevent us altogether from directing our attention to it, and has debarred us from everything that leads only to excessive desire and lust. This is an important thing included in the objects of our Law. See how the Law commanded to slay a person from whose conduct it is evident that he will go too far in seeking the enjoyment of eating and drinking. I mean "the rebellious and stubborn son"; he is described as "a glutton and a drunkard" (Deut. xxi. 20). The Law commands to stone him and to remove him from society lest he grow up in this character, and kill many, and injure the condition of good men by his great lust....

Similarly one of the intentions of the Law is purity and sanctification; I mean by this renouncing and avoiding sexual intercourse and causing it to be as infrequent as possible, as I shall make

clear. Thus, when He, may He be exalted, commanded the religious community to be sanctified with a view to receiving the Torah, and He said: *And sanctify them today and tomorrow*—He said; *Come not near a woman.* Consequently He states clearly that sanctity consists in renouncing sexual intercourse, just as He also states explicitly that the giving-up of the drinking of wine constitutes sanctity, in what He says about the Nazarite: *He shall be saintly....*

Chapter XXXIV

It is also important to note that the Law does not take into account exceptional circumstances; it is not based on conditions which rarely occur. Whatever the Law teaches, whether it be of an intellectual, a moral, or a practical character, is founded on that which is the rule and not on that which is the exception; it ignores the injury that might be caused to a single person through a certain maxim or a certain divine precept.... If the Law depended on the varying conditions of man, it would be imperfect in its totality, each precept being left indefinite. For this reason it would not be right to make the fundamental principles of the Law dependent on a certain time or a certain place; on the contrary, the statutes and the judgments must be definite, unconditional, and general....

After having premised these introductory remarks I will now proceed to the exposition of that which I intended to explain.

Chapter XXXV

In accordance with this intention I find it convenient to divide all precepts into fourteen classes.

The first class comprises those precepts which form fundamental principles....

The second class comprises the precepts which are connected with the prohibition of idolatry....

The third class is formed by commandments which are connected with the improvement of the moral condition [of mankind]....

The fourth class includes precepts relating to charity, loans, gifts, and the like.... The object of these precepts is clear; their benefit concerns all people by turns; for he who is rich to-day may one day be poor—either he himself or his descendants; and he who is now poor, he himself or his son may be rich to-morrow.

The fifth class contains those precepts which relate to the prevention of wrong and violence.... Their beneficial character is evident.

The sixth class is formed of precepts respecting fines, e.g., the laws on theft and robbery, on false witnesses....Their benefit is apparent; for if sinners and robbers were not punished, injury would not be prevented at all: and persons scheming evil would not become rarer. They are wrong who suppose that it would be an act of mercy to abandon the laws of compensation for injuries; on the contrary, it would be perfect cruelty and injury to the social state of the country. It is an act of mercy that God commanded "judges and officers thou shalt appoint to thee in all thy gates" (Deut. xvi. 18).

The seventh class comprises those laws which regulate the business transactions of men with each other; e.g., laws about loans, hire, trust, buying, selling, and the like; the rules about inheritance belong to this class.... The object of these precepts is evident, for monetary transactions are necessary for the peoples of all countries, and it is impossible to have these transactions without a proper standard of equity and without useful regulations.

The eighth class includes those precepts which relate to certain days, as Sabbaths and holydays....

The ninth class comprises the general laws concerning religious rites and ceremonies....

The object of these laws is apparent; they all prescribe actions which firmly establish the love of God in our minds, as also the right belief concerning Him and His attributes.

The tenth class is formed of precepts which relate to the Sanctuary, its vessels, and its ministers....

The eleventh class includes those precepts which related to Sacrifices....

The twelfth class comprises the laws concerning things unclean and clean ...

The thirteenth class includes the precepts concerning forbidden food and the like ...

The fourteenth class comprises the precepts concerning forbidden sexual intercourse; they are given in the section *Nashim* and *Hilkot issurebiah.* The laws concerning the intermixture of cattle belong to this class. The object of these precepts is likewise to diminish sexual intercourse, to restrain as much as possible indulgence in lust, and [to teach] that this enjoyment is not, as foolish people think, the final cause of man's existence....

As is well known, the precepts are also divided into two classes, viz., precepts concerning the relation between man and God, and precepts concerning the relation between man and man. Of the classes into which we divide the precepts and which we have enumerated, the fifth, sixth, and seventh, and part of the third, include laws concerning the relation of man to man. The other classes contain the laws about the relation of man to God, i.e., positive or negative precepts, which tend to improve the moral or intellectual condition of mankind, or to regulate such of each man's actions which [directly] only concern him and lead him to perfection. For these are called laws concerning man's relation to God, although in reality they lead to results which concern also his fellow-men; because these results become only apparent after a long series of intermediate links, and from a general point of view; whilst directly these laws are not intended to prevent man from injuring his fellow-man. Note this....

Chapter XL

The precepts of the fifth class, enumerated in the Section "On Damages" (*Sepher nezikin*), aim at the removal of wrong and the prevention of injury. As we are strongly recommended to prevent damage, we are responsible for every damage caused by our property or through our work in so far as it is in our power to take care and to guard it from becoming injurious. We are, therefore, responsible for all damage caused by our cattle; we must guard them. The same is the case with fire and pits; they are made by man, and he can be careful that they do not cause damage. . . .

This class includes also the duty of killing him who pursues another person; that is to say, if a person is about to commit a crime we may prevent it by killing him. Only in two cases is this permitted; viz., when a person runs after another in order to murder him, or in order to commit fornication; because in these two cases the crime, once committed; cannot be remedied. . . .

The beneficial character of the law concerning "the breaking of the neck of a heifer" (Deut. xxi. 1–8) is evident. For it is the city that is nearest to the slain person that brings the heifer, and in most cases the murderer comes from that place. The elders of the place call upon God as their witness, according to the interpretation of our Sages, that they have always kept the roads in good condition, have protected them, and have directed everyone that asked his way; that the person has not been killed because they were careless in these general provisions, and they do not know who has slain him. As a rule the investigation, the procession of the elders, the measuring, and the taking of the heifer, make people talk about it, and by making the event public, the murdered may be found out, and he who knows of him, or has heard of him, or has discovered him by any clue, will now name the person that is the murderer, and as soon as a man, or even a woman or handmaid, rises up and names a certain person as having committed the murder, the heifer is not killed. It is well known that it is considered great wickedness and guilt on the part of a person who knows the murderer, and is silent about him whilst the elders call upon God as witness that they know nothing about the mur-

derer. Even a woman will, therefore, communicate whatever knowledge she has of him. When the murderer is discovered, the benefit of the law is apparent. . . . Force is added to the law by the rule that the place in which the neck of the heifer is broken should never be cultivated or sown. The owner of the land will therefore use all means in his power to search and to find the murderer, in order that the heifer be not killed and his land be not made useless to him.

Chapter XLI

The precepts of the sixth class comprise the different ways of punishing the sinner. Their general usefulness is known and has also been mentioned by us. . . .

The law concerning false witnesses (Deut. xix. 19) prescribes that they shall suffer exactly the same loss which they intended to inflict upon another. If they intended to bring a sentence of death against a person, they are killed; if they aimed at the punishment of stripes, they receive stripes; and if they desire to make a person pay money, they are sentenced to pay exactly the same sum. The object of all these laws is to make the punishment equal to the crime; and it is also on this account that the judgments are "righteous" (Deut. iv. 8). . . .—Whether the punishment is great or small, the pain inflicted intense or less intense, depends on the following four conditions.

1. The greatness of the sin. Actions that cause great harm are punished severely, whilst actions that cause little harm are punished less severely.

2. The frequency of the crime. A crime that is frequently committed must be put down by severe punishment; crimes of rare occurrence may be suppressed by a lenient punishment considering that they are rarely committed.

3. The amount of temptation. Only fear of a severe punishment restrains us from

actions for which there exists a greater temptation, either because we have a great desire for these actions, or are accustomed to them, or feel unhappy without them.

4. The facility of doing the thing secretly, and unseen and unnoticed. From such acts we are deterred only by the fear of a great and terrible punishment. . . .

Death by the court of law is decreed in important cases: when faith is undermined, or a great crime is committed, viz., idolatry, incest, murder, or actions that lead to these crimes. It is further decreed for breaking the Sabbath (Exod. xxxi. 15); because the keeping of Sabbath is a confirmation of our belief in the Creation; a false prophet and a rebellious elder are put to death on account of the mischief which they cause; he who strikes his father or his mother is killed on account of his great audacity, and because he undermines the constitution of the family, which is the foundation of the state. A rebellious and disobedient son is put to death (Deut. xxi. 18

seq.) on account of what he might become, because he will likely be a murderer; he who steals a human being is killed, because he is also prepared to kill him whom he steals (Exod. xxi. 16). Likewise he who is found breaking into a house is prepared for murder (*ibid.* xxii. 1), as our Sages stated. These three, the rebellious and disobedient son, he who steals and sells a human being, and he who breaks into a house, become murderers in the course of time, as is well known. Capital punishment is only decreed for these serious crimes, and in no other case. Not all forbidden sexual intercourse is visited with the penalty of death, but only in those cases in which the criminal act can easily be done, is of frequent occurrence, is base and disgraceful, and of a tempting character; otherwise excision is the punishment. Likewise not all kinds of idolatry are capital crimes, but only the principal acts of idolatry, such as praying to an idol, prophesying in its name, passing a child through the fire, consulting with familiar spirits, and acting as a wizard or witch. . . .

RECOMMENDED READINGS

Texts

Coppleston, Frederick. *Aquinas.* London: Penguin, 1955.
Finnis, John. *Natural Law and Natural Rights.* Oxford: Oxford University Press, 1982.
Gilson, Etienne. *The Christian Philosophy of St. Thomas Aquinas.* New York: Random House, 1956.
Kenny, Anthony, ed. *Aquinas.* Notre Dame, IN: Notre Dame Press, 1976.
Lisska, Anthony. *Aquinas's Theory of Natural Law,* Oxford: Oxford University Press, 1996.
McInerny, R. *St. Thomas Aquinas.* Notre Dame, IN: Notre Dame Press, 1982.
Sigmund, Paul, ed. *St. Thomas Aquinas on Politics and Ethics.* New York: W. W. Norton, 1988.

Feminist Perspective

Lucas, Angela. *Women in the Middle Ages: Religion, Marriage and Letters.* Brighton: Harvester Press, 1984.
Pierce, Christine. "Natural Law Language and Women." In *Women in Sexist Society,* edited by Vivian Gornick and Barbara K. Moran. New York: Basic Books, 1971.

Multicultural Perspective

Kraemer, Joel. *Perspectives on Maimonides.* Oxford: Oxford University Press, 1991.
Weiss, Raymond. *Maimonides' Ethics: The Encounter of Philosophic and Religious Morality.* Chicago: University of Chicago Press, 1991.

PART V

❧❧

HUME

INTRODUCTION

David Hume was born in Edinburgh in 1711, four years after the union of England and Scotland. He died in 1776 at the beginning of the American Revolutionary War. Hume confessed that a desire for literary fame was the ruling passion of his life. Unfortunately, his first philosophical work, *A Treatise of Human Nature,* written when he was twenty-six, by his own admission "fell stillborne from the press," and he was never able to secure a university position. For a time, he served as a companion to a nobleman who turned out to be insane. A little later, he became aide-de-camp to General James St. Clair, a distant relative, who was planning an invasion of French Canada, which was then aborted in favor of an ill-fated assault on the coast of France. After that, Hume was appointed as a librarian in Edinburgh but was later discharged for stocking the shelves with obscene books. Late in life, he served as secretary in the British embassy in Paris. Fortunately, he did experience literary fame during his lifetime, but it was based on his multi-volume *History of England* rather than on his philosophical works It was only years later, after his death, that his philosophical greatness was recognized.

In our selection from his *A Treatise of Human Nature,* Hume argues against the view that morality can be justified by reason. According to Hume, "Reason is, and ought only to be the slave of the passions." Reason, according to Hume, has only two functions—to discover relations among abstract ideas (as in mathematics) and to discover truths about matters of fact (as in science and everyday affairs). According to Hume, reason gives us knowledge about things we want and how best to attain them, but it cannot cause us to want anything and therefore, it cannot by itself move us to act. Only in conjunction with our passions can it do that. In addition, Hume claims that there are only two senses in which any passion can be called unreasonable. First, when it is founded on a false supposition. Second, when we choose means insufficient to our end. Thus, according to Hume, "it is not contrary to reason to prefer the destruction of the whole world to the scratching of my finger." Nevertheless, there could be other ways to reject certain passions as unreasonable, for example, if the views that they support are question-begging.

Hume also maintains that it is impossible to move from "is" to "ought" or from factual claims to normative claims. But Hume's argument here is based on the mistaken assumption that "is" statements can only support "ought" statements if they entail them. But there is no general requirement that "is" statements can only support "ought" statements by entailing them.[1] For example, that Jones's fingerprints are on the murder weapon can support the conclusion that we ought to arrest Jones for the murder without entailing that conclusion. Moreover, even if Hume were right about their being an "is-ought" gap, we may still be able to begin our moral arguments with at least partially evaluative premises that all parties hold in common.

According to Hume, it is sympathy that produces our moral sentiments. It is the principle that takes us far out of ourselves, so as to give us the same pleasure or uneasiness in what happens to others as if it were happening to ourselves.

Annette Baier in "Hume, the Women's Moral Theorist?" argues that a number of features of Hume's moral theory—for example, his limited place for conformity to general rules and the thesis that morality depends on passions and sentiments more than reason—are similar to the respects in which Carol Gilligan found girls' and women's versions of morality to differ from men's. Baier claims that many of the apparently sexist comments that Hume makes about women are simply meant to be descriptive of actual inequalities between men and women. Baier claims that Hume did not necessarily endorse those inequalities and sometimes even suggests how they might be removed. For these reasons, Baier claims that Hume is a woman's moral theorist. But the question we must ask ourselves here is whether there are others, other theories or theorists, that might still better serve a feminist agenda.

The Ewe Proverbs selected here are compiled and explained by N. K. Dzobo, a professor of education in Ghana and a member of the Ewe tribe. The Ewe tribe lives in what is now southern Ghana, Togo, and Benin. As one reads these proverbs, one cannot but be impressed by the universality of the moral experience they convey. Those who think that all morality is relative and contextual need to explain why these proverbs seem to have such universal moral authority.

NOTES

1. See Kurt Baier, *The Rational and the Moral Order* (La Salle, Ill.: Open Court, 1995), pp. 31–4.

18. A Treatise of Human Nature

DAVID HUME

Of the Influencing Motives of the Will

Nothing is more usual in philosophy, and even in common life, than to talk of the combat of passion and reason, to give the preference to reason, and to assert that men are only so far virtuous as they conform themselves to its dictates. Every rational creature, 'tis said, is oblig'd to regulate his actions by reason; and if any other motive or principle challenge the direction of his conduct, he ought to oppose it, 'till it be entirely subdu'd, or at least brought to a conformity with that superior principle. On this method of thinking the greatest part of moral philosophy, ancient and modern, seems to be founded; nor is there an ampler field, as well for metaphysical arguments, as popular declamations, than this suppos'd pre-eminence of reason above passion. The eternity, invariableness, and divine origin of the former have been display'd to the best advantage: The blindness, unconstancy and deceitfulness of the latter have been as strongly insisted on. In order to shew the fallacy of all this philosophy, I shall endeavour to prove *first,* that reason alone can never be a motive to any action of the will; and *secondly,* that it can never oppose passion in the direction of the will.

The understanding exerts itself after two different ways, as it judges from demonstration or probability; as it regards the abstract relations of our ideas, or those relations of objects, of which experience only gives us information. I believe it scarce will be asserted, that the first species of reasoning alone is ever the cause of any action.

Reprinted from *Treatise of Human Nature.* edited by L. A. Selby-Bigge (Oxford: Oxford University Press, 1888).

As it's proper province is the world of ideas, and as the will always places us in that of realities, demonstration and volition seem, upon that account, to be totally remov'd, from each other. Mathematics, indeed, are useful in all mechanical operations, and arithmetic in almost every art and profession: But 'tis not of themselves they have any influence. Mechanics are the art of regulating the motions of bodies *to some design'd end or purpose;* and the reason why we employ arithmetic in fixing the proportions of numbers, is only that we may discover the proportions of their influence and operation. A merchant is desirous of knowing the sum total of his accounts with any person: Why? but that he may learn what sum will have the same *effects* in paying his debt, and going to market, as all the particular articles taken together. Abstract or demonstrative reasoning, therefore, never influences any of our actions, but only as it directs our judgment concerning causes and effects; which leads us to the second operation of the understanding.

'Tis obvious, that when we have the prospect of pain or pleasure from any object, we feel a consequent emotion of aversion or propensity, and are carry'd to avoid or embrace what will give us this uneasiness or satisfaction. 'Tis also obvious, that this emotion rests not here, but making us cast our view on every side, comprehends whatever objects are connected with its original one by the relation of cause and effect. Here then reasoning takes place to discover this relation; and according as our reasoning varies, our actions receive a subsequent variation. But 'tis evident in this case, that the impulse arises not from reason, but is only directed by it. 'Tis from the prospect of pain or pleasure that the aversion or propensity arises towards any object: And these emotions extend themselves to the causes and effects of that object, as they are pointed out to us by reason and experience. It can never in the least concern us to know, that such objects are causes, and such others effects, if both the causes and effects be indifferent to us. Where the objects themselves do not affect us, their connexion can never give them any influence; and 'tis plain, that as reason is nothing but the discovery of this connexion, it cannot be by its means that the objects are able to affect us.

Since reason alone can never produce any action, or give rise to volition, I infer, that the same faculty is as incapable of preventing volition, or of disputing the preference with any passion or emotion. This consequence is necessary. 'Tis impossible reason cou'd have the latter effect of preventing volition, but by giving an impulse in a contrary direction to our passion; and that impulse, had it operated alone, wou'd have been able to produce volition. Nothing can oppose or retard the impulse of passion, but a contrary impulse; and if this contrary impulse ever arises from reason, that latter faculty must have an original influence on the will, and must be able to cause, as well as hinder any act of volition. But if reason has no original influence, 'tis impossible it can withstand any principle, which has such an efficacy, or ever keep the mind in suspence a moment. Thus it appears, that the principle, which opposes our passion, cannot be the same with reason, and is only call'd so in an improper sense. We speak not strictly and philosophically when we talk of the combat of passion and of reason. Reason is, and ought only to be the slave of the passions, and can never pretend to any other office than to serve and obey them. As this opinion may appear somewhat extraordinary, it may not be improper to confirm it by some other considerations.

A passion is an original existence, or, if you will, modification of existence, and contains not any representative quality, which renders it a copy of any other existence or modification. When I am angry, I am actually possest with the passion, and in that emotion have no more a reference to any other object, than when I am thirsty, or sick, or more than five foot high. 'Tis impossible, therefore, that this passion can be oppos'd by, or be contradictory to truth and reason; since this contradiction consists in the disagreement of ideas, consider'd as copies, with those objects, which they represent.

What may at first occur on this head, is, that as nothing can be contrary to truth or reason, except what has a reference to it, and as the judgments of our understanding only have this reference, it must follow, that passions can be contrary to reason only so far as they are *accompany'd* with some judgment or opinion. According to this principle, which is so obvious and natural, 'tis only in two senses, that any affection can be call'd unreasonable. First, When a passion, such as hope or fear, grief or joy, despair or security, is founded on the supposition of the existence of objects, which really do not exist. Secondly, When in exerting any passion in action, we chuse means insufficient for the design'd end, and deceive ourselves in our judgment of causes and effects. Where a passion is neither founded on false suppositions, nor chuses means insufficient for the end, the understanding can neither justify nor condemn it. 'Tis not contrary to reason to prefer the destruction of the whole world to the scratching of my finger. 'Tis not contrary to reason for me to chuse my total ruin, to prevent the least uneasiness of an *Indian* or person wholly unknown to me. 'Tis as little contrary to reason to prefer even my own acknowledg'd lesser good to my greater, and have a more ardent affection for the former than the latter. A trivial good may, from certain circumstances, produce a desire superior to what arises from the greatest and most valuable enjoyment; nor is there any thing more extraordinary in this, than in mechanics to see one pound weight raise up a hundred by the advantage of its situation. In short, a passion must be accompany'd with some false judgment, in order to its being unreasonable; and even then 'tis not the passion, properly speaking, which is unreasonable, but the judgment.

The consequences are evident. Since a passion can never, in any sense, be call'd unreasonable, but when founded on a false supposition, or when it chuses means insufficient for the design'd end, 'tis impossible, that reason and passion can ever oppose each other, or dispute for the government of the will and actions. The moment we perceive the falshood of any supposition, or the insufficiency of any means our passions yield to our reason without any opposition. I may desire any fruit as of an excellent relish; but whenever you convince me of my mistake, my longing ceases. I may will the performance of certain actions as means of obtaining any desir'd good; but as my willing of these actions is only secondary, and founded on the supposition, that they are causes of the propos'd effect; as soon as I discover the falshood of that supposition, they must become indifferent to me.

'Tis natural for one, that does not examine objects with a strict philosophic eye, to imagine, that those actions of the mind are entirely the same, which produce not a different sensation, and are not immediately distinguishable to the feeling and perception. Reason, for instance, exerts itself without producing any sensible emotion; and except in the more sublime disquisitions of philosophy, or in the frivolous subtilties of the schools, scarce ever conveys any pleasure or uneasiness. Hence it proceeds, that every action of the mind, which operates with the same calmness and tranquillity, is confounded with reason by all those, who judge of things from the first view and appearance. Now 'tis certain, there are certain calm desires and tendencies, which, tho' they be real passions, produce little emotion in the mind, and are more known by their effects than by the immediate feeling or sensation. These desires are of two kinds; either

certain instincts originally implanted in our natures, such as benevolence and resentment, the love of life, and kindness to children; or the general appetite to good, and aversion to evil, consider'd merely as such. When any of these passions are calm, and cause no disorder in the soul, they are very readily taken for the determinations of reason, and are suppos'd to proceed from the same faculty, with that, which judges of truth and falshood. Their nature and principles have been suppos'd the same, because their sensations are not evidently different.

Beside these calm passions, which often determine the will, there are certain violent emotions of the same kind, which have likewise a great influence on that faculty. When I receive any injury from another, I often feel a violent passion of resentment, which makes me desire his evil and punishment, independent of all considerations of pleasure and advantage to myself. When I am immediately threaten'd with any grievous ill, my fears, apprehensions, and aversions rise to a great height, and produce a sensible emotion.

The common error of metaphysicians has lain in ascribing the direction of the will entirely to one of these principles, and supposing the other to have no influence. Men often act knowingly against their interest: For which reason the view of the greatest possible good does not always influence them. Men often counter-act a violent passion in prosecution of their interests and designs: 'Tis not therefore the present uneasiness alone, which determines them. In general we may observe, that both these principles operate on the will; and where they are contrary, that either of them prevails, according to the *general* character or *present* disposition of the person. What we call strength of mind, implies the prevalence of the calm passions above the violent; tho' we may easily observe, there is no man so constantly possess'd of this virtue, as never on any occasion to yield to the solicitations of passion and desire. From these variations of temper proceeds the great difficulty of deciding concerning the actions and resolutions of men, where there is any contrariety of motives and passions. . . .

Moral Distinctions not deriv'd from Reason

Reason is the discovery of truth or falshood. Truth or falshood consists in an agreement or disagreement either to the *real* relations of ideas, or to *real* existence and matter of fact. Whatever, therefore, is not susceptible of this agreement or disagreement, is incapable of being true or false, and can never be an object of our reason. Now 'tis evident our passions, volitions, and actions, are not susceptible of any such agreement or disagreement; being original facts and realities, compleat in themselves, and implying no reference to other passions, volitions, and actions. 'Tis impossible, therefore, they can be pronounced either true or false, and be either contrary or conformable to reason.

This argument is of double advantage to our present purpose. For it proves *directly,* that actions do not derive their merit from a conformity to reason, nor their blame from a contrariety to it; and it proves the same truth more *indirectly,* by shewing us, that as reason can never immediately prevent or produce any action by contradicting or approving of it, it cannot be the source of moral good and evil, which are found to have that influence. Actions may be laudable or blameable; but they cannot be reasonable or unreasonable: Laudable or blameable, therefore, are not the same with reasonable or unreasonable. The merit and demerit of actions frequently contradict, and sometimes controul our natural propensities. But reason has no such influence. Moral distinctions, therefore, are not the offspring of reason. Reason is wholly inactive, and can never be the source of so active a principle as conscience, or a sense of morals.

But perhaps it may be said, that tho' no will or action can be immediately contradictory to reason, yet we may find such a contradiction in some of the attendants of the action, that is, in its causes or effects. The action may cause a judgment, or may be *obliquely* caus'd by one, when the judgment concurs with a passion; and by an abusive way of speaking, which philosophy will scarce allow of, the same contrariety may, upon that account, be ascrib'd to the actions. How far this truth or falshood may be the source of morals, 'twill now be proper to consider.

It has been observ'd, that reason, in a strict and philosophical sense, can have an influence on our conduct only after two ways: Either when it excites a passion by informing us of the existence of something which is a proper object of it; or when it discovers the connexion of causes and effects, so as to afford us means of exerting any passion. These are the only kinds of judgment, which can accompany our actions, or can be said to produce them in any manner; and it must be allow'd, that these judgments may often be false and erroneous. A person may be affected with passion, by supposing a pain or pleasure to lie in an object, which has no tendency to produce either of these sensations, or which produces the contrary to what is imagin'd. A person may also take false measures for the attaining his end, and may retard, by his foolish conduct, instead of forwarding the execution of any project. These false judgments may be thought to affect the passions and actions, which are connected with them, and may be said to render them unreasonable, in a figurative and improper way of speaking. But tho' this be acknowledg'd, 'tis easy to observe, that these errors are so far from being the source of all immorality, that they are commonly very innocent, and draw no manner of guilt upon the person who is so unfortunate as to fall into them. They extend not beyond a mistake of *fact,* which moralists have not generally suppos'd criminal, as being perfectly involuntary. I am more to be lamented than blam'd, if I am mistaken with regard to the influence of objects in producing pain or pleasure, or if I know not the proper means of satisfying my desires. No one can ever regard such errors as a defect in my moral character. A fruit, for instance, that is really disagreeable, appears to me at a distance, and thro' mistake I fancy it to be pleasant and delicious. Here is one error. I choose certain means of reaching this fruit, which are not proper for my end. Here is a second error; nor is there any third one, which can ever possibly enter into our reasonings concerning actions. I ask, therefore, if a man, in this situation, and guilty of these two errors, is to be regarded as vicious and criminal, however unavoidable they might have been? Or if it be possible to imagine, that such errors are the sources of all immorality? . . .

As to those judgments which are the *effects* of our actions, and which, when false, give occasion to pronounce the actions contrary to truth and reason; we may observe, that our actions never cause any judgment, either true or false, in ourselves, and that 'tis only on others they have such an influence. 'Tis certain, that an action, on many occasions, may give rise to false conclusions in others; and that a person, who thro' a window sees any lewd behaviour of mine with my neighbour's wife, may be so simple as to imagine she is certainly my own. In this respect my action resembles somewhat a lye or falshood; only with this difference, which is material, that I perform not the action with any intention of giving rise to a false judgment in another, but merely to satisfy my lust and passion. It causes, however, a mistake and false judgment by accident; and the falshood of its effects may be ascribed, by some odd figurative way of speaking, to the action itself. But still I can see no pretext of reason for asserting, that the tendency to cause such an error is the first spring or original source of all immorality.

Thus upon the whole, 'tis impossible, that the distinction betwixt moral good and evil, can be made by reason; since that distinction has an influence upon our actions, of which reason alone is incapable. Reason and judgment may, indeed, be the mediate cause of an action, by prompting, or by directing a passion: But it is not pretended, that a judgment of this kind, either

in its truth or falshood, is attended with virtue or vice. . . .

But can there be any difficulty in proving, that vice and virtue are not matters of fact, whose existence we can infer by reason? Take any action allow'd to be vicious: Wilful murder, for instance. Examine it in all lights, and see if you can find that matter of fact, or real existence, which you call *vice*. In which-ever way you take it, you find only certain passions, motives, volitions and thoughts. There is no other matter of fact in the case. The vice entirely escapes you, as long as you consider the object. You never can find it, till you turn your reflexion into your own breast, and find a sentiment of disapprobation, which arises in you, towards this action. Here is a matter of fact; but 'tis the object of feeling, not of reason. It lies in yourself, not in the object. So that when you pronounce any action or character to be vicious, you mean nothing, but that from the constitution of your nature you have a feeling or sentiment of blame from the contemplation of it. Vice and virtue, therefore, may be compar'd to sounds, colours, heat and cold, which, according to modern philosophy, are not qualities in objects, but perceptions in the mind: And this discovery in morals, like that other in physics, is to be regarded as a considerable advancement of the speculative sciences; tho', like that too, it has little or no influence on practice. Nothing can be more real, or concern us more, than our own sentiments of pleasure and uneasiness; and if these be favourable to virtue, and unfavourable to vice, no more can be requisite to the regulation of our conduct and behaviour.

I cannot forbear adding to these reasonings an observation, which may, perhaps, be found of some importance. In every system of morality, which I have hitherto met with, I have always remark'd, that the author proceeds for some time in the ordinary way of reasoning, and establishes the being of a God, or makes observations concerning human affairs; when of a sudden I am surpriz'd to find, that instead of the usual copulations of propositions, *is,* and *is not,* I meet with no proposition that is not connected with an *ought,* or an *ought not.* This change is imperceptible; but is, however, of the last consequence. For as this *ought,* or *ought not,* expresses some new relation or affirmation, 'tis necessary that it shou'd be observ'd and explain'd; and at the same time that a reason should be given, for what seems altogether inconceivable, how this new relation can be a deduction from others, which are entirely different from it. But as authors do not commonly use this precaution, I shall presume to recommend it to the readers; and am persuaded, that this small attention wou'd subvert all the vulgar systems of morality, and let us see, that the distinction of vice and virtue is not founded merely on the relations of objects, nor is perceiv'd by reason.

Moral Distinctions Deriv'd from a Moral Sense

Thus the course of the argument leads us to conclude, that since vice and virtue are not discoverable merely by reason, or the comparison of ideas, it must be by means of some impression or sentiment they occasion, that we are able to mark the difference betwixt them. Our decisions concerning moral rectitude and depravity are evidently perceptions; and as all perceptions are either impressions or ideas, the exclusion of the one is a convincing argument for the other. Morality, therefore, is more properly felt than judg'd of; tho' this feeling or sentiment is commonly so soft and gentle, that we are apt to confound it with an idea, according to our common custom of taking all things for the same, which have any near resemblance to each other.

The next question is, Of what nature are these impressions, and after what manner do they operate upon us? Here we cannot remain long in suspense, but must pronounce the impression arising from virtue, to be agreeable, and that proceeding from vice to be uneasy. Every moment's experience must convince us of this. There is no spectacle so fair and beautiful as a noble and generous action; nor any which gives us more abhorrence than one that is cruel and treacherous. No enjoyment equals the satisfaction we receive from the company of those we love and esteem; as the greatest of all punishments is to be oblig'd to pass our lives with those we hate or contemn. A very play or romance may afford us instances of this pleasure, which virtue conveys to us; and pain, which arises from vice.

Now since the distinguishing impressions, by which moral good or evil is known, are nothing but *particular* pains or pleasures; it follows, that in all enquiries concerning these moral distinctions, it will be sufficient to shew the principles, which make us feel a satisfaction or uneasiness from the survey of any character, in order to satisfy us why the character is laudable or blameable. An action, or sentiment, or character is virtuous or vicious; why? because its view causes a pleasure or uneasiness of a particular kind. In giving a reason, therefore, for the pleasure or uneasiness, we sufficiently explain the vice or virtue. To have the sense of virtue, is nothing but to *feel* a satisfaction of a particular kind from the contemplation of a character. The very *feeling* constitutes our praise or admiration. We go no farther; nor do we enquire into the cause of the satisfaction. We do not infer a character to be virtuous, because it pleases: But in feeling that it pleases after such a particular manner, we in effect feel that it is virtuous. The case is the same as in our judgments concerning all kinds of beauty, and tastes, and sensations. Our approbation is imply'd in the immediate pleasure they convey to us. . . .

Of the Origin of the Natural Virtues and Vices

We come now to the examination of such virtues and vices as are entirely natural, and have no dependence on the artifice and contrivance of men. The examination of these will conclude this system of morals.

The chief spring or actuating principle of the human mind is pleasure or pain; and when these sensations are remov'd, both from our thought and feeling, we are, in a great measure, incapable of passion or action, of desire or volition. The most immediate effects of pleasure and pain are the propense and averse motions of the mind; which are diversified into volition, into desire and aversion, grief and joy, hope and fear, according as the pleasure or pain changes its situation, and becomes probable or improbable, certain or uncertain, or is consider'd as out of our power for the present moment. But when along with this, the objects, that cause pleasure or pain, acquire a relation to ourselves or others; they still continue to excite desire and aversion, grief and joy: But cause, at the same time, the indirect passions of pride or humility, love or hatred, which in this case have a double relation of impressions and ideas to the pain or pleasure.

We have already observ'd, that moral distinctions depend entirely on certain peculiar sentiments of pain and pleasure, and that whatever mental quality in ourselves or others gives us a satisfaction, by the survey or reflexion, is of course virtuous; as every thing of this nature, that gives uneasiness, is vicious. Now since every quality in ourselves or others, which gives pleasure, always causes pride or love; as every one, that produces uneasiness, excites humility or hatred: It follows, that these two particulars are to be consider'd as equivalent, with regard to our mental qualities, *virtue* and the power of producing love or pride, *vice* and the power of producing humility or hatred. In every case, therefore, we must judge of the one by the other; and may pronounce any *quality* of the mind virtuous, which causes love or pride; and any one vicious, which causes hatred or humility.

If any *action* be either virtuous or vicious, 'tis only as a sign of some quality or character. It must depend upon durable principles of the mind, which extend over the whole conduct, and enter into the personal character. Actions themselves, not proceeding from any constant principle, have no influence on love or hatred, pride or humility; and consequently are never consider'd in morality.

This reflexion is self-evident, and deserves to be attended to, as being of the utmost importance in the present subject. We are never to consider any single action in our enquiries concerning the origin of morals; but only the quality or character from which the action proceeded. These alone are *durable* enough to affect our sentiments concerning the person. Actions are, indeed, better indications of a character than words, or even wishes and sentiments; but 'tis only so far as they are such indications, that they are attended with love or hatred, praise or blame.

To discover the true origin of morals, and of that love or hatred, which arises from mental qualities, we must take the matter pretty deep and compare some principles.

We may begin with considering a-new the nature and force of *sympathy*. The minds of all men are similar in their feelings and operations, nor can any one be actuated by any affection, of which all others are not, in some degree, susceptible. As in strings equally wound up, the motion of one communicates itself to the rest; so all the affections readily pass from one person to another, and beget correspondent movements in every human creature. When I see the *effects* of passion in the voice and gesture of any person, my mind immediately passes from these effects to their causes, and forms such a lively idea of the passion, as is presently converted into the passion itself. In like manner, when I perceive the *causes* of any emotion, my mind is convey'd to the effects, and is actuated with a like emotion. Were I present at any of the more terrible operations of surgery, 'tis certain, that even before it begun, the preparation of the instruments, the laying of the bandages in order, the heating of the irons, with all the signs of anxiety and concern in the patients and assistants, wou'd have a great effect upon my mind, and excite the strongest sentiments of pity and terror. No passion of another discovers itself immediately to the mind. We are only sensible of its causes or effects. From *these* we infer the passion: And consequently *these* give rise to our sympathy.

Our sense of beauty depends very much on this principle; and where any object has a tendency to produce pleasure in its possessor, it is always regarded as beautiful; as every object, that has a tendency to produce pain, is disagreeable and deform'd. Thus the conveniency of a house, the fertility of a field, the strength of a horse, the capacity, security, and swift-sailing of a vessel, form the principal beauty of these several objects. Here the object, which is denominated beautiful, pleases only by its tendency to produce a certain effect. That effect is the pleasure or advantage of some other person. Now the pleasure of a stranger, for whom we have no friendship, pleases us only by sympathy. To this principle, therefore, is owing the beauty, which we find in every thing that is useful. How considerable a part this is of beauty will easily appear upon reflexion. Wherever an object has a tendency to produce pleasure in the possessor, or in other words, is the proper *cause* of pleasure, it is sure to please the spectator, by a delicate sympathy with the possessor. Most of the works of art are esteem'd beautiful, in proportion to their fitness for the use of man, and even many of the productions of nature derive their beauty from that source. Handsome and beautiful, on most occasions, is not an absolute but a relative quality, and pleases us by nothing but its tendency to produce an end that is agreeable.

The same principle produces, in many instances, our sentiments of morals, as well as those of beauty. No virtue is more esteem'd than justice, and no vice more detested than injustice; nor are there any qualities, which go farther to the fixing the character, either as amiable or odious. Now justice is a moral virtue, merely because it has that tendency to the good of mankind; and, indeed, is nothing but an artificial invention to that purpose. The same may be said of allegiance, of the laws of nations, of mod-

esty, and of goodmanners. All these are mere human contrivances for the interest of society. And since there is a very strong sentiment of morals, which in all nations, and all ages, has attended them, we must allow, that the reflecting on the tendency of characters and mental qualities, is sufficient to give us the sentiments of approbation and blame. Now as the means to an end can only be agreeable, where the end is agreeable; and as the good of society, where our own interest is not concern'd, or that of our friends, pleases only by sympathy: It follows, that sympathy is the source of the esteem, which we pay to all the artificial virtues.

Thus it appears, *that* sympathy is a very powerful principle in human nature, *that* it has a great influence on our taste of beauty, and *that* it produces our sentiment of morals in all the artificial virtues. From thence we may presume, that it also gives rise to many of the other virtues; and that qualities acquire our approbation, because of their tendency to the good of mankind. This presumption must become a certainty, when we find that most of those qualities, which we *naturally* approve of, have actually that tendency, and render a man a proper member of society: While the qualities, which we *naturally* disapprove of, have a contrary tendency, and render any intercourse with the person dangerous or disagreeable. For having found, that such tendencies have force enough to produce the strongest sentiment of morals, we can never reasonably, in these cases, look for any other cause of approbation or blame; it being an inviolable maxim in philosophy, that where any particular cause is sufficient for an effect, we ought to rest satisfied with it, and ought not to multiply causes without necessity. We have happily attain'd experiments in the artificial virtues, where the tendency of qualities to the good of society, is the *sole* cause of our approbation, without any suspicion of the concurrence of another principle. From thence we learn the force of that principle. And where that principle may take place, and the quality approv'd of is really beneficial to society, a true philosopher will never require any other principle to account for the strongest approbation and esteem.

That many of the natural virtues have this tendency to the good of society, no one can doubt of. Meekness, beneficence, charity, generosity, clemency, moderation, equity, bear the greatest figure among the moral qualities, and are commonly denominated the *social* virtues, to mark their tendency to the good of society. This goes so far, that some philosophers have represented all moral distinctions as the effect of artifice and education, when skilful politicians endeavour'd to restrain the turbulent passions of men, and make them operate to the public good, by the notions of honour and shame. This system, however, is not consistent with experience. For, *first,* there are other virtues and vices beside those which have this tendency to the public advan-

tage and loss. *Secondly,* had not men a natural sentiment of approbation and blame, it cou'd never be excited by politicians; nor wou'd the words *laudable* and *praise-worthy, blameable* and *odious,* be any more intelligible, than if they were a language perfectly unknown to us, as we have already observ'd. But tho' this system be erroneous, it may teach us, that moral distinctions arise, in a great measure, from the tendency of qualities and characters to the interests of society, and that 'tis our concern for that interest, which makes us approve or disapprove of them. Now we have no such extensive concern for society but from sympathy; and consequently 'tis that principle, which takes us so far out of ourselves, as to give us the same pleasure or uneasiness in the characters of others, as if they had a tendency to our own advantage or loss.

19. Hume, the Women's Moral Theorist?

Annette C. Baier

In his brief autobiography, David Hume tells us that "as I took particular pleasure in the company of modest women, I had no reason to be displeased with the reception I met with from them." This double-edged remark is typical of Hume's references to women. Suggesting as it does that what pleased Hume was the women's pleasure in his pleasure in *their* company, it both diminishes the significance of their welcome to

him, since "whoever can find the means either by his services, his beauty or his flattery to render himself useful or agreeable to us is sure of our affections" (Hume 1978, p. 388) and makes us wonder about the sources of his particular pleasure in their company. Pleasure in the ample returns he got for a little flattery? Yet his flattery of women, in his writings, is itself double-edged, as much insult as appreciation. Their "insinuation, charm and address" he tells us, in the section on justice in his *Enquiry Concerning the Principles of Morals,* will enable them to break up any incipient male conspiracy

Reprinted from *Women and Moral Theory* by permission of the Rowman and Littlefield.

against them. His archness of tone in "Of love and Marriage," the patronizing encouragement to the greater intellectual effort of reading history instead of romances in "Of the Study of History," were reason enough for him to suppress those two essays (as he did, but for unclear reasons, and along with the more interesting and more radical "Of Moral Prejudices" where he describes a man who is totally dependent, emotionally, on his wife and daughter, and a woman who makes herself minimally dependent on the chosen father of her child).[1] It is not surprising that despite his popularity with the women, modest and less modest, who knew him, his writings have not met with a very positive reception from contemporary feminists. They fix on his references to the "fair" and the "weak and pious" sex, on his defense in the essay on "The Rise of the Arts and Sciences" of the claim that male gallantry is as natural a virtue as respect for one's elders, both being ways of generously allaying others' well founded sense of inferiority or infirmity: "As nature has given *man* the strength above *women,* by endowing him with greater strength both of mind and body, it is his part to alleviate that superiority, as much as possible, by a studied deference and complaisance for all her inclinations and opinions." Hume's "polite" displays of concern for the sex that he saw to be weaker in mind and body are not likely to encourage feminists to turn to him for moral inspiration any more than Kant's exclusion, in the *Metaphysical Elements of Justice,* §46, of all women from the class of those with "civil personality," fit to vote, will encourage them to look to him....

Our central concern is with the concept of morality many women have, and the sort of experience, growth, and reflection on it, which lead them to have it. Our interest in a moral theory like Hume's in this context then, should primarily be with the extent to which the version of morality he works out squares or does not square with women's moral wisdom. Should the main lines of his account prove to be true to

morality as women conceive of it, then it will be an ironic historical detail if he showed less respect than we would have liked for those of his fellow persons who were most likely to find his moral theory in line with their own insights. And whatever the root causes of women's moral outlook, of the tendency of the care perspective to dominate over the justice perspective in their moral deliberations, be it difference in childhood situation, or natural "inferiority" of mind and body, natural superiority of mind and heart, or just difference in mind, heart, and body, now that we have, more or less, social equality with men, women's moral sense should be made as explicit as men's moral sense, and as influential in structuring our practices and institutions. One way, not of course the only or the best way, to help make it explicit is to measure the influential men's moral theories against it. That is what I propose to do with Hume's theory. This can be seen as a prolegomenon to making wise women's theories influential. Then, once I have examined Hume's theory and its fit or misfit with women's moral wisdom, I shall briefly return to the question of how his own attitude to women relates to his moral theory....

Hume's ethics, unlike Kant's, make morality a matter not of obedience to universal law, but of cultivating the character traits which give a person "inward peace of mind, consciousness of integrity," (Hume 1975, p. 283) and at the same time make that person good company to other persons, in a variety of senses of "company," ranging from the relatively impersonal and "remote" togetherness of fellow citizens, to the more selective but still fairly remote relations of parties to a contract, to the closer ties between friends, family, lovers. To become a good fellow-person one doesn't consult some book of rules, but cultivates one's capacity for sympathy, or fellow feeling, as well as for that judgment needed when conflicts arise between the different demands on us such sympathy may lead us to feel. Hume's ethics requires us to be able to be rule-followers, in some contexts, but do not reduce morality to rule-following. Corrected (sometimes rule-corrected) sympathy, not law-discerning reason, is the fundamental moral capacity.

Secondly, there is Hume's difference from Kant about the source of what general rules he does recognize as morally binding, namely the rules of justice. Where Kant sees human reason as the sole author of these moral rules, and sees them as universal, Hume sees them as authored by self-interest, instrumental reason, and rationally "frivolous" factors such as historical chance, human fancy and what it selects as salient, and by custom and tradition. He does not see these rules, such as property rules, as universal, but as varying from community to community and changeable by human will, as conditions or needs, wishes, or human fancy change. His theory of social "artifice," and his account of justice as obedience to the rules of these social artifices, formed by "convention," and subject to historical variation and change, stands in stark opposition to rationalist accounts, like Aquinas's and Kant's, of justice as obedience to laws of pure practical reason, valid for all people at all times and places. Hume has a historicist and conventionalist account of the moral rules which we find ourselves expected to obey, and which, on reflection, we usually see it to be sensible for us to obey, despite their elements of arbitrariness and despite the inequalities their working usually produces. He believes it is sensible for us to conform to the rules of our group, those rules which specify obligations and rights, as long as these do redirect the dangerous destructive workings of self-interest into more mutually advantageous channels, thereby giving all the "infinite advantages" of increased force, stability, and security (compared with what we would have in the absence of any such rules), although some may receive *more* benefits of a given sort, say wealth or authority, than others. . . . The moral and critical stance Hume encourages us to adopt to, say, the property rules of our society, before seeing the rights they recognize as *moral*

rights, comes not from our ability to test them by higher more general rules, but from our capacity for sympathy, from our ability to recognize and sympathetically share the reactions of others to that system of rights, to communicate feelings and understand what our fellows are feeling, so realize what resentments and satisfactions the present social scheme generates. Self-interest, and the capacity to sympathize with the self-interested reactions of others, plus the rational, imaginative, and inventive ability to think about the likely human consequences of any change in the scheme, rather than an acquaintance with a higher law, are what a Humean appeals to at the post-conventional stage.

This difference from Kantian views about the role of general principles in grounding moral obligations goes along in Hume with a downplaying of the role of reason, and a playing up of the role of feeling in moral judgment. Agreeing with the rationalists that when we use our reason we all appeal to universal rules (the rules of arithmetic, or of logic, or of causal inference) and and failing to find any such universal rules of morality, as well as failing to see how, even if we found them, they should be able, alone, to *motivate* us to act as they tell us to act, he claims that morality rests ultimately on sentiment, on a special motivating feeling we come to have once we have exercised our capacity for sympathy with others' feelings, and also learned to overcome the emotional conflicts which arise in a sympathetic person when the wants of different fellow-persons clash, or when one's own wants clash with those of one's fellows. Morality, on Hume's account, is the outcome of a search for ways of eliminating contradictions in the "passions" of sympathetic persons who are aware both of their own and their fellows' desires and needs, including emotional needs. Any moral progress or development a person undergoes will be, for Hume, a matter of "the correction of sentiment," where what corrects it will be contrary sentiments, plus the cognitive-cum-passionate drive to minimize conflict both between and within persons. Reason and logic are indispensable "slaves" to the passions in this achievement, since reason enables us to think clearly about consequences or likely consequences of alternative actions, to foresee outcomes and avoid self-defeating policies. But "the ultimate ends of human actions can never, in any case, be accounted for by *reason,* but recommend themselves entirely to the sentiments and affections of mankind, without any dependence upon intellectual faculties" (Hume 1975, p. 293). A lover of conflict will have no reason, since he will have no motive, to cultivate the moral sentiment, and nor will that man of "cold insensibility" who is "unaffected with the images of human happiness or misery" (Hume 1975, p. 225). A human heart, as well as human reason, is needed for the understanding of morality, and the heart's responses are to particular persons, not to universal principles of abstract justice. Such immediate responses may be corrected by general rules (as they will be when justice demands that the good poor man's debt to the less good miser be paid) and by more reflective feeling responses, such as dismay and foreboding at unwisely given love and trust, or disapproval of excessive parental indulgence, but what controls and regulates feeling will be a wider web of feelings, which reason helps us apprehend and understand, not any reason holding authority over all feelings.

The next point to note is that Hume's version of what a typical human heart desires is significantly different from that both of egoists and of individualists. "The interested passion," or self-interest, plays an important role, but so does sympathy, and concern for others. Even where self-interest is of most importance in his theory, namely in his account of justice, it is the self-interest of those with fairly fluid ego boundaries, namely of family members, concerned with "acquiring goods and possessions for ourselves and our nearest friends", (Hume 1978, pp. 491–2). This is the troublesome passion that needs to be redirected by agreed rules, whereby it can control itself so as to avoid socially destructive conflict over scarce goods. Its self-control, in a society-wide cooperative scheme, which establishes property rights, is possible because the persons involved in it have already learned, in the family, the advantages that can come both from self-control and from cooperation (Hume 1978, p. 486). Had the rough corners of "untoward" and uncontrolled passions, selfish or unselfish, not been already rubbed off by growing up under some parental discipline, and were there no minimally sociable human passions such as love between man and woman, love of parents for their children, love of friends, sisters and brothers, the Human artifice of justice could not be constructed. Its very possibility as an artificial virtue depends upon human nature containing the natural passions, which make family life natural for human beings, which make parental solicitude, grateful response to that, and the restricted cooperation thereby resulting, phenomena that do not need to be contrived by artifice. At the very heart of Hume's moral theory lies his celebration of family life and of parental love. Justice, the chief artificial virtue, is the offspring of family cooperativeness and inventive self-interested reason, which sees how such a *mutually beneficial cooperative* scheme might be extended. And when Hume lists the natural moral virtues, those not consisting in obedience to agreed rules, and having point even if not generally possessed, his favourite example is parental love and solicitude. The good person, the possessor of the natural virtues, is the one who is "a safe companion, an easy friend, a gentle master, an agreeable husband, an indulgent father" (Hume 1978, p. 606). We may deplore that patriarchal combination of roles—master, husband, father, but we should also note the virtues these men are to display—gentleness, agreeability, indulgence. These were more traditionally expected from mistresses, wives, and mothers than from masters, husbands, and fathers. Of course, they are not the only virtues Humean good characters show, there is also due pride, or self-esteem, and the proper ambition and courage that that may involve, as well as generosity, liberality, zeal, gratitude, compassion, patience, industry, perseverance, activity, vigilance, application, integrity, constancy, temperance, frugality, economy, resolution, good temper, charity, clemency, equity, honesty, truthfulness, fidelity, discretion, caution, presence of mind, "and a thousand more of the same kind" (Hume 1975, p. 243).

In Hume's frequent lists of virtues, some are conspicuous by their absence, or by the qualifications accompanying them, namely the martial "virtues" and the monastic or puritan "virtues." Martial bravery and military glory can threaten "the sentiment of humanity" and lead to "infinite confusions and disorders ... the devastation of provinces, the sack of cities" (Hume 1978, p. 601), so cool reflection leads the Humean moral judge to hesitate to approve of these traditionally masculine traits. The monastic virtues receive more forthright treatment. They, namely celibacy, fasting, penance, mortification, self-denial, humility, silence, solitude "are everywhere rejected by men of sense, because they serve no manner of purpose. We observe, on the contrary, that they cross all these desirable ends, stupify the understanding and harden the heart, obscure the fancy and sour the temper" (Hume 1975, p. 270). Here speaks Hume the good companion, the one who enjoyed cooking for supper parties for his Edinburgh friends, the darling, or perhaps the intellectual mascot, of the pleasure-loving Parisian salons. Calvinist upbringing and the brief taste he had in youth of the military life seem to have left him convinced of the undesirability of such styles of life; and his study of history convinced him of the dangers for society both of religious dedication, "sacred zeal and rancor," and of military zeal and rancor. So his list of virtues is a remarkably unaggressive, uncompetitive, one might almost say, womanly list.

Although many of the virtues on his list are character traits that would show in a great range of contexts, most of those contexts are social contexts, involving relations to others, and many of them involve particular relationships such as

parent-child, friend to friend, colleagues to each other, fellow conversationalists. Even when he tries to list virtues that are valued because they are useful and agreeable to their possessor, rather than valued primarily for their contribution to the quality of life of the virtuous person's fellows, the qualities he lists are ones involving relations to others—the ability to get and keep the trust of others, sexual self-command and modesty, (as well as sexual promise, that is the capacity to derive "so capital a pleasure in life" and to "communicate it" to another (Hume 1975, p. 245)), temperance, patience, and sobriety, are virtues useful (long term) to their possessor; while among those he lists as immediately agreeable to their possessor are contagious serenity and cheerfulness, "a proper sense of what is due to oneself in society and the common intercourse of life" (Hume 1975, p. 253), friendliness and an avoidance of "perpetual wrangling, and scolding and mutual reproaches" (Hume 1975, p. 257), amorous adventurousness, at least in the young, liveliness of emotional response and expressive powers—all agreeable traits which presuppose that their possessor is in company with others, reacting to them and the object of their reactions. There may be problems in seeing how a person is to combine the various Humean virtues—to be frugal yet liberal, to be sufficiently chaste yet show amorous enterprise, to have a proper sense of what is due one yet avoid wrangling and reproaches. Hume may, indeed, be depending on a certain sexual division of moral labor, allocating chastity to the women and amorous initiative to the men, more self-assertion to the men and more avoidance of wrangling to the women, but we should not exaggerate the extent to which he did this.

The title page of Book Three of the *Treatise* invokes Lucan's words referring to the lover of difficult virtue, and Humean virtues may be difficult to unify. Only in some social structures, indeed, may they turn out to be a mutually compatible set. Some investigation not only into what virtue is and what the true virtues are, but into the social precondition of their joint exemplification, may be needed in the lover of difficult virtue. Indeed everything Hume says suggests that these are not independent enterprises, since what counts as useful and agreeable virtues will depend in part on the social and economic conditions in which their possessors live, just as the acceptability of those social and economic conditions depends on what sort of virtues can flourish there, and how they are distributed within the population. Hume points out that the usefulness of a trait like good memory will be more important in Cicero's society than in his own, given the lesser importance in the latter of making well turned speeches without notes, and given the general encouraged reliance there on written records in most spheres of life. The availability, accessibility, and portability of memory substitutes will vary with the customs and technological development of a society, and Hume is aware that such facts are relevant to the recognition of character traits as functional virtues. The ease of simulation or perversion of such traits will also affect virtue-recognition—in an age when private ambition is easily masked as public spirit, or tax exemption as benevolence, the credit given to such easily pretended virtues may also understandably sink. The status of a character trait as a virtue need not be a fixed matter, but a matter complexly interrelated with the sort of society in which it appears. This makes good sense, if moral virtues are the qualities that enable one to play an acceptable part in an acceptable network of social roles, to relate to people in the variety of ways that a decent society will require, facilitate, encourage, or merely permit.

The next point I want to stress in Hume's moral theory is that in his attention to various interpersonal relations, in which our Humean virtues or vices show, he does not give any special centrality to relationships between equals, let alone autonomous equals. Since his analysis of social cooperation starts from cooperation within the family, relations between those who are necessarily unequals, namely parents and children, is at the center of the picture. He starts from a bond which he considers "the strongest and most indissoluble bond in nature" (Hume 1975, p. 240), "the strongest tie the mind is capable of" (Hume 1978, p. 352), namely the love of parents for children, and in his moral theory he works out, as it were, from there. This relationship, and the obligations and virtues it involves, lack three central features of relations between moral agents as understood by Kantians and contractarians—it is intimate, it is unchosen, and is between unequals. Of course, the intimacy need not be "indissoluble," the inequality may be temporary, or later reversed, and the extent to which the initial relationship is unchosen will vary from that of unplanned or contrary-to-plan parenthood, to intentional parenthood (although not intentional parenting of a given particular child) to that highest degree of voluntariness present when, faced with an actual newborn child, a decision is taken not to let it be adopted by others, or, when a contrary decision is taken by the biological parent or parents, by the decision of adoptive parents to adopt such an already encountered child. Such fully chosen parenthood is rare, and the norm is for parents to *find themselves* with a given child, perhaps with any child at all, and for parental affection to attach itself fairly indiscriminately to its unselected objects. The contractarian model of morality as a matter of living up to self-chosen commitments gets into obvious trouble both with duties of young children to their unchosen parents, to whom no binding commitments have been made, and of initially involuntary parents to their children. Hume has no problem with such unchosen moral ties, since he takes them as the paradigm moral ties, one's giving rise to moral obligations more self-evident than any obligation to keep contracts.

The last respect in which I wish to contrast Hume's moral philosophy with its more Kantian alternative is in his version of what problem morality is supposed to solve, what its point is. For Kantians and contractarians, the point is freedom, the main problem how to achieve it given that other freedom-aspirants exist and that conflict between them is likely. The Rousseau-

Kant solution is obedience to collectively agreed-to general law, where each freedom-seeker can console himself with the thought that the legislative will he must obey is as much his own as it is anyone else's. For Hume, that problem, of the coexistence of would-be unrestrained self-assertors, is solved by the invention of social artifices and the recognition of the virtue of justice, namely of conformity to the rules of such mutually advantageous artifices. But the problem morality solves is deeper; it is as much intrapersonal as interpersonal. It is the problem of contradiction, conflict, and instability in any one person's desires, over time, as well as conflict between persons. Morality, in theory, saves us from internally self-defeating drives as well as from self-defeating interpersonal conflict. Nor is it just an added extra to Hume's theory that the moral point of view overcomes contradictions in our individual sentiments over time. ("Our situation, with regard to both persons and things, is in continual fluctuation; and a man that lies at a distance from us, may, in a little time, become a familiar acquaintance." (Hume 1978, p. 581). His whole account of our sentiments has made them intrinsically reactive to other persons' sentiments. Internal conflict in a sympathetic and reassurance-needing person will not be independent of conflicts between the various persons in his or her emotional world. "We can form no wish, which has not a reference to society. A perfect solitude is, perhaps, the greatest punishment we can suffer. Every pleasure languishes when enjoy'd apart from company, and every pain is more cruel and intolerable. Whatever other passions we may be actuated by, pride, ambition, avarice, revenge, or lust the soul or animating principle of them all is sympathy; nor would they have any force were we to abstract entirely from the thoughts and sentiments of others" (Hume 1978, p. 363).

I have drawn attention ot the limited place of conformity to general rules in Hume's version of morality, to the historicist conventionalist account he gives of such rules, to his thesis that morality depends upon self-corrected senti-

ments, or passions, as much or more than it depends upon the reason that concurs with and serves those passions; to the nonindividualist, nonegoistic version of human passions he advances, to the essentially interpersonal or social nature of those passions which are approved as virtues, the central role of the family, at least at its best, as an exemplar of the cooperation and interdependency morality preserves and extends, the fact that moral cooperation, for him, includes cooperation in unchosen schemes, with unchosen partners, with unequal partners, in close initmate relations as well as distanced and more formal ones. And finally, I emphasized that the need for morality arises for Hume from conflicts within each person, as well as from interpersonal conflict. It is a fairly straightforward matter to relate these points to at least some of the respects in which Gilligan found girls' and women's versions of morality to differ from men's. Hume turns out to be uncannily womanly in his moral wisdom. "Since the reality of interconnexion is experienced by women as given rather than freely contracted, they arrive at an understanding of life that reflects the limits of autonomy and control" (Gilligan 1982, p. 172). Hume lived before autonomy became an obsession with moral and social philosophers, or rather lived while Rousseau was making it their obsession, but his attack on contractarian doctrines of political obligation, and his clear perception of the given-ness of interconnection, in the family and beyond, his emphasis on our capacity to make others' joys and sorrows our own, on our need for a "seconding" of sentiments, and the inescapable mutual vulnerability and mutual enrichment that the human psychology and the human condition, when thus understood, entail, make autonomy not even an ideal, for Hume. A certain sort of freedom is an ideal, namely freedom of thought and expression, but to "live one's own life in one's own way" is not likely to be among the aims of persons whose every pleasure languishes when not shared and seconded by some other person or persons. "The concept of identity expands to include the experience of interconnexion" (Giligan 1982, p. 173).

The women Gilligan studied saw morality as primarily a matter of responsibilities arising out of their attachment to others, often stemming from originally given rather than chosen relations. The men spoke more of their rights than of their responsibilities, and saw those rights as arising out of a freely accepted quasi-agreement between self-interested equals. Hume does in his account of justice have a place for quasi-agreement-based rights serving the long run interests of those respecting them, but he also makes room for a host of responsibilities which presuppose no prior agreement or quasi-agreement to shoulder them. The responsibilities of parents are the paramount case of such duties of care, but he also includes cases of mutual care, and duties of gratitude where "I do services to such persons as I love, and am particularly acquainted with, without any prospect of advantage; and they may make me a return in the same manner" (Hume 1978, p. 521). Here there is no right to a return, merely the reasonable but unsecured trust that it will be forthcoming. (There may even be something of an either/or, duck-rabbit effect, between his "artificial virtues," including justice, and his "natural virtues," including mercy and equity, in all those contexts where both seem to come in to play.) . . .

Hume is a realist about the historical givenness and inevitable arbitrariness of most of the general rules there is any chance of our all observing. Like Carol Gilligan's girls and women, he takes moral problems in concrete historical settings, where the past history as well as the realistic future prospects for a given group are seen as relevant to their moral predicaments, and their solutions. Even the fairly abstract and historical social artifices of the *Treatise* are given a quasi-historical setting, and give way in the *Essays* and *History of England* to detailed looks at actual concrete social and moral predicaments, in full narrative depth.

The distrust of abstract ahistorical principles,

the girls' need to fill out Kohlberg's puzzle questions with a story, before answering them, led to the suspicion that this poor performance on the application of universal principles to sketchily indicated particular cases, shorn of full narrative context, showed that their "reason" was less well developed than the boys' (Gilligan 1982, p. 28). It might rather have been, as it was in Hume's case, a conviction that this was a false model of how moral judgments are made. He endorses the emotional response to a fully realized situation as moral reflection at its best, not as one of its underdeveloped stages, and he mocks those rationalists who think abstract universal rules will ever show why, say, killing a parent is wrong for human beings but not for oak trees (Hume 1978, pp. 466–7). . . .

I end with the question of how this wise moral theory of Hume's could allow its author to make the apparently sexist remarks he did. Now, I think, we are in a position to see how harmless they might be, a display of his social realism, his unwillingness to idealize the actual. Women in his society *were* inferior in bodily strength and in intellectual achievement. Neither of these, however, for someone who believes that reason should be the slave of reflective and moralized passions, are the capacities that matter most. What matters most, for judging moral wisdom, are corrected sentiments, imagination, and cooperative genius. There Hume never judges women inferior. He does call them the "timorous and pious" sex, and that is for him a criticism, but since he ties both of these characteristics with powerlessness, his diagnoses here are of a piece with his more direct discussions of how much power women have. In those discussions he is at pains to try to point out not just the subordination of their interests to those of men in the existing institutions (marriage in particular) but also to show women where their power lies, should they want to change the situation.

As he points out, a concern for "the propagation of our kind" is a normal concern of men and women, but each of us needs the cooperation of a member of the other sex to further this concern, and "a trivial and anatomical observation" (Hume 1978, p. 571) shows us that no man can know that his kind has been propagated unless he can trust some woman either to be sexually "faithful" to him, or to keep track of and tell him the truth about the paternity of any child she bears. This gives women great, perhaps dangerously great, threat advantage in any contest with men, a power very different from any accompanying the "insinuation, charm and address" (Hume 1975, p. 191) that Hume had invoked as sufficient to break any male confederacy against them. The non self-sufficiency of persons in reproductive respects that he goes on in the next paragraphs to emphasize, and the need of the male for a trustworthy female, in order to satisfy his postulated desire for offspring he can recognize as his (a desire Hume had emphasized in the *Treatise* section "Of Chastity and Modesty,") put some needed iron into the gloved hands of the fair and charming sex. Hume gives many descriptions in his *History* and *Essays* of strong independent women, and he dwells on the question of whether the cost of their iron wills and their independence is a loss of the very moral virtues he admires in anyone but finds more often in women than in men—the "soft" non-martial compassionate virtues. Need women, in ceasing to be timorous and servile, cease also to be experts at care and mutual care? His moral tale of a liberated woman who chooses to be a single mother, (in "Of Moral Prejudices") suggests not—that avoidance of servile dependence on men can be combined with the virtues of the

caring and bearing responsibility, that pride and at least some forms of love can be combined.

NOTES

1. The three essays referred to in this section were published by Hume in the first edition of *Essays Moral and Political* 1741–2, but removed by him in subsequent editions. They can be found in Hume, ed. Miller, 1985, in an appendix "Essays Withdrawn and Unpublished."

REFERENCES

Gilligan, Carol. 1982. *In a Different Voice: Psychological Theory and Women's Development*. Cambridge, Mass., London: Harvard University Press

Hall, Judith A. 1984. *Non Verbal Sex Differences*. Baltimore: The Johns Hopkins University Press.

Hume, David. 1975. *Enquiries*. L. A. Selby-Bigge and P. H. Nidditch, eds. Oxford: Clarendon Press.

———. 1978. *A Treatise of Human Nature*. L. A. Selby-Bigge and P. H. Nidditch, eds. Oxford: Clarendon Press.

———. 1985. *Essays Moral, Political and Literary*. Ed. Eugene F. Millar. Indianapolis: Liberty Classics.

———. *History of England*. any edition.

Kant, Immanuel. 1965. *The Metaphysical Elements of Justice*. John Ladd, trans., Indianapolis, New York, Kansas City: Bobbs-Merrill.

Kohlberg, Lawrence. 1971. *Collected Papers on Moral Development and Moral Education*. Harvard University: Moral Education Research Foundation.

———. 1981. *The Philosophy of Moral Development*. San Francisco, Calif.: Harper & Row.

Rosenthal, Robert, J. A. Hall, M. R. DiMatteo, P. L. Rogers, and D. Archer, 1979. *Sensitivity to Nonverbal Communication: The PONS Test*. Baltimore: The Johns Hopkins University Press.

20. EWE PROVERBS

"The child who breaks a snail's shell cannot break a tortoise's shell."

Moral Teaching: There are certain things any human being can do and others he cannot because his powers are limited, therefore you must know the limit of your powers and keep your ambitions within them. Do not be over-ambitious. . . .

"The game that you miss, i.e. runs away from a hunter, is always a big one."

Moral Teaching: There is always a tendency to overvalue things that we want but we do not have, and so this proverb is warning against the danger of overvaluing the real worth of what we want badly but cannot get. We must rather learn to appreciate whatever we have.

"Suffering and happiness are twins."

Moral Teaching: Life is a mixture of joy and suffering and so we must learn to accept both, and the acceptance of both is a sign of maturity.

"The crab says that when you see it walking clumsily it does not mean that it has lost its way."

Moral Teaching: This proverb can be used by anybody whose actions are misunderstood, to warn those who judge him that he had not forgotten the essential principles that guide his behaviour. The proverb warns against the practice of misjudging the basic principles that guide the behaviour of people. . . .

Reprinted from *African Proverbs: Guide to Conduct.* by permission of N. K. Dzoba.

"The virtue cannot cure baldness" (because if it can it would have cured its own baldness).

Moral Teaching: In the traditional society some people lay claim to certain powers to cure diseases, to make others wealthy or to make barren women productive. The problem is, how do you test the validity of the claims that they make? This proverb establishes a standard for evaluating such claims. Whatever powers a person claims to have, such powers must be seen to make a practical difference to his own life before his claims could be accepted as valid, and so anybody who accepts such claims without this test of their validity will be considered gullible. The proverb is counselling against the tendency to be gullible in such matters and recommends critical assessment and discernment instead of gullibility. . . .

"There is no rain whose flood can submerge all mountains" i.e. there is an end to every fall of rain.

Moral Teaching: There is an end to everything and people are supposed to use this knowledge to guide their behaviour or to comfort themselves in their sufferings. . . .

"A lazy man's farm is a breeding ground for snakes."

Explanation: A lazy farmer does not keep his farm clear of weeds and so snakes can easily live there and he may be bitten by them, and this will be regarded as a punishment for his laziness.
Moral Teaching: Laziness has its own appropriate punishment and so people must learn to be hardworking so as to avoid the inevitable punishment for laziness.

"The person who goes to draw water does not drink mud."

Explanation: In many African homes women and children go out to draw water from common wells or from nearby streams, and in the big towns from public hydrants. Since water-drawers provide water for their homes they themselves will get good water to drink at all cost.

Moral Teaching: Those who work will always eat the fruits of their labour. Every just toil will be rewarded and the traditional society uses the truth of the saying as a motivation for hard work....

"A child who resembles his father does not necessarily take after his father."

Moral Teaching: Children must *learn to behave* themselves because any physical resemblances between them and their parents will not automatically help them maintain the good name of their parents.

"The antelope does not wear the shoes of an elephant."

Moral Teaching: Accept your humble status and do not aspire after greatness that is beyond your reach. This proverb offers a lesson also in the importance of self-acceptance and warns against unrealistic and inordinate aspirations....

"The salt does not praise itself." (It is others who say that salt is good.)

Moral Teaching: Do not brag about your goodness but be modest about it. This proverb therefore teaches people to have a humble estimate about their merits.

"However good the hair may be a hat is worn on it."

Moral Teaching: This proverb again emphasises the importance of submission to authority. No individual is so good that he cannot be subjected to some kind of authority. Every individual must be prepared to submit himself to one form of authority or another, be it human or divine.

"When you are carrying beef on your head you do not use your feet to catch grasshoppers."

Explanation: Beef is a better meat than grasshopper and so if you have beef you do not go after a grasshopper.

Moral Teaching: Be able to tell the relative value of things you have and do not spend your energy on less valuable things. This proverb teaches the importance of the right judgment of the relative value of things....

"You clean the ceiling before you clean the floor."

Moral Teaching: The simple truth of this statement is used to teach the need for doing things according to a specific form of procedure. Orderly procedure is a social value.

"You do not take a big gourd to a farm that is close by."

Explanation: Farmers take water pots or gourds to their farms and usually the size of the pot will depend upon how far the farm is from the village. If the farm is close by you take a small pot of water and if not you take a big one.

Moral Teaching: The ability to size up the seriousness of a problem and to work out the appropriate solution to it is at a premium in a society where nothing is allowed to disrupt human relationships. Members of a traditional society are expected to learn to assess accurately the seriousness of a problem, and work out an appropriate solution to it. Over-estimation or under-estimation is considered as a serious defect in an assessment of problems.

"If you are patient enough you can cook a stone and it will become soft."

Moral Teaching: With patience you can achieve seemingly impossible tasks....

"A stump that stays in a river for a hundred years does not become a crocodile."

Moral Teaching: The Ewe on the whole are very patriotic and they teach their children to love their places of birth. This proverb ... warns people who go to live in foreign lands that they will never become real citizens of those lands. Even if they stay abroad for a long time they will be regarded as "strangers" and because of this they must learn to love and honour their homelands. . . .

> "Knowledge is like a baobab tree (monkey-bread tree) and no one person can embrace it with both arms."

Explanation: The baobab tree usually has a very huge base stem and cannot be embraced by the two arms of any human being.

Moral Teaching: Knowledge and truth are like the unbounded ocean and so no one individual can claim to have a corner on them. Individuals must therefore be humble in their claims to knowledge and in such a humble frame of mind they can always acquire more knowledge since there is no limit to what any man can know. . . .

> "Love is like an egg, it breaks easily" (and so it should be handled carefully).

Moral Teaching: The loving relationship is very vulnerable and so must be carefully handled otherwise it will turn into hate or indifference. . . .

> "You do not grumble about self-imposed or self-chosen tasks."

Moral Teaching: This proverb also teaches cheerfulness and endurance in discharging self-chosen projects. . . .

> "The chicken is never declared innocent in the court of hawks" (because the chicken is a prey to hawks).

Moral Teaching: This proverb is advising on how to relate to one's enemies and the relationship should be one of non-interference in their affairs. . . .

> "The new is woven on to the old."

Moral Teaching: In this proverb "the old" stands for the "traditions of the past," and it is maintained that the traditions of the past form the foundation of the present and so traditions should be respected. The proverb is meant to develop a positive attitude to and respect for traditional practices. . . .

> "The cotton thread says that it is only as a team that you carry a stone."

Explanation: This proverb comes from the practice of kente weavers who, to straighten their cotton threads, make them into a loop and hang them down with a heavy stone from a transverse wooden bar. The loop of many threads can stand the weight of a heavy stone while one single thread cannot.

Moral Teaching: There is strength in unity, therefore learn to work together with others.

> "One hand cannot hold a bull's horns."

Explanation: The "bull's horn" represents any difficult task which cannot be done by one man alone but as he teams up with others they could do it.

Moral Teaching: This proverb stresses the need for a united effort in solving difficult problems, and it also advises individuals who trust too much in their own strengths to learn to co-operate with others in solving difficult tasks. The two virtues commended by the two preceding proverbs are *unity* and *cooperation*. . . .

RECOMMENDED READINGS

Texts

Ayer, A. J. *Hume.* Oxford, England: Oxford University Press, 1980.

Basson, A. H. *David Hume.* London: Penguin Books, 1958.

Chappell, V. C., ed. *Hume: A Collection of Critical Essays.* Garden City, NY: Doubleday 7 Co., 1966.

Knight, William. *Hume*. Port Washington, NY: Kennikat Press, 1970.

Merrill, Kenneth R., and Robert W. Shahan, eds. *David Hume: Many-sided Genius*. Norman: University of Oklahoma Press, 1976.

Norton, David Fate, ed. *The Cambridge Companion to Hume*. New York: Cambridge University Press, 1993.

Pears, David. *Hume's System*. New York: Oxford University Press, 1990.

Stroud, Barry. *Hume*. London: Routledge & Kegan Paul, 1977.

Feminist Perspective

Battersby, Christine. "An Enquiry Concerning the Humean Woman." *Philosophy* 56 (1981): 303–312.

Burns, Steven A. Macleod. "The Humean Female." In *The Sexism of Social and Political Theory: Women and Reproduction from Plato to Nietzsche*. Eds. Lorenne M. G. Clark and Lynda Lange. Toronto: University of Toronto Press, 1979.

Lacoste, Louise Marcil. "Hume's Method in Moral Reasoning." In *The Sexism of Social and Political Theory: Women and Reproduction from Plato to Nietzsche*. Eds. Lorenne M. G. Clark and Lynda Lange. Toronto: University of Toronto Press, 1979.

Lloyd, Genevieve. *The Man of Reason: "Male" and "Female" in Western Philosophy*, Chapter 3. Minneapolis: University of Minnesota Press, 1984.

Multicultural Perspective

Appiah, Anthony Kwame. *In My Father's House*. Oxford: Oxford University Press, 1992.

Serequeberhan, Tsenay. *African Philosophy*. New York: Paragon, 1991.

PART VI

❦

KANT

INTRODUCTION

Immanuel Kant was born in 1724 in Konigsberg, East Prussia (now called Kaliningrad, and part of Russia) and he never journeyed more than seventy miles from the city. Kant appears to have seriously entertained the possibility of marriage at least twice during his life. On one occasion, he was in the process of assessing his financial situation to determine whether to propose to a young widow, when the woman accepted a marriage proposal from someone else. On another occasion, a Westphialian visitor to Konigsberg, in whom Kant was interested, left town with her employer before Kant could make up his mind.

Kant was educated in Leibniz's philosophy, but later was profoundly influenced by Hume and Rousseau. By Kant's own admission, Hume awakened him from his dogmatic slumbers. However, Rousseau seemed to have had an even stronger influence on him. When he received a copy of Rousseau's *Emile* in 1762, his rigid schedule (rising, coffee-drinking, writing, lecturing, dining, walking, each at a set time) was thrown out of kilter for two whole days while he read the book. At the University of Konigsberg, Kant was a popular lecturer; his public lectures were so well attended that students often had to arrive early to get seats.

Kant published *Observations on the Feeling of the Beautiful and Sublime* in 1766. His most important work, his *Critique of Pure Reason,* was not published until 1781. After that, his other famous writings followed in quick succession. In 1783, he published the *Prologomena to any Future Metaphysics;* in 1785, the *Foundations of a Metaphysics of Morals;* in 1786, the *Metaphysical First Principles of Natural Science;* in 1787, the second edition of the *Critique of Pure Reason;* in 1788, the *Critique of Practical Reason;* in 1790, the *Critique of Judgment;* in 1792, *Theory and Practice;* in 1793, *Religion within the Bounds of Reason Alone;* in 1795, *Perpetual Peace;* and in 1797 *the Metaphysics of Morals.*

Only once did Kant come into collision with political authority. That was in connection with his *Religion within the Bounds of Reason Alone.* The work was approved by the theological faculty of Konigsberg in 1793. But in 1794, the work was censured by Frederick William II, and Kant was forbidden to write or lecture on any religious subject. Kant accepted this censure, an act for which he was widely criticized.

Kant died in 1804. He was already fifty-seven years old when he published his *Critique of Pure Reason.* Consequently, his literary production from 1781 to the time of his death constitutes a remarkable performance. He was working on a restatement of his philosophy at the time of his death.

In our selection from the *Foundations of a Metaphysics of Morals,* Kant argues for the importance of acting from duty. According to Kant, the only thing good without qualification is a good will, and a person acquires both a good will and moral worth by acting from duty. In addition, a person acts from duty by acting with the motive of doing one's duty. By contrast, a person acts according to duty by simply doing one's duty with whatever motive one happens to have. Kant further contends that one's duty is to act in accord with objective moral laws. For Kant, such laws are categorical rather than hypothetical imperatives.

Hypothetical imperatives either have the form "If one wants x one ought to do y" or "Since one wants x one ought to do y." Whereas categorical imperatives have the form "One ought to do y irrespective of what one wants."

According to Kant, we can determine which moral imperatives are valid, i.e., objective moral laws, by applying the test of the Categorical Imperative. This test requires:

- Act only on that maxim which you can at the same time will to be a universal law.

Kant thinks there are alternative formulations of this test which are all equivalent. They are:

- *The Formula of Universal Law:* Act only on that maxim whereby it were to become by your will a universal law of nature.

- *The Formula of Humanity:* Act so that you treat humanity, whether in your own person or in that of another, always as an end and never as a means only.

- *Formula of the Kingdom of Ends:* Act as if you were by your maxims in every case a legislating member in the universal kingdom of ends.

Commentators have disputed whether these formulations are actually equivalent, as well as how the Categorical Imperative should be applied to practical cases.

In our selection from Kant's *Observations on the Feeling of the Beautiful and Sublime,* we actually find many of the views that Jean Jacques Rousseau expressed about women. Thus, Kant agreed with Rousseau that there is a basic and pervasive difference between the sexes. Kant thought that the fair sex is properly named not only because woman is more comely than man in looks and manner but also because beauty is a woman's most dominant feature, just as man's is to be noble or sublime. Woman's understanding is also different from man's—it is a fine understanding as opposed to the deep or profound understanding of a man. And woman's virtue is a beautiful virtue as opposed to the noble virtue of a man. Even many of a woman's faults, such as tearfulness, vanity, and coquetry, are beautiful.

Kant claims that though a woman may succeed in rigorous study, this takes away from the excellence peculiar to her sex. Hence, disciplines, such as geometry, geography, philosophy, astronomy, history, and physics are not for her. A woman is not to reason but to feel. Since a woman tends to be resistant to restraint, incapable of principles, and motivated by pleasure, virtue is best instilled in her by using examples rather than universal principles and by making what is good pleasing to her. In marriage, Kant thought, husband and wife are like a single moral person, guided by the understanding of the husband and the taste of the wife. In the contemporary scene, these views of Kant are not without their contemporary defenders.

In our second selection from his *Observations on the Feeling of the Beautiful and Sublime,* Kant claims that while the feeling for the beautiful predominates among Frenchmen and the feeling for the sublime predominates among Britons, among his fellow Germans happily both these feelings can be found. Kant goes on to claim that "Negroes of Africa have by nature no feeling which rises above the trifling," and that the differences between the races "appears to be equally great with regard to the mental capabilities as with regard to color." Certainly, Kant's expression of prejudice here should make one doubt that his native Konigsberg was "an appropriate place for enlarging one's knowledge of people as well as the world at large."[1] Yet later in the same section, Kant does note that among Canadian Indians respect for women may "surpass even our civilized part of the world."

In "Maria von Herbert's Challenge to Kant," Rae Langton presents an exchange of letters between Kant and Maria von Herbert, who had been rejected by her lover as a result of having told him the truth about a past affair. In despair, Herbert contemplates suicide, which Kant maintains is immoral, and she writes Kant for guidance. Kant replies that she must never regret having done her duty by being truthful and that the breakup of the relationship with her lover must be for the best. Now withdrawn into a state of apathy, Herbert again writes Kant, this time asking for permission to visit him. Kant does not reply to her. Instead, he sends the exchange of letters to a female acquaintance as a warning of how one can be "capsized on the reef of romantic love," and refers to Herbert as mentally deranged. Langton disagrees and faults Kant for not being a friend to Herbert. Eventually, Herbert did commit suicide.

What this exchange of letters shows, assuming that Langton is right, is not only how difficult it is even for Kant to apply his own theory, but also how difficult it is, in general, for men, when applying any such theory, to fully appreciate the different circumstances in which women find themselves in society.

The *Bhagavad Gita* (Song of God), composed more than two thousand years ago as part of the massive epic *Mahabharata,* is India's single most influential religious text. Like Kant's view, it emphasizes the importance of acting from duty and not from inclination. Our selection opens with Arjuna, a great warrior, reflecting on a battlefield just before a battle is to begin. He sees his teachers, friends, and relatives lined up on the opposing side, and even though he believes his cause is just, he has no desire to kill them. Krishna, the embodiment of the god Vishnu, then reminds Arjuna of his duty, and when Arjuna still protests, Krishna explains that one must distinguish between ordinary things in the world and the unchanging ultimate reality (Brahman), noting that it is just the *"bodies* of the indestructible, immeasurable, and eternal embodied self that are characterized as coming to an end." Therefore Arjuna should fight. But if what is important is to recognize and identify with the unchanging ultimate reality (Brahman), why, asks Arjuna, should he be concerned to do his duty? Krishna's reply is that no one can avoid action, but if one is to achieve identity with the unchanging ultimate reality (Brahman), then one must do one's duty without attachment, without desires, without inclinations.

NOTES

1. Immanuel Kant, *Anthropology from a Pragmatic Point of View,* trans. Victor Lyle Dowdell (Carbondale, Southern Illinois University, 1978) pp. 4–5n

21. FUNDAMENTAL PRINCIPLES OF THE METAPHYSICS OF MORALS

❦

IMMANUEL KANT

TRANSITION FROM THE COMMON RATIONAL KNOWLEDGE OF MORALITY TO THE PHILOSOPHICAL

Nothing can possibly be conceived in the world, or even out of it, which can be called good, without qualification, except a Good Will. Intelligence, wit, judgment, and the other *talents* of the mind, however they may be named, or courage, resolution, perseverance, as qualities of temperament, are undoubtedly good and desirable in many respects; but these gifts of nature may also become extremely bad and mischievous if the will which is to make use of them, and which, therefore, constitutes what is called *character,* is not good. It is the same with the *gifts of fortune.* Power, riches, honor, even health, and the general well-being and contentment with one's condition which is called *happiness,* inspire pride, and often presumption, if there is not a good will to correct the influence of these on the mind, and with this also to rectify the whole principle of acting, and adapt it to its end. The sight of a being who is not adorned with a single feature of a pure and good will, enjoying unbroken prosperity, can never give pleasure to an impartial rational spectator. Thus a good will appears to constitute the indispensable condition even of being worthy of happiness.

Reprinted from *Kant's Critique of Practical Reason and Other Writings on the Theory of Ethics*, 6th ed. trans. by Thomas Kingmil Abbott (London: Longmans, 1909).

There are even some qualities which are of service to this good will itself, and may facilitate its action, yet which have no intrinsic unconditional value, but always presuppose a good will, and this qualifies the esteem that we justly have for them, and does not permit us to regard them as absolutely good. Moderation in the affections and passions, self-control, and calm deliberation are not only good in many respects, but even seem to constitute part of the intrinsic worth of the person; but they are far from deserving to be called good without qualification, although they have been so unconditionally praised by the ancients. For without the principles of a good will, they may become extremely bad; and the coolness of a villain not only makes him far more dangerous, but also directly makes him more abominable in our eyes than he would have been without it.

A good will is good not because of what it performs or effects, not by its aptness for the attainment of some proposed end, but simply by virtue of the volition, that is, it is good in itself, and considered by itself is to be esteemed much higher than all that can be brought about by it in favor of any inclination, nay, even of the sum total of all inclinations. Even if it should happen that, owing to special disfavor of fortune, or the niggardly provision of a stepmotherly nature, this will should wholly lack power to accomplish its purpose, if with its greatest efforts it should yet achieve nothing, and there should remain only the good will (not, to be sure, a mere wish, but the summoning of all means in our power), then, like a jewel, it would still shine by its own light, as a thing which has its whole value in itself. Its usefulness or fruitlessness can neither add to nor take away anything from this value. It would be, as it were, only the setting to enable us to handle it the more conveniently in common commerce, or to attract to it the attention of those who are not yet connoisseurs, but not to recommend it to true connoisseurs, or to determine its value. . . .

We have then to develop the notion of a will which deserves to be highly esteemed for itself, and is good without a view to anything further, a notion which exists already in the sound natural understanding, requiring rather to be cleared up than to be taught, and which in estimating the value of our actions always takes the first place, and constitutes the condition of all the rest. In order to do this, we will take the notion of duty, which includes that of a good will, although implying certain subjective restrictions and hindrances. These, however, far from concealing it, or rendering it unrecognizable, rather bring it out by contrast, and make it shine forth so much the brighter.

I omit here all actions which are already recognized as inconsistent with duty, although they may be useful for this or that purpose, for with these the question whether they are done *from duty* cannot arise at all, since they even conflict with it. I also set aside those actions which really conform to duty, but to which men have *no* direct *inclination,* performing them because they are impelled thereto by some other inclination. For in this case we can readily distinguish whether the action which agrees with duty is done *from duty,* or from a selfish view. It is much harder to make this distinction when the action accords with duty, and the subject has besides a *direct* inclination to it. For example, it is always a matter of duty that a dealer should not overcharge an inexperienced purchaser; and whenever there is much commerce the prudent tradesman does not overcharge, but keeps a fixed price for everyone, so that a child buys of him as well as any other. Men are thus *honestly*

served; but this is not enough to make us believe that the tradesman has so acted from duty and from principles of honesty: his own advantage required it; it is out of the question in this case to suppose that he might besides have a direct inclination in favor of the buyers, so that, as it were, from love he should give no advantage to one over another. Accordingly the action was done neither from duty nor from direct inclination, but merely with a selfish view.

On the other hand, it is a duty to maintain one's life; and, in addition, everyone has also a direct inclination to do so. But on this account the often anxious care which most men take for it has no intrinsic worth, and their maxim has no moral import. They preserve their life *as duty requires* no doubt, but not *because duty requires.* On the other hand, if adversity and hopeless sorrow have completely taken away the relish for life; if the unfortunate one, strong in mind, indignant at his fate rather than desponding or dejected, wishes for death, and yet preserves his life without loving it—not from inclination or fear, but from duty—then his maxim has a moral worth.

To be beneficent when we can is a duty; and besides this, there are many minds so sympathetically constituted that, without any other motive of vanity or self-interest, they find a pleasure in spreading joy around them, and can take delight in the satisfaction of others so far as it is their own work. But I maintain that in such a case an action of this kind, however proper, however amiable it may be, has nevertheless no true moral worth, but is on a level with other inclinations, e.g. the inclination to honor, which, if it is happily directed to that which is in fact of public utility and accordant with duty, and consequently honorable, deserves praise and encouragement, but not esteem. For the maxim lacks the moral import, namely, that such actions be done *from duty,* not from inclination. Put the case that the mind of that philanthropist was clouded by sorrow of his own, extinguishing all sympathy with the lot of others, and that while he still has the power to benefit others in distress, he is not touched by their trouble because he is absorbed with his own; and now suppose that he tears himself out of this dead insensibility, and performs the action without any inclination to it, but simply from duty, then first has his action its genuine moral worth. Further still; if nature has put little sympathy in the heart of this or that man; if he, supposed to be an upright man, is by temperament cold and indifferent to the sufferings of others, perhaps because in respect of his own he is provided with the special gift of patience and fortitude, and supposes, or even requires, that others should have the same—and such a man would certainly not be the meanest product of nature—but if nature had not specially framed him for a philanthropist, would he not still find in himself a source from whence to give himself a far higher worth than that of a good-natured temperament could be? Unquestionably. It is just in this that the moral worth of the character is brought out which is incomparably the highest of all, namely, that he is beneficent, not from inclination, but from duty.

To secure one's own happiness is a duty, at least indirectly; for discontent with one's condition, under a pressure of many anxieties and amidst unsatisfied wants, might easily become a great *temptation to transgression of duty*. But here again, without looking to duty, all men have already the strongest and most intimate inclination to happiness, because it is just in this idea that all inclinations are combined in one total. But the precept of happiness is often of such a sort that it greatly interferes with some inclinations, and yet a man cannot form any definite and certain conception of the sum of satisfaction of all of them which is called happiness. It is not then to be wondered at that a single inclination, definite both as to what it promises and as to the time within which it can be gratified, is often able to overcome such a fluctuating idea, and that a gouty patient, for instance, can choose to enjoy what he likes, and to suffer what he may, since, according to his calculation, on this occa-

sion at least, he has [only] not sacrificed the enjoyment of the present moment to a possible mistaken expectation of a happiness which is supposed to be found in health. But even in this case, if the general desire for happiness did not influence his will, and supposing that in his particular case health was not a necessary element in this calculation, there yet remains in this, as in all other cases, this law, namely, that he would promote his happiness not from inclination but from duty, and by this would his conduct first acquire true moral worth.

It is in this manner, undoubtedly, that we are to understand those passages of Scripture also in which we are commanded to love our neighbor, even our enemy. For love, as an affection, cannot be commanded, but beneficence for duty's sake may; even though we are not impelled to it by any inclination—nay, are even repelled by a natural and unconquerable aversion. This is *practical* love, and not *pathological*—a love which is seated in the will, and not in the propensions of sense—in principles of action and not of tender sympathy; and it is this love alone which can be commanded.

The second[1] proposition is: That an action done from duty derives its moral worth, *not from the purpose* which is to be attained by it, but from the maxim by which it is determined, and therefore does not depend on the realization of the object of the action, but merely on the *principle of volition* by which the action has taken place, without regard to any object of desire. It is clear from what precedes that the purposes which we may have in view in our actions, or their effects regarded as ends and springs of the will, cannot give to actions any unconditional or moral worth. In what, then, can their worth lie, if it is not to consist in the will and in reference to its expected effect? It cannot lie anywhere but in the *principle of the will* without regard to the ends which can be attained by the action. For the will stands between its a priori principle, which is formal, and its a posteriori spring, which is material, as between two roads, and as it must be determined by something, it follows that it must be determined by the formal principle of volition when an action is done from duty, in which case every material principle has been withdrawn from it.

The third proposition, which is a consequence of the two preceding, I would express thus: *Duty is the necessity of acting from respect for the law.* I may have *inclination* for an object as the effect of my proposed action, but I cannot have respect for it, just for this reason, that it is an effect and not an energy of will. Similarly, I cannot have respect for inclination, whether my own or another's; I can at most, if my own, approve it; if another's, sometimes even love it; i.e. look on it as favorable to my own interest. It is only what is connected with my will as a principle, by no means as an effect—what does not subserve my inclination, but overpowers it, or at least in case of choice excludes it from its calculation—in other words, simply the law of itself, which can be an object of respect, and hence a command. Now an action done from duty must wholly exclude the influence of inclination, and with it every object of the will, so that nothing remains which can determine the will except objectively the *law,* and subjectively *pure respect* for this practical law, and consequently the maxim[2] that I should follow this law even to the thwarting of all my inclinations.

Thus the moral worth of an action does not lie in the effect expected from it, nor in any principle of action which requires to borrow its motive from this expected effect. For all these effects—agreeableness of one's condition, and even the promotion of the happiness of others—could have been also brought about by other causes, so that for this there would have been no need of the will of a rational being; whereas it is in this alone that the supreme and unconditional good can be found. The pre-eminent good which we call moral can therefore consist in nothing else than *the conception of law* in itself, *which certainly is only possible in a rational being,* so far as this conception, and not the expected effect, determines the will. This is a good which is already present in the person who acts accordingly, and we have not to wait for it to appear first in the result.[3] . . .

TRANSITION FROM POPULAR MORAL PHILOSOPHY TO THE METAPHYSIC OF MORALS

. . . Everything in nature works according to laws. Rational beings alone have the faculty of acting according *to the conception* of laws, that is according to principles, i.e. have a *will.* Since the deduction of actions from principles requires *reason,* the will is nothing but practical reason. If reason infallibly determines the will, then the actions of such a being which are recognized as objectively necessary are subjectively necessary also, i.e. the will is a faculty to choose *that only* which reason independent of inclination recognizes as practically necessary, i.e. as good. But if reason of itself does not sufficiently determine the will, if the latter is subject also to subjective conditions (particular impulses) which do not always coincide with the objective conditions; in a word, if the will does not *in itself* completely accord with reason (which is actually the case with men), then the actions which objectively are recognized as necessary are subjectively contingent, and the determination of such a will according to objective laws is *obligation,* that is to say, the relation of the objective laws to a will that is not thoroughly good is conceived as the determination of the will of a rational being by principles of reason, but which the will from its nature does not of necessity follow.

The conception of an objective principle, in so far as it is obligatory for a will, is called a command (of reason), and the formula of the command is called an Imperative.

All imperatives are expressed by the word *ought* [or *shall*], and thereby indicate the relation of an objective law of reason to a will, which from its subjective constitution is not necessarily determined by it (an obligation). They say that something would be good to do or to forbear, but they say it to a will which does not always do a thing because it is conceived to be good to do it. That is practically *good,* however, which determines the will by means of the conceptions of reason, and consequently not from subjective causes, but objectively, that is on principles which are valid for every rational being as such. It is distinguished from the *pleasant,* as that which influences the will only by means of sensation from merely subjective causes, valid only for the sense of this or that one, and not as a principle of reason, which holds for every one.[4]

A perfectly good will would therefore be equally subject to objective laws (viz. laws of good), but could not be conceived as *obliged* thereby to act lawfully, because of itself from its subjective constitution it can only be determined by the conception of good. Therefore no imperatives hold for the Divine will, or in general for a *holy* will; *ought* is here out of place, because the volition is already of itself necessarily in unison with the law. Therefore imperatives are only formulae to express the relation of objective laws of all volition to the subjective imperfection of the will of this or that rational being, e.g. the human will.

Now all *imperatives* command either *hypothetically* or *categorically.* The former represent the practical necessity of a possible action as means to something else that is willed (or at least which one might possibly will). The categorical imperative would be that which represented an action as necessary of itself without reference to another end, i.e. as objectively necessary.

Since every practical law represents a possible action as good, and on this account, for a subject who is practically determinable by reason, necessary, all imperatives are formulae determining an action which is necessary according to the principle of a will good in some respects. If now the action is good only as a means *to something else,* then the imperative is *hypothetical;* if it is conceived as good *in itself* and consequently as

being necessarily the principle of a will which of itself conforms to reason, then it is *categorical.*

Thus the imperative declares what action possible by me would be good, and presents the practical rule in relation to a will which does not forthwith perform an action simply because it is good, whether because the subject does not always know that it is good, or because, even if it know this, yet its maxims might be opposed to the objective principles of practical reason.

Accordingly the hypothetical imperative only says that the action is good for some purpose, *possible* or *actual.* In the first case it is a Problematical, in the second an Assertorial practical principle. The categorical imperative which declares an action to be objectively necessary in itself without reference to any purpose, i.e. without any other end, is valid as an Apodictic (practical) principle.

Whatever is possible only by the power of some rational being may also be conceived as a possible purpose of some will; and therefore the principles of action as regards the means necessary to attain some possible purpose are in fact infinitely numerous. All sciences have a practical part, consisting of problems expressing that some end is possible for us, and of imperatives directing how it may be attained. These may, therefore, be called in general imperatives of Skill. Here there is no question whether the end is rational and good, but only what one must do in order to attain it. The precepts for the physician to make his patient thoroughly healthy, and for a poisoner to ensure certain death, are of equal value in this respect, that each serves to effect its purpose perfectly. Since in early youth it cannot be known what ends are likely to occur to us in the course of life, parents seek to have their children taught a *great many things,* and provide for their *skill* in the use of means for all sorts of arbitrary ends, of none of which can they determine whether it may not perhaps hereafter be an object to their pupil, but which it is at all events *possible* that he might aim at; and this anxiety is so great that they commonly neglect to form and correct their judgment on the value of the things which may be chosen as ends.

There is *one* end, however, which may be assumed to be actually such to all rational beings (so far as imperatives apply to them, viz. as dependent beings), and, therefore, one purpose which they not merely *may* have, but which we may with certainty assume that they all actually *have* by a natural necessity, and this is *happiness*. The hypothetical imperative which expresses the practical necessity of an action as means to the advancement of happiness is Assertorial. We are not to present it as necessary for an uncertain and merely possible purpose, but for a purpose which we may presuppose with certainty and a priori in every man, because it belongs to his being. Now skill in the choice of means to his own greatest wellbeing may be called *prudence*[5] in the narrowest sense. And thus the imperative which refers to the choice of means to one's own happiness, i.e. the precept of prudence, is still always *hypothetical;* the action is not commanded absolutely, but only as means to another purpose.

Finally, there is an imperative which commands a certain conduct immediately, without having as its condition any other purpose to be attained by it. This imperative is Categorical. It concerns not the matter of the action, or its intended result, but its form and the principle of which it is itself a result; and what is essentially good in it consists in the mental disposition, let the consequence be what it may. This imperative may be called that of Morality.

There is a marked distinction also between the volitions on these three sorts of principles in the *dissimilarity* of the obligation of the will. In order to mark this difference more clearly, I think they would be most suitably named in their order if we said they are either *rules* of skill, or *counsels* of prudence, or *commands* (*laws*) of morality. For it is *law* only that involves the conception of an *unconditional* and objective necessity, which is consequently universally valid; and commands are laws which must be obeyed, that is, must be followed, even in opposition to incli-

nation. *Counsels,* indeed, involve necessity, but one which can only hold under a contingent subjective condition, viz. they depend on whether this or that man reckons this or that as part of his happiness; the categorical imperative, on the contrary, is not limited by any condition, and as being absolutely, although practically, necessary, may be quite properly called a command. We might also call the first kind of imperatives *technical* (belonging to art), the second *pragmatic*[6] (to welfare), the third *moral* (belonging to free conduct generally, that is, to morals).

Now arises the question, how are all these imperatives possible? This question does not seek to know how we can conceive the accomplishment of the action which the imperative ordains, but merely how we can conceive the obligation of the will which the imperative expresses. No special explanation is needed to show how an imperative of skill is possible. Whoever wills the end, wills also (so far as reason decides his conduct) the means in his power which are indispensably necessary thereto. This proposition is, as regards the volition, analytical for, in willing an object as my effect, there is already thought the causality of myself as an acting cause, that is to say, the use of the means; and the imperative educes from the conception of volition of an end the conception of actions necessary to this end. Synthetical propositions must no doubt be employed in defining the means to a proposed end; but they do not concern the principle, the act of the will, but the object and its realization. E.g., that in order to bisect a line on an unerring principle I must draw from its extremities two intersecting arcs; this no doubt is taught by mathematics only in synthetical propositions; but if I know that it is only by this process that the intended operation can be performed, then to say that if I fully will the operation, I also will the action required for it, is an analytical proposition; for it is one and the same thing to conceive something as an effect which I can produce in a certain way, and to conceive myself as acting in this way.

If it were only equally easy to give a definite conception of happiness, the imperatives of prudence would correspond exactly with those of skill, and would likewise be analytical. For in this case as in that, it could be said, whoever wills the end, wills also (according to the dictate of reason necessarily) the indispensable means thereto which are in his power. But, unfortunately, the notion of happiness is so indefinite that although every man wishes to attain it, yet he never can say definitely and consistently what it is that he really wishes and wills. The reason of this is that all the elements which belong to the notion of happiness are altogether empirical, i.e. they must be borrowed from experience, and nevertheless the idea of happiness requires an absolute whole, a maximum of welfare in my present and all future circumstances. Now it is impossible that the most clear-sighted and at the same time most powerful being (supposed finite) should frame to himself a definite conception of what he really wills in this. Does he will riches, how much anxiety, envy, and snares might he not thereby draw upon his shoulders? Does he will knowledge and discernment, perhaps it might prove to be only an eye so much the sharper to show him so much the more fearfully the evils that are now concealed from him, and that cannot be avoided, or to impose more wants on his desires, which already give him concern enough. Would he have long life? Who guarantees to him that it would not be a long misery? Would he at least have health? How often has uneasiness of the body restrained from excesses into which perfect health would have allowed one to fall? And so on. In short, he is unable, on any principle, to determine with certainty what would make him truly happy; because to do so he would need to be omniscient. We cannot therefore act on any definite principles to secure happiness, but only on empirical counsels, e.g. of regimen, frugality, courtesy, reserve, etc., which experience teaches do, on the average, most promote well-being. Hence it follows that the imperatives of prudence do not, strictly speaking, command at all, that is, they cannot present actions objectively as practically *necessary*, that they are rather to be regarded as counsels (*consilia*) than precepts (*praecepta*) of reason, that the problem to determine certainly and universally what action would promote the happiness of a rational being is completely insoluble, and consequently no imperative respecting it is possible which should, in the strict sense, command to do what makes happy; because happiness is not an ideal of reason but of imagination, resting solely on empirical grounds, and it is vain to expect that these should define an action by which one could attain the totality of a series of consequences which is really endless. This imperative of prudence would, however, be an analytical proposition if we assume that the means to happiness could be certainly assigned; for it is distinguished from the imperative of skill only by this, that in the latter the end is merely possible, in the former it is given; as, however, both only ordain the means to that which we suppose to be willed as an end, it follows that the imperative which ordains the willing of the means to him who wills the end is in both cases analytical. Thus there is no difficulty in regard to the possibility of an imperative of this kind either.

On the other hand, the question, how the imperative of *morality* is possible, is undoubtedly one, the only one, demanding a solution, as this is not at all hypothetical, and the objective necessity which it presents cannot rest on any hypothesis, as is the case with the hypothetical imperatives. Only here we must never leave out of consideration that we *cannot* make out *by any example*, in other words empirically, whether there is such an imperative at all; but it is rather to be feared that all those which seem to be categorical may yet be at bottom hypothetical. For instance, when the precept is: Thou shalt not promise deceitfully; and it is assumed that the necessity of this is not a mere counsel to avoid some other evil, so that it should mean: Thou shalt not make a lying promise, lest if it become known thou shouldst destroy thy credit, but that an action of this kind must be regarded as evil in itself, so that the imperative of the prohibition is categorical; then we cannot show with certainty in any example that the will was determined merely by the law, without any other spring of action, although it may appear to be so. For it is always possible that fear of disgrace, perhaps also obscure dread of other dangers, may have a secret influence on the will. Who can prove by experience the non-existence of a cause when all that experience tells us is that we do not perceive it? But in such a case the so-called moral imperative, which as such appears to be categorical and unconditional, would in reality be only a pragmatic precept, drawing our attention to our own interests, and merely teaching us to take these into consideration.

We shall therefore have to investigate a priori the possibility of a categorical imperative, as we have not in this case the advantage of its reality being given in experience, so that [the elucidation of] its possibility should be requisite only for its explanation, not for its establishment. In the meantime it may be discerned beforehand that the categorical imperative alone has the purport of a practical law: all the rest may indeed be called *principles* of the will but not laws, since whatever is only necessary for the attainment of some arbitrary purpose may be considered as in itself contingent, and we can at any time be free from the precept if we give up the purpose: on the contrary, the unconditional command leaves the will no liberty to choose the opposite; consequently it alone carries with it that necessity which we require in a law.

Secondly, in the case of this categorical imperative or law of morality, the difficulty (of discerning its possibility) is a very profound one. It is an a priori synthetical practical proposition;[7] and as there is so much difficulty in discerning the possibility of speculative propositions of this kind, it may readily be supposed that the difficulty will be no less with the practical.

In this problem we will first inquire whether the mere conception of a categorical imperative may not perhaps supply us also with the formula of it, containing the proposition which alone can be a categorical imperative; for even if we know the tenor of such an absolute command, yet how it is possible will require further special and laborious study, which we postpone to the last section.

When I conceive a hypothetical imperative, in general I do not know beforehand what it will contain until I am given the condition. But when I conceive a categorical imperative, I know at once what it contains. For as the imperative contains besides the law only the necessity that the maxims[8] shall conform to this law, while the law contains no conditions restricting it, there remains nothing but the general statement that the maxim of the action should conform to a universal law, and it is this conformity alone that the imperative properly represents as necessary.

There is therefore but one categorical imperative, namely, this: *Act only on that maxim whereby thou canst at the same time will that it should become a universal law.*

Now if all imperatives of duty can be deduced from this one imperative as from their principle, then, although it should remain undecided whether what is called duty is not merely a vain notion, yet at least we shall be able to show what we understand by it and what this notion means.

Since the universality of the law according to which effects are produced constitutes what is properly called *nature* in the most general sense (as to form), that is the existence of things so far as it is determined by general laws, the imperative of duty may be expressed thus: *Act as if the maxim of the action were to become by thy will a universal law of nature.*

We will now enumerate a few duties, adopting the usual division of them into duties to ourselves and to others, and into perfect and imperfect duties.[9]

1. A man reduced to despair by a series of misfortunes feels wearied of life, but is still so far in possession of his reason that he can ask him-

self whether it would not be contrary to his duty to himself to take his own life. Now he inquires whether the maxim of his actions could become a universal law of nature. His maxim is: From self-love I adopt it as a principle to shorten my life when its longer duration is likely to bring more evil than satisfaction. It is asked then simply whether this principle founded on self-love can become a universal law of nature. Now we see at once that a system of nature of which it should be a law to destroy life by means of the very feeling whose special nature it is to impel to the improvement of life would contradict itself, and therefore could not exist as a system of nature; hence that maxim cannot possibly exist as a universal law of nature, and consequently would be wholly inconsistent with the supreme principle of all duty.

2. Another finds himself forced by necessity to borrow money. He knows that he will not be able to repay it, but sees also that nothing will be lent to him, unless he promises stoutly to repay it in a definite time. He desires to make this promise, but he has still so much conscience as to ask himself: Is it not unlawful and inconsistent with duty to get out of a difficulty in this way? Suppose, however, that he resolves to do so, then the maxim of his action would be expressed thus: When I think myself in want of money, I will borrow money and promise to repay it, although I know that I never can do so. Now this principle of self-love or of one's own advantage may perhaps be consistent with my whole future welfare; but the question now is, Is it right? I change then the suggestion of self-love into a universal law, and state the question thus: How would it be if my maxim were a universal law? Then I see at once that it could never hold as a universal law of nature, but would necessarily contradict itself. For supposing it to be a universal law that everyone when he thinks himself in a difficulty should be able to promise whatever he pleases, with the purpose of not keeping his promise, the promise itself would become impossible, as well as the end that one might have in view in it, since no

one would consider that anything was promised to him, but would ridicule all such statements as vain pretenses.

3. A third finds in himself a talent which with the help of some culture might make him a useful man in many respects. But he finds himself in comfortable circumstances, and prefers to indulge in pleasure rather than to take pains in enlarging and improving his happy natural capacities. He asks, however, whether his maxim of neglect of his natural gifts, besides agreeing with his inclination to indulgence, agrees also with what is called duty. He sees then that a system of nature could indeed subsist with such a universal law although men (like the South Sea Islanders) should let their talents rest, and resolve to devote their lives merely to idleness, amusement, and propagation of their species— in a word, to enjoyment; but he cannot possibly *will* that this should be a universal law of nature, or be implanted in us as such by a natural instinct. For, as a rational being, he necessarily wills that his faculties be developed, since they serve him, and have been given him, for all sorts of possible purposes.

4. A fourth, who is in prosperity, while he sees that others have to contend with great wretchedness and that he could help them, thinks: What concern is it of mine? Let everyone be as happy as Heaven pleases, or as he can make himself; I will take nothing from him nor even envy him, only I do not wish to contribute anything to his welfare or to his assistance in distress! Now no doubt if such a mode of thinking were a universal law, the human race might very well subsist, and doubtless even better than in a state in which everyone talks of sympathy and goodwill, or even takes care occasionally to put it into practice, but, on the other side, also cheats when he can, betrays the rights of men, or otherwise violates them. But although it is possible that a universal law of nature might exist in accordance with that maxim, it is impossible to *will* that such a principle should have the universal validity of a law of nature. For a will

which resolved this would contradict itself, inasmuch as many cases might occur in which one would have need of the love and sympathy of others, and in which, by such a law of nature, sprung from his own will, he would deprive himself of all hope of the aid he desires.

These are a few of the many actual duties, or at least what we regard as such, which obviously fall into two classes on the one principle that we have laid down. We must be *able to will* that a maxim of our action should be a universal law. This is the canon of the moral appreciation of the action generally. Some actions are of such a character that their maxim cannot without contradiction be even *conceived* as a universal law of nature, far from it being possible that we should *will* that it *should* be so. In others this intrinsic impossibility is not found, but still it is impossible to *will* that their maxim should be raised to the universality of a law of nature, since such a will would contradict itself. It is easily seen that the former violate strict or rigorous (inflexible) duty; the latter only laxer (meritorious) duty. Thus it has been completely shown by these examples how all duties depend as regards the nature of the obligation (not the object of the action) on the same principle.

If now we attend to ourselves on occasion of any transgression of duty, we shall find that we in fact do not will that our maxim should be a universal law, for that is impossible for us; on the contrary, we will that the opposite should remain a universal law, only we assume the liberty of making an *exception* in our own favor or (just for this time only) in favor of our inclination. Consequently if we considered all cases from one and the same point of view, namely, that of reason, we should find a contradiction in our own will, namely, that a certain principle should be objectively necessary as a universal law, and yet subjectively should not be universal, but admit of exceptions. As, however, we at one moment regard our action from the point of view of a will wholly conformed to reason, and

then again look at the same action from the point of view of a will affected by inclination, there is not really any contradiction, but an antagonism of inclination to the precept of reason, whereby the universality of the principle is changed into a mere generality, so that the practical principle of reason shall meet the maxim half way. Now, although this cannot be justified in our own impartial judgment, yet it proves that we do really recognize the validity of the categorical imperative and (with all respect for it) only allow ourselves a few exceptions, which we think unimportant and forced from us. . . .

Supposing, however, that there were something *whose existence* has *in itself* an absolute worth, something which, being *an end in itself,* could be a source of definite laws, then in this and this alone would lie the source of a possible categorical imperative, i.e. a practical law.

Now I say: man and generally any rational being *exists* as an end in himself, *not merely as a means* to be arbitrarily used by this or that will, but in all his actions, whether they concern himself or other rational beings, must be always regarded at the same time as an end. All objects of the inclinations have only a conditional worth; for if the inclinations and the wants founded on them did not exist, then their object would be without value. But the inclinations themselves being sources of want are so far from having an absolute worth for which they should be desired, that, on the contrary, it must be the universal wish of every rational being to be wholly free from them. Thus the worth of any object which is *to be acquired* by our action is always conditional. Beings whose existence depends not on our will but on nature's, have nevertheless, if they are not rational beings, only a relative value as means, and are therefore called things; rational beings, on the contrary, are called *persons,* because their very nature points them out as ends in themselves, that is as something which must not be used merely as means, and so far therefore restricts freedom of action (and is an object of respect). These, therefore, are not merely subjective ends whose existence has a worth *for us* as an effect of our action, but *objective ends,* that is things whose existence is an end in itself: an end moreover for which no other can be substituted, which they should subserve *merely* as means, for otherwise nothing whatever would possess *absolute worth;* but if all worth were conditioned and therefore contingent, then there would be no supreme practical principle of reason whatever.

If then there is a supreme practical principle or, in respect of the human will, a categorical imperative, it must be one which, being drawn from the conception of that which is necessarily an end for everyone because it is *an end in itself,* constitutes an *objective* principle of will, and can therefore serve as a universal practical law. The foundation of this principle is: *rational nature exists as an end in itself.* Man necessarily conceives his own existence as being so: so far then this is a *subjective* principle of human actions. But every other rational being regards its existence similarly, just on the same rational principle that holds for me: so that it is at the same time an objective principle, from which as a supreme practical law all laws of the will must be capable of being deduced. Accordingly the practical imperative will be as follows: *So act as to treat humanity whether in thine own person or in that of any other, in every case as an end withal, never as means only.* We will now inquire whether this can be practically carried out.

To abide by the previous examples:

Firstly, under the head of necessary duty to oneself: He who contemplates suicide should ask himself whether his action can be consistent with the idea of humanity *as an end in itself.* If he destroys himself in order to escape from painful circumstances, he uses a person merely as *a mean* to maintain a tolerable condition up to the end of life. But a man is not a thing, that is to say, something which can be used merely as means, but must in all his actions be always considered as an end in himself. I cannot, therefore, dispose in any way of a man in my own person so as to mutilate, to damage or kill him. It belongs to ethics proper to define this principle more precisely, so as to avoid all misunderstanding, e.g. as to the amputation of the limbs in order to preserve myself; as to exposing my life to danger with a view to preserve it, etc. This question is therefore omitted here.)

Secondly, as regards necessary duties, or those of strict obligation, toward others; he who is thinking of making a lying promise to others will see at once that he would be using another man *merely as a mean,* without the latter containing at the same time the end in himself. For he whom I propose by such a promise to use for my own purposes cannot possibly assent to my mode of acting toward him, and therefore cannot himself contain the end of this action. This violation of the principle of humanity in other men is more obvious if we take in examples of attacks on the freedom and property of others. For then it is clear that he who transgresses the rights of men intends to use the person of others merely as means, without considering that as rational beings they ought always to be esteemed also as ends, that is, as beings who must be capable of containing in themselves the end of the very same action.

Thirdly, as regards contingent (meritorious) duties to oneself; it is not enough that the action does not violate humanity in our own person as an end in itself, it must also *harmonize with it.* Now there are in humanity capacities of greater perfection which belong to the end that nature has in view in regard to humanity in ourselves as the subject: to neglect these might perhaps be consistent with the *maintenance* of humanity as an end in itself, but not with the *advancement* of this end.

Fourthly, as regards meritorious duties toward others: the natural end which all men have is their own happiness. Now humanity might indeed subsist, although no one should contribute anything to the happiness of others, provided he did not intentionally withdraw anything from it; but after all, this would only harmonize negatively, not positively, with *humanity as an end in itself,* if everyone does not also endeavor, as far as in him lies, to forward the ends of others. For the ends of any subject which is an end in himself, ought as far as possible to be *my* ends also, if that conception is to have its *full* effect with me. . . .

Looking back now on all previous attempts to discover the principle of morality, we need not wonder why they all failed. It was seen that man was bound to laws by duty, but it was not observed that the laws to which he is subject are *only those of his own giving,* though at the same time they are *universal.* And that he is only bound to act in conformity with his own will; a will, however, which is designed by nature to give universal laws. For when one has conceived man only as subject to a law (no matter what), then this law required some interest, either by way of attraction or constraint, since it did not originate as a law from *his own* will, but this will was according to a law obliged by *something else* to act in a certain manner. Now by this necessary consequence all the labor spent in finding a supreme principle of *duty* was irrevocably lost. For men never elicited duty, but only a necessity of acting from a certain interest. Whether this interest was private or otherwise, in any case the imperative must be conditional, and could not by any means be capable of being a moral command. I will therefore call this the principle of *Autonomy* of the will, in contrast with every other which I accordingly reckon as *Heteronomy.*

The conception of every rational being as one which must consider itself as giving in all the maxims of its will universal laws, so as to judge itself and its actions from this point of view— this conception leads to another which depends on it and is very fruitful, namely, that of a *kingdom of ends.*

By a *kingdom* I understand the union of different rational beings in a system by common laws. Now since it is by laws that ends are determined as regards their universal validity, hence, if we abstract from the personal differences of rational beings, and likewise from all the content of their private ends, we shall be able to conceive all ends combined in a systematic whole (including both rational beings as ends in themselves, and also the special ends which each may propose to himself), that is to say, we can conceive a kingdom of ends, which on the preceding principles is possible.

For all rational beings come under the *law* that each of them must treat itself and all others *never merely as means,* but in every case *at the same time as ends in themselves.* Hence results a systematic union of rational beings by common objective laws, i.e. a kingdom which may be called a kingdom of ends, since what these laws have in view is just the relation of these beings to one another as ends and means. It is certainly only an ideal.

A rational being belongs as a *member* to the kingdom of ends when, although giving universal laws in it, he is also himself subject to these laws. He belongs to it *as sovereign* when, while giving laws, he is not subject to the will of any other.

A rational being must always regard himself as giving laws either as member or as sovereign in a kingdom of ends which is rendered possible by the freedom of will. He cannot, however, maintain the latter position merely by the maxims of his will, but only in case he is a completely independent being without wants and with unrestricted power adequate to his will. . . .

We can now end where we started at the beginning, namely, with the conception of a will unconditionally good. *That will* is *absolutely good* which cannot be evil—in other words, whose maxim, if made a universal law, could never contradict itself. This principle, then, is its supreme law: Act always on such a maxim as thou canst at the same time will to be a universal law; this is the sole condition under which a will can never contradict itself; and such an imperative is categorical. Since the validity of the will as a universal law for possible actions is analogous to the universal connection of the existence of things by general laws, which is the formal notion of nature in general, the categorical imperative can also be expressed thus; *Act on maxims which can at the same time have for their object themselves as universal laws of nature.* Such then is the formula of an absolutely good will.

Rational nature is distinguished from the rest of nature by this, that it sets before itself an end. This end would be the matter of every good will. But since in the idea of a will that is absolutely good without being limited by any condition (of attaining this or that end) we must abstract wholly from every end *to be effected* (since this would make every will only relatively good), it follows that in this case the end must be conceived, not as an end to be effected, but as an *independently* existing end. Consequently it is conceived only negatively, i.e. as that which we must never act against, and which, therefore, must never be regarded merely as means, but must in every volition be esteemed as an end likewise. Now this end can be nothing but the subject of all possible ends, since this is also the subject of a possible absolutely good will; for such a will cannot without contradiction be postponed to any other object. This principle: So act in regard to every rational being (thyself and others), that he may always have place in thy maxim as an end in himself, is accordingly essentially identical with this other; Act upon a maxim which, at the same time, involves its own universal validity for every rational being. For that in using means for every end I should limit my maxim by the condition of its holding good as a law for every subject, this comes to the same thing as that the fundamental principle of all maxims of action must be that the subject of all ends, i.e. the rational being himself, be never employed merely as means, but as the supreme condition restricting the use of all means, that is in every case as an end likewise.

It follows incontestably that, to whatever laws any rational being may be subject, he being an end in himself must be able to regard himself as also legislating universally in respect of these same laws, since it is just this fitness of his max-

ims for universal legislation that distinguishes him as an end in himself; also it follows that this implies his dignity (prerogative) above all mere physical beings, that he must always take his maxims from the point of view which regards himself, and likewise every other rational being, as lawgiving beings (on which account they are called persons). In this way a world of rational beings (*mundus intelligibilis*) is possible as a kingdom of ends, and this by virtue of the legislation proper to all persons as members. Therefore every rational being must so act as if he were by his maxims in every case a legislating member in the universal kingdom of ends. The formal principle of these maxims is: So act as if thy maxim were to serve likewise as the universal law (of all rational beings). A kingdom of ends is thus only possible on the analogy of a kingdom of nature, the former, however, only by maxims, that is self-imposed rules, the latter only by the laws of efficient causes acting under necessitation from without. Nevertheless, although the system of nature is looked upon as a machine, yet so far as it has reference to rational beings as its ends, it is given on this account the name of a kingdom of nature. Now such a kingdom of ends would be actually realized by means of maxims conforming to the canon which the categorical imperative prescribes to all rational beings, *if they were universally followed.* But although a rational being, even if he punctually follows this maxim himself, cannot reckon upon all others being therefore true to the same, nor expect that the kingdom of nature and its orderly arrangements shall be in harmony with him as a fitting member, so as to form a kingdom of ends to which he himself contributes, that is to say, that it shall favor his expectation of happiness, still that law: Act according to the maxims of a member of a merely possible kingdom of ends legislating in it universally, remains in its full force, inasmuch as it commands categorically. And it is just in this that the paradox lies; that the mere dignity of man as a rational creature, without any other end or advantage to be attained thereby, in other words, respect for a mere idea, should yet serve as an inflexible precept of the will, and that it is precisely in this independence of the maxim on all such springs of action that its sublimity consists; and it is this that makes every rational subject worthy to be a legislative member in the kingdom of ends: for otherwise he would have to be conceived only as subject to the physical law of his wants. And although we should suppose the kingdom of nature and the kingdom of ends to be united under one sovereign, so that the latter kingdom thereby ceased to be a mere idea and acquired true reality, then it would no doubt gain the accession of a strong spring, but by no means any increase of its intrinsic worth. For this sole absolute lawgiver must, notwithstanding this, be always conceived as estimating the worth of rational beings only by their disinterested behavior, as prescribed to themselves from that idea [the dignity of man] alone. The essence of things is not altered by their external relations, and that which, abstracting from these, alone constitutes the absolute worth of man, is also that by which he must be judged, whoever the judge may be, and even by the Supreme Being. *Morality,* then, is the relation of actions to the autonomy of the will, that is, to the potential universal legislation by its maxims. An action that is consistent with the autonomy of the will is *permitted;* one that does not agree therewith is *forbidden.* A will whose maxims necessarily coincide with the laws of autonomy is a *holy* will, good absolutely. The dependence of a will not absolutely good on the principle of autonomy (moral necessitation) is obligation. This, then, cannot be applied to a holy being. The objective necessity of actions from obligation is called *duty.*

From what has just been said, it is easy to see how it happens that although the conception of duty implies subjection to the law, we yet ascribe a certain *dignity* and sublimity to the person who fulfills all his duties. There is not, indeed, any sublimity in him, so far as he is *subject* to the moral law; but inasmuch as in regard to that very

law he is likewise a *legislator,* and on that account alone subject to it, he has sublimity. We have also shown above that neither fear nor inclination, but simply respect for the law, is the spring which can give actions a moral worth. Our own will, so far as we suppose it to act only under the condition that its maxims are potentially universal laws, this ideal will which is possible to us is the proper object of respect; and the dignity of humanity consists just in this capacity of being universally legislative, though with the condition that it is itself subject to this same legislation.

NOTES

1. The first proposition was that to have moral worth an action must be done from duty.
2. A *maxim* is the subjective principle of volition. The objective principle (i.e. that which would also serve subjectively as a practical principle to all rational beings if reason had full power over the faculty of desire) is the practical *law.*
3. It might be here objected to me that I take refuge behind the word *respect* in an obscure feeling, instead of giving a distinct solution of the question by a concept of the reason. But although respect is a feeling, it is not a feeling *received* through influence, but is *self-wrought* by a rational concept, and, therefore, is specifically distinct from all feelings of the former kind, which may be referred either to inclination or fear. What I recognize immediately as a law for me, I recognize with respect. This merely signifies the consciousness that my will is *subordinate* to a law, without the intervention of other influences on my sense. The immediate determination of the will by the law, and the consciousness of this, is called *respect,* so that this is regarded as an *effect* of the law on the subject, and not as the *cause* of it. Respect is properly the conception of a worth which thwarts my self-love. Accordingly it is something which is considered neither as an object of inclination nor of fear, although it has something analogous to both. The *object* of respect is the *law* only, and that, the law which we impose on *ourselves,* and yet recognize as necessary in itself. As a law, we are subjected to it without consulting self-love; as imposed by us on ourselves, it is a result of our will. In the former

aspect it has an analogy to fear, in the latter to inclination. Respect for a person is properly only respect for the law (of honesty, etc.) of which he gives us an example. Since we also look on the improvement of our talents as a duty, we consider that we see in a person of talents, as it were, the *example of a law* (viz. to become like him in this by exercise), and this constitutes our respect. All so-called moral *interest* consists simply in *respect* for the law.

4. The dependence of the desires on sensations is called inclination, and this accordingly always indicates a *want*. The dependence of a contingently determinable will on principles of reason is called an *interest*. This, therefore, is found only in the case of a dependent will which does not always of itself conform to reason; in the Divine will we cannot conceive any interest. But the human will can also *take an interest* in a thing without therefore acting *from interest*. The former signifies the *practical* interest in the action, the latter the *pathological* in the object of the action. The former indicates only dependence of the will on principles of reason in themselves; the second, dependence on principles of reason for the sake of inclination, reason supplying only the practical rules how the requirement of the inclination may be satisfied. In the first case the action interests me; in the second the object of the action (because it is pleasant to me). We have seen in the first section that in an action done from duty we must look not to the interest in the object, but only to that in the action itself, and in its rational principle (viz. the law).

5. The word *prudence* is taken in two senses: in the one it may bear the name of knowledge of the world, in the other that of private prudence. The former is a man's ability to influence others so as to use them for his own purposes. The latter is the sagacity to combine all these purposes for his own lasting benefit. This latter is properly that to which the value even of the former is reduced, and when a man is prudent in the former sense, but not in the latter, we might better say of him that he is clever and cunning, but, on the whole, imprudent.

6. It seems to me that the proper signification of the word *pragmatic* may be most accurately defined in this way. For *sanctions* are called pragmatic which flow properly, not from the law of the states as necessary enactments, but from precaution for the general welfare. A history is composed pragmatically when it teaches prudence, i.e. instructs the world how it can provide for its interests better, or at least as well as the men of former time.

7. I connect the act with the will without presupposing any condition resulting from any inclination, but a priori, and therefore necessarily (though only objectively, i.e. assuming the idea of a reason possessing full power over all subjective motives). This is accordingly a practical proposition which does not deduce the willing of an action by mere analysis from another already presupposed (for we have not such a perfect will), but connects it immediately with the conception of the will of a rational being, as something not contained in it.

8. A maxim is a subjective principle of action, and must be distinguished from the *objective principle,* namely, practical law. The former contains the practical rule set by reason according to the conditions of the subject (often its ignorance or its inclinations), so that it is the principle on which the subject *acts,* but the law is the objective principle valid for every rational being, and is the principle on which it *ought to act* that is an imperative.

9. It must be noted here that I reserve the division of duties for a future *metaphysic of morals,* so that I give it here only as an arbitrary one (in order to arrange my examples). For the rest, I understand by a perfect duty one that admits no exception in favor of inclination, and then I have not merely external but also internal perfect duties. This is contrary to the use of the word adopted in the schools; but I do not intend to justify it here, as it is all one for my purpose whether it is admitted or not. [*Perfect* duties are usually understood to be those which can be enforced by external law; *imperfect,* those which cannot be enforced. They are also called respectively *determinate* and *indeterminate, officio juris* and *officio virtutis.*]

22. ON THE SUBLIME AND THE BEAUTIFUL

❧

IMMANUEL KANT

OF THE DIFFERENCE OF THE SUBLIME AND OF THE BEAUTIFUL IN THE COUNTERRELATION OF BOTH SEXES

He, who first comprehended the women under the name of the *fair sex,* wished perhaps to say something flattering: but he has hit it better, than he himself may have imagined. For, without taking into consideration, that their form is in general finer, their features softer and more delicate, their mien in the expression of friendliness, of joking, of kindness and humanity more significant and engaging, than that of the male sex, not forgetting, however, that which must be deducted for the secret magic power, whereby they render our passion favourable to the most advantageous judgment of them, there lie chiefly in the character of mind of this sex peculiar strokes, which clearly distinguish it from ours, and which principally tend to make it known by the criterion, *fair.* We, on the other hand, lay claim to the denomination of the *noble sex,* were it not required of a noble disposition of mind, to decline names of honour and rather to bestow than to receive them. By this is not to be understood, that women want noble properties, or that the male sex must totally dispense with the beauties: it is rather expected, that each sex shall unite both, yet so, that all other excellencies of a woman shall unite themselves but in order to elevate the character of the *beautiful,* which is the proper point of reference; whereas among the male properties the *sublime,* as the criterion

of his sex, must be the most eximious. To this must refer all judgments of these two sexes, as well the commendable, as the blameable. This must all education and instruction, and all endeavours to forward the moral perfection of both, have in view; unless the charming distinction, which nature intended to make between two human sexes, shall be rendered indiscernible. For it is here not enough to represent men to one's self, it must at the same time be noticed that these men are not of the same nature.

Women have an innate strong feeling for all that is beautiful, ornamented and embellished. Already in youth they are willingly dressed and take a pleasure in being set off. They are cleanly and very delicate with regard to every thing that occasions disgust. They love jesting, and can be entertained with trifles, if they are but sprightly and agreeable. They acquire very early a modest behaviour, know to assume a polite carriage or manner, and possess themselves; and this at an age, when our wellbred male youth is yet untoward, awkward and embarrassed. They have many sympathetic feelings, much goodheartedness and compassion, prefer the beautiful to the useful, and willingly turn the superfluity of maintenance into parsimony, in order to support the expence of glitter and dress. They are very sensible of the smallest offence, and in general acute in observing the smallest want of attention and reverence for them. In fine, they contain the chief ground of the contrast of the beautiful properties with the noble in human nature, and even refine the male sex.

I hope I may be excused from the enumeration of the male properties, so far as they run

---

Reprinted from *Essays and Treatises* trans. by James Beck (London: W. Richardson, 1797).

parallel with those, as it may suffice to contemplate both in the comparison. The female sex have understanding, as well as the male, yet is it but a *fine understanding;* our understanding must be a *profound* one, which is an expression of the same signification with a sublime.

To the beauty of all actions it belongs, chiefly, that they show an easiness in themselves and seem to be accomplished without a painful exertion; whereas efforts and surmounted difficulties excite admiration and belong to the sublime. Deep reflection and a long continued contemplation are noble, but difficult, and are not suitable to a person, in whom ought to appear charms without constraint and a beautiful nature. Laborious study, or painful investigation, though a woman should succeed in it, destroys the excellencies peculiar to her sex, and may because of the singularity render her an object of cold admiration; but it at the same time weakens the charms, by which she exercises her great power over the other sex. Woman, who have their heads stuffed with Greek, like Mrs. Dacier, or carry on profound disputes about mechanics, like the marchioness of Chastelet, might have a beard to boot; for this would perhaps express more remarkably the air of penetration, to which they aspire. The fine understanding chuses for its objects all that is nearly connected with the fine feeling, and leaves abstract speculations and knowledge, which are useful but dry, to the diligent, solid and profound understanding. Ladies consequently do not study geometry; they know but as much of the position of sufficient reason, or of monades, as is necessary, in order to perceive the salt in the satires of the shallow fancymongers of our sex. The fair may let Cartesius' vortices continue to revolve, without giving themselves any trouble on that account, even should the agreeable Fontenelle bear them company among the planets, and the attraction of their charms loses nothing of its power, though they should know nothing of all that Algarotti endeavoured to point out, for their use, of the powers of attraction of coarse matter according to Newton. They should fill their heads neither with battles from history, nor with forts from geography; for it becomes them as little to smell of gunpowder, as men of musk.

It seems to be a wicked artifice of men to have wished to mislead the fair sex to this perverted taste. For, well aware of their weakness with regard to its natural charm, and that a single waggish look throws them into more confusion, than the most difficult question of the schools, they find themselves, as soon as the sex gives into this taste, decidedly superior, and in the advantage, which they otherwise would scarcely have, assist the weaknesses of its vanity with a generous indulgence. The subject of the great science of women is rather a husband, and of men, man. The philosophy of women is not to reason, but to feel. In the opportunity that is afforded them to cultivate their beautiful nature, this relation must always be had in view. One must endeavour to enlarge their whole moral feeling, but not their memory, and that not by universal rules, but by some judgments on the conduct which they see around them. The examples that are borrowed from other times in order to perspect the influence that the fair sex have had in the affairs of the world, the various relations, in which they stood towards the male sex in other ages, as well as in foreign countries; the character of both, so far as it may be hereby illustrated, and the variable taste of pleasures, constitute their whole history and geography. It is proper, that the view of a map, which represents either the whole globe, or the chief parts of the world, should be rendered agreeable to women. This may be done by presenting it but for the purpose of describing the various characters of nations that inhabit them, the differences of their taste and moral feeling, especially with regard to the effect which these have on the relations of the sexes; with a few easy dilucidations from the difference of climates, of their liberty or slavery. It is of little moment, whether or not they know the particular divisions of these countries, their commerce, potency and rulers. In like manner it will not be useful for them to know more of the fabric of the world, than is necessary to render moving to them the aspect of the heavens in a beautiful evening, if they have in some measure comprehended, that there are to be met with still more worlds and in them other beautiful creatures. Feeling for expressive descriptions, and for music, not so far as it shews art, but sentiment, all this forms and refines the taste of this sex, and has always some connexion with moral emotions. Never a cold and speculative instruction, always sentiments or feelings, which remain as near as possible to their relation of sex. This instruction is so rare, because it requires talents, experience and a feeling heart, and women may do without every other, as even without these they commonly cultivate or improve themselves very well.

The virtue of the female sex is a *beautiful virtue.* That of the male must be a *noble one.* Those avoid the bad, not because it is wrong, but because it is ugly, and virtuous actions signify, with them, such as are morally beautiful. Nothing of *ought,* nothing of *must,* nothing of *due.* All orders and all surly compulsion are to women insupportable. They do something but because they are pleased so to do, and the art consists but in making that which is good pleasing to them. I hardly believe that the fair sex are capable of principles, and in this I hope I do not offend, for these are very rare with men. Instead of which, however, Providence hath implanted in their breasts humane and benevolent sentiments, a fine feeling for becomingness, and a complaisant soul. Let not sacrifices and magnanimous self-compulsion be required. A man must never tell his wife, when he risks a part of his fortune on account of a friend. Why should he fetter her sprightly affability by burdening her mind with a weighty secret, the keeping of which is incumbent on him only? Even many of their weaknesses are, so to speak, *beautiful faults.* Injury or misfortune moves their delicate souls to sorrow. A man must never shed but generous tears.

Those which he sheds in pain or for circumstances of fortune render him contemptible. The *vanity,* with which the fair sex is so often upbraided, if it be a fault in them, it is but a beautiful one. For not to mention, that men, who so willingly flatter the fair, would be in a sad case, were these not inclined to take it well; they really animate thereby their charms. This inclination is an incitement, to show agreeableness and good grace, to give play to their sprightly wit, as also to glitter by the variable sensations occasioned by dress, and to heighten their beauty. In this now there is nothing so offensive to others, but rather, when it is done with good taste, something so comely and elegant, that it is very unmannerly to inveigh severely against it. A woman, who flirts and dazzles too much with this, is named a *fool;* which term, however, has no such harsh meaning, as when applied to a man, insomuch that, when persons understand one another, it may sometimes denote even a familiar flattery. If vanity is a fault which in a woman well merits excuse; to be puffed up with pride is not only blameable in them, as in men in general, but totally disfigures the character of their sex. For this property is stupid, ugly, and totally opposite to the engaging, insinuating, modest charm. Then such a person is in a slippery situation. She must be content to be judged severely and without the smallest indulgence; for whoever boasts of meriting esteem, invites all around her to censure. Each discovery of even the smallest fault affords a real joy to every body, and the word fool here loses it softened signification. Vanity and haughtiness must always be distinguished. The former seeks applause and in some measure honours those, on whose account it gives itself this trouble; the latter believes itself already in its full possession, and as it does not endeavour to acquire it, it gains none. A few ingredients of vanity by no means disfigure a woman in the eyes of the male sex; yet they serve, the more evident they are, the more to disunite the fair sex among one another, They then judge one another very sharply, because the one seems to eclipse the charms of the other, and those who have great pretension to conquest, are seldom friends in the true sense.

To the beautiful there is nothing so opposite as the disgustful, and nothing sinks more beneath the sublime than the ridiculous. Hence no abuse can be more cutting to a man, than to name him a fool, and to a woman, than that she is disgusting. The spectator takes it, that no reproach can be more mortifying to a man, than to be held a liar, and to a woman none bitterer, than that she is unchaste. I shall let this, so far as it is judged according to strict morality, remain valid. But here the question is not, what in itself merits the greatest blame, but what is actually the most severely felt. And I put the question to the reader, whether, when he has reflected on this case, he does not coincide with my opinion. Miss Ninon Lenclos laid not the smallest claim to the honour of chastity, and yet she would have been irreconcilably offended, had one of her lovers transgressed so much in his judgment: and we all know the cruel fate of Monaldeschi, on account of an insulting expression of this nature, from a princess, who did not even wish to represent a Lucretia. It is insupportable, that one should not even be able to do bad, though he had a mind to it, as the forbearance from it is never but a very ambiguous virtue.

In order to avoid this disgustfulness as much as possible, *cleanliness* is necessary, which indeed becomes every person, but in the fair sex is among the virtues of the first rank, and by them cannot easily be carried too far, men, however, sometimes carry it to excess and it is then named trifling.

Modesty is a secret of nature, to set bounds to an inclination which is very ungovernable, and, as it has the call of nature for it, always seems, though it rambles, to agree with good moral properties. It, therefore, as a supplement to principles, is highly necessary; for there is no case where the inclination becomes so easily a sophist, to invent agreeable principles, as here. But modesty serves at the same time to throw a mysteri-

ous veil even over the fittest and most necessary ends of nature, in order that the too intimate acquaintance with them may not occasion disgust, or at least indifference, with regard to the final designs of an instinct, upon which are grafted the finest and most lively inclinations of human nature. This property is chiefly peculiar to the fair sex, and very beseeming to them. . . .

At last however age, the great destroyer of beauty, threatens all these charms, and, if the natural order is to be followed, the sublime and noble properties must gradually occupy the place of the beautiful, in order to render a person, as she ceases to be lovely, always worthy of a greater reverence. In my opinion the whole perfection of the fair sex ought in the bloom of years to consist in the beautiful simplicity, elevated by a refined feeling in all that is charming and noble. As the pretensions to charms remit, the reading of books and the enlarging of knowledge might insensibly supply the vacant place of the Graces by the Muses, and the husband ought to be the first instructor. However, when old age, an epoch so terrible to all women, advances, they even then still belong to the fair sex and they disfigure themselves, when, in a sort of despair to maintain this character longer, they give themselves up to a morose and waspish humour.

A woman advanced in years, who graces a society with her modest and friendly behaviour, is affable in a cheerful and rational manner, favours with decency the pleasure of youth, in which she herself has no share, and, while she takes care of every thing, betrays contentment and complacency in the joy she sees around her, is still a finer person, than a man of the same age, and perhaps more amiable than a young woman though in another sense. Indeed the platonic love, which an ancient philosopher pretended, when he said of the object of his inclination, *the Graces reside in her wrinkles, and my very soul seems to hover on my lips, when I kiss her withered mouth,* may be somewhat too mystical; but such claims must then be relinquished. An old man in love is a gawk, and similar pretensions of the other sex are disgustful. It is never the fault of nature if we appear not with a good grace, but of our endeavouring to pervert nature.

In order not to lose sight of my text, I shall yet make a few observations on the influence which the one sex may have on the other, either to embellish or to ennoble its feeling. Women have chiefly a feeling for the *beautiful,* so far as it belongs to themselves; but for the *noble,* so far as it is to be met with in the male sex. Man on the other hand has a decided feeling for the *noble* that pertains to his properties; but for the *beautiful,* so far as it is to be met with in the women. Hence must follow, that the ends of nature tend still more to *ennoble* the man by the inclination to sex and still more to *embellish* the woman by the very same inclination. A woman is at no loss, because she does not possess certain deep introspections, because she is timid and not fit for weighty affairs &c. &c.; she is beautiful, she is engaging, and that is enough. Whereas, she requires all these properties in a man and the sublimity of her soul discovers itself but by her knowing to value these noble properties, so far as they are to be met with in him. How would it otherwise be possible, that so many male apish faces, though they may have merit, could get so handsome and fine wives? Man, on the other side, is much more delicate with regard to the beautiful charms of the woman. He is by their fine figure, their sprightly *naiveté* and their charming friendliness, sufficiently indemnified for the want of book-learning and for other wants, which he must supply by his own talents. Vanity and modes may easily give a false direction to these natural impulses and of many a man make a *beau,* but of many a woman a *pedant* or an *amazon;* but nature always endeavours to return to her own order. From this may be judged, what potent influence the inclination to sex would have chiefly on the male sex, in order to ennoble them, if, instead of much dry instruction, the moral sentiment of the women were early developed, in order to feel sufficiently what belongs to the dignity and the sublime properties of the other sex, and they were thereby prepared to consider the trifling fops with contempt, and to be attached to no other property than merit. It is beyond a doubt that the power of their charms would thereby gain in general; for it is obvious, that their magic for the most part acts but on noble souls, others are not fine enough to feel it. As the poet Simonides, when he was advised to let the Thessaliens hear his fine cantatas, said, These fellows are too stupid to be deceived by such a man as I am. It has always been considered as an effect of the intercourse with the fair sex, that the manners of the men are grown softer, their behaviour more agreeable and more polite; and their address more elegant; however this is but a secondary matter. The greatest consequence is, that the man as a man grow more perfect and the woman as a woman, that is, that the springs of the inclination to sex act conformably to the hint of nature, to ennoble the one still more and to embellish the properties of the other. When things come to the extreme, the man may boldly say of his merit, Though you do not love me, I will compel you to esteem me, and the women, sure of the might of their charms, answer, Though you do not esteem us profoundly, we will compel you to love us. For want of such principles men may be seen to adopt effeminacies, in order to please, and women sometimes, (though much seldomer) to affect a masculine air, in order to inspire esteem; but what is done contrary to the course of nature is always very badly done.

In the connubial life the united pair must in a manner constitute one single moral person, who is animated and governed by the understanding of the man and by the taste of the woman. For not only that more insight grounded upon experience may be attributed to him, and to her more freedom and justness of feeling, but a disposition of mind, the more sublime it is, is the more inclined to place the greatest design of the exertions in the contentment of a beloved object, and on the other hand the more beautiful it is, the more it endeavours to retaliate this exertion. In such a relation therefore a contest for preference is trifling and, where it happens, the surest criterion either of a coarse, or of an unequally matched taste. When it comes to that pass, that the question is concerning the right to command, the matter is already highly spoiled; for, where the whole union is founded but upon inclination, it is, as soon as *shall* begins to be heard, immediately dissolved. The pretension of the woman in this harsh tone is extremely ugly, and of the man in the highest degree ignoble and contemptible. The wise order of things, however, will have it, that all these finenesses and delicacies of feeling shall have their whole strength in the beginning only, but afterwards by commerce and domestic affairs grow insensibly blunter, and then degenerate into familiar love, where at last the great art consists in preserving sufficient rests of those, in order that indifference and disgust may not destroy the whole value of the pleasure, by which only is requited the entering into such a conjunction. . . .

OF NATIONAL CHARACTERS, SO FAR AS THEY REST UPON THE DISTINCT FEELING OF THE BEAUTIFUL AND OF THE SUBLIME

The *Frenchman* has a predominant feeling for the moral beautiful. He is agreeable, polite and complaisant. He grows very quickly familiar, is jocular and free in conversation, and the expression he or she is *du bon ton* can be understood but by those, who have acquired the delicate sentiments of a Frenchman. Even his sublime feelings, of which he has not few, are subordinate to the feeling of the beautiful, and receive their force but by the consension with the latter. He is very willingly witty and sacrifices, without hesitation, something of the truth to a sally. Whereas, where one cannot be witty, he shows solid introspection, as well as any person of another nation, for instance, in the mathematics and in the other dry or profound arts and sci-

ences. A *bon mot* with him has not the transitory value as with others, it is eagerly promulgated, and carefully treasured up in books, like the most momentous event. He is a peaceable citizen and revenges himself for the oppression of the Farmers General by satires, or by remonstrances to parliament, which, after they have conformably to their design given a beautiful patriotic appearance to the fathers of the nation, are of no farther consequence, than that they are crowned by an honourable mention and celebrated in ingenious panegyrics. The object, to which refer the most the merit and national abilities of the French, are the women. Not as if they were more loved or esteemed here than elsewhere, but because it affords the best occasion to display the most favourite talents of wit, of agreeableness and of good breeding; besides, a vain person of either sex never loves but himself: others are merely his playthings. As the French by no means want noble properties, only that these can be animated but by the feeling of the beautiful; the fair sex here, were it endeavoured to favour a little this bent of the national spirit, might have a more powerful influence to awake and to stir up the noblest action of the other sex, than any thing else in the world. It's a pity that the lilies spin not.

The fault, on which this national character borders the nearest, is, trifling, or, if you chuse a more polite expression, levity. Important matters are treated as sport, and bagatelles serve for a serious occupation. At an advanced period of life the Frenchman still sings lively airs, and is, as much as he can, gallant towards the ladies. In these remarks I have for me great guarantees of this same nation, and shelter myself behind a Montesquieu and a d'Alambert, in order to be secure against every apprehended indignation.

The *Briton* at the beginning of every acquaintance is cold, and indifferent towards a stranger. He has little inclination to small complaisances; on the other hand, as soon as he becomes a friend, he is disposed to render great services. In society he is not solicitous to be witty, or to show a polite behaviour, but he is intelligent and composed. He is a bad imitator, inquires little about what others judge, and follows his own taste entirely. Relatively to the fair he is not of the French agreeableness, but shows far more reverence for them, and carries this perhaps too far, as in the conjugal state he commonly grants his wife an unlimited authority. He is steadfast, sometimes to obstinacy, bold and resolute, frequently to temerity, and commonly acts according to principles, even to inflexibility. He easily becomes singular, not through vanity, but because he gives himself little trouble about others, and does not easily do violence to his own taste out of complaisance, or imitation; and on that account is seldom so much beloved as the Frenchman, but, when he is known, commonly more esteemed.

The *German* has a mixed feeling of that of a Briton and of a Frenchman, but seems to come the nearest to the former, and the greater similarity with the latter is but artificial and imitated. He has a happy mixture in the feeling as well of the sublime as of the beautiful; and though he does not equal the Briton in the one, or the Frenchman in the other, he, so far as he unites them, surpasses both. He shows more complaisance in society than the former, and does not bring into it so much agreeable vivacity and wit as the Frenchman, yet he manifests therein more discretion and understanding. He is, as in every sort of taste, so in love, pretty methodical and, by combining the beautiful with the noble, in the sentiment of both cool enough, to occupy his head about the considerations of understanding, of magnificence and shaw. Hence with him are family, title and rank in the civil relation as well as in love affairs of great importance. He inquires more than the others, What people think of him, and if there is any thing in his character that can excite the wish of a principal amendment; it is this weakness, by which he dares not be original, though he has all the talents fit for being so, and enters too much into the opinion of others; which, by making the moral

properties inconstant and affected, deprives them of all support. . . .

The *Negroes* of Africa have by nature no feeling, which rises above the trifling. Mr. (David) Hume challenges every body, to produce a single example where a Negro has shown talents, and maintains, That among a hundred thousand Blacks, who are transported from their native home, though many of them are emancipated, not a single one of them has ever been found that has performed any thing great, either in the arts or sciences, or shown any other commendable property, though among the Whites there are constantly some, who raise themselves up from among the populace, and acquire consideration in the world by distinguished talents. So essential is the difference between these two races of men, and it appears to be equally great with regard to the mental capacities, as with regard to the colour. The Fetiche-religion so widely diffused among them is a species of idolatry, which perhaps sinks as deep into the trifling, as it seems possible for human nature to admit of. A feather, a cow-horn, a muscle, or any other common thing, the moment it is consecrated by muttering a few words, is an object of adoration, and of invocation in making oath. The blacks are remarkably vain, but in a negro manner, and so loquacious, that they must absolutely be separated by the cogent and conclusive argument of caning. . . .

In the countries of the blacks, what can be expected to be met with, but a thorough and most abject slavery of the female sex? A coward is always a strict master of the weak, as with us those, who have scarcely dared to appear before any one out of their own house, are always tyrants of the kitchen. Father Labat mentions, that a negro carpenter, whom he upbraided with high-minded procedure towards his wives, returned for answer: You whites are great fools, for ye first allow your wives too much, and afterwards complain, when they put you mad. It would seem as if there were in this something, which perhaps merits to be taken into consideration; but this fellow was from the crown of his head to the very soles of his feet jet-black; a direct proof, that what he said was stupid. Among all savages there are none, by whom the female sex are more really respected, than by those of Canada. In this they perhaps surpass even our civilized part of the world. Not as if one did the women there humble services; these are but compliments. No, they actually command. They assemble and deliberate concerning the most weighty affairs of the nation, concerning peace and war. On this they send their delegates to the counsel of the men and their voice commonly decides. But they purchase this prerogative dear enough. They have the whole burden of the household affairs, and take a share in all the hardships of the men.

23. MARIA VON HERBERT'S CHALLENGE TO KANT

RAE LANGTON

This is a paper about two philosophers who wrote to each other. One is famous; the other is not. It is about two practical standpoints, the strategic and the human, and what the famous philosopher said of them. And it is about friendship and deception, duty and despair. That is enough by way of preamble.[1]

FRIENDSHIP

In 1791 Kant received a letter from an Austrian lady whom he had never met. She was Maria von Herbert, a keen and able student of Kant's philosophy, and sister to Baron Franz Paul von Herbert, another zealous Kantian disciple. The

Reprinted from "Maria von Herbert's Challenge to Kant," with the permission of the author and Cambridge University Press.

zeal of her brother the Baron was indeed so great that he had left his lead factory, and his wife, for two years in order to study Kant's philosophy in Weimar and Jena. Upon his return, the von Herbert household had become a centre, a kind of *salon*, where the critical philosophy was intensely debated, against the backdrop of vehement opposition to Kant in Austria as in many German states. The household was, in the words of a student of Fichte's, "a new Athens," an oasis of Enlightenment spirit, devoted to preaching and propagating the Kantian gospel, reforming religion, and replacing dull unthinking piety with a morality based on reason.[2] Here is the letter.

1. *To Kant, from Maria von Herbert, August 1791*

Great Kant,
    As a believer calls to his God, I call to you for help, for comfort, or for counsel to prepare me for death. Your writings prove that there is a

future life. But as for this life, I have found nothing, nothing at all that could replace the good I have lost, for I loved someone who, in my eyes, encompassed within himself all that is worthwhile, so that I lived only for him, everything else was in comparison just rubbish, cheap trinkets. Well, I have offended this person, because of a long drawn out lie, which I have now disclosed to him, though there was nothing unfavourable to my character in it, I had no vice in my life that needed hiding. The lie was enough though, and his love vanished. As an honourable man, he doesn't refuse me friendship. But that inner feeling that once, unbidden, led us to each other, is no more—oh my heart splinters into a thousand pieces! If I hadn't read so much of your work I would certainly have put an end to my life. But the conclusion I had to draw from your theory stops me—it is wrong for me to die because my life is tormented, instead I'm supposed to live because of my being. Now put yourself in my place, and either damn me or comfort me. I've read the metaphysic of morals, and the categorical imperative, and it doesn't help a bit. My reason abandons me just when I need it. Answer me, I implore you—or you won't be acting in accordance with your own imperative.

My address is Maria Herbert of Klagenfurt, Carinthia, care of the white lead factory, or perhaps you would rather send it via Reinhold because the mail is more reliable there.

Kant, much impressed by this letter, sought advice from a friend as to what he should do. The friend advised him strongly to reply, and to do his best to distract his correspondent from "the object to which she [was] enfettered."[3] We have the carefully prepared draft of Kant's response.

2. *To Maria von Herbert, Spring 1792 (Kant's rough draft)*

Your deeply felt letter comes from a heart that must have been created for the sake of virtue and honesty, since it is so receptive to instruction in those qualities. I must do as you ask, namely, put myself in your place, and prescribe for you a pure moral sedative. I do not know whether your relationship is one of marriage or friendship, but it makes no significant difference. For love, be it for one's spouse or for a friend, presupposes the same mutual esteem for the other's character, without which it is no more than perishable, sensual delusion.

A love like that wants to communicate itself completely, and it expects of its respondent a similar sharing of heart, unweakened by distrustful reticence. That is what the ideal of friendship demands. But there is something in us which puts limits on such frankness, some obstacle to this mutual outpouring of the heart, which makes one keep some part of one's thoughts locked within oneself, even when one is most intimate. The sages of old complained of this secret distrust—"My dear friends, there is no such thing as a friend!"

We can't expect frankness of people, since everyone fears that to reveal himself completely would be to make himself despised by others. But this lack of frankness, this reticence, is still very different from dishonesty. What the honest but reticent man says is true, but not the whole truth. What the dishonest man says is something he knows to be false. Such an assertion is called, in the theory of virtue, a lie. It may be harmless, but it is not on that account innocent. It is a serious violation of a duty to oneself; it subverts the dignity of humanity in our own person, and attacks the roots of our thinking. As you see, you have sought counsel from a physician who is no flatterer. I speak for your beloved and present him with arguments that justify his having wavered in his affection for you.

Ask yourself whether you reproach yourself for the imprudence of confessing, or for the immorality intrinsic to the lie. If the former, then you regret having done your duty. And why? Because it has resulted in the loss of your friend's confidence. This regret is not motivated by anything moral, since it is produced by an awareness not of the act itself, but of its consequences. But if your reproach is grounded in a moral judgment of your behaviour, it would be a poor moral physician who would advise you to cast it from your mind.

When your change in attitude has been revealed to your beloved, only time will be needed to quench, little by little, the traces of his justified indignation, and to transform his coldness into a more firmly grounded love. If this doesn't happen, then the earlier warmth of his affection was more physical than moral, and would have disappeared anyway—a misfortune which we often encounter in life, and when we do, must meet with composure. For the value of life, insofar as it consists of the enjoyment we get from people, is vastly overrated.

Here then, my dear friend, you find the customary divisions of a sermon: instruction, penalty and comfort. Devote yourself to the first two; when they have had their effect, comfort will be found by itself.

Kant's letter has an enormously interesting and sensitive discussion of friendship and secrecy, much of which turns up word for word in *The Doctrine of Virtue,* published some six years later.[4] But what Kant's letter fails to say is as at least as interesting as what it says. Herbert writes that she has lost her love, that her heart is shattered, that there is nothing left to make life worth living, and that Kant's moral philosophy hasn't helped a bit. Kant's reply is to suggest that the love is deservedly lost, that misery is an appropriate response to one's own moral failure, and that the really interesting moral question here is the one that hinges on a subtle but necessary scope distinction: the distinction between telling a lie and failing to tell the truth, between *saying "not-p,"* and *not saying "p."* Conspicuously absent is an acknowledgement of Herbert's more than theoretical interest in the question: is suicide compatible with the moral law? And perhaps this is just as well from a practical point of view. The sooner she gives up those morbid thoughts the better; the less said on the morbid subject, the less likely the morbid thoughts will

arise. Perhaps it is also just as well, for Kant, from a theoretical point of view. Kant's conviction that suicide is incompatible with the moral law is not nearly as well founded as he liked to think; so here too, the less said, the better. Having posted his moral sedative off to Austria, and receiving no reply from the patient in more than a year, Kant enquired of a mutual friend who often saw her about the effect his letter had had. Herbert then wrote back, with apologies for her delay. This is her second letter.

3. *To Kant, from Maria von Herbert, January 1793*

Dear and revered sir,

Your kindness, and your exact understanding of the human heart, encourage me to describe to you, unshrinkingly, the further progress of my soul. The lie was no cloaking of a vice, but a sin of keeping something back out of consideration for the friendship (still veiled by love) that existed then. There was a struggle, I was aware of the honesty friendship demands, and at the same time I could foresee the terribly wounding consequences. Finally I had the strength and revealed the truth to my friend, but so late—and when I told him, the stone in my heart was gone, but his love was torn away in exchange. My friend hardened in his coldness, just as you said in your letter. But then afterwards he changed towards me, and offered me again the most intimate friendship. I'm glad enough about it, for his sake—but I'm not really content, because it's just amusement, it doesn't have any point.

My vision is clear now. I feel that a vast emptiness extends inside me, and all around me—so that I almost find my self to be superfluous, unnecessary. Nothing attracts me. I'm tormented by a boredom that makes life intolerable. Don't think me arrogant for saying this, but the demands of morality are too easy for me. I would eagerly do twice as much as they command. They only get their prestige from the attractiveness of sin, and it costs me almost no effort to resist that.

I comfort myself with the thought that, since the practice of morality is so bound up with sensuality, it can only count for this world. I can hope that the afterlife won't be yet another life ruled by these few, easy demands of morality, another empty and vegetating life. Experience wants to take me to task for this bad temper I have against life by showing me that nearly everyone finds his life ending much too soon, everyone is so glad to be alive. So as not to be a queer exception to the rule, I shall tell you of a remote cause of my deviation, namely my chronic poor health, which dates from the time I first wrote to you. I don't study the natural sciences or the arts any more, since I don't feel that I'm genius enough to extend them; and for myself, there's no need to know them. I'm indifferent to everything that doesn't bear on the categorical imperative, and my transcendental consciousness—although I'm all done with those thoughts too.

You can see, perhaps, why I only want one thing, namely to shorten this pointless life, a life which I am convinced will get neither better nor worse. If you consider that I am still young and that each day interests me only to the extent that it brings me closer to death, you can judge what a great benefactor you would be if you were to examine this question closely. I ask you, because my conception of morality is silent here, whereas it speaks decisively on all other matters. And if you cannot give me the answer I seek, I beg you to give me something that will get this intolerable emptiness out of my soul. Then I might become a useful part of nature, and, if my health permits, would make a trip to Königsberg in a few years. I want to ask permission, in advance, to visit you. You must tell me your story then, because I would like to know what kind of life your philosophy has led you to—whether it never seemed to you to be worth the bother to marry, or to give your whole heart to anyone, or to reproduce your likeness. I have an engraved portrait of you by Bause, from Leipzig. I see a profound calm there, and moral depth—but not the astuteness of which the *Critique of Pure Reason* is proof.

And I'm dissatisfied not to be able to look you right in the face.

Please fulfill my wish, if it's not too inconvenient. And I need to remind you: if you do me this great favour and take the trouble to answer, please focus on specific details, not on the general points, which I understand, and already understood back when I happily studied your works at the side of my friend. You would like him, I'm sure. He is honest, goodhearted, and intelligent—and besides that, fortunate enough to fit this world.

I am with deepest respect and truth, Maria Herbert.

Herbert's letter speaks for itself. The passion, the turbulence, has vanished. Desolation has taken its place, a "vast emptiness," a vision of the world and the self that is chilling in its clarity, chilling in its nihilism. Apathy reigns. Desire is dead. Nothing attracts. Bereft of inclination, the self is "superfluous," as Herbert so starkly puts it. Nothing has any point—except of course the categorical imperative. But morality itself has become a torment, not because it is too difficult, but because it is too easy. Without the counterweight of opposing inclination, what course could there be but to obey? The moral life is the empty, vegetating life, where one sees at a glance what the moral law requires and simply does it, unhampered by the competing attractions of sin. Herbert concludes that morality must be bound up with sensuality, that moral credit depends on the battle of the will with the sensual passions, a battle which, when there are no passions, is won merely, and tediously, by default—and where can be the credit in that? The imperative requires us never to treat persons merely as means to one's own ends. But if one has no ends, if one is simply empty, what could be easier than to obey? Herbert draws hope from her conclusion: if morality is bound to sensuality, with luck the next life will not be thus accursed.

This sounds like heresy. Is it? If so, Kant is blind to it. But perhaps it is not heresy at all. What Kant fails to see—what Herbert herself fails to see—is that her life constitutes a profound challenge to his philosophy, at least construed one way. Consider Kant's views on duty and inclination.

An action has moral worth when it is done for the sake of duty; it is not sufficient that the action conforms with duty.[5] Now, inclinations are often sufficient to make us perform actions that conform with our duty. To preserve one's life is a duty; and most of us have strong inclinations to preserve our lives. To help others where one can is a duty; and most of us are sympathetic enough and amiable enough to be inclined to help others, at least some of the time. But—if we take Kant at his word here—actions thus motivated have no moral worth. The action of moral worth is that of "the wretched man . . . [for whom] disappointments and hopeless misery have quite taken away the taste for life, who longs for death" but who, notwithstanding, preserves his life. The action that has moral worth is that of the misanthropist, "the man cold in temperament and indifferent to the sufferings of others" who nonetheless helps others "not from inclination but from duty."[6]

This looks as though moral credit depends on both the absence of coinciding inclinations, such as sympathy; and the presence of opposing inclinations, like misanthropy. If so, Herbert is right: morality depends on there being inclinations to defeat. It is important to see though that even here, what Kant says is not motivated by a kind of blind rule worship, but by a sense of the gulf between the two standpoints from which we must view ourselves. We are at once cogs in the grand machine of nature, and free agents in the Kingdom of Ends. We are persons, members of an intelligible world, authors of our actions; and at the same time animals, puppets of our genes and hormones, buffeted about by our lusts and loathings. Inclinations are *passions* in the sense that they *just happen* to us. And insofar as we let our actions be driven by them we allow ourselves to be puppets, not persons. We allow ourselves, to use Kant's own metaphors, to become mari-

onettes or automatons, which may appear to be initiators of action, but whose freedom is illusory, "no better than the freedom of a turnspit, which, when once wound up also carries out its motions by itself."[7] The inclinations are effects on us, they are *pathe,* and for that reason pathological. If we let them be causes of our behaviour, we abandon our personhood.

Whether they lead us towards the action of duty or away from it, inclinations are among virtue's chief obstacles. When inclination opposes duty, it is an obstacle to duty's performance. When inclination coincides with duty, it is an obstacle at least to knowledge of the action's worth. "Inclination, be it good-natured or otherwise, is blind and slavish . . . The feeling of sympathy and warmhearted fellow-feeling . . . is burdensome even to right-thinking persons, confusing their considered maxims and creating the wish to be free from them and subject only to law-giving reason."[8] In the battle against the inclinations we can enlist the aid of that strange thing, respect, or reverence for the moral law. Reverence for the law serves to "weaken the hindering influence of the inclinations."[9] Reverence is a kind of feeling, but it is not something we "passively feel," something inflicted upon us from outside. It is the sensible correlate of our own moral activity, the "consciousness of the direct constraint of the will through law."[10] Its function is not to motivate our moral actions, for that would still be motivation by feeling. Rather, its function is to remove the obstacles, to silence inclinations, something we should all look forward to. For inclinations are "so far from having an absolute value . . . that it must . . . be the universal wish of every rational being to be wholly free from them."[11]

Kant goes so far as to say we have a *duty of apathy,* a duty he is less than famous for. "Virtue necessarily presupposes apathy," he says in *The Doctrine of Virtue.* "The word 'apathy' has fallen into disrepute," he continues, "as if it meant lack of feeling and so subjective indifference regarding objects of choice: it has been taken for weakness. We can prevent this misunderstanding by giving the name 'moral apathy' to that freedom from agitation which is to be distinguished from indifference, for in it the feelings arising from sensuous impressions lose their influence on moral feeling only because reverence for the law prevails over all such feelings."[12] Something rather similar to apathy is described in the *Critique of Practical Reason,* but this time it is called not apathy, but "bliss" (*Seligkeit*). Bliss is the state of "complete independence from inclinations and desires."[13] While it must be the universal wish of every rational being to achieve bliss, can we in fact achieve it? Apparently not, or not here. Bliss is "the self-sufficiency which can be ascribed only to the Supreme Being."[14] The Supreme Being has no passions and inclinations. His intuition is intellectual, and not sensible. He can be affected by nothing, not even our prayers. He can have no *pathe.* God is the being more apathetic than which cannot be conceived.

What of Kant's moral patient? She is well beyond the virtue of apathy that goes with mastery of the inclinations. She has no inclinations left to master. She respects the moral law, and obeys it. But she needn't battle her passions to do so. She has no passions. She is empty—but for the clear vision of the moral law and unshrinking obedience to it. She is well on the way to bliss, lucky woman, and, if Kant is right about bliss, well on the way to Godhead. No wonder she feels that she—unlike her unnamed friend—does not quite "fit the world." She obeys the moral law in her day to day dealings with people from the motive of duty alone. She has no other motives. She is no heretic. She is a Kantian saint. Oh brave new world, that has such moral saints in it.[15]

What should Kant have said about inclinations? I have no clear view about this, but some brief remarks may be in order. A saner view is arguably to be found in Kant's own writings. In the *Doctrine of Virtue*[16] Kant apparently advocates the cultivation of natural sentiment to back up the motive of duty. It is hard, though, to rec-

oncile this with his other teachings, which tell us that inclinations, all inclinations, are to be abjured, as "blind and slavish," in the graphic phrase from the *Critique of Practical Reason.* "Blind" is an evocative word in the Kantian context, associated as it is with the blind workings of nature, with the sensual as opposed to the intellectual. It calls to mind the famous slogan of the first *Critique:* thoughts without content are empty, intuitions without concepts are *blind.* That slogan famously captures the synthesis of rationalism and empiricism Kant thought necessary for knowledge. It acknowledges the twin aspects of human creatures, as Kant sees us: we have a *sensible* intuition, a *passive* intuition, through which we are affected by the world; and an active intellect. *We need both.* If only Kant had effected a similar synthesis in the moral sphere: for if it is true, as he says, that inclinations without reasons are blind, it seems equally true that reasons without inclinations are empty. The moral life without inclinations is a life of "intolerable emptiness," as Herbert found. We need both.

I said that Herbert has no inclinations: but there are two exceptions. She wants to die. And she wants to visit Kant. She is, it seems, like the would-be suicide Kant describes in *The Groundwork:* her persistence with life has moral worth, because it is so opposed to her inclinations. But is she really like him? Not quite. For she is not even sure that duty points to persistence with life. Notice the change here. In her first letter she believed that self-respect, respect for "her own being" required her to persist with life. But as her "being" has begun to contract, as the self has withered, sloughed off, become superfluous—as the emptiness has grown—so too has her doubt. Now her conception of morality is "silent" on the question of suicide. She wants to die. She has almost no opposing inclinations. And morality is silent. It takes no expert to wonder if she is in danger.

Why does she want to visit Kant? She says (letter 3): "I would like to know what kind of life your philosophy has led you to." In the *Critique of Practical Reason* Kant cites approvingly what he took to be the practice of the ancients: no one was justified in calling himself a philosopher—a lover of wisdom—"unless he could show [philosophy's] infallible effect on his own person as an example."[17] Kant thinks we are justified in inquiring after the effect of philosophy on the philosopher, daunting as the prospect seems today. But what does Herbert have in mind? She wonders, perhaps, whether Kant's life is as empty as her own, and for the same reason. She discovered that love is "pointless" when inclinations have withered, when you have no passions of your own and therefore no passions to share. And she wonders whether Kant's life reflects this discovery. She wonders whether Kant's philosophy has led him to think that it was simply "not worth the bother" to marry, or to "give his whole heart" to anyone. Perhaps she is right to wonder.

SHIPWRECK

In reply to an inquiry, Kant received this explanatory letter from a mutual friend, Erhard.

4. To Kant, from J. B. Erhard, January 17, 1793

I can say little of Miss Herbert. She has capsized on the reef of romantic love. In order to realize an idealistic love, she gave herself to a man who misused her trust. And then, trying to achieve such love with another, she told her new lover about the previous one. That is the key to her letter. If my friend Herbert had more delicacy, I think she could still be saved.

Yours, Erhard.

Kant writes again, not to Herbert, but to someone about whom we know little:

5. From Kant, to Elisabeth Motherby, February 11, 1793

I have numbered the letters[18] which I have the honour of passing on to you, my dear mademoiselle, according to the dates I received

them. The ecstatical little lady didn't think to date them. The third letter, from another source, provides an explanation of the lady's curious mental derangement. A number of expressions refer to writings of mine that she read, and are difficult to understand without an interpreter.

You have been so fortunate in your upbringing that I do not need to commend these letters to you as an example of warning, to guard you against the wanderings of a sublimated fantasy. But they may serve nonetheless to make your perception of that good fortune all the more lively.

I am, with the greatest respect, my honoured lady's most obedient servant, I. Kant.

Kant is unaware that he has received a letter from a Kantian saint. Indeed, it is hard to believe that he has read her second letter. He relies on the opinion of his friend, whose diagnosis of the patient resorts to that traditional and convenient malady of feminine hysteria. Herbert "has capsized on the reef of romantic love." The diagnosis is exactly wrong. Herbert has no passions. Her vision is clear. Her life is empty. But it is easier not to take this in, easier to suppose a simpler illness. She is at the mercy (aren't all women?) of irrational passions. She is evidently beyond the reach of instruction, beyond the reach of his moral sedatives; so Kant abandons her. It is hard to imagine a more dramatic shift from the interactive stance to the objective.[19] In Kant's first letter, Herbert is "my dear friend," she is the subject for moral instruction, and reprimand. She is responsible for some immoral actions, but she has a "heart created for the sake of virtue," capable of seeing the good and doing it. Kant is doing his best to communicate, instruct, and console. He is not very good at it, hardly surprising if he believes—as I think he does—that he should master rather than cultivate his moral sentiments. But there is little doubt that the good will is there. He treats her as a human being, as an end, as a person. This is the standpoint of interaction.

But now? Herbert is *die kleine Schwärmerin,* the little dreamer, the ecstatical girl, suffering a "curious mental derangement," lost in the "wanderings of a sublimated fantasy," who doesn't think, especially about important things like dating letters. Kant is here forgetting an important aspect of the duty of respect, which requires something like a Davidsonian principle of charity. We have "a duty of respect for man *even in the logical use of his reason:* a duty not to censure his error by calling it absurdity . . . but rather to suppose that his error must yet contain some truth and to seek this out."[20] Herbert, now deranged, is no longer guilty. She is merely unfortunate. She is not responsible for what she does. She is the pitiful product of a poor upbringing. She is an item in the natural order, a ship wrecked on a reef. She is a thing.

And, true to Kant's picture, it now becomes appropriate to use her as a means to his own ends. He bundles up her letters, private communications from a "dear friend," letters that express thoughts, philosophical and personal, some of them profound. He bundles them up and sends them to an acquaintance under the title, "Example of Warning." The end is obscure and contradictory: it seems it is to warn somebody who, in Kant's own view, needs no warning. Is it gossip? Ingratiation? But the striking thing is that the letters are no longer seen as human communications. Far from it: Kant's presumption is that they *will not be understood* by their new recipient. For the letters "refer to writings of mine that she read, and are difficult to understand without an interpreter." This is not the speech of persons, to be understood and debated; this is derangement, to be feared and avoided. These are not thoughts, but symptoms. Kant is doing something with her as one does something with a tool: Herbert cannot share the end of the action. She cannot be co-author. Kant's deceiving of her—neatly achieved by reticence—has made sure of that. Her action of pleading for help, asking advice, arguing philosophy, her action of writing to a well-loved

philosopher and then to a friend—these have become the action of warning of the perils of romantic love. She did not choose to do *that.* Well may Kant have warned "My dear friends, there is no such thing as a friend."

STRATEGY FOR THE KINGDOM'S SAKE

Enough. This is not a cautionary tale of the inability of philosophers to live by their philosophy. What interests me is what interested Kant at the outset: friendship and deception. What interests me is the very first problem: the "long drawn out lie, disclosed." Was it wrong for Herbert to deceive? Is it always wrong to deceive? Apparently, yes, from the Kantian perspective. In deceiving we treat our hearers as less than human. We act from the objective standpoint. We force others to perform actions they don't choose to perform. We make them things. If I reply to the murderer, "No, my friend is not here," I deceive a human being, use his reasoning ability as a tool, do something that has a goal (saving my friend) that I make impossible for him to share, make him do something (abandon his prey) that he did not choose to do. I have made him, in this respect, a thing.

But this is too simple. Recall that Herbert puts her dilemma like this: "I was aware of *the honesty friendship demands* and at the same time I could see the terribly wounding consequences . . . The lie . . . was a . . . keeping something back *out of consideration for the friendship.*"[21] She is torn. Friendship demands honesty; and friendship demands dishonesty. Is she confused? Is she in contradiction? Not at all. It is an old dilemma: having an ideal you want to live by, and an ideal you want to seek and preserve. You owe honesty to your friend; but the friendship will vanish if you are honest. Friendship is a very great good: it is the Kingdom of Ends made real and local. Kant says that the man who is without a friend is the man who "must shut himself up in himself," who must remain "completely alone with his thoughts, as in a prison."[22] One of the goods of friendship is that it makes possible the kind of relationship where one can unlock the prison of the self, reveal oneself to the compassionate and understanding eye of the other. But Kant sees true friendship to be a very rare thing, rare, he says as a black swan.[23] And what threatens friendship most is asymmetry, inequality with regard to love or respect, which can result in the partial breakdown of the interactive stance. This asymmetry can be brought about by the very act of self revelation: if one person "reveals his failings while the other person concealed his own, he would lose something of the other's respect by presenting himself so candidly."[24] What Kant is pointing to is the very problem encountered, far more acutely, by Herbert: in being a friend, in acting in the way that friendship demands, one can sometimes threaten friendship. To act as a member of the Kingdom can make the Kingdom more, and not less, remote. How should we think of Kant's ideal: is the Kingdom an ideal to be lived by, or a goal to be sought? If it is ever the latter, then sometimes—in evil circumstances—it will be permissible, and even required, to act strategically for the Kingdom's sake.[25] There is a question about what evil is. But for Kant it must, above all, be this: the reduction of persons to things. Now consider Herbert's position. There is something we have been leaving out. Herbert is a *woman* in a society in which women start out on an unequal footing and then live out their lives that way, where women—especially women—must perpetually walk a tightrope between being treated as things and treated as persons. She must make her choices against a backdrop of social institutions and habits that strip her of the dignity due to persons, where what she does and what she says will always be interpreted in the light of that backdrop, so that even if she says "my vision is clear," and speaks in a manner consistent with that claim, her speech will be read as the speech of the deranged, a mere plaything of the passions. Central among the institutions she must encounter

in her life is that of the sexual marketplace, where human beings are viewed as having a *price,* and not a dignity, and where the price of women is fixed in a particular way. Women, as things, as items in the sexual marketplace, have a market value that depends in part on whether they have been used. Virgins fetch a higher price than second hand goods. Such are the background circumstances in which Herbert finds herself. They are, I suggest, evil circumstances, evil by Kantian lights (though Kant himself never saw it).

Despite these handicaps, Herbert has achieved a great thing: she has achieved something like a friendship of mutual love and respect, found someone with whom she can share her activities and goals, become a partner in a relationship where ends are chosen in such a way that the ends of both agents coincide (prominent among which was, it seems, the happy study of Kant's works!). She has achieved a relationship where frankness and honesty prevail—with one exception. Her lie is the lie of "keeping something back for the sake of the friendship." If she tells the truth, evil circumstance will see to it that her action will not be taken as the honest self-revelation of a person, but the revelation of her thing-hood, her hitherto unrecognized status as used merchandise, as item with a price that is lower than the usual. If she tells the truth, she becomes a thing, and the friendship—that small neighbourhood of the Kingdom—will vanish. Should she lie? Perhaps. If her circumstances are evil, she is permitted to have friendship as her goal, to be sought and preserved, rather than a law to be lived by. So she is permitted to lie. Then other considerations come in. She has a duty to "humanity in her own person," of which Kant says: "By virtue of this worth we are not for sale at any price; we possess an inalienable dignity which instills in us reverence for ourselves." She has a duty of self esteem: she must respect her own person and demand such respect of others, abjuring the vice of servility.[26] I think she may have a duty to lie.

This is strategy, for the Kingdom's sake. Kant would not allow it. He thinks we should act as if the Kingdom of Ends is with us now. He thinks we should rely on God to make it all right in the end. But God will not make it all right in the end. And the Kingdom of Ends is not with us now. Perhaps we should do what we can to bring it about.

Coda

Kant never replied, and his correspondent, as far as I know, did not leave Austria.[27] In 1803 Maria von Herbert killed herself, having worked out at last an answer to that persistent and troubling question—the question to which Kant, and her own moral sense, had responded with silence. Was that a vicious thing to do? Not entirely. As Kant himself concedes, "Self murder requires courage, and in this attitude there is always room for reverence for humanity in one's own person."[28]

NOTES

1. This paper is a shortened version of "Duty and Desolation," which appeared in *Philosophy, 67* (1992). As the original version makes evident, my interpretation of Kant owes a great debt to the work of P. F. Strawson ("Freedom and Resentment," in *Freedom and Resentment* [Methuen: London, 1974], 1–25), and Christine Korsgaard, whose views on Kant and lying are developed in "The Right to Lie: Kant on Dealing with Evil," *Philosophy and Public Affairs,* 15, 4 (1986), 325–49; and, on Kant and friendship, in "Creating the Kingdom of Ends: Responsibility and Reciprocity in Personal Relations," *Philosophical Perspectives 6: Ethics,* ed. James Tomberlin (The Ridgeview Publishing Company: Atascadero, Calif., 1992). "Duty and Desolation" was first read at a conference on moral psychology at Monash, Aug. 1991, and has been read at the University of Queensland, the Australian National University, and the University of Delhi. I am indebted to those present on all these occa-

sions for stimulating and searching comments. I am especially grateful to Philip Pettit and Richard Holton for helpful discussion, and to Margaret Wilson and Christine Korsgaard for written comments on an early draft.

2. According to Arnulf Zweig, in his introduction to *Kant: Philosophical Correspondence, 1759–1799* (University of Chicago Press: Chicago, 1967), 24.

3. Letter to Kant from Ludwig Ernst Borowski, probably Aug. 1791. The correspondence between Kant and Maria von Herbert, and the related letters, are in volume 11 of the edition of Kant's work published by the Prussian Academy of Sciences (Walter de Gruyter: Berlin, 1922). The English translations given in this paper are closely based on those of Arnulf Zweig, partly revised in the light of the Academy edition, and very much abridged. See Zweig, *Kant: Philosophical Correspondence, 1759–1799,* © 1967 by the University of Chicago. All Rights Reserved. (I make use of the translations with the kind permission of Prof. Zweig and the University of Chicago Press. Readers who would like to see fuller versions of the letters should consult the Academy edition, or the Zweig translations.)

4. Immanuel Kant, *The Doctrine of Virtue,* (part II of *The Metaphysic of Morals*), trans. Mary Gregor (Harper and Row: London, 1964). One wonders whether these parts of *The Doctrine of Virtue* may have been influenced by Kant's thoughts about Herbert's predicament. An alternative explanation might be that *The Doctrine of Virtue* and Kant's letter to Herbert are both drawing on Kant's lecture notes.

5. *The Groundwork of the Metaphysic of Morals,* trans. M. J. Paton (Harper and Row: London, 1964), 397.

6. Ibid. 398.

7. Immanuel Kant, *Critique of Practical Reason,* trans. L. W. Beck (Macmillan: London, 1956), 97, 101.

8. Ibid. 119.

9. Ibid. 80.

10. Ibid. 117.

11. *Groundwork,* 428.

12. *Doctrine of Virtue,* 407.

13. *Critique of Practical Reason,* 118.

14. Ibid.

15. See Susan Wolf, "Moral Saints," *The Journal of Philosophy,* 79 (1982), 419–39, on the perils of sainthood.

16. See e.g. *Doctrine of Virtue,* 456.
17. *Critique of Practical Reason,* 190.
18. Letters 1, 3, and 4 above. Elisabeth Motherby was the daughter of Kant's friend Robert Motherby, an English merchant in Königsberg.
19. This is Strawson's way of characterizing the two standpoints in Kant's moral philosophy ("Freedom and Resentment").
20. *Doctrine of Virtue,* 462, my italics.
21. Letter 3, my italics.
22. *Doctrine of Virtue,* 471. This is a remarkable metaphor for a philosopher who finds in the autonomous human self, and its self-legislating activity, the only source of intrinsic value.
23. Ibid. 471. Kant's ignorance of Antipodean bird life is (just) forgivable.
24. Ibid. 471.
25. This development of Kant's philosophy is proposed by Korsgaard as a way of addressing the problem of lying to the murderer at the door (Korsgaard, "The Right to Lie"). I discuss it in more detail in the original version of this paper.
26. *Doctrine of Virtue,* 434, 435.
27. There is one final letter from her on the record, dated early 1794, in which she expresses again a wish to visit Kant, and reflects upon her own desire for death.
28. Ibid. 424.

24. THE BHAGAVAD GITA

CHAPTER 1

[...]

26   There Arjuna saw, standing their ground, fathers, grandfathers, teachers, maternal uncles, brothers, sons, grandsons, friends,

27   Fathers-in-law, and companions in both armies. And looking at all these kinsmen so arrayed, Arjuna, the son of Kunti,

28   Was overcome by deep compassion; and in despair he said: 'Krishna, when I see these my own people eager to fight, on the brink,

29   My limbs grow heavy, and my mouth is parched, my body trembles and my hair bristles,

30   My bow, Gandiva, falls from my hand, my skin's on fire, I can no longer stand—my mind is reeling,

31   I see evil omens, Krishna: nothing good can come from slaughtering one's own family in battle—I foresee it!

32   I have no desire for victory, Krishna, or kingship, or pleasures. What should we do with kingship, Govinda? What are pleasures to us? What is life?

33   The men for whose sake we desire kingship, enjoyment and pleasures are precisely those drawn up for this battle, having abandoned their lives and riches.

34   Teachers, fathers, sons, as well as grandfathers, maternal uncles, fathers-in-law, grandsons, brothers-in-law, and kinsmen—

35   I have no desire to kill them, Madhusudana, though they are killers themselves— no, not for the lordship of the three worlds,[1] let alone the earth!

Reprinted from *Bhagavad Gita* trans. W. J. Johnson by permission of Oxford University Press.

36   Where is the joy for us, Janardana, in destroying Dhritarashtra's people? Having killed these murderers, evil would attach itself to us.

37   It follows, therefore, that we are not required to kill the sons of Dhritarashtra—they are our own kinsmen, and having killed our own people, how could we be happy, Madhava?

38   And even if, because their minds are overwhelmed by greed, *they* cannot see the evil incurred by destroying one's own family, and the degradation involved in the betrayal of a friend,

39   How can *we* be so ignorant as not to recoil from this wrong? The evil incurred by destroying one's own family is plain to see, Janardana.

40   With the destruction of family the eternal family laws are lost; when the law is destroyed, lawlessness overpowers the entire family.

41   Krishna, because of overpowering lawlessness, the women of the family are corrupted; when women are corrupted, Varshneya, there is intermingling of the four estates.[2]

42   And intermingling leads to hell for the family-destroyers *and* the family, for their ancestors, robbed of their rice-ball and water offerings, fall back.

43   Through these evils of the family-destroyers, which cause intermingling of the four estates, caste laws and the eternal family laws are obliterated.

44   For men whose family laws have been obliterated we have heard that a place in hell is certain, Janardana.

45   Oh, ignominy! We are about to perpetrate a great evil—out of sheer greed for kingdoms and pleasures, we are prepared to kill our own people.

46   It would be better for me if Dhritarashtra's armed men were to kill me in battle, unresisting and unarmed.'

47   Having spoken this on the field of conflict, Arjuna sank down into the chariot, letting slip his bow and arrow, his mind distracted with grief.

Chapter 2

Sanjaya said:

1   Then, Krishna, the destroyer of the demon Madhu, spoke these words to the dejected Arjuna, who, eyes blurred and brimming with tears, was so overcome by pity:
The Lord said:

2   Arjuna, where do you get this weakness from at a moment of crisis? A noble should not experience this. It does not lead to heaven, it leads to disgrace.

3   No impotence, Partha, it does not become you. Abandon this base, inner weakness. Get up, Incinerator of the Foe!
Arjuna said:

4   Destroyer of Madhu, destroyer of the enemy, how can I shoot arrows at Bhishma and Drona in battle when they should be honoured?

5   Better to eat begged food among common people than to kill such worthy teachers. For having killed my teachers, who desire legitimate worldly ends, I should be consuming food smeared with blood.

6   And we do not know which is better for us—that we should overcome Dhritarashtra's men, standing there before us, or that they should overcome us. For if we were to kill them, we should have no desire to go on living.

7   My inner being is disabled by that vice of dejection. My mind is bewildered as to what is right. I ask you, which would be better? Tell me for certain. I am your student, I have come to you for help. Instruct me!

8   Though I were to obtain a prosperous, unrivalled kingdom on earth, and even mastery

over the gods, I cannot imagine what could dispel my grief, which withers the senses.

Sanjaya said:

9 And having spoken thus to Krishna, to Govinda, having said 'I will not fight!' Arjuna, the Incinerator of the Foe, fell silent.

10 O Dhritarashtra, between the two armies, Krishna, with the shadow of a smile, spoke these words to that dejected man:

The Lord said:

11 You utter wise *words,* yet you have been mourning those who should not be mourned; the truly wise do not grieve for the living or the dead.

12 There never was a time when I was not, or you, or these rulers of men. Nor will there ever be a time when we shall cease to be, all of us hereafter.

13 Just as within this body the embodied self passes through childhood, youth and old age, so it passes to another body. The wise man is not bewildered by this.

14 But contacts with matter, Son of Kunti, give rise to cold and heat, pleasure and pain. They come and go, Bharata; they are impermanent and you should endure them.

15 For these things, Bull among men, do not perturb that wise man for whom pleasure and pain are the same; he is ready for immortality.

16 For the non-existent there is no coming into existence, for the existent there is no lapsing into non-existence; the division between them is observed by those who see the underlying nature of things.

17 But know that that on which all this is stretched is indestructible. No one can destroy this imperishable one.

18 It is just these *bodies* of the indestructible, immeasurable, and eternal embodied self that are characterized as coming to an end—therefore fight, Bharata!

19 Anyone who believes this a killer, and anyone who thinks this killed, they do not understand: it does not kill, it is not killed.

20 It is not born, it never dies; being, it will never again cease to be. It is unborn, invariable, eternal, primeval. It is not killed when the body is killed.

21 Partha, how can that man who knows it to be indestructible, invariable, unborn and imperishable bring about the death of anyone? Whom does he kill?

22 Just as a man casting off worn-out clothes takes up others that are new, so the embodied self, casting off its worn-out bodies, goes to other, new ones.

23 Blades do not pierce it, fire does not burn it, waters do not wet it, and the wind does not parch it.

24 It cannot be pierced, it cannot be burned, it cannot be wetted, it cannot be parched. It is invariable, everywhere, fixed, immovable, eternal.

25 It is said to be imperceptible, unthinkable and immutable; knowing it to be so, you should not therefore grieve.

26 And even if you believe that it is regularly born and regularly dead, you should not grieve for it, Great Arm.

27 Death is inevitable for those who are born; for those who are dead birth is just as certain. Therefore you must not grieve for what is ineluctable.

28 Bharata, beings have imperceptible beginnings; the interim is clear; their ends are again indistinct. What is there to lament in this?

29 Quite exceptionally does anyone see it, and quite exceptionally does anyone speak of it; it is quite exceptional for anyone to hear of it, but even when they have heard of it, no one in fact knows it.

30 Bharata, this embodied self in the body of everyone is eternally unkillable. Therefore you must not grieve for any beings at all.

31 Recognizing your inherent duty, you must

not shrink from it. For there is nothing better for a warrior than a duty-bound war.

32 It is a door to heaven, opened fortuitously. Fortunate are the warriors, Partha, who are presented with such a war.

33 But if, careless of your inherent duty and renown, you will not undertake this duty-bound conflict, you shall transgress.

34 Moreover, people will recount your limitless disgrace—and disgrace is worse than death for the man who has once been honoured.

35 The great warriors will suppose that you withdrew from the battle out of fear. And you will fade from their high regard into insignificance.

36 Then your enemies will say many things that would be better unsaid, slighting your strength—and what could be more painful than that?

37 You will either be killed and attain heaven, or conquer and enjoy the earth. So rise, Son of Kunti, determined to fight.

38 Making yourself indifferent to pleasure and pain, gain and loss, victory and defeat, commit yourself to battle. And in that way you shall not transgress.

39 You have received this intelligence according to Sankhya theory,[3] now hear it as it applies to practice. Disciplined with such intelligence, Partha, you shall throw off the bondage of action.

40 In this there is no wasted effort, no reverse; just a little of this truth saves from great danger.

41 Son of the Kurus, in this the resolute intelligence is one, the intellects of the irresolute are without limit and many-branched.

42 Partha, that florid speech the uninspired utter, addicted to the words of the Veda,[4] claiming that there is nothing else.

43 Their nature desire, their aim heaven— that speech which produces rebirth as the fruit of action, and which is dense with specific ritual acts aimed at the attainment of enjoyment and power,

44 Robs those addicted to enjoyment and power of their minds. For them no resolute intelligence is established in concentration.

45 The Vedas' sphere of activity is the three constituents of material nature. Arjuna, be free from the three constituents, free from duality, forever grounded in purity, beyond getting and keeping, possessed of the self.

46 For the brahmin who knows, there is no more purpose in all the Vedas than in a water-tank surrounded by a flood.

47 You are qualified simply with regard to action, never with regard to its results. You must be neither motivated by the results of action nor attached to inaction.

48 Grounded in yogic discipline, and having abandoned attachment, undertake actions, Dhananjaya, evenly disposed as to their success or failure. Yoga is defined as evenness of mind.

49 For action in itself is inferior by far to the discipline of intelligence, Dhananjaya. You must seek refuge in intelligence. Those motivated by results are wretched.

50 The man disciplined in intelligence renounces in this world the results of both good and evil actions. Therefore commit yourself to yogic discipline; yogic discipline is skill in actions.

51 For, having abandoned the result produced from action, those who understand, who are disciplined in intelligence, are freed from the bondage of rebirth and achieve a state without disease.

52 When your intelligence emerges from the thicket of delusion, then you will become disenchanted with what is to be heard and has been heard in the Veda.

53 When, turned away from the Veda, your intelligence stands motionless, immovable in concentration, then you will attain yogic discipline.

Arjuna said:

54 O Keshava, how do you describe that man whose mentality is stable, whose concentra-

tion is fixed? What should the man whose thought is settled say? How should he sit? How should he walk?

The Lord said:

55 Partha, when he abandons every desire lodged in the mind, by himself content within the self, then he is called a man of stable mentality.

56 He is called a holy man, settled in thought, whose mind is not disturbed in the midst of sorrows, who has lost the desire for pleasures, whose passion, fear and anger have disappeared.

57 His mentality is stabilized who feels no desire for anything, for getting this or that good or evil, and who neither rejoices in nor loathes anything.

58 When this man, like a tortoise retracting its limbs, entirely withdraws his senses from the objects of sense, his mentality is stabilized.

59 For the embodied being who does not feed on them the objects of sense disappear, except flavour; flavour fades too for the one who has seen the highest.

60 Son of Kunti, even for the man of discernment who strives, the harassing senses forcibly seize the mind.

61 Restraining all the senses, one should sit, yogically disciplined, focused on me; for if one's senses are under control one's mentality is grounded.

62 When a man meditates on the objects of sense he becomes attached to them; from attachment desire is born, from desire anger.

63 Out of anger confusion arises, through confusion memory wanders, from loss of memory the intelligence is destroyed; from the destruction of intelligence a man is lost.

64 But engaging the objects of sense with his senses separated from desire and loathing, and subject to the will of the self, a man who is self-controlled attains calmness.

65 In calm all his miseries are ended, for the intelligence of the man whose mind is calm is immediately stabilized.

66 The undisciplined man has no intelligence, and no capacity to produce anything, and one who has no capacity is without serenity. And how can there be happiness for the man who lacks serenity?

67 For a mind conforming to the wandering senses carries away one's insight, as the wind a ship on the water.

68 Therefore, Great Arm, whoever has entirely withheld the senses from the objects of sense has stabilized his insight.

69 When it is night for all creatures, the man who restrains himself is awake; when creatures are awake, it is night for the perceptive seer.

70 Just as waters enter the sea, which is forever being filled although its depths are unmoving, so the man whom all desires enter in the same way attains peace—but not the desirer of desires.

71 The man who, having abandoned all desires, lives free from longing, unpossessive and unegoistical, approaches peace.

72 This, Partha, is the Brahman state; having attained it, one is not deluded; fixed in it, even at the moment of death one reaches the nirvana of Brahman.[5]

CHAPTER 3

Arjuna said:

1 Krishna, if it is your belief that the way of intelligence is superior to action, then why do you enjoin me, Keshava, to this terrible undertaking?

2 With such equivocal words you seem to confuse my intelligence. Describe clearly an unambiguous way through which I may attain what is best.

The Lord said:

3 Blameless one, I have taught of old that in this world two ways are open: the discipline

of knowledge for Sankhya theorists, and the discipline of action for yogis.

4 A man does not attain freedom from the results of action by abstaining from actions, and he does not approach perfection simply by renunciation.

5 For no one ever, even for a moment, exists without acting; everyone, regardless of their will, is made to perform actions by the constituents which originate from material nature.

6 The man who, having restrained his action organs, then sits with his mind preoccupied with sense objects, is called a self-deluding hypocrite.

7 But the man who, controlling his senses with his mind, undertakes through his action organs the discipline of action without attachment, distinguishes himself, Arjuna.

8 You should perform enjoined action, for action is better than non-action; even the minimum of bodily subsistence would be impossible without action.

9 The entire world is bound by actions; the only exception is action undertaken for sacrificial purposes. Therefore, Son of Kunti, free from attachment, you should perform that kind of action.

10 When he created creatures in the beginning, along with the sacrifice, Prajapati[6] said: 'May you be fruitful by this sacrifice, let this be the cow which produces all you desire.

11 'You should nourish the gods with this so that the gods may nourish you; nourishing each other, you shall achieve the highest good.

12 'For nourished by the sacrifice, the gods will give you the pleasures you desire. The man who enjoys these gifts without repaying them is no more than a thief.'

13 The virtuous who eat the remainder of the sacrifice are released from all faults; the wicked who cook for the sake of themselves consume impurity.

14 Beings exist through food, the origin of food is rain, rain comes from sacrifice, sacrifice derives from action.

15 Know that action originates from Brahman—Brahman whose source is the imperishable. Therefore all-pervading Brahman is eternally established in the sacrifice.

16 Whoever in this world does not turn the wheel thus set in motion, Partha, lives in vain, making a pleasure garden of his senses, intent upon evil.

17 But it is clear that, for the man who delights in the self, and is satisfied with the self, and fulfilled only in the self, there is nothing that has to be done.[7]

18 For him there is no significance whatsoever in what has been done or has not been done in this world, and he has no kind of dependence at all on any being.

19 Therefore, without attachment, always do whatever action has to be done; for it is through acting without attachment that a man attains the highest.

20 Indeed, it was by action alone that King Janaka and others attained perfection. Looking only to what maintains the world, you too must act.

21 Whatever the superior man does, so do the rest; whatever standard he sets, the world follows it.

22 Partha, as for me there is nothing whatever that has to be done in the three worlds; there is nothing unaccomplished to be accomplished. Yet I still engage in action.

23 For were I not to engage tirelessly in action, humans everywhere would follow in my wake, Partha.

24 If I did not engage in action, these worlds would fall into ruin; I should be the instrument of anarchy; I should destroy these creatures.

25 Just as the ignorant act out of attachment to action, Bharata, so the wise should also act, but without attachment, intent upon maintaining the world.

26 The wise man should not disturb the minds of those ignorant people who are attached to action; acting in a disciplined manner himself, he should encourage involvement in all actions.

27 In every case, actions are performed by the constituents of material nature; although the man who is deluded by egotism thinks to himself, 'I am the actor.'

28 But he who knows the principle underlying the division of constituents and actions, understanding that it is constituents that are acting on constituents, is not attached, Great Arm.

29 The person whose knowledge is comprehensive should not agitate those dullards whose knowledge is not so great—those who are deluded by the constituents of material nature and attached to the actions of the constituents.

30 Giving up all actions to me, with your mind on what relates to the self, desireless and not possessive, fight! Your fever is past.

31 Faithful, uncontentious men, who constantly practise this doctrine of mine, are also released from the results of action.

32 But you should know that those who object to this, who do not follow my doctrine, and who are blind to all knowledge, are mindless and lost.

33 Even the one who knows acts in accordance with his own material nature. Creatures conform to material nature—what good will repression do?

34 In the case of a sense, desire and aversion adhere to the object of that sense; you should not fall into the power of those two, for they will block your path.

35 It is better to practise your own inherent duty deficiently than another's duty well. It is better to die conforming to your own duty; the duty of others invites danger.

Arjuna said:

36 So what is it that impels a man to do evil, Varshneya, even unwillingly, as though compelled to it by force?

The Lord said:

37 It is desire, it is anger, produced from the constituent of passion, all-consuming, all-injuring; know that that is the enemy here.

38 As a fire is covered by smoke and a mirror by dust; as an embryo is covered by a sac, this world is enveloped by that.

39 By this perpetual enemy of the wise, by this insatiable fire in the form of desire, knowledge is obscured, Son of Kunti.

40 It is said that the senses, the mind and the intelligence are its locality; having obscured a man's knowledge with these, it deludes the embodied self.

41 Therefore, having first restrained the senses, Bull of the Bharatas, strike down this evil thing, the destroyer of insight and knowledge.

42 They say that the senses are great; the mind is greater than the senses. Yet greater than the mind is the intelligence; but he [i.e. the true self—Ed.] is that which is still greater than the intelligence.

43 So, Great Arm, having learned what is higher than the intelligence, and having strengthened yourself through the self, kill that enemy in the shape of desire, so difficult to pin down.

NOTES

1. Heaven, earth, and the atmosphere or sometimes the lower regions.
2. I.e. the four castes of Indian society: priests (*brahmins*), warrior-nobles, merchants and labourers.
3. The two main tenets of the Sankhya school of philosophy to which the *Gita* appeals are (a) the sepa-

ration of the true self or soul from the natural world, and (b) the explanation of the natural world in terms of three material constituents (*gunas*).

4. The revealed texts of Brahminical religion and mainstream Hinduism.

5. The *Gita* is an eclectic work. Sankhyan and Yogic thought figures large, and in this verse we find a reference to the Buddhist notion of *nirvana* and the Vedantic concept of *Brahman*.

6. The 'Lord of Creatures' . . . protector of life and procreation.

7. The reference here is clearly to the 'pure' or 'true' self, to be distinguished from the empirical ego, the psychological subject of desires, motives etc.

RECOMMENDED READINGS

Texts

Allison, Henry. *Kant's Theory of Freedom*. Cambridge: Cambridge University Press, 1990.

Cummiskey, David. *Kantian Consequentialism* (Oxford: Oxford University Press, 1996).

Herman, Barbara. *The Practice of Moral Judgment* (Cambridge: Harvard University Press, 1993).

Korsgaard, Christine. *Creating the Kingdom of Ends* (Cambridge: Harvard University Press, 1996).

Sherman, Nancy. *Making a Necessity of Virtue* (Cambridge: Cambridge University Press, 1997)

Feminist Perspective

Blum, Lawrence A. "Kant's and Hegel's Moral Rationalism: A Feminist Perspective." *Canadian Journal of Philosophy* 12, no. (182): 287–302.

Cartwright, David. "Kant's View of the Moral Significance of Kindhearted Emotions and the Moral Insignificance of Kant's View." *The Journal of Value Inquiry* 21 (1987): 291–304.

Multicultural Perspective

Crawford, S. Cromwell. *Dilemmas of Life and Death: Hindu Ethics in a North American Context*. Albany: SUNY, 1994.

Radhakrishman, Sarvapalli, *Hindu View of Life*. New York: Macmillan, 1964.

PART VII

❧

MILL AND HARRIET TAYLOR

INTRODUCTION

John Stuart Mill was born in London in 1806. He was educated at home by his father, a prominent economist, and by Jeremy Bentham, both of whom were eager for a subject on whom to test out their educational theories. At three, Mill learned Greek, by seven he was reading the Platonic dialogues. All the while, he was treated to an intensive regimen of mathematics and logic. Later, when he was twenty, Mill experienced a deep depression. He came to recognize that his education had provided him with little opportunity for emotional development, and he turned to Wordsworth and Coleridge, the great Romantic poets, and in other ways tried to compensate for this lack.

In 1823, Mill became clerk with the East India Company and rose to the office of Chief Examiner. Fortunately for Mill's other interests, his work at the East India Company only required a few hours each day on official business. In 1830, he was introduced to Harriet Taylor, who was then married with two children. She became his closest friend and confidant, and Mill credits her with inspiring much of his own thinking and writing. This unconventional relationship, lasting twenty years, estranged Mill from his family and most of their friends. In 1851, Mill married Taylor, two years after her husband died. Seven years later, Harriet died from tuberculosis, probably contracted from Mill, who was suffering from the disease. In 1865, Mill was elected to Parliament, despite his refusal to campaign, and served one term.

Mill published *On Liberty* in 1859, claiming that more than anything else he had written, this book was a joint production with Harriet Taylor. In 1863, he published *Utilitarianism*, and in 1869, *The Subjection of Women*. Harriet Taylor's *Enfranchisement of Women* was published earlier in 1851.[1] Cared for in his last years by his stepdaughter, Helen, Mill died in Avignon in 1873 and was buried alongside Harriet.

In the selection from *Utilitarianism,* Mill argues that actions are right in proportion as they tend to promote happiness: wrong as they tend to produce the reverse of happiness. By happiness, Mill means pleasure and the absence of pain: by unhappiness, pain and the privation of pleasure. Mill differs from Bentham in maintaining that pleasures can be evaluated in terms of quality as well as quantity. According to Mill, the more desirable pleasures are those that would be preferred by competent judges who have experienced the alternatives. Applying this standard for evaluating pleasures, Mill contends that it is better to be a human being dissatisfied than a pig satisfied. While most people tend to share Mill's preference for being human, it is not clear how that preference could be supported by a competent judge who had experienced both alternatives. Experiencing what it is like to be a pig is not the same as imagining what it is like to be a human trapped in a pig's body!

In the selections from *The Subjection of Women,* Mill contends that the subjection of women was never justified but was imposed on them because they were physically weaker than men and that later this subjection was confirmed by law. Mill argues that society must remove the legal restrictions that deny women the same opportunities that are enjoyed by men. However, Mill does not consider whether, because of past discrimination against women, it may be necessary to do more than simply remove legal restrictions to provide women with the same opportunities that men enjoy. He doesn't consider whether positive assistance may also be required.

Usually it is not enough simply to remove unequal restrictions to make a competition fair among those who have been participating. Positive assistance to those who have been disadvantaged in the past may also be required, as would be the case if one were running a race in which one was unfairly impeded by having to carry a ten-pound weight. Similarly, positive assistance, such as affirmative action programs, may be necessary if women who have been disadvantaged in the past are now for the first time to enjoy equal opportunity with men.

In *The Subjection of Women,* Mill does not see any need to compensate women for the work they do in the home, whereas in the selection from her *Enfranchisement of Women,* Taylor does see such a need. She contends that it would be preferable "if women both earned and had a right to possess, a part of the income of the family." In this work, Taylor also speaks out more strongly in favor of married women having a life and career of their own. In these respects, Taylor is clearly more in accord with present day feminism than Mill is.

In "Utility and Perfect Equality," Maria Morales argues that a correct understanding of Mill's conception of utility requires taking the fundamental aim of a utilitarian ethic to be the development of human beings' sympathetic dispositions and sentiments. To be a Millian utilitarian, it is not enough that our actions tend to promote the general happiness; our character must also be constituted in a certain way. Morales further points out that, according to Mill, human happiness required perfect equality, and so he was opposed to the unequal gender roles in society as being harmful to both men and women.

Mo Tzu was born of very humble origins in 470 B.C. shortly after Confucius' death, and he went on to found a rival school of philosophy known as Moism. In the selection from Mo Tzu's *Universal Love* similarities to utilitarianism are striking. In Moism, as in utilitarianism, actions are evaluated in terms of their overall consequences. Mo Tzu argues that the best overall consequences are achieved through the practice of universal, mutual love. He goes on to consider various objections to the practice of universal, mutual love and finds them wanting. There are also obvious similarities between Moism and the later Christian doctrine of universal love.

Historically, however, Moism did not fair very well. Up until the beginning of the Han Empire, Moism, and its doctrine of universal mutual love, was the main rival to Confucianism, with its emphasis on particular duties to particular people, but after the third century B.C., other views, such as Taoism, sprang up to rival Confucianism, and Moism all but disappeared, only to be revived in the nineteenth and twentieth centuries. Two factors that contributed to the decline of Moism were the turning of Confucianism into a state cult during the Han dynasty, and Moism's uncompromising condemnation of war, which obviously did not endear it to the powers that be. For better or for worse, the modern revival has not endorsed Moism's uncompromising condemnation of war.

NOTES

1. For the discussion of the authorship of this work, see Alice Rossi's introductory essay to John Stuart Mill and Harriet Taylor Mill, *Essays on Sex Equality* (Chicago, 1970). p.41ff.

25. UTILITARIANISM

JOHN STUART MILL

CHAPTER I: GENERAL REMARKS

There are few circumstances among those which make up the present condition of human knowledge more unlike what might have been expected, or more significant of the backward state in which speculation on the most important subjects still lingers, than the little progress which has been made in the decision of the controversy respecting the criterion of right and wrong. From the dawn of philosophy, the question concerning the *summum bonum,* or, what is the same thing, concerning the foundation of morality, has been accounted the main problem in speculative thought, has occupied the most gifted intellects and divided them into sects and schools carrying on a vigorous warfare against one another. And after more than two thousand years the same discussions continue, philosophers are still ranged under the same contending banners, and neither thinkers nor mankind at large seem nearer to being unanimous on the subject than when the youth Socrates listened to the old Protagoras and asserted (if Plato's dialogue be grounded on a real conversation) the theory of utilitarianism against the popular morality of the so-called sophist.

It is true that similar confusion and uncertainty and, in some cases, similar discordance exist respecting the first principles of all the sciences, not excepting that which is deemed the most certain of them—mathematics, without much impairing, generally indeed without impairing at all, the trustworthiness of the con-clusions of those sciences. An apparent anomaly, the explanation of which is that the detailed doctrines of a science are not usually deduced from, nor depend for their evidence upon, what are called its first principles. Were it not so, there would be no science more precarious, or whose conclusions were more insufficiently made out, than algebra, which derives none of its certainty from what are commonly taught to learners as its elements, since these, as laid down by some of its most eminent teachers, are as full of fictions as English law, and of mysteries as theology. The truths which are ultimately accepted as the first principles of a science are really the last results of metaphysical analysis practiced on the elementary notions with which the science is conversant; and their relation to the science is not that of foundations to an edifice, but of roots to a tree, which may perform their office equally well though they be never dug down to and exposed to light. But though in science the particular truths precede the general theory, the contrary might be expected to be the case with a practical art, such as morals or legislation. All action is for the sake of some end, and rules of action, it seems natural to suppose, must take their whole character and color from the end to which they are subservient. When we engage in a pursuit, a clear and precise conception of what we are pursuing would seem to be the first thing we need, instead of the last we are to look forward to. A test of right and wrong must be the means, one would think, of ascertaining what is right or wrong, and not a consequence of having already ascertained it.

The difficulty is not avoided by having recourse to the popular theory of a natural fac-

Reprinted from *Utilitarianism*. First published in 1863.

ulty, a sense of instinct, informing us of right and wrong. For—besides that the existence of such a moral instinct is itself one of the matters in dispute—those believers in it who have any pretensions to philosophy have been obliged to abandon the idea that it discerns what is right or wrong in the particular case in hand, as our other senses discern the sight or sound actually present. Our moral faculty, according to all those of its interpreters who are entitled to the name of thinkers, supplies us only with the general principles of moral judgments; it is a branch of our reason, not of our sensitive faculty, and must be looked to for the abstract doctrines of morality, not for perception of it in the concrete. The intuitive, no less than what may be termed the inductive, school of ethics insists on the necessity of general laws. They both agree that the morality of an individual action is not a question of direct perception, but of the application of a law to an individual case. They recognize also, to a great extent, the same moral laws, but differ as to their evidence and the source from which they derive their authority. According to the one opinion, the principles of morals are evident a priori, requiring nothing to command assent except that the meaning of the terms be understood. According to the other doctrine, right and wrong, as well as truth and falsehood, are questions of observation and experience. But both hold equally that morality must be deduced from principles; and the intuitive school affirm as strongly as the inductive that there is a science of morals. Yet they seldom attempt to make out a list of the a priori principles which are to serve as the premises of the science; still more rarely do they make any effort to reduce those various principles to one first principle or common ground of obligation. They either assume the ordinary precepts of morals as of a priori authority, or they lay down as the common groundwork of those maxims some generality much less obviously authoritative than the maxims themselves, and which has never succeeded in gaining popular acceptance. Yet to support their pretensions there ought either to be some one fundamental principle or law at the root of all morality, or, if there be several, there should be a determinate order of precedence among them; and the one principle, or the rule for deciding between the various principles when they conflict, ought to be self-evident.

To inquire how far the bad effects of this deficiency have been mitigated in practice, or to what extent the moral beliefs of mankind have been vitiated or made uncertain by the absence of any distinct recognition of an ultimate standard, would imply a complete survey and criticism of past and present ethical doctrine. It would, however, be easy to show that whatever steadiness or consistency these moral beliefs have attained has been mainly due to the tacit influence of a standard not recognized. Although the non-existence of an acknowledged first principle has made ethics not so much a guide as a consecration of men's actual sentiments, still, as men's sentiments, both of favor and of aversion, are greatly influenced by what they suppose to be the effects of things upon their happiness, the principle of utility, or, as Bentham latterly called it, the greatest happiness principle, has had a large share in forming the moral doctrines even of those who most scornfully reject its authority. Nor is there any school of thought which refuses to admit that the influence of actions on happiness is a most material and even predominant consideration in many of the details of morals, however unwilling to acknowledge it as the fundamental principle of morality and the source of moral obligation. I might go much further and say that to all those a priori moralists who deem it necessary to argue at all, utilitarian arguments are indispensable. It is not my present purpose to criticize these thinkers; but I cannot help referring, for illustration, to a systematic treatise by one of the most illustrious of them, the *Metaphysics of Ethics* by Kant. This remarkable man, whose system of thought will long remain one of the landmarks in the history of philosophical speculation, does, in the treatise in question, lay down a universal first principle as the origin and ground of moral obligation; it is this: "So act that the rule on which thou actest would admit of being adopted as a law by all rational beings." But when he begins to deduce from this precept any of the actual duties of morality, he fails, almost grotesquely, to show that there would be any contradiction, any logical (not to say physical) impossibility, in the adoption by all rational beings of the most outrageously immoral rules of conduct. All he shows is that the *consequences* of their universal adoption would be such as no one would choose to incur.

On the present occasion, I shall, without further discussion of the other theories, attempt to contribute something toward the understanding and appreciation of the "utilitarian" or "happiness" theory, and toward such proof as it is susceptible of. It is evident that this cannot be proof in the ordinary and popular meaning of the term. Questions of ultimate ends are not amenable to direct proof. Whatever can be proved to be good must be so by being shown to be a means to something admitted to be good without proof. The medical art is proved to be good by its conducing to health; but how is it possible to prove that health is good? The art of music is good, for the reason, among others, that it produces pleasure; but what proof is it possible to give that pleasure is good? If, then, it is asserted that there is a comprehensive formula, including all things which are in themselves good, and that whatever else is good is not so as an end but as a means, the formula may be accepted or rejected, but is not a subject of what is commonly understood by proof. We are not, however, to infer that its acceptance or rejection must depend on blind impulse or arbitrary choice. There is a larger meaning of the word "proof," in which this question is as amenable to it as any other of the disputed questions of philosophy. The subject is within the cognizance of the rational faculty; and neither does that faculty deal with it solely in the way of intuition. Con-

siderations may be presented capable of determining the intellect either to give or withhold its assent to the doctrine; and this is equivalent to proof.

We shall examine presently of what nature are these considerations; in what manner they apply to the case, and what rational grounds, therefore, can be given for accepting or rejecting the utilitarian formula. But it is a preliminary condition of rational acceptance or rejection that the formula should be correctly understood. I believe that the very imperfect notion ordinarily formed of its meaning is the chief obstacle which impedes its reception, and that, could it be cleared even from only the grosser misconceptions, the question would be greatly simplified and a large proportion of its difficulties removed. Before, therefore, I attempt to enter into the philosophical grounds which can be given for assenting to the utilitarian standard, I shall offer some illustrations of the doctrine itself, with the view of showing more clearly what it is, distinguishing it from what it is not, and disposing of such of the practical objections to it as either originate in, or are closely connected with, mistaken interpretations of its meaning. Having thus prepared the ground, I shall afterwards endeavor to throw such light as I can call upon the question considered as one of philosophical theory.

CHAPTER II: WHAT UTILITARIANISM IS

A passing remark is all that needs be given to the ignorant blunder of supposing that those who stand up for utility as the test of right and wrong use the term in that restricted and merely colloquial sense in which utility is opposed to pleasure. An apology is due to the philosophical opponents of utilitarianism for even the momentary appearance of confounding them with anyone capable of so absurd a misconception; which is the more extraordinary, inasmuch as the contrary accusation, of referring everything to pleasure, and that, too, in its grossest form, is another of the common charges against utilitarianism: and, as has been pointedly remarked by an able writer, the same sort of persons, and often the very same persons, denounce the theory "as impracticably dry when the word 'utility' precedes the word 'pleasure,' and as too practically voluptuous when the word 'pleasure' precedes the word 'utility.'" Those who know anything about the matter are aware that every writer, from Epicurus to Bentham, who maintained the theory of utility meant by it, not something to be contradistinguished from pleasure, but pleasure itself, together with exemption from pain; and instead of opposing the useful to the agreeable or the ornamental, have always declared that the useful means these, among other things. Yet the common herd, including the herd of writers, not only in newspapers and periodicals, but in books of weight and pretension, are perpetually falling into this shallow mistake. Having caught up the word "utilitarian," while knowing nothing whatever about it but its sound, they habitually express by it the rejection or the neglect of pleasure in some of its forms: of beauty, of ornament, or of amusement. Nor is the term thus ignorantly misapplied solely in disparagement, but occasionally in compliment, as though it implied superiority to frivolity and the mere pleasures of the moment. And this perverted use is the only one in which the word is popularly known, and the one from which the new generation are acquiring their sole notion of its meaning. Those who introduced the word, but who had for many years discontinued it as a distinctive appellation, may well feel themselves called upon to resume it if by doing so they can hope to contribute anything toward rescuing it from this utter degradation.[1]

The creed which accepts as the foundation of morals "utility" or the "greatest happiness principle" holds that actions are right in proportion as they tend to promote happiness; wrong as they tend to produce the reverse of happiness. By happiness is intended pleasure and the absence of pain; by unhappiness, pain and the privation of pleasure. To give a clear view of the moral standard set up by the theory, much more requires to be said; in particular, what things it includes in the ideas of pain and pleasure, and to what extent this is left an open question. But these supplementary explanations do not affect the theory of life on which this theory of morality is grounded—namely, that pleasure and freedom from pain are the only things desirable as ends; and that all desirable things (which are as numerous in the utilitarian as in any other scheme) are desirable either for pleasure inherent in themselves or as means to the promotion of pleasure and the prevention of pain.

Now such a theory of life excites in many minds, and among them in some of the most estimable in feeling and purpose, inveterate dislike. To suppose that life has (as they express it) no higher end than pleasure—no better and nobler object of desire and pursuit—they designate as utterly mean and groveling, as a doctrine worthy only of swine, to whom the followers of Epicurus were, at a very early period, contemptuously likened; and modern holders of the doctrine are occasionally made the subject of equally polite comparisons by its German, French, and English assailants.

When thus attacked, the Epicureans have always answered that it is not they, but their accusers, who represent human nature in a degrading light, since the accusation supposes human beings to be capable of no pleasures except those of which swine are capable. If this supposition were true, the charge could not be gainsaid, but would then be no longer an imputation; for if the sources of pleasure were precisely the same to human beings and to swine, the rule of life which is good enough for the one would be good enough for the other. The comparison of the Epicurean life to that of beasts is felt as degrading, precisely because a beast's pleasures do not satisfy a human being's conceptions of happiness. Human beings have faculties more elevated than the animal appetites and, when once made conscious of them, do not regard anything as happiness which does not include their gratification. I do not, indeed, consider the Epicureans to have been by any means faultless in drawing out their scheme of consequences from the utilitarian principle. To do this in any sufficient manner, many Stoic, as well as Christian, elements require to be included. But there is no known Epicurean theory of life which does not assign to the pleasures of the intellect, of the feelings and imagination, and of the moral sentiments a much higher value as pleasures than to those of mere sensation. It must be admitted, however, that utilitarian writers in general have placed the superiority of mental over bodily pleasures chiefly in the greater permanency, safety, uncostliness, etc., of the former—that is, in their circumstantial advantages rather than in their intrinsic nature. And on all these points utilitarians have fully proved their case; but they might have taken the other and, as it may be called, higher ground with entire consistency. It is quite compatible with the principle of utility to recognize the fact that some kinds of pleasure are more desirable and more valuable than others. It would be absurd that, while in estimating all other things quality is considered as well as quantity, the estimation of pleasure should be supposed to depend on quantity alone.

If I am asked what I mean by difference of quality in pleasures, or what makes one pleasure more valuable than another, merely as a pleasure, except its being greater in amount, there is but one possible answer. Of two pleasures, if there be one to which all or almost all who have experience of both give a decided preference, irrespective of any feeling of moral obligation to prefer it, that is the more desirable pleasure. If one of the two is, by those who are competently acquainted with both, placed so far above the other that they prefer it, even though knowing it to be attended with a greater amount of discontent, and would not resign it for any quantity of the other pleasure which their nature is capable of, we are justified in ascribing to the preferred enjoyment a superiority in quality so far outweighing quantity as to render it, in comparison, of small account.

Now it is an unquestionable fact that those who are equally acquainted with and equally capable of appreciating and enjoying both do give a most marked preference to the manner of existence which employs their higher faculties. Few human creatures would consent to be changed into any of the lower animals for a promise of the fullest allowance of a beast's pleasures; no intelligent human being would consent to be a fool, no instructed person would be an ignoramus, no person of feeling and conscience would be selfish and base, even though they should be persuaded that the fool, the dunce, or the rascal is better satisfied with his lot than they are with theirs. They would not resign what they possess more than he for the most complete satisfaction of all the desires which they have in common with him. If they ever fancy they would, it is only in cases of unhappiness so extreme that to escape from it they would exchange their lot for almost any other, however undesirable in their own eyes. A being of higher faculties requires more to make him happy, is capable probably of more acute suffering, and certainly accessible to it at more points, than one of an inferior type; but in spite of these liabilities, he can never really wish to sink into what he feels to be a lower grade of existence. We may give what explanation we please of this unwillingness; we may attribute it to pride, a name which is given indiscriminately to some of the most and to some of the least estimable feelings of which mankind are capable; we may refer it to the love of liberty and personal independence, an appeal to which was with the Stoics one of the most effective means for the inculcation of it; to the love of power or to the love of excitement, both of which do really enter into and contribute to it; but its most appropriate appellation is a sense of dignity, which all human beings possess in one form or other, and in some, though by no means in exact, proportion to their higher faculties, and which is so essential a part of the happiness of those in whom it is strong that nothing which conflicts with it could be otherwise than momentarily an object of desire to them. Whoever supposes that this preference takes place at a sacrifice of happiness—that the superior being, in anything like equal circumstances, is not happier than the inferior—confounds the two very different ideas of happiness and content. It is indisputable that the being whose capacities of enjoyment are low has the greatest chance of having them fully satisfied; and a highly endowed being will always feel that any happiness which he can look for, as the world is constituted, is imperfect. But he can learn to bear its imperfections, if they are at all bearable; and they will not make him envy the being who is indeed unconscious of the imperfections, but only because he feels not at all the good which those imperfections qualify. It is better to be a human being dissatisfied than a pig satisfied; better to be Socrates dissatisfied than a fool satisfied. And if the fool, or the pig, are of a different opinion, it is because they only know their own side of the question. The other party to the comparison knows both sides.

It may be objected that many who are capable of the higher pleasures occasionally, under the influence of temptation, postpone them to the lower. But this is quite compatible with a full appreciation of the intrinsic superiority of the higher. Men often, from infirmity of character, make their election for the nearer good, though they know it to be the less valuable; and this no less when the choice is between two bodily pleasures than when it is between bodily and mental. They pursue sensual indulgences to the injury of health, though perfectly aware that health is the greater good. It may be further objected that many who begin with youthful enthusiasm for everything noble, as they advance in years, sink into indolence and selfishness. But I do not believe that those who undergo this very common change voluntarily choose the lower description of pleasures in preference to the higher. I believe that, before they devote themselves exclusively to the one, they have already become incapable of the other. Capacity for the nobler feelings is in most natures a very tender plant, easily killed, not only by hostile influences, but by mere want of sustenance; and in the majority of young persons it speedily dies away if the occupations to which their position in life has devoted them, and the society into which it has thrown them, are not favorable to keeping that higher capacity in exercise. Men lose their high aspirations as they lose their intellectual tastes, because they have not time or opportunity for indulging them; and they addict themselves to inferior pleasures, not because they deliberately prefer them, but because they are either the only ones to which they have access or the only ones which they are any longer capable of enjoying. It may be questioned whether anyone who has remained equally susceptible to both classes of pleasures ever knowingly and calmly preferred the lower, though many, in all ages, have broken down in an ineffectual attempt to combine both.

From this verdict of the only competent judges, I apprehend there can be no appeal. On a question which is the best worth having of two pleasures, or which of two modes of existence is the most grateful to the feelings, apart from its moral attributes and from its consequences, the judgment of those who are qualified by knowledge of both, or, if they differ, that of the majority among them, must be admitted as final. And there needs be the less hesitation to accept this judgment respecting the quality of pleasures, since there is no other tribunal to be referred to even on the question of quantity. What means are there of determining which is the acutest of two pains, or the intensest of two pleasurable sensations, except the general suffrage of those who are familiar with both? Neither pains nor pleasures are homogeneous, and pain is always heterogeneous with pleasure. What is there to decide whether a particular pleasure is worth purchasing at the cost of a particular pain, except the feelings and judgment of the experienced? When, therefore, those feelings and judgment declare the pleasures derived from the higher faculties to be preferable *in kind,* apart from the question of intensity, to those of which the animal nature, disjoined from the higher faculties, is susceptible, they are entitled on this subject to the same regard.

I have dwelt on this point as being a necessary part of a perfectly just conception of utility or happiness considered as the directive rule of human conduct. But it is by no means an indispensable condition to the acceptance of the utilitarian standard; for that standard is not the agent's own greatest happiness, but the greatest amount of happiness altogether; and if it may possibly be doubted whether a noble character is always the happier for its nobleness, there can be no doubt that it makes other people happier, and that the world in general is immensely a gainer by it. Utilitarianism, therefore, could only attain its end by the general cultivation of nobleness of character, even if each individual were only benefited by the nobleness of others, and his own, so far as happiness is concerned, were a sheer deduction from the benefit. But the bare enunciation of such an absurdity as this last renders refutation superfluous.

According to the greatest happiness principle, as above explained, the ultimate end, with reference to and for the sake of which all other things are desirable—whether we are considering our own good or that of other people—is an existence exempt as far as possible from pain, and as rich as possible in enjoyments, both in point of quantity and quality; the test of quality and the rule for measuring it against quantity being the preference felt by those who, in their opportunities of experience, to which must be added their habits of self-consciousness and self-observation, are best furnished with the means of comparison. This, being according to the utilitarian opinion the end of human action, is necessarily also the standard of morality, which may accordingly be defined "the rules and precepts for human conduct," by the observance of which an existence such as has been described might be, to the greatest extent possible, secured to all mankind; and not to them only, but, so far as the nature of things admits, to the whole sentient creation. . . .

Unquestionably it is possible to do without happiness; it is done involuntarily by nineteen-twentieths of mankind, even in those parts of our present world which are least deep in barbarism; and it often has to be done voluntarily by the hero or the martyr, for the sake of something which he prizes more than his individual happiness. But this something, what is it, unless the happiness of others or some of the requisites of happiness? It is noble to be capable of resigning entirely one's own portion of happiness, or chances of it; but, after all, this self-sacrifice must be for some end; it is not its own end; and if we are told that its end is not happiness but virtue, which is better than happiness, I ask, would the sacrifice be made if the hero or martyr did not believe that it would earn for others immunity from similar sacrifices? Would it be made if he thought that his renunciation of happiness for himself would produce no fruit for any of his fellow creatures, but to make their lot like his and place them also in the condition of persons who have renounced happiness? All honor to those who can abnegate for themselves the personal enjoyment of life when by such renunciation they contribute worthily to increase the amount of happiness in the world; but he who does it or professes to do it for any other purpose is no more deserving of admiration than the ascetic mounted on his pillar. He may be an inspiriting proof of what men *can* do, but assuredly not an example of what they *should.*

Though it is only in a very imperfect state of the world's arrangements that anyone can best serve the happiness of others by the absolute sacrifice of his own, yet, so long as the world is in that imperfect state, I fully acknowledge that the readiness to make such a sacrifice is the highest virtue which can be found in man. I will add that in this condition of the world, paradoxical as the assertion may be, the conscious ability to do without happiness gives the best prospect of realizing such happiness as is attainable. For nothing except that consciousness can raise a person above the chances of life by making him feel that, let fate and fortune do their worst, they have not power to subdue him; which, once felt, frees him from excess of anxiety concerning the evils of life and enables him, like many a Stoic in the worst times of the Roman Empire, to cultivate in tranquility the sources of satisfaction accessible to him, without concerning himself about the uncertainty of their duration any more than about their inevitable end.

Meanwhile, let utilitarians never cease to claim the morality of self-devotion as a possession which belongs by as good a right to them as either to the Stoic or to the Transcendentalist. The utilitarian morality does recognize in human beings the power of sacrificing their own greatest good for the good of others. It only refuses to admit that the sacrifice is itself a good. A sacrifice which does not increase or tend to increase the sum total of happiness, it considers as wasted. The only self-renunciation which it applauds is devotion to the happiness, or to some of the means of happiness, of others, either of mankind collectively or of individuals within the limits imposed by the collective interests of mankind.

I must again repeat what the assailants of utilitarianism seldom have the justice to acknowledge, that the happiness which forms the utilitarian standard of what is right in conduct is not the agent's own happiness but that of all concerned. As between his own happiness and that of others, utilitarianism requires him to be as strictly impartial as a disinterested and benevolent spectator. In the golden rule of Jesus of Nazareth, we read the complete spirit of the ethics of utility. "To do as you would be done by," and "to love your neighbor as yourself," constitute the ideal perfection of utilitarian moral-

ity. As the means of making the nearest approach to this ideal, utility would enjoin, first, that laws and social arrangements should place the happiness or (as, speaking practically, it may be called) the interest of every individual as nearly as possible in harmony with the interest of the whole; and, secondly, that education and opinion, which have so vast a power over human character, should so use that power as to establish in the mind of every individual an indissoluble association between his own happiness and the good of the whole, especially between his own happiness and the practice of such modes of conduct, negative and positive, as regard for the universal happiness prescribes; so that not only he may be unable to conceive the possibility of happiness to himself, consistently with conduct opposed to the general good, but also that a direct impulse to promote the general good may be in every individual one of the habitual motives of action, and the sentiments connected therewith may fill a large and prominent place in every human being's sentient existence. If the impugners of the utilitarian morality represented it to their own minds in this its true character, I know not what recommendation possessed by any other morality they could possibly affirm to be wanting to it; what more beautiful or more exalted developments of human nature any other ethical system can be supposed to foster, or what springs of action, not accessible to the utilitarian, such systems rely on for giving effect to their mandates.

The objectors to utilitarianism cannot always be charged with representing it in a discreditable light. On the contrary, those among them who entertain anything like a just idea of its disinterested character sometimes find fault with its standard as being too high for humanity. They say it is exacting too much to require that people shall always act from the inducement of promoting the general interests of society. But this is to mistake the very meaning of a standard of morals and confound the rule of action with the motive of it. It is the business of ethics to tell us what are our duties, or by what test we may know them; but no system of ethics requires that the sole motive of all we do shall be a feeling of duty; on the contrary, ninety-nine hundredths of all our actions are done from other motives, and rightly so done if the rule of duty does not condemn them. It is the more unjust to utilitarianism that this particular misapprehension should be made a ground of objection to it, inasmuch as utilitarian moralists have gone beyond almost all others in affirming that the motive has nothing to do with the morality of the action, though much with the worth of the agent. He who saves a fellow creature from drowning does what is morally right, whether his motive be duty or the hope of being paid for his trouble; he who betrays the friend that trusts him is guilty of a crime, even if his object be to serve another friend to whom he is under greater obligations.[2] But to speak only of actions done from the motive of duty, and in direct obedience to principle: it is a misapprehension of the utilitarian mode of thought to conceive it as implying that people should fix their minds upon so wide a generality as the world, or society at large. The great majority of good actions are intended not for the benefit of the world, but for that of individuals, of which the good of the world is made up; and the thoughts of the most virtuous man need not on these occasions travel beyond the particular persons concerned, except so far as is necessary to assure himself that in benefiting them he is not violating the rights, that is, the legitimate and authorized expectations, of anyone else. The multiplication of happiness is, according to the utilitarian ethics, the object of virtue: the occasions on which any person (except one in a thousand) has it in his power to do this on an extended scale—in other words, to be a public benefactor—are but exceptional; and on these occasions alone is he called on to consider public utility; in every other case, private utility, the interest or happiness of some few persons, is all he has to attend to. Those alone the influence of whose actions extends to society in general need concern themselves habitually about so large an object. In the case of abstinences indeed—of things which people forbear to do from moral considerations, though the consequences in the particular case might be beneficial—it would be unworthy of an intelligent agent not to be consciously aware that the action is of a class which, if practiced generally, would be generally injurious, and that this is the ground of the obligation to abstain from it. The amount of regard for the public interest implied in this recognition is no greater than is demanded by every system of morals, for they all enjoin to abstain from whatever is manifestly pernicious to society. . . .

It may not be superfluous to notice a few more of the common misapprehensions of utilitarian ethics, even those which are so obvious and gross that it might appear impossible for any person of candor and intelligence to fall into them; since persons, even of considerable mental endowment, often give themselves so little trouble to understand the bearings of any opinion against which they entertain a prejudice, and men are in general so little conscious of this voluntary ignorance as a defect that the vulgarest misunderstandings of ethical doctrines are continually met with in the deliberate writings of persons of the greatest pretensions both to high principle and to philosophy. We not uncommonly hear the doctrine of utility inveighed against as a *godless* doctrine. If it be necessary to say anything at all against so mere an assumption, we may say that the question depends upon what idea we have formed of the moral character of the Deity. If it be a true belief that God desires, above all things, the happiness of his creatures, and that this was his purpose in their creation, utility is not only not a godless doctrine, but more profoundly religious than any other. If it be meant that utilitarianism does not recognize the revealed will of God as the supreme law of morals, I answer that a utilitarian who believes in the perfect goodness and wisdom of *God* necessarily believes that whatever God has thought fit to reveal on the subject of morals must fulfill the requirements of utility in a supreme degree. But others besides utilitarians have been of opinion that the Christian revelation was intended, and is fitted, to inform the hearts and minds of mankind with a spirit which should enable them to find for themselves what is right, and incline them to do it when found, rather than to tell them, except in a very general way, what it is; and that we need a doctrine of ethics, carefully followed out, to *interpret* to us the will of God. Whether this opinion is correct or not, it is superfluous here to discuss; since whatever aid religion, either natural or revealed, can afford to ethical investigation is as open to the utilitarian moralist as to any other. He can use it as the testimony of God to the usefulness or hurtfulness of any given course of action by as good a right as others can use it for the indication of a transcendental law having no connection with usefulness or with happiness. . . .

Again, defenders of utility often find themselves called upon to reply to such objections as this—that there is not time, previous to action, for calculating and weighing the effects of any line of conduct on the general happiness. This is exactly as if anyone were to say that it is impossible to guide our conduct by Christianity because there is not time, on every occasion on which anything has to be done, to read through the Old and New Testaments. The answer to the objection is that there has been ample time, namely, the whole past duration of the human species. During all that time mankind have been learning by experience the tendencies of actions; on which experience all the prudence as well as all the morality of life are dependent. People talk as if the commencement of this course of experience had hitherto been put off, and as if, at the moment when some man feels tempted to meddle with the property or life of another, he had to begin considering for the first time whether murder and theft are injurious to human happiness. Even then I do not think that he would find the question very puzzling; but, at all events, the matter is now done to his hand. It is truly a whimsical supposition that, if mankind were agreed in considering utility to be the test of morality, they would remain without any agreement as to what *is* useful, and would take no measures for having their notions on the subject taught to the young and enforced by law and opinion. There is no difficulty in proving any ethical standard whatever to work ill if we suppose universal idiocy to be conjoined with it; but on any hypothesis short of that, mankind must by this time have acquired positive beliefs as to the effects of some actions on their happiness; and the beliefs which have thus come down are the rules of morality for the multitude, and for the philosopher until he has succeeded in finding better. That philosophers might easily do this, even now, on many subjects; that the received code of ethics is by no means of divine right; and that mankind have still much to learn as to the effects of actions on the general happiness, I admit or rather earnestly maintain. The corollaries from the principle of utility, like the precepts of every practical art, admit of indefinite improvement, and, in a progressive state of the human mind, their improvement is perpetually going on. But to consider the rules of morality as improvable is one thing; to pass over the intermediate generalization entirely and endeavor to test each individual action directly by the first principle is another. It is a strange notion that the acknowledgment of a first principle is inconsistent with the admission of secondary ones. To inform a traveler respecting the place of his ultimate destination is not to forbid the use of landmarks and direction-posts on the way. The proposition that happiness is the end and aim of morality does not mean that no road ought to be laid down to that goal, or that persons going thither should not be advised to take one direction rather than another. Men really ought to leave off talking a kind of nonsense on this subject, which they would neither talk nor listen to on other matters of practical concernment. Nobody argues that the art of navigation is not founded on astronomy because sailors cannot wait to calculate the Nautical Almanac. Being rational creatures, they go to sea with it ready calculated; and all rational creatures go out upon the sea of life with their minds made up on the common questions of right and wrong, as well as on many of the far more difficult questions of wise and foolish. And this, as long as foresight is a human quality, it is to be presumed they will continue to do. Whatever we adopt as the fundamental principle of morality, we require subordinate principles to apply it by; the impossibility of doing without them, being common to all systems, can afford no argument against any one in particular; but gravely to argue as if no such secondary principles could be had, and as if mankind had remained till now, and always must remain, without drawing any general conclusions from the experience of human life is as high a pitch, I think, as absurdity has ever reached in philosophical controversy.

The remainder of the stock arguments against utilitarianism mostly consist in laying to its charge the common infirmities of human nature, and the general difficulties which embarrass conscientious persons in shaping their course through life. We are told that a utilitarian will be apt to make his own particular case an exception to moral rules, and, when under temptation, will see a utility in the breach of a rule, greater than he will see in its observance. But is utility the only creed which is able to furnish us with excuses for evil-doing and means of cheating our own conscience? They are afforded in abundance by all doctrines which recognize as a fact in morals the existence of conflicting considerations, which all doctrines do that have been believed by sane persons. It is not the fault of any creed, but of the complicated nature of human affairs, that rules of conduct cannot be so framed as to require no exceptions, and that hardly any kind of action can safely be laid down as either always obligatory or always condemnable. There is no ethical creed which does not temper the rigidity of its laws by giving a certain latitude, under the moral responsibility of

the agent, for accommodation to peculiarities of circumstances; and under every creed, at the opening thus made, self-deception and dishonest casuistry get in. There exists no moral system under which there do not arise unequivocal cases of conflicting obligation. These are the real difficulties, the knotty points both in the theory of ethics and in the conscientious guidance of personal conduct. They are overcome practically, with greater or with less success, according to the intellect and virtue of the individual; but it can hardly be pretended that anyone will be the less qualified for dealing with them, from possessing an ultimate standard to which conflicting rights and duties can be referred. If utility is the ultimate source of moral obligations, utility may be invoked to decide between them when their demands are incompatible. Though the application of the standard may be difficult, it is better than none at all; while in other systems, the moral laws all claiming independent authority, there is no common umpire entitled to interfere between them; their claims to precedence one over another rest on little better than sophistry, and, unless determined, as they generally are, by the unacknowledged influence of consideration of utility, afford a free scope for the action of personal desires and partialities. We must remember that only in these cases of conflict between secondary principles is it requisite that first principles should be appealed to. There is no case of moral obligation in which some secondary principle is not involved; and if only one, there can seldom be any real doubt which one it is, in the mind of any person by whom the principle itself is recognized.

Chapter IV: Of What Sort of Proof the Principle of Utility Is Susceptible

It has already been remarked that questions of ultimate ends do not admit of proof, in the ordinary acceptation of the term. To be incapable of proof by reasoning is common to all first principles; to the first premises of our knowledge, as well as to those of our conduct. But the former, being matters of fact, may be the subject of a direct appeal to the faculties which judge of fact—namely, our senses and our internal consciousness. Can an appeal be made, to the same faculties on questions of practical ends? Or by what other faculty is cognizance taken of them?

Questions about ends are, in other words, questions about what things are desirable. The utilitarian doctrine is that happiness is desirable, and the only thing desirable, as an end; all other things being only desirable as means to that end. What ought to be required of this doctrine— what conditions is it requisite that the doctrine should fulfill—to make good its claim to be believed?

The only proof capable of being given that an object is visible, is that people actually see it. The only proof that a sound is audible, is that people hear it: and so of the other sources of our experience. In like manner, I apprehend, the sole evidence it is possible to produce that anything is desirable, is that people do actually desire it. If the end which the utilitarian doctrine proposes to itself were not, in theory and in practice, acknowledged to be an end, nothing could ever convince any person that it was so. No reason can be given why the general happiness is desirable, except that each person, so far as he believes it to be attainable, desires his own happiness. This, however, being a fact, we have not only all the proof which the case admits of, but all which it is possible to require, that happiness is a good: that each person's happiness is a good to that person, and the general happiness, therefore, a good to the aggregate of all persons. Happiness has made out its title as *one* of the ends of conduct, and consequently one of the criteria of morality.

But it has not, by this alone, proved itself to be the sole criterion. To do that, it would seem, by the same rule, necessary to show, not only that people desire happiness, but that they never desire anything else. Now it is palpable that they do desire things which, in common language, are decidedly distinguished from happiness. They desire, for example, virtue, and the absence of vice, no less really than pleasure and the absence of pain. The desire of virtue is not as universal; but it is as authentic a fact, as the desire of happiness. And hence the opponents of the utilitarian standard deem that they have a right to infer that there are other ends of human action besides happiness, and that happiness is not the standard of approbation and disapprobation.

But does the utilitarian doctrine deny that people desire virtue, or maintain that virtue is not a thing to be desired? The very reverse. It maintains not only that virtue is to be desired, but that it is to be desired disinterestedly, for itself. Whatever may be the opinion of utilitarian moralists as to the original conditions by which virtue is made virtue; however they may believe (as they do) that actions and dispositions are only virtuous because they promote another end than virtue; yet this being granted, and it having been decided, from considerations of this description, what *is* virtuous, they not only place virtue at the very head of the things which are good as means to the ultimate end, but they also recognize as a psychological fact the possibility of its being, to the individual, a good in itself, without looking to any end beyond it; and hold, that the mind is not in a right state, not in a state conformable to utility, not in the state most conducive to the general happiness, unless it does love virtue in this manner—as a thing desirable in itself, even although, in the individual instance, it should not produce those other desirable consequences which it tends to produce and on account of which it is held to be virtue. This opinion is not, in the smallest degree, a departure from the happiness principle. The ingredients of happiness are very various, and each of them is desirable in itself, and not merely when considered as swelling an aggregate. The principle of utility does not mean that any given pleasure, as music for instance, or any given exemption from pain, as for example health, are to be looked upon as a means to a collective something termed happiness, and to be desired on that account. They are desired and desirable in and for themselves; besides being means, they are part of the end. Virtue, according to the utilitarian doctrine, is not naturally and originally part of the end, but it is capable of becoming so; and in those who love it disinterestedly it has become so, and is desired and cherished, not as a means to happiness, but as a part of their happiness.

To illustrate this farther, we may remember that virtue is not the only thing, originally a means, and which if it were not a means to anything else, would be and remain indifferent, but which by association with what it is a means to, comes to be desired for itself, and that too with the utmost intensity. What, for example, shall we say of the love of money? There is nothing originally more desirable about money than about any heap of glittering pebbles. Its worth is solely that of the things which it will buy; the desires for other things than itself, which it is a means of gratifying. Yet the love of money is not only one of the strongest moving forces of human life, but money is, in many cases, desired in and for itself; the desire to possess it is often stronger than the desire to use it, and goes on increasing when all the desires which point to ends beyond it, to be encompassed by it, are falling off. It may be then said truly, that money is desired not for the sake of an end, but as part of the end. From being a means to happiness, it has come to be itself a principal ingredient of the individual's conception of happiness. The same may be said of the majority of the great objects of human life—power, for example, or fame; except that to each of these there is a certain amount of immediate pleasure annexed, which has at least the semblance of being naturally inherent in them; a thing which cannot be said of money. Still, however, the strongest natural attraction, both of power and of fame, is the immense aid they give to the attainment of our other wishes; and it is the strong association thus generated between them and all our objects of desire, which gives to the direct desire of them the intensity it often assumes, so as in some characters to surpass in strength all other desires. In these cases the means have become a part of the end, and a more important part of it than any of the things which they are means to. What was once desired as an instrument for the attainment of happiness, has come to be desired for its own sake. In being desired for its own sake it is, however, desired as *part* of happiness. The person is made, or thinks he would be made, happy by its mere possession; and is made unhappy by failure to obtain it. The desire of it is not a different thing from the desire of happiness, any more than the love of music or the desire of health. They are included in happiness. They are some of the elements of which the desire of happiness is made up. Happiness is not an abstract idea, but a concrete whole; and these are some of its parts. And the utilitarian standard sanctions and approves their being so. Life would be a poor thing, very ill provided with sources of happiness, if there were not this provision of nature, by which things originally indifferent, but conducive to, or otherwise associated with, the satisfaction of our primitive desires, become in themselves sources of pleasure more valuable than the primitive pleasures, both in permanency, in the space of human existence than they are capable of covering, and even in intensity.

Virtue, according to the utilitarian conception, is a good of this description. There was no original desire of it, or motive to it, save its conduciveness to pleasure, and especially to protection from pain. But through the association thus formed, it may be felt a good in itself, and desired as such with as great intensity as any other good; and with this difference between it and the love of money, of power, or of fame, that all of these may, and often do, render the individual noxious to the other members of the society to which he belongs, whereas there is nothing which makes him so much a blessing to them as the cultivation of the disinterested love of virtue. And consequently, the utilitarian standard, while it tolerates and approves those other acquired desires, up to the point beyond which they would be more injurious to the general happiness than promotive of it, enjoins and requires the cultivation of the love of virtue up to the greatest strength possible, as being above all things important to the general happiness.

It results from the preceding considerations, that there is in reality nothing desired except happiness. Whatever is desired otherwise than as a means to some end beyond itself, and ultimately to happiness, is desired as itself a part of happiness, and is not desired for itself until it has become so. Those who desire virtue for its own sake, desire it either because the consciousness of it is a pleasure, or because the consciousness of being without it is a pain, or for both reasons united; as in truth the pleasure and pain seldom exist separately, but almost always together, the same person feeling pleasure in the degree of virtue attained, and pain in not having attained more. If one of these gave him no pleasure, and the other no pain, he would not love or desire virtue, or would desire it only for the other benefits which it might produce to himself or to persons whom he cared for.

We have now, then, an answer to the question, of what sort of proof the principle of utility is susceptible. If the opinion which I have now stated is psychologically true—if human nature is so constituted as to desire nothing which is not either a part of happiness or a means of happiness, we can have no other proof, and we require no other, that these are the only things desirable. If so, happiness is the sole end of human action, and the promotion of it the test by which to judge of all human conduct; from whence it necessarily follows that it must be the criterion of morality, since a part is included in the whole.

And now to decide whether this is really so; whether mankind do desire nothing for itself but that which is a pleasure to them, or of which the absence is a pain; we have evidently arrived at a question of fact and experience, dependent like all similar questions, upon evidence. It can only be determined by practiced self-consciousness and self-observation, assisted by observation of others. I believe that these sources of evidence, impartially consulted, will declare that desiring a thing and finding it pleasant, aversion to it and thinking of it as painful, are phenomena entirely inseparable, or rather two parts of the same phenomenon; in strictness of language, two different modes of naming the same psychological fact: that to think of an object as desirable (unless for the sake of its consequences), and to think of it as pleasant, are one and the same thing; and that to desire anything, except in proportion as the idea of it is pleasant, is a physical and metaphysical impossibility.

So obvious does this appear to me, that I expect it will hardly be disputed: and the objection made will be, not that desire can possibly be directed to anything ultimately except pleasure and exemption from pain, but that the will is a different thing from desire; that a person of confirmed virtue, or any other person whose purposes are fixed, carries out his purposes without any thought of the pleasure he has in contemplating them, or expects to derive from their fulfillment; and persists in acting on them, even though these pleasures are much diminished, by changes in his character or decay of his passive sensibilities, or are outweighed by the pains which the pursuit of the purposes may bring upon him. All this I fully admit, and have stated it elsewhere, as positively and emphatically as any one. Will, the active phenomenon, is a different thing from desire, the state of passive sensibility, and though originally an offshoot from it, may in time take root and detach itself from the parent stock; so much so that in the case of an habitual purpose, instead of willing the thing because we desire it, we often desire it only because we will it. This, however, is but an instance of that familiar fact, the power of habit, and is nowise confined to the case of virtuous actions. Many indifferent things, which men originally did from a motive of some sort, they continue to do from habit. Sometimes this is done unconsciously, the consciousness coming only after the action; at other times with conscious volition, but volition which has become habitual, and is put into operation by the force of habit, in opposition perhaps to the deliberate preference, as often happens with those who have contracted habits of vicious or hurtful indulgence. Third and last comes the case in which the habitual act of will in the individual instance is not in contradiction to the general intention prevailing at other times, but in fulfillment of it; as in the case of the person of confirmed virtue, and of all who pursue deliberately and consistently any determinate end. The distinction between will and desire thus understood, is an authentic and highly important psychological fact; but the fact consists solely in this—that will, like all other parts of our constitution, is amenable to habit, and that we may will from habit what we no longer desire for itself, or desire only because we will it. It is not the less true that will, in the beginning, is entirely produced by desire; including in that term the repelling influence of pain as well as the attractive one of pleasure. Let us take into consideration, no longer the person who has a firmed will to do right, but him in whom that virtuous will is still feeble, conquerable by temptation, and not to be fully relied on; by what means can it be strengthened? How can the will to be virtuous, where it does not exist in sufficient force, be implanted or awakened? Only by making the person *desire* virtue—by making him think of it in a pleasurable light, or of its absence in a painful one. It is by associating the doing right with pleasure, or the doing wrong with pain, or by eliciting and impressing and bringing home to the person's experience the pleasure naturally involved in the one or the pain in the other, that it is possible to call forth that will to be virtuous, which, when confirmed, acts without any thought of either pleasure or pain. Will is the child of desire, and passes out of habit. That which is the result of habit affords no presumption of being intrinsically good; and

there would be no reason for wishing that the purpose of virtue should become independent of pleasure and pain, were it not that the influence of the pleasurable and painful associations which prompt to virtue is not sufficiently to be depended on for unerring constancy of action until it has acquired the support of habit. Both in feeling and in conduct, habit is the only thing which imparts certainty; and it is because of the importance to others of being able to rely absolutely on one's feelings and conduct, and to oneself of being able to rely on one's own, that the will to do right ought to be cultivated into this habitual independence. In other words, this state of the will is a means to good, not intrinsically a good; and does not contradict the doctrine that nothing is a good to human beings but in so far as it is either itself pleasurable, or a means of attaining pleasure or averting pain.

But if this doctrine be true, the principle of utility is proved. Whether it is so or not, must now be left to the consideration of the thoughtful reader.

NOTES

1. The author of this essay has reason for believing himself to be the first person who brought the word "utilitarian" into use. He did not invent it, but adopted it from a passing expression in Mr [John] Galt's *Annals of the Parish*. After using it as a designation for several years, he and others abandoned it from a growing dislike to anything resembling a badge or watchword of sectarian distinction. But as a name for one single opinion,—not a set of opinions—to denote the recognition of utility as a standard, not any particular way of applying it—the term supplies a want in the language, and offers, in many cases, a convenient mode of avoiding tiresome circumlocution.
2. An opponent, whose intellectual and moral fairness it is a pleasure to acknowledge (the Revd. J. Llewellyn Davies), has objected to this passage, saying, "Surely the rightness or wrongness of saving a man from drowning does depend very much upon the motive with which it is done. Suppose

that a tyrant, when his enemy jumped into the sea to escape from him, saved him from drowning simply in order that he might inflict upon him more exquisite tortures, would it tend to clearness to speak of that rescue as 'a morally right action'? Or suppose again, according to one of the stock illustrations of ethical inquiries, that a man betrayed a trust received from a friend, because the discharge of it would fatally injure that friend himself or someone belonging to him, would utilitarianism compel one to call the betrayal 'a crime' as much as if it had been done from the meanest motive?"

I submit that he who saves another from drowning in order to kill him by torture afterwards does not differ only in motive from him who does the same thing from duty or benevolence; the act itself is different. The rescue of the man is, in the case supposed, only the necessary first step of an act far more atrocious than leaving him to drown would have been. Had Mr Davies said, "The rightness or wrongness of saving a man from drowning does depend very much"—not upon the motive, but—"upon the *intention*," no utilitarian would have differed from him. Mr Davies, by an oversight too common not to be quite venial, has in this case confounded the very different ideas of Motive and Intention. There is no point which utilitarian thinkers (and Bentham pre-eminently) have taken more pains to illustrate than this. The morality of the action depends entirely upon the intention—that is, upon what the agent *wills to do*. But the motive, that is, the feeling which makes him will so to do, if it makes no difference in the act, makes none in the morality: though it makes a great difference in our moral estimation of the agent, especially if it indicates a good or a bad habitual *disposition*—a bent of character from which useful, or from which hurtful actions are likely to arise.

26. THE SUBJECTION OF WOMEN

JOHN STUART MILL

CHAPTER 1

The object of this essay is to explain as clearly as I am able, the grounds of an opinion which I have held from the very earliest period when I had formed any opinions at all on social or political matters, and which, instead of being weakened or modified, has been constantly growing stronger by the progress of reflection and the experience of life: That the principle which regulates the existing social relations between the two sexes—the legal subordination of one sex to the other—is wrong in itself, and now one of the chief hindrances to human improvement; and that it ought to be replaced by a principle of perfect equality, admitting no power or privilege on the one side, nor disability on the other.

The very words necessary to express the task I have undertaken show how arduous it is. But it would be a mistake to suppose that the difficulty of the case must lie in the insufficiency or obscurity of the grounds of reason on which my conviction rests. The difficulty is that which exists in all cases in which there is a mass of feeling to be

Reprinted from *The Subjection of Women*, First published in 1869.

contended against. So long as an opinion is strongly rooted in the feelings, it gains rather than loses in stability by having a preponderating weight of argument against it. For if it were accepted as a result of argument, the refutation of the argument might shake the solidity of the conviction; but when it rests solely on feeling, the worse it fares in argumentative contest, the more persuaded its adherents are that their feeling must have some deeper ground, which the arguments do not reach; and while the feeling remains, it is always throwing up fresh intrenchments of argument to repair any breach made in the old. And there are so many causes tending to make the feelings connected with this subject the most intense and most deeply-rooted of all those which gather round and protect old institutions and customs, that we need not wonder to find them as yet less undermined and loosened than any of the rest by the progress of the great modern spiritual and social transition; nor suppose that the barbarisms to which men cling longest must be less barbarisms than those which they earlier shake off. . . .

In the first place, the opinion in favour of the present system, which entirely subordinates the weaker sex to the stronger, rests upon theory only; for there never has been trial made of any other; so that experience, in the sense in which it is vulgarly opposed to theory, cannot be pretended to have pronounced any verdict. And in the second place, the adoption of this system of inequality never was the result of deliberation, or forethought, or any social ideas, or any notion whatever of what conducted to the benefit of humanity or the good order of society. It arose simply from the fact that from the very earliest twilight of human society, every woman (owing to the value attached to her by men, combined with her inferiority in muscular strength) was found in a state of bondage to some man. Laws and systems of polity always begin by recognising the relations they find already existing between individuals. They convert what was a mere physical fact into a legal right, give it the sanction of society, and principally aim at the substitution of public and organized means of asserting and protecting these rights, instead of the irregular and lawless conflict of physical strength. Those who had already been compelled to obedience became in this manner legally bound to it. Slavery, from being a mere affair of force between the master and the slave, became regularized and a matter of compact among the masters, who, binding themselves to one another for common protection, guaranteed by their collective strength the private possessions of each, including his slaves. In early times, the great majority of the male sex were slaves, as well as the whole of the female. And many ages elapsed, some of them ages of high cultivation, before any thinker was bold enough to question the rightfulness and the absolute social necessity, either of the one slavery or of the other. . . .

If people are mostly so little aware how completely, during the greater part of the duration of our species, the law of force was the avowed rule of general conduct, any other being only a special and exceptional consequence of peculiar ties—and from how very recent a date it is that the affairs of society in general have been even pretended to be regulated according to any moral law; as little do people remember or consider, how institutions and customs which never had any ground but the law of force, last on into ages and states of general opinion which never would have permitted their first establishment. Less than forty years ago, Englishmen might still by law hold human beings in bondage as saleable property; within the present century they might kidnap them and carry them off, and work them literally to death. This absolutely extreme case of the law of force, condemned by those who can tolerate almost every other form of arbitrary power, and which, of all others, presents features the most revolting to the feelings of all who look at it from an impartial position, was the law of civilized and Christian England within the memory of persons now living: and in one half of Anglo-Saxon America three or four years ago, not only did slavery exist, but the slave trade, and the breeding of slaves expressly for it, was a general practice between slave states. Yet not only was there a greater strength of sentiment against it, but, in England at least, a less amount either of feeling or of interest in favour of it, than of the other of the customary abuses of force: for its motive was the love of gain, unmixed and undisguised; and those who profited by it were a very small numerical fraction of the country, while the natural feeling of all who were not personally interested in it was unmitigated abhorrence. So extreme an instance makes it almost superfluous to refer to any other; but consider the long duration of absolute monarchy. In England at present it is the almost universal conviction that military despotism is a case of the law of force having no other origin or justification. Yet in all the great nations of Europe except England it either still exists, or has only just ceased to exist, and has even now a strong party favourable to it in all ranks of the people, especially among persons of station and consequence. Such is the power of an established system, even when far from universal, when not only in almost every period of history there have been great and well-known examples of the contrary system, but these have almost invariably been afforded by the most illustrious and most prosperous communities. In this case, too, the possessor of the undue power, the person directly interested in it, is only one person, while those who are subject to it and suffer from it are literally all the rest. The yoke is naturally and necessarily humiliating to all persons, except the one who is on the throne, together with, at most, the one who expects to succeed to it. How different are these cases from that of the power of men over women! I am not now prejudging the question of its justifiableness. I am showing how vastly more permanent it could not but be, even if not justifiable, than these other dominations which have nevertheless lasted down to our own time. Whatever gratification of pride there is in the possession of power, and whatever personal interest in its exercise, is in this case not confined to a limited class, but common to the whole male sex. Instead of being, to most of its supporters, a thing desirable chiefly in the abstract, or, like the political ends usually contended for by factions, of little private importance to any but the leaders; it comes home to the person and hearth of every male head of a family, and of everyone who looks forward to being so. The clodhopper exercises, or is to exercise, his share of the power equally with the highest nobleman. And the case is that in which the desire of power is the strongest: for everyone who desires power, desires it most over those who are nearest to him, with whom his life is passed, with whom he has most concerns in common, and in whom any independence of his authority is oftenest likely to interfere with his individual preferences. If in the other cases specified, power manifestly grounded only on force, and having so much less to support them, are so slowly and with so much difficulty got rid of, much more must it be so with this, even if it rests on no better foundation than those. We must consider, too, that the possessors of the power have facilities in this case, greater than in any other, to prevent any uprising against it. Every one of the subjects lives under the very eye, and almost, it may be said, in the hands of one of the masters—in closer intimacy with him than with any of her fellow-subjects; with no means of combining against him, no power of even locally overmastering him, and, on the other hand, with the strongest motives for seeking his favour and avoiding to give him offence. In struggles for political emancipation, everybody knows how often its champions are bought off by bribes, or daunted by terrors. In the case of women, each individual of the subject-class is in a chronic state of bribery and intimidation combined. In setting up the standard of resistance, a large number of the leaders, and still more of the followers, must make an almost complete sacrifice of the pleasures or the alleviations of their own individual lot. If ever any system of privilege and enforced subjection had its yoke tightly riveted on the necks of those who are kept down by it, this has. . . .

But, it will be said, the rule of men over women differs from all these others in not being a rule of force: it is accepted voluntarily; women make no complaint, and are consenting parties to it. In the first place, a great number of women do not accept it. Ever since there have been women able to make their sentiments known by their writings (the only mode of publicity which society permits to them), an increasing number of them have recorded protests against their present social condition: and recently many thousands of them, headed by the most eminent women known to the public, have petitioned Parliament for their admission to the Parliamentary Suffrage. The claim of women to be educated as solidly, and in the same branches of knowledge, as men, is urged with growing intensity, and with a great prospect of success; while the demand for their admission into professions and occupations hitherto closed against them, becomes every year more urgent. Though there are not in this country, as there are in the United States, periodical Conventions and an organized party to agitate for the Rights of Women, there is a numerous and active Society organized and managed by women, for the more limited object of obtaining the political franchise. Nor is it only in our own country and in America that women are beginning to protest, more or less collectively, against the disabilities under which they labour. France, and Italy, and Switzerland, and Russia now afford examples of the same thing. How many more women there are who silently cherish similar aspirations, no one can possibly know; but there are abundant tokens how many *would* cherish them, were they not so strenuously taught to repress them as contrary to the proprieties of their sex. It must be remembered, also, that no enslaved class ever asked for complete liberty at once. When Simon de Montfort called the deputies of the commons to sit for the first time in Parliament, did any of them dream of demanding that an assembly, elected by their constituents, should make and destroy ministries, and dictate to the king in affairs of state? No such thought entered into the imagination of the most ambitious of them. The nobility had already these pretensions; the commons pretended to nothing but to be exempt from arbitrary taxation, and from the gross individual oppression of the king's officers. It is a political law of nature that those who are under any power of ancient origin, never begin by complaining of the power itself, but only of its oppressive exercise. There is never any want of women who complain of ill usage by their husbands. There would be infinitely more, if complaint were not the greatest of all provocatives to a repetition and increase of the ill usage. It is this which frustrates all attempts to maintain the power but protect the woman against its abuses. In no other case (except that of a child) is the person who has been proved judicially to have suffered an injury, replaced under the physical power of the culprit who inflicted it. Accordingly wives, even in the most extreme and protracted cases of bodily ill usage, hardly ever dare avail themselves of the laws made for their protection: and if, in a moment of irrepressible indignation, or by the interference of neighbours, they are induced to do so, their whole effort afterwards is to disclose as little as they can, and to beg off their tyrant from his merited chastisement.

All men, except the most brutish, desire to have, in the woman most nearly connected with them, not a forced slave but a willing one, not a slave merely, but a favourite. They have therefore put everything in practice to enslave their minds. The masters of all other slaves rely, for maintaining obedience, on fear; either fear of themselves, or religious fears. The masters of women wanted more than simple obedience, and they turned the whole force of education to effect their purpose. All women are brought up from the very earliest years in the belief that their ideal of character is the very opposite to that of men;

not self-will, and government by self-control, but submission, and yielding to the control of others. All the moralities tell them that it is the duty of women, and all the current sentimentalities that it is their nature, to live for others; to make complete abnegation of themselves, and to have no life but in their affections. And by their affections are meant the only ones they are allowed to have—those to the men with whom they are connected, or to the children who constitute an additional and indefeasible tie between them and a man. When we put together three things—first, the natural attraction between opposite sexes; secondly, the wife's entire dependence on the husband, every privilege or pleasure she has being either his gift, or depending entirely on his will; and lastly, that the principal object of human pursuit, consideration, and all objects of social ambition, can in general be sought or obtained by her only through him, it would be a miracle if the object of being attractive to men had not become the polar star of feminine education and formation of character. And, this great means of influence over the minds of women having been acquired, an instinct of selfishness made men avail themselves of it to the utmost as a means of holding women in subjection, by representing to them meekness, submissiveness, and resignation of all individual will into the hands of a man, as an essential part of sexual attractiveness. Can it be doubted that any of the other yokes which mankind have succeeded in breaking, would have subsisted till now if the same means had existed, and had been as sedulously used, to bow down their minds to it? If it had been made the object of the life of every young plebeian to find personal favour in the eyes of some patrician, of every young serf with some seigneur; if domestication with him, and a share of his personal affections, had been held out as the prize which they all should look out for, the most gifted and aspiring being able to reckon on the most desirable prizes; and if, when this prize had been obtained, they had been shut out by a wall of brass from all interests not centering in him, all feelings and desires but those which he shared or inculcated; would not serfs and seigneurs, plebeians and patricians, have been as broadly distinguished at this day as men and women are? and would not all but a thinker here and there, have believed the distinction to be a fundamental and unalterable fact in human nature?

The preceding considerations are amply sufficient to show that custom, however universal it may be, affords in this case no presumption, and ought not to create any prejudice, in favour of the arrangements which place women in social and political subjection to men. But I may go farther, and maintain that the course of history, and the tendencies of progressive human society, afford not only no presumption in favour of this system of inequality of rights, but a strong one against it; and that, so far as the whole course of human improvement up to this time, the whole stream of modern tendencies, warrants any inference on the subject, it is, that this relic of the past is discordant with the future, and must necessarily disappear.

For, what is the peculiar character of the modern world—the difference which chiefly distinguishes modern institutions, modern social ideas, modern life itself, from those of times long past? It is, that human beings are no longer born to their place in life, and chained down by an inexorable bond to the place they are born to, but are free to employ their faculties, and such favourable chances as offer, to achieve the lot which may appear to them most desirable. Human society of old was constituted on a very different principle. All were born to a fixed social position, and were mostly kept in it by law, or interdicted from any means by which they could emerge from it. As some men are born white and others black, so some were born slaves and others freemen and citizens; some were born patricians, others plebeians; some were born feudal nobles, others commoners and *roturiers*. A slave or serf could never make himself free, nor, except by the will of his master, become so. In most European countries it was not till towards the close of the middle ages, and as a consequence of the growth of regal power, that commoners could be ennobled. Even among nobles, the eldest son was born the exclusive heir to the paternal possessions, and a long time elapsed before it was fully established that the father could disinherit him. Among the industrious classes, only those who were born members of a guild, or were admitted into it by its members, could lawfully practise their calling within its local limits; and nobody could practise any calling deemed important, in any but the legal manner—by processes authoritatively prescribed. Manufacturers have stood in the pilory for presuming to carry on their business by new and improved methods. In modern Europe, and most in those parts of it which have participated most largely in all other modern improvements, diametrically opposite doctrines now prevail. Law and government do not undertake to prescribe by whom any social or industrial operation shall or shall not be conducted, or what modes of conducting them shall be lawful. These things are left to the unfettered choice of individuals. Even the laws which required that workmen should serve an apprenticeship, have in this country been repealed: there being ample assurance that in all cases in which an apprenticeship is necessary, its necessity will suffice to enforce it. The old theory was, that the least possible should be left to the choice of the individual agent; that all he had to do should, as far as practicable, be laid down for him by superior wisdom. Left to himself he was sure to go wrong. The modern conviction, the fruit of a thousand years of experience is, that things in which the individual is the person directly interested, never go right but as they are left to his own discretion; and that any regulation of them by authority, except to protect the rights of others, is sure to be mischievous. This conclusion, slowly arrived at, and not adopted until almost every possible application of the contrary theory had been made with disastrous result, now (in the industrial department) prevails universally in the most advanced countries, almost universally in all that have pretensions to any sort of advancement. It is not that all processes are supposed to be equally good, or all persons to be equally qualified for everything; but that freedom of individual choice is now known to be the only thing which procures the adoption of the best processes, and throws each operation into the hands of those who are best qualified for it. Nobody thinks it necessary to make a law that only a strong-armed man shall be a blacksmith. Freedom and competition suffice to make blacksmiths strong-armed men, because the weak-armed can earn more by engaging in occupations for which they are more fit. In consonance with this doctrine, it is felt to be an overstepping of the proper bounds of authority to fix beforehand, on some general presumption, that certain persons are not fit to do certain things. It is now thoroughly known and admitted that if some such presumptions exist, no such presumption is infallible. Even if it be well grounded in a majority of cases, which it is very likely not to be, there will be a minority of exceptional cases in which it does not hold; and in those it is both an injustice to the individuals, and a detriment to society, to place barriers in the way of their using their faculties for their own benefit and for that of others. In the cases, on the other hand, in which the unfitness is real, the ordinary motives of human conduct will on the whole suffice to prevent the incompetent person from making, or from persisting in, the attempt.

If this general principle of social and economical science is not true; if individuals, with such help as they can derive from the opinion of those who know them, are not better judges than the law and the government, of their own capacities and vocation; the world cannot too soon abandon this principle, and return to the old system of regulations and disabilities. But if the principle is true, we ought to act as if we believed it, and not to ordain that to be born a girl instead of a boy, any more than to be born black instead of white, or a commoner instead of a nobleman, shall decide the person's position through all life—shall interdict people from all the more elevated social positions, and from all, except a few, respectable occupations. Even were we to admit the utmost that is ever pretended as to the superior fitness of men for all the functions now reserved to them, the same argument applies which forbids a legal qualification for members of Parliament. If only once in a dozen years the conditions of eligibility exclude a fit person, there is a real loss, while the exclusion of thousands of unfit persons is no gain; for if the constitution of the electoral body disposes them to choose unfit persons, there are always plenty of such persons to choose from. In all things of any difficulty and importance, those who can do them well are fewer than the need, even with the most unrestricted latitude of choice; and any limitation of the field of selection deprives society of some chances of being served by the competent, without ever saving it from the incompetent.

At present, in the more improved countries, the disabilities of women are the only case, save one, in which laws and institutions take persons at their birth, and ordain that they shall never in all their lives be allowed to compete for certain things. . . .

The social subordination of women thus stands out an isolated fact in modern social institutions; a solitary breach of what has become their fundamental law; a single relic of an old world of thought and practice exploded in everything else, but retained in the one thing of most universal interest. . . .

The least that can be demanded is that the question should not be considered as prejudged by existing fact and existing opinion, but open to discussion on its merits, as a question of justice and expediency; the decision on this, as on any of the other social arrangements of mankind, depending on what an enlightened estimate of tendencies and consequences may show to be most advantageous to humanity in general without distinction of sex. And the discussion must be a real discussion, descending to foundations, and not resting satisfied with vague and general assertions. It will not do, for instance, to assert in general terms, that the experience of mankind has pronounced in favour of the existing system. Experience cannot possibly have decided between two courses, so long as there has only been experience of one. If it be said that the doctrine of the equality of the sexes rests only on theory, it must be remembered that the contrary doctrine also has only theory to rest upon. All that is proved in its favour by direct experience, is that mankind have been able to exist under it, and to attain the degree of improvement and prosperity which we now see; but whether that prosperity has been attained sooner, or is now greater, than it would have been under the other system, experience does not say. On the other hand, experience does say, that every step in improvement has been so invariably accompanied by a step made in raising the social position of women, that historians and philosophers have been led to adopt their elevation or debasement as on the whole the surest test and most correct measure of the civilization of a people or an age. Through all the progressive period of human history, the condition of women has been approaching nearer to equality with men. This does not of itself prove that the assimilation must go on to complete equality; but it assuredly affords some presumption that such is the case.

Neither does it avail anything to say that the *nature* of the two sexes adapts them to their present functions and position, and renders these appropriate to them. Standing on the ground of common sense and the constitution of the human mind, I deny that anyone know, or can know, the nature of the two sexes, as long as they have only been seen in their present relation to one another. If men had ever been found in society without women, or women without men, or if there had been a society of men and women in which the women were not under the control of the men, something might have been positively known about the mental and moral differences which may be inherent in the nature of each.

What is now called the nature of women is an eminently artificial thing—the result of forced repression in some directions, unnatural stimulation in others. It may be asserted without scruple, that no other class of dependents have had their character so entirely distorted from its natural proportions by their relation with their masters; for, if conquered and slave races have been, in some respects, more forcibly repressed, whatever in them has not been crushed down by an iron heel has generally been let alone, and if left with any liberty of development, it has developed itself according to its own laws; but in the case of women, a hot-house and stove cultivation has always been carried on of some of the capabilities of their nature, for the benefit and pleasure of their masters. . . .

Hence, in regard to that most difficult question, what are the natural differences between the two sexes—a subject on which it is impossible in the present state of society to obtain complete and correct knowledge—while almost everybody dogmatizes upon it, almost all neglect and make light of the only means by which any partial insight can be obtained into it. This is, an analytic study of the most important department of psychology, the laws of the influences of circumstances on character. For, however great and apparently ineradicable the moral and intellectual differences between men and women might be, the evidence of their being natural differences could only be negative. Those only could be inferred to be natural which could not possibly be artificial—the residuum, after deducting every characteristic of either sex which can admit of being explained from education or external circumstances. The profoundest knowledge of the laws of the formation of character is indispensable to entitle anyone to affirm even that there is any difference, much more what the difference is, between the two sexes considered as moral and rational beings; and since no one, as yet, has that knowledge (for there is hardly any subject which, in proportion to its importance, has been so little studied), no one is thus far enti-

tled to any positive opinion on the subject. Conjectures are all that can at present be made; conjectures more or less probable, according as more or less authorized by such knowledge as we yet have of the laws of psychology, as applied to the formation of character.

Even the preliminary knowledge, what the differences between the sexes now are, apart from all questions as to how they are made what they are, is still in the crudest and most incomplete state. . . .

One thing we may be certain of—that what is contrary to women's nature to do, they never will be made to do by simply giving their nature free play. The anxiety of mankind to interfere in behalf of nature, for fear lest nature should not succeed in effecting its purpose, is an altogether unnecessary solicitude. What women by nature cannot do, it is quite superfluous to forbid them from doing. What they can do, but not so well as the men who are their competitors, competition suffices to exclude them from; since nobody asks for protective duties and bounties in favour of women; it is only asked that the present bounties and protective duties in favour of men should be recalled. If women have a greater natural inclination for some things than for others, there is no need of laws or social inculcation to make the majority of them do the former in preference to the latter. Whatever women's services are most wanted for, the free play of competition will hold out the strongest inducements to them to undertake. And, as the words imply, they are most wanted for the things for which they are most fit; by the apportionment of which to them, the collective faculties of the two sexes can be applied on the whole with the greatest sum of valuable result.

The general opinion of men is supposed to be, that the natural vocation of a woman is that of a wife and mother. I say, is supposed to be, because, judging from acts—from the whole of the present constitution of society—one might infer that their opinion was the direct contrary. They might be supposed to think that the alleged natural vocation of women was of all things the most repugnant to their nature; insomuch that if they are free to do anything else—if any other means of living, or occupation of their time and faculties, is open, which has any chance of appearing desirable to them—there will not be enough of them who will be willing to accept the condition said to be natural to them. If this is the real opinion of men in general, it would be well that it should be spoken out. I should like to hear somebody openly enunciating the doctrine (it is already implied in much that is written on the subject)—"It is necessary to society that women should marry and produce children. They will not do so unless they are compelled. Therefore it is necessary to compel them." The merits of the case would then be clearly defined. It would be exactly that of the slaveholders of South Carolina and Louisiana. "It is necessary that cotton and sugar should be grown. White men cannot produce them, Negroes will not, for any wages which we choose to give, *Ergo* they must be compelled." An illustration still closer to the point is that of impressment. Sailors must absolutely be had to defend the country. It often happens that they will not voluntarily enlist. Therefore there must be the power of forcing them. How often has this logic been used! and, but for one flaw in it, without doubt it would have been successful up to this day. But it is open to the retort—First pay the sailors the honest value of their labour. When you have made it as well worth their while to serve you, as to work for other employers, you will have no more difficulty than others have in obtaining their services. To this there is no logical answer except "I will not": and as people are now not only ashamed, but are not desirous, to rob the labourer of his hire, impressment is no longer advocated. Those who attempt to force women into marriage by closing all other doors against them, lay themselves open to a similar retort. If they mean what they say, their opinion must evidently be, that men do not render the married condition so desirable to

women, as to induce them to accept it for its own recommendations. It is not a sign of one's thinking the boon one offers very attractive, when one allows only Hobson's choice, "that or none." And here, I believe, is the clue to the feelings of those men, who have a real antipathy to the equal freedom of women. I believe they are afraid, not lest women should be unwilling to marry, for I do not think that anyone in reality has that apprehension; but lest they should insist that marriage should be on equal conditions; lest all women of spirit and capacity should prefer doing almost anything else, not in their own eyes degrading, rather than marry, when marrying is giving themselves a master, and a master too of all their earthly possessions. And truly, if this consequence were necessarily incident to marriage, I think that the apprehension would be very well founded. I agree in thinking it probable that few women, capable of anything else, would, unless under an irresistible *entrainement,* rendering them for the time insensible to anything but itself, choose such a lot, when any other means were open to them of filling a conventionally honourable place in life: and if men are determined that the law of marriage shall be a law of despotism, they are quite right, in point of mere policy, in leaving to women only Hobson's choice. But, in that case, all that has been done in the modern world to relax the chain on the minds of women, has been a mistake. They never should have been allowed to receive a literary education. Women who read, much more women who write, are, in the existing constitution of things, a contradiction and a disturbing element: and it was wrong to bring women up with any acquirements but those of an odalisque, or of a domestic servant. . . .

CHAPTER IV

There remains a question, not of less importance than those already discussed, and which will be asked the most importunately by those opponents whose conviction is somewhat shaken on the main point. What good are we to expect from the changes proposed in our customs and institutions? Would mankind be at all better off if women were free? If not, why disturb their minds, and attempt to make a social revolution in the name of an abstract right?

It is hardly to be expected that this question will be asked in respect to the change proposed in the condition of women in marriage. The sufferings, immoralities, evils of all sorts, produced in innumerable cases by the subjection of individual women to individual men, are far too terrible to be overlooked. Unthinking or uncandid persons, counting those cases alone which are extreme, or which attain publicity, may say that the evils are exceptional; but no one can be blind to their existence, nor, in many cases, to their intensity. And it is perfectly obvious that the abuse of power cannot be very much checked while the power remains. It is a power given, or offered, not to good men, or to decently respectable men, but to all men; the most brutal, and the most criminal. There is no check but that of opinion, and such men are in general within the reach of no opinion but that of men like themselves. If such men did not brutally tyrannize over the one human being whom the law compels to bear everything from them, society must already have reached a paradisiacal state. There could be no need any longer of laws to curb men's vicious propensities. Astraea must not only have returned to earth, but the heart of the worst man must have become her temple. The law of servitude in marriage is a monstrous contradiction to all the principles of the modern world, and to all the experience through which those principles have been slowly and painfully worked out. It is the sole case, now that negro slavery has been abolished, in which a human being in the plenitude of every faculty is delivered up to the tender mercies of another human being, in the hope forsooth that this other will use the power solely for the good of the person subjected to it. Marriage is the only actual bondage known to our law. There remain no legal slaves, except the mistress of every house.

It is not, therefore, on this part of the subject, that the question is likely to be asked, *Cui bono?* ["For the good of whom?"] We may be told that the evil would outweigh the good, but the reality of the good admits of no dispute. In regard, however, to the larger question, the removal of women's disabilities—their recognition as the equals of men in all that belongs to citizenship—the opening to them of all honourable employments, and of the training and education which qualifies for those employments—there are many persons for whom it is not enough that the inequality has no just or legitimate defence; they require to be told what express advantage would be obtained by abolishing it.

To which let me first answer, the advantage of having the most universal and pervading of all human relations regulated by justice instead of injustice. The vast amount of this gain to human nature, it is hardly possible, by any explanation or illustration, to place in a stronger light than it is placed by the bare statement, to anyone who attaches a moral meaning to words. All the selfish propensities, the self-worship, the unjust self-preference, which exist among mankind, have their source and root in, and derive their principal nourishment from, the present constitution of the relation between men and women. Think what it is to a boy, to grow up to manhood in the belief that without any merit or any exertion of his own, though he may be the most frivolous and empty or the most ignorant and stolid of mankind, by the mere fact of being born a male he is by right the superior of all and everyone of an entire half of the human race: including probably some whose real superiority to himself he has daily or hourly occasion to feel; but even if in his whole conduct he habitually follows a woman's guidance, still, if he is a fool, he thinks that of course she is not, and cannot be, equal in ability and judgment to himself; and if he is not a fool, he does worse—he sees that she is superior to him, and believes that, notwithstanding her superiority, he is entitled to command and she is bound to obey. What must be the effect on his character, of this lesson? And men of the cultivated classes are often not aware how deeply it sinks into the immense majority of male minds. For, among right-feeling and well-bred people, the inequality is kept as much as possible out of sight; above all, out of sight of the children. As much obedience is required from boys to their mother as to their father: they are not permitted to domineer over their sisters, nor are they accustomed to see these postponed to them, but the contrary; the compensations of the chivalrous feeling being made prominent, while the servitude which requires them is kept in the background. Well brought-up youths in the higher classes thus often escape the bad influences of the situation in their early years, and only experience them when, arrived at manhood, they fall under the dominion of facts as they really exist. Such people are little aware, when a boy is differently brought up, how early the notion of his inherent superiority to a girl arises in his mind; how it grows with his growth and strengthens with his strength; how it is inoculated by one schoolboy upon another; how early the youth thinks himself superior to his mother, owing her perhaps forbearance, but no real respect; and how sublime and sultan-like a sense of superiority he feels, above all, over the woman whom he honours by admitting her to a partnership of his life. Is it imagined that all this does not pervert the whole manner of existence of the man, both as an individual and as a social being? It is an exact parallel to the feeling of a hereditary king that he is excellent above others by being born a king, or a noble by being born a noble. The relation between husband and wife is very like that between lord and vassal, except that the wife is held to more unlimited obedience than the vassal was. However the vassal's character may have been affected, for better and for worse, by his subordination, who can help seeing that the lord's was affected greatly for the worse? whether he was led to believe that his vassals were really

superior to himself, or to feel that he was placed in command over people as good as himself, for no merits or labours of his own, but merely for having, as Figaro says, taken the trouble to be born. The self-worship of the monarch, or of the feudal superior is matched by the self-worship of the male. Human beings do not grow up from childhood in the possession of unearned distinctions, without pluming themselves upon them. Those whom privileges not acquired by their merit, and which they feel to be disproportioned to it, inspire with additional humility, are always the few, and the best few. The rest are only inspired with pride, and the worst sort of pride, that which values itself upon accidental advantages, not of its own achieving. Above all, when the feeling of being raised above the whole of the other sex is combined with personal authority over one individual among them; the situation, if a school of conscientious and affectionate forbearance to those whose strongest points of character are conscience and affection, is to men of another quality a regularly constituted Academy or Gymnasium for training them in arrogance and overbearingness; which vices, if curbed by the certainty of resistance in their intercourse with other men, their equals, break out towards all who are in a position to be obliged to tolerate them, and often revenge themselves upon the unfortunate wife for the involuntary restraint which they are obliged to submit to elsewhere.

The example afforded, and the education given to the sentiments, by laying the foundation of domestic existence upon a relation contradictory to the first principles of social justice, must, from the very nature of man, have a perverting influence of such magnitude, that it is hardly possible with our present experience to raise our imaginations to the conception of so great a change for the better as would be made by its removal. All that education and civilization are doing to efface the influences on character of the law of force, and replace them by those of justice, remains merely on the surface, as long as the citadel of the enemy is not attacked. The principle of the modern movement in morals and politics, is that conduct, and conduct alone, entitles to respect: that not what men are, but what they do, constitutes their claim to deference; that, above all, merit, and not birth, is the only rightful claim to power and authority. If no authority, not in its nature temporary, were allowed to one human being over another, society would not be employed in building up propensities with one hand which it has to curb with the other. The child would really, for the first time in man's existence on earth, be trained in the way he should go, and when he was old there would be a chance that he would not depart from it. But so long as the right of the strong to power over the weak rules in the very heart of society, the attempt to make the equal right of the weak the principle of its outward actions will always be an uphill struggle; for the law of justice, which is also that of Christianity, will never get possession of men's inmost sentiments; they will be working against it, even when bending to it. . . .

Any society which is not improving, is deteriorating: and the more so, the closer and more familiar it is. Even a really superior man almost always begins to deteriorate when he is habitually (as the phrase is) king of his company: and in his most habitual company the husband who has a wife inferior to him is always so. While his self-satisfaction is incessantly ministered to on the one hand, on the other he insensibly imbibes the modes of feeling, and of looking at things, which belong to a more vulgar or a more limited mind than his own. This evil differs from many of those which have hitherto been dwelt on, by being an increasing one. The association of men with women in daily life is much closer and more complete than it ever was before. Men's life is more domestic. Formerly, their pleasures and chosen occupations were among men, and in men's company: their wives had but a fragment of their lives. At the present time, the progress of civilization, and the turn of opinion against the rough amusements and convivial excesses which formerly occupied most men in their hours of relaxation—together with (it must be said) the improved tone of modern feeling as to the reciprocity of duty which binds the husband towards the wife—have thrown the man very much more upon home and its inmates, for his personal and social pleasures: while the kind and degree of improvement which has been made in women's education, has made them in some degree capable of being his companions in ideas and mental tastes, while leaving them, in most cases, still hopelessly inferior to him. His desire of mental communication is thus in general satisfied by a communion from which he learns nothing. An unimproving and unstimulating companionship is substituted for (what he might otherwise have been obliged to seek) the society of his equals in powers and his fellows in the higher pursuits. We see, accordingly, that young men of the greatest promise generally cease to improve as soon as they marry, and, not improving, inevitably degenerate. If the wife does not push the husband forward, she always holds him back. He ceases to care for what she does not care for; he no longer desires, and ends by disliking and shunning, society congenial to his former aspirations, and which would now shame his falling-off from them; his higher faculties both of mind and heart cease to be called into activity. And this change coinciding with the new and selfish interests which are created by the family, after a few years he differs in no material respect from those who have never had wishes for anything but the common vanities and the common pecuniary objects.

What marriage may be in the case of two persons of cultivated faculties, identical in opinions and purposes, between whom there exists that best kind of equality, similarity of powers and capacities with reciprocal superiority in them—so that each can enjoy the luxury of looking up to the other, and can have alternately the pleasure of leading and of being led in the path of development—I will not attempt to describe. To those who can conceive it, there is no need; to those who cannot, it would appear the dream of an enthusiast. But I maintain, with the profoundest conviction, that this, and this only, is the ideal of marriage; and that all opinion, customs, and institutions which favour any other notion of it, or turn the conceptions and aspirations connected with it into any other direction, by whatever pretences they may be coloured, are relics of primitive barbarism. The moral regeneration of mankind will only really commence, when the most fundamental of the social relations is placed under the rule of equal justice, and when human beings learn to cultivate their strongest sympathy with an equal in rights and in cultivation.

27. THE ENFRANCHISEMENT OF WOMEN

HARRIET TAYLOR

... Concerning the fitness, then, of women for politics, there can be no question: but the dispute is more likely to turn upon the fitness of politics for women. When the reasons alleged for excluding women from active life in all its higher departments are stripped of their garb of declamatory phrases, and reduced to the simple expression of a meaning, they seem to be mainly three: first, the incompatibility of active life with maternity, and with the cares of a household; secondly, its alleged hardening effect on the character; and thirdly, the inexpediency of making an addition to the already excessive pressure of competition in every kind of professional or lucrative employment.

The first, the maternity argument, is usually laid most stress upon: although (it needs hardly be said) this reason; if it be one, can apply only to mothers. It is neither necessary nor just to make imperative on women that they shall be either mothers or nothing; or that if they have been mothers once, they shall be nothing else during the whole remainder of their lives. Neither women nor men need any law to exclude them from an occupation, if they have undertaken another which is incompatible with it. No one proposes to exclude the male sex from Parliament because a man may be a soldier or sailor in active service, or a merchant whose business requires all his time and energies. Nine-tenths of the occupations of men exclude them *de facto* from public life, as effectually as if they were excluded by law; but that is no reason for making laws to exclude even the nine-tenths, much less the remaining tenth. The reason of the case is the same for women as for men. There is no need to make provision by law that woman shall not carry on the active details of a household, or of the education of children, and at the same time practise a profession, or be elected to parliament. Where incompatibility is real, it will take care of itself: but there is gross injustice in making the incompatibility a pretence for the exclusion of those in whose case it does not exist. And these, if they were free to choose, would be a very

Reprinted from *The Enfranchisement of Women*. First published in 1851.

large proportion. The maternity argument deserts its supporters in the case of single women, a large and increasing class of the population; a fact which, it is not irrelevant to remark, by tending to diminish the excessive competition of numbers, is calculated to assist greatly the prosperity of all. There is no inherent reason or necessity that all women should voluntarily choose to devote their lives to one animal function and its consequences. Numbers of women are wives and mothers only because there is no other career open to them, no other occupation for their feelings or their activities. Every improvement in their education, and enlargement of their faculties, everything which renders them more qualified for any other mode of life, increases the number of those to whom it is an injury and an oppression to be denied the choice. To say that women must be excluded from active life because maternity disqualifies them for it, is in fact to say, that every other career should be forbidden them in order that maternity may be their only resource.

But secondly, it is urged, that to give the same freedom of occupation to women as to men, would be an injurious addition to the crowd of competitors, by whom the avenues to almost all kinds of employment are choked up, and its remuneration depressed. This argument, it is to observed, does not reach the political question. It gives no excuse for withholding from women the rights of citizenship. The suffrage, the jury-box, admission to the legislature and to office, it does not touch. It bears only on the industrial branch of the subject. Allowing it, then, in an economical point of view, its full force; assuming that to lay open to women the employments now monopolized by men, would tend, like the breaking down of other monopolies, to lower the rate of remuneration in those employments; let us consider what is the amount of this evil consequence, and what the compensation is for it. The worst ever asserted, much worse than is at all likely to be realized, is that if women competed with men, a man and a woman could not together earn more than is now earned by the man alone. Let us make this supposition, the most unfavourable supposition possible: the joint income of the two would be the same as before, while the woman would be raised from the position of a servant to that of a partner. Even if every woman, as matters now stand, had a claim on some man for support, how infinitely preferable is it that part of the income should be of the woman's earning, even if the aggregate sum were but little increased by it, rather than that she should be compelled to stand aside in order that men may be the sole earners, and the sole dispensers of what is earned. Even under the present laws respecting the property of women, a woman who contributes materially to the support of the family, cannot be treated in the same contemptuously tyrannical manner as one who, however she may toil as a domestic drudge, is a dependent on the man for subsistence.[1] As for the depression of wages by increase of competition, remedies will be found for it in time. Palliatives might be applied immediately; for instance, a more rigid exclusion of children from industrial employment, during the years in which they ought to be working only to strengthen their bodies and minds for later life. Children are necessarily dependent, and under the power of others; and their labour, being not for themselves but for the gain of their parents, is a proper subject for legislative regulation. With respect to the future, we neither believe that improvident multiplication, and the consequent excessive difficulty of gaining a subsistence, will always continue, nor that the division of mankind into capitalists and hired labourers, and the regulation of the reward of labourers mainly by demand and supply, will be for ever, or even much longer, the rule of the world. But so long as competition is the general law of human life, it is tyranny to shut out one-half of the competitors. All who have attained the age of self-government have an equal claim to be permitted to sell whatever kind of useful labour they are capable of, for the price which it will bring.

The third objection to the admission of women to political or professional life, its alleged hardening tendency, belongs to an age now past, and is scarcely to be comprehended by people of the present time. There are still, however, persons who say that the world and its avocations render men selfish and unfeeling; that the struggles, rivalries, and collisions of business and of politics make them harsh and unamiable; that if half the species must unavoidably be given up to these things, it is the more necessary that the other half should be kept free from them; that to preserve women from the bad influences of the world, is the only chance of preventing men from being wholly given up to them.

There would have been plausibility in this argument when the world was still in the age of violence; when life was full of physical conflict, and every man had to redress his injuries or those of others, by the sword or by the strength of his arm. Women, like priests, by being exempted from such responsibilities, and from some part of the accompanying dangers, may have been enabled to exercise a beneficial influence. But in the present condition of human life, we do not know where those hardening influences are to be found, to which men are subject and from which women are at present exempt. Individuals now-a-days are seldom called upon to fight hand to hand, even with peaceful weapons; personal enmities and rivalries count for little in worldly transactions; the general pressure of circumstances, not the adverse will of individuals, is the obstacle men now have to make head against. That pressure, when excessive, breaks the spirit, and cramps and sours the feelings, but not less of women than of men, since they suffer certainly not less from its evils. There are still quarrels and dislikes, but the sources of them are changed. The feudal chief once found his bitterest enemy in his powerful neighbour, the minister or courtier in his rival for place: but opposition of interest in active life, as a cause of personal animosity, is out of date; the enmities of the present day arise not from great things but small, from what people say of one another, more than from what they do; and if there are hatred, malice, and all uncharitable-

ness, they are to be found among women fully as much as among men. In the present state of civilization, the notion of guarding women from the hardening influences of the world, could only be realized by secluding them from society altogether. The common duties of common life, as at present constituted, are incompatible with any other softness in women than weakness. Surely weak minds in weak bodies must ere long cease to be even supposed to be either attractive or amiable.

But, in truth, none of these arguments and considerations touch the foundations of the subject. The real question is, whether it is right and expedient that one-half of the human race should pass through life in a state of forced subordination to the other half. If the best state of human society is that of being divided into two parts, one consisting of persons with a will and a substantive existence, the other of humble companions to these persons, attached, each of them to one, for the purpose of bring up *his* children, and making *his* home pleasant to him; if this is the place assigned to women, it is but kindness to educate them for this; to make them believe that the greatest good fortune which can befall them, is to be chosen by some man for this purpose; and that every other career which the world deems happy or honourable, is closed to them by the law, not of social institutions, but of nature and destiny.

When, however, we ask why the existence of one-half the species should be merely ancillary to that of the other—why each woman should be a mere appendage to a man, allowed to have no interests of her own, that there may be nothing to compete in her mind with his interests and his pleasure; the only reason which can be given is, that men like it. It is agreeable to them that men should live for their own sake, women for the sake of men: and the qualities and conduct in subjects which are agreeable to rulers, they succeed for a long time in making the subjects themselves consider as their appropriate virtues. Helvetius has met with much obloquy for asserting, that persons usually mean by virtues the qualities which are useful or convenient to themselves. How truly this is said of mankind in general, and how wonderfully the ideas of virtue set afloat by the powerful, are caught and imbibed by those under their dominion, is exemplified by the manner in which the world were once persuaded that the supreme virtue of subjects was loyalty to kings, and are still persuaded that the paramount virtue of womanhood is loyalty to men. Under a nominal recognition of a moral code common to both, in practice self-will and self-assertion form the type of what are designated as manly virtues, while abnegation of self, patience, resignation, and submission to power, unless when resistance is commanded by other interests than their own, have been stamped by general consent as preeminently the duties and graces required of women. The

meaning being merely, that power makes itself the centre of moral obligation, and that a man likes to have his own will, but does not like that his domestic companion should have a will different from his. . . .

NOTES

1. The truly horrible effects of the present state of the law among the lowest of the working population, is exhibited in those cases of hideous maltreatment of their wives by working men, with which every newspaper, every police report, teems. Wretches unfit to have the smallest authority over any living thing, have a helpless woman for their household slave. These excesses could not exist if women both earned, and had the right to possess, a part of the income of the family.

28. UTILITY AND PERFECT EQUALITY

MARIA H. MORALES

The true virtue of human beings is fitness to live together as equals; claiming nothing for themselves but what they as freely concede to everyone else; regarding command of any kind as an exceptional necessity, and in all cases a temporary one; and preferring, whenever possible, the society of those with whom leading and following can be alternate and reciprocal.
John Stuart Mill, *The Subjection of Women*, 1861

I. INTRODUCTION

John Stuart Mill's moral theory defies categorization. Although Mill was in his youth principally influenced by the classical utilitarianism of Bentham, his mature moral philosophy so revolutionized the orthodox utilitarian position as to render calling him a utilitarian problematic, if not misleading. There is a strong undercurrent in his moral and political writings of virtue ethics, which, given the classical bent of his early education, is not surprising. Utilitarianism and

Reprinted from "Utility and Perfect Equality" by permission of the author.

virtue ethics had already met in Hume's moral theory, which we should view as closer in spirit to Mill's mature outlook than Bentham's. In fact, Bentham was much less concerned with ethics than with legislation, the engine of politics, and Mill criticized his focus on the "public" realm as falling short of what an "enlarged" understanding of utility requires.[1]

Millean utility provides us with a richer paradigm of morality than is found anywhere else in the utilitarian tradition, with which he decided to remain associated despite its shortcomings.[2] Given the complexity of the utilitarian standard as Mill understood it, it is particularly imperative to examine it in context, as part of an overall conception of human improvement and social progress. Narrower renditions of Millean utility, particularly those that construe it exclusively or primarily as a standard for individual action,[3] run the risk of neglecting what were for Mill significant *moral* considerations, for example, those having to do with character.[4] Worse still: these renditions come close to misrepresenting Mill's moral theory by failing to take into account, *when attempting to elucidate what sort of standard utility is,* the foundational role that moral sentiments play in his reflections on ethics. Chief among these sentiments, for Mill, is sympathy, which, as in Hume's moral theory, paves the way in Mill's theory for the central role that sociability plays in the moral life. Sympathy and sociability, which are at the core of Mill's enlarged understanding of utility, propel us to engage in cooperative and egalitarian relationships with others in various domains of human social life. The significance of "shared goods"[5] to Millean morality is hard to grasp from the perspective of narrow readings of Mill's utilitarianism.

My approach to thinking about Mill's ethics is unconventional. I do not find it fruitful to analyze his utilitarianism by itself, as it were, and only then proceed to unravel the relationship of utility to his other commitments as a moral and political thinker—for example, liberty, human development, social progress, justice, equality, and democracy. Instead, I take these values—notably the value of equality, which, I have argued elsewhere,[6] unifies his other moral and social ideals—and use *them* to illuminate the character of his utilitarianism. This interpretive strategy is consonant with Mill's own approach: Mill viewed utility as the most general axiom of value and specified its requirements by introducing various secondary principles of practice. Millean utility does not have action-guiding force by itself: it does not tell us what to do, but what to strive for. It is a complex general axiological standard embodying the ideal of value that other, particular ideals and principles—including principles of action—must aim to realize. This way of conceiving of the ultimate source of value, as unpacked by and pursued by means of, secondary ideals and principles, renders Mill's utilitarianism *indirect* and *two-tiered* in character. The interpreter must provide an account of what the tiers are and explain the interrelationships, logical and substantive, between secondary ideals and principles. These tasks are daunting for at least two reasons. First, Mill's texts are not precise on either point. Second, *Mill* might have had a clear conception both of what the secondary principles are and of how, together, they constitute a unified system. But since he did not tell, the interpreter can at most venture an informed, yet necessarily speculative, account of his conception. Given our data, the outcome of interpretation will be both less precise and less final than some philosophers might care to tolerate.[7] Yet recent scholarship on Mill has finally established that where "older" critics used to find rampant philosophical confusion or fallacious reasoning, there is in fact "subtlety and respect for the complexity of our moral concepts."[8]

I shall proceed as follows. In Section (II), I shall explain what I take to be Mill's conception of utility and, at the outset, dispel some serious misunderstandings that continue to dominate discussions of his utilitarianism. In Section (III), I shall address the connections between the cultivation of the moral sentiments and our participation in good human relationships, which are key to Mill's conception of the moral life. Finally, in my concluding remarks, I shall weave together my suggestions as to what it is to be a utilitarian in Mill's sense of the term.

II. MILLEAN UTILITY

I have intimated that Millean utility is not easy to grasp. The standard interpretation, still found among otherwise "revisionary" Mill scholars, is that Mill's conception of morality is a version, albeit "improved," of Bentham's. This interpretation fails to provide a satisfactory account of the Millean standard. A close examination of Mill's Herculean attempt to salvage orthodox utilitarianism from its doctrinal failures yields a wholly different account of a good human life than we find in Bentham. Given the appeal of this alternative not only to classical utilitarianism, but to many other competing moral theories, elucidating the elusive notion of utility in Mill is a worthwhile labor.

The classical formulation of the utilitarian standard is Bentham's: the principle of utility "approves or disapproves of every action whatsoever, according to the tendency which it appears to have to augment or diminish the happiness of the party whose interest is in question."[9] By "utility" Bentham meant pleasure, and he used the terms "benefit," "advantage," "good," and "happiness" as equivalent to pleasure. When we turn to Mill for a definition of the principle of utility, matters are not quite so straightforward. At least one scholar has found some fifteen formulations of the standard in *Utilitarianism* alone.[10] Yet it turns out, none of these formulations, by itself or together, actually captures Millean utility! Despite good arguments to the contrary,[11] however, it is still not unusual for commentators to interpret Mill in *Utilitarianism* as beginning his reflections on the principle of utility with something akin to the Benthamite standard.[12] The relevant passage in *Utilitarianism* reads:

The creed which accepts as the foundation of morals "utility" or the "greatest happiness principle" holds that actions are right in proportion as they tend to promote happiness; wrong as they tend to produce the reverse of happiness. By happiness is intended pleasure and the absence of pain; by unhappiness, pain and the privation of pleasure. To give a clear view of the moral standard set up by the theory, much more requires to be said; in particular, what things it includes in the ideas of pain and pleasure, and to what extent this is left an open question. But these supplementary explanations do not affect the theory of life on which this theory of morality is grounded—namely, that pleasure and freedom from pain are the only things desirable as ends; and that all desirable things (which are as numerous in the utilitarian theory as in any other scheme) are desirable either for pleasure inherent in themselves or as means to the promotion of pleasure and the prevention of pain. (U, II, 2)[13]

In this passage, Mill was paraphrasing *Bentham's* definition of the principle of utility and the theory of life on which it rests. To appreciate that this is what Mill was doing, we must look at the passage that immediately precedes the introduction of "the creed." In *that* passage, Mill addressed those who hold two "absurd misconceptions," supposing that utility is opposed to pleasure or referring everything to pleasure, and proceed to reject the first as "impractically dry" and the second as "too practically voluptuous." (U, II, 1) According to Mill, the term "utilitarian" has been consistently and "ignorantly misapplied" by utilitarianism's opponents, so much so that he himself "had for many years discontinued it as a distinctive appellation" and now found himself "called upon to resume it if by doing so [he] can hope to contribute anything toward rescuing it from this utter degradation."

The first two paragraphs of chapter II of *Utilitarianism,* then, are to be interpreted as follows: in the first, Mill explained that he intended to resume the appellation "utilitarian" to rescue utilitarianism from the "utter degradation" into which it had fallen in the hands of Bentham's critics; and in the second, Mill began the rescue mission by paraphrasing Bentham's creed in a way that does not involve the "ignorant" misapplication of the term "utility" as is found in "the creed" as Bentham understood it. The second paragraph *does not give us Mill's version of the creed,* nor does it begin to hint at the theory of life that underlies the utilitarian creed as *he* understood it. In fact, it is not until the fourth paragraph, where Mill began his response to the objection that utilitarianism is "a doctrine worthy only of swine," that we find *Millean* doctrines: the doctrine of the higher faculties and the doctrine of the higher pleasures. Even after the introduction of these doctrines, we do not know what Mill took "utility" to be or the utilitarian standard to require. The first hint comes in paragraph nine, where Mill remarked that the utilitarian standard is "the greatest amount of happiness altogether," as opposed to the greatest amount of the agent's own happiness. Admittedly, this remark falls short of an account, explanation, and surely of a definition of the principle of utility, and does not tell us much about what utility is. It is painfully general and vague, not to mention unhelpful if what we are looking for is an action-guiding principle. The eleventh paragraph gives us the best candidate in *Utilitarianism:*

> According to the greatest happiness principle ... the ultimate end, with reference to and for the sake of which all other things are desirable—whether we are considering our own good or that of other people—is an existence exempt as far as possible from pain, and as rich as possible in enjoyments, both in point of quantity and quality; the test of quality and the rule for measuring it against quantity being the preference felt by those who, in their opportunities of experience, to which must be added their habits of self-consciousness and self-observation, are best furnished with the means of comparison. (U, II, 11)

This "definition," despite its convolutedness, begins to point us in the right direction by introducing ideas that are key to Mill's conception of morality: it is directed toward an end, which accounts for the value ("desirability") of other ends; it involves a certain kind of existence, rich in various sorts of enjoyments and open to all human beings (and, to some lesser extent, to all sentient creatures); it is empirical, its test the "decided preference" of reflective human beings with experience of alternatives (U, II, 5); and it is the ultimate end of human action. Since Mill did not fill in the gaps in the rest of chapter two of *Utilitarianism,* we shall have to do it ourselves. First, we shall turn to the last book of the *Logic,* which concerns the general structure of the "moral sciences."

Utility and The Art of Life

In Book VI, chapter twelve, of the *Logic,* Mill argued that morality is not a science, but an "art."[14] Art frames a conception of the effects to be produced by action, which is based on a definition of an end to be sought and an affirmation that the end is desirable. Science finds the causes that will produce the desired effects on the basis of reasoning that connects the end of art with the means for its realization, which constitutes the general "scientific theory" of the art. Like Aristotle, Mill believed that every art has "one first principle, or general major premise, not borrowed from science," which determines its proper province. The first principles of art "enjoin or recommend that something should be"—the builder's art, that it is desirable to have buildings; the medical art, that it is desirable to preserve health.[15] These propositions of art "are a class by themselves," namely *axiological* propositions, which are "generically different" from factual ones. For Mill, it is key to distinguish the language of "*ought* or *should be*" from the language of "*is* or *will be*." The former is the language of morals.

How do arts decide what ends are desirable?

Mill did not deem it sufficient to claim that the end recommended "excites in the speaker's mind the feeling of approbation," because this feeling does not capture why *others* should approve of it. Only general premises can provide the justification of these feelings and "[t]hese general premises, together with the principal conclusions which may be deduced from them, form (or rather might form) a body of doctrine, which is properly the Art of Life, in its three departments, Morality, Prudence or Policy, and Aesthetics; the Right, the Expedient, and the Beautiful or Noble, in human conduct and works." To this art all others are subordinate.[16]

The ultimate principle of the Art of Life is "that of conduciveness to the happiness of mankind, or rather, of all sentient beings: in other words, ... the promotion of happiness is the ultimate principle of Teleology."[17] We should understand Mill's principle of utility as functioning at the critical level of reasoning about conduct: it is the principle that provides us with the "major premise" of practical reasoning, which is a premise about value. The principle of utility is an axiological principle that oversees the entire Art of Life. It is neither exclusively nor primarily a moral principle.[18] Mill argued that utility should be sought through secondary principles of practice,[19] which specify utility's requirements. Each of the departments of the Art of Life has such principles: there is a division of labor among these departments regarding the promotion of utility. The objects of each branch—the right, the expedient, and the beautiful—constitute the differentiae, which determine what requirements are the concern of each branch. Mill supposed that people generally agree on what principles fall under the different branches even when they disagree about what constitutes the ultimate end or standard of value.

Since Mill did not specify the matter, exactly what *he* took these secondary principles to be for each branch is open to a great deal of interpretation. Moreover, his supposition about the general agreement over these principles is problematic:

even utilitarians disagreed with him about the status of some of his values.[20] In addition, even if people agreed about what the secondary principles are, those who disagree that happiness is the ultimate end will disagree also with their "ranking" on a scale of "desirability," because the criterion for the ranking is the promotion of the ultimate end construed as happiness. So, it is far from clear that the general agreement Mill assumed would yield substantive agreement about the relationship between these principles. Even sympathetic scholars find it maddeningly difficult to provide a unified account of what Mill himself took this relationship to be, given how indirect his remarks are throughout his corpus. He did address the possibility of there arising incompatible demands from secondary principles, which, he said, would be "overcome practically, with greater or with less success, according to the intellect and virtue of the individual." (U, II, 24) *Only* in such cases, he maintained, "utility may be invoked" directly as a "common umpire" to decide which demand takes priority in the particular case. According to Mill, it is a strength of utilitarianism that it can rely on an "objective" ultimate standard for the resolution of conflicts of obligation, even if the application of utility to these cases depends heavily on the agent's "intellect" and "virtue." Other moral systems, in his view, either fail completely to provide a common umpire (perhaps on the assumption that such conflicts can never arise) or provide an arbitrary one, thus affording "a free scope for the action of personal desires and partialities." Although the utilitarian resolution of conflicts between secondary principles must be undertaken on a case-by-case basis, *Millean moral agents are well-equipped to undertake the reflection necessary to arrive at the "right" decision because they have developed their intellectual and moral capacities.* Mill's position on this subject might still not convince (by itself, at any rate) detractors of happiness as the ultimate end. Yet for the purposes of understanding his view, it is helpful: it points straightforwardly to the importance of character development, including virtue, to utilitarian ethics. I shall return to this topic in section (III).

It would be useful to recapitulate what we have learned so far about Mill's principle of utility. First, it is *teleological,* that is, it concerns the end toward which practice in general ought to be directed. Second, and relatedly, it is *axiological,* as opposed to directly (and in the first instance) practical, or concerned with conduct. Third, it is *general* in the sense that it rules over not only morality, but also policy and aesthetics. Finally, it is *fundamental* both in that it provides the most general principle of practical reasoning and in that it is the justification for all other principles of practice, including moral principles. Utilitarianism, in Mill's view, is *not* a moral theory concerned with the criterion for right (and wrong) action, although morality is one of its departments.[21] Specifically, the ultimate principle of teleology, or the principle of utility, is *not* a moral principle with action-guiding force: it does not function at the practical, but rather at the critical or reflective, level.[22] To know what is *right,* which is the province of morality, we need to turn to specifically moral principles (or rules or standards), which act as "intermediaries" between the principle of utility and agency and are themselves justified with reference to the principle of utility. Neither is the principle of utility a principle of expediency, that is, a principle that tells us how most efficiently to bring about some desired result. This is a crucial point: Mill *disagreed strongly with Bentham's conflation of the principle of utility with the principle of expediency,* or of "specific consequences."[23] The principle of expediency, on Mill's model, is not even a moral principle: it is a principle ("the" principle, if we wish) of the department of prudence or policy. As we have seen, Mill sharply *separated* the right, which is the object of morality, from the expedient, which is the object of prudence/policy. This important distinction should lead us in the direction of understanding Mill's moral theory more on the model of Aristotle's, as teleological and

eudaimonistic, than on the model of Bentham's consequentialist aggregative utilitarianism.

Mill himself stressed the importance of conceiving of the utilitarian standard as having a fundamentally justificatory aim right after introducing "the ultimate principle of Teleology":

> I do not mean to assert that the promotion of happiness should be itself the end of all actions, or even of all rules of action. It is the justification, and ought to be the controller, of all ends, but is not itself the sole end. There are many virtuous actions, and even virtuous modes of action, (though the cases are, I think, less frequent than is often supposed,) by which happiness in the particular instance is sacrificed, more pain being produced than pleasure. But conduct of which this can be truly asserted admits of justification only because it can be shown that on the whole more happiness will exist in the world *if feelings are cultivated* which make people, in certain cases, regardless of happiness. I fully admit that this is true: that *the cultivation of an ideal nobleness of will and conduct should be to individual human beings an end,* to which the specific pursuit either of their own happiness or of that of others (except so far as it is included in that idea) should, in any case of conflict, give way. But I hold that the very question, what constitutes this elevation of character, is itself to be decided by a reference to happiness as the standard.[24]

This passage does more than speak to the general relationship between secondary principles and the principle of utility. Some of what it does should strike careful readers of *Utilitarianism* as problematic: in the infamous section on the "proof" of the principle of utility in chapter four of that work, Mill claimed that the principle of utility is the end of all actions and the *sole* end for which all other ends are pursued. (U, IV, 2–3) This claim squarely contradicts the one in the *Logic* at the beginning of the above quote. What should we make of this conflict? I suggest that we take the claim in the *Logic* as reflecting Mill's position. I further suggest that doing so is consistent with the spirit, although not with the written word, of his views in *Utilitarianism*. The conflict arises because of a difference of emphasis in the latter (and later) work, where Mill was polemically arguing against Bentham's detractors rather than advancing a philosophical account of morality. Unfortunately, Mill did not do the latter in any one place as completely as one would want.

What *is* Mill's philosophical position? The preponderance of the evidence favors the following interpretation: Mill believed that the principle of utility is *the* end of the Art of Life, which does not entail that it is the *only* end of practice. On the contrary, there are many other ends to which agency in general ought to be directed if it is to promote the general happiness. All of these ends *are justified* with reference to the principle of utility, but cannot be *reduced* to that principle (as in Bentham). In other words, utility is always "the controller" of all ends, but these ends are distinct from utility: what they do is *promote* utility as a "super-end," as it were. In *Utilitarianism* Mill emphasized this super-end character of utility in two ways: (i) by reiterating the distinction between ultimate and secondary principles, and (ii) by providing "considerations capable of determining the intellect" (that is, a proof in the loose sense of the term) to the effect that happiness is the ultimate end to which all other ends are subservient. The "proof" in chapter four should be seen to serve the polemical role of stressing the character of utility as the overarching end of the Art of Life as a whole. In fact, after introducing the principle of utility in the *Logic* Mill referred to his "little volume" (read: *Utilitarianism*) for "an express discussion and vindication" of it,[25] which suggests that *he* took the discussion in the *Logic* to be consistent with that in *Utilitarianism*. Charging Mill with committing fallacies that philosophy undergraduates are trained to avoid is both preposterous and futile for the purposes of understanding Mill's sophisticated moral thought.

The passage that we have been examining mentions a crucial element of Mill's conception of morality we have still to discuss: the importance of moral character to human well-being. His claim is that cultivating feelings that make up a noble character and characterize noble actions is "an end" that human beings ought to embrace. Mill's account of character formation and its "laws" occupies an important chapter of the *Logic*.[26] Rather than discussing it, however, I shall provide a general account of the place of character in Mill's moral theory, which includes an interpretation of what *virtues* make up his ideal of moral character. My account here is based mainly on portions of *Utilitarianism* and of *The Subjection of Women*. I shall argue that Mill conceived of fraternity (in the guise of sympathy) and equality not only as moral ideals with important implications for politics, but also, and most importantly, as virtues of character whose cultivation is necessary for the promotion of human well-being. These values are among the "permanent" interests of humans considered as "progressive." The progressiveness of societies is tied closely to the formation of a sympathetic character.

III. THE MORAL SENTIMENTS AND SHARED GOODS

Before specifying what virtues make up Mill's ideal of moral character, we must at least briefly discuss the general relationship between virtue and utility in his moral theory.[27] In *Utilitarianism* Mill maintained that the general object of virtue is "the multiplication of happiness." (U, II, 17) In his view, "the utilitarian doctrine" (read: his own) "maintains not only that virtue is to be desired, but that it is to be desired disinterestedly, for itself." (U, IV, 5) Virtue is not only "at the head" of things that are good as means to utility. More importantly, for Mill, it is "a psychological fact" that virtue can be "to the individual, a good in itself, without looking to any end beyond it." In fact, Mill claimed, the mind is not in a right state, not in a state conformable to utility, not in the state most conducive to the general happiness, *unless it loves virtue in this manner*—as a thing desirable in itself, even although, in the individual instance, it should not produce those other desirable consequences which it tends to produce, and on account of which it is held to be virtue. (U, IV, 5, my emphasis)

Mill took the disinterested cultivation of virtue to be not only consistent with, but *required by,* utilitarianism. It is a mistake, he maintained, to suppose that the principle of utility requires that any given pleasure or exemption from pain "is to be looked upon as a means to a collective something termed happiness, and to be desired on that account." In the case of virtue, the utilitarian standard requires that it become for the moral agent a part of the end, that is, "something desired and cherished, not as a means to happiness, but as part of [the moral agent's] happiness." In other words, the Millean utilitarian is someone for whom virtue is not something to be "balanced" against considerations of "utility" and rejected when it fails to bring about "good" consequences. Rather, virtue is part of the utilitarian's good and, in that sense, inseparable from what it is to be a good person, *regardless* of consequences. Once acquired,[28] virtue is part of what is involved in being happy and inseparable from our conception of our own good. For Mill, part of what is involved in *desiring* happiness, then, is desiring virtue for its intrinsic goodness. In this sense, virtue is one "of the elements of which the desire for happiness is made up," and in this way, via the pursuit of goods that come to be desired for their intrinsic value, happiness becomes not "an abstract idea but a concrete whole."

How can virtue fail to have good consequences? Virtue, for Mill, can fail to have good consequences for *the agent* and when the object of action is supposed to be *the agent's own interest.* In other words, being virtuous does not always "pay" if the "returns" are to be cashed out in self-love currency. But self-love, or the agent's own good, is not the object of utilitarian morality. Utilitarians are concerned with the happiness of the whole, and virtue always "pays" in general happiness currency. Mill contended that the utilitarian standard "enjoins and requires the cultivation of the love of virtue up to the greatest strength possible, as being above all things important to the general happiness." (U, IV, 7) Unlike the love of money, the love of power, and the love of fame, which "may, and often do, render the individual noxious to the other members of the society to which he belongs," the disinterested love of virtue makes him "a blessing" to others. Although it may be doubted whether a virtuous person is always happier for her virtue, "there can be no doubt that [virtue] makes other people happier, and that the world in general is immensely a gainer for it." (U, II, 9) In *On Liberty* Mill made it clear that only other-regarding dispositions are virtues.[29] Similarly, only dispositions that are harmful to others enter into Mill's list of vices, notably:

> [c]ruelty of disposition; malice and ill-nature; that most antisocial and odious of all passions, envy; dissimulation and insincerity, irascibility on insufficient cause, and resentment disproportioned to the provocation; the love of domineering over others; the desire to engross more than one's share of advantages (the *pleonexia* of the Greeks); the pride which derives gratification from the abasement of others; the egotism which thinks self and its concerns more important than everything else, and decides all doubtful questions in its own favor. . . . (L, IV, 6)

By contrast to these, we can formulate a set of basic virtues that render life "a blessing," rather than a curse, to others: a benevolent, calm, and good-natured disposition; sympathy; sincerity or truthfulness; an egalitarian spirit; respectfulness of others' needs and humanity; and altruism, or a disinterested concern with others' good. I take these virtues to be part of the ideal of "nobleness of character" bound up with the utilitarian standard.

Mill's ideal of character is tied to human beings' capability of moral improvement. In *On Liberty,* we find a "definition" of utility quite different from the one we have examined so far: utility embodies, Mill maintained, "the permanent interests of man as a progressive being." (L, I, 11) The "spin" this definition puts on utility is different from, but consistent with, the more general ones in *Utilitarianism* and the *Logic.* In fact, the definition in *On Liberty* helps us further to elucidate the nature of the abstract utilitarian standard. The relevant initial questions to ask are, (i) Who is "man as a progressive being"? and (ii) What interests are permanent (and what did Mill mean by "permanent")? I have argued elsewhere that Millean utility is a progressive and historical standard.[30] "Progressiveness" is Mill's term for tendencies toward improvement (though not synonymous with improvement), which are exhibited both by human beings and by societies as a whole (the latter depending on the former). A progressive being is someone with the capacity to improve—cultivate, develop, and exercise—his or her higher faculties, namely, the intellect, the emotions, the imagination, and the moral sentiments. A progressive society is one that fosters and sustains this improvement in all of its members by means of the educative effects of its institutional and social arrangements. Progressiveness is tied to utility quite clearly: a progressive being is someone whose interests advance the general happiness, as opposed to someone concerned only with his or her own happiness (and that of close others); and a progressive society is one that promotes and preserves the interests of humans as progressive by providing the institutional and social conditions that make human improvement possible.

Progressive beings, Mill believed, have "permanent" interests. What explains these interests' permanence is that they are objective standards against which human flourishing must be measured under modern conditions.[31] The interests of human beings under modern conditions include morality, benevolence, democracy based on equality, liberty, active development, and human worth. In *Utilitarianism* Mill stressed the importance of security to human well-being by according it the status of "the most vital" human interest. (U, V, 25)[32] Yet I would suggest that this interest is of a different sort than the others: it functions as a precondition for the pursuit of our other interests or ends, by "making safe for us the very groundwork of our existence." The reason that security is so important is that no one can do without it, whereas, although it might not be desirable, we can, if necessary, do without other interests. Security has to do with protection ("immunity") from evil generally, which is for human beings a "most indispensable [necessary], after physical nutriment." Because of the very basic status of this interest—which, as its place next to physical nourishment suggests, is actually more a *basic need* than an interest in Mill's sense[33]—the rules of justice, with which he was concerned in this chapter of *Utilitarianism,* are the "chief part, and incomparably the most sacred and binding part," of morality. (U, V, 32) Both the principle of liberty and the principle of equality are parts of Mill's theory of justice[34] and, hence, among those "classes of moral rules which concern the essentials of human well-being more nearly, and are therefore of more absolute obligation, than any other rules for the guidance of human life."

According to Mill, orthodox utilitarians neglected the importance of human beings' permanent interests to utilitarian ethics and politics. As he attempted his rescue mission, Mill introduced these values as inextricably tied to the utilitarian standard. In *On Liberty* the focus is on liberty as a constituent of an ideal of character that has active development as its progressive engine. In *Utilitarianism* the focus is on the moral sentiments, notably sympathy, and the importance of their cultivation to progressiveness. And in *The Subjection of Women* the focus is on the value of "perfect equality," which complements the ideal of liberty and depends on the development of sympathy, which is the most important moral sentiment. I shall focus on how two of these, sympathy and equality, are interrelated in Mill's conception of moral character.

The importance of cultivating the "social"[36] part of our natures is not derivative for Mill: it is what characterizes us as human and makes it possible for us to flourish in social life, which involves cooperative and reciprocally rewarding human relations. In *Utilitarianism* sociability becomes the "internal sanction" of utility, that is, the basis of "powerful natural sentiment" that provides the motivation to be moral. (U, III, 10) In other words, the question, Why be moral? is, for Mill, answered with reference to morality's grounding on "the social feelings of mankind," notably "the desire to be in unity with our fellow creatures, which is already a powerful principle in human nature, and happily one of those which tend to become stronger, even without express inculcation, from the influences of advancing civilization." Mill's view is that the advancement of civilization can be measured by the degree to which is fostered our capacity for benevolent regard of other people's interests; for cooperation with others in promoting our "collective" interest, that is, the general happiness; and for equality. Mill added:

> Not only does all strengthening of social ties, and all healthy growth of society, give to each individual a stronger personal interest in practically consulting the welfare of others, it also leads him to identify *his feelings* more and more with their good, or at least with an even greater degree of practical consideration for it. He comes, as though instinctively, to be conscious of himself as a being who *of course* pays regard to others. The good of others becomes to him a thing naturally and necessarily to be attended to, like any of the physical conditions of our existence. (U, III, 10)

The "contagion of sympathy" and the influence of education (broadly understood) are the forces that propel the social feelings forward.

The role of sympathy in Mill's moral theory is apparent in his discussion of moral education in *Utilitarianism*. First, Mill argued, *as a remedy for selfishness* moral education should foster people's moral sentiments and their interests in the public good. He asserted that "[t]here is no reason why any human being should be a selfish egotist, devoid of every feeling or care but those which center in his own miserable individuality." (U, II, 12) People who structure their lives around their own "miserable individualities" cannot form cooperative and reciprocally rewarding associations with others. Second, Mill claimed, sympathetic benevolence, or "a direct impulse to promote the general good," must come to be among a person's habitual motives of action, and the sentiments connected with these sympathetic aims must come to "fill a large and prominent place in every human being's sentient existence." Utility does not render human beings "cold and unsympathizing," as objectors to Bentham's standard supposed. When responding to this objection, Mill described the utilitarian ethic *in terms of sympathy and love.* "In the golden rule of Jesus of Nazareth," Mill maintained,

> we read the complete spirit of the ethics of utility. "To do as you would be done by," and "to love your neighbor as yourself," constitute the ideal perfection of utilitarian morality. As the means of making the nearest approach to this ideal, utility would enjoin, first, that laws and social arrangements should place the happiness or (as, speaking practically, it may be called) the interest of every individual as nearly as possible in harmony with the interest of the whole; and, secondly, that education and opinion, which have so vast a power over human character, should so use that power as to establish in the mind of every individual an indissoluble association between his own happiness and the good of the whole, especially between his own happiness and the practice of such modes of conduct, negative and positive, as regard for the universal happiness prescribes. (U, II, 16)

Only those "whose mind is a moral blank" will be unmoved by the argument that it would not be good to be entirely without sympathy and consider it "a superstition of education or a law despotically imposed by the power of society." In fact, for Mill, as for Hume before him,[39] only sympathy can provide "a powerful internal binding force" to morality—what Mill referred to as utility's "ultimate sanction"—and counteract the dissolving force of analysis.

What is the peculiar contribution of sympathy to Mill's conception of moral character? Sympathy is the distinctive moral excellence or, more appropriately, the emotional basis for moral excellence. It is the sentiment upon which is built the edifice of one's moral personality, so to speak. Sympathy provides the "raw material" for the development of morality via sympathetic feelings, which are part of our constitution and "natural" in this sense. Given the importance of cultivating this sentiment, we can formulate the following prescription: both for the agent's sake and for the sake of others, the calling forth and cultivation of sympathy should be pursued as an end and to the utmost degree encouraged in others. As we have seen, Mill broke down this utilitarian requirement into two: one part concerns the harmony between individual and social interests achieved by good laws and social arrangements; and the other, the proper end of moral education, is achieved by instilling in people the right sorts of associations between their good and the good of others. It is the latter part that is encapsulated in the prescription above, which is phrased with character-formation in mind.

Now I want to turn to the remaining ideal, equality, as it pertains to the formation of a confirmed character. This ideal is the most important, yet perhaps the most difficult to make sense of *as an ideal of character.* Typically, equality is followed by the question, Of what? Some answers might be of opportunity, of resources, or of consideration before the law. This formulation of the ideal does not fit the model of excellence of character. Neither does what seems to be equality's relational character: equality is a rela-

tion that holds between two things (say, two sticks), or between portions of something divided into similar units (say, parcels of land ten acres each), or even between people, given some criterion (say, Donna is equal to Ray in that they are both autonomous rational agents). But what can equality mean when construed as an excellence of character? I suggest that it means the opposite of pride, understood as a vice premised on a false sense of superiority over others. On this construal, equality is a kind of moral humility premised on the full recognition of others as progressive beings with permanent interests. In addition, on this construal, liberty and equality as excellences of character are complementary: both are opposed to power. I shall now argue that this construal is the one Mill had in mind in *The Subjection of Women,* the work where he systematically discussed and defended the value of perfect equality as among the essentials of human well-being.

One of Mill's central concerns was with what power can do to individuals: how it can distort their characters and prevent them from living a flourishing life. Power, construed as dominating (or "domineering") power,[40] is not only the nemesis of perfect equality, a moral ideal that requires sympathy and reciprocity in human relations, but also of liberty. Mill believed that "the love of liberty and the love of power are in eternal antagonism." (S, IV, 19) The love of power has a corrupting influence on human beings: it leads them to perceive as virtues what are really vices of character.[41] In *The Subjection of Women* Mill argued that because men are trained from early on to feel superior to all women, they develop into self-centered tyrants who view their social power as natural and appropriate to their sex, and women's lack of selfhood as fitting to their natural lot in life, which is to serve and please men (by the way they look, as well as by their dispositions toward abnegation). Similarly, because women are trained from infancy to believe that their "nature" is to be passive in all affairs of life, they develop into meek "slaves" who view their lack of social power as natural and appropriate to their sex, and men's pride as fitting to their natural lot in life, which is to rule and protect women. Both "ideals" of character are morally odious: the former encourages the vices of selfishness, which promote social fragmentation; the latter encourages the vices of selflessness, which promote social apathy. These "artificial,"[42] gender-specific "ideals" of character—which we would call "masculinity" and "femininity" respectively—harm everyone: men, women, and society as a whole. To the extent that these false ideals are substituted by the ideal of perfect equality, Mill claimed, the fountain of human happiness will not dry up. Less metaphorically, Mill believed that the significant harms of inequality, which undermine the realization of the utilitarian ideal, are removable by human effort. In particular, Mill focused on two institutions: marriage, which instead of "the state of slavery lasting on" could be a paradigm for good human relationships based on the model of friendship,[43] or what Aristotle called friendship based on virtue[44] (S, I, 5); and the family, which instead of a "school of despotism" could be a "school of sympathy" based on egalitarian relationships between the adults. (S, II, 11) Mill's emphasis on the relational aspects of a good human life shows his commitment to a substantive ideal of equality, embodied not in abstract rules for counting utilities (roughly, the Benthamite formal standard of "everyone to count for one, no one for more than one") but rather in the character of *concrete human relations*. In the case of marriage, a woman and a man become equal partners when they are bound not by the "rule of force" and control,[45] but instead by sympathetic ties that move them to share a life together that is mutually enhancing and reciprocal in the distribution of benefits as well as burdens. The motive of sympathy that is cultivated in egalitarian relations is *the same motive* that underlies Mill's "progressive" understanding of utility.

Mill's principle of perfect equality prescribes shared power and privilege, as well as reciprocity and mutuality in social, not only legal, relations between women and men.[46] Mill contrasted the egalitarian ethic as a requirement of justice with the "command and obedience" ethic that requires fixed hierarchies in human relations. The command and obedience ethic places each person either "above" or "below" others. Where this ethic is the rule of life, human beings tend to view themselves and others in terms of the superior/inferior or better/worse categories. In other words, we tend to judge our own and others' worth on the basis of where we stand with respect to these categories. The command and obedience ethic, which fosters this tendency, is the antithesis of perfect equality: "to be an equal is to be an enemy." (S, II, 12) This ethic is the egoistic and competitive ethic that Mill condemned in *Utilitarianism* for rendering people cold and unsympathizing, for inducing them to regard their fellows as "struggling rivals for the means of happiness," and, as a result, for undermining their well-being. (U, II, 16) Complementing these criticisms, we find in *The Subjection of Women* Mill's argument that the command and obedience ethic in personal relations fosters vices of character, thereby sabotaging the quest for a flourishing life. This ethic encourages people to prefer "command of any kind" to the position of a subject, or *some* command over others even when one is in a position of a subject vis a vis someone else. (S, II, 12) In *The Subjection of Women* Mill focused on the command and obedience ethic in relations between women and men, both in and outside of the family (and marriage). But the ideal of perfect equality requires the complete overthrow of the command and obedience ethic *as a general ethic defining fundamentally inegalitarian relations in all aspects of social life.*[47]

The ideal of perfect equality is an ideal of human relations inseparable from an ideal of moral character. Human excellence, Mill maintained, is like a tree's: capable of self-development and good growth only if well-tended to and rightly nurtured from the outside. (L, III, 4; S, I, 16) Foremost among the right conditions for full self-development and good growth is cultivating confirming associations with others. Human flourishing is impossible apart from the blooming of other-regarding sentiments and affections. The strongest argument in *The Subjection of Women* is that perfect equality is a central element of the human good. The corrupting influence of power undermines the possibility of human happiness by frustrating the pursuit of key constituents of a good human life: unfeigned bonds of cooperation, friendship, and love. Human beings cannot be fully happy without relations of sympathetic unity with others. Despotism inhibits the prospect of forming and sustaining such relations. Thus, despotism renders the life of despots and subjects emotionally barren and incomplete. The cultivation of sympathy, which Mill took to play an important role in self-knowledge as well as in knowledge of others, is the antidote to the alienation of self, and of self from others, to which the command and obedience ethic lead.

My analysis of the relative contributions of fraternity and equality to Mill's conception of moral character renders them complementary values backed by the same strong impulse, the desire to be in unity with others. This desire expresses a fundamental psychological function: the need for confirmation of our own worth. This need can only be satisfied in the context of life-affirming relationships with others. Mill's account of the moral life underscores the irreplaceable value to human beings of shared goods, whose value depends in part in that each party to a relationship appreciates that the other values it. Mill was keenly sensitive to how our concrete attachments to others affect the kind of life we can expect to live. The life of the self-centered, selfish, or self-serving human being is an *impoverished* life. Mill's conception of a good human life as requiring qualitatively good relations with others ultimately rests on the (plausi-

ble) assumption that, given the sorts of creatures that we are, we cannot live *well* without others.

IV. CONCLUDING REMARKS: THE MILLEAN UTILITARIAN

I have offered an account of Mill's conception of utility that depends on taking the fundamental aim of a utilitarian ethic to be the burgeoning of human beings' sympathetic dispositions and sentiments. To be a Millean utilitarian it is not sufficient that our actions tend to promote the general happiness. Also necessary is that our character be constituted in a certain way: we must become beings who honor our own permanent interests and recognize others as beings of the same sort. Millean utilitarians strive to expand their sympathetic ties to others, because they recognize the value of sympathetic feelings to their lives and the life of society as a whole. Unlike Bentham, Mill stressed that we have fundamentally other-regarding needs, for example, to develop and maintain confirming associations with others. These needs can be satisfied only if we actualize our capabilities to become moral, that is, sympathetic people who appreciate the intrinsic value of conceiving of our good as intertwined with the good of others. Because we come to regard the cultivation of moral sentiments as part of what it is to be human, we do not dismiss moral education, particularly as concerns character formation, as despotic social conditioning or sheer brainwashing. As Mill put it, these traits are such that "it would not be well for [us] to be without" them. Unless our minds are morally blank, their absence tends to kindle a real sense of loss and longing. The greatest weakness of Benthamite utilitarianism, from this perspective, is that in denouncing the cultivation of moral sentiments as despotic, it *induces* minds to become moral blanks and so (in a self-defeating way) undermines the pursuit of human happiness.

Furthermore, from Mill's perspective, Bentham focused on the morality of actions (or, more appropriately, rules of actions that the legislator is charged with formulating) without taking into consideration that there is a crucial link between moral *character* and agency. He dismissed character as falling under the province of "private" utility and also relegated to this realm (if to any) considerations of the morality of human relations, which, as Mill recognized, fundamentally shape character formation. The nature of human relations was so important to Mill precisely because of their educative effect. Utilitarians, in his view, cannot disregard questions about what kind of persons we should be, because what kind of person we are determines to a great extent how we view and relate to others. They cannot disregard how we view and relate to others, because external sanctions—the fear of punishment, blame, social ostracism, and even eternal damnation—often fail to sustain morality. Also necessary is to cultivate the internal source of morality, sympathetic feelings, which form the basis for the moral sentiments. These sentiments are far from idiosyncrasies of taste: our capacity to be moral is the salient feature of our constitution. The moral sentiments are the most important of the "higher faculties" because on their development and exercise hinges the possibility of human well-being. Consequently, the most important form of human development for a Millean utilitarian is the development of the moral part of human nature.

NOTES

1. John Stuart Mill, "Remarks on Bentham's Philosophy," *Collected Works of John Stuart Mill,* ed. John Robson, (Toronto: University of Toronto Press, 1963–1991) Vol. X, p. 7.
2. For an important varied collection of essays on Mill's *Utilitarianism,* see *Mill's* Utilitarianism: *Critical Essays,* ed. David Lyons (Lanham, Maryland and Oxford, England: Rowman & Littlefield Publishers, Inc., 1997). Hereinafter *Critical Essays.*
3. For an interpretation of Mill's ethics as a form of act-utilitarianism, see *Mill's Ethical Writings,* ed. Jerome Schneewind (New York: Collier Books, 1965), pp. 7–39. The "classical" interpretation of Mill as a rule-utilitarian is found in J. O. Urmson, "The Interpretation of the Moral Philosophy of J.S. Mill," in *Critical Essays,* pp. 1–8. Variations of this theme are too many to cite in this context.
4. For an insightful discussion of the connection between character and utilitarianism, see Peter Railton, "How Thinking About Character and Utilitarianism Might Lead to Rethinking the Character of Utilitarianism," in *Critical Essays,* pp. 99–121.
5. For my conception of shared goods, see Maria H. Morales, *Perfect Equality: John Stuart Mill on Well-Constituted Communities* (Lanham, Maryland and Oxford, England: Rowman & Littlefield Publishers, Inc., 1996), p. 6. Hereinafter *Perfect Equality.*
6. Ibid., especially chapters 3–4 and 7.
7. Mill himself, like Aristotle before him, stressed that "the science of human nature" falls short of "the standard of exactness" realized in what we might call the *hard* sciences. This "inherent" imprecision is due (i) to the subject-matter of ethics, namely "the thoughts, feelings, and actions of human beings"; (ii) to the myriad of influences that shape our circumstances and characters at any given time; and (iii) to the fact that "the data are never all given, nor ever precisely alike in different cases." From these constraints it follows, according to Mill, that we can "neither make positive predictions, nor lay down universal propositions" in ethics, what we *can* do is make *verifiable* predictions and arrive at *approximate* generalizations resting on what Mill called "the universal laws of human nature," which suffices for the purposes of social inquiry—in fact, they are "equivalent" in the moral sciences to the "final" conclusions of the hard sciences. (See John Stuart Mill, *The Logic of the Moral Sciences* (LaSalle, Illinois: Open Court, 1987), p. 32; cf Aristotle, *Nicomachean Ethics,* Book I, chapter 3.)
8. David Lyons, ed., *Critical Essays,* Preface, p. ix.
9. Jeremy Bentham, *Introduction to the Principles of Morals and Legislation,* Chapter I, paragraph 2 (any edition).

10. D. G. Brown, "What is Mill's Principle of Utility?," in *Critical Essays*, pp. 10–14.

11. See, for example, D. G. Brown, "What is Mill's Principle of Utility?"; John Baker, "*Utilitarianism* and Secondary Principles," *Philosophical Quarterly*, 21 (1971, 69–71); and Maria H. Morales, *Perfect Equality*, pp. 80–81.

12. See, for example, Wendy Donner, "Mill's Utilitarianism," in *The Cambridge Companion to Mill*, ed. John Skorupski (Cambridge, England: Cambridge University Press, 1998), pp. 255–292.

13. I shall include references to Mill's *Utilitarianism* (U), *On Liberty* (L), and *The Subjection of Women* (S) in the text by chapter and paragraph number in any edition.

14. John Stuart Mill, *The Logic of the Moral Sciences*, pp. 135–136.

15. Ibid., p. 140.

16. Ibid., p. 141.

17. Ibid., pp. 142–143.

18. The "classical" arguments against interpreting Mill's ethics as involving a commitment to a "maximizing" standard are in David Lyons, "Mill's Theory of Justice," in *Values and Morals: Essays in Honor of William Frankena, Charles Stevenson, and Richard Brandt*, ed. Alvin Goldman and Jaegwon Kim (Dordrecht: D. Reidel, 1978), pp. 1–20.

19. John Stuart Mill, *The Logic of the Moral Sciences*, pp. 139–140.

20. Bentham certainly would have rejected Mill's construal of utilitarianism as based on substantive values and as requiring the cultivation of the moral sentiments. His critic James Fitzjames Stephen directly rejected Mill's interpretation of the "humanistic" creed in his *Liberty, Equality, Fraternity* (London: Smith Elden, 1873).

21. See David Lyons, "Mill's Theory of Justice," p. 12; "Mill's Theory of Morality," *Nous* 10 (1976), pp. 101–20; and "Human Rights and the General Welfare," in *Critical Essays*, pp. 29–43. See also John Gray, *Mill on Liberty: A Defence* (London: Routlege & Kegan Paul, 1983), pp. 30–34.

22. John Gray, *Mill on Liberty: A Defence*, p. 41.

23. John Stuart Mill, "Bentham," *Collected Works of John Stuart Mill, Vol. X*, pp. 98–99.

24. John Stuart Mill, *The Logic of the Moral Sciences*, p. 143.

25. Ibid., footnote.

26. Ibid., chapters three to five in particular.

27. For a detailed examination of this connection, see, for example, Semmel's interpretation in his *John Stuart Mill and The Pursuit of Virtue* (New Haven: Yale University Press, 1984).

28. For Mill, virtue is acquired by association (with ideas of pleasure and pain) and through habituation, as in Aristotle. See U, IV, 6; cf Aristotle, *Nicomachean Ethics*, Book II, chapter 1.

29. "Self-regarding" dispositions are not moral virtues, for Mill, but signs of a prudent character or of self-respect and a desire for self-development. Conversely, "self-regarding" faults are not moral vices, but signs of weakness or lack of self-control. However, I doubt that any of these dispositions is wholly self-regarding: prudence has "effects" on other people, and so does lack of self-control.

30. Maria H. Morales, *Perfect Equality*, pp. 75–83.

31. Ibid., pp. 77–78.

32. I thank Dale Miller for raising in conversation a question regarding the place of security among all these values.

33. I take "interest" in Mill to be linked to human progressiveness in a way that basic needs are not; the latter we share with all sentient creatures.

34. For an account of the place of liberty in Mill's conception of justice, see Fred Berger, *Happiness, Justice, and Freedom* (Berkley and Los Angeles: University of California Press, 1934). I discuss this connection in chapter 4 of *Perfect Equality* and the connection between equality and justice in chapters 5 and 6.

35. For a superb discussion of Mill's conception of the good, see Elizabeth Anderson, "Mill and Experiments of Living" in *Critical Essays*, pp. 123–147.

36. John Stuart Mill, *A System of Logic: Ratiocinative and Inductive, Collected Works of John Stuart Mill*, Vol. VII, pp. 842–43.

37. Mill's mature view is that moral development is the yardstick of progress, although earlier on he had suggested that intellectual improvement is key. See, Maria H. Morales, *Perfect Equality*, pp. 77–78.

38. Mill often slipped into using the term "social" in what Bentham would have called a "eulogistic" sense, that is, as carrying moral connotations. But the desire for domineering power over others, for example, is as "social" as the desire to live with them in terms of equality. Thus, it is better to use the term "social" as neutral and to use the

term "sympathetic" when moral connotations are sought.

39. David Hume, *A Treatise of Human Nature,* ed. Sir Amherst Selby-Bigge (rev. 2nd ed.), (Oxford, England: Oxford University Press, 1978), p. 457.

40. Maria H. Morales, *Perfect Equality,* chapters four and five, and "The Corrupting Influence of Power" in *Philosophical Perspectives on Power and Domination: Theories and Practices,* eds. Laura Duhan Kaplan and Lawrence F. Bove (Rodopi, 1997), pp. 41–53.

41. Maria H. Morales, *Perfect Equality,* pp. 122–126.

42. Mill's distinction between the natural and the artificial does not have normative content. The problem with the ideals of femininity and masculinity is not that they distort women's and men's underlying "real" natures, but rather that they prevent women and men from developing sentiments, aspirations, and skills that are good for anyone who has them. See Ibid., pp. 133–135.

43. For an insightful discussion of the ideal of marital friendship, see Mary Lyndon Shanley, "The Subjection of Women," in *The Cambridge Companion to Mill,* pp. 396–422, and Maria H. Morales, *Perfect Equality,* chapter six.

44. Aristotle, *Nicomachean Ethics,* Book IX, chapter 12.

45. The relevant respect in which the marriage is a form of "slavery" for women, for Mill, is that both involve the rule of force. The slavery analogy illustrates the role of force in women's subjection in several ways. First, the law enforced women's virtual inability to withdraw from marriage and all but condoned men's use of physical force against them. Second, like slaves properly so-called, married women owed absolute obedience to their masters and were told that their subjection is "natural." Thus, like slavery, he command and obedience marriage is an example of a social relation characterized by absolute power on the one hand and complete submission on the other.

46. I have argued that it is a mistake to interpret the principle of perfect equality as a formal principle that regulates only *legal* relations between women and men. See, in particular, Maria H. Morales, *Perfect Equality,* pp. 105–107 and chapters 5–6.

47. I have argued for this claim in chapters 3, 4 and 7 of *Perfect Equality.*

29. Universal Love

❧❦

MO TZU

Chapter 1

It is the business of the sages to effect the good government of the world. They must know,

Reprinted from *The Four Books,* edited and translated by James Legge. Originally Published in *The Chinese Classics,* Volume II (Oxford: Clarendon, 1895).

therefore, whence disorder and confusion arise, for without this knowledge their object cannot be effected. We may compare them to a physician who undertakes to cure men's diseases:—he must ascertain whence a disease has arisen, and then he can assail it with effect, while, without such knowledge, his endeavors will be in vain. Why should we except the case of those who have to regulate disorder from this rule? They must know whence it has arisen, and then they can regulate it.

It is the business of the sages to effect the good government of the world. They must examine therefore into the cause of disorder; and when they do so they will find that it arises from the want of mutual love. When a minister and a son are not filial to their sovereign and their father, this is what is called disorder. A son loves himself, and does not love his father;—he therefore wrongs his father, and seeks his own advantage: a younger brother loves himself and does not love his elder brother;—he therefore wrongs his elder brother, and seeks his own advantage: a minister loves himself, and does not love his sovereign;—he therefore wrongs his sovereign, and seeks his own advantage:—all these are cases of what is called disorder. Though it be the father who is not kind to his son, or the elder brother who is not kind to his younger brother, or the sovereign who is not gracious to his minister:—the case comes equally under the general name of disorder. The father loves himself, and does not love his son:—he therefore wrongs his son, and seeks his own advantage: the elder brother loves himself, and does not love his younger brother;—he therefore wrongs his younger brother, and seeks his own advantage: the sovereign loves himself, and does not love his minister;—he therefore wrongs his minister, and seeks his own advantage. How do these things come to pass? They all arise from the want of mutual love. Take the case of any thief or robber:—it is just the same with him. The thief loves his own house, and does not love his neighbour's house:—he therefore steals from his neighbour's house to benefit his own: the robber loves his own person, and does not love his neighbour;—he therefore does violence to his neighbour to benefit himself. How is this? It all arises from the want of mutual love. Come to the case of great officers throwing each other's Families into confusion, and of princes attacking one another's States:—it is just the same with them. The great officer loves his own Family, and does

not love his neighbour's;—he therefore throws the neighbour's Family into disorder to benefit his own: the prince loves his own State, and does not love his neighbour's:—he therefore attacks his neighbour's State to benefit his own. All disorder in the kingdom has the same explanation. When we examine into the cause of it, it is found to be the want of mutual love.

Suppose that universal, mutual love prevailed throughout the kingdom;—if men loved others as they love themselves, disliking to exhibit what was unfilial....And moreover would there be those who were unkind? Looking on their sons, younger brothers, and ministers as themselves, and disliking to exhibit what was unkind . . . the want of filial duty would disappear. And would there be thieves and robbers? When every man regarded his neighbour's house as his own, who would be found to steal? When everyone regarded his neighbour's person as his own, who would be found to rob? Thieves and robbers would disappear. And would there be great officers throwing one another's Families into confusion, and princes attacking one another's States? When officers regarded the families of others as their own, what one would make confusion? When princes regarded other States as their own, what one would begin an attack? Great officers throwing one another's Families into confusion, and princes attacking one another's States, would disappear.

If, indeed, universal, mutual love prevailed throughout the kingdom; one State not attacking another, and one Family not throwing another into confusion; thieves and robbers nowhere existing; rulers and ministers, fathers and sons, all being filial and kind:—in such a condition the nation would be well governed. On this account, how many sages, whose business it is to effect the good government of the kingdom, do but prohibit hatred and advise to love? On this account it is affirmed that universal mutual love throughout the country will lead to its happy order, and that mutual hatred leads to confusion. This was what our master, the philosopher Mo, meant, when he said, "We must above all inculcate the love of others."

CHAPTER II

Our Master, the philosopher Mo, said, "That which benevolent men consider to be incumbent on them as their business, is to stimulate and promote all that will be advantageous to the nation, and to take away all that is injurious to it. This is what they consider to be their business."

And what are the things advantageous to the nation, and the things injurious to it? Our master said, "The mutual attacks of State on State; the mutual usurpation of Family on Family; the mutual robberies of man on man; the want of kindness on the part of the ruler and of loyalty on the part of the minister; the want of tenderness and filial duty between father and son and of harmony between brothers:—these, and such as these, are the things injurious to the kingdom."

And from what do we find, on examination, that these injurious things are produced? Is it not from the want of mutual love?

Our Master said, "Yes, they are produced by the want of mutual love. Here is a prince who only knows to love his own State, and does not love his neighbour's;—he therefore does not shrink from raising all the power of his State to attack his neighbour. Here is the chief of a Family who only knows to love it, and does not love his neighbour's;—he therefore does not shrink from raising all his powers to seize on that other Family. Here is a man who only knows to love his own person, and does not love his neighbour's;—he therefore does not shrink from using all his resources to rob his neighbour. Thus it happens, that the princes, not loving one another, have their battle-fields; and the chiefs of Families, not loving one another, have their mutual usurpations; and men, not loving one another, have their mutual robberies; and rulers and ministers, not loving one another, become unkind and disloyal; and fathers and sons, not loving one another, lose their affection and filial duty; and brothers, not loving one another, con-

tract irreconcilable enmities. Yea, men in general not loving one another, the strong make prey of the weak; the rich do despite to the poor; the noble are insolent to the mean; and the deceitful impose upon the stupid. All the miseries, usurpations, enmities, and hatreds in the world, when traced to their origin, will be found to arise from the want of mutual love. On this account, the benevolent condemn it."

They may condemn it; but how shall they change it?

Our Master said, "They may change it by the law of universal mutual love and by the interchange of mutual benefits."

How will this law of universal mutual love and the interchange of mutual benefits accomplish this?

Our Master said, "It would lead to the regarding another's kingdom as one's own: another's family as one's own: another's person as one's own. That being the case, the princes, loving one another, would have no battle-fields; the chiefs of families, loving one another, would attempt no usurpations; men, loving one another, would commit no robberies; rulers and ministers, loving one another, would be gracious and loyal; fathers and sons, loving one another, would be kind and filial; brothers, loving one anther, would be harmonious and easily reconciled. Yea, men in general loving one another, the strong would not make prey of the weak; the many would not plunder the few; the rich would not insult the poor; the noble would not be insolent to the mean; and the deceitful would not impose upon the simple. The way in which all the miseries, usurpations, enmities, and hatreds in the world, may be made not to arise, is universal mutual love. On this account, the benevolent value and praise it."

Yes; but the scholars of the kingdom and superior men say, "True; if there were this universal love, it would be good. It is, however, the most difficult thing in the world."

Our Master said, "This is because the scholars and superior men simply do not understand the advantageousness of the law, and to conduct their reasonings upon that. Take the case of assaulting a city, or of a battle-field, or of the sacrificing one's life for the sake of fame:—this is felt by the people everywhere to be a difficult thing. Yet, if the ruler be pleased with it, both officers and people are able to do it:—how much more might they attain to universal mutual love, and the interchange of mutual benefits, which is different from this! When a man loves others, they respond to and love him; when a man benefits others, they respond to and benefit him; when a man injures others, they respond to and injure him; when a man hates others, they respond to and hate him:—what difficulty is there in the matter? It is only that rulers will not carry on the government on this principle, and so officers do not carry it out in their practice. . . ."

Yes; but now the officers and superior men say, "Granted; the universal practice of mutual love would be good; but it is an impracticable thing. It is like taking up the T'ai mountain, and leaping with it over the Ho or the Chi."

Our Master said, "That is not the proper comparison for it. To take up the T'ai mountain and leap with it over the Ho or the Chi, may be called an exercise of most extraordinary strength; it is, in fact, what no one, from antiquity to the present time, has ever been able to do. But how widely different from this is the practice of universal mutual love, and the interchange of mutual benefits!"

"Anciently, the sage kings practised this. . . ."

If, now, the rulers of the kingdom truly and sincerely wish all in it to be rich, and dislike any being poor; if they desire its good government, and dislike disorder; they ought to practice universal mutual love, and the interchange of mutual benefits. This was the law of the sage kings; it is the way to effect the good government of the nation; it may not but be striven after.

CHAPTER III

Our Master, the philosopher Mo, said, "The business of benevolent men requires that they should strive to stimulate and promote what is advantageous to the kingdom, and to take away what is injurious to it."

Speaking, now, of the present time, what are to be accounted the most injurious things to the kingdom? They are such as the attacking of small States by great ones; the inroads on small Families by great ones; the plunder of the weak by the strong; the oppression of the few by the many; the scheming of the crafty against the simple; the insolence of the noble to the mean. To the same class belong the ungraciousness of rulers, and the disloyalty of ministers; the unkindness of fathers, and the want of filial duty on the part of sons. Yea, there is to be added to these the conduct of the mean men, who employ their edged weapons and poisoned stuff, water and fire, to rob and injure one another.

Pushing on the inquiry now, let us ask whence all these injurious things arise. Is it from loving others and advantaging others? It must be answered "No"; and it must likewise be said, "They arise clearly from hating others and doing violence to others." If it be further asked whether those who hate and do violence to others hold the principle of loving all, or that of making distinctions, it must be replied, "They make distinctions." So then, it is the principle of making distinctions between man and man, which gives rise to all that is most injurious in the kingdom. On this account we conclude that the principle is wrong.

Our Master said, "He who condemns others must have means whereby to change them." To condemn men, and have no means of changing them, is like saving them from fire by plunging them in water. A man's language in such a case must be improper. On this account our Master said, "There is the principle of loving all, to take the place of that which makes distinctions." If, now, we ask, "And how is it that universal love can change the consequences of that other principle which makes distinctions?" the answer is, "If princes were as much for the States of others as for their own, what one among them would raise the forces of his State to attack that of another?—he is for that other as much as for himself. If they were for the capitals of others as much as for their own, what one would raise the forces of his capital to attack that of another?— he is for that as much as for his own. If chiefs regarded the families of others as their own, what one would lead the power of his Family to throw that of another into confusion?—he is for that other as much as for himself. If, now, States did not attack, nor holders of capitals smite, one another, and if Families were guilty of no mutual aggressions, would this be injurious to the kingdom, or its benefit? It must be replied, "This would be advantageous to the kingdom." Pushing on the inquiry, now, let us ask whence all these benefits arise. Is it from hating others and doing violence to others? It must be answered, "No"; and it must likewise be said, "They arise clearly from loving others and doing good to others." If it be further asked whether those who love others and do good to others hold the principle of making distinctions between man and man, or that of loving all, it must be replied, "They love all." So then it is this principle of universal mutual love which really gives rise to all that is most beneficial to the nation. On this account we conclude that that principle is right.

Our Master said, a little while ago, "The business of benevolent men requires that they should strive to stimulate and promote what is advantageous to the kingdom, and to take away what is injurious to it." We have now traced the subject up, and found that it is the principle of universal love which produces all that is most beneficial to the kingdom, and the principle of making distinctions which produces all that is injurious to it. On this account what our Master said, "The principle of making distinctions between man and man is wrong, and the principle of universal love is right," turns out to be correct as the sides of a square.

If, now, we just desire to promote the benefit of the kingdom, and select for that purpose the principle of universal love, then the acute ears and piercing eyes of people will hear and see for one another; and the strong limbs of people will move and be ruled for one another; and men of principle will instruct one another. It will come about that the old, who have neither wife nor children, will get supporters who will enable them to complete their years; and the young and weak, who have no parents, will yet find helpers that shall bring them up. On the contrary, if this principal of universal love is held not to be correct, what benefits will arise from such a view? What can be the reason that the scholars of the kingdom, whenever they hear of this principle of universal love, go on to condemn it? Plain as the case is, their words in condemnation of this principle do not stop;—they say "It may be good, but how can it be carried into practice?"

Our Master said, "Supposing that it could not be practiced, it seems hard to go on likewise to condemn it. But how can it be good, and yet incapable of being put into practice?"

Let us bring forward two instances to test the matter—Let anyone suppose the case of two individuals, the one of whom shall hold the principle of making distinctions, and the other shall hold the principle of universal love. The former of these will say, "How can I be for the person of my friend as much as for my own person? How can I be for the parents of my friend as much as for my own parents?" Reasoning in this way, he may see his friend hungry, but he will not feed him; cold, but he will not clothe him; sick, but he will not nurse him; dead, but he will not bury him. Such will be the language of the individual holding the principle of distinction, and such will be his conduct. He will say, "I have heard that he who wishes to play a lofty part among men, will be for the person of his friend as much as for his own person, and for the parents of his friend as much as for his own parents. It is only thus that he can attain his distinction?" Reasoning in this way, when he sees his friend hungry, he will feed him; cold, he will clothe him; sick, he will nurse him; dead, he will bury him. Such will be the language of him who holds the principle of universal love, and such will be his conduct.

The words of the one of these individuals are a condemnation of those of the other, and their conduct is directly contrary. Suppose now that their words are perfectly sincere, and that their conduct will be carried out,—that their words and actions will correspond like the parts of a token, every word being carried into effect; and let us proceed to put the following questions on the case:—Here is a plain in the open country, and an officer, with coat of mail, gorget, and helmet, is about to take part in a battle to be fought in it, where the issue, whether for life or death, cannot be foreknown; or here is an officer about to be dispatched on a distant commission from Pa to Yüeh, or from Ch'i to Ching, where the issue of the journey, going and coming, is quite uncertain—on either of these suppositions, to whom will the officer entrust the charge of his house, the support of his parents, and the care of his wife and children?—to one who holds the principle of universal love? or to one who holds that which makes distinctions? I apprehend there is no one under heaven, man or woman, however stupid, though he may condemn the principle of universal love, but would at such a time make one who holds it the subject of his trust. This is in words to condemn the principle, and when there is occasion to choose between it and the opposite, to approve it;—words and conduct are here in contradiction. I do not know how it is that throughout the kingdom scholars condemn the principle of universal love, whenever they hear it.

Plain as the case is, their words in condemnation of it do not cease, but they say, "This principle may suffice perhaps to guide in the choice of an officer, but it will not guide in the choice of a sovereign."

Let us test this by taking two illustrations:—Let anyone suppose the case of two sovereigns, the one of whom shall hold the principle of mutual love, and the other shall hold the principle which makes distinctions. In this case, the latter of them will say, "How can I be as much for the persons of all my people as for my own? This is much opposed to human feelings. The life of man upon the earth is but a very brief space; it may be compared to the rapid movement of a team of horses whirling past a small chink." Rea-

soning in this way, he may see his people hungry, but he will not feed them; cold, but he will not clothe them; sick, but he will not nurse them; dead, but he will not bury them. Such will be the language of the sovereign who holds the principle of distinctions, and such will be his conduct. Different will be the language and conduct of the other who holds the principle of universal love. He will say, "I have heard that he who would show himself a virtuous and intelligent sovereign, ought to make his people the first consideration, and think of himself only after them." Reasoning in this way, when he sees any of the people hungry, he will feed them; cold he will clothe them; sick, he will nurse them; dead, he will bury them. Such will be the language of the sovereign who holds the principle of universal love, and such his conduct. If we compare the two sovereigns, the words of the one are condemnatory of those of the other, and their actions are opposite. Let us suppose that their words are equally sincere, and that their actions will make them good—that their words and actions will correspond like the parts of a token, every word being carried into effect; and let us proceed to put the following questions on the case:—Here is a year when a pestilence walks abroad among the people; many of them suffer from cold and famine; multitudes die in the ditches and water-channels. If at such a time they might make an election between the two sovereigns whom we have supposed, which would they prefer? I apprehend there is no one under heaven, however stupid, though he may condemn the principle of universal love, but would at such a time prefer to be under the sovereign who holds it. This is in words to condemn the principle, and, when there is occasion to choose between it and the opposite, to approve it;—words and conduct are here in contradiction. . . .

. . . How is that the scholars throughout the kingdom condemn this universal love, whenever they hear of it? Plain as the case is, the words of those who condemn the principle of universal love do not cease. They say, "It is not advantageous to the entire devotion to parents which is required:—it is injurious to filial piety." Our Master said, "Let us bring this objection to the test:—A filial son, having the happiness of his parents at heart, considers how it is to be secured. Now, does he, so considering, wish men to love and benefit his parents? or does he wish them to hate and injure his parents?" On this view of the question, it must be evident that he wishes men to love and benefit his parents. And what must he himself first do in order to gain this object? If I first address myself to love and benefit men's parents, will they for that return love and benefit to my parents? or if I first address myself to hate men's parents, will they for that return love and benefit to my parents? It is clear that I must first address myself to love and benefit men's parents, and they will return to me love and benefit to my parents. The conclusion is that a filial son has no alternative.—He must address himself in the first place to love and do good to the parents of others. If it be supposed that this is an accidental course, to be followed on emergency by a filial son, and not sufficient to be regarded as a general rule, let us bring it to the test to what we find in the Books of the ancient kings.—It is said in the Ta Ya,

Every word finds its answer;
    Every action its recompense
    He threw me a peach;
    I returned him a plum.

These words show that he who loves others will be loved, and that he who hates others will be hated. How is it that the scholars throughout the kingdom condemn the principle of universal love, when they hear it?. . . .

. . . And now, as to universal mutual love, it is an advantageous thing and easily practiced—beyond all calculation. The only reason why it is not practised is, in my opinion, because superiors do not take pleasure in it. If superiors were to take pleasure in it, stimulating men to it by rewards and praise, and awing them from opposition to it by punishments and fines, they would, in my opinion, move to it—the practice of universal mutual love, and the interchange of mutual benefits—as fire rises upwards, and as water flows downwards:—nothing would be able to check them. This universal love was the way of the sage kings; it is the principle to secure peace for kings, dukes, and great men; it is the means to secure plenty of food and clothes for the myriads of the people. The best course for the superior man is to well understand the principle of universal love, and to exert himself to practice it. It requires the sovereign to be gracious, and the minister to be loyal; the father to be kind and the son to be filial; the elder brother to be friendly, and the younger to be obedient. Therefore the superior man,—with whom the chief desire is to see gracious sovereigns and loyal ministers; kind fathers and filial sons; friendly elder brothers and obedient younger ones—ought to insist on the indispensableness of the practice of universal love. It was the way of the sage kings; it would be the most advantageous thing for the myriads of the people.

RECOMMENDED READINGS

Texts

Berger, Fred. *Happiness, Justice and Freedom.* Berkeley: University of California Press, 1985.
Brittain, Karl. *John Stuart Mill.* Harmondsworth: Penguin, 1953.
Donner, Wendy. *The Liberal Self: John Stuart Mill's Moral and Political Philosophy.* Ithaca, NY: Cornell University Press, 1991.
Gorowitz, S., ed. *Utilitarianism and Critical Essays.* Indianapolis: Bobbs-Merrill, 1971.

Gray, John. *Mill on Liberty: A Defence.* London: Routledge, 1983.
Plamenatz, John. *The English Utilitarians.* Oxford: Blackwell, 1949.
Radcliff, Peter, ed. *Limits of Liberty.* Belmont, CA: Wadsworth, 1966.
Ryan, Alan. *Mill.* London: Routledge, 1974.
Thomas, William. *J. S. Mill.* Oxford University Press, 1985.

Feminist Perspective

Annas, Julia. "Mill and the Subjection of Women," *Philosophy* 52 (1977).
Boralevi, Lea Campos. "Utilitarianism and Feminism." In *Women in Western Political Philosophy,* edited by Ellen Kennedy and Susan Mendus. Brighton: Wheatsheaf Books, 1987.
Held, Virginia. "Justice and Harriet Taylor." *The Nation* (October 25, 1971): 405–406.
Mill, John Stuart, and Harriet Taylor. *Essays on Sex Equality,* edited by Alice C. Rossi. Chicago: University of Chicago Press, 1970.
Morales, Maria. *Perfect Equality: John Stuart Mill on Well-Constituted Communities.* New York: Rowman and Littlefield, 1996.

Multicultural Perspective

Fang, Thomas, *The Chinese View of Life and Creativity in Man and Nature.* Taipei: Linking, 1980.
Schwartz, Benjamin, *The World of Thought in Ancient China.* Cambridge, MA: Harvard University Press, 1985.

PART VIII

❦

NIETZSCHE

INTRODUCTION

Friedrich Nietzsche was born near Leipzig, Germany in 1844. His father was a Lutheran minister and the son of a minister; his mother was the daughter of a Lutheran minister. A number of Nietzsche's ancestors had been butchers; none of them seem to have been Polish noblemen as Nietzsche believed. His was christened Friedrich Wilhelm after King Friedrich Wilhelm IV of Prussia on whose birthday he was born. The king became insane a few years later, as did Nietzsche's father. Nietzsche later shed his middle name, along with his family's patriotism and religion, but in 1889, he too became insane, probably from syphilis contracted during his university years.

Nietzsche studied theology and classical philology at the University of Bonn, transferring in 1865 to the University of Leipzig to study philology with Friedrich Ritschl. When the chair of classical philology at Basel became vacant, Ritschl recommended Nietzsche, even though he had neither received his degree nor written a dissertation. The result was that Nietzsche found himself appointed a university professor before he had taken his doctorate, something very unusual for his time. He taught at Basel for ten years, until he had to retire because of poor health. During this stay at Basel, Nietzsche became very friendly with Richard Wagner, the famous composer. In his first major work, *The Birth of Tragedy,* in 1872, Nietzsche argued that contemporary German culture could be saved only if it were permeated with the spirit of Wagner.

Although there are many negative remarks about women in Nietzsche's writings, there were two women whom he both loved and admired. One was Cosima Wagner, the wife of Richard Wagner, and the other was Lou Solomé, a younger woman, whom he met in the spring of 1882. Nietzsche thought of Solomé as a disciple who could carry on his work: "I conceived the plan of leading you step by step to the final consequences of my philosophy—you as the first person I took to be fit for this." The relationship went on for ten months, and it ended apparently because Solomé thought that although Nietzsche proposed marriage, what he was really interested in was "secretarial use and sexual abuse." During the time of the relationship, however, Nietzsche wrote differently about women:

> A powerful contralto voice, as we occasionally hear it in the theatre, raises suddenly for us the curtain on possibilities in which we usually do not believe; all at once we are convinced that somewhere in the world there may be women with high, heroic, royal souls, capable and prepared for domination over men, because in them the best in man, superior to sex has become a corporeal ideal.[1]

One can only wonder whether Nietzsche's views on women would have continued to develop in this different direction if he had been able to sustain his relationship with Lou Solomé. But after the breakup with Solomé, he never again wrote in this way about women.[2]

After leaving the university, Nietzsche recovered his health somewhat and was extremely prolific. He wrote *Human all too Human* in 1880, *The Dawn of Day* in 1881, *The Gay Science* in 1882, *Thus Spoke Zarathustra* in 1884, *Beyond Good and Evil* in 1886, *Genealogy of Morals* in 1887, *The AntiChrist* in 1889, and his final work—a collection of fragments—*The Will to Power* also in 1889. In that same year in Turin, Nietzsche, excited by the effort of trying to protect a horse from being beaten, had a violent seizure and lapsed into insanity. He died the next year.

In our selection from *Beyond Good and Evil,* Nietzsche attacks traditional Western morality, the morality of "good and evil." But he begins by attacking the theoreticians of morality, those who have tried to squeeze all of the varieties of morality into a single mold, and have thereby tried to justify their own "moral prejudices." Nietzsche asks why people should adopt a morality at all. He thinks we have currently adopted a morality of timidity, or a herd morality, because of our commitment to democracy (the equality of all persons) and Christianity (compassion for the weak and suffering).

Nietzsche favors a different morality, a morality of nobility in which a few people are, and are recognized to be, superior to all the rest. A morality of nobility is a master morality. It is a morality of self-assertion and respect for excellence. By contrast, a slave morality is a morality of weakness. It requires those who are superior to "level" themselves, to bring themselves down to everyone else and so become wholly nonthreatening; it praises the mediocre.

In "Nietzsche and Moral Change," Kathryn Pyne Addelson argues that the narrow focus of traditional ethics enables it to understand moral reform but not moral revolution of the sort Nietzsche was advocating. She claims that a Nietzschean typology of morals is more adequate because it incorporates both the notions of moral reform and moral revolution. She illustrates the usefulness of Nietzsche's typology by applying it to a particular case of moral revolution—the women's revolution of the nineteenth century She also claims that this way of understanding Nietzsche's work helps to put his views about women in proper focus.

In "Nietzsche's Trans-European Eye," Mervyn Sprung explores the nature and extent of Nietzsche's use of Indian thought. Nietzsche himself speaks of his "transEuropean eye," which enables him to see that "Indian philosophy is the only major parallel to our European philosophy." After surveying the various references that Nietzsche made to Indian thought in his works, as well as the resources for learning Indian thought that were available to him at the time, Sprung concludes that although Nietzsche's understanding of Indian thought was less than adequate, he definitely did try to use what he knew to undermine traditional European categories.

NOTES

1. Friedrich Nietzsche, *The Gay Science* 103#70
2. For a discussion of Nietzsche's views about women, see Christine Garside Allen, "Nietzsche's Ambivalence about Women," in *The Sexism of Social and Political Theory* edited by Lorenne Clark and Lynda Lange (Toronto: University of Toronto Press, 1979). pp. 117–133.

30. BEYOND GOOD AND EVIL

FRIEDRICH NIETZSCHE

THE NATURAL HISTORY OF MORALS

The moral sentiment in Europe at present is perhaps as subtle, belated, diverse, sensitive, and refined, as the "Science of Morals" belonging thereto is recent, initial, awkward, and coarse-fingered:—an interesting contrast, which sometimes becomes incarnate and obvious in the very person of a moralist. Indeed, the expression, "Science of Morals" is, in respect to what is designated thereby, far too presumptuous and counter to *good* taste,—which is always a foretaste of more modest expressions. One ought to avow with the utmost fairness *what* is still necessary here for a long time, *what* is alone proper for the present: namely, the collection of material, the comprehensive survey and classification of an immense domain of delicate sentiments of worth, and distinctions of worth, which live, grow, propagate, and perish—and perhaps attempts to give a clear idea of the recurring and more common forms of these living crystallisations—as preparation for a *theory of types* of morality. To be sure, people have not hitherto been so modest. All the philosophers, with a pedantic and ridiculous seriousness, demanded of themselves something very much higher, more pretentious, and ceremonious, when they concerned themselves with morality as a science: they wanted to *give a basis* to morality—and every philosopher hitherto has believed that he has given it a basis; morality itself, however, has been regarded as something "given." How far

Reprinted from *The Complete Works of Nietzsche* trans. by Helen Zimmern. First published in 1907.

from their awkward pride was the seemingly insignificant problem—left in dust and decay—of a description of forms of morality, notwithstanding that the finest hands and senses could hardly be fine enough for it! It was precisely owing to moral philosophers knowing the moral facts imperfectly, in an arbitrary epitome, or an accidental abridgment—perhaps as the morality of their environment, their position, their church, their *Zeitgeist,* their climate and zone—it was precisely because they were badly instructed with regard to nations, eras, and past ages, and were by no means eager to know about these matters, that they did not even come in sight of the real problems of morals—problems which only disclose themselves by a comparison of *many* kinds of morality. In every "Science of Morals" hitherto, strange as it may sound, the problem of morality itself has been *omitted;* there has been no suspicion that there was anything problematic there! That which philosophers called "giving a basis to morality," and endeavoured to realise, has, when seen in a right light, proved merely a learned form of good *faith* in prevailing morality, a new means of its *expression,* consequently just a matter-of-fact within the sphere of a definite morality, yea, in its ultimate motive, a sort of denial that it is *lawful* for this morality to be called in question—and in any case the reverse of the testing, analysing, doubting, and vivisecting of this very faith. Hear, for instance, with what innocence—almost worthy of honour—Schopenhauer represents his own task, and draw your conclusions concerning the scientificalness of a "Science" whose latest master still talks in the strain of children and old wives: "The principle," he says (page 136 of the *Grund-*

probleme der Ethik[1], "the axiom about the purport of which all moralists are *practically* agreed: *neminem læde, immo omnes quantum potes juva*—is *really* the proposition which all moral teachers strive to establish, ... the *real* basis of ethics which has been sought, like the philosopher's stone, for centuries."—The difficulty of establishing the proposition referred to may indeed be great—it is well known that Schopenhauer also was unsuccessful in his efforts; and whoever has thoroughly realised how absurdly false and sentimental this proposition is, in a world whose essence is Will to Power, may be reminded that Schopenhauer, although a pessimist, *actually*—played the flute ... daily after dinner: one may read about the matter in his biography. A question by the way: a pessimist, a repudiator of God and of the world, who *makes a halt* at morality—who assents to morality, and plays the flute to *læde-neminem* morals, what? Is that really—a pessimist?

Apart from the value of such assertions as "there is a categorical imperative in us," one can always ask: What does such an assertion indicate about him who makes it? There are systems of morals which are meant to justify their author in the eyes of other people; other systems of morals are meant to tranquillise him, and make him self-satisfied; with other systems he wants to crucify and humble himself; with others he wishes to take revenge; with others to conceal himself; with others to glorify himself and gain superiority and distinction;—this system of morals helps its author to forget, that system makes him, or something of him, forgotten; many a moralist would like to exercise power and creative arbitrariness over mankind; many another, perhaps, Kant especially, gives us to understand by his morals that "what is estimable in me, is that I know how to obey—and with you it *shall* not be otherwise than with me!" In short, systems of morals are only a *sign-language of the emotions.*

In contrast to *laisser-aller,* every system of morals is a sort of tyranny against "nature" and also against "reason"; that is, however, no objection, unless one should again decree by some system of morals, that all kinds of tyranny and unreasonableness are unlawful. What is essential and invaluable in every system of morals, is that it is a long constraint. In order to understand Stoicism, or Port-Royal, or Puritanism, one should remember the constraint under which every language has attained to strength and freedom—the metrical constraint, the tyranny of rhyme and rhythm. How much trouble have the poets and orators of every nation given themselves!—not excepting some of the prose writers of to-day, in whose ear dwells an inexorable conscientiousness—"for the sake of a folly," as utilitarian bunglers say, and thereby deem themselves wise—"from submission to arbitrary laws," as the anarchists say, and thereby fancy themselves "free," even free-spirited. The singular fact remains, however, that everything of the nature of freedom, elegance, boldness, dance, and masterly certainty, which exists or has existed, whether it be in thought itself, or in administration, or in speaking and persuading, in art just as in conduct, has only developed by means of the tyranny of such arbitrary law; and in all seriousness, it is not at all improbable that precisely this is "nature" and "natural"—and *not laisser-aller!* Every artist knows how different from the state of letting himself go, is his "most natural" condition, the free arranging, locating, disposing, and constructing in the moments of "inspiration"—and how strictly and delicately he then obeys a thousand laws, which, by their very rigidness and precision, defy all formulation by means of ideas (even the most stable idea has, in comparison therewith, something floating, manifold, and ambiguous in it). The essential thing "in heaven and in earth" is, apparently (to repeat it once more), that there should be long *obedience* in the same direction; there thereby results, and has always resulted in the long run, something which has made life worth living; for instance, virtue, art, music, dancing, reason, spirituality—anything whatever that is transfiguring, refined, foolish, or divine. The long bondage of the spirit, the distrustful constraint in the communicability of ideas, the discipline which the thinker imposed on himself to think in accordance with the rules of a church or a court, or conformable to Aristotelian premises, the persistent spiritual will to interpret everything that happened according to a Christian scheme, and in every occurrence to rediscover and justify the Christian God:—all this violence, arbitrariness, severity, dreadfulness, and unreasonableness, has proved itself the disciplinary means whereby the European spirit has attained its strength, its remorseless curiosity and subtle mobility; granted also that much irrecoverable strength and spirit had to be stifled, suffocated, and spoilt in the process (for here, as everywhere, "nature" shows herself as she is, in all her extravagant and *indifferent* magnificence, which is shocking, but nevertheless noble). That for centuries European thinkers only thought in order to prove something—nowadays, on the contrary, we are suspicious of every thinker who "wishes to prove something"—that it was always settled beforehand what *was to be* the result of their strictest thinking, as it was perhaps in the Asiatic astrology of former times, or as it is still at the present day in the innocent, Christian-moral explanation of immediate personal events "for the glory of God," or "for the good of the soul":—this tyranny, this arbitrariness, this severe and magnificent stupidity, has *educated* the spirit; slavery, both in the coarser and the finer sense, is apparently an indispensable means even of spiritual education and discipline. One may look at every system of morals in this light: it is "nature" therein which teaches to hate the *laisser-aller,* the too great freedom, and implants the need for limited horizons, for immediate duties—it teaches the *narrowing of perspectives,* and thus, in a certain sense, that stupidity is a condition of life and development. "Thou must obey some one, and for a long time; *otherwise* thou wilt come to grief, and lose all respect for thyself"—this seems to me to be the moral imperative of nature, which is certainly neither "categorical," as old Kant wished (consequently the "otherwise"), nor does it address itself to the individual (what does nature care for the individual!), but to nations, races, ages, and ranks, above all, however, to the animal "man" generally, to *mankind.* . . .

The old theological problem of "Faith" and "Knowledge," or more plainly, of instinct and reason—the question whether, in respect to the valuation of things, instinct deserves more authority than rationality, which wants to appreciate and act according to motives, according to a "Why," that is to say, in conformity to purpose and utility—it is always the old moral problem that first appeared in the person of Socrates, and had divided men's minds long before Christianity. Socrates himself, following, of course, the taste of his talent—that of a surpassing dialectician—took first the side of reason; and, in fact, what did he do all his life but laugh at the awkward incapacity of the noble Athenians, who were men of instinct, like all noble men, and could never give satisfactory answers concerning the motives of their actions? In the end, however, though silently and secretly, he laughed also at himself: with his finer conscience and introspection, he found in himself the same difficulty and incapacity. "But why"—he said to himself—"should one on that account separate oneself from the instincts! One must set them right, and the reason *also*—one must follow the instincts, but at the same time persuade the reason to support them with good arguments." This was the real *falseness* of that great and mysterious ironist; he brought his conscience up to the point that he was satisfied with a kind of self-outwitting: in fact, he perceived the irrationality in the moral judgment.—Plato, more innocent in such matters, and without the craftiness of the plebeian, wished to prove to himself, at the expenditure of all his strength—the greatest strength a philosopher had ever expended—that reason and instinct lead spontaneously to one goal, to the good, to "God"; and since Plato, all theologians and philosophers have followed the same path—which means that in matters of morality, instinct (or as Christians call it, "Faith," or as I call it, "the herd") has hitherto triumphed. Unless one should make an exception in the case of Descartes, the father of rationalism (and consequently the grandfather of the Revolution), who recognised only the authority of reason: but reason is only a tool, and Descartes was superficial. . . .

Inasmuch as in all ages, as long as mankind has existed, there have also been human herds (family alliances, communities, tribes, peoples, states, churches), and always a great number who obey in proportion to the small number who command—in view, therefore, of the fact that obedience has been most practised and fostered among mankind hitherto, one may reasonably suppose that, generally speaking, the need thereof is now innate in every one, as a kind of *formal conscience* which gives the command: "Thou shalt unconditionally do some thing, unconditionally refrain from something"; in short, "Thou shalt." This need tries to satisfy itself and to fill its form with a content; according to its strength, impatience, and eagerness, it at once seizes as an omnivorous appetite with little selection, and accepts whatever is shouted into its ear by all sorts of commanders—parents, teachers, laws, class prejudices, or public opinion. The extraordinary limitation of human development, the hesitation, protractedness, frequent retrogression, and turning thereof, is attributable to the fact that the herd-instinct of obedience is transmitted best, and at the cost of the art of command. If one imagine this instinct increasing to its greatest extent, commanders and independent individuals will finally be lacking altogether; or they will suffer inwardly from a bad conscience, and will have to impose a deception on themselves in the first place in order to be able to command: just as if they also were only obeying. This condition of things actually exists in Europe at present—I call it the moral hypocrisy of the commanding class. They know no other way of protecting themselves from their bad conscience than by playing the rôle of executors of older and higher orders (of predecessors, of the constitution, of justice, of the law, or of God himself), or they even justify themselves by maxims from the current opinions of the herd, as "first servants of their people," or "instruments of the public weal." On the other hand, the gregarious European man nowadays assumes an air as if he were the only kind of man that is allowable; he glorifies his qualities, such as public spirit, kindness, deference, industry, temperance, modesty, indulgence, sympathy, by virtue of which he is gentle, endurable, and useful to the herd, as the peculiarly human virtues. In cases, however, where it is believed that the leader and bell-wether cannot be dispensed with, attempt after attempt is made nowadays to replace commanders by the summing together of clever gregarious men: all representative constitutions, for example, are of this origin. In spite of all, what a blessing, what a deliverance from a weight becoming unendurable, is the appearance of an absolute ruler for these gregarious Europeans—of this fact the effect of the appearance of Napoleon was the last great proof: the history of the influence of Napoleon is almost the history of the higher happiness to which the entire century has attained in its worthiest individuals and periods. . . .

After the fabric of society seems on the whole established and secured against external dangers, it is this fear of our neighbour which again creates new perspectives of moral valuation. Certain strong and dangerous instincts, such as the love of enterprise, foolhardiness, revengefulness, astuteness, rapacity, and love of power, which up till then had not only to be honoured from the point of view of general utility—under other names, of course, than those here given—but had to be fostered and cultivated (because they were perpetually required in the common danger against the common enemies), are now felt in their dangerousness to be doubly strong—when the outlets for them are lacking—and are gradually branded as immoral and given over to calumny. The contrary instincts and inclinations now attain to moral honour; the gregarious instinct gradually draws its conclusions. How much or how little dangerousness to the community or to equality is contained in an opinion, a condition, an emotion, a disposition, or an endowment—that is now the moral perspective; here again fear is the mother of morals. It is by the loftiest and strongest instincts, when they break out passionately and carry the individual far above and beyond the average, and the low level of the gregarious conscience, that the self-reliance of the community is destroyed; its belief in itself, its backbone, as it were, breaks; consequently these very instincts will be most branded and defamed. The lofty independent spirituality, the will to stand alone, and even the cogent reason, are felt to be dangers; everything that elevates the individual above the herd, and is a source of fear to the neighbour, is henceforth called *evil;* the tolerant, unassuming, self-adapting, self-equalising disposition, the *mediocrity* of desires, attains to moral distinction and honour. Finally, under very peaceful circumstances, there is always less opportunity and necessity for training the feelings to severity and rigour; and now every form of severity, even in justice, begins to disturb the conscience; a lofty and rigorous nobleness and self-responsibility almost offends, and awakens distrust, "the lamb," and still more "the sheep," wins respect. There is a point of diseased mellowness and effeminacy in the history of society, at which society itself takes the part of him who injures it, the part of the *criminal,* and does so, in fact, seriously and honestly. To punish, appears to it to be somehow unfair—it is certain that the idea of "punishment" and "the obligation to punish" are then painful and alarming to people. "Is it not sufficient if the criminal be rendered *harmless?* Why should we still punish? Punishment itself is terrible!"—with these questions gregarious morality, the morality of fear, draws its ultimate conclusion. If one could at all do away with danger, the cause of fear, one would have done away with this morality at the same time, it would no longer be necessary, it would not consider itself any longer necessary!—Whoever examines the conscience of the present-day European, will always elicit the same imperative from its thousand moral folds and hidden recesses, the imperative of the timidity of the herd: "we wish that some time or other there may be *nothing more to fear!*" Some time or other—the will and the way *thereto* is nowadays called "progress" all over Europe.

Let us at once say again what we have already said a hundred times, for people's ears nowadays are unwilling to hear such truths—*our* truths. We know well enough how offensively it sounds when any one plainly, and without metaphor, counts man amongst the animals; but it will be accounted to us almost a *crime,* that it is precisely in respect to men of "modern ideas" that we have constantly applied the terms "herd," "herd-instincts," and such like expressions. What avail is it? We cannot do otherwise, for it is precisely here that our new insight is. We have found that in all the principal moral judgments Europe has become unanimous, including likewise the countries where European influence prevails: in Europe people evidently *know* what Socrates thought he did not know, and what the famous serpent of old once promised to teach—they "know" to-day what is good and evil. It must then sound hard and be distasteful to the ear, when we always insist that that which here thinks it knows, that which here glorifies itself with praise and blame, and calls itself good, is the instinct of the herding human animal: the instinct which has come and is ever coming more and more to the front, to preponderance and supremacy over other instincts, according to the increasing physiological approximation and resemblance of which it is the symptom. *Morality in Europe at present is herding-animal morality;* and therefore, as we understand the matter, only one kind of human morality, beside which, before which, and after which many other moralities, and above all *higher* moralities, are or should be possible. Against such a "possibility," against such a "should be," however, this morality defends itself with all its strength; it says obstinately and inexorably: "I am morality itself and nothing else is morality!" Indeed, with the help of a religion which has humoured and flattered the sublimest desires of the herding-animal, things have reached such a point that we always find a more visible expression of this morality even in political and social arrangements: the *democratic* movement is the inheritance of the Christian movement. That its *tempo,* however, is much too slow and sleepy for the more impatient ones, for those who are sick and distracted by the herding-instinct, is indicated by the increasingly furious howling, and always less disguised teeth-gnashing of the anarchist dogs, who are now roving through the highways of European culture. Apparently in opposition to the peacefully industrious democrats and Revolution-ideologues, and still more so to the awkward philosophasters and fraternity-visionaries who call themselves Socialists and want a "free society," those are really at one with them all in their thorough and instinctive hostility to every form of society other than that of the *autonomous* herd (to the extent even of repudiating the notions "master" and "servant"—*ni dieu ni maître,* says a socialist formula); at one in their tenacious opposition to every special claim, every special right and privilege (this means ultimately opposition to *every* right, for when all are equal, no one needs "rights" any longer); at one in their distrust of punitive justice (as though it were a violation of the weak, unfair to the *necessary* consequences of all former society); but equally at one in their religion of sympathy, in their compassion for all that feels, lives, and suffers (down to the very animals, up even to "God"—the extravagance of "sympathy for God" belongs to a democratic age); altogether at one in the cry and impatience of their sympathy, in their deadly hatred of suffering generally, in their almost feminine incapacity for witnessing it or *allowing* it; at one in their involuntary beglooming and heart-softening, under the spell of which Europe seems to be threatened with a new Buddhism; at one in their belief in the morality of *mutual* sympathy, as though it were morality in itself, the climax, the *attained* climax of mankind, the sole hope of the future, the con-

solation of the present, the great discharge from all the obligations of the past; altogether at one in their belief in the community as the *deliverer,* in the herd, and therefore in "themselves."

We, who hold a different belief—we, who regard the democratic movement, not only as a degenerating form of political organisation, but as equivalent to a degenerating, a waning type of man, as involving his mediocrising and depreciation: where have *we* to fix our hopes? In *new philosophers*—there is no other alternative: in minds strong and original enough to initiate opposite estimates of value, to transvalue and invert "eternal valuations"; in forerunners, in men of the future, who in the present shall fix the constraints and fasten the knots which will compel millenniums to take *new* paths. To teach man the future of humanity as his *will,* as depending on human will, and to make preparation for vast hazardous enterprises and collective attempts in rearing and educating, in order thereby to put an end to the frightful rule of folly and chance which has hitherto gone by the name of "history" (the folly of the "greatest number" is only its last form)—for that purpose a new type of philosophers and commanders will some time or other be needed, at the very idea of which everything that has existed in the way of occult, terrible, and benevolent beings might look pale and dwarfed. The image of such leaders hovers before *our* eyes:—is it lawful for me to say it aloud, ye free spirits? The conditions which one would partly have to create and partly utilise for their genesis; the presumptive methods and tests by virtue of which a soul should grow up to such an elevation and power as to feel a *constraint* to these tasks; a transvaluation of values, under the new pressure and hammer of which a conscience should be steeled and a heart transformed into brass, so as to bear the weight of such responsibility; and on the other hand the necessity for such leaders, the dreadful danger that they might be lacking, or miscarry and degenerate:— these are *our* real anxieties and glooms, ye know it well, ye free spirits! these are the heavy distant thoughts and storms which sweep across the heaven of *our* life. There are few pains so grievous as to have seen, divined, or experienced how an exceptional man has missed his way and deteriorated; but he who has the rare eye for the universal danger of "man" himself *deteriorating,* he who like us has recognised the extraordinary fortuitousness which has hitherto played its game in respect to the future of mankind—a game in which neither the hand, nor even a "finger of God" has participated!—he who divines the fate that is hidden under the idiotic unwariness and blind confidence of "modern ideas," and still more under the whole of Christo-European morality—suffers from an anguish with which no other is to be compared. He sees at a glance all that could still *be made out of man* through a favourable accumulation and augmentation of human powers and arrangements; he knows with all the knowledge of his conviction how unexhausted man still is for the greatest possibilities, and how often in the past the type man has stood in presence of mysterious decisions and new paths:—he knows still better from his painfulest recollections on what wretched obstacles promising developments of the highest rank have hitherto usually gone to pieces, broken down, sunk, and become contemptible. The *universal degeneracy of mankind* to the level of the "man of the future"—as idealised by the socialistic fools and shallowpates—this degeneracy and dwarfing of man to an absolutely gregarious animal (or as they call it, to a man of "free society"), this brutalising of man into a pigmy with equal rights and claims, is undoubtedly *possible!* He who has thought out this possibility to its ultimate conclusion knows *another* loathing unknown to the rest of mankind—and perhaps also a new *mission!*

WHAT IS NOBLE?

Every elevation of the type "man," has hitherto been the work of an aristocratic society—and so will it always be—a society believing in a long scale of gradations of rank and differences of worth among human beings, and requiring slavery in some form or other. Without the *pathos of distance,* such as grows out of the incarnated difference of classes, out of the constant outlooking and down-looking of the ruling caste on subordinates and instruments, and out of their equally constant practice of obeying and commanding, of keeping down and keeping at a distance—that other more mysterious pathos could never have arisen, the longing for an ever new widening of distance within the soul itself, the formation of ever higher, rarer, further, more extended, more comprehensive states, in short, just the elevation of the type "man," the continued "self-surmounting of man," to use a moral formula in a supermoral sense. To be sure, one must not resign oneself to any humanitarian illusions about the history of the origin of an aristocratic society (that is to say, of the preliminary condition for the elevation of the type "man"): the truth is hard. Let us acknowledge unprejudicedly how every higher civilisation hitherto has *originated!* Men with a still natural nature, barbarians in every terrible sense of the word, men of prey, still in possession of unbroken strength of will and desire for power, threw themselves upon weaker, more moral, more peaceful races (perhaps trading or cattle-rearing communities), or upon old mellow civilisations in which the final vital force was flickering out in brilliant fireworks of wit and depravity. At the commencement, the noble caste was always the barbarian caste: their superiority did not consist first of all in their physical, but in their *psychical power*—they were more *complete men* (which at every point also implies the same as "more complete beasts").

Corruption—as the indication that anarchy threatens to break out among the instincts, and that the foundation of the emotions, called "life," is convulsed—is something radically different according to the organisation in which it manifests itself. When, for instance, an aristocracy like that of France at the beginning of the Revolution, flung away its privileges with sublime disgust and sacrificed itself to an excess of its moral sentiments, it was corruption:—it was really only the closing act of the corruption which had existed for centuries, by virtue of which that aristocracy had abdicated step by step its lordly prerogatives and lowered itself to a *function* of royalty (in the end even to its decoration and parade-dress). The essential thing, however, in a good and healthy aristocracy is that it should *not* regard itself as a function either of the kingship or the commonwealth, but as the *significance* and highest justification thereof—that it should therefore accept with a good conscience the sacrifice of a legion of individuals, who, *for its sake,* must be suppressed and reduced to imperfect men, to *slaves* and instruments. Its fundamental belief must be precisely that society is *not* allowed to exist for its own sake, but only as a foundation and scaffolding, by means of which a select class of beings may be able to elevate themselves to their higher duties, and in general to a higher *existence:* like those sun-seeking climbing plants in Java—they are called *Sipo Matador,*—which encircle an oak so long and so often with their arms, until at last, high above it, but supported by it, they can unfold their tops in the open light, and exhibit their happiness.

To refrain mutually from injury, from violence, from exploitation, and put one's will on a par with that of others: this may result in a certain rough sense in good conduct among individuals when the necessary conditions are given (namely, the actual similarity of the individuals in amount of force and degree of worth, and their co-relation within one organisation). As soon, however, as one wished to take this principle more generally, and if possible even as *the fundamental principle of society,* it would immediately disclose what it really is—namely, a Will to the *denial* of life, a principle of dissolution and decay. Here one must think profoundly to the very basis and resist all sentimental weakness: life itself is *essentially* appropriation, injury, con-

quest of the strange and weak, suppression, severity, obtrusion of peculiar forms, incorporation, and at the least, putting it mildest, exploitation;—but why should one for ever use precisely these words on which for ages a disparaging purpose has been stamped? Even the organisation within which, as was previously supposed, the individuals treat each other as equal—it takes place in every healthy aristocracy—must itself, if it be a living and not a dying organisation, do all that towards other bodies, which the individuals within it refrain from doing to each other: it will have to be the incarnated Will to Power, it will endeavour to grow, to gain ground, attract to itself and acquire ascendency—not owing to any morality or immorality, but because it *lives,* and because life *is* precisely Will to Power. On no point, however, is the ordinary consciousness of Europeans more unwilling to be corrected than on this matter; people now rave everywhere, even under the guise of science, about coming conditions of society in which "the exploiting character" is to be absent:—that sounds to my ears as if they promised to invent a mode of life which should refrain from all organic functions. "Exploitation" does not belong to a depraved, or imperfect and primitive society: it belongs to the *nature* of the living being as a primary organic function; it is a consequence of the intrinsic Will to Power, which is precisely the Will to Life.—Granting that as a theory this is a novelty—as a reality it is the *fundamental fact* of all history: let us be so far honest towards ourselves!

In a tour through the many finer and coarser moralities which have hitherto prevailed or still prevail on the earth, I found certain traits recurring regularly together and connected with one another, until finally two primary types revealed themselves to me, and a radical distinction was—brought to light. There is *master-morality* and *slave-morality*—I would at once add, however, that in all higher and mixed civilisations, there are also attempts at the reconciliation of the two moralities; but one finds still oftener the confusion and mutual misunderstanding of them, indeed, sometimes their close juxtaposition—even in the same man, within one soul. The distinctions of moral values have either originated in a ruling caste, pleasantly conscious of being different from the ruled—or among the ruled class, the slaves and dependents of all sorts. In the first case, when it is the rulers who determine the conception "good," it is the exalted, proud disposition which is regarded as the distinguishing feature, and that which determines the order of rank. The noble type of man separates from himself the beings in whom the opposite of this exalted, proud disposition displays itself: he despises them. Let it at once be noted that in this first kind of morality the antithesis "good" and "bad" means practically the same as "noble" and "despicable";—the antithesis "good" and "*evil*" is of a different origin. The cowardly, the timid, the insignificant, and those thinking merely of narrow utility are despised; moreover, also, the distrustful, with their constrained glances, the self-abasing, the dog-like kind of men who let themselves be abused, the mendicant flatterers, and above all the liars:—it is a fundamental belief of all aristocrats that the common people are untruthful. "We truthful ones"—the nobility in ancient Greece called themselves. It is obvious that everywhere the designations of moral value were at first applied to *men,* and were only derivatively and at a later period applied to *actions;* it is a gross mistake, therefore, when historians of morals start with questions like, "Why have sympathetic actions been praised?" The noble type of man regards *himself* as a determiner of values; he does not require to be approved of; he passes the judgment: "What is injurious to me is injurious in itself"; he knows that it is he himself only who confers honour on things; he is a *creator of values.* He honours whatever he recognises in himself: such morality is self-glorification. In the foreground there is the feeling of plenitude, of power, which seeks to overflow, the happiness of

high tension, the consciousness of a wealth which would fain give and bestow:—the noble man also helps the unfortunate, but not—or scarcely—out of pity, but rather from an impulse generated by the superabundance of power. The noble man honours in himself the powerful one, him also who has power over himself, who knows how to speak and how to keep silence, who takes pleasure in subjecting himself to severity and hardness, and has reverence for all that is severe and hard. "Wotan placed a hard heart in my breast," says an old Scandinavian Saga: it is thus rightly expressed from the soul of a proud Viking. Such a type of man is even proud of *not* being made for sympathy; the hero of the Saga therefore adds warningly: "He who has not a hard heart when young, will never have one." The noble and brave who think thus are the furthest removed from the morality which sees precisely in sympathy, or in acting for the good of others, or in *désintéressement,* the characteristic of the moral; faith in oneself, pride in oneself, a radical enmity and irony towards "selflessness," belong as definitely to noble morality, as do a careless scorn and precaution in presence of sympathy and the "warm heart."— It is the powerful who *know* how to honour, it is their art, their domain for invention. The profound reverence for age and for tradition—all law rests on this double reverence,—the belief and prejudice in favour of ancestors and unfavourable to newcomers, is typical in the morality of the powerful; and if, reversely, men of "modern ideas" believe almost instinctively in "progress" and the "future," and are more and more lacking in respect for old age, the ignoble origin of these "ideas" has complacently betrayed itself thereby. A morality of the ruling class, however, is more especially foreign and irritating to present-day taste in the sternness of its principle that one has duties only to one's equals; that one may act towards beings of a lower rank, towards all that is foreign, just as seems good to one, or "as the heart desires," and in any case "beyond good and evil": it is here that sympathy and similar sentiments can have a place. The ability and obligation to exercise prolonged gratitude and prolonged revenge—both only within the circle of equals,—artfulness in retaliation, *raffinement* of the idea in friendship, a certain necessity to have enemies (as outlets for the emotions of envy, quarrelsomeness, arrogance—in fact, in order to be a good *friend*): all these are typical characteristics of the noble morality, which, as has been pointed out, is not the morality of "modern ideas," and is therefore at present difficult to realise, and also to unearth and disclose.—It is otherwise with the second type of morality, *slave-morality*. Supposing that the abused, the oppressed, the suffering, the unemancipated, the weary, and those uncertain of themselves, should moralise, what will be the common element in their moral estimates? Probably a pessimistic suspicion with regard to the entire situation of man will find expression, perhaps a condemnation of man, together with his situation. The slave has an unfavourable eye for the virtues of the powerful; he has a scepticism and distrust, a *refinement* of distrust of everything "good" that is there honoured—he would fain persuade himself that the very happiness there is not genuine. On the other hand, *those* qualities which serve to alleviate the existence of sufferers are brought into prominence and flooded with light; it is here that sympathy, the kind, helping hand, the warm heart, patience, diligence, humility, and friendliness attain to honour; for here these are the most useful qualities, and almost the only means of supporting the burden of existence. Slave-morality is essentially the morality of utility. Here is the seat of the origin of the famous antithesis "good" and "evil":—power and dangerousness are assumed to reside in the evil, a certain dreadfulness, subtlety, and strength, which do not admit of being despised. According to slave-morality, therefore, the "evil" man arouses fear; according to master-morality, it is precisely the "good" man who arouses fear and seeks to arouse it, while the bad man is regarded as the despicable

being. The contrast attains its maximum when, in accordance with the logical consequences of slave-morality, a shade of depreciation—it may be slight and well-intentioned—at last attaches itself even to the "good" man of this morality; because, according to the servile mode of thought, the good man must in any case be the *safe* man: he is good-natured, easily deceived, perhaps a little stupid, *un bonhomme*. Everywhere that slave-morality gains the ascendency, language shows a tendency to approximate the significations of the words "good" and "stupid."—A last fundamental difference: the desire for *freedom*, the instinct for happiness and the refinements of the feeling of liberty belong as necessarily to slave-morals and morality, as artifice and enthusiasm in reverence and devotion are the regular symptoms of an aristocratic mode of thinking and estimating.—Hence we can understand without further detail why love *as a passion*—it is our European speciality—must absolutely be of noble origin; as is well known, its invention is due to the Provençal poet-cavaliers, those brilliant ingenious men of the "*gai saber*," to whom Europe owes so much, and almost owes itself. . . .

A *species* originates, and a type becomes established and strong in the long struggle with essentially constant *unfavourable* conditions. On the other hand, it is known by the experience of breeders that species which receive superabundant nourishment, and in general a surplus of protection and care, immediately tend in the most marked way to develop variations, and are fertile in prodigies and monstrosities (also in monstrous vices). Now look at an aristocratic commonwealth, say an ancient Greek *polis*, or Venice, as a voluntary or involuntary contrivance for the purpose of *rearing* human beings; there are there men beside one another, thrown upon their own resources, who want to make their species prevail, chiefly because they *must* prevail, or else run the terrible danger of being exterminated. The favour, the superabundance, the protection are there lacking under which variations are fostered; the species needs itself as species, as something which, precisely by virtue of its hardness, its uniformity, and simplicity of structure, can in general prevail and make itself permanent in constant struggle with its neighbours, or with rebellious or rebellion-threatening vassals. The most varied experience teaches it what are the qualities to which it principally owes the fact that it still exists, in spite of all Gods and men, and has hitherto been victorious: these qualities it calls virtues, and these virtues alone it develops to maturity. It does so with severity, indeed it desires severity; every aristocratic morality is intolerant in the education of youth, in the control of women, in the marriage customs, in the relations of old and young, in the penal laws (which have an eye only for the degenerating): it counts intolerance itself among the virtues, under the name of "justice." A type with few, but very marked features, a species of severe, warlike, wisely silent, reserved and reticent men (and as such, with the most delicate sensibility for the charm and *nuances* of society) is thus established, unaffected by the vicissitudes of generations; the constant struggle with uniform *unfavourable* conditions is, as already remarked, the cause of a type becoming stable and hard. Finally, however, a happy state of things results, the enormous tension is relaxed; there are perhaps no more enemies among the neighbouring peoples, and the means of life, even of the enjoyment of life, are present in superabundance. With one stroke the bond and constraint of the old discipline severs: it is no longer regarded as necessary, as a condition of existence—if it would continue, it can only do so as a form of *luxury,* as an archaïsing *taste.* Variations, whether they be deviations (into the higher, finer, and rarer), or deteriorations and monstrosities, appear suddenly on the scene in the greatest exuberance and splendour; the individual dares to be individual and detach himself. At this turningpoint of history there manifest themselves, side by side, and often mixed and entangled together, a magnificent, manifold, virgin—forest—like upgrowth and up-striving, a kind of *tropical tempo* in the rivalry of growth, and an extraordinary decay and self-destruction, owing to the savagely opposing and seemingly exploding egoisms, which strive with one another "for sun and light," and can no longer assign any limit, restraint, or forbearance for themselves by means of the hitherto existing morality. It was this morality itself which piled up the strength so enormously, which bent the bow in so threatening a manner:—it is now "out of date," it is getting "out of date." The dangerous and disquieting point has been reached when the greater, more manifold, more comprehensive life *is lived beyond* the old morality; the "individual" stands out, and is obliged to have recourse to his own law-giving, his own arts and artifices for self-preservation, self-elevation, and self-deliverance. Nothing but new "Whys," nothing but new "Hows," no common formulas any longer, misunderstanding and disregard in league with each other, decay, deterioration, and the loftiest desires frightfully entangled, the genius of the race overflowing from all the cornucopias of good and bad, a portentous simultaneousness of Spring and Autumn, full of new charms and mysteries peculiar to the fresh, still inexhausted, still unwearied corruption. Danger is again present, the mother of morality, great danger; this time shifted into the individual, into the neighbour and friend, into the street, into their own child, into their own heart, into all the most personal and secret recesses of their desires and volitions. What will the moral philosophers who appear at this time have to preach? They discover, these sharp onlookers and loafers, that the end is quickly approaching, that everything around them decays and produces decay, that nothing will endure until the day after to-morrow, except one species of man, the incurably *mediocre.* The mediocre alone have a prospect of continuing and propagating themselves—they will be the men of the future, the sole survivors; "be like them! become mediocre!" is now the only morality which has still a significance, which still obtains a hearing.—But it is difficult to preach this morality of mediocrity! it can never avow what it is and what it desires! it has to talk of moderation and dignity and duty and brotherly love—it will have difficulty *in concealing its irony!*

There is an *instinct for rank,* which more than anything else is already the sign of a *high* rank; there is a *delight* in the *nuances* of reverence which leads one to infer noble origin and habits. The refinement, goodness, and loftiness of a soul are put to a perilous test when something passes by that is of the highest rank, but is not yet protected by the awe of authority from obtrusive touches and incivilities: something that goes its way like a living touchstone, undistinguished, undiscovered, and tentative, perhaps voluntarily veiled and disguised. He whose task and practice it is to investigate souls, will avail himself of many varieties of this very art to determine the ultimate value of a soul, the unalterable, innate order of rank to which it belongs: he will test it by its *instinct for reverence. Différence engendre haine:* the vulgarity of many a nature spurts up suddenly like dirty water, when any holy vessel, any jewel from closed shrines, any book bearing the marks of great destiny, is brought before it; while on the other hand, there is an involuntary silence, a hesitation of the eye, a cessation of all gestures, by which it is indicated that a soul *feels* the nearness of what is worthiest of respect. The way in which, on the whole, the reverence for the *Bible* has hitherto been maintained in Europe, is perhaps the best example of discipline and refinement of manners which Europe owes to Christianity: books of such profoundness and supreme significance require for their protection an external tyranny of authority, in order to acquire the *period* of thousands of years which is necessary to exhaust and unriddle them. Much has been achieved when the sentiment has been at last instilled into the masses (the shallow-pates and the boobies of every kind) that they are not allowed to touch everything, that there are holy experiences before which they must take off their shoes and keep away the unclean hand—it is almost their highest advance towards humanity. On the contrary, in the so-called cultured classes, the believers in "modern ideas," nothing is perhaps so repulsive as their lack of shame, the easy insolence of eye and hand with which they touch, taste, and finger everything; and it is possible that even yet there is more *relative* nobility of taste, and more tact for reverence among the people, among the lower classes of the people, especially among peasants, than among the newspaper-reading *demimonde* of intellect, the cultured class. . . .

At the risk of displeasing innocent ears, I submit that egoism belongs to the essence of a noble soul, I mean the unalterable belief that to a being such as "we," other beings must naturally be in subjection, and have to sacrifice themselves. The noble soul accepts the fact of his egoism without question, and also without consciousness of harshness, constraint, or arbitrariness therein, but rather as something that may have its basis in the primary law of things:—if he sought a designation for it he would say: "It is justice itself." He acknowledges under certain circumstances, which made him hesitate at first, that there are other equally privileged ones; as soon as he has settled this question of rank, he moves among those equals and equally privileged ones with the same assurance, as regards modesty and delicate respect, which he enjoys in intercourse with himself—in accordance with an innate heavenly mechanism which all the stars understand. It is an *additional* instance of his egoism, this artfulness and self-limitation in intercourse with his equals—every star is a similar egoist; he honours *himself* in them, and in the rights which he concedes to them, he has no doubt that the exchange of honours and rights, as the *essence* of all intercourse, belongs also to the natural condition of things. The noble soul gives as he takes, prompted by the passionate and sensitive instinct of requital, which is at the root of his nature. The notion of "favour" has, *inter pares,* neither significance nor good repute; there may be a sublime way of letting gifts as it were light upon one from above, and of drinking them thirstily like dew-drops; but for those arts and displays the noble soul has no aptitude. His egoism hinders him here: in general, he looks "aloft" unwillingly—he looks either *forward,* horizontally and deliberately, or downwards— *he knows that he is on a height.*

NOTES

1. Pages 54–55 of Schopenhauer's *Basis of Morality,* translated by Arthur B. Bullock, M.A. (1903).

31. NIETZSCHE AND MORAL CHANGE

KATHRYN PYNE ADDELSON

What is moral change? An answer to this question is necessary if we are to answer the question, "What is essential to morality?" But among moral philosophers, Nietzsche stands almost alone in trying to examine the full structure of moral change.

There is a reason for this. The main body of tradition in ethics has occupied itself with the notions of obligation, moral principle, justification of acts under principle, justification of principle by argument. When moral change was considered at all, it was seen as change to bring our activities into conformity with our principles, as change to dispel injustice, as change to alleviate suffering. In short, moral change was seen as moral reform, with no other sort of moral change acknowledged or even imagined.

Reprinted with permission of the author and Robert Solomon, ed., *Nietzsche* (Doubleday, 1973).

But moral reform is not the only sort of moral change. There is also moral revolution. Moral revolution has not to do with making our principles consistent, not to do with greater application of what we *now* conceive as justice. That is the task of moral reform, because its aim is the preservation of values. But the aim of moral revolution is the creation of values.

The traditional view in ethics has been unable to see this because moral creativity cannot be understood when the theory of morality is exhausted by the notions of obligation, principle, and justification. Nor can certain types of morality be understood, those which don't concern themselves (or those which concern themselves very little) with the notions of obligation, rightness of act, justification of principle.

By paying attention to moral revolution, Nietzsche was able to understand some of these things. I'd like to work with his insights and develop some of the points I think he was trying to make. This means that I shall not be doing "Nietzsche scholarship" but rather trying to apply some of his insights to theoretical and practical problems which face us. Given his views on the interpretation of literature, I don't believe this is against the Nietzschean spirit.

I shall argue that the narrow focus of traditional ethics makes it impossible to account for the behavior of the moral revolutionary *as* moral behavior. In seeing this, we shall see that the traditional view misrepresents the structure of morality, and why a Nietzschean typology of morals offers us new moral notions which are more adequate. In the end, we shall be able to distinguish moral revolution from moral reform on the basis of his typology and have greater insight into moral phenomena. . . .

I shall argue from a particular case of moral revolution—the women's revolution of the nineteenth century. This is one of the clearest examples of a moral revolution, and it offers ideal illustrations of some of the moral phenomena Nietzsche discusses.

In using this example, I shall go beyond Nietzsche—and perhaps in a direction he would not endorse. This is not because it is a *women's* revolution. Despite its name, it was a human revolution, affecting men, women, and children. And despite his remarks, Nietzsche was no simple misogynist. His distaste for women was a distaste for the slavish character shown by nineteenth-century women. It was this slave morality in women which the women's revolution hoped to overthrow.

But the women's revolution was a revolution of the people, and Nietzsche looked sourly upon such things. His highest moral categories are aimed at capturing moral revolution in the *individual*. However, I think that these categories can be used to understand the individual moral revolutionary and, through him, moral revolution itself. In the end, I think such a use of Nietzsche's categories reveals the phenomena of morality in a way he himself was unable to reveal it. . . .

Part II takes up some central arguments given by conservatives and revolutionaries in the nineteenth century to show that the traditional views in ethics cannot account for the behavior of the moral revolutionary as moral, while Part III suggests a new understanding of the women's revolution in light of Nietzschean explanations.

Part IV considers a typology of morals based on certain Nietzschean distinctions. With the aid of the typology, a separation is made between moral revolution and moral reform in Part V, and it is suggested that Nietzsche is correct in taking the essential parts of morality to consist in creation and self-overcoming. . . .

II

[Morality] works against our acquiring new experiences and correcting morality accordingly, which means that morality works against a better, newer morality.

The traditional philosopher of science explains the structure of science in terms of theories, scientific principles, observations, and, in addition, all the scientific methods of justification which he is at pains to explicate. The traditional moral philosopher explains the structure of morality in terms of moral principles, as well as all the moral methods of justification which he is at pains to explicate. In both cases, change is said to take place by reform.

According to the traditional view, it is through moral principles that situations are categorized as morally relevant or not. For example, the principle "One ought to tell the truth" picks out situations in which I am reporting facts to others as morally relevant but leaves situations in which I am not (situations in which I am alone and eating supper, for example) as morally neutral. This means that moral principles enter into our activities in two ways. They enter *internally,* in that I categorize the world of my possible actions in their terms and act in accord with them or not. They enter *externally* in that others see and judge my acts in their terms, and I justify my own acts to others in part by their means. It is a fundamental assumption here that morally proper behavior must be morally *justifiable* behavior.

Moral principles themselves must be justified. Sometimes this is done in terms of higher-level moral principles. But there are *very* high-level moral principles ("One ought to act so as to bring about the greatest happiness. . . .") which require metaphysical or philosophical justification.

It is important to look at moral justifications which are actually given to see how all of these elements enter. I shall do this in some detail, to show that the conservative fares well and the revolutionary fares very ill indeed under this traditional view of morality.

During the nineteenth century in the United States, there was an attempt to bring about a moral revolution—an attempt which was in part successful. The main attack was on those values which operated to keep women in a morally, culturally, and socially subordinate position, as well as a legally subordinate one. That is, the thrust was against the *humanly* subordinate position of women, against a double standard of humanity, one which adversely affected the moral being of *both* men and women. The organized part of this moral revolution deteriorated into a movement toward mere reform as the twentieth century began, with the increased emphasis on woman suffrage. So its earlier phases are the ones of interest to us. But these earlier phases constitute one of the clearest examples of moral revolution there is, and they offer admirable illustrations of some of the moral phenomena which Nietzsche emphasized but which philosophers in ethics generally overlook.

There was an argument presented by Senator Frelinghuysen of New Jersey shortly after the Civil War which captures the essence of the conservative position against the women's revolution.

It seems to me as if the God of our race has stamped upon [the women of America] a milder, gentler nature, which not only makes them shrink from, but disqualifies them for the turmoil and battle of public life. They have a higher and holier mission. It is in retiracy to make the character of coming men. Their mission is at home, by their blandishments and their love to assuage the passions of men as they come in from the battle of life, and not themselves by joining in the contest to add fuel to the very flames. It will be a sorry day for this country when those vestal fires of love and piety are put out.[1]

Eleanor Flexner, an historian of the women's rights struggle, says that emotional arguments like this characterized all debates down to 1919, and that no rational argument was able to make a dent in them. But she is mistaken in dubbing this a mere emotional argument. It is a perfectly rational justification of the moral claim that one ought to oppose the attempts of the women's rights workers, and there are reasons that the moral revolutionaries couldn't make a dent in it. Let's look more carefully at the argument.

1. Senator Frelinghuysen's justification uses the scientific claim that women differ by nature from men. We might call this the "Aristotelian claim," after an early espouser of it. It is supported on the one hand by a vague, "Aristotelian" scientific theory (still held in the nineteenth century) about the natures of individuals and the relations of these to their natural capacities. One's nature attaches to him as a member of a kind. For example, all women have the same nature in this sense.

The claim that women differ by nature from men is overwhelmingly supported by differences in their behavior. In ancient Greece, nineteenth-century America, and even twentieth-century America, women did not show the abilities to command or the abilities to reason which men showed. They were in fact timid and dependent, better followers than leaders. Of contributions to human development deemed worthy of report in the history books, virtually all were made by men. What great women statesmen, scientists, musicians, painters, religious leaders, or philosophers does history show? Such data not only support the claim that there is a difference between men and women, they show what the difference is.

In addition, the claim for the difference was supported on religious grounds, for example, on the basis of standard interpretations of Genesis. Woman's place, and her tasks, were taken to have been intended by "the God of our race."

2. Senator Frelinghuysen's justification presupposes the moral claim that *one ought to act according to his or her nature.* This claim is essential, since some women showed better abilities to lead and reason than the senator did.

This moral principle was a central one, and it was considered generally impeccable down to our own time. It has been used, for example, to justify condemnation of sexual deviates and to justify monstrous treatment of homosexuals on grounds of "unnaturalness" even in our own day.

The principle can be given religious support—we ought to act as God intended. But even in the nineteenth century, it was given other support. It is *harmful* to the person to act against his nature.[2] As a worthy group of Massachusetts ministers said in attacking the Grimké sisters' efforts toward women's liberation,

We invite your attention to the dangers which at present seem to threaten the FEMALE CHARACTER with widespread and permanent injury.[3]

This indicates that Senator Frelinghuysen's case rests ultimately on the high-level moral principle that one should act so as to promote the highest moral character in oneself and in others.[4]

Through the senator's argument itself, we see that the traditional view would classify his activity as morally relevant, and it appears that he has justified his behavior. But what of the moral rev-

olutionary? We need to look at her behavior through the glasses of the traditional moral philosopher. I'd like to take Sarah Grimké as protagonist here and consider some of the moral reasoning and argument she used in 1837, in her *Letters on the Equality of the Sexes and the Condition of Women.* Like Senator Frelinghuysen's arguments, hers involve claims that were put forward throughout the nineteenth century—for example, we find their echo in Mill's later and better-known paper "The Subjection of Women."

In brief, Miss Grimké argued that what appear to be natural differences between men and women are due to differences in education, training, and expectation. She claimed that "women are educated from childhood to regard themselves as inferior," and that "our powers of mind have been crushed, as far as man could do it, our sense of morality has been impaired by his interpretation of our duties." She argued directly against the interpretation of the Bible used to support the "natural difference" view, saying that Genesis actually shows that God created men and women equal.

There is also an egalitarian principle underlying the arguments in her *Letters,* one which is clearly present in her argument in favor of equal pay for equal work. We might make it explicit in Mill's terms:

The principle of the modern movement in morals and politics, is that conduct, and conduct alone, entitles to respect . . . that, above all, merit and not birth, is the only rightful claim to power and authority.[5]

Now these remarks seem directly aimed at conservative arguments against the women's movement. [Today], most of us would accept them. But that fact is not at all to the point, for the question is whether they constituted arguments which could serve as a justification for Miss Grimké's behavior in 1837, and whether they could serve as a basis for counting her behavior as moral behavior—much less morally *proper* behavior. I shall argue that they could not so serve, that they are at best calls for a new paradigm.

(1) Miss Grimké's claim that nurture, not nature, determines the difference in behavior and ability in men and women is meant to undermine the claim that the Aristotelian theory is data-supported. The form of the argument here is exactly correct: to undermine the empirical support for the Aristotelian theory, the data must be reinterpreted, explained by a different scientific theory. Unfortunately, Miss Grimké was ahead of her time in her scientific as well as her moral views. There was no scientific theory to support her interpretation of the data. This point is important, but perhaps difficult to grasp in this case because we now accept a scientific view properly interpreting her hypothesis. But merely putting a scientific hypothesis into *words* does not constitute giving a justification.

If the hypothesis is understood against the background of the conservative paradigm, then "education" and "nature" will be understood as interpreted under that paradigm, and evidence for the hypothesis will be construed as it is construed under that paradigm. What Miss Grimké needs is an alternate theory on nature and education and their effects on human capacity and behavior. Her argument at best *suggests* that a scientific justification for her position can be developed. It is not itself a justification but rather a call for a new scientific paradigm.

One might object here that the Aristotelian sort of theory is subject to a direct test which does not require development of an alternative theory. Miss Grimké herself suggests such a test:

All I ask of our brethren is that they will take their feet from off our necks and permit us to stand upright on that ground which God designed us to occupy. If he has not given us the rights which have, as I conceive, been wrested from us, we shall soon give evidence of our inferiority . . . (see 3).

Such a "direct test" would no more falsify the

Aristotelian theory than it did the more recent Freudian one. Freudian theory postulated a difference in nature for men and women too, a difference which was strikingly similar to that postulated under the Aristotelian theory. Behavior of women which might falsify the theory was accommodated by altering the theory slightly, to admit that some few women had "masculine natures" (and were thus natural anomalies). But the vast majority of women were supposed to have natural feminine natures. Aggressiveness and "unwomanly" behavior among these are explained by saying that they are driven by penis envy into a neurotic emulation of men. Such emulation was judged to be an illness requiring treatment to bring the woman to accept her nature. To change the educational process so as to develop these unnatural characteristics in all women would be, in Freudian eyes as well as the eyes of the Massachusetts ministers, "to threaten the FEMALE CHARACTER with widespread and permanent injury" (see 3).

But of course in asking that "our brethren . . . take their feet from off our necks," Miss Grimké is not merely suggesting a test for the conservative theory. She is making a call for the moral revolution.

(2) The claim that merit, not birth, is the only rightful claim to power and authority is aimed at overthrowing the moral principle that one ought to act according to his nature as it limits the participation of women in society. However, rather than relying on that principle as it is understood under the conservative moral paradigm, Mill is suggesting a *reinterpretation* of it. For that principle was understood to mean that birth into a particular social *class* should not disqualify an adult male. The principle cannot support Mill's position because it presupposes his position on women. Again, we have merely a call to bring about the revolution, and an example of how a particular moral principle would be reinterpreted under the new paradigm.

In the case of legal principles, we have a formal structure (the court system) to take care of interpretation of their meaning. An examination of the changes in interpretation of the Bill of Rights, for example, shows how paradigm dependent our legal and governmental principles are for their interpretation. My claim here is that an analogous situation exists with regard to scientific and moral principles, even so-called "trans-societal" principles. It may be less well noticed only because we lack a formal structure to take care of their interpretation.

There is, however, one principle which does not seem quite so paradigm-dependent for its understanding, and that is the hedonistic act utilitarian principle. The principle might be stated roughly in this way: One ought to choose that act which produces a greater surplus of happiness over unhappiness than any alternative act. What *makes* people happy before and after the revolution will be different. But a utilitarian would hope for psychological tests of happiness which are independent of the *moral* paradigm at least.

There are general difficulties in applying this principle, since a comparison of possible acts and their possible consequences is necessary. This is particularly difficult in the case of moral revolution, since calculating the consequences of the revolutionary's acts requires knowing what *would* make people happy after the revolution as well as calculating their degrees of happiness.

These difficulties are not the major ones. It is more important that there is scarcely a person who would hold the unmodified hedonistic act utilitarian principle. This is because the resultant *quantity* of happiness is at best only one element we're concerned with. Fairness in the distribution of happiness is also important. The methods used to bring about the happiness are important. To be acceptable, this utilitarian principle needs to be "restricted" by other principles, particularly a principle of justice. But other principles, *particularly* the principle of justice, are heavily dependent on the paradigm for their interpretation.

If a revolutionary wishes, he may give some justification to his actions by using the hedonistic act utilitarian principle. If he cannot himself accept that principle unsupplemented—and I am sure that there is scarcely one who will accept it—then there seems to be no way for him to give a justification.

The revolutionary must, then, proceed without proper justification. But this is not all. Most philosophers holding a traditional view don't feel that moral principles merely enter after the fact, merely enter in giving a justification. One doesn't merely act willy-nilly, then fish about for some principle which will justify the act. One assesses the situation morally before acting. But even to assess the situation as moral requires the use of moral categories, thus principles of one sort or another (or so it seems, on the traditional view).

The moral revolutionary cannot do this. If he is to be seen as acting under principles at all, they must be principles interpreted under the new paradigm. Principles as understood under the old paradigm will not properly characterize the moral features of the current situation. But the new paradigm is not yet in existence. So even if the revolutionary cites principles, even if he himself says the words to himself, he has only a limited understanding of those words. Let me support this by a quotation from Paul Feyerabend:

> One often takes it for granted that a clear and distinct understanding of new ideas precedes and should precede any formulation and any institutional expression of them. . . . [but] we must expect, for example, that the idea of liberty could be made clear only by means of the very same actions which were supposed to create liberty. Creation of a thing, and creation plus full understanding of a correct idea of the thing, are very often parts of one and the same indivisible process and they cannot be separated without bringing the process to a standstill.

The arguments of the moral revolutionary constitute a call for change, not a justification. But even as a call, they are not statements of principles interpreted fully under the new paradigm but a *hint* at a direction in which to go in the creative process.

III

> That the value of the world lies in our interpretation...; that previous interpretations have been perspective valuations by virtue of which we can survive in life, i.e., in the will to power for the growth of power...[6e]

Some traditional philosophers will not be surprised that the moral revolutionary cannot justify himself and, if he is seen as acting morally at all, he is seen as being *evil*. A contemporary Hobbesian might grant that revolution is sometimes necessary (though he would see any such revolution as political). But since the only way to judge rightness and wrongness and obligation is under the laws and rules of the existing system, the revolutionary must be a traitor or subversive. It is only after the revolution that he can justify what he has done—if the revolution is a success, that is. Here, as with Nietzsche's morality of custom (*Sitte*), change is immoral (*unsittlich*) ([6b] 18).

But this is unsatisfactory so far as moral theory goes, and it is certainly unsatisfactory if we try to apply moral theory to practice. It allows no adequate explanation of the structure of moral revolution *as moral*. And it sacrifices whatever light may be shed on normal morality and the traditional view itself by the phenomenon of moral revolution....

Seen in a Nietzschean light, moral revolution contains what is essential to morality in a way that morality in stasis does not. In focusing on morality in stasis, and especially on morality as it concerns justification and principle, the traditional philosopher is "human, all too human." He offers the rationalization that is necessary to the herd, the rationalization which operates *against* creation and change. This will become more evident in Part IV. Here, we might look again at the women's revolution to put traditional ethics in perspective.

I mentioned in Part II that the data that supported Senator Frelinghuysen's conservative view on women were *facts*. Women understood themselves and their lives in terms of the way they were characterized under this view. Miss Grimké saw this when she said that women are "educated from earliest childhood, to regard themselves as inferior creatures..." (see 3).

This picture of women was not one which was imposed from outside by a sexist science. Kuhn would say that the science created the world picture and created its facts. But the adequate characterization of the situation is given far better by Nietzsche than by Kuhn. For it was Nietzsche's insight that our science does not operate independently of our morality. Science and morality work together not only in giving us a picture of a world but also in creating that world and the human beings in it.[4] I think that this is evident from the discussions in Part II. But those discussions were concerned with principle and argument, and there is more to the matter than that.

Throughout written history, the structure of the family has been closely integrated with the structure of the society, the one supporting the other. Revolutionaries and conservatives in the nineteenth century used two radically different analogies in describing the family and the relationship of husband and wife within it. Revolutionaries see the family structure on analogy with a tyrant-slave or master-servant relationship ("The Subjection of Women"). Conservatives see it roughly on analogy with a parent-child relationship. The husband protects the weaker wife. There is a biological basis for the parent-child relationship, and they see one in the relationship of husband to wife.[7]

The family was seen by conservatives as a unit made up of individuals with specialized functions—the social closely following the biological. Each individual must fulfill his function, for that is necessary for the survival of the unit. And survival of the family unit is necessary for the survival of the society. Conservatives argued that the whole theory of government and society presupposed this view of the family, in terms of this division of functions.[8]

Women were different from men in their capacities and personalities because it was *necessary* for them to be different from men. The survival of the family and state depended on it. This offers a striking confirmation of Nietzsche's claim that what is necessary for our survival we see as truth. Of course, to take something as truth doesn't make it true. But Nietzsche remarks on this,

> 'No matter how strongly a thing may be believed, strength of belief is no criterion of truth.' But what is truth? Perhaps a kind of belief that has become a condition of life? (see 6e)

Without departing from Nietzsche, we might say that what is necessary for our survival *becomes truth.* Theory follows fact, and human facts of this sort follow need. The traditional view has stood the matter on its head.

The *way* in which our principles are embedded in fact makes it clear that a moral revolution cannot be one based on principle, with its major struggle one to make act conform with principle. That is at best the task of moral reform. The women's revolution had to proceed by making the facts different. The revolutionaries had to proceed by bringing a new paradigm into being. Principles followed. They followed as they always have, as a rationalization of what is and what is necessary. Traditionalists overlook this because they focus on "normal morality," morality in *stasis.* Of that, Nietzsche says, "Whatever lives long is gradually so saturated with reason that its irrational origins become improbable" (see 6b). But what seems improbable may nonetheless not be.

A moral, social, and scientific paradigm (the paradigm of a conceptual scheme) is not merely something through which we see the world. It is something which shapes the facts of the human world. The traditional view deals only with a certain sort of *post hoc* rationalization, taking this rationalization as what is essential to morality. Accepting it as the whole story, we cannot understand the moral revolutionary and we cannot understand normal morality either.

To understand these things, and to understand how morality might be liberated from necessity, we need to look at *other* views on morality, or rather, other *moralities* alternative to those picked out by the traditional view. In Nietzsche's writings, we find alternatives.

IV

> *The* beautiful exists just as little as does *the* good, or *the* true. In every case it is a question of the conditions of preservation of a certain type of man . . . (see 6e).

Nietzsche's interest in psychological and developmental aspects of morality, his emphasis on transvaluation of values and on self-overcoming make him one of the few philosophers who have put "normal morality" in perspective. But in understanding this, it's important to put aside the dogmatism of the traditional view. Otherwise, the transvaluation is seen merely as the replacement of one set of values by another (all encapsulated in principles), and self-overcoming is seen merely as self-discipline of the usual moral sort.

If we look at a (somewhat) Nietzschean categorization of different varieties of morality, I think it's possible to understand the varieties of moral revolution and of normal morality more fully. In doing this, I'd like to consider "slave morality," "morality of the person of conscience," and what I shall call "noble morality" as varieties.[9] Using these notions to pick out varieties of morality requires leaving aside negative or positive connotations of "slave" or "noble."

What might slave morality be? A slave's life, *qua* slave, is full of duties. Freedom is essential to any moral agent, but the slave's freedom consists in his freedom to obey or disobey. Because there are sanctions which follow upon disobedience of a rule, the slave must be able to *justify* what he does. Sometimes the sanctions are external. If the slave cannot give an acceptable justification, he may be punished by the law courts (a political sanction) or by the ill opinion and acts of his compatriots (a moral sanction). But sometimes the sanctions are internalized, and conscience and feelings of guilt are the instruments ensuring obedience. In fact, the primary value in slave morality is obedience, and it's axiomatic that the moral person is the obedient person: obedient to the moral rule.

It should be evident that what Nietzsche calls "slave morality" comes very close, as a *type* of morality, to what I've been calling "morality on the traditional view."

Nietzsche felt that a fairly widespread sort of morality which grew out of the Christian tradition was a slave morality—a morality of the weak, with their fear of strength and their resentment. Women constituted slaves *par excellence* in this sense, and that fact may explain some of Nietzsche's diatribes against them. It was *this* sort of slave morality which the women's rights workers had to root out of themselves. But for our typology, it is better to abstract from these characteristics and see slave morality as one involving principle, rule, and justification, with acts taken as the basic moral units and with obedience to rule the cardinal virtue.

What I shall call "noble morality" differs essentially from slave morality, not in being a morality of the strong, but in being a different *type* of morality. It happens that strength of one sort or another is required in this morality, and that the weak find protection under slave morality, and this is morally and psychologically important. But more important to us is the difference in their structures.

Within noble morality, there is no concern with rules, obedience, and justification. The person, not the act, is the basic moral unit. Nietzsche says, "It is obvious that moral designations were everywhere applied to *human beings* and only later, derivatively, to actions" (6a). But this shouldn't be taken to mean that in noble morality it is the *person* who is judged, justified, etc., instead of the act. Rather, "The noble type of man experiences *itself* as determining values; it does not need approval" (6a). The noble person apprehends himself as worthy, and he *confers* values in his acts.

I have called this sort of morality "noble morality" rather than "master morality" because, in Nietzsche's discussions, master morality is sometimes not clearly distinct from what I shall call "the morality of the person of conscience." It is not clearly a type which Nietzsche himself set out, although some readers of Nietzsche seem to interpret his master morality in this way.

In discussing the noble distinction "good-bad" (which contrasts with the slave distinction "good-evil"), Nietzsche explicitly mentions the very ancient Greeks (6c). These "noble ones" do not have a noble morality in my sense because they have not attained the necessary, partial "self-overcoming" (see their behavior in 6c). But we might take a later development of this morality, as exemplified by some ideals in classical Greece, to represent noble morality.

Here, the noble person sees himself as worthy (see Aristotle's "great-souled person"). He confers value in his acts. He has overcome himself in the sense Kaufmann stresses: He has triumphed over his impulses (2). He is disciplined, so much so that his triumph and discipline flow from his nature. He is not a slave to a moral code. In fact, on a somewhat Aristotelian analysis, his valuations are the *foundation* of values for the society. A just act is one which the just person would do, and to act justly is to do such an act as the just person would do it.

There is a third type of morality, the morality of the person of conscience (following Nietzsche, 6c). This individual is "master of a free will." He is free *not* to obey or disobey, as the slave is free. Like the noble person, he is free from the slavery to the moral codes and opinions of his society. But in addition, he is free to create.

The person of conscience creates values, but only by creating himself. Here, I think self-overcoming has a different import from that which it has under noble morality. Noble morality involves only a partial self-overcoming. Self-overcoming in the person of conscience requires a self-disciplining, it is true. But it cannot properly be described as reason overcoming impulse, as Kaufmann describes self-overcoming (2). Rather, an overcoming of the *entire* old self is involved, of the old ways of perceiving oneself and the world, of the old ways of *being*. It is an overcoming which is *necessarily* a creation of oneself. It involves, in part, a phenomenon analogous to what is currently called "consciousness raising." One overcomes the old self which is structured within the old paradigm and becomes "The sovereign individual, like only to himself" (6c). In this self-overcoming, one creates himself anew, and creates values.

Given these unfortunately sketchy remarks on types of morality, we might use them to look at moral phenomena.

First, we might see (as Nietzsche did) that different societies emphasize one sort of morality over others. Greek society emphasized noble morality. Nineteenth-century Anglo-American society emphasized slave or rule morality. It is only a myopia induced by the traditional view on morality that would bring us to see these differences as a mere difference in *moral code.*

Second, we might use the typology to investigate different sorts of moral phenomena which occur within a single society. Nietzsche himself suggests that master and slave morality "at times . . . occur directly along side each other—even in the same human being, within a *single* soul" (6a). Our own society seems to be a mixed one.

Finally, we might use the typology to look at moral change. The first thing we would learn is

that a moral revolution need not result in replacement of one set of principles by another, or in the reinterpretation of principles held under the old paradigm. It might result in *a morality of a new type.* This parallels the way a political revolution might result not in the replacement of one form of government by another, but in an anarchistic society.

The second thing we would learn is that the moral revolutionary *is* behaving morally, but under a different type of morality from that which the traditional view recognizes. I mentioned in Part II that the women's revolution workers had to *change the way they were as women* in bringing about their revolution. I don't want to claim that all—or even that any—of these women became "persons of conscience." But it is *that* sort of morality which best captures the moral behavior of each of them, as revolutionaries.

Each of the serious workers in this revolution had to overcome herself in the sense of morally disciplining herself. But she also had to create herself as an individual like only to herself. That she later met others like her is irrelevant. The southern aristocrat who was Sarah Grimké, the overworked farm girl who was Lucy Stone, the slave mother of thirteen who became Sojourner Truth, all had to be overcome. Each woman had to create herself anew, in a process of self-overcoming which took no models (there were none to take) and which continued as long as she was a revolutionary. Today we have example after example of black young people who have gone through this self-overcoming, and many others of us have gone through it in a more modest way.

Nietzsche's morality of the person of conscience captures the morality of individual revolutionaries far better than the traditional view does. It offers a beginning for understanding how moral revolutions take place. As we saw in Part III, it is necessary to change the world, to create new facts and a new paradigm, in bringing about the revolution. The process of self-overcoming explains some of this, and it indicates that the creation of values begins with the creation of the individual revolutionary as a new sort of human being.

But this is individual morality. It is not the aim of the moral revolutionary to become the "sovereign individual" when this brings with it the *isolation* of uniqueness. And given Nietzsche's attitude toward revolutions of the people, we would not expect his favorite moral type to fit revolutionaries too well.

The revolutionary cannot create himself in isolation as a sovereign individual. Rather, he must begin to create himself as the "first of his kind." This creation, this self-overcoming, continues throughout the revolutionary process. But it is part of his task as a revolutionary of the people to help *them* to overcome themselves, to help each create himself as a new kind of individual. In the course of this process, the new paradigm comes into being—that is, the new values are created.

V

... art is *worth more* than truth (6e).

Given all of this, we can begin to see the difference between the moral revolutionary and the moral reformer. Both activities involve a struggle against the conservative forces in power. But the moral revolutionary is like the scientific revolutionary in struggling to overthrow some part of the present structure. In doing this, he must overcome himself in the process of the revolution. He must work to help his people overcome themselves. And this is a necessary process to the end that a new kind of human being may be brought into being, and thus a new paradigm and new values as well. For a moral revolution essentially involves creation of a new human being. It was one of Nietzsche's insights that moralities determine *kinds* of persons.

The reformer, on the other hand, is doing "normal morality." Like the scientist doing normal science, he operates within the present paradigm. He finds contradictions in held principles, or contradictions between principle and application of principle; he acts to eliminate suffering or injustice (as justice is understood under the prevailing paradigm). He makes those demands which the minority group he represents wants *now*.[10] And this is necessary so that the principles of his paradigm are consistent and so that practice follows principle. Reform essentially involves the *preservation* of values.

The behavior of the moral reformer *seems* to be explicable under the traditional view on morality—after all, he is doing "normal morality." But because the behavior of the moral revolutionary is not explicable under the traditional view, all moral change is seen as reform. This may explain why so many contemporary Anglo-American philosophers find virtue in the reformer but not in the revolutionary.

Of course, the moral revolutionary may sometimes *feel* he wants to relieve suffering and injustice. But it is creation, and not the relief of suffering and injustice, which must serve as his foundation. And there are reasons for this.

Workers in the women's revolution might have *felt* that injustice was being done, but according to the notion of justice within their paradigm, it was not. They may have *felt* that women were suffering under a sexist society, but the vast majority of nineteenth-century women *did not feel* they were suffering from sexism. It's difficult to make a case that one is struggling to relieve suffering when the "sufferers" themselves deny the suffering.

It is of the reformer that we might say,

> Either his reforms will be acceptable to the people, or they will not: if they are acceptable, the people have in principle the power to implement them, and it will be a question not of overthrowing the system but of making it function; if they are not, he has no business to impose them.[11]

The revolutionary will not (generally, cannot) impose his demands. But he ceases to be a revolutionary if he makes only those demands which are acceptable to the people at the time. *That* is not a way to creation of values, to creation of a new human being.

I have spoken of "normal morality" and "moral revolution." But the condition which is normal to human life is not a state of stasis but a state of revolution. Stasis is less painful, more easy to rationalize, more *sure,* more safe. It encourages us to believe we can rest, because we have the truth. But if we think in terms of Nietzschean epistemology, . . . we see that in science and morality, it is a continued state of revolution which expresses our humanity best. Nietzsche says, in *Zarathustra,*

> And life itself confided this secret to me: "Behold," it said, "I am *that which must always overcome itself.* Indeed, you call it a will to procreate or a drive to an end, to something higher, farther, more manifold: but all this is one. . . . whatever I create and however much I love it—soon I must oppose it and my love . . ." (6d).

NOTES AND BIBLIOGRAPHY

1. Eleanor Flexner, *Century of Struggle,* Atheneum, New York (1971).
2. Walter Kaufmann, *Nietzsche: Philosopher, Psychologist, Antichrist,* Vintage Books, New York (1968). In our own day, the whole Freudian view on neurosis has operated to support Frelinghuysen's moral principle.
3. Sarah M. Grimké, *Letters on the Equality of the Sexes and the Condition of Women.*
4. Thomas S. Kuhn, The Structure of Scientific Revolutions, University of Chicago Press, Chicago (1970). There is also a means-ends argument included by the senator. It involves the evaluative claim that maintenance of the home is good, and the factual claim that granting the women's demands will lead to the destruction of the home. It is a long-lived argument and was used by Illinois House Majority Leader Henry Hyde, who opposed ratification of the Equal Rights Amendment on the grounds that it constitutes "an attack on the home and motherhood"
    (Chicago *Sun-Times,* Friday, May 19, 1972). Frelinghuysen and Hyde are correct.
5. John Stuart Mill, "The Subjection of Women," in (8). Grimké's sociological and psychological analyses in the *Letters* are remarkable. See her remarks on the "butterflies of the fashionable world" in the Old South (pp. 43–44). Many people, including Nietzsche, have criticized these "butterflies," but Grimké's analysis could have been written in the mid-twentieth century. Her criticism is very positive and gets at the roots of the difficulty.
6. Rule utilitarianism (under which rules are justified by the consequences of adopting them, and acts justified by the rules) and pure act utilitarianism (under which acts are justified by the goodness resulting) won't do as principles under which the revolutionary can justify himself. The understanding of the rules and the understanding of "goodness" (except where this is happiness or pleasure) are thoroughly paradigm-dependent.

    Friedrich Nietzsche
    a. *Beyond Good and Evil,* W. Kaufmann, transl., Vintage Books, New York (1966).
    b. *The Dawn,* selections appearing in (9c), pp. 186–90.
    c. *On the Genealogy of Morals,* W. Kaufmann, ed., Vintage Books, New York (1969).
    d. *Thus Spoke Zarathustra,* in *The Portable Nietzsche,* W. Kaufmann, ed., The Viking Press, New York (1968).
    e. *The Will to Power,* W. Kaufmann, ed., Vintage Books, New York (1968).
7. This difference in analogies constitutes one of the core differences between the conservative and the revolutionary. The basic vision of the revolutionary springs from seeing the family structure in light of the master-servant analogy. It is the beginnings of their new way of seeing the world. In this regard, we might notice the importance of analogies in science on the one hand, and the use of analogies by Nietzsche on the other (his use of master and slave as analogies in setting out types of moralities is one striking example). Overemphasis on principles leads to overlooking the importance of analogies.
8. Miriam Schneir (ed.), *Feminism: The Essential Historical Writings,* Vintage Books, New York (1972). This structural interdependence was explicitly brought out by many conservatives.

Consider a remark made by Senator Williams of Oregon shortly after the Civil War: "When God married our first parents in the garden according to that ordinance they were made 'bone of one bone and flesh of one flesh' and the whole theory of government and society proceeds upon the assumption that their interests are one ..." Revolutionaries tended to ignore this interdependence, although it is stressed by Engels in "The Origin of the Family, Private Property, and the State." That work, of course, was too late for our revolutionaries to use (1884), and even if it had not been, it was far too politically radical.

9. I speak of "noble morality" rather than "master morality" for reasons given below.

10. Michael Walzer, "The Obligations of Oppressed Minorities," *Commentary,* May 1970. See Walzer's remark: "I should think the immediate goals of the activists must be set by the general consciousness of the oppressed group rather than by their own ideology. The effects can only be judged by those who will feel them. 'Helping' someone usu-

ally means doing something for him that he regards or seems likely to regard (*given his present state of mind*) as helpful" (my italics). The women's revolution never would have come about if its "activists" had followed this advice. The fact that these remarks have only to do with reform is also evident in the title of the article: "The Obligations of Oppressed Minorities." I think one of Nietzsche's major contributions to the understanding of change lies in his insight that change need not take place only to relieve oppression. In fact, the claim that a change is necessary to relieve oppression is very often merely a rationalization to explain and justify the natural and creative drive which is essential to human beings. The people see themselves oppressed when their consciousness is raised, i.e., when they begin to look at things from the perspective of the budding new paradigm.

11. Peter Caws, "Reform and Revolution," in *Philosophy and Political Action,* V. Held, K. Nielsen, and C. Parsons, eds., Oxford University Press (1972), p. 98.

32. NIETZSCHE'S TRANS-EUROPEAN EYE

❦

MERVYN SPRUNG

According to a tenacious tradition, still apparently alive in our day—though Eastern allusions are not quite the popular fashion they were a few years ago—Nietzsche had a lifelong interest in Sanskrit philosophy and Indian thought. His early adoration of Schopenhauer, who *was* a serious student of Buddhism and the Upanishads, and his persistent, if broken, acquaintance with Paul Deussen, who *was* an academic sanskritist

and comparative philosopher, from their schooldays until after Nietzsche's breakdown, have fed this tradition with plausibility. Most convincing, however, is Nietzsche's own use of passages and sayings from Sanskrit texts and his recurrent adductions, some repudiative, some grudgingly favourable, of Buddhism.

In a vivacious letter to Paul Deussen of 3 January 1888 Nietzsche speaks of his "trans-European eye" which enables him to see that "Indian philosophy is the only major parallel to our European philosophy." Some thirteen years earlier (January 1875) he had assured Deussen of his

Reprinted from *Nietzsche and Asian Thought* by permission of the University of Chicago Press and the author.

"eagerness, myself to drink from the spring of Indian philosophy which you will one day open up for all of us." A normal reading of such passages would suggest a persistent concern for Indian philosophy on Nietzsche's part throughout this span of years, and most of those who have been aware of the question have indeed so inferred. Alsdorf[1] relied heavily on the widely held belief that Deussen and Nietzsche were "life-long close friends" and yet offered Nietzsche's praise of the *Laws of Manu* (with which Deussen had nothing to do and which he must have found repugnant) as evidence of his interest in India. Even Glasenapp, despite his straight-laced criticism of Nietzsche, found it encumbent to praise his serious and penetrating study of Indian thought: "He penetrated deeply into its essence"; "He reflected a great deal on Buddhism."[2]

Quite recently the common presumption has been both tacitly and explicitly reinforced. Ryōgi Ōkōchi in *Nietzsche-Studien,*[3] though remarking on Nietzsche's limitations as a scholar of Buddhism, believes he was, through Deussen, in direct contact with the findings of German Sanskrit philosophy of his time and had a rather large number of books on Indian philosophy and Buddhism in his personal library (which is, regrettably, not the case: Hermann Oldenberg's *Buddha: Sein Leben, sein Lehre, seine Gemeinde,* the *only* book on Buddhism still there, appears never to have been opened). A current note[4] on Nietzsche and Deussen accepts the statements and protestations in letters and the use of Indian concepts in Nietzsche's published work at face value, and quite naturally concludes to a major impact of Indian thought on Nietzsche due to his "life-long friendship" with Deussen.

When we recall that the rhetoric, if not the argument in *The Birth of Tragedy* virtually turns on the Sanskrit term *māyā* (world illusion), that the title page of *Daybreak* carries a line from the *R̥g Veda,* and that, in a note to Rohde a few days after his final collapse, the underlayers of Nietzsche's mind could produce the sentence "Taine composed the Vedas," the impression is virtually irresistible that Indian thought was formative in Nietzsche's intellectual destiny, although to a much lesser extent than Greek and German philosophy, Judaism, and Christianity. Sharing this impression, I thought it worthwhile to search out whatever might tell us more about this area of Nietzsche's thought. During a few weeks in Weimar, assisted invaluably by my wife, I worked through the dossiers of letters between Nietzsche and Deussen and searched Nietzsche's personal library for any trace of his interest in or knowledge of Indian thought. This included leafing through every relevant book to note marginal comments, underlinings, and any other indicator of interest or lack of it, such as uncut pages.

The reflections stimulated by this brief search easily broadened to form a set of related questions. It seems to me now that these questions have some interest for Nietzsche research in general.

1. What was the nature and extent of Nietzsche's interest in Indian thought?

2. What Indian texts did Nietzsche *know?*

3. How adequate was Nietzsche's understanding of Indian thought?

4. What importance did Indian thought have in the formation of Nietzsche's own thought? . . .

Though he speaks of or alludes to Indian thought frequently enough to arouse the presumption that it was alive in his mind, Nietzsche seldom quotes from an Indian text: I have found some nine or ten such quotations, though this is perhaps not exhaustive. Precise references are, of course, never given, and what Nietzsche puts between quotation marks is more often than not drawn from several points in the original text and composed by him into one quotation to intensify the power of his argument.

In his *Untimely Meditation* on Schopenhauer, Nietzsche introduced the Upanishadic sentence

"Men are born, in accordance with their deeds, stupid, dumb, deaf, misshapen"[5] (*UM* III, 8) to beat German academics with, but without a flicker of interest in the principle of *karma*, a *leitmotive* of Indian philosophy. The title page of *Daybreak* carries the line "There are so many days that have not broken" from the *Rg Veda*. This verse fragment is, I judge, drawn from *Rg Veda* VII 76, although Nietzsche's version of this obscure passage does not correspond to the interpretation of the German and English translators. Geldner and Griffith agree that the thought is rather "There are so many dawns that have *already* dawned," a version not quite so appropriate to Nietzsche's mood of 1881. In the *The Gay Science* Nietzsche uses the mantras "*om mane padme hum*" and "*Ram, Ram, Ram,*" though they are hardly quotations, derisively, to belittle prayer (*GS* 128). With the approval often vouchsafed Buddha, the admonition "Do not flatter your benefactor" (*GS* 142) is quoted in disparagement of Christian practice.

The only passage in which Nietzsche quotes substantially from Indian philosophy is in *On the Genealogy of Morals* during his discussion of asceticism. He first introduces a Buddhist statement "Good and evil, both are fetters: the Perfect One became master over both"; then the *Vedanta* believer is said to hold "What is done and what is not done give him no pain; as a sage he shakes good and evil from himself; no deed can harm his kingdom; he has gone beyond both good and evil" (*GM* III, 17). This latter quotation is drawn from the *Kauṣītakī a Upaniṣad* but is Nietzsche's own composition.

Immediately following this Nietzsche adduces three considerable "quotations" from Deussen's *Das System des Vedanta*. They are all taken from Shankara's Commentary on the *Brahma Sūtras* and consist, in fact, of passages from the *Chāndogya Upaniṣad* (VIII 3, 4, 11, 12) with one sentence unidentified: "For the man of knowledge there is no duty." Nietzsche finds praise for the Indians' recognition that virtue does not suffice for redemption, but believes that their doctrine of release is at bottom Epicurean, a valuation of the hypnotic experience of nothingness as supreme. In this passage Nietzsche, uncharacteristically, names Deussen and praises his work.

In *Twilight of the Idols* Nietzsche reports on the *Laws of Manu* (which he had read in French translation) and composes a "quotation" from it (*TI* VI, 3). He focuses exclusively on the genetic engineering (*Züchtung*) implicit in Manu's decrees casting out the *Chaṇḍālas alas* from normal communal life. Finally, in *Ecce Homo*, discussing *ressentiment* Nietzsche praises Buddha as the physiologist whose teachings are more a hygiene than a religion and quotes from the *Dhammapada:* "Not by enmity is enmity ended; by friendliness enmity is ended" (*EH* I, 6).

Thus the meagre list of Nietzsche's quotations from Indian texts so far as I can find them. What do these quotations tell us about his reading? Excepting the three brief Buddhist quotes and the line from the *Rg Veda* in *Daybreak*, none presupposes more than Deussen's book *Das System des Vedanta* backed up by DuPerron's Latin version of the Upaniṣads, and a French translation of the *Laws of Manu*. Compared with the assiduous and persistent efforts of Schopenhauer to keep himself abreast of the lively Indian scholarship of the day, the evidence from quotations does not support the view that Nietzsche's "trans-European eye" was scanning the Indian horizon with much interest.

But then Nietzsche *quotes* little from any source. It is the frequency, spontaneity, and unpredictability of his naming of ideas, philosophical schools, and religions of India, invariably with a strong argumentative twist, that persuades the casual reader that Nietzsche drew substantially on a strong, if nontechnical, sympathy with Indian thought. *The Birth of Tragedy*, studded as it is with "the veil of *Māyā*" and "Buddhistic denial of the will" and structured on the key concept of "Buddhistic culture," reads as if the author were *approaching* the Greeks from a point of departure in classical India. This impression is, of course, not sustained in the pieces that followed. "On Truth and Lie in the Extra-Moral Sense," the early piece which Nietzsche never published, though its theme longs for nurture and support from the skeptical epistemologies of India, is written as if classical Sanskrit did not exist. In his *Untimely Mediation* on Schopenhauer Nietzsche does of course have India in the background much of the time. He thinks Indian history is virtually the history of Indian philosophy; he beats at the German philologists for ignoring Indian philosophy "as an animal [ignores] music"; he sees Schopenhauer as a hero of the spirit whose will should find its end in nirvana. The comment which, unwittingly, reveals most about Nietzsche himself is his opinion that Schopenhauer, in expounding his own philosophy, resorted to Buddhist and Christian mythology simply as "an extraordinary rhetorical instrument" (*UM* III, 7).

Daybreak not only carries the *Ṛg Veda* quote mentioned earlier but has a fine passage (aph. 96) on the religious history of India, which praises a height of culture capable of abolishing gods and priests and of producing a religion of *self*-liberation (Buddhism), an achievement Nietzsche urges Europe to emulate. In *The Gay Science* it is clear that neither Buddhism nor Vedanta, however "scientific," qualifies as "gay." Nirvana is "The oriental nothing," "rigid resignation . . . self extinction" (*GS* Prologue, 3), which nevertheless can induce a new self-mastery and stronger will to live, and which is the condition of a higher humanity. Nietzsche seems to imply he has made this passage himself. A tendency to positivistic sociology and history is unmistakable in Nietzsche's use of the vegetarian diet to explain oriental lethargy and indulgence in opium, and in relating these to the spread of Buddhism (*GS* 145).

From *Beyond Good and Evil* on, the influence of Deussen's first major book, *Das System des Vedanta* (the copy in Nietzsche's library bears, in some sections, the marginal marks of his attentive reading) is quite unmistakable. Nietzsche recognizes that the liberated man of Vedanta is beyond good and evil, but regrets that he is still within the framework of morality; he finds Vedanta an example of the way dogmatic philosophy becomes "a mask," as Platonism did in Europe (*BGE*, Preface); he believes that Europe is threatened by a softening of the mind, "a new Buddhism" (*BGE* 202); he approves of the Brahmins using religion to win power over kings (*BGE* 61). In *On the Genealogy of Morals* Nietzsche continues his attack on nirvana as a "nihilistic turning away from existence" which is creeping into Europe (*GM* II, 21); he writes vehemently against Vedanta asceticism, holding it to be Epicurean, "a hypnotic feeling of nothingness," but again praises the Indian schools for going beyond good and evil (*GM* III, 17).

The last of Nietzsche's published works, including the notebooks, are dominated, so far as India is concerned, by his reading, in the spring of 1888, a French translation of the *Laws of Manu*. In *Twilight of the Idols* he says the Bible should not be mentioned in the same breath with it; it is "*vornehm*" (noble) and has a philosophy behind it; the caste system reflects the order of nature and excretes useless products; it is a "holy lie"; "the sun shines upon the entire book." Only this once in all his writing does Nietzsche speak unreserved praise of anything Indian. He acquired the concept of *chaṇḍālas*—an outcast misbegotten—and uses it liberally during the last year of his work, even seeing himself as chaṇḍāla (*TI* VII, 2). In *The Antichrist* Nietzsche uses Buddhism to make disparaging comment on Christianity the easier. Buddhism is the only positivistic religion we know of; it ripens after a long tradition of philosophic thought; it has transcended the self-deception of morality: it is beyond good and evil; and all this in spite of its being a religion of decadence (*AC* 20). In *Ecce Homo* Buddha is praised as a great physiologist and Buddhism is said to be more a hygiene than a morality (*EH* I, 6). The notebooks of the last years contain a number of observations that emphasize much the same conclusions as we have already noted. Buddhism is more frequently taken up than Vedanta, and Nietzsche more than once draws a historical parallel between Buddha's position in Indian cultural history and his own position in Europe, implying that the doctrine of the eternal recurrence, in its negative aspect, is analogous to Buddhist nihilism (or perhaps vice versa) (*WP* 55).

This hasty scanning of Nietzsche's writings supports, in the main, the impressions gained from reviewing the quotations themselves. Noteworthy is the absence of India from the two works which are most spontaneous and least historically argumentative: *Human, All Too Human* and *Zarathustra*.[6] Nowhere are there references to Vedanta which imply wider reading than the quotations did: i.e., Deussen and at least two or three Upanishads. The case of Buddhism is slightly more complex. Though Nietzsche's grasp of Buddhism does not go beyond Schopenhauer, so that he betrays no awareness of a Buddhist philosophy beyond the doctrine of release from suffering, nonetheless the perspicacity he shows in sensing the freedom from moral self-deception in the words of Buddha suggest some reading of the original discourses, although there is no hint left us which ones, if any, he may have read. He quotes from the *Dhammapada* and quite conceivably knew nothing else. . . .

The outward signs of a "life-long friendship" between Nietzsche and Deussen have been universally accepted as evidence of Nietzsche's life-long interest in Indian thought. However trustworthy these outward signs may prove to be, it is true that the acid test of Nietzsche's interest in Indian thought must be his relationship to Deussen. The long acquaintance of the two men, from schooldays to the years after Nietzsche's collapse, is a theme worthy of a monograph, and until that has been written perhaps the last word about the significance of India for Nietzsche cannot be spoken. Restricting my survey to the exchange of letters between the two, and drawing on Deussen's two autobiographical books[7] marginally, I find that the evidence here is not different from that so far noted, and indeed is surprisingly confirmatory.

The Weimar Archives hold twenty-seven letters and two postcards from Nietzsche to Deussen and thirty-two letters from Deussen to Nietzsche. The bulk of this correspondence dates from their *Studentenzeit* up to Deussen's disastrous visit to Nietzsche in Basel in July of 1871. During the next sixteen years—the creative period in the lives of both men—Nietzsche wrote Deussen four letters, two of which were gracious acknowledgements of the receipt of Deussens's first two books. In the last year of his activity, 1888, Nietzsche wrote Deussen four letters and one postcard, the fresh stimulus being Deussen's visit to Sils Maria the previous summer, the first meeting of the two since 1872, and his offer of an anonymous gift of two thousand Deutschmarks.

Apart from gracious and perspicacious words of recognition and praise on receipt of Deussen's books—followed of course immediately by a blunt rejection of their content for himself—Nietzsche never in the course of twenty-four years broaches the subject of India and never asks one question, nor ever solicits Deussen's opinion, about Indian philosophy. The two revert again and again to Schopenhauer, and Deussen reports from time to time on his progress in Sanskrit studies, referring on one occasion to the "clear, luminous Indo-German world" without touching a sympathetic nerve in his classical friend.[8] Nietzsche was quite aware of Deussen's eminence and unique ability to interpret Indian ideas in European terms, but never once bothered to seek information from or discuss issues with him. In short, the correspondence gives no evidence not available from his own writing of any reading Nietzsche may have done, and no indication of a more active or wider interest. The correspondence, indeed, does rather the reverse: it suggests a much lesser interest than the published writings do. Without the latter as corrective, one could study the letters of Nietzsche to Deussen and conclude that his interest was not so much in the subject matter of Deussen's work as it was in remaining loyal to an old school friend.

And indeed this is the final, if surprising, impression which Nietzsche's relation to Deussen makes on one. Nietzsche never takes Deussen seriously as a thinker; he often scolds him, lectures him on the elements of philosophy, sometimes barely, sometimes not at all, concealing his slight regard for, not to say scorn of Deussen's ideas. Nietzsche plays the part of the impatient teacher and imperious father. During a breathless midnight visit of Deussen to Basel in the summer of 1871, Nietzsche told him "You are not gifted philosophically."[9] Deussen, although himself a man of great ambition and self-esteem, never fights back; he humbles himself in front of his great friend and, when deeply hurt, suffers in prolonged, tortured silence.

It may, of course, have been precisely this unhappy lack of respect which made it impossible for Nietzsche to learn from Deussen; one cannot say. But the fact is that Nietzsche made no attempt to exploit his acquaintance with the most competent comparative philosopher of the time in order to study critically the ideas of the Sanskrit philosophers. Oddly, Deussen, who has generally been seen as concrete evidence of Nietzsche's "trans-European vision," and whom I certainly so regarded before working through his correspondence with Nietzsche, turns out to be, as I now believe, the most crucial evidence we have of Nietzsche's lack of interest in trans-European ideas. . . .

There may well be much more to say than this sketchy survey of the complex material has turned up; and I may have too easily inferred an absence of interest from an absence of documentary evidence; again my initial assumption of a substantial, if minor, concern with Indian thought on Nietzsche's part may have led me to undervalue or overlook anything less than this. However this may be, a summing up of my impressions from the sources used turns out something like this.

We can conveniently name four areas of Nietzsche's interest—Buddhism, Vedanta, *Laws of Manu,* historical parallels—in descending order of frequency of reference.

Buddhism means to Nietzsche essentially what it meant to Schopenhauer, though his appreciation is more superficial: a religion of release from the inevitable suffering of human existence; a religion of pity based on the refined hedonism of the experience of nothingness. Nietzsche praises Buddhism for showing no trace of Semitic *ressentiment,* for being more a hygiene than a morality, and for rejecting the ultimacy of good and evil (though he quite fails to grasp the radical nature of this rejection). Often the word Buddhism can be read as a synonym for pessimism and this in turn as shorthand for Schopenhauer. One can apply Nietzsche's comment on Schopenhauer, that he used Buddhist mythology as a "rhetorical instrument," to himself. The term "Buddhism" functions most frequently as a focus of Nietzsche's abuse, as a counterpole to his own Dionysian ideas, as a device for saying succinctly what it is he disapproves of and thinks must be overcome ("European Buddhism"). That Buddhism is so often a scapegoat derives perhaps from Nietzsche's tendency to attack most relentlessly what he most feared as his own weakness.

Vedanta served Nietzsche as the perfect model of a world-denying way of thought. It was conveniently remote, and the swift perusal of two of Deussen's books confirmed his suspicion that Schopenhauer's pessimism was rooted in such philosophy. He made little attempt to grapple with the mysteries of negation as a strong form of affirmation, the "pivotal point" of Indian philosophy. He found the asceticism of Vedanta too extreme; in denying the body as well as subject and object, it was guilty of an "assault on reason." Its rejection of good and evil as ultimates was however a saving mark of its realism, Nietzsche thought. Here, too, as in the case of Buddhism, one must conclude from Nietzsche's disinclination to penetrate the issues raised by Vedanta, that the term served him more as a shibboleth, useful for denouncing what he believed to be his arch-enemy.

Little can be added to what has already been said about the *Laws of Manu:* Nietzsche seized on it as a happy and unexpected confirmation of an aspect of his own thinking. It was the radical hierarchy of human worth that aroused his enthusiasm; one has to admire Nietzsche's sensitive "nose," when he says "Plato reads like one who had been well instructed by a Brahmin."

The explicit references to Indian history attempt either to apply a blunt materialist theory or to draw parallels with the Europe of Nietzsche's own time. Both Buddhism and Vedanta as historical phenomena are accounted for by the rice and vegetarian diet of the Indians, which so enfeebles that it exposes those who follow it to the temptations of opium, and thus to a withdrawal from life. Such comments are, however, merely thrown off in passing. More than once Nietzsche sees in the rise of atheistic, amoral Buddhism, at a time of crumbling Vedic religions, a parallel to his efforts to create a new basis for humans in the face of the collapse of Christian culture in Europe, a parallel which does not quite extend to the philosophic content of the two doctrines. That Nietzsche accorded Indian history and ideas so much importance that he found it worthwhile to draw them into his own thinking, even if only in an impressionistic way, is perhaps the appropriate concluding observation on the nature and extent of his interest in these matters.

This perhaps somewhat pedantic exposure of Nietzsche's acquaintance with Indian philosophical literature leaves the remaining questions, stated at the beginning of this paper, for further and more probing consideration: (1) The adequacy of Nietzsche's grasp of Indian thinking; (2) the nature and importance of any influence Indian thinking may have had on Nietzsche's own work; (3) the extent to which, or at least the possibility that Nietzsche, in spite of his fragmentary and second-hand knowledge of the

Sanskrit texts, has made Western access to them easier. These questions demand a fully-rounded grasp of Nietzsche's own life-long thought struggles, no less than a careful study of the reluctant rapprochement of Western thought since Nietzsche, and the available texts from India's classical age. Indeed they demand a sure grasp of the volcanic changes in Western thought itself since Nietzsche. There can be no question of these matters being discussed here. If I can give a useful edge to the questions themselves, based on the limited research of this paper, that will be all.

1. Nietzsche's conceptions were probably not greatly different from those prevailing in his time, or at least not greatly less adequate. After all, Max Müller argued that nirvana did not exclude the possibility of personal immortality in heaven! Nietzsche's hard and courageous comments have the merit of silhouetting the contrast between the European Faustian man and the Indian liberated man. At the same time they reveal the inadequacy of setting up an absolute polarity between yes and no in philosophical thought. The Indians are wary of this and would remind us that Nietzsche's enthused yes-saying Dionysian is suppressing human capacities no less, perhaps more, than the composed Bodhisattva who is master of his enthusiasms. No injunction is more common in Buddhist literature than to summon the courage and the virility to make passions one's servants, not one's master. Nietzsche's repudiation of Buddhism and Hinduism as "life-denying" is hardly adequate to the Indian conception.

2. How important was Nietzsche's knowledge of Indian thought for the development of his own thought? This must remain a problem for a full-length study of the growth of Nietzsche's thought from Röcken to Sils Maria. However, the first impression one has is that ideas from India penetrated Nietzsche as little as drops of water penetrate a goose's feathers. Certainly the conclusions of this study appear to

support that impression. When one re-reads the *The Birth of Tragedy,* however, one can be struck by the force of Nietzsche's conviction that the person conventionally understood as *das Ich* (the "I")—the free agent of thinking and of action—was purely phenomenal, a part of *māyā,* and was not a metaphysical absolute. This conviction never weakened, I believe, in spite of the primary place he accords the individual. Nietzsche tried to be sceptical toward all Greek-European categories, but the one he attacks most vehemently and which he appears to regard as the key is the Cartesian and Kantian *ich,* the grammatical subject of the *cogito.* The hallowed concepts "being," "knowledge," and many others are equally repudiated. Could it be that Nietzsche was sustained in these heresies by knowing that Indian thinkers shared them with him? Perhaps, but I would not hazard an opinion.

3. Finally, has Nietzsche, in spite of his inadequacies or even misconceptions, made Western access to Indian thought any easier? It is difficult to believe that he understood himself in this way, but often enough a thinker's influence is quite other than his intentions. Nietzsche was the first European to sweep through the inherited systems of Greek categories with a disconcerting, disintegrating scepsis. Being, truth, causality, person, whatever he found in use, he rejects as "fictions, unusable." This is a striking parallel to the Vedantist and Buddhist treatment of concepts, a treatment which Westerners, almost without exception, take to be irresponsible or eccentric, and at the very least irrelevant. That a great Western thinker has been driven to this conclusion must shake our complacency some-what and alert us to the odd fact that in some matters Nietzsche is in substantial agreement with thinkers from another, remote, tradition. Ironically, he denied this throughout, with vehemence. Is it possible that Nietzsche's historical sense was acute when he surmised that Europe might now be in a cultural phase comparable to India at the time of the Upanishads and Buddha, a phase in which a radically altered self-understanding is needed if humans are to continue to believe in themselves?

NOTES

1. Ludwig Alsdorf, *Deutsch-Indisch Geistesbeziehungen* (Heidelberg, 1944).
2. H. Von Glasenapp, *Das Indienbild Deutscher Denker* (Stuttgart, 1960), pp. 102, 106.
3. Ryōgi Ōkōchi, "Nietzsches Amor Fati im Lichte von Karma des Buddhismus," *Nietzsche-Studien* 1 (1972): 36–94.
4. Hans Rollmann, "Deussen, Nietzsche and Vedanta," *Journal of the History of Ideas* 39/1 (1978): 125–32.
5. I cannot locate this precise sentence, but it reminds one of the *Kauṣītakī Upaniṣad* I, 2.
6. Freny Mistry, *Nietzsche and Buddhism* (Berlin, 1981), p. 142, note 9, draws attention to an entry in the note books from the time of *Zarathustra*—*KSA* 11, 26[220]. Nietzsche mentions pages in Oldenberg's *Buddha* which deal with the Upanishadic problem of suffering, infinite rebirth, and freedom, in connection with his own thinking about the eternal return.
7. Paul Deussen, *Erinnerungen an Friedrich Nietzsche* (Leipzig, 1901); *Mein Leben* (Leipzig, 1922).
8. Deussen to Nietzsche, 6 January 1867.
9. Deussen to Nietzsche, 5 January 1872.

RECOMMENDED READINGS

Texts

Hollingdale, R. J. *Nietzsche.* London: Routledge & Kegan Paul, 1973.
Kaufmann, W. *Nietzsche, Philosopher, Psychologist, Anti-Christ,* 3d ed. Princeton: Princeton University Press, 1968.

Jaspers, K. *Nietzsche: An Introduction to the Understanding of His Philosophical Activity.* Tucson: University of Arizona Press, 1965.

Nietzsche, Friedrich. *The Portable Nietzsche.* New York: Viking Press, Inc., 1954.

Morgan, G. A. *What Nietzsche Means.* Cambridge: Harvard University Press, 1943.

Solomon, R. ed. *A Collection of Critical Essays.* Notre Dame: University of Notre Dame Press, 1980.

Stern, J. *A Study of Nietzsche.* Cambridge: Cambridge University Press, 1979.

Feminist Perspective

Allen, Christine Garside. "Nietzsche's Ambivalence About Women." In *The Sexism of Social and Political Philosophy.* Ed. Lorenne Clark and Lynda Lange. Toronto: University of Toronto Press, 1979.

Frisbe, Sandra. "Women and the Will to Power," *Gnosis* (1975): 1–10.

Multicultural Perspective

Panikkar, Raimundo. *The Vedic Experience: Mantramanjari.* Los Angeles: University of California Press, 1977.

Parkes, Graham. *Nietzsche and Asian Thought.* Chicago: University of Chicago Press, 1991.

PART IX

❦

SARTRE AND DE BEAUVOIR

INTRODUCTION

Jean-Paul Sartre was born in Paris in 1905. His father, who died when Jean-Paul was little more than a year old, was a naval officer. His mother was a cousin of Albert Schweitzer, the well-known Christian missionary doctor. Sartre was brought up in the home of his maternal grandparents, who pampered and indulged him. He studied at the École Normale Supériéure, concentrating in philosophy and literature. It was here he met Simone de Beauvoir in 1929 when they were both studying for the final agrégation exam. Sartre took first place in the exam, Beauvoir second, although "everyone agreed that *she* was the true philosopher."[1] For the next few years, Sartre taught at a number of lycées both in Paris and elsewhere, and from 1933 to 1936, he was a research student at the Institute Francais in Berlin and the University of Freiburg. In 1938, he published his philosophical novel, *Nausea,* which he later judged to be "the best thing I've done." At the outbreak of World War II, he joined the Army, was captured and later escaped from a German prison camp. He resumed his teaching in Neuilly while working within the resistance. In 1943, he published *Being and Nothingness,* his major philosophical work. In 1945, Sartre delivered his famous lecture, "Existentialism is a Humanism," in Paris at the Club Maintenant. It was this work that popularized existentialism.

As one of the founders, along with Simone de Beauvoir and Maurice Merleau-Ponty, of *Les Temps Modernes,* a review devoted to the discussion of political and literary questions from a generally existentialist point of view, Sartre took an active part in the political controversies of the time. While he viewed himself as a Marxist, Sartre never joined the French Communist party, although at times he did endorse their political agenda. In his *Critique of Dialectical Reason* (1960), he argued for an underlying harmony between Marxism and existentialism, and in favor of a situated freedom rather than the absolute freedom he had defended in his earlier works. In a long interview in June of 1975 reflecting on his life, Sartre described Simone de Beauvoir as the central person of his adult life, emphasizing the equality of their relationship, and that each had been helpfully critical of the other's writings. When he died in 1980, French President Giscard d'Estaing came to pay his respects.

In our selection from "Existentialism is a Humanism." Sartre explains that the central thesis of existentialism is that existence precedes essence. For Sartre, whether or not there is a God, there is no one or nothing to give an "essence," a distinctive purpose or reason, to our existence. Thus, we have no fixed nature or essence and so are free to make of ourselves what we will. Our only essence is the one we make for ourselves by our actions. But this freedom, Sartre argues, also requires responsibility. To have choices and to be able to make a difference requires that we take responsibility for what we choose and for the differences we make. Moreover, Sartre argues that in choosing for ourselves, we also choose for all humankind because in choosing for ourselves we affirm what we think is valuable for anyone else in our circumstances. In so choosing, we legislate for the world. In this respect, Sartre's view is very much like the view of Immanuel Kant.

Simone de Beauvoir was born in Paris in 1908. Her father was an atheist, her mother a pious Catholic. She was educated at a conservative Catholic girls' preparatory school, where she met Zaza, the first love of her life. In 1927, de Beauvoir was one of the three top recipients of the certificat in general philosophy. Simon Weil was first and Maurice Merleau-Ponty third. She taught in a lycée in Marseilles and then in Rouen, where an intimate relationship with a former student became a trio that included Sartre.

She published a novel, *She Came to Stay,* in 1943, which Sartre read in manuscript and which influenced his views in *Being and Nothingness.* In addition to a number of novels and collections of essays, she published *The Ethics of Ambiguity* (1947), in which she argues for a situated freedom as opposed to the absolute freedom that Sartre defended in *Being and Nothingness.* In *America Day by Day* (1948), de Beauvoir presented an analysis of racial segregation in the United States, influenced by the work of the African-American writer Richard Wright, which provided the model for her analysis of women's oppression in *The Second Sex* (1949). In her autobiographies, she disguised her lesbian relationships and went along with the critics who described her as Sartre's philosophical follower. However, the publication of her letters and notebooks in 1990, four years after her death, has served to undermine the conventional myths about her private life and her contributions to philosophy as well.[2]

In our selections from *The Second Sex,* Simon de Beauvoir seeks to answer the question: What is a woman? The answer she gives is that woman is the Other, man is the One. Men are active, transcendent, able to transform their environment; women are passive and immanent, that is, existing within themselves, with little capacity to affect the outside world. Men are the "subjects" of their own lives; women are the "objects," the acted upon. However, de Beauvoir argues that this state of affairs is not an immutable state of nature. Rather it is socially constructed, and it can be changed. De

Beauvoir goes on to explain why women have been defined as the Other, and what has to be done if they are to escape from the sphere hitherto assigned to them and aspire to full membership in the human race.

In "Simone de Beauvoir and Women: Just Who Does She Think "We" Is?" Elizabeth Spelman argues that de Beauvoir has all the essential ingredients of a feminist account of "women's lives" that would not conflate "woman" with a small group of women—namely, white, middle-class women in Western countries. Yet unfortunately, Spelman argues, de Beauvoir ends up doing just that. According to Spelman, de Beauvoir thinks that sexism is nullified by race or class oppression and thus can only be experienced by white, middle-class women in Western countries, since only they are not subject to any class or racial oppression.

Suppose, however, we interpret de Beauvoir as holding the more plausible view that sexism is only sometimes and only in some respects nullified by class and racial oppression. We could infer that she also holds the more plausible view that sexism shares common features in many times and places, yet takes distinctive forms as well. Hence, it would follow, for example, that sexism in African-American culture is somewhat the same and somewhat different from sexism in white, middle-class American culture. Interpreted in this way, it would seem that de Beauvoir would be able to meet Spelman's criticism.

In "We Are All Related," Eagle Man (Ed McGaa), an Oglala Sioux, argues for a situated freedom that is different from the situated freedom defended by de Beauvoir and later by Sartre himself. According to Eagle Man, we are to respect individual freedom provided that it does not threaten the tribe, or the people, or Mother Earth. Eagle Man introduces a concern for Mother Earth because, he says, we are all related. We all come from this Mother Earth and we all will return to her. Accordingly, Eagle Man contends, we should use no more resources than we need, and we should be sharing and generous with other living beings, including nonhuman living beings. What we need to ask ourselves is whether this American Indian perspective provides a more morally defensible account of situated freedom.

NOTES

1. Claude Francis and Fermande Gontier, *Simone de Beauvoir: A Life . . . A Love Story.* Translated by L. Nesselson. New York: St Martin's (1987), p. 69
2. See *Feminist Interpretations of Simone de Beauvoir,* edited by Margaret A Simon. Penn State University Press, 1995.

33. EXISTENTIALISM IS A HUMANISM

❧

JEAN-PAUL SARTRE

What is meant by the term *existentialism?*

It can be defined easily. What complicates matters is that there are two kinds of existentialist; first, those who are Christian, among whom I would include Jaspers and Gabriel Marcel, both Catholic; and on the other hand the atheistic existentialists, among whom I class Heidegger, and then the French existentialists and myself. What they have in common is that they think that existence precedes essence, or, if you prefer, that subjectivity must be the starting point.

Just what does that mean? Let us consider some object that is manufactured, for example, a book or a paper-cutter: here is an object which has been made by an artisan whose inspiration came from a concept. He referred to the concept of what a paper-cutter is and like-wise to a known method of production, which is part of the concept, something which is, by and large, a routine. Thus, the paper-cutter is at once an object produced in a certain way and, on the other hand, one having a specific use; and one can not postulate a man who produces a paper-cutter but does not know what it is used for. Therefore, let us say that, for the paper-cutter, essence—that is, the ensemble of both the production routines and the properties which enable it to be both produced and defined—precedes existence. Thus, the presence of the paper-cutter or book in front of me is determined. Therefore, we have here a technical view of the world whereby it can be said that production precedes existence.

Reprinted from *Existentialism Is a Humanism*, trans. by Bernard Frechtman, by permission of Philosophical Library.

When we conceive God as the Creator, He is generally thought of as a superior sort of artisan. Whatever doctrine we may be considering, whether one like that of Descartes or that of Leibnitz, we always grant that will more or less follows understanding or, at the very least, accompanies it, and that when God creates He knows exactly what He is creating. Thus, the concept of man in the mind of God is comparable to the concept of paper-cutter in the mind of the manufacturer, and, following certain techniques and a conception, God produces man, just as the artisan, following a definition and a technique, makes a paper-cutter. Thus, the individual man is the realisation of a certain concept in the divine intelligence.

In the eighteenth century, the atheism of the *philosophes* discarded the idea of God, but not so much for the notion that essence precedes existence. To a certain extent, this idea is found everywhere; we find it in Diderot, in Voltaire, and even in Kant. Man has a human nature; this human nature, which is the concept of the human, is found in all men, which means that each man is a particular example of a universal concept, man. In Kant, the result of this universality is that the wild-man, the natural man, as well as the bourgeois, are circumscribed by the same definition and have the same basic qualities. Thus, here too the essence of man precedes the historical existence that we find in nature.

Atheistic existentialism, which I represent, is more coherent. It states that if God does not exist, there is at least one being in whom existence precedes essence, a being who exists before he can be defined by any concept, and that this being is man, or, as Heidegger says, human reality. What is meant here by saying that existence precedes essence? It means that, first of all, man exists, turns up, appears on the scene, and, only afterwards, defines himself. If man, as the existentialist conceives him, is indefinable, it is because at first he is nothing. Only afterward will he be something, and he himself will have made what he will be. Thus, there is no human nature, since there is no God to conceive it. Not only is man what he conceives himself to be, but he is also only what he wills himself to be after this thrust toward existence.

Man is nothing else but what he makes of himself. Such is the first principle of existentialism. It is also what is called subjectivity, the name we are labeled with when charges are brought against us. But what do we mean by this, if not that man has a greater dignity than a stone or table? For we mean that man first exists, that is, that man first of all is the being who hurls himself toward a future and who is conscious of imagining himself as being in the future. Man is at the start a plan which is aware of itself, rather than a patch of moss, a piece of garbage, or a cauliflower; nothing exists prior to this plan; there is nothing in heaven; man will be what he will have planned to be. Not what he will want to be. Because by the word "will" we generally mean a conscious decision, which is subsequent to what we have already made of ourselves. I may want to belong to a political party, write a book, get married; but all that is only a manifestation of an earlier, more spontaneous choice that is called "will." But if existence really does precede essence, man is responsible for what he is. Thus, existentialism's first move is to make every man aware of what he is and to make the full responsibility of his existence rest on him. And when we say that a man is responsible for himself, we do not only mean that he is responsible for his own individuality, but that he is responsible for all men.

The word subjectivism has two meanings, and our opponents play on the two. Subjectivism means, on the one hand, that an individual chooses and makes himself; and, on the other, that it is impossible for man to transcend human subjectivity. The second of these is the essential meaning of existentialism. When we say that man chooses his own self, we mean that every one of us does likewise; but we also mean by that that in making this choice he also chooses all men. In fact, in creating the man that we want to be, there is not a single one of our acts which does not at the same time create an image of man as we think he ought to be. To choose to be this or that is to affirm at the same time the value of what we choose, because we can never choose evil. We always choose the good, and nothing can be good for us without being good for all.

If, on the other hand, existence precedes essence, and if we grant that we exist and fashion our image at one and the same time, the image is valid for everybody and for our whole age. Thus, our responsibility is much greater than we might have supposed, because it involves all mankind. If I am a workingman and choose to join a Christian trade-union rather than be a communist, and if by being a member I want to show that the best thing for man is resignation, that the kingdom of man is not of this world, I am not only involving my own case—I want to be resigned for everyone. As a result, my action has involved all humanity. To take a more individual matter, if I want to marry, to have children; even if this marriage depends solely on my own circumstances or passion or wish, I am involving all humanity in monogamy and not merely myself. Therefore, I am responsible for myself and for everyone else. I am creating a certain image of man of my own choosing. In choosing myself, I choose man.

This helps us understand what the actual content is of such rather grandiloquent words as anguish, forlornness, despair. As you will see, it's all quite simple.

First, what is meant by anguish? The existentialists say at once that man is anguish. What that means is this: the man who involves himself and who realizes that he is not only the person he chooses to be, but also a law-maker who is, at the same time, choosing all mankind as well as himself, can not help escape the feeling of his total and deep responsibility. Of course, there are many people who are not anxious; but we claim that they are hiding their anxiety, that they are fleeing from it. Certainly, many people believe that when they do something, they themselves are the only ones involved, and when someone says to them, "What if everyone acted that way?" they shrug their shoulders and answer, "Everyone doesn't act that way." But really, one should always ask himself, "What would happen if everybody looked at things that way?" There is no escaping this disturbing thought except by a kind of double-dealing. A man who lies and makes excuses for himself by saying "not everybody does that," is someone with an uneasy conscience, because the act of lying implies that a universal value is conferred upon the lie.

Anguish is evident even when it conceals itself. This is the anguish that Kierkegaard called the anguish of Abraham. You know the story: an angel has ordered Abraham to sacrifice his son; if it really were an angel who has come and said, "You are Abraham, you shall sacrifice your son," everything would be all right. But everyone might first wonder, "Is it really an angel, and am I really Abraham? What proof do I have?"

There was a madwoman who had hallucinations; someone used to speak to her on the telephone and give her orders. Her doctor asked her, "Who is it who talks to you?" She answered, "He says it's God." What proof did she really have that it was God? If an angel comes to me, what proof is there that it's an angel? And if I hear voices, what proof is there that they come from heaven and not from hell, or from the subconscious, or a pathological condition? What proves that they are addressed to me? What proof is there that I have been appointed to impose my choice and my conception of man on humanity? I'll never find any proof or sign to convince me of that. If a voice addresses me, it is

always for me to decide that this is the angel's voice; if I consider that such an act is a good one, it is I who will choose to say that it is good rather than bad.

Now, I'm not being singled out as an Abraham, and yet at every moment I'm obliged to perform exemplary acts. For every man, everything happens as if all mankind had its eyes fixed on him and were guiding itself by what he does. And every man ought to say to himself, "Am I really the kind of man who has the right to act in such a way that humanity might guide itself by my actions?" And if he does not say that to himself, he is masking his anguish.

There is no question here of the kind of anguish which would lead to quietism, to inaction. It is a matter of a simple sort of anguish that anybody who has had responsibilities is familiar with. For example, when a military officer takes the responsibility for an attack and sends a certain number of men to death, he chooses to do so, and in the main he alone makes the choice. Doubtless, orders come from above, but they are too broad; he interprets them, and on this interpretation depend the lives of ten or fourteen or twenty men. In making a decision he can not help having a certain anguish. All leaders know this anguish. That doesn't keep them from acting; on the contrary, it is the very condition of their action. For it implies that they envisage a number of possibilities, and when they choose one, they realize that it has value only because it is chosen. We shall see that this kind of anguish, which is the kind that existentialism describes, is explained, in addition, by a direct responsibility to the other men whom it involves. It is not a curtain separating us from action, but is part of action itself.

When we speak of forlornness, a term Heidegger was fond of, we mean only that God does not exist and that we have to face all the consequences of this. The existentialist is strongly opposed to a certain kind of secular ethics which would like to abolish God with the least possible expense. About 1880, some French teachers tried to set up a secular ethics which went something like this: God is a useless and costly hypothesis; we are discarding it; but, meanwhile, in order for there to be an ethics, a society, a civilization, it is essential that certain values be taken seriously and that they be considered as having an *a priori* existence. It must be obligatory, *a priori,* to be honest, not to lie, not to beat your wife, to have children, etc., etc. So we're going to try a little device which will make it possible to show that values exist all the same, inscribed in a heaven of ideas, though otherwise God does not exist. In other words-and this, I believe, is the tendency of everything called reformism in France-nothing will be changed if God does not exist. We shall find ourselves with the same norms of honesty, progress, and humanism, and we shall have made of God an outdated hypothesis which will peacefully die off by itself.

The existentialist, on the contrary, thinks it very distressing that God does not exist, because all possibility of finding values in a heaven of ideas disappears along with Him; there can no longer be an *a priori* Good, since there is no infinite and prefect consciousness to think it. Nowhere is it written that the Good exists, that we must be honest, that we must not lie; because the fact is we are on a plane where there are only men. Dostoievsky said, "If God didn't exist, everything would be possible." That is the very starting point of existentialism. Indeed, everything is permissible if God does not exist, and as a result man is forlorn, because neither within him nor without does he find anything to cling to. He can't start making excuses for himself.

If existence really does precede essence, there is no explaining things away by reference to a fixed and given human nature. In other words, there is no determinism, man is free, man is freedom. On the other hand, if God does not exist, we find no values or commands to turn to which legitimize our conduct. So, in the bright realm of values, we have no excuse behind us, nor justification before us. We are alone, with no excuses.

That is the idea I shall try to convey when I say that man is condemned to be free. Condemned, because he did not create himself, yet, in other respects is free; because, once thrown into the world, he is responsible for everything he does. The existentialist does not believe in the power of passion. He will never agree that a sweeping passion is a ravaging torrent which fatally leads a man to certain acts and is therefore an excuse. He thinks that man is responsible for his passion.

The existentialist does not think that man is going to help himself by finding in the world some omen by which to orient himself. Because he thinks that man will interpret the omen to suit himself. Therefore, he thinks that man, with no support and no aid, is condemned every moment to invent man. Ponge, in a very fine article, has said, "Man is the future of man." That's exactly it. But if it is taken to mean that this future is recorded in heaven, that God sees it, then it is false, because it would really no longer be a future. If it is taken to mean that, whatever a man may be, there is a future to be forged, a virgin future before him, then this remark is sound. But then we are forlorn.

To give you an example which will enable you to understand forlornness better, I shall cite the case of one of my students who came to see me under the following circumstances: his father was on bad terms with his mother, and, moreover, was inclined to be a collaborationist; his older brother had been killed in the German offensive of 1940, and the young man, with somewhat immature but generous feelings, wanted to avenge him. His mother lived alone with him, very much upset by the half-treason of her husband and the death of her older son; the boy was her only consolation.

The boy was faced with the choice of leaving for England and joining the Free French Forces—that is, leaving his mother behind—or remaining with his mother and helping her to carry on. He was fully aware that the woman lived only for him and that his going-off—and perhaps his death—would plunge her into despair. He was also aware that every act that he did for his mother's sake was a sure thing, in the sense that it was helping her to carry on, whereas every effort he made toward going off and fighting was an uncertain move which might run aground and prove completely useless; for example, on his way to England he might, while passing through Spain, be detained indefinitely in a Spanish camp; he might reach England or Algiers and be stuck in an office at a desk job. As a result, he was faced with two very different kinds of action: one, concrete, immediate, but concerning only one individual; the other concerned an incomparably vaster group, a national collectivity, but for that very reason was dubious, and might be interrupted en route. And, at the same time, he was wavering between two kinds of ethics. On the one hand, an ethics of sympathy, of personal devotion; on the other, a broader ethics, but one whose efficacy was more dubious. He had to choose between the two.

Who could help him choose? Christian doctrine? No. Christian doctrine says, "Be charitable, love your neighbor, take the more rugged path, etc., etc." But which is the more rugged path? Whom should he love as a brother? The fighting man or his mother? Which does the greater good, the vague act of fighting in a group, or the concrete one of helping a particular human being to go on living? Who can decide a priori? Nobody. No book of ethics can tell him. The Kantian ethics says, "Never treat any person as a means, but as an end." Very well, if I stay with my mother, I'll treat her as an end and not as a means; but by virtue of this very fact, I'm running the risk of treating the people around me who are fighting, as means; and, conversely, if I go to join those who are fighting, I'll be treating them as an end, and, by doing that, I run the risk of treating my mother as a means.

If values are vague, and if they are always too broad for the concrete and specific case that we are considering, the only thing left for us is to trust our instincts. That's what this young man tried to do; and when I saw him, he said, "In the end; feeling is what counts. I ought to choose whichever pushes me in one direction. If I feel that I love my mother enough to sacrifice everything else for her—my desire for vengeance, for action, for adventure—then I'll stay with her. If, on the contrary, I feel that my love for my mother isn't enough, I'll leave."

But how is the value of a feeling determined? What gives his feeling for his mother value? Precisely the fact that he remained with her. I may say that I like so-and-so well enough to sacrifice a certain amount of money for him, but I may say so only if I've done it. I may say "I love my mother well enough to remain with her" if I have remained with her. The only way to determine the value of this affection is, precisely, to perform an act which confirms and defines it. But, since I require this affection to justify my act, I find myself caught in a vicious circle.

On the other hand, Gide has well said that a mock feeling and a true feeling are almost indistinguishable; to decide that I love my mother and will remain with her, or to remain with her by putting on an act, amount somewhat to the same thing. In other words, the feeling is formed by the acts one performs; so, I can not refer to it in order to act upon it. Which means that I can neither seek within myself the true condition which will impel me to act, nor apply to a system of ethics for concepts which will permit me to act. You will say, "At least, he did go to a teacher for advice." But if you seek advice from a priest, for example, you have chosen this priest; you already knew, more or less, just about what advice he was going to give you. In other words, choosing your adviser is involving yourself. The proof of this is that if you are a Christian, you will say, "Consult a priest." But some priests are collaborating, some are just marking time, some are resisting. Which to choose? If the young man chooses a priest who is resisting or collaborating, he has already decided on the kind of advice he's going to get. Therefore, in coming to see me he knew the answer I was going to give him, and I had only one answer to give: "You're free, choose, that is, invent." No general ethics can show you what is to be done; there are no omens in the world. The Catholics will reply, "But there are." Granted—but, in any case, I myself choose the meaning they have.

When I was a prisoner, I knew a rather remarkable young man who was a Jesuit. He had entered the Jesuit order in the following way: he had had a number of very bad breaks; in childhood, his father died, leaving him in poverty, and he was a scholarship student at a religious institution where he was constantly made to feel that he was being kept out of charity; then, he failed to get any of the honors and distinctions that children like; later on, at about eighteen, he bungled a love affair; finally, at twenty-two, he failed in military training, a childish enough matter, but it was the last straw.

This young fellow might well have felt that he had botched everything. It was a sign of something, but of what? He might have taken refuge in bitterness or despair. But he very wisely looked upon all this as a sign that he was not made for secular triumphs, and that only the triumphs of religion, holiness, and faith were open to him. He saw the hand of God in all this, and so he entered the order. Who can help seeing that he alone decided what the sign meant?

Some other interpretation might have been drawn from this series of setbacks; for example, that he might have done better to turn carpenter or revolutionist. Therefore, he is fully responsible for the interpretation. Forlornness implies that we ourselves choose our being. Forlornness and anguish go together. . . .

Besides, if it is impossible to find in every man some universal essence which would be human nature, yet there does exist a universal human condition. It's not by chance that today's thinkers speak more readily of man's condition than of his nature. By condition they mean, more or less definitely, the *a priori* limits which outline man's fundamental situation in the universe. Historical situations vary; a man may be born a slave in a pagan society or a feudal lord or a proletarian.

What does not vary is the necessity for him to exist in the world, to be at work there, to be there in the midst of other people, and to be mortal there. The limits are neither subjective nor objective, or, rather, they have an objective and a subjective side. Objective because they are to be found everywhere and are recognizable everywhere; subjective because they are *lived* and are nothing if man does not live them, that is, freely determine his existence with reference to them. And though the configurations may differ, at least none of them are completely strange to me, because they all appear as attempts either to pass beyond these limits or recede from them or deny them or adapt to them. Consequently, every configuration, however individual it may be, has a universal value.

Every configuration, even the Chinese, the Indian, or the Negro, can be understood by a Westerner. "Can be understood" means that by virtue of a situation that he can imagine, a European of 1945 can, in like manner, push himself to his limits and reconstitute within himself the configuration of the Chinese, the Indian, or the African. Every configuration has universality in the sense that every configuration can be understood by every man. This does not at all mean that this configuration defines man forever, but that it can be met with again. There is always a way to understand the idiot, the child, the savage, the foreigner, provided one has the necessary information.

In this sense we may say that there is a universality of man; but it is not given, it is perpetually being made. I build the universal in choosing myself; I build it in understanding the configuration of every other man, whatever age he might have lived in. This absoluteness of choice does not do away with the relativeness of each epoch. . . .

Existentialism is nothing else than an attempt to draw all the consequences of a coherent atheistic position. It isn't trying to plunge man into despair at all. But if one calls every attitude of unbelief despair, like the Christians, then the word is not being used in its original sense. Existentialism isn't so atheistic that it wears itself out showing that God doesn't exist. Rather, it declares that even if God did exist, that would change nothing. There you've got our point of view. Not that we believe that God exists, but we think that the problem of His existence is not the issue. In this sense existentialism is optimistic, a doctrine of action, and it is plain dishonesty for Christians to make no distinction between their own despair and ours and then to call us despairing.

34. THE SECOND SEX

SIMONE DE BEAUVOIR

For a long time I have hesitated to write a book on woman. The subject is irritating, especially to women; and it is not new. Enough ink has been spilled in the quarreling over feminism, now practically over, and perhaps we should say no more about it. It is still talked about, however, for the voluminous nonsense uttered during the last century seems to have done little to illuminate the problem. After all, is there a problem? And if so, what is it? Are there women, really? Most assuredly the theory of the eternal feminine still has its adherents who will whisper in your ear: "Even in Russia women still are *women*"; and other erudite persons—sometimes the very same—say with a sigh: "Woman is losing her way, woman is lost." One wonders if women still exist, if they will always exist, whether or not it is desirable that they should, what place they occupy in this world, what their place should be. "What has become of women?" was asked recently in an ephemeral magazine.[1]

But first we must ask: what is a woman? *"Tota mulier in utero,"* says one, "woman is a womb." But in speaking of certain women, connoisseurs declare that they are not women, although they are equipped with a uterus like the rest. All agree in recognizing the fact that females exist in the human species; today as always they make up about one half of humanity. And yet we are told that femininity is in danger; we are exhorted to be women, remain women, become women. It would appear, then, that every female human being is not necessarily a woman; to be so considered she must share in that mysterious and threatened reality known as femininity. Is this attribute something secreted by the ovaries? Or is it a Platonic essence, a product of the philosophic imagination? Is a rustling petticoat enough to bring it down to earth? Although some women try zealously to incarnate this essence, it is hardly patentable. It is frequently described in vague and dazzling terms that seem to have been borrowed from the vocabulary of the seers, and indeed in the times of St. Thomas it was considered an essence as certainly defined as the somniferous virtue of the poppy. . . .

In truth, to go for a walk with one's eyes open is enough to demonstrate that humanity is divided into two classes of individuals whose clothes, faces, bodies, smiles, gaits, interests, and occupations are manifestly different. Perhaps these differences are superficial, perhaps they are destined to disappear. What is certain is that right now they do most obviously exist.

If her functioning as a female is not enough to define woman, if we decline also to explain her through "the eternal feminine," and if nevertheless we admit, provisionally, that women do exist, then we must face the question: what is a woman?

To state the question is, to me, to suggest, at once, a preliminary answer. The fact that I ask it is in itself significant. A man would never get the notion of writing a book on the peculiar situation of the human male.[2] But if I wish to define myself, I must first of all say: "I am a woman"; on this truth must be based all further discussion. A man never begins by presenting himself as an individual of a certain sex; it goes without saying that he is a man. The terms *masculine* and *feminine* are used symmetrically only as a matter of form, as on legal papers. In actuality the relation of the two sexes is not quite like that of two electrical poles, for man represents both the positive and the neutral, as is indicated by the common use of *man* to designate human beings in general; whereas woman represents only the negative, defined by limiting criteria, without reciprocity. In the midst of an abstract discussion it is vexing to hear a man say: "You think thus and so because you are a woman"; but I know that my only defense is to reply: "I think thus and so because it is true," thereby removing my subjective self from the argument. It would be out of the question to reply: "And you think the contrary because you are a man," for it is understood that the fact of being a man is no peculiarity. A man is in the right in being a man; it is the woman who

is in the wrong. It amounts to this: just as for the ancients there was an absolute vertical with reference to which the oblique was defined, so there is an absolute human type, the masculine. Woman has ovaries, a uterus; these peculiarities imprison her in her subjectivity, circumscribe her within the limits of her own nature. It is often said that she thinks with her glands. Man superbly ignores the fact that his anatomy also includes glands, such as the testicles, and that they secrete hormones. He thinks of his body as a direct and normal connection with the world, which he believes he apprehends objectively, whereas he regards the body of woman as a hindrance, a prison, weighed down by everything peculiar to it. "The female is a female by virtue of a certain *lack* of qualities," said Aristotle; "we should regard the female nature as afflicted with a natural defectiveness." And St. Thomas for his part pronounced woman to be an "imperfect man," an "incidental" being. This is symbolized in Genesis where Eve is depicted as made from what Bossuet called "a supernumerary bone" of Adam.

Thus humanity is male and man defines woman not in herself but as relative to him; she is not regarded as an autonomous being. Michelet writes: "Woman, the relative being. . . ." And Benda is most positive in his *Rapport d' Uriel:* "The body of man makes sense in itself quite apart from that of woman, whereas the latter seems wanting in significance by itself. . . . Man can think of himself without woman. She cannot think of herself without man." And she is simply what man decrees; thus she is called "the sex," by which is meant that she appears essentially to the male as a sexual being. For him she is sex—absolute sex, no less. She is defined and differentiated with reference to man and not he with reference to her; she is the incidental, the inessential as opposed to the essential. He is the Subject, he is the Absolute—she is the Other.[3]

The category of the *Other* is as primordial as consciousness itself. In the most primitive societies, in the most ancient mythologies, one finds the expression of a duality—that of the Self and the Other. This duality was not originally attached to the division of the sexes; it was not dependent upon any empirical facts. . . . Otherness is a fundamental category of human thought.

Thus it is that no group ever sets itself up as the One without at once setting up the Other over against itself. If three travelers chance to occupy the same compartment, that is enough to make vaguely hostile "others" out of all the rest of the passengers on the train. In small-town eyes all persons not belonging to the village are "strangers" and suspect; to the native of a country all who inhabit other countries are "foreigners"; Jews are "different" for the anti-Semite, Negroes are "inferior" for American racists, aborigines are "natives" for colonists, proletarians are the "lower class" for the privileged. . . .

No subject will readily volunteer to become the object, the inessential; it is not the Other who, in defining himself as the Other, establishes the One. The Other is posed as such by the One in defining himself as the One. But if the Other is not to regain the status of being the One, he must be submissive enough to accept this alien point of view. . . .

If woman seems to be the inessential which never becomes the essential, it is because she herself fails to bring about this change. Proletarians say "We"; Negroes also. Regarding themselves as subjects, they transform the bourgeois, the whites, into "others." But women do not say "We," except at some congress of feminists or similar formal demonstration; men say "women," and women use the same word in referring to themselves. They do not authentically assume a subjective attitude. The proletarians have accomplished the revolution in Russia, the Negroes in Haiti, the Indo-Chinese are battling for it in Indo-China; but the women's effort has never been anything more than a symbolic agitation. They have gained only what men have been willing to grant; they have taken nothing, they have only received.

The reason for this is that women lack concrete means for organizing themselves into a unit which can stand face to face with the correlative unit. They have no past, no history, no religion of their own; and they have no such solidarity of work and interest as that of the proletariat. They are not even promiscuously herded together in the way that creates community feeling among the American Negroes, the ghetto Jews, the workers of Saint-Denis, or the factory hands of Renault. They live dispersed among the males, attached through residence, housework, economic condition, and social standing to certain men—fathers or husbands—more firmly than they are to other women. If they belong to the bourgeoisie, they feel solidarity with men of that class, not with proletarian women; if they are white, their allegiance is to white men, not to Negro women. The proletariat can propose to massacre the ruling class, and a sufficiently fanatical Jew or Negro might dream of getting sole possession of the atomic bomb and making humanity wholly Jewish or black; but woman cannot even dream of exterminating the males. The bond that unites her to her oppressors is not comparable to any other. The division of the sexes is a biological fact, not an event in human history. Male and female stand opposed within a primordial *Mitsein,* and woman has not broken it. The couple is a fundamental unity with its two halves riveted together, and the cleavage of society along the line of sex is impossible. Here is to be found the basic trait of woman: she is the Other in a totality of which the two components are necessary to one another.

One could suppose that this reciprocity might have facilitated the liberation of woman. When Hercules sat at the feet of Omphale and helped with her spinning, his desire for her held him captive; but why did she fail to gain a lasting power? To revenge herself on Jason, Medea killed their children; and this grim legend would seem to suggest that she might have obtained a formidable influence over him through his love for his offspring. In *Lysistrata* Aristophanes gaily depicts a band of women who joined forces to gain social ends through the sexual needs of their men; but this is only a play. In the legend of the Sabine women, the latter soon abandoned their plan of remaining sterile to punish their ravishers. In truth woman has not been socially emancipated through man's need—sexual desire and the desire for offspring—which makes the male dependent for satisfaction upon the female.

Master and slave, also, are united by a reciprocal need, in this case economic, which does not liberate the slave. In the relation of master to slave the master does not make a point of the need that he has for the other; he has in his grasp the power of satisfying this need through his own action; whereas the slave, in his dependent condition, his hope and fear, is quite conscious of the need he has for his master. Even if the need is at bottom equally urgent for both, it always works in favor of the oppressor and against the oppressed. That is why the liberation of the working class, for example, has been slow.

Now, woman has always been man's dependent, if not his slave; the two sexes have never shared the world in equality. And even today woman is heavily handicapped, though her situation is beginning to change. Almost nowhere is her legal status the same as man's[4] and frequently it is much to her disadvantage. Even when her rights are legally recognized in the abstract, long-standing custom prevents their full expression in the mores. In the economic sphere men and women can almost be said to make up two castes; other things being equal, the former hold the better jobs, get higher wages, and have more opportunity for success than their new competitors. In industry and politics men have a great many more positions and they monopolize the most important posts. In addition to all this, they enjoy a traditional prestige that the education of children tends in every way to support, for the present enshrines the past—and in the past all history has been made by men. At the present time, when women are beginning to take part in the affairs of the world, it is still a world that belongs to men—they have no doubt of it at all and women have scarcely any. To decline to be the Other, to refuse to be a party to the deal—this would be for women to renounce all the advantages conferred upon them by their alliance with the superior caste. Man-the-sovereign will provide woman-the-liege with material protection and will undertake the moral justification of her existence; thus she can evade at once both economic risk and the metaphysical risk of a liberty in which ends and aims must be contrived without assistance. Indeed, along with the ethical urge of each individual to affirm his subjective existence, there is also the temptation to forgo liberty and become a thing. This is an inauspicious road, for he who takes it—passive, lost, ruined—becomes henceforth the creature of another's will, frustrated in his transcendence and deprived of every value. But it is an easy road; on it one avoids the strain involved in undertaking an authentic existence. When man makes of woman the *Other,* he may, then, expect her to manifest deep-seated tendencies toward complicity. Thus, woman may fail to lay claim to the status of subject because she lacks definite resources, because she feels the necessary bond that ties her to man regardless of reciprocity, and because she is often very well pleased with her role as the *Other.*

But it will be asked at once: how did all this begin? It is easy to see that the duality of the sexes, like any duality, gives rise to conflict. And doubtless the winner will assume the status of absolute. But why should man have won from the start? It seems possible that women could have won the victory; or that the outcome of the conflict might never have been decided. How is it that this world has always belonged to the men and that things have begun to change only recently? Is this change a good thing? Will it bring about an equal sharing of the world between men and women?

These questions are not new, and they have often been answered. But the very fact that woman *is the Other* tends to cast suspicion upon all the justifications that men have ever been able to provide for it. These have all too evidently been dictated by men's interest. A little-known feminist of the seventeenth century, Poulain de la Barre, put it this way: "All that has been written about women by men should be suspect, for the men are at once judge and party to the lawsuit." Everywhere, at all times, the males have displayed their satisfaction in feeling that they are the lords of creation. "Blessed be God . . . that He did not make me a woman," say the Jews in their morning prayers, while their wives pray on a note of resignation: "Blessed be the Lord, who created me according to His will." The first among the blessings for which Plato thanked the gods was that he had been created free, not enslaved; the second, a man, not a woman. But the males could not enjoy this privilege fully unless they believed it to be founded on the absolute and the eternal; they sought to make the fact of their supremacy into a right. "Being men, those who have made and compiled the laws have favored their own sex, and jurists have elevated these laws into principles," to quote Poulain de la Barre once more.

Legislators, priests, philosophers, writers, and scientists have striven to show that the subordinate position of woman is willed in heaven and advantageous on earth. The religions invented by men reflect this wish for domination. In the legends of Eve and Pandora men have taken up arms against women. They have made use of philosophy and theology, as the quotations from Aristotle and St. Thomas have shown. Since ancient times satirists and moralists have delighted in showing up the weaknesses of women. We are familiar with the savage indictments hurled against women throughout French literature. Montherlant, for example, follows the tradition of Jean de Meung, though with less gusto. This hostility may at times be well founded, often it is gratuitous; but in truth it more or less successfully conceals a desire for self-justification. As Montaigne says, "It is easier to accuse one sex than to excuse the other." Sometimes what is going on is clear enough. For instance, the Roman law limiting the rights of woman cited "the imbecility, the instability of the sex" just when the weakening of family ties seemed to threaten the interests of male heirs. And in the effort to keep the married woman under guardianship, appeal was made in the sixteenth century to the authority of St. Augustine, who declared that "woman is a creature neither decisive nor constant," at a time when the single woman was thought capable of managing her property. Montaigne understood clearly how arbitrary and unjust was woman's appointed lot: "Women are not in the wrong when they decline to accept the rules laid down for them, since the men make these rules without consulting them. No wonder intrigue and strife abound." But he did not go so far as to champion their cause.

It was only later, in the eighteenth century, that genuinely democratic men began to view the matter objectively. Diderot, among others, strove to show that woman is, like man, a human being. Later John Stuart Mill came fervently to her defense. But these philosophers displayed unusual impartiality. In the nineteenth century the feminist quarrel became again a quarrel of partisans. One of the consequences of the industrial revolution was the entrance of women into productive labor, and it was just here that the claims of the feminists emerged from the realm of theory and acquired an economic basis, while their opponents became the more aggressive. Although landed property lost power to some extent, the bourgeoisie clung to the old morality that found the guarantee of private property in the solidity of the family. Woman was ordered back into the home the more harshly as her emancipation became a real menace. Even within the working class the men endeavored to restrain woman's liberation, because they began to see the women as dangerous competitors—the more so because they were accustomed to work for lower wages.

In proving woman's inferiority, the antifeminists then began to draw not only upon religion, philosophy, and theology, as before, but also upon science—biology, experimental psychology, etc. At most they were willing to grant "equality in difference" to the *other* sex. That profitable formula is most significant; it is precisely like the "equal but separate" formula of the Jim Crow laws aimed at the North American Negroes. As is well known, this so-called equalitarian segregation has resulted only in the most extreme discrimination. The similarity just noted is in no way due to chance, for whether it is a race, a caste, a class, or a sex that is reduced to a position of inferiority, the methods of justification are the same. "The eternal feminine" corresponds to "the black soul" and to "the Jewish character." True, the Jewish problem is on the whole very different from the other two—to the anti-Semite the Jew is not so much an inferior as he is an enemy for whom there is to be granted no place on earth, for whom annihilation is the fate desired. But there are deep similarities between the situation of woman and that of the Negro. Both are being emancipated today from a like paternalism, and the former master class wishes to "keep them in their place"—that is, the place chosen for them. In both cases the former masters lavish more or less sincere eulogies, either on the virtues of "the good Negro" with his dormant, childish, merry soul—the submissive Negro—or on the merits of the woman who is "truly feminine"—that is, frivolous, infantile, irresponsible—the submissive woman. In both cases the dominant class bases its argument on a state of affairs that it has itself created. As George Bernard Shaw puts it, in substance, "The American white relegates the black to the rank of shoeshine boy; and he concludes from this that the black is good for nothing but shining shoes." This vicious circle is met with in all analogous circumstances; when an individual (or a group of individuals) is kept in a situation of inferiority, the fact is that he *is* inferior. But the significance of the verb *to be* must be rightly understood here; it is in bad faith to give it a static value when it

really has the dynamic Hegelian sense of "to have become." Yes, women on the whole *are* today inferior to men; that is, their situation affords them fewer possibilities. The question is: should that state of affairs continue? . . .

People have tirelessly sought to prove that woman is superior, inferior, or equal to man. Some say that, having been created after Adam, she is evidently a secondary being; others say on the contrary that Adam was only a rough draft and that God succeeded in producing the human being in perfection when He created Eve. Woman's brain is smaller; yes, but it is relatively larger. Christ was made a man; yes, but perhaps for his greater humility. Each argument at once suggests its opposite, and both are often fallacious. If we are to gain understanding, we must get out of these ruts; we must discard the vague notions of superiority, inferiority, equality which have hitherto corrupted every discussion of the subject and start afresh. . . .

But it is doubtless impossible to approach any human problem with a mind free from bias. The way in which questions are put, the points of view assumed, presuppose a relativity of interest; all characteristics imply values, and every objective description, so called, implies an ethical background. Rather than attempt to conceal principles more or less definitely implied, it is better to state them openly at the beginning. This will make it unnecessary to specify on every page in just what sense one uses such words as *superior, inferior, better, worse, progress, reaction,* and the like. If we survey some of the works on woman, we note that one of the points of view most frequently adopted is that of the public good, the general interest; and one always means by this the benefit of society as one wishes it to be maintained or established. For our part, we hold that the only *public good* is that which assures the private good of the citizens; we shall pass judgment on institutions according to their effectiveness in giving concrete opportunities to individuals. But we do not confuse the idea of private interest with that of happiness, although that is another common point of view. Are not women of the harem more happy than women voters? Is not the housekeeper happier than the workingwoman? It is not too clear just what the word *happy* really means and still less what true values it may mask. There is no possibility of measuring the happiness of others, and it is always easy to describe as happy the situation in which one wishes to place them.

In particular those who are condemned to stagnation are often pronounced happy on the pretext that happiness consists in being at rest. This notion we reject, for our perspective is that of existentialist ethics. Every subject plays his part as such specifically through exploits or projects that serve as a mode of transcendence; he achieves liberty only through a continual reaching out toward other liberties. There is no justification for present existence other than its expansion into an indefinitely open future. Every time transcendence falls back into immanence, stagnation, there is a degradation of existence into the *"en-soi"*—the brutish life of subjection to given conditions—and of liberty into constraint and contingence. This downfall represents a moral fault if the subject consents to it; if it is inflicted upon him, it spells frustration and oppression. In both cases it is an absolute evil. Every individual concerned to justify his existence feels that his existence involves an undefined need to transcend himself, to engage in freely chosen projects.

Now, what peculiarly signalizes the situation of woman is that she—a free and autonomous being like all human creatures—nevertheless finds herself living in a world where men compel her to assume the status of the Other. They propose to stabilize her as object and to doom her to immanence since her transcendence is to be overshadowed and forever transcended by another ego (*conscience*) which is essential and sovereign. The drama of woman lies in this conflict between the fundamental aspirations of every subject (ego)—who always regards the self as the essential—and the compulsions of a situa-

tion in which she is the inessential. How can a human being in woman's situation attain fulfillment? What roads are open to her? Which are blocked? How can independence be recovered in a state of dependency? What circumstances limit woman's liberty and how can they be overcome? These are the fundamental questions on which I would fain throw some light. This means that I am interested in the fortunes of the individual as defined not in terms of happiness but in terms of liberty.

Quite evidently this problem would be without significance if we were to believe that woman's destiny is inevitably determined by physiological, psychological, or economic forces. . . .

In spite of legends no physiological destiny imposes an eternal hostility upon Male and Female as such; even the famous praying mantis devours her male only for want of other food and for the good of the species: it is to this, the species, that all individuals are subordinated, from the top to the bottom of the scale of animal life. Moreover, humanity is something more than a mere species: it is a historical development; it is to be defined by the manner·in which it deals with its natural, fixed characteristics, its *facticité*. Indeed, even with the most extreme bad faith in the world, it is impossible to demonstrate the existence of a rivalry between the human male and female of a truly physiological nature. Further, their hostility may be allocated rather to that intermediate terrain between biology and psychology: psychoanalysis. Woman, we are told, envies man his penis and wishes to castrate him; but the childish desire for the penis is important in the life of the adult woman only if she feels her femininity as a mutilation; and then it is as a symbol of all the privileges of manhood that she wishes to appropriate the male organ. We may readily agree that her dream of castration has this symbolic significance: she wishes, it is thought, to deprive the male of his transcendence.

But her desire, as we have seen, is much more ambiguous: she wishes, in a contradictory fashion, *to have* this transcendence, which is to suppose that she at once respects it and denies it, that she intends at once to throw herself into it and keep it within herself. This is to say that the drama does not unfold on a sexual level; further, sexuality has never seemed to us to define a destiny, to furnish in itself the key to human behavior, but to express the totality of a situation that it only helps to define. The battle of the sexes is not immediately implied in the anatomy of man and woman. The truth is that when one evokes it, one takes for granted that in the timeless realm of Ideas a battle is being waged between those vague essences the Eternal Feminine and the Eternal Masculine; and one neglects the fact that this titanic combat assumes on earth two totally different forms, corresponding with two different moments of history.

The woman who is shut up in immanence endeavors to hold man in that prison also; thus the prison will be confused with the world, and woman will no longer suffer from being confined there: mother, wife, sweetheart are the jailers. Society, being codified by man, decrees that woman is inferior: she can do away with this inferiority only by destroying the male's superiority. She sets about mutilating, dominating man, she contradicts him, she denies his truth and his values. But in doing this she is only defending herself; it was neither a changeless essence nor a mistaken choice that doomed her to immanence, to inferiority. They were imposed upon her. All oppression creates a state of war. And this is no exception. The existent who is regarded as inessential cannot fail to demand the re-establishment of her sovereignty.

Today the combat takes a different shape; instead of wishing to put man in a prison, woman endeavors to escape from one; she no longer seeks to drag him into the realms of immanence but to emerge, herself, into the light of transcendence. Now the attitude of the males creates a new conflict: it is with a bad grace that the man lets her go. He is very well pleased to remain the sovereign subject, the absolute superior, the essential being; he refuses to accept his companion as an equal in any concrete way. She replies to his lack of confidence in her by assuming an aggressive attitude. It is no longer a question of a war between individuals each shut up in his or her sphere: a caste claiming its rights goes over the top and it is resisted by the privileged caste. Here two transcendences are face to face; instead of displaying mutual recognition, each free being wishes to dominate the other.

This difference of attitude is manifest on the sexual plane as on the spiritual plane. The "feminine" woman in making herself prey tries to reduce man, also, to her carnal passivity; she occupies herself in catching him in her trap, in enchaining him by means of the desire she arouses in him in submissively making herself a thing. The emancipated woman, on the contrary, wants to be active, a taker, and refuses the passivity man means to impose on her. Thus Elise and her emulators deny the values of the activities of virile type; they put the flesh above the spirit, contingence above liberty, their routine wisdom above creative audacity. But the "modern" woman accepts masculine values: she prides herself on thinking, taking action, working, creating, on the same terms as men; instead of seeking to disparage them, she declares herself their equal.

In so far as she expresses herself in definite action, this claim is legitimate, and male insolence must then bear the blame. But in men's defense it must be said that women are wont to confuse the issue. A Mabel Dodge Luhan intended to subjugate D. H. Lawrence by her feminine charms so as to dominate him spiritually thereafter; many women, in order to show by their successes their equivalence to men, try to secure male support by sexual means; they play on both sides, demanding old-fashioned respect and modern esteem, banking on their old magic and their new rights. It is understandable that a man becomes irritated and puts himself on the defensive; but he is also double-dealing when he requires woman to play the game fairly while he denies them the indispensable trump cards through distrust and hostility. Indeed, the struggle cannot be clearly drawn between them, since woman is opaque in her very being; she stands before man not as a subject but as an object paradoxically endued with subjectivity; she takes herself simultaneously as *self* and as *other,* a contradiction that entails baffling consequences. When she makes weapons at once of her weakness and of her strength, it is not a matter of designing calculation: she seeks salvation spontaneously in the way that has been imposed on her, that of passivity, at the same time when she is actively demanding her sovereignty; and no doubt this procedure is unfair tactics, but it is dictated to her by the ambiguous situation assigned her. Man, however, becomes indignant when he treats her as a free and independent being and then realizes that she is still a trap for him; if he gratifies and satisfies her in her posture as prey, he finds her claims to autonomy irritating; whatever he does, he feels tricked and she feels wronged.

The quarrel will go on as long as men and women fail to recognize each other as peers; that is to say, as long as femininity is perpetuated as such. Which sex is the more eager to maintain it? Woman, who is being emancipated from it, wishes none the less to retain its privileges; and man, in that case, wants her to assume its limitations. "It is easier to accuse one sex than to excuse the other," says Montaigne. It is vain to apportion praise and blame. The truth is that if the vicious circle is so hard to break, it is because the two sexes are each the victim at once of the other and of itself. Between two adversaries confronting each other in their pure liberty, an agreement could be easily reached: the more so as the war profits neither. But the complexity of the whole affair derives from the fact that each camp is giving aid and comfort to the enemy; woman is pursuing a dream of submission, man a dream of identification. Want of authenticity does not pay: each blames the other for the unhappiness he or she has incurred in yielding to the temptations of the easy way; what man and woman loathe in each other is the shattering frustration of each one's own bad faith and baseness.

We have seen why men enslaved women in the first place; the devaluation of femininity has been a necessary step in human evolution, but it might have led to collaboration between the two sexes; oppression is to be explained by the tendency of the existent to flee from himself by means of identification with the other, whom he oppresses to that end. In each individual man that tendency exists today; and the vast majority yield to it. The husband wants to find himself in his wife, the lover in his mistress, in the form of a stone image; he is seeking in her the myth of his virility, of his sovereignty, of his immediate reality. "My husband never goes to the movies," says his wife, and the dubious masculine opinion is graved in the marble of eternity. But he is himself the slave of his double: what an effort to build up an image in which he is always in danger! In spite of everything his success in this depends upon the capricious freedom of women: he must constantly try to keep this propitious to him. Man is concerned with the effort to appear male, important, superior; he pretends so as to get pretense in return; he, too, is aggressive, uneasy; he feels hostility for women because he is afraid of them, he is afraid of them because he is afraid of the personage, the image, with which he identifies himself. What time and strength he squanders in liquidating, sublimating, transferring complexes, in talking about women, in seducing them, in fearing them! He would be liberated himself in their liberation. But this is precisely what he dreads. And so he obstinately persists in the mystifications intended to keep woman in her chains.

That she is being tricked, many men have realized. "What a misfortune to be a woman! And yet the misfortune, when one is a woman, is at bottom not to comprehend that it is one," says Kirkegaard.[5] For a long time there have been efforts to disguise this misfortune. For example, guardianship has been done away with: women have been given "protectors," and if they are invested with the rights of the old-time guardians, it is in woman's own interest. To forbid her working, to keep her at home, is to defend her against herself and to assure her happiness. We have seen what poetic veils are thrown over her monotonous burdens of housekeeping and maternity: in exchange for her liberty she has received the false treasures of her "femininity." Balzac illustrates this maneuver very well in counseling man to treat her as a slave while persuading her that she is a queen. Less cynical, many men try to convince themselves that she is really privileged. There are American sociologists who seriously teach today the theory of "low-class gain." In France, also, it has often been proclaimed—although in a less scientific manner—that the workers are very fortunate in not being obliged to "keep up appearances" and still more so the bums who can dress in rags and sleep on the sidewalks, pleasures forbidden to the Count de Beaumont and the Wendels. Like the carefree wretches gaily scratching at their vermin, like the merry Negroes laughing under the lash and those joyous Tunisian Arabs burying their starved children with a smile, woman enjoys that incomparable privilege: irresponsibility. Free from troublesome burdens and cares, she obviously has "the better part." But it is disturbing that with an obstinate perversity—connected no doubt with original sin—down through the centuries and in all countries, the people who have the better part are always crying to their benefactors: "It is too much! I will be satisfied with yours!" But the munificent capitalists, the generous colonists, the superb males, stick to their guns: "Keep the better part, hold on to it!"

It must be admitted that the males find in woman more complicity than the oppressor usually finds in the oppressed. And in bad faith they take authorization from this to declare that she has *desired* the destiny they have imposed on her. We have seen that all the main features of her training combine to bar her from the roads of revolt and adventure. Society in general—beginning with her respected parents—lies to her by praising the lofty values of love, devotion, the gift of herself, and then concealing from her the fact that neither lover nor husband nor yet her children will be inclined to accept the burdensome charge of all that. She cheerfully believes these lies because they invite her to follow the easy slope: in this others commit their worst crime against her; throughout her life from childhood on, they damage and corrupt her by designating as her true vocation this submission, which is the temptation of every existent in the anxiety of liberty. If a child is taught idleness by being amused all day long and never being led to study, or shown its usefulness, it will hardly be said, when he grows up, that he chose to be incapable and ignorant; yet this is how woman is brought up, without ever being impressed with the necessity of taking charge of her own existence. So she readily lets herself come to count on the protection, love, assistance, and supervision of others, she lets herself be fascinated with the hope of self-realization without *doing* anything. She does wrong in yielding to the temptation; but man is in no position to blame her, since he has led her into the temptation. When conflict arises between them, each will hold the other responsible for the situation; she will reproach him with having made her what she is: "No one taught me to reason or to earn my own living"; he will reproach her with having accepted the consequences: "You don't know anything, you are an incompetent," and so on. Each sex thinks it can justify itself by taking the offensive; but the wrongs done by one do not make the other innocent.

The innumerable conflicts that set men and women against one another come from the fact that neither is prepared to assume all the consequences of this situation which the one has offered and the other accepted. The doubtful concept of "equality in inequality," which the one uses to mask his despotism and the other to mask her cowardice, does not stand the test of experience: in their exchanges, woman appeals to the theoretical equality she has been guaranteed, and man the concrete inequality that exists. The result is that in every association an endless debate goes on concerning the ambiguous meaning of the words *give* and *take:* she complains of giving her all, he protests that she takes his all. Woman has to learn that exchanges—it is a fundamental law of political economy—are based on the value the merchandise offered has for the buyer, and not for the seller: she has been deceived in being persuaded that her worth is priceless. The truth is that for man she is an amusement, a pleasure, company, an inessential boon; he is for her the meaning, the justification of her existence. The exchange, therefore, is not of two items of equal value.

This inequality will be especially brought out in the fact that the time they spend together—which fallaciously seems to be the same time—does not have the same value for both partners. During the evening the lover spends with his mistress he could be doing something of advantage to his career, seeing friends, cultivating business relationships, seeking recreation; for a man normally integrated in society, time is a positive value: money, reputation, pleasure. For the idle, bored woman, on the contrary, it is a burden she wishes to get rid of; when she succeeds in killing time, it is a benefit to her: the man's presence is pure profit. In a liaison what most clearly interests the man, in many cases, is the sexual benefit he gets from it: if need be, he can be content to spend no more time with his mistress than is required for the sexual act; but—with exceptions—what she, on her part, wants is to kill all the excess time she has on her hands; and—like the storekeeper who will not sell potatoes unless the customer will take turnips also—she will not yield her body unless her lover will take hours of conversation and "going out" into the bargain. A balance is reached if, on the whole, the cost does not seem too high to the man, and this depends, of course, on the strength of his desire and the importance he gives to what is to be sacrificed. But if the woman demands—

offers—too much time, she becomes wholly intrusive, like the river overflowing its banks, and the man will prefer to have nothing rather than too much. Then she reduces her demands; but very often the balance is reached at the cost of a double tension: she feels that the man has "had" her at a bargain, and he thinks her price is too high. This analysis, of course, is put in somewhat humorous terms; but—except for those affairs of jealous and exclusive passion in which the man wants total possession of the woman—this conflict constantly appears in cases of affection, desire, and even love. He always has "other things to do" with his time; whereas she has time to burn; and he considers much of the time she gives him not as a gift but as a burden.

As a rule he consents to assume the burden because he knows very well that he is on the privileged side, he has a bad conscience; and if he is of reasonable good will he tries to compensate for the inequality by being generous. He prides himself on his compassion, however, and at the first clash he treats the woman as ungrateful and thinks, with some irritation: "I'm too good to her." She feels she is behaving like a beggar when she is convinced of the high value of her gifts, and that humiliates her.

Here we find the explanation of the cruelty that woman often shows she is capable of practicing; she has a good conscience because she is on the unprivileged side; she feels she is under no obligation to deal gently with the favored caste, and her only thought is to defend herself. She will even be very happy if she has occasion to show her resentment to a lover who has not been able to satisfy all her demands: since he does not give her enough, she takes savage delight in taking back everything from him. At this point the wounded lover suddenly discovers the value *in toto* of a liaison each moment of which he held more or less in contempt: he is ready to promise her everything, even though he will feel exploited again when he has to make good. He accuses his mistress of blackmailing him: she calls him stingy; both feel wronged.

Once again it is useless to apportion blame and excuses: justice can never be done in the midst of injustice. A colonial administrator has no possibility of acting rightly toward the natives, nor a general toward his soldiers; the only solution is to be neither colonist nor military chief; but a man could not prevent himself from being a man. So there he is, culpable in spite of himself and laboring under the effects of a fault he did not himself commit; and here she is, victim and shrew in spite of herself. Sometimes he rebels and becomes cruel, but then he makes himself an accomplice of the injustice, and the fault becomes really his. Sometimes he lets himself be annihilated, devoured, by his demanding victim; but in that case he feels duped. Often he stops at a compromise that at once belittles him and leaves him ill at ease. A well-disposed man will be more tortured by the situation than the woman herself: in a sense it is always better to be on the side of the vanquished; but if she is well-disposed also, incapable of self-sufficiency, reluctant to crush the man with the weight of her destiny, she struggles in hopeless confusion.

In daily life we meet with an abundance of these cases which are incapable of satisfactory solution because they are determined by unsatisfactory conditions. A man who is compelled to go on materially and morally supporting a woman whom he no longer loves feels he is victimized; but if he abandons without resources the woman who has pledged her whole life to him, she will be quite as unjustly victimized. The evil originates not in the perversity of individuals—and bad faith first appears when each blames the other—it originates rather in a situation against which all individual action is powerless. Women are "clinging," they are a dead weight, and they suffer for it; the point is that their situation is like that of a parasite sucking out the living strength of another organism. Let them be provided with living strength of their own, let them have the means to attack the world and wrest from it their own subsistence,

and their dependence will be abolished—that of man also. There is no doubt that both men and women will profit greatly from the new situation.

A world where men and women would be equal is easy to visualize, for that precisely is what the Soviet Revolution *promised:* women raised and trained exactly like men were to work under the same conditions[6] and for the same wages. Erotic liberty was to be recognized by custom, but the sexual act was not to be considered a "service" to be paid for; woman was to be *obliged* to provide herself with other ways of earning a living; marriage was to be based on a free agreement that the spouses could break at will; maternity was to be voluntary, which meant that contraception and abortion were to be authorized and that, on the other hand, all mothers and their children were to have exactly the same rights, in or out of marriage; pregnancy leaves were to be paid for by the State, which would assume charge of the children, signifying not that they would be *taken away* from their parents, but that they would not be *abandoned* to them.

But is it enough to change laws, institutions, customs, public opinion, and the whole social context, for men and women to become truly equal? "Women will always be women," say the skeptics. Other seers prophesy that in casting off their femininity they will not succeed in changing themselves into men and they will become monsters. This would be to admit that the woman of today is a creation of nature; it must be repeated once more that in human society nothing is natural and that woman, like much else, is a product elaborated by civilization. The intervention of others in her destiny is fundamental: if this action took a different direction, it would produce a quite different result. Woman is determined not by her hormones or by mysterious instincts, but by the manner in which her body and her relation to the world are modified through the action of others than herself. The abyss that separates the adolescent boy and girl has been deliberately opened out between them since earliest childhood; later on, woman could not be other than what she *was made,* and that past was bound to shadow her for life. If we appreciate its influence, we see clearly that her destiny is not predetermined for all eternity.

We must not believe, certainly, that a change is woman's economic condition alone is enough to transform her, though this factor has been and remains the basic factor in her evolution; but until it has brought about the moral, social, cultural, and other consequences that it promises and requires, the new woman cannot appear. At this moment they have been realized nowhere, in Russia no more than in France or the United States; and this explains why the woman of today is torn between the past and the future. She appears most often as a "true woman" disguised as a man, and she feels herself as ill at ease in her flesh as in her masculine garb. She must shed her old skin and cut her own new clothes. This she could do only through a social evolution. No single educator could fashion a *female human being* today who would be the exact homologue of the *male human being;* if she is raised like a boy, the young girl feels she is an oddity and thereby she is given a new kind of sex specification. Stendhal understood this when he said: "The forest must be planted all at once." But if we imagine, on the contrary, a society in which the equality of the sexes would be concretely realized, this equality would find new expression in each individual.

If the little girl were brought up from the first with the same demands and rewards, the same severity and the same freedom, as her brothers, taking part in the same studies, the same games, promised the same future, surrounded with women and men who seemed to her undoubted equals, the meanings of the castration complex and of the oedipus complex would be profoundly modified. Assuming on the same basis as the father the material and moral responsibility of the couple, the mother would enjoy the same lasting prestige; the child would perceive around her an androgynous world and not a masculine world. Were she emotionally more attracted to her father—which is not even sure—her love for him would be tinged with a will to emulation and not a feeling of powerlessness; she would not be oriented toward passivity. Authorized to test her powers in work and sports, competing actively with the boys, she would not find the absence of the penis—compensated by the promise of a child—enough to give rise to an inferiority complex; correlatively, the boy would not have a superiority complex if it were not instilled into him and if he looked up to women with as much respect as to men.[7] The little girl would not seek sterile compensation in narcissism and dreaming, she would not take her fate for granted; she would be interested in what she was *doing,* she would throw herself without reserve into undertakings.

I have already pointed out how much easier the transformation of puberty would be if she looked beyond it, like the boys, toward a free adult future: menstruation horrifies her only because it is an abrupt descent into femininity. She would also take her young eroticism in much more tranquil fashion if she did not feel a frightened disgust for her destiny as a whole; coherent sexual information would do much to help her over this crisis. And thanks to coeducational schooling, the august mystery of Man would have no occasion to enter her mind: it would be eliminated by everyday familiarity and open rivalry.

Objections raised against this system always imply respect for sexual taboos; but the effort to inhibit all sex curiosity and pleasure in the child is quite useless; one succeeds only in creating repressions, obsessions, neuroses. The excessive sentimentality, homosexual fervors, and platonic crushes of adolescent girls, with all their train of silliness and frivolity, are much more injurious than a little childish sex play and a few definite sex experiences. It would be beneficial above all for the young girl not to be influenced against taking charge herself of her own existence, for then she would not seek a demigod in the male—merely a comrade, a friend, a partner. Eroticism and love would take on the nature of free transcendence and not that of resignation; she could experience them as a relation between equals. There is no intention, of course, to remove by a stroke of the pen all the difficulties that the child has to overcome in changing into an adult; the most intelligent, the most tolerant education could not relieve the child of experiencing things for herself; what could be asked is that obstacles should not be piled gratuitously in her path. Progress is already shown by the fact that "vicious" little girls are no longer cauterized with a red-hot iron. Psychoanalysis has given parents some instruction, but the conditions under which, at the present time, the sexual training and initiation of woman are accomplished are so deplorable that none of the objections advanced against the idea of a radical change could be considered valid. It is not a question of abolishing in woman the contingencies and miseries of the human condition, but of giving her the means for transcending them.

Woman is the victim of no mysterious fatality; the peculiarities that identify her as specifically a woman get their importance from the significance placed upon them. They can be surmounted, in the future, when they are regarded in new perspectives. Thus, as we have seen, through her erotic experience woman feels—and often detests—the domination of the male; but this is no reason to conclude that her ovaries condemn her to live forever on her knees. Virile aggressiveness seems like a lordly privilege only within a system that in its entirety conspires to affirm masculine sovereignty; and woman *feels* herself profoundly passive in the sexual act only because she already *thinks* of herself as such. Many modern women who lay claim to their dignity as human beings still envisage their erotic life from the standpoint of a tradition of slavery: since it seems to them humiliating to lie beneath the man, to be penetrated by him, they grow tense in frigidity. But if the reality were different, the meaning expressed symbolically in amorous

gestures and postures would be different, too: a woman who pays and dominates her lover can, for example, take pride in her superb idleness and consider that she is enslaving the male who is actively exerting himself. And here and now there are many sexually well-balanced couples whose notions of victory and defeat are giving place to the idea of an exchange.

As a matter of fact, man, like woman, is flesh, therefore passive, the plaything of his hormones and of the species, the restless prey of his desires. And she, like him, in the midst of the carnal fever, is a consenting, a voluntary gift, an activity; they live out in their several fashions the strange ambiguity of existence made body. In those combats where they think they confront one another, it is really against the self that each one struggles, projecting into the partner that part of the self which is repudiated; instead of living out the ambiguities of their situation, each tries to make the other bear the abjection and tries to reserve the honor for the self. If, however, both should assume the ambiguity with a clear-sighted modesty, correlative of an authentic pride, they would see each other as equals and would live out their erotic drama in amity. The fact that we are human beings is infinitely more important than all the peculiarities that distinguish human beings from one another; it is never the given that confers superiorities: "virtue," as the ancients called it, is defined at the level of "that which depends on us." In both sexes is played out the same drama of the flesh and the spirit, of finitude and transcendence; both are gnawed away by time and laid in wait for by death, they have the same essential need for one another; and they can gain from their liberty the same glory. If they were to taste it, they would no longer be tempted to dispute fallacious privileges, and fraternity between them could then come into existence.

I shall be told that all this is utopian fancy, because woman cannot be "made over" unless society has first made her really the equal of man. Conservatives have never failed in such circumstances to refer to that vicious circle; history, however, does not revolve. If a caste is kept in a state of inferiority, no doubt it remains inferior; but liberty can break the circle. Let the Negroes vote and they become worthy of having the vote; let woman be given responsibilities and she is able to assume them. The fact is that oppressors cannot be expected to make a move of gratuitous generosity; but at one time the revolt of the oppressed, at another time even the very evolution of the privileged caste itself, creates new situations; thus men have been led, in their own interest, to give partial emancipation to woman: it remains only for women to continue their ascent, and the successes they are obtaining are an encouragement for them to do so. It seems almost certain that sooner or later they will arrive at complete economic and social equality, which will bring about an inner metamorphosis.

However this may be, there will be some to object that if such a world is possible it is not desirable. When woman is "the same" as her male, life will lose its salt and spice. This argument, also, has lost its novelty: those interested in perpetuating present conditions are always in tears about the marvelous past that is about to disappear, without having so much as a smile for the young future. It is quite true that doing away with the slave trade meant death to the great plantations, manificent with azaleas and camellias, it meant ruin to the whole refined Southern civilization. The attics of time have received its rare old laces along with the clear pure voices of the Sistine *castrati*,[8] and there is a certain "feminine charm" that is also on the way to the same dusty repository. I agree that he would be a barbarian indeed who failed to appreciate exquisite flowers, rare lace, the crystal-clear voice of the eunuch, and feminine charm.

When the "charming woman" shows herself in all her splendor, she is a much more exalting object than the "idiotic paintings, over-doors, scenery, showman's garish signs, popular chromos," that excited Rimbaud; adorned with the most modern artifices, beautified according to the newest techniques, she comes down from the remoteness of the ages, from Thebes, from Crete, from Chichén-Itzá; and she is also the totem set up deep in the African jungle; she is a helicopter and she is a bird; and there is this, the greatest wonder of all: under her tinted hair the forest murmur becomes a thought, and words issue from her breasts. Men stretch forth avid hands toward the marvel, but when they grasp it it is gone; the wife, the mistress, speak like everybody else through their mouths: their words are worth just what they are worth; their breasts also. Does such a fugitive miracle—and one so rare—justify us in perpetuating a situation that is baneful for both sexes? One can appreciate the beauty of flowers, the charm of women, and appreciate them at their true value; if these treasures cost blood or misery, they must be sacrificed.

But in truth this sacrifice seems to men a peculiarly heavy one; few of them really wish in their hearts for woman to succeed in making it; those among them who hold woman in contempt see in the sacrifice nothing for them to gain, those who cherish her see too much that they would lose. And it is true that the evolution now in progress threatens more than feminine charm alone: in beginning to exist for herself, woman will relinquish the function as double and mediator to which she owes her privileged place in the masculine universe; to man, caught between the silence of nature and the demanding presence of other free beings, a creature who is at once his like and a passive thing seems a great treasure. The guise in which he conceives his companion may be mythical, but the experiences for which she is the source or the pretext are none the less real: there are hardly any more precious, more intimate, more ardent. There is no denying that feminine dependence, inferiority, woe, give women their special character; assuredly woman's autonomy, if it spares men many troubles, will also deny them many conveniences; assuredly there are certain forms of the sexual adventure which will be lost in the world of tomorrow. But this does not mean that love, happiness, poetry, dream, will be banished from it.

Let us not forget that our lack of imagination always depopulates the future; for us it is only an abstraction; each one of us secretly deplores the absence there of the one who was himself. But the humanity of tomorrow will be living flesh and in its conscious liberty; that time will be its present and it will in turn prefer it. New relations of flesh and sentiment of which we have no conception will arise between the sexes; already, indeed, there have appeared between men and women friendships, rivalries, complicities, comradeships—chaste or sensual—which past centuries could not have conceived. To mention one point, nothing could seem to me more debatable than the opinion that dooms the new world to uniformity and hence to boredom. I fail to see that this present world is free from boredom or that liberty ever creates uniformity.

To begin with, there will always be certain differences between man and woman; her eroticism, and therefore her sexual world, have a special form of their own and therefore cannot fail to engender a sensuality, a sensitivity, of a special nature. This means that her relations to her own body, to that of the male, to the child, will never be identical with those the male bears to his own body, to that of the female, and to the child; those who make much of "equality in difference" could not with good grace refuse to grant me the possible existence of differences in equality. Then again, it is institutions that create uniformity. Young and pretty, the slaves of the harem are always the same in the sultan's embrace; Christianity gave eroticism its savor of sin and legend when it endowed the human female with a soul; if society restores her sovereign individuality to woman, it will not thereby destroy the power of love's embrace to move the heart.

It is nonsense to assert that revelry, vice, ecstasy, passion, would become impossible if man and woman were equal in concrete matters; the contradictions that put the flesh in opposition to the spirit, the instant to time, the swoon of immanence to the challenge of transcendence, the absolute of pleasure to the nothingness of forgetting, will never be resolved; in sexuality will always be materialized the tension, the

anguish, the joy, the frustration, and the triumph of existence. To emancipate woman is to refuse to confine her to the relations she bears to man, not to deny them to her; let her have her independent existence and she will continue none the less to exist for him *also:* mutually recognizing each other as subject, each will yet remain for the other an *other.* The reciprocity of their relations will not do away with the miracles—desire, possession, love, dream, adventure—worked by the division of human beings into two separate categories; and the words that move us—giving, conquering, uniting—will not lose their meaning. On the contrary, when we abolish the slavery of half of humanity, together with the whole system of hypocrisy that it implies, then the "division" of humanity will reveal its genuine significance and the human couple will find its true form. "The direct, natural, necessary relation of human creatures is the *relation of man to woman,*" Marx has said.[9] "The nature of this relation determines to what point man himself is to be considered as a *generic being,* as mankind; the relation of man to woman is the most natural relation of human being to human being. By it is shown, therefore, to what point the *natural* behavior of man has become *human* or to what point the *human* being has become his *natural* being, to what point his *human nature* has become his *nature.*"

The case could not be better stated. It is for man to establish the reign of liberty in the midst of the world of the given. To gain the supreme victory, it is necessary, for one thing, that by and through their natural differentiation men and women unequivocally affirm their brotherhood.

NOTES

1. *Franchise,* dead today.
2. The Kinsey Report [Alfred C. Kinsey and others: *Sexual Behavior in the Human Male* (W. B. Saunders Co., 1948)] is no exception, for it is limited to describing the sexual characteristics of American men, which is quite a different matter.

3. E. Lévinas expresses this idea most explicitly in his essay *Temps et l'Autre*. "Is there not a case in which otherness, alterity [*altérité*], unquestionably marks the nature of a being, as its essence, an instance of otherness not consisting purely and simply in the opposition of two species of the same genus? I think that the feminine represents the contrary in its absolute sense, this contrariness being in no wise affected by any relation between it and its correlative and thus remaining absolutely other. Sex is not a certain specific difference . . . no more is the sexual difference a mere contradiction. . . . Nor does this difference lie in the duality of two complementary terms, for two complementary terms imply a pre-existing whole. . . . Otherness reaches its full flowering in the feminine, a term of the same rank as consciousness but of opposite meaning."

I suppose that Lévinas does not forget that woman, too, is aware of her own consciousness, or ego. But it is striking that he deliberately takes a man's point of view, disregarding the reciprocity of subject and object. When he writes that woman is mystery, he implies that she is mystery for man. Thus his description, which is intended to be objective, is in fact an assertion of masculine privilege.

4. At the moment an "equal rights" amendment to the Constitution of the United States is before Congress.—Tr.

5. In *Vino Veritas*. He says further: "Politeness is pleasing—essentially—to woman, and the fact that she accepts it without hesitation is explained by nature's care for the weaker, for the unfavored being, and for one to whom an illusion means more than a material compensation. But this illusion, precisely, is fatal to her. . . . To feel oneself freed from distress thanks to something imaginary, to be the dupe of something imaginary, is that not a still deeper mockery? . . . Woman is very far from being *verwahrlost* (neglected), but in another sense she is, since she can never free herself from the illusion that nature has used to console her."

6. That certain too laborious occupations were to be closed to women is not in contradiction to this project. Even among men there is an increasing effort to obtain adaptation to profession; their varying physical and mental capacities limit their possibilities of choice; what is asked is that, in any case, no line of sex or caste be drawn.

7. I knew a little boy of eight who lived with his mother, aunt, and grandmother, all independent and active women, and his weak old half-crippled grandfather. He had a crushing inferiority complex in regard to the feminine sex, although he made efforts to combat it. At school he scorned comrades and teachers because they were miserable males.

8. Eunuchs were long used in the male choirs of the Sistine Chapel in Rome, until the practice was forbidden by Pope Leo XIII in 1880. The operation of castration caused the boy's soprano voice to be retained into adulthood, and it was performed for this purpose.—Tr.

9. *Philosophical Works,* Vol. VI (Marx's italics).

35. Simone de Beauvoir and Women: Just Who Does She Think "We" Is?

❧

Elizabeth V. Spelman

> The critics often repeat in new contexts versions of the old assumptions they set out to contest.
>
> *Martha Minow*

In *The Second Sex,* Simone de Beauvoir explores the many ways in which men have depicted women as ruled by forces in human nature that men can neither fully accept nor fully deny.[1] *The Second Sex* is a landmark work in contemporary feminist thought (even though for many years de Beauvoir apparently resisted being identified as a feminist).[2] She attempted to give an account of the situation of women in general and to include proposals for the conditions that would have to change if women were to become free. Although not all feminists subsequent to de Beauvoir referred to her work, or even necessarily knew about it, there is hardly any issue that feminists have come to deal with that she did not address. Indeed, she touched on issues such as attitudes towards lesbianism that some later feminists didn't dare to think about.[3]

De Beauvoir explicitly recognized that we live in a world in which there are a number of forms of oppression, and she tried to locate sexism in that context. In her work, we have all the essential ingredients of a feminist account of "women's lives" that would not conflate "woman" with a small group of women—namely, white middle-class heterosexual Christian women in Western countries. Yet de Beauvoir ends up producing an account which does just that. Here I shall explore how both de Beauvoir's theoretical perspective and her empirical observations lend themselves to a far richer account of "women's nature" than she herself ends up giving. (I am not going to argue about the strengths or weaknesses of her theory or the accuracy of her observations, but rather raise some questions about why she took them to lead in one direction rather than another.) Then I want to suggest reasons for the serious discrepancy between the potential broad scope of her views and the actual narrow focus of her position. De Beauvoir is a thinker of great perspicacity, so to explain the discrepancy simply in terms of a kind of race and class privilege that makes it easy for her to think of her own experience as representative of the experience of others is not enough. We need to ask what it might be in the language or methodology or theory employed by de Beauvoir that enables her to disguise from herself the assertion of privilege she so keenly saw in women of her own position.

I

Human beings aren't satisfied merely to live, de Beauvoir insists: we aspire to a meaningful exis-

From *Inessential Woman* by Elizabeth V. Spelman. Copyright © 1988 by Elizabeth V. Spelman. Reprinted by permission of Beacon Press, Boston.

tence.[4] But much about our constitution conspires against the possibility of such an existence: our being creatures of the flesh entails the ever-present possibility that our grand projects will be mocked. It is not only the facts of our birth and death that give the lie to our being pure, unembodied, immortal spirit. Our bodies need tending to each day, and there is nothing meaningful in the many activities involved in this tending. The feeding and cleaning of bodies, the maintenance of shelter against the powerful vagaries of the natural world, are necessary if we are to live. But if that is all we did, or all we thought we could do, we wouldn't find anything valuable about human life. As de Beauvoir says, unless we can engage in activities that "transcend [our] animal nature," we might as well be brute animals: "On the biological level a species is maintained only by creating itself anew; but this creation results only in repeating the same Life in more individuals. But man assures the repetition of Life while transcending Life through Existence; by this transcendence he creates values that deprive pure repetition of all value."[5]

"Existing," as opposed to merely "living," is best expressed in those aspects of life that are the function of "the loftiest human attitudes: heroism, revolt, disinterestedness, imagination, creation."[6] Only "existing" gives any reason for life; mere living "does not carry within itself its reasons for being, reasons that are more important than life itself."[7] To exist is to be a creative subject, not a passive object of the forces of nature; it is to be molding a new future through the power of one's intelligence, rather than being at the play of the repetitive rhythms of one's animal nature. Existing is as different from living as consciousness is from matter, will from passivity, transcendence from immanence, spirit from flesh.[8]

But life is necessary for existence, and we must preserve life even while we struggle against its demands. Descent into life is possible because of the never fully eradicated allure of dumbness and unfreedom, the ever-present possibility of forgoing (or seeming to forgo) the

responsibilities, uncertainties, and risks of intelligence and freedom. Men, de Beauvoir says, make women the repository of the multiform threats to a life of transcendence, agency, freedom, spirit; woman remains "in bondage to life's mysterious processes," "doomed to immanence."[9] Her life "is not directed towards ends: she is absorbed in producing or caring for things that are never more than means, such as food, clothing, and shelter. These things are inessential intermediaries between animal life and free existence."[10] Though woman is no less capable of real "existence" than man, it is in her corporeality rather than his own that man sees palpable and undeniable reminders of his own animal nature, of his own deeply regrettable and undignified contingency. Desirous of seeing no part of himself in her, he regards her as thoroughly Other, or as thoroughly Other as he can, given that he nevertheless needs her as a companion who is neither merely an animal nor merely a thing: "Man knows that to satisfy his desires, to perpetuate his race, woman is indispensable."[11]

Although women are constitutionally no less desirous or capable than men of "existing" rather than merely "living," historically most women have not resisted men's definition of them as embodying mysterious, dumb forces of nature. They have done little to try to undermine the economic, social, and political institutions that reinforce and are reinforced by such attitudes. In this, de Beauvoir says, women are unlike other oppressed groups—for example, Blacks, Jews, workers.

There are two reasons for this. First, women are spread throughout the population, across racial, class, ethnic, national, and religious lines, and this presents huge obstacles to their working together politically. They don't share the same economic and social position, nor do they have a shared consciousness. Moreover, "the division of the sexes is a biological fact, not an event in human history."[12] In all other cases of oppression, she claims, both the oppressors and the oppressed have taken their relative positions to be the result of historical events or social change and hence in principle capable of alteration: "A condition brought about at a certain time can be abolished at some other time, as the Negroes of Haiti and others have proved." Similarly, "proletarians have not always existed, whereas there have always been women."[13]

De Beauvoir's point here presumably is not that whites never have taken racial differences to be biological; rather she seems to be pointing out that the idea that biological differences entitle whites to dominate Blacks has been undermined in theory (to the extent that differences between Black and white are held to be less significant than their similarities as human beings) and nullified in political struggles (through which Blacks make clear their capacity to regard themselves as "subjects" and whites as "others").[14] De Beauvoir seems to be saying here that owing to a deep and apparently unbridgeable biological divide, women constitute for men the Other, whereas Blacks or the proletariat, for example, have not always constituted an Other for those by whom they may be dominated.

At the same time, despite these differences among women and between women and other oppressed groups, women do share something in common—but what they share paradoxically works against any possible solidarity. They "identify with each other" but do not communicate, as men do, "through ideas and projects of personal interest," and are only "bound together by a kind of immanent complicity."[15] By this de Beauvoir means that women are aware of inhabiting a special domain separate from men—in which they discuss recipes, frigidity, children, clothing—but nevertheless they regard each other as rivals for the attention of the masculine world. They are capable of ceasing to be Other. Despite what men find it convenient to believe, the difference between men and women is no more a biological given and historical necessity than the difference between bourgeoisie and proletariat. There is, however, a difference between the biological condition of being female and the social condition of being woman. So despite the differences among women, their different social and political locations, they could join in resisting the domination of men. But they haven't.[16]

And why haven't they? Sometimes de Beauvoir suggests that it is because being a "true woman" is inseparable from being the Other, so that it is logically impossible both to be a real woman and to be a subject, while there is no definitional problem, whatever other problems there are, in being a Black, or a worker, or a Jew, and also a subject. But this does not explain why women don't refuse to be "true women." And indeed sometimes de Beauvoir suggests that women simply choose to take the less arduous path: "No doubt it is more comfortable to submit to a blind enslavement than to work for liberation"; to "decline to be the Other, to refuse to be a party to the deal—this would be for women to renounce all the advantages conferred upon them by their alliance with the superior caste."[17]

Hence sometimes when she says that economic independence is the necessary condition of women's liberation, there is the suggestion that only if women are forced by circumstance to provide for themselves will they embrace their transcendence rather than fall into their immanence, see themselves as subjects rather than objects, as Self rather than Other. Women recognize the importance and value of transcendence, but only enough to search for men whose creative and productive flights will rub off on them, metaphysically speaking. Women want what men have, but only in wanting the men who have it. What we need, de Beauvoir is saying, is a world in which if women are to get it at all, they must do it on their own.

In short, de Beauvoir argues that there are at least three things that help to explain the fact of women's domination by men:

1. Men's having the attitudes they do toward women;
2. the existence of economic, social, and political institutions through which such atti-

tudes are expressed, enforced and perpetuated;

3. women's failure to resist such attitudes and institutions.

II

Differences among women

As noted above, de Beauvoir more than once remarks on class, racial, and national differences among women and how such differences bear on the economic, social, and political positions of women thus variously situated. Her comments on the lack of a sense of shared concerns among women are quite arresting: "If [women] belong to the bourgeoisie, they feel solidarity with men of that class, not with proletarian women; if they are white, their allegiance is to white men, not to Negro women."[18] The housewife is hostile toward her "servant [and toward] the teachers, governesses, nurses and nursemaids who attend to her children."[19] "Freed from the male, [the middle-class woman] would have to work for a living; she felt no solidarity with working-women, and she believed that the emancipation of bourgeois women would mean the ruin of her class."[20] De Beauvoir, then, is saying that the women least prepared to have their status changed have been white middle-class women, who are willing to keep the sexual status quo in return for the privileges of their class and race.

In all such examples, she cites the unwillingness of women with race or class privileges to give them up as the main obstacle to women's all doing something together to resist the domination of men. That is, what prevents a white middle-class woman from attacking sexism is her awareness that if she undermines sexism she will thereby undermine her race and class privilege. This ties in with de Beauvoir's point about the difference class makes to privilege based on sex. She argues that the less class privilege men and women enjoy, the less sexual privilege men of that class have; the more extreme class oppression is, the less extreme sex oppression is. So according to de Beauvoir sexism and classism are deeply intertwined. An important way in which class distinctions can be made is in terms of male-female relationships: we can't describe the sexism women are subject to without specifying their class; nor can we understand how sexism works without looking at its relation to class privilege. What makes middle-class women dependent on men of their class is the same as what distinguishes them from working-class women.[21]

But de Beauvoir does not heed her own insights here. On the contrary, she almost always describes relations between men and women as if the class or race or ethnic identity of the men and women made no difference to the truth of statements about "men and women." This poses some very serious difficulties for her attempt to give a general account of "woman." On her own terms it ought to be misleading to say, as she does, that we live "in a world that belongs to men,"[22] as if all differences between princes and paupers, masters and slaves, can be canceled out by the fact that they are all male.[23] In describing the psychological development of girls, she remarks on the ways in which everything in a girl's life "confirms her in her belief in masculine superiority."[24] And yet she later makes clear that a white girl growing up in the United States hardly believes that Black men are superior to her: "During the War of Secession no Southerners were more passionate in upholding slavery than the women." She describes ways in which girls of the upper classes are taught to believe in their superiority to working-class men: "In the upper classes women are eager accomplices of their masters because they stand to profit from the benefits provided. . . . The women of the upper middle classes and the aristocracy have always defended their class interests even more obstinately than have their husbands."[25] Whether or not de Beauvoir is entirely accurate in her descriptions of some women's passionate insistence on preserving privilege—were they really more fierce about it than the men of their race and class?[26]—the point is that these descriptions undermine her claims elsewhere about the common position of women.

De Beauvoir's perceptiveness about class and race inequality should make us wonder about her account of the "man" as "citizen" and "producer" with "economic independence" and all "the advantages attached to masculinity" in contrast to the "woman," who is "before all, and often exclusively, a wife," "shut up in the home," enjoying "vast leisure," and entertaining at tables "laden with fine food and precious wines."[27]

> Since the husband is the productive worker, he is the one who goes beyond family interest to that of society, opening up a future for himself through cooperation in the building of the future: he incarnates transcendence. Woman is doomed to the continuation of the species and the care of the home—that is, to immanence.[28]

Here de Beauvoir, despite evidence she provides to the contrary, makes it look as if racism, for example, had never existed and never affected the conditions under which a man can "incarnate transcendence." Here and elsewhere when she points to the role women play in reproducing family and species—"the oppression of woman has its cause in the will to perpetuate the family and to keep the patrimony intact"[29]—she chooses to ignore questions about legitimacy even while alluding to them elsewhere. She quotes Demosthenes: "We have hetairas for the pleasures of the spirit, concubines for sensual pleasure, and wives to give us sons";[30] and her argument implies among other things that human beings typically do not "continue the species" randomly or without regard to what kinds of beings will populate the future. Both Plato and Aristotle were concerned about joining the right kind of men with the right kind of women to produce philosopher-rulers and citizens of the *polis*. De Beauvoir surely was aware of the extent to which racial, class, and religious

conventions dictate what comprises appropriate sexual behavior and "legitimate" reproduction. Indeed, as we shall see below, she explicitly points out but does not consider the implications of the fact that everything she says about sexual privilege only works when the man and woman belong to the same race and class.[31]

De Beauvoir sabotages her insights about the political consequences of the multiple locations of women in another way: she frequently compares women to other groups—in her language, "Jews, the Black, the Yellow, the proletariat, slaves, servants, the common people." For example, she asks us to think about the differences between the situation of women, on the one hand, and, on the other "the scattering of the Jews, the introduction of slavery into America, the conquests of imperialism." She discusses with considerable appreciation Bebel's comparison of "women and the proletariat." She remarks that some of what Hegel says about "master and slave" better applies to "man and woman." In reflecting on slavery in the United States, she says that there was a "great difference" between the case of American Blacks and that of women: "the Negroes submit with a feeling of revolt, no privileges compensating for their hard lot, whereas woman is offered inducements to complicity." She speaks of the role of religion in offering "women" and "the common people" the hope of moving out of immanence: "When a sex or a class is condemned to immanence, it is necessary to offer it the mirage of some form of transcendence." She compares the talk of women about their husbands to conversations "of domestics talking about their employers critically in the servants' quarters."[32]

I bring up these comparisons not in order to assess their historical accuracy but to note that in making them de Beauvoir obscures the fact that half of the populations to whom she compares women consists of women. This is particularly puzzling in light of her recognition of the ways in which women are distributed across race, class, religious, and ethnic lines. She sometimes contrasts "women" to "slaves," sometimes describes women as "slaves,"[33] but she never really talks about those women who according to her own categories belonged to slave populations—for example, Black female slaves in the United States. She does say at one point that "there were women among the slaves, to be sure, but there have always been free women"[34] and then she proceeds to make clear that it is free women whom she will examine. She also says that in "classes in which women enjoyed some economic independence and took part in production ... women workers were enslaved even more than the male workers."[35] But in contrasting "women" to a number of other groups, and in choosing not to pay attention to the women in those other groups, she expresses her determination to use "woman" only in reference to those females not subject to racism, anti-Semitism, classism, imperialism.

Perhaps she is aware at some level that this is the price she must pay for consistency: for where she does describe briefly the situation of females who belong to the groups she contrasts to "women," what she says does not follow from her account of "women." For example, she claims that in the Middle Ages peasant men and women lived on a "footing of equality," and that "in the working classes economic oppression nullified the inequality of the sexes."[36] If she believes this, then of course she has to restrict her use of the word "woman" to those females not subject to the other forms of oppression she refers to; otherwise her large claims about the subordination of women to men would be undermined by her own account. And yet at the same time, she subjects them to question, which we see as we turn to a third way in which de Beauvoir fails to pay attention to her own significant insights.

Toward the end of The Second Sex, de Beauvoir acknowledges that the differences in privilege and power between men and women she has been referring to are "in play" only when men and women are of the same class and race.[37]

This is a logical conclusion for someone who holds, as we have seen she does, that the wives of white slaveowners in the United States fought even harder than their husbands to preserve the privileges of race; since she thought of "slaves" as male, she could hardly maintain that men who were slaves dominated women who were not. But there is a problem even in the way she signals here that claims about privilege based on sex apply only within the same class or race. For that suggests that sexism within one class or race is just like that within any other class or race. If so, her claims do have a kind of generality after all—for example, what characterizes relations between white men and white women would also characterize those between Black men and Black women. But we've seen that de Beauvoir also holds that sexual oppression is essentially nullified when men and women are subject to other forms of oppression. In that case, her claim is not really that the sexism she describes operates only when class and race are constant, but rather that she is talking about the sexism in effect only when the men and women involved are not subject to class or racial oppression. She herself leads us to the conclusion that the sexism she is concerned with in The Second Sex is that experienced by white middle-class women in Western countries.

The creation of women

"One is not born, but rather becomes, a woman." This opening sentence from Book 2 of The Second Sex has come to be the most often cited and perhaps most powerful of de Beauvoir's insights. Among other things it offers a starting point for the distinction between sex and gender. It is one thing to be biologically female, quite another to be shaped by one's culture into a "woman"—a female with feminine qualities, someone who does the kinds of things "women," not "men," do, someone who has the kinds of thoughts and feelings that make doing these things seem an easy expression of one's feminine nature.

If being a woman is something one can become, then it also is something one can fail to become. De Beauvoir insists that while being or not being female is a biological matter, becoming or not becoming a woman is not. "Civilization as a whole" produces women. In the absence of other humans, no female would become a woman; particular human "intervention in her destiny is fundamental" to who and what she becomes: "Woman is determined not by her hormones or by mysterious instincts, but by the manner in which her body and her relation to the world are modified through the action of others than herself." In particular, "in men's eyes—and for the legion of women who see it through men's eyes—it is not enough to have a woman's body nor to assume the female function as mistress or mother in order to be 'true woman.'"[38] What she has to do to become a "true woman" is to be seen and to see herself as Other in contrast to the Self of the male, as inessential in contrast to the essential, as object in contrast to the subject. Females of the species don't come created in this way; they are made this way by the concerted efforts of men and women.

Moreover, de Beauvoir insists that humans create whatever significance is attached to having a body and more particularly to having a male or female body. She directs us to thinking about "the body as lived in by the subject" as opposed to the body as described by the biologist. The consciousness one has of one's body in this way is acquired "under circumstances dependent upon the society of which [one] is a member" or indeed even upon the class one belongs to. De Beauvoir suggests, for example, that the physical event of having an abortion is experienced differently by conventional middle-class women and by those "schooled by poverty and misery to disdain bourgeois morality." Along similar lines, she claims that the biological changes that take place during menopause are experienced differently by those "true women" who have "staked everything on their femininity" and by "the peasant woman, the work man's

wife," who, "constantly under the threat of new pregnancies, are happy when, at long last, they no longer run this risk."[39]

Biology is not destiny in at least two senses, according to de Beauvoir. First, being female is not the same thing as being a "woman"; nor does it determine whether and how one will become a "woman." Second, different women experience biological events associated with being female differently, depending on how their bodies are otherwise employed and their beliefs about what are the proper things to do with or to their bodies. But de Beauvoir doesn't take this insight as far as she might in the directions to which her own comments lead. She seems to be saying that there is no particular significance that must be given to biological facts about our bodies, that whether or how a female becomes a "woman" depends upon human consciousness and human action. But she is well aware of the fact that in many ways human consciousness and human action take quite different forms in different societies. We get a hint of this in her comment quoted above about how a woman's consciousness of femininity is dependent on the society in which she lives, as well as in her reminder that the intervention of others is so crucial a factor in the creation of a "woman" out of a female that "if this action took a different direction, it would produce a quite different result."[40]

This surely points to the variability in the creation of "women" across and within cultures. Here is where de Beauvoir's lack of attention to females belonging to the populations she contrasts to "women" is particularly disappointing. She doesn't reflect on what her own theoretical perspective strongly suggests and what her own language mirrors: namely, that different females are constructed into different kinds of "women"; that under some conditions certain females count as "women," others don't.

Moreover, de Beauvoir's analysis of racial oppression, cursory as it is, tells us that she believes people have attached different significance to racial differences at different times. She counts as successful social change those economic and political reversals in which a people once regarded as Other no longer are regarded as such by those who formerly dominated them. When she comments, early in the book, on the change of status of Blacks in Haiti after the revolution,[41] and much later on how Black suffrage helped to lead to the perception of Blacks as worthy of having the vote,[42] she is alluding to changes in the significance attached by whites to what they take to be biological differences between whites and Blacks. If we follow up her insistence that we pay attention to "the body as lived in by the subject," we might begin to ask not only about living in a male or female body in the context of sexism but also about living in a black or white or brown or yellow or red body in the context of racism. Though de Beauvoir refers to the variability in ideals of feminine beauty[43] and, as we've seen, is certainly aware of racial oppression, she does not speak at length about women subject to racism and so does not talk about the ways in which notions of beauty are racially coded. While she certainly is aware of the significance attached to skin color, she does not join that to her point about the distinction between other physical differences among human bodies (i.e., sexual differences) and what humans make of those differences.

The real and the ideal woman

A third promising ingredient of de Beauvoir's analysis is her attack on the discrepancy between the reality of actual women and a static ideal of "woman." The latter is not an empirical generalization based on observations of specific women but a male myth about the nature of femininity:

> As against the dispersed, contingent, and multiple existences of actual women, mythical thought opposes the Eternal Feminine, unique and changeless. If the definition provided for this concept is contradicted by the behavior of flesh-and-blood women, it is the latter who are

wrong; we are told not that Femininity is a false entity, but that the women concerned are not feminine.[44]

De Beauvoir believes that this mythical ideal reaches deep into the idea of woman as Other, and as we've seen, she sometimes speaks as if men's treatment of women as Other is inevitable. But on the other hand, it is clear that she thinks that if political and economic conditions change in the right direction, women will be seen in their historical specificity—that is, women might come to be truly known by men rather than being the occasion for men's projection of a mythic ideal of femininity.

> It is noteworthy that the feminine comrade, colleague, and associate are without mystery [being "mysterious" is one version of the mythic ideal]; on the other hand, if the vassal is male, if, in the eyes of a man or a woman who is older, or richer, a young fellow, for example, plays the role of the inessential object, then he too becomes shrouded in mystery. And this uncovers for us a substructure under the feminine mystery which is economic in nature.[45]
>
> The more relationships are concretely lived, the less they are idealized. The fellah of ancient Egypt, the Bedouin peasant, the artisan of the Middle Ages, the worker of today has in the requirements of work and poverty relations with his particular woman companion which are too definite for her to be embellished with an aura either auspicious or inauspicious.[46].

De Beauvoir seems to be making a brief here for establishing a set of conditions under which people can see each other as they actually are. The liberation of women depends upon establishing economic and political conditions under which men won't simply project their notion of "woman" onto women but will look at who women in fact are, observing "the behavior of flesh-and blood women." De Beauvoir has high regard for what she refers to as "knowledge," "empirical law," "laws of nature," "scientific explanation."[47] Though she does not explain exactly what she means by these terms, it is clear that she accuses men of not being very scientific in their claims about women. Men are right to look for universally true statements about women, but they don't realize that the only solid grounds for such claims are empirical observations. Clear thinking about women would lead to universally true statements about them.

De Beauvoir has not of course laid out a full-blown epistemology here, but the hints of one point to the potential richness of her account of women. As we have noted on several occasions, de Beauvoir at one level is quite aware of the diverse historical, economic, and political situations of women, of the differences class and race make to women's relationships with men and to their relationships with other women. She likens the notion of the "Eternal Feminine" to a Platonic "Idea, timeless, unchangeable." As an existentialist, she has no truck with the idea of an "essence" of anything—of humanity, of man, of woman. We are not who or what we are by virtue of being particular instances of some transcendental entity; rather, "an existent *is* nothing other than what he does . . . he is to be measured by his acts."[48]

De Beauvoir suggests that a search for some essence of "woman" is deeply misplaced: we would look in vain for some metaphysical nugget of pure womanhood that defines all women as women. We have to look at what women do to find out who they are. This means that we cannot decide prior to actual investigation of women's lives what they do or do not have in common; and this means that we cannot assume that what we find to be true about the lives of women of one class or race or nationality or historical period will be true about the lives of other women. De Beauvoir warns us against any inclination to assume that the lives of women of one race or class are representative of the lives of all other women. Both existentialism and "scientific thinking" tell us we have to look and see what women are really like.

But at the same time, de Beauvoir also warns, neither existentialism nor "scientific reasoning" will lead us to the viewpoint of "woman," who "lacks the sense of the universal" and takes the world to be "a confused conglomeration of special cases." So while we can't assume, ahead of time, that any particular universal truth about "humanity" or "men" or "women" will be true, we can assume that investigation of women's lives will lead to such a truth or truths about women. Women's isolation from one another—the very isolation that de Beauvoir cites as one reason for their not constituting a likely political class—accounts in large part for their lacking "the sense of the universal": "She feels she is a special case because she is isolated in her home and hence does not come into active contact with other women."[49] If she had the opportunity to know about other women's lives, she might come to see the grounds for universal truths in the similarities in cases she earlier had taken to be special, unique, *sui generis*.

De Beauvoir has a lively concern that views about women be based neither on the assumption that women necessarily share some metaphysical essence nor on the assumption that women share nothing at all. Yet the universal truths she claims to be noting about "women" do not follow from the observations she makes about differences among women.

III

What might explain the contradictory pulls in de Beauvoir's account of women? The point of asking this is not to exonerate her from the charge of inconsistency or of misrepresenting the situation of white middle-class women as that of "women in general." The point, rather, is to see where white middle-class privilege has to lodge in order to make itself resistant to observations and theoretical perspectives that tell against it.

Certain strands of de Beauvoir's thought lead inexorably in the direction of a central focus on white middle-class women to illuminate the condition of "woman." As we've seen, at least some of the time she holds the following conditions to be true:

1. If one is not a "man," one is either a woman or a Black, a woman or Jewish, a woman or a poor person, etc.

2. Sexism is different from racism and other forms of oppression: sexism is the oppression women suffer as women, racism the oppression Blacks, for example, suffer as Blacks.

3. Sexism is most obvious in the case of women not otherwise subject to oppression (i.e., not subject to racism, classism, anti-Semitism, etc.).

Now insofar as de Beauvoir takes these conditions to be true, it is quite logical for her to take the examination of white middle-class women to be the examination of all women. Indeed, anyone who assumes the truth of these three conditions will take it to be the most logical thing in the world for feminists to focus on white middle-class women. De Beauvoir certainly is not alone in this position. To the degree that conditions 1, 2, and 3 seem logical, we ought to think of the white middle-class privilege her work expresses, not as a personal quirk in de Beauvoir, but as part of the intellectual and political air she and many of us breathe.

There are two important features of what we might call the 1-2-3 punch. First, it has the status of near truism: points 1 and 2 may appear to be true by definition (de Beauvoir, as we saw it, at times took them utterly for granted), and 3 may seem just to be a matter of common sense, something not even needing the confirmation of historical inquiry (aren't the effects of sexism on women more distinct and hence easier to investigate when other forms of oppression don't affect the women in question?). Second, it leads to the focus on white middle-class women *without mentioning white middle-class women.*

These two features are crucial to the way in which white middle-class privilege works in feminist theory and hence crucial to understanding why we would miss a golden opportunity if we simply dismissed de Beauvoir's focus as an individual expression of her privilege and left it at that. (Indeed, it would also be an expression of that privilege to mention its presence but not bother to explore and expose its depth and pervasiveness.) Privilege cannot work if it has to be noted and argued for. For someone to have privilege is precisely *not* to have to beg for attention to one's case. For feminist theory to express white middle-class privilege is for it to ensure that white middle-class women will automatically receive attention. How can it ensure this without making explicit what it is doing? Conditions 1–3 do the trick, by making the default position of feminist inquiry an examination of white middle-class women: unless otherwise noted, that's who we are going to be talking about.

De Beauvoir was very attuned to the expression of privilege in women's behavior: as we saw, she took note of the desire of white slaveowners' wives to preserve the racial status quo; she talked about the hostile treatment of female domestic workers by their middle- and upper-class female employers. But privilege, we well know, can lodge almost anywhere, and since it works best when it is least obvious, it is not surprising that we should find it reflected in what appear to be axioms of her inquiry into the condition of "women."

Insofar as any of us agree to points 1–3 (and the agreement is likely to be implicit, not explicit), we are not likely to give much weight to those strands in de Beauvoir's thought that might give us reason to question their status. For example, we aren't likely to be struck by the fact that if, as de Beauvoir claims, one of the reasons women don't seem to form a natural political class is that we are found in every population, then, contra 1, it is very odd to contrast women with Blacks, Jews, the poor. Nor are we likely to notice the force of de Beauvoir's saying that we ought always to ask about the race and class of any men and women we are talking about, since claims about sexual hierarchy hold only when race and class are kept constant: if this is so, the sexism women are subject to will vary in accordance with their race and class privilege. But in that case, contra 2, there is no simple form of sexism the same for all women as women. Thus even if, as condition 3 claims, sexism is easier to track in the case of women not otherwise subject to oppression, it doesn't mean the sexism one finds is just like the sexism one would find in the case of women who are subject to other forms of oppression. We have to be very careful: the oppression white middle-class women are subject to is not the oppression women face "as women" but the oppression white middle-class women face. Their race and class are not irrelevant to the oppression they face even though they are not oppressed on account of their race and class.

IV

We have been trying to see what might explain the discrepancy between the implicit complexity of de Beauvoir's assessment of the lives of women and the oversimplification in her explicit rendering of "woman's situation" and of gender relations. We've suggested that while it is true that such oversimplification expresses the privileged tunnel vision of someone of de Beauvoir's race and class, we must also take the task of unmasking privilege seriously by trying to locate the places it finds a home, rather than simply noting that it must be at work. Since de Beauvoir herself was highly attuned to and bothered by the presence of such privilege, we honor her work by asking how such privilege functions in her own thinking.

There's no doubt that the case de Beauvoir makes about "woman" would be less compelling, at least to many of her readers, if she were to wonder aloud whether there is any diffi-

culty posed for her account by the fact that there are women among the populations she contrasts to "woman"; if she were to say, "Notice, by the way, that the account I give of relations between middle-class men and women is not the same one I give of relations between working-class men and women"; if she did not hide away on page 605 of a 689-page book the reminder that any time we speak of male-female relations we must make sure that the men and women are of the same race and class.[50]

Such explicit musings would produce a less forceful argument for anyone who thinks that if we cannot talk about "woman" or about "women in general," then no case can be made about the injustice done to women, no strategy devised for the liberation of women. According to this line of thinking, a coherent feminist political analysis and agenda requires that we be able to talk about the history of the treatment of all women, as women. In order to be taken seriously, feminists have to make a case that they are speaking about more than a small group of people and that those referred to have been mistreated. So, for example, a group of white middle-class women would not claim that harm has come to them for being white or middle-class, but for being women. And they might well believe that not only would it be irrelevant to refer to being white and middle-class, but it would suggest that the group is not as representative as it otherwise would appear. So were de Beauvoir to make more explicit than she does who "woman" refers to in her analysis, she would defuse its potential impact: the case would not be that of "woman" but of particular women.

Furthermore, as we've seen, de Beauvoir thinks women lack a "sense of the universal." This has been a crucial part of their failure to resist the domination of men: not caring to notice the similarities in their experiences, each one given to "overestimat[ing] the value of her smile" because "no one has told her that all women smile." They fail to "sum . . . up in a valid conclusion" the many instances that ground claims about the conditions of "woman's" existence. Until women see beyond their own individual cases, they will not "succeed in building up a solid counter-universe whence they can challenge the males."[51] De Beauvoir may well regard it as a kind of weakness on her part were she to resist generalizing from the case of a woman like herself.

But it is one thing to urge women to look beyond their own cases; it is quite another to assume that if one does one will find a common condition or a common hope shared by all women. Perhaps there is a common condition or hope, but de Beauvoir's own work speaks against it. Given her insistence on the different social and economic positions occupied by women, she suggests not that similarities among women's various conditions are there to be found, but rather that they need to be created.

NOTES

1. Simone de Beauvoir, *The Second Sex,* trans. and ed. H. M. Parshley (New York: Knopf, 1953).
2. See, for example, Judith Okely, *Simone de Beauvoir* (London: Virago, 1986).
3. This is not to say that feminists have not found reason to disagree with her. For a recent extended critique, see Mary Evans, *Simone de Beauvoir: A Feminist Mandarin* (London and New York: Tavistock, 1985).
4. Though de Beauvoir's terminology is certainly different from Aristotle's, there are echoes here of his distinction between a group of cattle grazing and a vibrant human *polis.*
5. *Second Sex,* pp. 58, 59.
6. Ibid., p. 588.
7. Ibid., p. 59. The translator here renders *l'existence* as "existing" and *la vie* as "living." "Living" carries more weight for contemporary English speakers than mere "existing."
8. Ibid., p. 134.
9. Ibid., pp. 72, 68.
10. Ibid., p. 569.
11. Ibid., p. 74.
12. Ibid., p. xix.
13. Ibid., p. xviii.
14. Ibid.
15. Ibid., pp. 513, 511.
16. De Beauvoir does say quickly in passing that only feminists have done this. Ibid., pp. xviii–xix.
17. Ibid., pp. 246, xx. But she also insists for example, that "woman's 'character' [is] to be explained by her situation" (p. 588).
18. Ibid., p. xix; cf. pp. 103, 566, 590.
19. Ibid., p. 513.
20. Ibid., p. 103.
21. The idea that white middle-class women might be more reluctant than other women to battle sexism—if doing so is to cost them the privileges they have over white working-class women and all women of color—appears to conflict with what has become a historical truism: that the nineteenth- and twentieth-century women's movements in England, Europe, and the United States were founded and maintained by white middle-class women. Two questions immediately arise. Did they perceive their activity to be something that would involve giving up race or class privilege? Was what they were fighting for in fact something that would lead to loss of privilege whether or not they so perceived it? Were white female abolitionists actually fighting to end race privilege? Did they think it could be ended without ending sex privilege in the white population? In any event, if middle-class women were as reluctant as de Beauvoir says, what might this tell us about those middle-class women who were not reluctant?
22. *Second Sex,* pp. xx, 512, 563.
23. Contemporary feminists now stick in the qualifying adjective "white," as if that took care of the problem. But if it matters whether a man is white, it surely also matters—even if not in the same way—that a woman is white.
24. *Second Sex,* p. 38.
25. Ibid., pp. 566, 590.
26. On this see Ann Firor Scott, *The Southern lady: From Pedestal to Politics* (Chicago: University of Chicago Press, 1971).
27. *Second Sex,* pp. 430, 443, 497, 508, 663.
28. Ibid., p. 404.
29. Ibid., p. 82.
30. Ibid., p. 81.
31. Ibid., p. 605.
32. Ibid., pp. xviii, 49, 59, 278, 585, 579.

33. For instance, ibid., pp. 454, 569.
34. Ibid., p. 131.
35. Ibid., pp. 119–20.
36. Ibid., pp. 94, 96.
37. Ibid., p. 605.
38. Ibid., pp. 249, 682, 245.
39. Ibid., pp. 33, 44, 461, 542.
40. Ibid., p. 682.
41. Ibid., pp. xviii–xix.
42. Ibid., p. 686.
43. Ibid., p. 146.
44. Ibid., p. 237.

45. Ibid., pp. 241–2.
46. Ibid., p. 244.
47. Ibid., pp. 237, 580.
48. Ibid., pp. 237, 241.
49. Ibid., p. 580.
50. As Margaret Simons has pointed out, the English translation of *The Second Sex* does not include all of the original French version. See "The Silencing of Simone de Beauvoir: Guess What's Missing from *The Second Sex*," *Women's Studies International Forum*, 6, 1983, pp. 559–64.
51. *Second Sex*, pp. 580–1.

36. WE ARE ALL RELATED

EAGLE MAN

The plight of the non-Indian world is that it has lost respect for Mother Earth, from whom and where we all come.

We all start out in this world as tiny seeds— no different from our animal brothers and sisters, the deer, the bear, the buffalo, or the trees, the flowers, the winged people. Every particle of our bodies comes from the good things Mother Earth has put forth. Mother Earth is our real mother, because every bit of us truly comes from her, and daily she takes care of us.

The tiny seed takes on the minerals and the waters of Mother Earth. It is fueled by *Wiyo*, the sun, and given a spirit by *Wakan Tanka*.

This morning at breakfast we took from Mother Earth to live, as we have done every day of our lives. But did we thank her for giving us the means to live? The old Indian did. When he drove his horse in close to a buffalo running at full speed across the prairie, he drew his bowstring back and said as he did so, "Forgive me, brother, but my people must live." After he butchered the buffalo, he took the skull and faced it toward the setting sun as a thanksgiving and an acknowledgment that all things come from Mother Earth. He brought the meat back to camp and gave it first to the old, the widowed, and the weak. For thousands of years great herds thrived across the continent because the Indian never took more than he needed. Today, the buffalo is gone.

You say *ecology*. We think the words *Mother Earth* have a deeper meaning. If we wish to survive, we must respect her. It is very late, but there is still time to revive and discover the old American Indian value of respect for Mother Earth. She is very beautiful, and already she is showing

---

us signs that she may punish us for not respecting her. Also, we must remember she has been placed in this universe by the one who is the All Powerful, the Great Spirit Above, or *Wakan Tanka*—God. But a few years ago, there lived on the North American continent people, the American Indians, who knew a respect and value system that enabled them to live on their native grounds without having to migrate, in contrast to the white brothers and sisters who migrated by the thousands from their homelands because they had developed a value system different from that of the American Indian. There is no place now to which we can migrate, which means we can no longer ignore the red man's value system.

Carbon-dating techniques say that the American Indian has lived on the North American continent for thousands upon thousands of years. If we did migrate, it was because of a natural phenomenon—a glacier. We did not migrate because of a social system, value system, and spiritual system that neglected its responsibility to the land and all living things. We Indian people say we were always here.

We, the American Indian, had a way of living that enabled us to live within the great, complete beauty that only the natural environment can provide. The Indian tribes had a common value system and a commonality of religion, without religious animosity, that preserved that great beauty that the two-leggeds definitely need. Our four commandments from the Great Spirit are: (1) respect for Mother Earth, (2) respect for the Great Spirit, (3) respect for our fellow man and woman, and (4) respect for individual freedom (provided that individual freedom does not threaten the tribe or the people or Mother Earth).

We who respect the great vision of Black Elk see the four sacred colors as red, yellow, black, and white. They stand for the four directions— red for the east, yellow for the south, black for the west, and white for the north.

From the east comes the rising sun and new knowledge from a new day.

From the south will come the warming south winds that will cause our Mother to bring forth the good foods and grasses so that we may live.

To the west where the sun goes down, the day will end, and we will sleep; and we will hold our spirit ceremonies at night, from where we will communicate with the spirit world beyond. The sacred color of the west is black; it stands for the deep intellect that we will receive from the spirit ceremonies. From the west come the life-giving rains.

From the north will come the white winter snow that will cleanse Mother Earth and put her to sleep, so that she may rest and store up energy to provide the beauty and bounty of springtime. We will prepare for aging by learning to create, through our arts and crafts, during the long winter season. Truth, honesty, strength, endurance, and courage also are represented by the white of the north. Truth and honesty in our relationships bring forth harmony.

All good things come from these sacred directions. These sacred directions, or four sacred colors, also stand for the four races of humanity: red, yellow, black, and white. We cannot be a prejudiced people, because all men and women are brothers and sisters and because we all have the same mother—Mother Earth. One who is prejudiced, who hates another because of that person's color, hates what the Great Spirit has put here. Such a one hates that which is holy and will be punished, even during this lifetime, as humanity will be punished for violating Mother Earth. Worse, one's conscience will follow into the spirit world, where it will be discovered that all beings are equal. This is what we Indian people believe.

We, the Indian people, also believe that the Great Spirit placed many people throughout this planet: red, yellow, black, and white. What about the brown people? The brown people evolved from the sacred colors coming together. Look at our Mother Earth. She, too, is brown because the four directions have come together. After the Great Spirit, *Wakan Tanka,* placed them in their respective areas, the *Wakan Tanka* appeared to each people in a different manner and taught them ways so that they might live in harmony and true beauty. Some men, some tribes, some nations have still retained the teachings of the Great Spirit. Others have not. Unfortunately, many good and peaceful religions have been assailed by narrow-minded zealots. Our religious beliefs and our traditional Indian people have suffered the stereotype that we are pagans, savages, or heathens; but we do not believe that only one religion controls the way to the spirit world that lies beyond. We believe that *Wakan Tanka* loves all of its children equally, although the Great Spirit must be disturbed at times with those children who have destroyed proven value systems that practiced sharing and generosity and kept Mother Earth viable down through time. We kept Mother Earth viable because we did not sell her or our spirituality!

Brothers and sisters, we must go back to some of the old ways if we are going to truly save our Mother Earth and bring back the natural beauty that every person seriously needs, especially in this day of vanishing species, vanishing rain forests, overpopulation, poisoned waters, acid rain, a thinning ozone layer, drought, rising temperatures, and weapons of complete annihilation.

Weapons of complete annihilation? Yes, that is how far the obsession with war has taken us. These weapons are not only hydraheaded; they are hydroheaded as well, meaning that they are the ultimate in hydrogen bomb destruction. We will have to divert our obsessions with defense and wasteful, all-life-ending weapons of war to reviving our environment. If such weapons are ever fired, we will wind up destroying ourselves. The Armageddon of war is something that we have all been very close to and exposed to daily. However, ever since that day in August when people gathered in fields and cities all across the planet to beseech for peace and harmony, it appears that we are seeing some positive steps toward solving this horror. *Maybe some day two-*

leggeds will read this book and missiles will no longer be pointed at them.

The quest for peace can be more efficiently pursued through communication and knowledge than by stealth and unending superior weaponry. If the nations of the world scale back their budgets for weaponry, we will have wealth to spend to solve our serious environmental problems. Our home planet is under attack. It is not an imagined problem. This calamity is upon us now. We are in a real war with the polluting, violating blue man of Black Elk's vision.

Chief Sitting Bull advised us to take the best of the white man's ways and to take the best of the old Indian ways. He also said, "When you find something that is bad, or turns out bad, drop it and leave it alone."

The fomenting of fear and hatred is something that has turned out very badly. This can continue no longer; it is a governmental luxury maintained in order to support pork-barrel appropriations to the Department of Defense, with its admirals and generals who have substituted their patriotism for a defense contractor paycheck after retirement. War has become a business for profit. In the last two wars, we frontline warriors—mostly poor whites and minorities—were never allowed to win our wars, which were endlessly prolonged by the politicians and profiteers, who had their warrior-aged sons hidden safely away or who used their powers, bordering on treason, to keep their offspring out of danger. The wrong was that the patriotic American or the poor had to be the replacement. The way to end wars in this day and age is to do like the Indian: put the chiefs and their sons on the front lines.

Sitting Bull answered a relative, "Go ahead and follow the white man's road and do whatever the [Indian] agent tells you. But I cannot so easily give up my old ways and Indian habits; they are too deeply ingrained in me."

My friends, I will never cease to be an Indian. I will never cease respecting the old Indian values, especially our four cardinal commandments and our values of generosity and sharing. It is true that many who came to our shores brought a great amount of good to this world. Modern medicine, transportation, communication, and food production are but a few of the great achievements that we should all appreciate. But it is also true that too many of those who migrated to North America became so greedy and excessively materialistic that great harm has been caused. We have seen good ways and bad ways. The good way of the non-Indian way I am going to keep. The very fact that we can hold peace-seeking communication and that world leaders meet and communicate for peace shows the wisdom of the brothers and sisters of this time. By all means, good technology should not be curtailed, but care must be taken lest our water, air, and earth become irreparably harmed. The good ways I will always respect and support. But, my brothers and sisters, I say we must give up this obsession with excess consumption and materialism, especially when it causes the harming of the skies surrounding our Mother and the pollution of the waters upon her. *She is beginning to warn us!*

Keep those material goods that you need to exist, but be a more sharing and generous person. You will find that you can do with less. Replace this empty lifestyle of hollow impressing of the shallow ones with active participation for your Mother Earth. At least then, when you depart into the spirit world, you can look back with pride and fulfillment. Other spirit beings will gather around you, other spirits of your own higher consciousness will gather around you and share your satisfaction with you. The eternal satisfaction of knowing you did not overuse your Mother Earth and that you were here to protect her will be a powerful satisfaction when you reach the spirit world.

Indian people do not like to say that the Great Mystery is exactly this or exactly that, but we do know there is a spirit world that lies beyond. We are allowed to know that through our ceremonies. We know that we will go into a much higher plane beyond. We know nothing of hell-fire and eternal damnation from some kind of unloving power that placed us here as little children. None of that has ever been shown to us in our powerful ceremonies, conducted by kind, considerate, proven, and very nonmaterialistic leaders. We do know that everything the Great Mystery makes is in the form of a circle. Our Mother Earth is a very large, powerful circle.

Therefore, we conclude that our life does not end. A part of it is within that great eternal circle. If there is a hell, then our concept of hell would be an eternal knowing that one violated or took and robbed from Mother Earth and caused this suffering that is being bestowed upon the generations unborn. This then, if it were to be imprinted upon one's eternal conscience, this would surely be a terrible, spiritual, mental hell. Worse, to have harmed and hurt one's innocent fellow beings, and be unable to alter (or conceal) the harmful actions would also be a great hell. Truth in the spirit world will not be concealed, nor will it be for sale. Lastly, we must realize that the generations unborn will also come into the spirit world. Let us be the ones that they wish to thank and congratulate, rather than eternally scorn.

While we are shedding our overabundant possessions, and linking up with those of like minds, and advancing spiritual and environmental appreciations, we should develop a respect for the aged and for family-centered traditions, even those who are single warriors, fighting for the revitalization of our Mother on a lone, solitary, but vital front. We should have more respect for an extended family, which extends beyond a son or daughter, goes beyond to grandparents and aunts and uncles, goes beyond to brothers, sisters, aunts, and uncles that we have adopted or made as relatives—and further beyond, to the animal or plant world as our brothers and sisters, to Mother Earth and Father Sky and then above to *Wakan Tanka,* the *Unci/Tankashilah,* the Grandparent of us all. When we pray directly to the Great Spirit, we say *Unci* (Grandmother) or *Tankashilah* (Grandfather) because we are so family-minded that we think of the Great Power above as a grandparent, and we are the grand-children. Of course, this is so because every particle of our being is from Mother Earth, and our energy and life force are fueled by Father Sky. This is a vital part of the great, deep feeling and spiritual psychology that we have as Indian people. It is why we preserved and respected our ecological environment for such a long period. *Mitakuye oyasin!* We are all related!

In conclusion, our survival is dependent on the realization that Mother Earth is a truly holy being, that all things in this world are holy and must not be violated, and that we must share and be generous with one another. You may call this thought by whatever fancy words you wish—psychology, theology, sociology, or philosophy—but you must think of Mother Earth as a living being. Think of your fellow men and women as holy people who were put here by the Great Spirit. Think of being related to all things! With this philosophy in mind as we go on with our environmental ecology efforts, our search for spirituality, and our quest for peace, we will be far more successful when we truly understand the Indians' respect for Mother Earth.

RECOMMENDED READINGS

Texts

Bergoffen, D. B. *The Philosophy of Simone de Beauvoir: Gendered Phenomenologies, Erotic Generosities.* Albany: State University of New York Press, 1997.
Cumming, Robert, ed. *The Philosophy of Jean-Paul Sartre.* New York: Modern Library, 1966.
Danto, Arthur C. *Jean-Paul Sartre.* New York: Viking, 1975.
Detmer, David. *Freedom as a Value.* LaSalle, IL: Open Court, 1988.
Grene, Marjorie. *Sartre.* New York: New Viewpoints, 1973.
Howells, Christina, ed. *The Cambridge Companion to Sartre.* New York: Cambridge University Press, 1992.
Santoni, Ronald E. *Bad Faith, Good Faith, and Authenticity in Sartre's Early Philosophy.* Philadelphia: Temple University Press, 1995.
Schilpp, Paul Arthur, ed. *The Philosophy of Jean-Paul Sartre.* LaSalle, IL: Open Court, 1981.
Warnock, Mary, ed. *Sartre: A Collection of Critical Essays.* Garden City, NY: Doubleday & Co., 1971.
Wenzel, H. V., ed. *Simone de Beauvoir: Witness to a Century.* New Haven: Yale University Press, 1986.

Feminist Perspective

Evans, M. *Simone de Beauvoir, A Feminist Mandarin.* New York: Tavistock, 1985.
Moi, T. *Feminist Theory and Simone de Beauvoir.* Oxford: Blackwell, 1990.
Noddings, N. *Caring: A Feminine Approach to Ethics and Moral Education.* Berkeley: University of California Press, 1984.
Peters, H. *The Existential Woman.* New York: P. Lang, 1990.

Multicultural Perspective

Booth, Annie L. and Harvey M. Jacobs. "Ties that Bind: Native American Beliefs as a Foundation for Environmental Consciousness." In *Earth Ethics,* 2nd. Ed. James P. Sterba. UpperSaddle, NJ: Prentice-Hall, 1999.
Hughes, J. Donald. *American Indian Ecology.* El Paso: Texas Western Press, 1983.

PART X

❦

RAWLS AND HARE

INTRODUCTION

John Rawls was born in Baltimore in 1921. He received his Ph.D. in philosophy from Princeton in 1950. He taught at Cornell University and MIT before going to Harvard University in 1962. In 1971, he published his best-known work, *A Theory of Justice*. It has been translated into every major European language, as well as Chinese, Japanese, and Korean. He was named James Bryant Conant University Professor in 1979. In 1993, he published *Political Liberalism*.

In *A Theory of Justice*, Rawls, like Kant, argues that principles of justice are those principles that free and rational persons who are concerned to advance their own interests would accept in an initial position of equality. Yet Rawls goes beyond Kant by interpreting the conditions of his "original position" to explicitly require a "veil of ignorance." This veil of ignorance, Rawls claims, has the effect of depriving persons in the original position of the knowledge they would need to advance their own interests in ways that are morally arbitrary.

The justification Rawls offers for the conditions he imposes on the original position takes two forms. First, Rawls claims that the conditions express weak but widely shared moral presumptions. Second, Rawls assures us that the choice of principles in the original position will always conform to our considered moral judgments. In cases of conflict, this will be accomplished either by revising our considered moral judgments or by revising the particular conditions on the original position that gave rise to them.

According to Rawls, the principles of justice that would be derived in the original position are the following:

I. Special Conception of Justice

1. Each person is to have an equal right to the most extensive total system of equal basic liberties compatible with a similar system of liberty for all.

2. Social and economic inequalities are to be arranged so that they are (a) to the greatest benefit of the least advantaged, consistent with the just savings principle and (b) attached to offices and position open to all under conditions of fair equality of opportunity.

II. General Conception of Justice

All social goods—liberty and opportunity, income and wealth, and the bases of self-respect—are to be distributed equally unless an unequal distribution of any or all of these goods is to the advantage of the least favored.

The general conception of justice differs from the special conception of justice by allowing trade-offs between liberty and other social goods. According to Rawls, persons in the original position would want the special conception of justice to be applied in place of the general conception of justice whenever social conditions allowed all representative persons to exercise their basic liberties.

Rawls holds that these principles of justice would be chosen in the original position because persons so situated would find it reasonable to follow the conservative dictates of the "maximin strategy" and *maxi*mize the *mini*mum, thereby securing for themselves the highest minimum payoff.

Rawls's defense of a welfare liberal conception of justice has been challenged in a variety of ways. Some critics have endorsed Rawls's contractual approach while disagreeing with Rawls over what principles of justice would be derived thereby. These critics usually attempt to undermine the use of a *maximin* strategy in the original position. Other critics, however, have found fault with the contractual approach itself. Libertarians, for example, have challenged the moral adequacy of the very ideal of contractual fairness.

This second challenge to the ideal of contractual fairness is potentially the more damaging because, if valid, it would force its supporters to embrace some other political ideal. This challenge, however, would fail if it can be shown that the libertarian's own ideal of liberty, when correctly interpreted, leads to much the same practical requirements as are usually associated with the welfare liberal ideal of contractual fairness.

R(ichard) M(erwyn) Hare was born in Backwell near Bristol in 1919. From 1939 to 1945 he served in Royal Artillery of the British Army, rising to the rank of lieutenant. He was a prisoner of war in Singapore and Siam (now Thailand) from 1942–1945. In 1947, he married Catherine Verney and received an M.A. degree from Balliol College, Oxford University. He was a fellow and tutor in philosophy at Balliol College from 1947–1966, university lecturer in philosophy from 1951–1966, and White's Professor of Moral Philosophy of Corpus Christi College from 1966 to 1983. In 1984, he became graduate research professor of philosophy at the University of Florida, Gainesville.

His most important publications in ethics are *The Language of Morals* (1952), *Freedom and Reason* (1963), *Moral Thinking* (1981), *Essays in Ethical Theory* (1989), and *Sorting Out Ethics* (1997).

In our selection from *Essays in Ethical Theory,* R. M. Hare argues that moral judgments have two logical features: prescriptivity and universalizability. Prescriptivity means that persons who say "I ought" should themselves act accordingly, if the judgment applies to them and if they can so act. Universalizability means that, by saying "I ought," persons commit themselves to agreeing that anybody ought who is in just those same circumstances. Hare further argues that if we are to assent rationally to ought judgments, we require correct factual information, and that we don't have correct factual information about other people's preferences unless it is the case that, were we ourselves in their shoes, we would prefer that their preferences be satisfied. What universalizability requires is that we use this knowledge and treat other people's preferences as if they were our own. In that case, if the preferences conflict, we would let the stronger preferences override the weaker ones. In this way, Hare thinks that he has arrived at essentially a utilitarian answer to what we should do morally: maximize the overall preference satisfaction of all people concerned. Furthermore, the best way to achieve this goal, Hare contends, is not to do a utilitarian cost-benefit analysis on each and every occasion, but rather to follow certain rules and dispositions, which experience has shown generally lead to the goal. Of course, when these rules and dispositions come into conflict, he argues that we have no alternative but to apply directly a utilitarian cost-benefit analysis to try to resolve those conflicts.

In "The Radical Future of Hare's Moral Theory," Lynne Arnault argues that for Hare's theory to meet his own criteria of prescriptivity and universalizability, it must abandon its liberal conception of the self, according to which people are not embedded in a social context, and its accompanying monological model of moral deliberation. Arnault argues that maintaining the internal coherence of Hare's theory requires allowing for the possibility that social divisions may be so embedded in the structure of things that it can be very difficult to put oneself in the situation of others who are quite different from us. To attempt to do this, we must enter into an extensive dialogue with people with different perspectives if we are to have any hope of coming to understand their preferences. In addition, Arnault points out that once we have come to an understanding of what are the relevant preferences that people have in a given situation, there are other options to maximizing simply the satisfaction overall. We could, for example, follow Rawls's approach and favor the preferences of the least advantaged.

In "Perversions of Justice: A Native-American Examination of the Doctrine of U.S. Rights to Occupancy in North America," Ward Churchill argues that the United States does not now possess, nor has it ever possessed, a legitimate right to occupancy in at least half the territory it claims as its own on this continent. He argues that the Supreme Court, through the Marshall Doctrine, subverted international law to gain control of Indian lands. He notes that the U.S. policies of extermination and assimilation of Indian populations would have succeeded, except for the fact that the ostensibly useless land to which Indians were consigned ironically turned out to be some of most mineral-rich land anywhere. Even so, given the way the Bureau of Indian

Affairs manages this land, Churchill point out, little of this wealth actually benefits American Indians. By U.S. figures, Indians have by far the lowest annual and lifetime per capita income of any group in the United States. Churchill draws analogies between the U.S. expansion over the North American continent and European colonial empires, the territorial ambitions of the Axis powers (Hitler explicitly anchored his concept of "politics of living space" on the United States treatment of American Indians) and Iraq's invasion and occupation of Kuwait. He claims that Iraq had a far better claim to Kuwait (its ninteenth province, separated from it by the British after World War I) than the U.S. government has to virtually any part of North America.

Suppose we were to apply Rawls's or Hare's theory to relations between the U.S. government and American Indians. Would Rawls's or Hare's theory support Churchill's contention that the U.S. government has no legitimate claim to at least half the territory it claims as its own on this continent? If so, what would this show, if anything, about the validity of their theories?

37. A THEORY OF JUSTICE

JOHN RAWLS

My aim is to present a conception of justice which generalizes and carries to a higher level of abstraction the familiar theory of the social contract as found, say, in Locke, Rousseau, and Kant.[1] In order to do this we are not to think of the original contract as one to enter a particular society or to set up a particular form of government. Rather, the guiding idea is that the principles of justice for the basic structure of society are the object of the original agreement. They are the principles that free and rational persons concerned to further their own interests would accept in an initial position of equality as defining the fundamental terms of their association. These principles are to regulate all further agreements; they specify the kinds of social cooperation that can be entered into and the forms of government that can be established. This way of regarding the principles of justice I shall call justice as fairness.

Thus we are to imagine that those who engage in social cooperation choose together, in one joint act, the principles which are to assign basic rights and duties and to determine the division of social benefits. Men are to decide in advance how they are to regulate their claims against one another and what is to be the foundation charter of their society. Just as each person must decide by rational reflection what constitutes his good—that is, the system of ends which it is rational for him to pursue—so a group of persons must decide once and for all

what is to count among them as just and unjust. The choice which rational men would make in this hypothetical situation of equal liberty, assuming for the present that this choice problem has a solution, determines the principles of justice.

In justice as fairness the original position of equality corresponds to the state of nature in the traditional theory of the social contract. This original position is not, of course, thought of as an actual historical state of affairs, much less as a primitive condition of culture. It is understood as a purely hypothetical situation characterized so as to lead to a certain conception of justice.[2] Among the essential features of this situation is that no one knows his place in society, his class position or social status, nor does any one know his fortune in the distribution of natural assets and abilities, his intelligence, strength, and the like. I shall even assume that the parties do not know their conceptions of the good or their special psychological propensities. The principles of justice are chosen behind a veil of ignorance. This ensures that no one is advantaged or disadvantaged in the choice of principles by the outcome of natural chance or the contingency of social circumstances. Since all are similarly situated and no one is able to design principles to favor his particular condition, the principles of justice are the result of a fair agreement or bargain. For given the circumstances of the original position, the symmetry of everyone's relations to each other, this initial situation is fair between individuals as moral persons; that is, as rational beings with their own ends and capable, I shall assume, of a sense of justice. The original position is, one might say, the appropriate initial status quo, and thus the fundamental agreements reached in it are fair. This explains the propriety of the name "justice as fairness"; it conveys the idea that the principles of justice are agreed to in an initial situation that is fair. The name does not mean that the concepts of justice and fairness are the same, any more than the phrase "poetry as metaphor" means that the concepts of poetry and metaphor are the same.

Justice as fairness begins, as I have said, with one of the most general of all choices which persons might make together, namely, with the choice of the first principles of a conception of justice which is to regulate all subsequent criticism and reform of institutions. Then, having chosen a conception of justice, we can suppose that they are to choose a constitution and a legislature to enact laws, and so on, all in accordance with the principles of justice initially agreed upon. Our social situation is just if it is such that by this sequence of hypothetical agreements we would have contracted into the general system of rules which defines it. Moreover, assuming that the original position does determine a set of principles (that is, that a particular conception of justice would be chosen), it will then be true that whenever social institutions satisfy these principles those engaged in them can say to one another that they are cooperating on terms to which they would agree if they were free and equal persons whose relations with respect to one another were fair. They could all view their arrangements as meeting the stipulations which they would acknowledge in an initial situation that embodies widely accepted and reasonable constraints on the choice of principles. The general recognition of this fact would provide the basis for a public acceptance of the corresponding principles of justice. No society can, of course, be a scheme of cooperation which men enter voluntarily in a literal sense; each person finds himself placed at birth in some particular position in some particular society, and the nature of this position materially affects his life prospects. Yet a society satisfying the principles

of justice as fairness comes as close as a society can to being a voluntary scheme, for it meets the principles which free and equal persons would assent to under circumstances that are fair. In this sense its members are autonomous and the obligations they recognize self-imposed.

One feature of justice as fairness is to think of the parties in the initial situation as rational and mutually disinterested. This does not mean that the parties are egoists; that is, individuals with only certain kinds of interests, say in wealth, prestige, and domination. But they are conceived as not taking an interest in one another's interests. They are to presume that even their spiritual aims may be opposed, in the way that the aims of those of different religions may be opposed. Moreover, the concept of rationality must be interpreted as far as possible in the narrow sense, standard in economic theory, of taking the most effective means to given ends. I shall modify this concept to some extent . . . but one must try to avoid introducing into it any controversial ethical elements. The initial situation must be characterized by stipulations that are widely accepted.

In working out the conception of justice as fairness one main task clearly is to determine which principles of justice would be chosen in the original position. To do this we must describe this situation in some detail and formulate with care the problem of choice which it presents. It may be observed, however, that once the principles of justice are thought of as arising from an original agreement in a situation of equality, it is an open question whether the principle of utility would be acknowledged. Offhand it hardly seems likely that persons who view themselves as equals, entitled to press their claims upon one another, would agree to a principle which may require lesser life prospects for some simply for the sake of a greater sum of advantages enjoyed by others. Since each desires to protect his interests, his capacity to advance his conception of the good, no one has a reason to acquiesce in an enduring loss for himself in order to bring about a greater net balance of satisfaction. In the absence of strong and lasting benevolent impulses, a rational man would not accept a basic structure merely because it maximized the algebraic sum of advantages irrespective of its permanent effects on his own basic rights and interests. Thus it seems that the principle of utility is incompatible with the conception of social cooperation among equals for mutual advantage. It appears to be inconsistent with the idea of reciprocity implicit in the notion of a well-ordered society. Or, at any rate, so I shall argue.

I shall maintain instead that the persons in the initial situation would choose two rather different principles: the first requires equality in the assignment of basic rights and duties, while the second holds that social and economic inequalities (for example, inequalities of wealth and authority) are just only if they result in compensating benefits for everyone, and in particular for the least advantaged members of society. These principles rule out justifying institutions on the grounds that the hardships of some are offset by a greater good in the aggregate. It may be expedient but it is not just that some should have less in order that others may prosper. But there is no injustice in the greater benefits earned by a few provided that the situation of persons not so fortunate is thereby improved. The intuitive idea is that since everyone's well-being depends upon a scheme of cooperation without which no one could have a satisfactory life, the division of advantages should be such as to draw forth the willing cooperation of everyone taking part in it, including those less well situated. Yet this can be expected only if reasonable terms are proposed. The two principles mentioned seem to be a fair agreement on the basis of which those better endowed, or more fortunate in their social position, neither of which we can be said to deserve, could expect the willing cooperation of others when some workable scheme is a necessary condition of the welfare of all.[3] Once we decide to look for a conception of justice that nullifies the accidents of natural endowment and the contingencies of social circumstance as counters in quest for political and economic advantage, we are led to these principles. They express the result of leaving aside those aspects of the social world that seem arbitrary from a moral point of view.

The problem of the choice of principles, however, is extremely difficult. I do not expect the answer I shall suggest to be convincing to everyone. It is, therefore, worth noting from the outset that justice as fairness, like other contract views, consists of two parts: (1) an interpretation of the initial situation and of the problem of choice posed there, and (2) a set of principles which, it is argued, would be agreed to. One may accept the first part of the theory (or some variant thereof), but not the other, and conversely. The concept of the initial contractual situation may seem reasonable although the particular principles proposed are rejected. To be sure, I want to maintain that the most appropriate conception of this situation does lead to principles of justice contrary to utilitarianism and perfectionism, and therefore that the contract doctrine provides an alternative to these views. Still, one may dispute this contention even though one grants that the contractarian method is a useful way of studying ethical theories and of setting forth their underlying assumptions.

Justice as fairness is an example of what I have called a contract theory. Now there may be an objection to the term "contract" and related expressions, but I think it will serve reasonably well. Many words have misleading connotations which at first are likely to confuse. The terms "utility" and "utilitarianism" are surely no exception. They too have unfortunate suggestions which hostile critics have been willing to exploit; yet they are clear enough for those prepared to study utilitarian doctrine. The same should be true of the term "contract" applied to moral theories. As I have mentioned, to understand it one has to keep in mind that it implies a certain level of abstraction. In particular, the content of the relevant agreement is not to enter a given society or to adopt a given form of government, but to accept certain moral principles. Moreover, the undertakings referred to are purely hypothetical: a contract view holds that certain principles would be accepted in a well-defined initial situation.

The merit of the contract terminology is that it conveys the idea that principles of justice may be conceived as principles that would be chosen by rational persons, and that in this way conceptions of justice may be explained and justified. The theory of justice is a part, perhaps the most significant part, of the theory of rational choice. Furthermore, principles of justice deal with conflicting claims upon the advantages won by social cooperation; they apply to the relations among several persons or groups. The word "contract" suggests this plurality as well as the condition that the appropriate division of advantages must be in accordance with principles acceptable to all parties. The condition of publicity for principles of justice is also connoted by the contract phraseology. Thus, if these principles are the outcome of an agreement, citizens have a knowledge of the principles that others follow. It is characteristic of contract theories to stress the public nature of political principles. Finally there is the long tradition of the contract doctrine. Expressing the tie with this line of thought helps to define ideas and accords with natural piety. There are then several advantages in the use of the term "contract." With due precautions taken, it should not be misleading.

A final remark. Justice as fairness is not a complete contract theory. For it is clear that the contractarian idea can be extended to the choice of more or less an entire ethical system; that is, to a system including principles for all the virtues and not only for justice. Now for the most part I shall consider only principles of justice and others closely related to them; I make no attempt to discuss the virtues in a systematic way. Obviously if justice as fairness succeeds reasonably well, a next step would be to study the more general view suggested by the name "rightness as fairness." But even this wider theory fails to embrace all moral relationships, since it would seem to include only our relations with other persons and to leave out of account how we are to conduct ourselves toward animals and the rest of nature. I do not contend that the contract notion offers a way to approach these questions, which are certainly of the first importance; and I shall have to put them aside. We must recognize the limited scope of justice as fairness and of the general type of view that it exemplifies. How far its conclusions must be revised once these other matters are understood cannot be decided in advance.

THE ORIGINAL POSITION AND JUSTIFICATION

I have said that the original position is the appropriate initial status quo which insures that the fundamental agreements reached in it are fair. This fact yields the name "justice as fairness." It is clear, then, that I want to say that one conception of justice is more reasonable than another, or justifiable with respect to it, if rational persons in the initial situation would choose its principles over those of the other for the role of justice. Conceptions of justice are to be ranked by their acceptability to persons so circumstanced. Understood in this way the question of justification is settled by working out a problem of deliberation: we have to ascertain which principles it would be rational to adopt given the contractual situation. This connects the theory of justice with the theory of rational choice.

If this view of the problem of justification is to succeed, we must, of course, describe in some detail the nature of this choice problem. A problem of rational decision has a definite answer only if we know the beliefs and interests of the parties, their relations with respect to one another, the alternatives between which they are to choose, the procedure whereby they make up their minds, and so on. As the circumstances are presented in different ways, correspondingly different principles are accepted. The concept of the original position, as I shall refer to it, is that of the most philosophically favored interpretation of this initial choice situation for the purposes of a theory of justice.

But how are we to decide what is the most favored interpretation? I assume, for one thing, that there is a broad measure of agreement that principles of justice should be chosen under certain conditions. To justify a particular description of the initial situation one shows that it incorporates these commonly shared presumptions. One argues from widely accepted but weak premises to more specific conclusions. Each of the presumptions should be itself be natural and plausible; some of them may seem innocuous or even trivial. The aim of the contract approach is to establish that taken together they impose significant bounds on acceptable principles of justice. The ideal outcome would be that these conditions determine a unique set of principles; but I shall be satisfied if they suffice to rank the main traditional conceptions of social justice.

One should not be misled, then, by the somewhat unusual conditions which characterize the original position. The idea here is simply to make vivid to ourselves the restrictions that it seems reasonable to impose on arguments for principles of justice, and therefore on these principles themselves. Thus it seems reasonable and generally acceptable that no one should be advantaged or disadvantaged by natural fortune or social circumstances in the choice of principles. It also seems widely agreed that it should be impossible to tailor principles to the circumstances of one's own case. We should ensure further that particular inclinations and aspirations, and persons' conceptions of their good, do not affect the principles adopted. The aim is to rule out those principles that it would be rational to propose for acceptance, however little the chance of success, only if one knew certain things that are irrelevant from the standpoint of justice. For example, if a man knew that he was wealthy, he might find it rational to advance the principle that various taxes for welfare measures be counted unjust; if he knew that he was poor, he would most likely propose the contrary principle. To represent the desired restrictions one imagines a situation in which everyone is deprived of this sort of information. One excludes the knowledge of those contingencies which sets men at odds and allows them to be guided by their prejudices. In this manner the veil of ignorance is arrived at in a natural way. This concept should cause no difficulty if we keep in mind the constraints on arguments that it is meant to express. At any time we can enter the original position, so to speak, simply by following a certain procedure; namely, by arguing for principles of justice in accordance with these restrictions.

It seems reasonable to suppose that the parties in the original position are equal. That is, all have the same rights in the procedure for choosing principles; each can make proposals, submit reasons for their acceptance, and so on. Obviously the purpose of these conditions is to represent equality between human beings as moral persons, as creatures having a conception of their good and capable of a sense of justice. The basis of equality is taken to be similarity in these two respects. Systems of ends are not ranked in value, and each man is presumed to have the requisite ability to understand and to act upon whatever principles are adopted. Together with the veil of ignorance, these conditions define the principles of justice as those which rational persons concerned to advance their interests would consent to as equals when none are known to be advantaged or disadvantaged by social and natural contingencies.

There is, however, another side to justifying a particular description of the original position. This is to see if the principles which would be chosen match our considered convictions of justice or extend them in an acceptable way. We can note whether applying these principles would lead us to make the same judgments about the basic structure of society which we now make intuitively and in which we have the greatest confidence; or whether, in cases where our present judgments are in doubt and given with hesitation, these principles offer a resolution which we can affirm on reflection. There are questions which we feel sure must be answered in a certain way. For example, we are confident that religious intolerance and racial discrimination are unjust. We think that we have examined these things with care and have reached what we believe is an impartial judgment not likely to be distorted by an excessive attention to our own interests. These convictions are provisional fixed points which we presume any conception of justice must fit. But we have much less assurance as to what is the correct distribution of wealth and authority. Here we may be looking for a way to remove our doubts. We can check an interpretation of the initial situation, then, by the capacity of its principles to accommodate our firmest convictions and to provide guidance where guidance is needed.

In searching for the most favored description of this situation we work from both ends. We begin by describing it so that it represents generally shared and preferably weak conditions. We then see if these conditions are strong enough to yield a significant set of principles. If not, we look for further premises equally reasonable. But if so, and these principles match our considered convictions of justice, then so far well and good. But presumably there will be discrepancies. In this case we have a choice. We can either modify the account of the initial situation or we can revise our existing judgments, for even the judgments we take provisionally as fixed points are liable to revision. By going back and forth, sometimes altering the conditions of the contractual circumstances, at others withdrawing our judgments and conforming them to principle, I assume that eventually we shall find a description of the initial situation that both expresses reasonable

conditions and yields principles which match our considered judgments duly pruned and adjusted. This state of affairs I refer to as reflective equilibrium.[4] It is an equilibrium because at last our principles and judgments coincide; and it is reflective since we know to what principles our judgments conform and the premises of their derivation. At the moment everything is in order. But this equilibrium is not necessarily stable. It is liable to be upset by further examination of the conditions which should be imposed on the contractual situation and by particular cases which may lead us to revise our judgments. Yet for the time being we have done what we can to render coherent and to justify our convictions of social justice. We have reached a conception of the original position.

I shall not, of course, actually work through this process. Still, we may think of the interpretation of the original position that I shall present as the result of such a hypothetical course of reflection. It represents the attempt to accommodate within one scheme both reasonable philosophical conditions on principles as well as our considered judgments of justice. In arriving at the favored interpretation of the initial situation there is no point at which an appeal is made to self-evidence in the traditional sense either of general conceptions or particular convictions. I do not claim for the principles of justice proposed that they are necessary truths or derivable from such truths. A conception of justice cannot be deduced from self-evident premises or conditions on principles; instead, its justification is a matter of the mutual support of many considerations, of everything fitting together into one coherent view.

A final comment. We shall want to say that certain principles of justice are justified because they would be agreed to in an initial situation of equality. I have emphasized that this original position is purely hypothetical. It is natural to ask why, if this agreement is never actually entered into, we should take any interest in these principles, moral or otherwise. The answer is that the conditions embodied in the description of the original position are ones that we do in fact accept. Or if we do not, then perhaps we can be persuaded to do so by philosophical reflection. Each aspect of the contractual situation can be given supporting grounds. Thus what we shall do is to collect together into one conception a number of conditions on principles that we are ready upon due consideration to recognize as reasonable. These constraints express what we are prepared to regard as limits on fair terms of social cooperation. One way to look at the idea of the original position, therefore, is to see it as an expository device which sums up the meaning of these conditions and helps us to extract their consequences. On the other hand, this conception is also an intuitive notion that suggests its own elaboration, so that led on by it we are drawn to define more clearly the standpoint from which we can best interpret moral relationships. We need a conception that enables us to envision our objective from afar: the intuitive notion of the original position is to do this for us. . . .

TWO PRINCIPLES OF JUSTICE

I shall now state in a provisional form the two principles of justice that I believe would be chosen in the original position. In this section I wish to make only the most general comments, and therefore the first formulation of these principles is tentative. As we go on I shall run through several formulations and approximate step by step the final statement to be given much later. I believe that doing this allows the exposition to proceed in a natural way.

The first statement of the two principles reads as follows:

First: each person is to have an equal right to the most extensive basic liberty compatible with a similar liberty for others.

Second: social and economic inequalities are to be arranged so that they are both (a) reasonably expected to be to everyone's advantage, and

(b) attached to positions and offices open to all.

There are two ambiguous phrases in the second principle, namely "everyone's advantage" and "open to all." Determining their sense more exactly will lead to a second formulation of the principle. . . .

By way of general comment, these principles primarily apply, as I have said, to the basic structure of society. They are to govern the assignment of rights and duties and to regulate the distribution of social and economic advantages. As their formulation suggests, these principles presuppose that the social structure can be divided into two more or less distinct parts, the first principle applying to the one, the second to the other. They distinguish between those aspects of the social system that define and secure the equal liberties of citizenship and those that specify and establish social and economic inequalities. The basic liberties of citizens are, roughly speaking, political liberty (the right to vote and to be eligible for public office) together with freedom of speech and assembly; liberty of conscience and freedom of thought; freedom of the person along with the right to hold (personal) property; and freedom from arbitrary arrest and seizure as defined by the concept of the rule of law. These liberties are all required to be equal by the first principle, since citizens of a just society are to have the same basic rights.

The second principle applies, in the first approximation, to the distribution of income and wealth and to the design of organizations that make use of differences in authority and responsibility, or chains of command. While the distribution of wealth and income need not be equal, it must be to everyone's advantage, and at the same time, positions of authority and offices of command must be accessible to all. One applies the second principle by holding positions open, and then, subject to this constraint, arranges social and economic inequalities so that everyone benefits.

These principles are to be arranged in a serial order with the first principle prior to the second. This ordering means that a departure from the institutions of equal liberty required by the first principle cannot be justified by, or compensated for, by greater social and economic advantages. The distribution of wealth and income, and the hierarchies of authority, must be consistent with both the liberties of equal citizenship and equality of opportunity.

It is clear that these principles are rather specific in their content, and their acceptance rests on certain assumptions that I must eventually try to explain and justify. A theory of justice depends upon a theory of society in ways that will become evident as we proceed. For the present, it should be observed that the two principles (and this holds for all formulations) are a special case of a more general conception of justice that can be expressed as follows:

> All social values—liberty and opportunity, income and wealth, and the bases of self-respect—are to be distributed equally unless an unequal distribution of any, or all, of these values is to everyone's advantage.

Injustice, then, is simply inequalities that are not to the benefit of all. Of course, this conception is extremely vague and requires interpretation.

As a first step, suppose that the basic structure of society distributes certain primary goods, that is, things that every rational man is presumed to want. These goods normally have a use whatever a person's rational plan of life. For simplicity, assume that the chief primary goods at the disposition of society are rights and liberties, powers and opportunities, income and wealth. (Later on . . . the primary good of self-respect has a central place.) These are the social primary goods. Other primary goods such as health and vigor, intelligence and imagination, are natural goods; although their possession is influenced by the basic structure, they are not so directly under its control. Imagine, then, a hypothetical initial arrangement in which all the social primary goods are equally distributed: everyone has similar rights and duties, and income and wealth are evenly shared. This state of affairs provides a benchmark for judging improvements. If certain inequalities of wealth and organizational powers would make everyone better off than in this hypothetical starting situation, then they accord with the general conception.

Now it is possible, at least theoretically, that by giving up some of their fundamental liberties men are sufficiently compensated by the resulting social and economic gains. The general conception of justice imposes no restrictions on what sort of inequalities are permissible; it only requires that everyone's position be improved. We need not suppose anything so drastic as consenting to a condition of slavery. Imagine instead that men forgo certain political rights when the economic returns are significant and their capacity to influence the course of policy by the exercise of these rights would be marginal in any case. It is this kind of exchange which the two principles as stated rule out; being arranged in serial order they do not permit exchanges between basic liberties and economic and social gains. The serial ordering of principles expresses an underlying preference among primary social goods. When this preference is rational so likewise is the choice of these principles in this order.

In developing justice as fairness I shall, for the most part, leave aside the general conception of justice and examine instead the special case of the two principles in serial order. The advantage of this procedure is that from the first the matter of priorities is recognized and an effort made to find principles to deal with it. One is led to attend throughout to the conditions under which the acknowledgment of the absolute weight of liberty with respect to social and economic advantages, as defined by the lexical order of the two principles, would be reasonable. Offhand, this ranking appears extreme and too special a case to be of much interest; but there is more justification for it than would appear at first sight. Or at any rate, so I shall maintain.... Furthermore, the distinction between fundamental rights and liberties and economic and social benefits marks a difference among primary social goods that one should try to exploit. It suggests an important division in the social system. Of course, the distinctions drawn and the ordering proposed are bound to be at best only approximations. There are surely circumstances in which they fail. But it is essential to depict clearly the main lines of a reasonable conception of justice; and under many conditions, anyway, the two principles in serial order may serve well enough. When necessary we can fall back on the more general conception.

The fact that the two principles apply to institutions has certain consequences. Several points illustrate this. First of all, the rights and liberties referred to by these principles are those that are defined by the public rules of the basic structure. Whether men are free is determined by the rights and duties established by the major institutions of society. Liberty is a certain pattern of social forms. The first principle simply requires that certain sorts of rules, those defining basic liberties, apply to everyone equally and that they allow the most extensive liberty compatible with a like liberty for all. The only reason for circumscribing the rights defining liberty and making men's freedom less extensive than it might otherwise be is that these equal rights as institutionally defined would interfere with one another.

Another thing to bear in mind is that when principles mention persons, or require that everyone gain from an inequality, the reference is to representative persons holding the various social positions, or offices, or whatever, established by the basic structure. Thus in applying the second principle I assume that it is possible to assign an expectation of well-being to representative individuals holding these positions. This expectation indicates their life prospects as viewed from their social station. In general, the expectations of representative persons depend upon the distribution of rights and duties throughout the basic structure. When this changes, expectations change. I assume, then, that expectations are connected: by raising the prospects of the representative man in one position we presumably increase or decrease the prospects of representative men in other positions. Since it applies to institutional forms, the second principle (or rather the first part of it) refers to the expectations of representative individuals. As I shall discuss below, neither principle applies to distributions of particular goods to particular individuals who may be identified by their proper names. The situation where someone is considering how to allocate certain commodities to needy persons who are known to him is not within the scope of the principles. They are meant to regulate basic institutional arrangements. We must not assume that there is much similarity from the standpoint of justice between an administrative allotment of goods to specific persons and the appropriate design of society. Our common sense intuitions for the former may be a poor guide to the latter.

Now the second principle insists that each person benefit from permissible inequalities in the basic structure. This means that it must be reasonable for each relevant representative man defined by this structure, when he views it as a going concern, to prefer his prospects with the inequality, to his prospects without it. One is not allowed to justify differences in income or organizational powers on the ground that the disadvantages of those in one position are outweighed by the greater advantages of those in another. Much less can infringements of liberty be counterbalanced in this way. Applied to the basic structure, the principle of utility would have us maximize the sum of expectations of representative men (weighted by the number of persons they represent, on the classical view); and this would permit us to compensate for the losses of some by the gains of others. Instead the two principles require that everyone benefit from economic and social inequalities.

The Reasoning Leading to the Two Principles of Justice

It will be recalled that the general conception of justice as fairness requires that all primary social goods be distributed equally unless an unequal distribution would be to everyone's advantage. No restrictions are placed on exchanges of these goods and therefore a lesser liberty can be compensated for by greater social and economic benefits. Now looking at the situation from the standpoint of one person selected arbitrarily, there is no way for him to win special advantages for himself. Nor, on the other hand, are there grounds for his acquiescing in special disadvantages. Since it is not reasonable for him to expect more than an equal share in the division of social goods, and since it is not rational for him to agree to less, the sensible thing for him to do is to acknowledge as the first principle of justice one requiring an equal distribution. Indeed, this principle is so obvious that we would expect it to occur to anyone immediately.

Thus, the parties start with a principle establishing equal liberty for all, including equality of opportunity, as well as an equal distribution of income and wealth. But there is no reason why this acknowledgment should be final. If there are inequalities in the basic structure that work to make everyone better off in comparison with the benchmark of initial equality, why not permit them? The immediate gain which a greater equality might allow can be regarded as intelligently invested in view of its future return. If, for example, these inequalities set up various incentives which succeed in eliciting more productive efforts, a person in the original position may look upon them as necessary to cover the costs of training and to encourage effective performance. One might think that ideally individ-

uals should want to serve one another. But since the parties are assumed not to take an interest in one another's interests, their acceptance of these inequalities is only the acceptance of the relations in which men stand in the circumstances of justice. They have no grounds for complaining of one another's motives. A person in the original position would, therefore, concede the justice of these inequalities. Indeed, it would be shortsighted of him not to do so. He would hesitate to agree to these regularities only if he would be dejected by the bare knowledge or perception that others were better situated; and I have assumed that the parties decide as if they are not moved by envy. In order to make the principle regulating inequalities determinate, one looks at the system from the standpoint of the least advantaged representative man. Inequalities are permissible when they maximize, or at least all contribute to, the long-term expectations of the least fortunate group in society.

Now this general conception imposes no constraints on what sorts of inequalities are allowed, whereas the special conception, by putting the two principles in serial order (with the necessary adjustments in meaning), forbids exchanges between basic liberties and economic and social benefits. I shall not try to justify this ordering here. . . . But roughly, the idea underlying this ordering is that if the parties assume that their basic liberties can be effectively exercised, they will not exchange a lesser liberty for an improvement in economic well-being. It is only when social conditions do not allow the effective establishment of these rights that one can concede their limitation; and these restrictions can be granted only to the extent that they are necessary to prepare the way for a free society. The denial of equal liberty can be defended only if it is necessary to raise the level of civilization so that in due course these freedoms can be enjoyed. Thus in adopting a serial order we are in effect making a special assumption in the original position, namely, that the parties know that the conditions of their society, whatever they are, admit the effective realization of the equal liberties. The serial ordering of the two principles of justice eventually comes to be reasonable if the general conception is consistently followed. This lexical ranking is the long-run tendency of the general view. For the most part I shall assume that the requisite circumstances for the serial order obtain.

It seems clear from these remarks that the two principles are at least a plausible conception of justice. The question, though, is how one is to argue for them more systematically. Now there are several things to do. One can work out their consequences for institutions and note their implications for fundamental social policy. In this way they are tested by a comparison with our considered judgments of justice. . . . But one can also try to find arguments in their favor that are decisive from the standpoint of the original position. In order to see how this might be done, it is useful as a heuristic device to think of the two principles as the maximum solution to the problem of social justice. There is an analogy between the two principles and the maximin rule for choice under uncertainty.[5] This is evident from the fact that the two principles are those a person would choose for the design of a society in which his enemy is to assign him his place. The maximin rule tells us to rank alternatives by their worst possible outcomes: we are to adopt the alternative the worst outcome of which is superior to the worst outcomes of the others. The persons in the original position do not, of course, assume that their initial place in society is decided by a malevolent opponent. As I note below, they should not reason from false premises. The veil of ignorance does not violate this idea, since an absence of information is not misinformation. But that the two principles of justice would be chosen if the parties were forced to protect themselves against such a contingency explains the sense in which this conception is the maximin solution. And this analogy suggests that if the original position has been

described so that it is rational for the parties to adopt the conservative attitude expressed by this rule, a conclusive argument can indeed be constructed for these principles. Clearly the maximin rule is not, in general, a suitable guide for choices under uncertainty. But it is attractive in situations marked by certain special features. My aim, then, is to show that a good case can be made for the two principles based on the fact that the original position manifests these features to the fullest possible degree, carrying them to the limit, so to speak.

Consider the gain-and-loss table below. It represents the gains and losses for a situation which is not a game of strategy. There is no one playing against the person making the decision; instead he is faced with several possible circumstances which may or may not obtain. Which circumstances happen to exist does not depend upon what the person choosing decides or whether he announces his moves in advance. The numbers in the table are monetary values (in hundreds of dollars) in comparison with some initial situation. The gain (g) depends upon the individual's decision (d) and the circumstances (c). Thus $g = f(d,c)$. Assuming that there are three possible decisions and three possible circumstances, we might have this gain-and-loss table.

Circumstances

Decisions	C1	C2	C3
d1	−7	8	12
d2	−8	7	14
d3	5	6	8

The maximin rule requires that we make the third decision. For in this case the worst that can happen is that one gains five hundred dollars, which is better than the worst for the other actions. If we adopt one of these we may lose either eight or seven hundred dollars. Thus, the choice of d_3 maximizes $f(d,c)$ for that value of c which for a given d, minimizes f. The term "maximin" means the *maximum minimorum*;

and the rule directs our attention to the worst that can happen under any proposed course of action, and to decide in the light of that.

Now there appear to be three chief features of situations that give plausibility to this unusual rule.[6] First, since the rule takes no account of the likelihoods of the possible circumstances, there must be some reason for sharply discounting estimates of these probabilities. Offhand, the most natural rule of choice would seem to be to compute the expectation of monetary gain for each decision and then to adopt the course of action with the highest prospect. (This expectation is defined as follows: let us suppose that g_{ij} represent the numbers in the gain-and-loss table, where i is the row index and j is the column index; and let p_j, j = 1, 2, 3, be the likelihoods of the circumstances, with Σp_j, = 1. Then the expectation for the ith decision is equal to $\Sigma p_j g_{ij}$.) Thus it must be, for example, that the situation is one in which a knowledge of likelihoods is impossible, or at best extremely insecure. In this case it is unreasonable not to be skeptical of probabilistic calculations unless there is no other way out, particularly if the decision is a fundamental one that needs to be justified to others.

The second feature that suggests the maximin rule is the following: the person choosing has a conception of the good such that he cares very little, if anything, for what he might gain above the minimum stipend that he can, in fact, be sure of by following the maximin rule. It is not worthwhile for him to take a chance for the sake of a further advantage, especially when it may turn out that he loses much that is important to him. This last provision brings in the third feature; namely, that the rejected alternatives have outcomes that one can hardly accept. The situation involves grave risks. Of course these features work most effectively in combination. The paradigm situation for following the maximin rule is when all three features are realized to the highest degree. This rule does not, then, generally apply, nor of course is it self-evident. Rather, it is a maxim, a rule of thumb, that comes into its

own in special circumstances. Its application depends upon the qualitative structure of the possible gains and losses in relation to one's conception of the good, all this against a background in which it is reasonable to discount conjectural estimates of likelihoods.

It should be noted, as the comments on the gain-and-loss table say, that the entries in the table represent monetary values and not utilities. This difference is significant since for one thing computing expectations on the basis of such objective values is not the same thing as computing expected utility and may lead to different results. The essential point, though, is that in justice as fairness the parties do not know their conception of the good and cannot estimate their utility in the ordinary sense. In any case, we want to go behind *de facto* preferences generated by given conditions. Therefore expectations are based upon an index of primary goods and the parties make their choice accordingly. The entries in the example are in terms of money and not utility to indicate this aspect of the contract doctrine.

Now, as I have suggested, the original position has been defined so that it is a situation in which the maximin rule applies. In order to see this, let us review briefly the nature of this situation with these three special features in mind. To begin with, the veil of ignorance excludes all but the vaguest knowledge of likelihoods. The parties have no basis for determining the probable nature of their society, or their place in it. Thus they have strong reasons for being wary of probability calculations if any other course is open to them. They must also take into account the fact that their choice of principles should seem reasonable to others, in particular their descendants, whose rights will be deeply affected by it. There are further grounds for discounting that I shall mention as we go along. For the present it suffices to note that these considerations are strengthened by the fact that the parties know very little about the gain-and-loss table. Not only are they unable to conjecture the likelihoods of the various possible circumstances, they cannot say much about what the possible circumstances are, much less enumerate them and foresee the outcome of each alternative available. Those deciding are much more in the dark than the illustration by a numerical table suggests. It is for this reason that I have spoken of an analogy with the maximin rule.

Several kinds of arguments for the two principles of justice illustrate the second feature. Thus, if we can maintain that these principles provide a workable theory of social justice, and that they are compatible with reasonable demands of efficiency, then this conception guarantees a satisfactory minimum. There may be, on reflection, little reason for trying to do better. Thus much of the argument ... is to show, by their application to the main questions of social justice, that the two principles are a satisfactory conception. These details have a philosophical purpose. Moreover, this line of thought is practically decisive if we can establish the priority of liberty, the lexical ordering of the two principles. For this priority implies that the persons in the original position have no desire to try for greater gains at the expense of the equal liberties. The minimum assured by the two principles in lexical order is not one that the parties wish to jeopardize for the sake of greater economic and social advantages. ...

Finally, the third feature holds if we can assume that other conceptions of justice may lead to institutions that the parties would find intolerable. For example, it has sometimes been held that under some conditions the utility principle (in either form) justifies, if not slavery or serfdom, at any rate serious infractions of liberty for the sake of greater social benefits. We need not consider here the truth of this claim, or the likelihood that the requisite conditions obtain. For the moment, this contention is only to illustrate the way in which conceptions of justice may allow for outcomes which the parties may not be able to accept. And having the ready alternative of the two principles of justice which

secure a satisfactory minimum, it seems unwise, if not irrational, for them to take a chance that these outcomes are not realized.

So much, then, for a brief sketch of the features of situations in which the maximin rule comes into its own and of the way in which the arguments for the two principles of justice can be subsumed under them. ...

THE FINAL FORMULATION OF THE PRINCIPLES OF JUSTICE

... I now wish to give the final statement of the two principles of justice for institutions. For the sake of completeness, I shall give a full statement including earlier formulations.

First principle

- Each person is to have an equal right to the most extensive total system of equal basic liberties compatible with a similar system of liberty for all.

Second principle

- Social and economic inequalities are to be arranged so that they are both:

    (a) to the greatest benefit of the least advantaged, consistent with the just savings principle, and

    (b) attached to offices and positions open to all under conditions of fair equality of opportunity.

First priority rule (the priority of liberty)

- The principles of justice are to be ranked in lexical order and therefore liberty can be restricted only for the sake of liberty. There are two cases:

    (a) a less extensive liberty must strengthen the total system of liberty shared by all;

    (b) a less than equal liberty must be acceptable to those with the lesser liberty.

Second priority rule (the priority of justice over efficiency and welfare)

- The second principle of justice is lexically prior to the principle of efficiency and to that of maximizing the sum of advantages; and fair opportunity is prior to the difference principle. There are two cases:

  (a) an inequality of opportunity must enhance the opportunities of those with the lesser opportunity;

  (b) an excessive rate of saving must on balance mitigate the burden of those bearing this hardship.

General conception

- All social primary goods—liberty and opportunity, income and wealth, and the bases of self-respect—are to be distributed equally unless an unequal distribution of any or all of these goods is to the advantage of the least favored.

By way of comment, these principles and priority rules are no doubt incomplete. Other modifications will surely have to be made, but I shall not further complicate the statement of the principles. It suffices to observe that when we come to non-ideal theory, we do not fall back straightway upon the general conception of justice. The lexical ordering of the two principles, and the valuations that this ordering implies, suggest priority rules which seem to be reasonable enough in many cases. By various examples I have tried to illustrate how these rules can be used and to indicate their plausibility. Thus the ranking of the principles of justice in ideal theory reflects back and guides the application of these principles to non-ideal situations. It identifies which limitations need to be dealt with first. The drawback of the general conception of justice is that it lacks the definite structure of the two principles in serial order. In more extreme and tangled instances of non-ideal theory there may be no alternative to it. At some point the priority of rules for non-ideal cases will fail; and indeed, we may be

able to find no satisfactory answer at all. But we must try to postpone the day of reckoning as long as possible, and try to arrange society so that it never comes. . . .

THE KANTIAN INTERPRETATION

Kant held, I believe, that a person is acting autonomously when the principles of his action are chosen by him as the most adequate possible expression of his nature as a free and equal rational being. The principles he acts upon are not adopted because of his social position or natural endowments, or in view of the particular kind of society in which he lives or the specific things that he happens to want. To act on such principles is to act heteronomously. Now the veil of ignorance deprives the persons in the original position of the knowledge that would enable them to choose heteronomous principles. The parties arrive at their choice together as free and equal rational persons knowing only that those circumstances obtain which give rise to the need for principles of justice.

To be sure, the argument for these principles does add in various ways to Kant's conception. For example, it adds the feature that the principles chosen are to apply to the basic structure of society; and premises characterizing this structure are used in deriving the principles of justice. But I believe that this and other additions are natural enough and remain fairly close to Kant's doctrine, at least when all of his ethical writings are viewed together. Assuming, then, that the reasoning in favor of the principles of justice is correct, we can say that when persons act on these principles they are acting in accordance with principles that they would choose as rational and independent persons in an original position of equality. The principles of their actions do not depend upon social or natural contingencies, nor do they reflect the bias of the particulars of their plan of life or the aspirations that motivate them. By acting from these principles persons express their nature as free and equal rational beings subject to the general conditions of human life. For to express one's nature as a being of a particular kind is to act on the principles that would be chosen if this nature were the decisive determining element. Of course, the choice of the parties in the original position is subject to the restrictions of that situation. But when we knowingly act on the principles of justice in the ordinary course of events, we deliberately assume the limitations of the original position. One reason for doing this, for persons who can do so and want to, is to give expression to one's nature.

The principles of justice are also categorical imperatives in Kant's sense. For by a categorical imperative Kant understands a principle of conduct that applies to a person in virtue of his nature as a free and equal rational being. The validity of the principle does not presuppose that one has a particular desire or aim. Whereas a hypothetical imperative by contrast does assume this: it directs us to take certain steps as effective means to achieve a specific end. Whether the desire is for a particular thing, or whether it is for something more general, such as certain kinds of agreeable feelings or pleasures, the corresponding imperative is hypothetical. Its applicability depends upon one's having an aim which one need not have as a condition of being a rational human individual. The argument for the two principles of justice does not assume that the parties have particular ends, but only that they desire certain primary goods. These are things that it is rational to want whatever else one wants. Thus given human nature, wanting them is part of being rational; and while each is presumed to have some conception of the good, nothing is known about his final ends. The preference for primary goods is derived, then, from only the most general assumptions about rationality and the conditions of human life. To act from the principles of justice is to act from categorical imperatives in the sense that they apply to us whatever in particular our aims are. This

simply reflects the fact that no such contingencies appear as premises in their derivation.

We may note also that the motivational assumption of mutual disinterest accords with Kant's notion of autonomy, and gives another reason for this condition. So far this assumption has been used to characterize the circumstances of justice and to provide a clear conception to guide the reasoning of the parties. We have also seen that the concept of benevolence, being a second-order notion, would not work out well. Now we can add that the assumption of mutual disinterest is to allow for freedom in the choice of a system of final ends.[7] Liberty in adopting a conception of the good is limited only by principles that are deduced from a doctrine which imposes no prior constraints on these conceptions. Presuming mutual disinterest in the original position carries out this idea. We postulate that the parties have opposing claims in a suitably general sense. If their ends were restricted in some specific way, this would appear at the outset as an arbitrary restriction on freedom. Moreover, if the parties were conceived as altruists, or as pursuing certain kinds of pleasures, then the principles chosen would apply, as far as the argument would have shown, only to persons whose freedom was restricted to choices compatible with altruism or hedonism. As the argument now runs, the principles of justice cover all persons with rational plans of life, whatever their content, and these principles represent the appropriate restrictions on freedom. Thus it is possible to say that the constraints on conceptions of the good are the result of an interpretation of the contractual situation that puts no prior limitations on what men may desire. There are a variety of reasons, then, for the motivational premise of mutual disinterest. This premise is not only a matter of realism about the circumstances of justice or a way to make the theory manageable. It also connects up with the Kantian idea of autonomy. . . .

The original position may be viewed, then, as a procedural interpretation of Kant's conception of autonomy and the categorical imperative. The principles regulative of the kingdom of ends are those that would be chosen in this position, and the description of this situation enables us to explain the sense in which acting from these principles expresses our nature as free and equal rational persons. No longer are these notions purely transcendent and lacking explicable connections with human conduct, for the procedural conception of the original position allows us to make these ties. . . .

NOTES

1. As the text suggests, I shall regard Locke's *The Second Treatise of Government,* Rousseau's *Social Contract,* and Kant's ethical works beginning with *The Foundations of the Metaphysics of Morals* as definitive of the contract tradition. For all of its greatness, Hobbes's *Leviathan* raises special problems. A general historical survey is provided by J. W. Gough, *The Social Contract,* 2nd edn (Oxford: The Clarendon Press, 1957), and Otto Gierke, *Natural Law and the Theory of Society,* trans. with an introduction by Ernest Barker (Cambridge: Cambridge University Press, 1934). A presentation of the contract view as primarily an ethical theory is to be found in G. R. Grice, *The Grounds of Moral Judgment* (Cambridge: Cambridge University Press, 1967). . . .

2. Kant is clear that the original agreement is hypothetical. See *The Metaphysics of Morals,* pt I (Rechtslehre), especially §§ 47, 52; and pt II of the essay "Concerning the Common Saying: This May Be True in Theory But It Does Not Apply in Practice," in *Kant's Political Writings,* ed. Hans Reiss and trans. by H. B. Nisbet (Cambridge: Cambridge University Press, 1970), pp. 73–87. See Georges Vlachos, *La Pensée politique de Kant* (Paris: Presses Universitaires de France, 1962), pp. 326–35; and J. G. Murphy, *Kant: The Philosophy of Right* (London: Macmillan, 1970), pp. 109–12, 133–6, for a further discussion.

3. For the formulation of this intuitive idea I am indebted to Allan Gibbard.

4. The process of mutual adjustment of principles and considered judgments is not peculiar to moral philosophy. See Nelson Goodman, *Fact, Fiction, and Forecast* (Cambridge, MA: Harvard University Press 1955), pp. 65–8, for parallel remarks concerning the justification of the principles of deductive and inductive inference.

5. An accessible discussion of this and other rules of choice under uncertainty can be found in W. J. Baumol, *Economic Theory and Operations Analysis,* 2nd ed. (Englewood Cliffs, NJ: Prentice-Hall, 1965), ch. 24. Baumol gives a geometric interpretation of these rules, including the diagram used . . . to illustrate the difference principle. See pp. 558–62. See also R. D. Luce and Howard Raiffa, *Games and Decisions* (New York: John Wiley, 1957), ch. XIII, for a fuller account.

6. Here I borrow from William Fellner, *Probability and Profit* (Homewood, IL: Richard D. Irwin, 1965), pp. 140–2, where these features are noted.

7. For this point I am indebted to Charles Fried.

38. THE STRUCTURE OF ETHICS AND MORALS

❦

R. M. HARE

I must start by saying what I think is the object of the enterprise called moral philosophy. It is to find a way of thinking better—that is, more rationally—about moral questions. The first step towards this is: *Understand the questions you are asking*. That might seem obvious; but hardly anybody tries to do it. We have to understand what we mean by expressions like 'I ought'. And to understand the meaning of a word like this involves understanding its logical properties, or in other words what it implies or what saying it commits us to. Then, if we find that we cannot accept what it commits us to, we shall have to give up saying it. And that is what moral argument essentially is. Ethics, the study of moral argument, is thus a branch of logic. This is one of the levels of thinking that are the concern of the moral philosopher. The others are about more substantial questions; but this first one, the logical or, as it is sometimes called, metaethical level is the foundation of the others.

Since the kind of ethics we are doing is a kind of logic, it has to use the methods of logic. But what are these? How do we find out what follows from what, what implies what, or what saying, for example, 'I ought to join the Army' or 'I ought to join the Revolution' commits me to? That is partly a general question about logical method, into which I shall not have room to go at all deeply. I can only declare what side I am on as regards some crucial questions. First, I think it is useful and indeed essential, and I hope it will not be thought pedantic, to distinguish between

Reprinted from "The Structure of Ethics and Morals" by permission of Oxford University Press.

two kinds of questions. I am going to call the first kind *formal* questions, and the second kind *substantial* questions. Formal questions are questions that can be answered solely by appeal to the form—that is, the purely logical properties—of proposed answers to them. That is the sort of question we are concerned with in meta-ethics. In this part of our work we are not allowed to bring in any substantial assumptions.

I will illustrate the distinction by an example which has nothing to do with ethics, because it is a clearer example and does not beg any ethical questions. It comes from a well-known paper by Professors Strawson and Grice (1956) refuting (in my view successfully) a claim made in an even better-known paper by Professor Quine (1951; some of Quine's claims may be all right, but it is pretty clear that Strawson and Grice have refuted this one). Suppose I say 'My three-year-old child understands Russell's Theory of Types'. Everyone will be sure that what I have said is false. But logically it could be true. On the other hand, suppose I say 'My three-year-old child is an adult'. We know that I cannot consistently say this, if we know what the words mean and nothing else; and this is obviously not the case with the first proposition.

This illustrates the distinction between what I am calling formal questions and what I am calling substantial questions. It applies equally to moral questions, which can also be divided into these two kinds. Suppose I say 'There is nothing wrong with flogging people for fun'. People's reasons for disagreeing with me (and I will come later to what these reasons might be) are of a quite different sort from what they would be if I had said 'There is nothing wrong in doing what one ought not to do'. We know that I cannot consistently say the latter if we just know the meanings of the words 'ought' and 'wrong'; whereas I could *consistently* utter the first proposition; we all think it is a dreadful thing to say—only a very wicked person would say it—but in saying it he would not be being *logically* inconsistent.

It is not necessary here to discuss Quine's rejection of the notion of analyticity and of that of synonymy. Strawson and Grice may be right in defending these notions; but even if they are not, the formal claims that I need to make about moral concepts do not have to be stated in terms of them, but only in terms of the notion of logical truth, which Quine in that paper accepts. This is because the moral concepts are formal in an even stricter sense than I have so far claimed. That is, they require for their explanation no material semantic stipulations but only reference to their purely logical properties. The semantic properties of moral words have to do with their particular descriptive meanings only, which are not part of their meaning in the narrow sense and do not affect their logic, though the fact that they have to have some descriptive meaning does affect it.

It will be noticed that the example I have just given of a moral statement which we should all reject on logical grounds, 'There is nothing wrong in doing what we ought not to do', is one whose contradictory ('There is something wrong in doing what we ought not to do') is a logical truth. This is because 'ought' and 'wrong' are interdefinable in terms purely of their logical properties without bringing in their descriptive meanings or semantics, just as are 'all' and 'some' in most systems of quantificational logic.

Next, I must mention a point which will turn out to be of fundamental importance for moral argument. When we are settling questions of the second kind in each case (that is, formal questions) we are not allowed to appeal to any other kind of consideration except those which can be established on the basis of our understanding of the words or concepts used. To take our two

examples: we know that we cannot say 'There is nothing wrong in doing what one ought not to do' because we know what 'wrong' and 'ought' mean; and we know that we cannot say 'My three-year-old child is an adult' because we know what 'child' and 'adult' mean. If, in order to establish that we could not say these things, we had to appeal to any other considerations than these, the questions of whether we could say them would not be formal questions.

In general, we establish theses in logic (or in the kind of logic I am speaking of, which includes the kind we use in ethics) by appeal to our understanding of the uses of words, and nothing else. It is because this logic is the foundation of moral argument that it is so important to understand the words. We must notice that this is a feature of the method I am advocating which distinguishes it quite radically from almost all the ethical theories which we find being proposed at the present time. All these theories appeal at some point or other, and often very frequently, to the substantial moral convictions which their proponents have, and which they hope their readers will share. Although I recognize that many people do not believe in the distinction that I have been making between formal and substantial moral questions, and therefore feel at liberty to use what I would call substantial convictions of theirs to support their theories, I still think that my way of proceeding provides a firmer basis for ethics.

Let me give very briefly my reasons for this confidence. If we are arguing about some moral question (for example about the question 'Ought I to join the Army?' or 'Ought I to join the Revolution?'), one of the things we have to get clear about at the beginning is what the *question* is. That is to say, if we are not to talk at cross purposes, we have to be meaning the same things by the words in which we are asking our question. But if we *are* meaning the same by the words, we have a solid basis of agreement (albeit formal and not substantial agreement) on which we can found our future arguments. If the distinction between formal and substantial holds, then we can have this formal agreement in spite of our substantial disagreement. We can then, as I hope to show, use the formal agreement to test the arguments either of us uses to support his views. We can ask, 'Can he consistently *say* this?', or 'Can he consistently say *this,* if he also says *that*?'.

On the other hand, if people import their own substantial convictions into the very foundations of their moral arguments, they will not be able to argue cogently against anybody who does not share those convictions. This is what the philosophers called *intuitionists* do; and I say with some confidence that my own position is much stronger than theirs, because I do not rely on anything except what everybody has to agree to who is asking the same questions as I am trying to answer. That was why I said that before an argument begins we have to agree on the meaning we attach to our questions. That is *all* I require to start off with.

So much, then, for the question of ethical method. I could say, and in order to plug all the holes would have to say, a great deal more about it, and have done this elsewhere, but now I wish to go on, and say what I hope to establish by this method and how it helps with real substantial questions. At the formal or meta-ethical level I need to establish just two theses; and for the sake of simplicity I shall formulate them as theses about the word 'ought' and its logic. I could have spoken instead about other words, such as 'right' and 'good'. But I prefer to talk about 'ought', because it is the simplest word that we use in our moral questionings.

Here, then, are two logical features of the word 'ought', as it occurs in the questions 'Ought I to join the Army?' and 'Ought I to join the Revolution?'. They are parts of what I commit myself to if I say 'Yes, I ought'. The first is sometimes called the *prescriptivity* of moral judgements. If I say 'Yes, I ought to join the Army', and mean it sincerely, and in its full sense—if I really think I ought—I shall join the Army. Of course there are plenty of less than full-blooded senses of 'ought', or of 'think that I ought', in which I could say 'I think that I ought, but I'm not going to', or 'I ought, but so what?'. But anyone who has been in this situation (as I have—it was one of the things that made me take up philosophy) will know that the whole point of asking 'Ought I?' is to help us decide the question 'Shall I?', and the answer to the first question, when asked in this sense, implies an answer to the second question. If it did not, what would have been the point of asking it?

The second feature of the word 'ought' that I shall be relying on is usually called *universalizability*. When I say that I ought, I commit myself to more than that *I* ought. Prescriptivity demands that the man who says 'I ought' should himself act accordingly, if the judgement applies to him and if he can so act. Universalizability means that, by saying 'I ought', he commits himself to agreeing that *anybody* ought who is in just those circumstances. If I say 'I ought, but there is someone else in exactly the same circumstances, doing it to someone who is just like the person I should be doing it to, but he ought not to do it', then logical eyebrows will be raised; it is *logically inconsistent* to say, of two exactly similar people in exactly similar situations, that the first ought to do something and the second ought not. I must explain that the similarity of the situations extends to the personal characteristics, and in particular to the likes and dislikes, of the people in them. If, for example, the person I was flogging actually liked being flogged (some people do) that would mean that the situation was not exactly similar to the normal case, and the difference might be relevant.

So, putting together these two features of prescriptivity and universalizability, we see that if I say 'I ought to do it to him', I commit myself to saying, not just that I should do it to him (and accordingly doing it), but that he should do it to me were our roles precisely reversed. That is, as we shall see, how moral argument gets its grip. I must repeat that it is not an essential part of my argument that *all* uses of 'ought' have these features. All I am maintaining now is that we do sometimes, when asking 'Ought I?', use the word in this way. I am addressing myself to those who are asking such questions, as I am sure many people do. If anybody wished to ask *different* questions, he might have to use a different logic. But I am quite sure that we do sometimes find ourselves asking, and disagreeing about, universal prescriptive questions—that is, about what to prescribe universally for all situations of a given kind, no matter who is the agent or the victim. I shall be content if I can show how we can validly argue about such questions, whose logical character is determined by their being *those* questions, i.e. universal prescriptive ones.

I might add that the whole point of having a moral language with these features—a language whose meaning is determined by its logical characteristics alone, and which can therefore be used in discussion by two people who have very different substantial moral convictions, is that then the words will mean the same to both of them, and they will be bound by the same logical rules in their argument. If their different moral convictions had somehow got written into the very meanings of their moral words (as does happen with *some* moral words, and as some philosophers mistakenly think happens with all of them) then they would be at cross purposes from the start; their moral argument would very quickly break down, and they would just have to fight it out. It is because of this formal character of my theory about the moral words that I think it more helpful than the theories of other philosophers who try to write their own moral convictions into the meanings of the words or the rules of argument. This is especially true when we come to deal with the kinds of moral problems about which people have radically different convictions. If the convictions have infected the words, they will not be able to communicate rationally with one another. That is indeed what we see happening all over the world (think of South Africa, for example, where I

gave an earlier version of this paper). In this situation the theories I am criticizing are of no help at all, because people will appeal to their opposing convictions, and serious, fruitful argument cannot even begin.

The next thing that I have to make clear is the place in moral argument of appeal to *facts*. If I ask 'Ought I to join the Army?', the first thing, as I said, is to be clear about what I mean by 'ought'. But that is not enough. I have to be clear what I am asking; but another important part of this is what the words 'join the Army' imply. In other words, what should I be doing if I joined the Army? There are some philosophers who use the word 'consequentialist' as a term of abuse for their opponents. Now I readily agree that there may be a sense in which we ought to do what is right and damn the consequences. But these philosophers are really very confused if they think that in deciding what we ought to do we can ignore what we should be doing if we did one or other of the things we could do. If someone thinks he ought not to join the Army, or that it would be wrong to do it, his reason (what in his view makes it wrong), must have something to do with what he would be doing if he joined the Army. That is the act or series of acts about whose morality we are troubled. Joining the Army means, in his circumstances (if that is the sort of regime he lives in, as in South Africa), committing himself to shooting people in the streets if the Government tells him to. That is what becoming a soldier involves in his present situation. Anyone who thinks that in this sense consequences are irrelevant to moral decisions cannot have understood what morality is about: it is about actions; that is, about what we do; and that is, what we are bringing about—the difference we are making to the course of events. These are the facts we have to know.

There are some ethical theories, known generally as *naturalistic* theories, which make facts relevant to moral decisions in a very direct way. They do it by saying that what moral words *mean* is something factual. To give a very crude example: if 'wrong' *meant* 'such as would endanger the State', then obviously it would be wrong to do anything that would endanger the State, and we ought not to do it. The trouble with such theories is the same, in effect, as with those I mentioned earlier. It makes a theory useless for the purposes of moral argument if its author writes his own moral convictions into the theory itself; and *one* of the ways of doing this is to write them into the meanings of the moral words. This makes communication and rational argument between people of different moral convictions impossible. If 'wrong' did mean what has just been suggested, somebody who thought that there were some things more important morally than the preservation of the State could not use the word to argue with a supporter of the regime. One of them would just have to join the Army and the other the Revolution; they would just have to fight.

I am not saying what naturalists say, because the account I have given of the meaning of 'ought' in terms of prescriptivity and universalizability does *not* incorporate any substantial moral convictions; it is *neutral* between the two participants in such a dispute, and both of them can therefore use the words, if I am right, in discussing their disagreement. I therefore have to give, and have already partly given, a different account of how facts are relevant to moral decisions. This goes via an account of rationality itself—of the notion of a reason.

It may be helpful if we start with something simpler than moral judgements: with plain imperatives. These two sorts of speech acts must not be confused, because there are important differences; but imperatives like 'Join the Army' do illustrate in a much simpler way the point I am trying to explain. They are the simplest kind of prescriptions (moral judgements are a much more complex kind because of universalizability). To take an even simpler example: suppose I say 'Give me tea' and not 'Give me coffee'. I say this because of *something about* drinking tea or drinking coffee just then. That is my reason for

saying it. If drinking tea were of a different character, I might not have said it. I want, or choose, to drink tea not coffee because I believe that that is what drinking tea would be like, i.e. because of a (supposed) fact about it. I hope that, if it is clear that, even in the case of simple imperatives like this, facts can be reasons for uttering them, it will be equally clear that moral judgements too can be uttered for reasons, even though they are not *themselves* (or not just) statements of fact, but are prescriptive. It would be irrational to ask for tea in complete disregard of what, in fact, it would be like to drink tea. Note that what I have just said in no way depends on universalizability; I have deliberately taken the case of plain simple imperatives which are *not* universalizable.

Now I wish to introduce another move, which does not depend on universalizability either, and indeed is independent of everything I have said so far. It too is a logical move, which depends on the meanings of words. It concerns the relation between *knowing* what it is to experience something, and experiencing it. The relevance of this to what I have been saying so far is that, if we are to know the facts about what we should be doing if we did something, one of the things we have to know is what we, or others, would experience if we did it. For example, if we are thinking of flogging somebody for fun, it is important that what we should be doing if we flogged him would be giving him *that* extremely unpleasant experience. If he did not mind it, or even liked it, our act would be different in a morally relevant respect. So it is important to consider what are the conditions for being said really to know what an experience (our own or somebody else's) which would be the result of our proposed act would be like.

Suppose that the experience in question is (as in this case) *suffering* of some kind. I wish to claim that we cannot suffer without knowing that we are suffering, nor know that we are suffering without suffering. The relation between having experiences and knowing that we are having them was noticed already by Aristotle. There are two distinct reasons for the last half of the thesis I have just put forward. The first is that we cannot know *anything* without its being the case (that is the sort of word that 'know' is). The second reason is a particular one, and more important for our argument: if we did not have the experience of suffering, there would be nothing to know, and no means of knowing it. The knowledge that we are having the experience of suffering is *direct* knowledge, not any kind of knowledge by inference, and so cannot exist without the object of knowledge (that is, the suffering) being present in our experience. That, indeed, is why it is so difficult to know what the sufferings of other people are like. As we shall see, imagination has to fill, in an inadequate way, the place of experience.

Next, we cannot be suffering without having the preference, *pro tanto,* so far as that goes, that we should not be. If we did not prefer, other things being equal, that it should stop, it is not suffering. The preference that it should stop is what would be expressed, if it were expressed in language, by means of a prescription that it should stop. So, putting all this together, if we are suffering, and therefore know that we are, we are bound to assent to the prescription that, other things being equal, it should stop. We must want it to stop, or it is not suffering.

So much for our own present sufferings. We have now to consider what is implied by the knowledge that we *shall,* or *would* under certain conditions, be suffering, or that *somebody else* is suffering. Let us take the last-mentioned case first. What am I committed to if I truly claim that I know how somebody else is suffering, or what it is like for him to suffer like that? The touchstone for this is, it seems to me, the question 'What are my preferences (or in other words, to what prescriptions do I assent) regarding a situation in which *I* was forthwith to be put into *his* exact situation, suffering just like that?' If he is suffering like that, he knows that he is, and has the preference that it should stop (a pref-

erence of a determinate strength, depending on how severe the suffering is). He thus assents, with a determinate strength of assent, to the prescription that it should stop. This preference and this assent are part of his situation, and therefore part of what I have to imagine myself experiencing, were I to be transferred forthwith into it.

I asked just now, 'What am I committed to if I truly claim that I know how he is suffering?' My thesis is going to be that I am committed to having myself a preference that, if I were myself to be transferred forthwith into his situation with his preferences, the suffering should stop; and the strength of this preference that I am committed to having is the same as the strength of his preference.

I said that that was going to be my thesis. But I have not yet argued for it, and the argument for it will be, I am sure, controversial. The move I am going to make is this: whether I am really thinking of the person who would be put forthwith into that situation as *myself* depends on whether I associate myself with, or take to myself, the preferences which that person (i.e. I myself) would have. Of course, as before, we have to add 'other things being equal'; there may well be other things which I prefer so strongly that they outweigh my preference that that person's preference (the person who I imagine myself being) should be satisfied. But *other things being equal* I have to be preferring that it be satisfied, with the same strength of preference as I should have were I in that situation with those preferences. If I am not, then either I do not really know what it is like to be in that situation with those preferences (I am not really fully representing it to myself), or I am not really thinking of the person who would be in that situation as myself.

Let me give an example to illustrate all this. Suppose that somebody has been tied up and a tyre put round his neck, and the tyre ignited with petrol. He is suffering to a certain extreme degree, and therefore knows that he is suffering. What is it for *me* to know what it is like for him to suffer like that? Or, to put it in terms of preferences: he prefers very much that he should stop being burnt in that way; what it is for me to know what it is like to have a preference like that for that outcome, or of that strength (to be saying 'Oh, stop! Stop!' with that degree of anguish)? And suppose then that I claim to know just what it is like for him to have such a preference and to be suffering like that; and then suppose that somebody offers to do the same to me without further delay, and I say 'I don't mind; it's all the same to me'. That would surely show that I do not know what it is like for him. This presumes that if I had it done to me, I should have the same experiences and the same preferences as the person to whom it is being done. I think that the same could be shown in less dramatic examples, and that, when we have made due allowance for other things not being equal (that is, for competing preferences), I could show convincingly that the thesis stands up; but I am not going to go on defending it now, because I want to draw conclusions from it for my main argument.

Let me first sum up the theses that I have advanced so far. We have the prescriptivity and the universalizability of moral judgements, which, I claim, can be established by arguments based on the meanings of words—logical arguments. Then we have the necessity, if we are to assent rationally to prescriptions, including prescriptions expressed with 'ought', of correct factual information. Lastly we have the thesis that we are *not* in possession of correct factual information about someone else's suffering, or in general about his preferences, unless we ourselves have preferences that, were *we* in his situation with his preferences, those preferences should be satisfied. Note, again, that although I claimed to be able to establish universalizability, I have not yet used it in the argument. That is what I am going to do now, in conjunction with the other theses.

Let us suppose that it is I who am causing the victim to suffer. He very much wants me to untie

him. That is to say, he assents with a certain very high strength of assent to the prescription that I should untie him. Already, without bringing in universalizability, we can say, on the strength of our previous theses, that I, if I know what it is like, for him, to be in that state (and if I do not know that, my moral judgement is faulted for lack of information)—I must myself have a preference that if I were in that state they should untie me. That is, I must be prescribing that they should, in those hypothetical circumstances, untie me. Now suppose that I ask myself what *universal* prescription I am prepared to assent to with regard to my present conduct which is causing him to suffer; that is, what I am prepared to say that I *ought* now to do to him. The 'ought' here expresses a universal prescription, so that, if I say 'I ought not to untie him', I am committed to the prescription that they should not untie me in similar circumstances.

I can of course say that I am not prepared to assent to *any* universal prescription. That is the position of the person whom I have elsewhere called the *amoralist,* and indicated how I would deal with him. But suppose I am not an amoralist, and am therefore prepared to assent to some universal prescription for people in precisely the present situation. The question is what this is going to be. If I universalize the prescription to go on making him suffer, then this entails prescribing that, if anybody were making me suffer in a precisely analogous situation, he should carry on doing it. But this runs counter to a prescription which, as we have seen, I already must be assenting to if I know what it is like to be in the situation of my victim: the prescription that if I were in that situation they should *not* carry on doing it, but should untie me. Thus I am in the predicament that Kant called a contradiction in the will.

How is the contradiction to be resolved? The answer becomes obvious if we notice that what is happening (what has to happen if I am trying to universalize my prescriptions) is that I am being constrained to treat other people's preferences as if they were my own. This is just another way of putting the requirement to universalize my prescriptions. But if in this situation the two preferences which have come into contradiction were both my own, what I would do would be to let the stronger of them override the weaker. And that is what I am constrained to do in the present case, where, as a result of the attempt to universalize, I have landed myself with two mutually contradictory preferences or prescriptions as to what should be done to me in the hypothetical situation in which I was in the other person's shoes. So the answer is that if my victim's preference that I should desist from tormenting him is stronger than my own preference that I should not desist (as it certainly will be), I should desist.

We have thus, in this simple bilateral case involving only two people, arrived at what is essentially a utilitarian answer to our moral problem; and we have arrived at it by a Kantian route. People talk as if Kant and the utilitarians were at opposite poles in moral philosophy; but this just shows how little they have understood either the utilitarians or Kant. We are led to give weight to the preferences of all the affected parties (in this case, two) in proportion to their strengths, and to say that we ought to act on the stronger. I could, if there were room, show how, by generalizing this argument to cover multilateral situations in which the preferences of many parties are affected, we should also adopt utilitarian answers, namely that we ought in each case so to act as to maximize the satisfactions of the preferences of all affected parties, treated impartially. But I am not going to attempt this now; I have done it elsewhere, and I have to go on to explain how this way of thinking is going to work out in the course of our actual moral lives, when we have to decide practical issues. I shall be able to do this only in very general terms.

It might be thought that what we have arrived at is a kind of act-utilitarianism; and this is in fact true. But it is not the kind of act-utilitarianism to which all beginner philosophy students are taught the standard objections. I will now try to explain how the kind of act-utilitarianism that I am advocating differs from the crude kind. The difference is not, strictly speaking, a theoretical one. It derives rather from a consideration of our actual human predicament when we are doing our moral thinking. To see this, let us think what it would be like if we had no human limitations. Suppose, that is to say, that we had infinite knowledge and clarity of thought and no partiality to self or other human weaknesses. Elsewhere I have called a being who has these superhuman powers the *archangel*. He really could think in an act-utilitarian way. But it would often be disastrous if we humans tried to do it, for obvious reasons. First of all, we lack the necessary information nearly always; in particular, we are very bad at putting ourselves in other people's shoes and imagining what it is like to be them. Secondly, we lack the time for acquiring and thinking about this information; and then we lack the ability to think clearly. These three handicaps make it all too easy for us to pretend to ourselves that some act is likely to be for the best (to satisfy preferences maximally and impartially) when in fact what commends it to us is our own self-interest. One sees this kind of special pleading going on all the time.

Suppose that, conscious of these handicaps, we went to an archangel for advice, not about a particular situation (for we shall not always have access to him, and therefore want him to give us advice for the future) but about how in general to minimize their bad effects. People think that they can appeal to God in this way; though what they say he tells them varies from one person to another. But let us suppose that we *had* immediate access to some supreme or at least superior being who could advise us. He would point out that the best we can do is on each occasion to make as great as possible the expectation of preference-satisfaction resulting from our actions. I am sure that this is what God would do, because he loves his creatures, and he wants us to do the best we can for them.

The expectation of preference-satisfaction (of

387 THE STRUCTURE OF ETHICS AND MORALS

utility, for short) is the sum of the products of the utility and the probability of the outcome for all the alternative possible outcomes of the action. This is what I mean by 'Acting for the best'. The question is, How shall we achieve this? Given our limitations, we shall not achieve it by doing a utilitarian calculation or a cost-benefit analysis on each occasion. The archangel will tell us, rather, to cultivate in ourselves a set of dispositions or principles, together with the attitudes or feelings or, if anybody wishes to use the word, intuitions that go with them: a set such that the cultivation of them is most likely on the whole to lead to the maximization of preference-satisfaction. The archangel, who can get the right answer on every single occasion, can do better than us; but that is the best that we can do.

It will be noticed that this, although in a sense it is a form of rule-utilitarianism, is a form which is not incompatible with act-utilitarianism. For what the archangel is advising us to do is to perform certain acts, namely acts of cultivating dispositions; and his reason for advising this is that these acts are the most likely to be for the best—which is exactly what an act-utilitarian would advise. However, this version of utilitarianism secures the advantages which older forms of rule-utilitarianism claimed, in particular the advantage of making our proposed system immune to objections based on the counter-intuitiveness of its consequences. For the intuitions which the act-utilitarian archangel will bid us cultivate are the *same* intuitions as those to which the objectors are appealing.

The effect of this move is to divide moral thinking into two levels (in addition to the third or meta-ethical level which is concerned, not with substantial moral thinking, but with the form of moral thinking (that is, with the logic of the moral language). I call these two levels the *intuitive* level and the *critical* level. If we follow the archangel's advice, we shall do nearly all our moral thinking at the intuitive level; in fact, for nearly all the time, we shall behave just as the intuitionists say we do and should. The difference, however, will be that because, as everyone realizes, the good dispositions and principles and attitudes that we rightly cultivate are to some degree general and simple and unspecific (if they were not, they would be unmanageable and unhelpful and unteachable), they will come into conflict in particular hard cases; and then, unlike intuitionists, we shall know what we have to try to do, difficult and dangerous as it is. Since we do not in fact have archangels on call, we have to do the best we can to think critically like archangels on those problematic occasions. But when our intuitions give us clear guidance, we shall follow them—at least that is what our utilitarian archangel will advise us during our once-for-all counselling session with him.

But, it will be said, this presumes that our intuitions are the right ones. Indeed it does. This gives us another reason for using critical thinking. It is dangerous to use it in crises; but when they are over, or in anticipation of them, it may be essential. Otherwise how shall we have any confidence that the intuitions we happen to have grown up with are the best ones? Intuitions about how Whites should treat Blacks, for example, or men women? So what the wise archangel will advise, and what wise human educators and self-educators will practise, will be a judicious admixture of intuitive and critical thinking, each employed on appropriate occasions. And this is what wise people do already.

39. THE RADICAL FUTURE OF HARE'S MORAL THEORY

LYNNE S. ARNAULT

For many philosophers in the American-British analytic tradition, radical feminist moral theory seems way out in left field. Feminist repudiation of essentialism and the autonomous self, its rejection of the "standpoint of exchange" and mind-centered definitions of moral reasoning, its emphasis on the influence of gender and gender politics in the construction of knowledge, including moral theory—all suggest to many analytic philosophers a radically different and problematic meta-ethical orientation. In this essay, I hope to gain support for radical feminist moral theory by taking a classic theory of moral reasoning—R. M. Hare's universal prescriptivism—and exposing its radical future.[1] I will attempt to show that in order to meet its own criteria of universalizability and prescriptivity, this formalist-dispositional account of morals must abandon the liberal conception of the self and its accompanying, monological model of moral deliberation. Maintaining the internal coherence of Hare's ideal of universal prescriptivism, I will argue, requires a trip to left field, endorsing a more radicalized conception of autonomy and allowing for the possibility that social divisions may be so embedded in the structure of things as to infect even the means of discourse.

I call Hare's theory of universal prescriptivism a "classic" moral theory for two reasons.

First, American-British analytic philosophers generally regard it as a major contribution to the development of "the novel issues and methods introduced into ethical theory in the twentieth century" (Kerner 1966:2). With the publication of G. E. Moore's *Principia Ethica* in 1903, American-British moral philosophy took a linguistic turn, involving itself with the logical analysis of moral terms, judgments, and modes of reasoning. Because Hare's theory that "the language of morals is one sort of prescriptive language" (Hare 1952:I) is usually included in analytic philosophy's canon of great theories, I have applied the honorific term "classic" to it.

Second, I call Hare's theory of universal prescriptivism a "classic" because I believe that if we put aside the particularities of the relatively new "linguistic turn" and the importance of Hare's theory within it, we find that the deep assumptions underlying Hare's theory are not really novel at all but have dominated western philosophy since the seventeenth century. Hare's moral theory embodies commitments to universalism, impersonality, detachment, dispassion, neutrality, and the social transcendency of language. It is representative of a tradition with certain enduring, dominating beliefs: that morality consists in respect for rules; that moral decision making is a matter of using the proper moral calculus; and that meta-ethics consists in identifying precisely the correct method for justifying moral judgments. These assumptions, I would argue, have systematically privileged the point of view of a particular group of people (white, middle-class males of European descent) and have reinforced dualistic ideologies of masculinity and femininity. By attempting to decanter some of Hare's fundamental theoretical assumptions and thereby to expose the radical future of a classic moral theory, I hope to encourage the reclamation of modalities too long suppressed.

To uncover the radical future of Hare's universal prescriptivism, we must first understand why Hare holds that universalizability and prescriptivity are the sine qua non of moral discourse and why he proposes that utilitarianism, which he views as a logical extension of universal prescriptivism, provides the proper method for resolving interpersonal moral disagreements. Hare contends that the logical properties of universalizability and prescriptivity[2] generate the rules that govern moral thinking at the critical level. By "universalizability" Hare means that "if we make different moral judgements about situations which we admit to be identical in their universal descriptive properties, we contradict ourselves" (Hare 1981:21). As he puts it more informally elsewhere, universalizability means that "if I now say that I ought to do a certain thing to a certain person, I am committed to the view that the very same thing ought to be done to me, were I in exactly his situation, including the same personal characteristics and in particular the same motivational states" (Hare 1981:108).

Hare insists that prescriptions must be universalizable to qualify as moral because he conceives of moral judgments as necessarily requiring "reasons" and sees this requirement as equivalent to requiring universalizability. One reason Hare insists that moral judgments have a reason-requiring function is that he believes they are prescriptive or action-guiding speech-acts, and he recognizes that a moral "prescriber" is able to influence conduct in a guiding rather than goading or coercive way only if "the answering of moral questions is . . . a rational activity" (Hare 1963:2).

By claiming that evaluative expressions are prescriptive, Hare wants to establish that normative judgments are necessarily connected with action; the common function of words like "ought" and "good," he believes, is to guide conduct, commend behavior. On Hare's view, then, accepting a moral judgment is necessarily connected with doing, or at least attempting to do, what the judgment enjoins. It is important, therefore, that he characterize moral judgments as necessarily requiring reasons because, although he wants to maintain that moral judgments involve assent to an imperative, he nevertheless wants to deny that these utterances are merely attempts at persuasion or goading; moral judgments, for Hare, involve a willingness to prescribe courses of action to others as rational self-guiding agents (Hare 1952:sec.1.7).

I will argue that Hare's theory of moral reasoning does not really secure the autonomy of the persons prescribed to, especially if they are members of a subordinated group. But before moving on to this critique, it is important to note that Hare gives a dispositional account of the criteria for right and wrong. The source of moral criteria, he believes, resides in the overriding dispositions or inclinations of the individual moral deliberator. What are to count as criteria for right conduct, he feels, ultimately boil down to a matter of individual choice. *Any* set of prescriptions subjected to the requirements of universalizability and prescriptivity constitutes a morality in good logical standing: as long as the moral deliberator has assumed the burden of universalizability, it is open to him or her to decide without logical error that a given set of facts does or does not constitute sufficient grounds for action (Hare 1963:195–196). Thus, for example, as long as a Nazi has assumed the burden of universalizability, he may decide without logical error that a person's being Jewish constitutes sufficient grounds for extermination. This follows from the fact that, on Hare's account, every moral judgment involves an implicit autonomous legislation of criteria.

Hare recognizes, of course, that people's inclinations may differ and thereby occasion moral dispute. People disagree about what ought to be done "because their different inclinations make one reject some singular prescription which the other can accept" (Hare 1963:97). According to Hare, moral disagreement can be resolved by rational deliberation in the majority of cases because "people's inclinations about most of the important matters in life tend to be the same (very few people, for example, like being starved or run over by motor-cars)" (Hare 1963:97). In particular, most human beings share the inclination or desire to have their own interests satisfied; as a result, they will not universalize prescriptions that disregard the desires of other people.

With the understanding that most people share the inclination to want their own interests respected, Hare claims that moral disagreements can be resolved by rational deliberation because the rules of moral reasoning, universalizability and prescriptivity, can be "generalized" to include the utilitarian principle "Everyone to count for one, nobody for more than one" (Hare 1963:118):

> For if my action is going to affect the interests of a number of people, and I ask myself what course of action I can prescribe universally for people in just this situation, then what I shall have to do, in order to answer this question, is to put myself imaginatively in the place of the other parties. ... And the considerations that weigh with me in this inquiry can only be, How much (as I imagine myself in the place of each man in turn) do I want to have this, or to avoid that? But when I have been the round of all the affected parties, and come back, in my own person, to make an impartial moral judgment giving equal weight to the interests of all parties, what can I possibly do except advocate that course which will, taken all in all, least frustrate the desires which I have imagined myself having? But this (it is plausible to go on) is to maximize satisfactions. (Hare 1963:123)

According to Hare, then, whenever there is a conflict of inclinations or interests, we must fully represent to ourselves the situation of each other party (Hare 1981:111); we must imagine ourselves in the place of the affected parties, not with our own likes and dislikes but with each of their likes and dislikes (Hare 1963:113). We must then accept only those prescriptions that impartially maximize satisfactions. By saying that our moral judgments must be impartial, Hare means that "whoever is in which role in the situation being judged ... [must not be] treated as relevant" (Hare 1981:211). Thus, according to Hare, whenever there is a moral dispute we must "put ourselves in the shoes of each of the affected persons" (Hare 1981:101), and we must accept only those prescriptions that count equal preferences equally, whatever their content (Hare 1981:145).

Hare argues that this procedure of implementing the ideal of universal prescriptivism is imposed on us by the logical properties of the moral concepts (Hare 1981:91). The steps in the argument from universal prescriptivism to utilitarianism are all based, he contends, on the logic of the concepts involved (Hare 1981:176).

The claim that utilitarian methodology follows from the logical features of moral discourse is not, I will argue, a well-founded claim, but it clearly reveals Hare's commitment to liberal individualism. Consider, for example, one assumption underlying Hare's account of interpersonal moral reasoning: most people will not universalize prescriptions that disregard the interests of other because they want to have their own interests satisfied. This implicitly articulates what Nancy Hartsock calls "the standpoint of exchange": it constitutes people as rational, self-interested, fundamentally isolated individuals who interact with one another when there is a momentary conjuncture of interest (Hare 1985:ch. 2). Despite their interdependence, individuals, as this model conceptualizes them, have no intrinsically fundamental relations with one another; interpersonal interactions are between Person and Other—the latter remaining "someone to whom Person has only instrumental and extrinsic ties and to whom he relates only to gain his own ends" (Hartsock 1985:24).

Hare seems to make allowances for the fact that we may have ties of affection and loyalty toward certain people that bind us less instrumentally to them than to humanity in general (Hare 1981:135–137). For example, Hare recognizes that mothers take an interest in the interests of their newborn children in a way that they do not with other people's children. But we should note that Hare endorses this partiality only because it "can be defended on utilitarian grounds by critical thinking, as having a high acceptance-utility" (Hare 1981:137). As he puts it:

> If mothers had the propensity to care equally for all the children in the world, it is unlikely that children would be as well provided for even as they are. The dilution of the responsibility would weaken it out of existence. . . . And evidently Evolution (if we may personify her) has had the same idea; there are, we are told, a great many of these particular loyalties and affections which are genetically transmitted, and have no doubt favoured the survival of the genes which transmit them (Hare 1981:137).

What is striking about this discussion, among other things, is that Hare ends up articulating the mother-child relationship from the standpoint of exchange. On his view, the "special" tie that binds a mother and her young child is not really so special after all. A mother's interest in the interests of her child turns out, upon critical inspection, to be a contingent feature of their relation: satisfying her child's interest in good care is a way for the mother to ensure that her own interests (in this case, her genes' "preference" for survival) will be satisfied.

It is not surprising, of course, that Hare ends up giving a kind of sociobiological account of the "special" connectedness of mothers and children in the modern nuclear family. A theory that constitutes people as rational, solitary, interest-driven monads whose every interpersonal action is an effort to maximize personal interests is not

especially well suited for representing experiences involving ongoing dependency. Nor, we should note, is it particularly well suited for giving voice to the forms of connectedness and solidarity that members of a subordinated group experience. Thus, in moral deliberation with members of dominant groups, women, people of color, and the poor would be at a disadvantage because they would be hindered from representing their experience, interests, and needs in a nondistorted, nonrepressed way.

Because Hare's theory of moral reasoning instructs us to imagine ourselves in the place of the affected parties, with each of their likes and dislikes, and to count equal preferences equally, it may seem as though everyone's interests—including those of women, people of color, and the poor—are equally well represented in his model of moral deliberation. But the fact that Hare presents "taking the standpoint of others" as a monological process belies that impression.

Hare characterizes "putting oneself in the shoes of others" as a matter of hypothetical role-playing, done singly by the moral deliberator. Getting to know the preferences of the people whom our actions will affect is a process, he suggests, of coming to identify with them: it involves imagining ourselves in the place of the affected parties and of representing to ourselves, by analogy with our own experience, what the experiences of these people would be like for them (Hare 1981:127).[3]

Hare gives what he calls a prescriptivist account of "extended" or "sympathetic identification" (Hare 1981:96f.). Identifying with another person, he claims, involves *acquiring* that person's inclinations, motivations, and preferences:

> If I have full knowledge of the other person's preferences, I shall myself have acquired preferences equal to his regarding what should be done to me were I in his situation; and these are the preferences which are now conflicting with my original prescription. So we have in effect not an interpersonal conflict of preferences or

prescriptions, but an intrapersonal one; both the conflicting preferences are mine. I shall therefore deal with the conflict in exactly the same way as with that between two original preferences of my own. (Hare 1981:110)

Even taken at his own word, that is, given his commitment to the liberal conception of the self and to a mind-centered definition of sympathetic identification, Hare's reduction of interpersonal moral conflict to intrapersonal conflict is a bold move. If I understand him correctly, Hare is claiming that it is possible *in practice* for me to acquire your preferences and dispositions. He admits that there are some "practical difficulties in getting to know the states of mind of other sentient beings, which increase with the remoteness of their experiences from ours," but he recommends that they are "to be overcome by getting as closely acquainted as we can with their circumstances, verbal and other behavior, anatomies, etc., and comparing them with our own"; and he dismisses the practical problem as secondary to the philosophical problem of other minds (Hare 1981:127).

On the grounds that it is possible in practice for me to acquire your preferences and dispositions, Hare claims that I can singly and impartially solve our interpersonal moral conflict by using a moral calculus: if I have gained full knowledge of your preferences, I have acquired your preferences as intensely or moderately as you hold them. The moral conflict, now, is therefore not as much *between us as within me*. The problem of being impartial in effect disappears: I can "impartially" determine how to maximize satisfactions because all that this procedure entails at this point is comparing the strengths of my own preferences.[4]

Because Hare characterizes the process of "putting oneself in the shoes of others" as a monological process, his model of moral deliberation articulates the liberal conception of the self. That is, it constitutes the social identity of the moral agent as being epistemically insignificant; the moral self is a disembodied and disembed-ded entity. We can acquire knowledge of other people's situations by a process of solitary hypothetical role-playing because membership in a particular social group or groups in an "accidental" or contingent feature of social life. Thus, on Hare's view, human beings approach the task of gaining knowledge of other people's situations, not as socially constituted members of historically changing groups, which have epistemologically distinctive vantage points, but as solitary individuals with essentially the same vantage point.

By discounting the effects of a person's social experience upon his or her motivations, interests, needs, and understandings of the world, Hare's monological model of moral deliberation makes no allowances for the possibilities that the forms of discourse may privilege the view point of dominant groups in society and that such forms could themselves become contested in moral deliberation. To be sure, Hare recognizes the difficulty, even the impossibility, of human beings reasoning in a perfectly unbiased manner. He explicitly acknowledges that his model of moral reasoning obligates us to try to think like "ideal observers" or "archangels," that is, like beings with superhuman powers of thought, superhuman knowledge, and no human weaknesses, in particular, no partiality to self, friends, or relations (Hare 1981:44). And he emphasizes the point that archangelic moral thinking is unattainable. But the fact that his model requires us to try to transcend human finitude is evidence of Hare's implicit commitment of viewing human individuals in abstraction from social circumstances. And it is significant, I want to suggest, that, although Hare acknowledges that archangelic thinking is unattainable, he does not recognize the possibility that the epistemological ideal embodied in "the archangel" reflects the experience and point of view of a particular social group, specifically, white male bourgeois property owners of European descent.

For Hare, the archangel's "virtue" consists precisely in his lack of social embeddedness: the ideal observer is ideal because "he" lacks a particular point of view. "His" is a disinterested, disembodied, value-neutral standpoint. In short, "his" is "a view from nowhere"[5]—a standpoint that bears no "social fingerprints." And, of course, if "his" point of view is really socially unsituated, then it is gender-neutral, and we could easily refer to him as "her."

The epistemological mandate embodied in the "ideal observer"—that the standpoint of the moral deliberator be "no-where"—has been criticized by radical feminists as both containing a deep gender bias and being highly implicated in projects of social domination, including projects of gender domination. According to feminist epistemologists,[6] what is problematic about the notion of a nonsituated, disembedded, disinterested standpoint is not simply that there can actually be no ideal observers. True, human individuals cannot be abstracted from their social circumstances, but what is more fundamentally problematic about the ideal observer, they believe, is that it is a masculinist ideal whose deployment structurally hinders members of subordinated groups from participating on a par with members of dominant groups in communicative interactions.

As Sandra Harding points out, for many feminist epistemologists, the gender-specificity of point-of-viewlessness is evidenced by the fact that this criterion of objectivity, with its emphasis on detachment, dispassion, and noninvolvement, relies upon three characteristically male conceptualizations: of *self* "as autonomous, individualistic, self-interested, fundamentally isolated from other people and from nature"; of *community* "as a collection of similarly autonomous, isolated, self-interested individuals having no intrinsically fundamental relations with one another"; and of *nature* as "an autonomous system from which the self is fundamentally separated and which must be dominated to alleviate the threat of the self's being controlled by it" (Harding 1986:171).[7] Underlying the epistemology embodied in the ideal of point-of-view-

lessness, feminists have argued, are the dualisms of mind versus body, reason versus emotion, culture versus nature, fact versus value, knowing versus being, objectivity versus subjectivity; these Cartesian dualisms historically have been regarded as gender-linked and have served, because of gender stratification, to stigmatize women's epistemic agency and to legitimize projects of gender domination.

Because the modalities against which reason has been defined—body, emotions, instincts, subjectivity—have traditionally been associated with the female and because the division of labor in western class societies is gender-based where women take primary responsibility for bodily processes, we should undoubtedly note that because the ideal observer functions in Hare's theory as a (disembodied) embodiment of "pure" reason, it is not easily referred to as a female. More important, however, we should recognize that the Cartesian ideal of point-of-viewlessness embodied in "the ideal observer" or "archangel" puts women and other subordinated people at a disadvantage in moral deliberation. By discounting the effects of people's social identity upon their understandings of the world, including theory of knowledge, Hare's archangel ideal obscures and mystifies the privileged relation that members of dominant groups occupy with respect to the sociocultural means of discourse.

From a radical perspective—that is, from a perspective that denies the autonomy or social transcendency of reason and the language of morals—a critical appreciation of the different levels of moral reflexivity is therefore crucial to moral theory. This brings us to the question of whether there is potential in Hare's theory, considered on its own terms, for a radicalization of its deepest assumptions. Given its monological form, its liberal conception of the self, and its commitment to both "the standpoint of exchange" and the neutrality of the forms of discourse, where, if at all, does the radical future of Hare's moral theory lie?

In what follows, I want to suggest that because Hare's notion of "taking the standpoint of others" is epistemically incoherent and because his argument for a utilitarian mode of reasoning contains a non sequitur—the fallacious inference that universal prescriptivism logically dictates utilitarianism—certain revisions are necessary that yield a more radicalized model of moral reasoning. I will argue that in order to make universalizability a viable criterion of morality and in order to take full account of the multiple ways of implementing the ideal of universal prescriptivism, Hare must abandon the liberal conception of the self and its accompanying, monological model of moral deliberation. These revisions, in turn, redefine the task of meta-ethics and call for a more radicalized, feminist notion of autonomy.

The epistemic incoherency of Hare's concept of "taking the standpoint of the other" is due, I want to argue, to his commitment to a liberal conception of the self. Given his emphasis on universalizability as a logical property of moral language, Hare clearly wants to maintain that adopting the moral point of view requires taking the preferences of others into account. The starting point for reflection and action in Hare's moral theory *seems* to be difference. But, as discussed above, Hare is implicitly committed to viewing the moral agency of human individuals in abstraction from social circumstances and all that belongs to them as embodied, historically situated beings. By bracketing the social experience of individuals, their historical situatedness and connectedness to specific human groups, Hare constitutes selves as being epistemologically and metaphysically prior to their individuating characteristics. This yields the following difficulty: how—if individuals are generalized abstractions—can the motivations, desires, needs, and interests of Person and Other be individuated? By assuming the standpoint of a disembodied, disembedded other means abstracting from the particularities that form an individual's identity, the difference between self and other disappears—and with it, the

coherency of Hare's concept of "taking the standpoint of the other."

Not surprisingly, Hare makes the essentialist statement that "people's inclinations about most of the important matters in life tend to be the same" (Hare 1963:97). But this claim, besides being empirically dubious, does not dissolve the problem of individuation that infects Hare's procedure of universalizability.

As I noted earlier, universalizability construed as a rule of moral reasoning requires that "if I now say that I ought to do a certain thing to a certain person, I am committed to the view that the very same thing ought to be done to me, were I in exactly his situation" (Hare 1981:108). The problem of individuating situations—of knowing that this situation is like or unlike that situation—arises for Hare because, on the one hand, situations do not have prepackaged descriptions or "people-independent" constructions and, on the other hand, Hare discounts the effects of a person's social experience upon his or her definition of a situation. Individuals define what the situation is, and their constructions depend upon their life-history, social experience and social situatedness. Thus, for example, a male manager may define the situation as simple flirtation, but a female secretary may construe it as sexual harassment. Similarly, a while male student may define his school's implementation of an affirmative action program as reverse discrimination, but a black student may construe the situation as the school's way of attempting to live up to egalitarian ideals.

There is interesting evidence in the research of Carol Gilligan that the way people see or understand a moral situation depends upon how they construe self, others, and the relationship between them—whether they assume that self and other are interdependent or whether, like classic liberals, they assume that the self is fundamentally isolated. Gilligan's findings suggest, moreover, that these constructions correlate according to gender. Hare's liberal understanding of the self and its connection with others, for example, may be characteristic of privileged white males. Important to the issue at hand is that the problem of individuation that infects Hare's procedure of universalizability cannot be dissolved by an a priori privileging of what is, according to Gilligan, a characteristically male orientation toward self and others. If one assumes the soundness of Gilligan's empirical findings, most women, and some men,[8] construe the self as fundamentally connected with others; this affects the way they frame or define a moral situation.

Because people may, and often do, dispute the definition of a moral situation, the universalizability requirement that we treat like situations alike can only be viable if the task of defining what constitutes a "like" situation is articulated as involving the viewpoints of moral deliberators who are not solitary, disembodied, point-of-viewless beings but rather who are socially constructed, embodied members of historically changing groups with epistemologically distinctive vantage points. This, in turn, requires characterizing "taking the standpoint of others" as an actual dialogic interaction with concrete others, rather than as a matter of hypothetical role-playing done singly by the moral deliberator. If the social identity of the moral deliberator is viewed as epistemologically significant, a moral theory must eschew a monological characterization of moral reasoning in order to ensure that taking the standpoint of others does not reduce de facto to projecting one's own perspective onto others, to defining others in one's own terms by putting oneself in their place.

I will argue that there is more to endorsing a dialogical model of moral deliberation than stipulating that moral agents sit down and talk to one another: unless one recognizes that the fairness of the conditions under which dialogue takes places is itself subject to dispute and evaluation, one's moral theory does not, I will contend, secure the moral autonomy of all the affected parties, especially members of subordinated groups. Before I turn to this point, how-

ever, I would like to demonstrate that it is necessary for Hare to articulate a dialogical ethic, not only to make universalizability a viable criterion of morality but also to take account of the fact that utilitarianism is not the only way of implementing the ideal of universal prescriptivism. Because the method of universalization, as well as conceptions of the good and definitions of the moral situation, can be the subject of moral disputation, the viability of Hare's moral theory depends, I want to argue, upon his characterizing moral reasoning as a dialogical process.

Because Hare asserts that moral thinking on the critical level consists "in making a choice under the constraints imposed by the logical properties of the moral concepts and by the non-moral facts, and by nothing else" (Hare 1981:40) and because he designates utilitarianism as the proper expedient for resolving moral conflicts, it is crucial to his theory that he demonstrate that a utilitarian mode of reasoning is logically generated by the requirement that we universalize our prescriptions. As the following passage reveals, Hare believes that utilitarianism is imposed on us by the logical properties of moral expressions because "the effect of universalizability is to compel us to find principles which impartially maximize the satisfaction of . . . [people's] preferences" (Hare 1981:226):

> We retain, all of us, the freedom to prefer whatever we prefer, subject to the constraint that we have, *ceteris paribus*, to prefer that, were we in others' exact positions, that should happen which *they* prefer should happen. The requirement of universalizability then demands that we adjust these preferences to accommodate the hypothetical preferences generated by this constraint, as if they were not hypothetical but for actual cases; and thus, each of us, arrive at a universal prescription which represents our total impartial preference (i.e., it is that principle which we prefer, all in all, should be applied in situations like this regardless of what position we occupy). What has happened is that the logical constraints have,

between them, compelled us, if we are to arrive at a moral judgement about the case, to coordinate our individual preferences into a total preference which is impartial between us. The claim is that this impartial preference will be the same for all, and will be utilitarian. (Hare 1981:227)

It is a mistake, I believe, for Hare to infer that accommodating the preferences of others means counting equal preferences equally or, as he puts it, arriving "at a universal prescription which represents our total impartial preference." Because he believes that moral principles are universal in application, Hare must hold—on pain of contradiction—that to advance a moral principle as universal is to prescribe that the principle be consistently followed by all parties. It does not follow from the claim that moral principles are binding on all people, however, that to advance a moral principle is to prescribe a principle that "coordinates our individual preferences into a total preference which is impartial between us" (Hare 1981:227). The mistake consists in overlooking the fact that universalizability is methodologically instantiable in more than one way. Insisting that principles of morality be universal in application does not commit us a priori to what the mode or way of operationalizing universalizability must be. As Kenneth Goodpaster points out, in principle there are no limits to the sorts of methods that a community of moral deliberators might agree upon as a way of operationalizing universalizability:

> One might resolve the conflict so as to maximize the satisfactions of the most gifted. Or the most influential. Or the most virtuous. Or, in the spirit of Rawls' recent theory of justice, the least advantaged. Or again, one might seek to maximize *average* utility, as against *total* utility. And the suggestions could be multiplied indefinitely.... At the very best, it seems to me, Hare might maintain plausibly that utilitarianism provides *one effective way* of implementing the ideal of universal prescriptivism. But it is

more than exaggeration to claim that universal prescriptivism in any way 'dictates' an utilitarian mode of reasoning or that such a mode of reasoning in any sense 'follows from' the logical features of moral expressions. For this suggests at the very least that one who rejects utilitarianism is in some way committed to rejecting universalizability (as a logical property)—and this is as implausible as it is unargued. (Goodpaster 1974:14, 15)

The objection, then, is that utilitarianism is not an expedient that *follows from* the logical properties of prescriptivity and universalizability. It is not, therefore, the only expedient that can be used to make prescriptivity and universalizability, construed as rules for moral reasoning, jointly sufficient in providing a method of moral reasoning. This consequence implies that moral reasoning may not be a single method for resolving conflicts of interest but rather a set of methods, each giving rise to principles of conduct that are prima facie justified (Goodpaster 1974:20–22). Without changing the rules of moral reasoning or ceasing to insist upon a monistic way of implementing the ideal of universal prescriptivism, then, Hare is not really warranted in designating utilitarianism as *the* method for resolving moral disagreements.

Of course, utilitarianism may provide one of the best ways of implementing the ideal of universal prescriptivism, and it might be chosen as the preferred method of universalization. But because universalizability is methodologically instantiable in more than one way, it would seem that in order to secure the autonomy[9] of the persons prescribed to, as well as the autonomy of the prescriber, Hare must add the proviso that if a set of facts is to constitute a reason or justification for moral action, it must be universalizable *and* the universalization must be intersubjectively acceptable. As I mentioned earlier, Hare wants to maintain that although moral judgments involve assent to an imperative, they are not merely attempts at persuasion or goading. Unless he introduces intersubjective constraints on the choice of a method or methods of universalization, however, it is difficult to see how Hare can coherently maintain that moral judgments involve a willingness to prescribe courses of action to others as rational self-guiding agents. The process of moral deliberation would turn out, ultimately, to be an act of solipsistic freedom on the part of individual moral prescribers. Thus, once one recognizes that no single method of universalization is guaranteed (or precluded) a priori by the requirement that moral principles be universalizable, in order to secure the autonomy of all affected parties, one must construe the process of choosing a method or methods of universalization as an actual dialogue in which the involved parties communicate with one another.

I would add, furthermore, that once one recognizes the different levels on which moral disputation may take place and the effects of a person's social experience upon his or her motivations, interests, needs, and understandings of the world, one must go deeper into "left field" and radicalize one's conceptions of both autonomy and meta-ethics. In the interests of showing that maintaining the internal coherence of Hare's theory of universal prescriptivism requires radicalizing some of its deep assumptions, I have followed Hare in privileging universalizability and prescriptivity as the rules of moral reasoning and in defining meta-ethics as the attempt "to give an account of the logical properties of . . . [moral language], and thus of the canons of rational thinking about moral questions" (Hare 1981:4). In the following discussion, I want to point out that the assumption that the forms of discourse are socially neutral underlies Hare's understanding of meta-ethics and the derivation of the rules of moral reasoning. This assumption, I will argue, is not tenable once we abandon the liberal conception of the self and a monological model of moral deliberation.

Hare maintains that when we operate on the meta-ethical level—that is, when we discuss the meanings of moral words and the logic of moral reasoning—we are not concerned with moral questions of substance (Hare 1981:26). Thus, according to Hare, because universalizability and prescriptivity are established as rules of moral reasoning by philosophical logic, they cannot be the subject matter of moral reasoning and dispute. Hare's theory, therefore, makes no allowances for the possibility that the meanings of moral expressions may themselves be entangled in a web of power relationships. He assumes the social neutrality of the means of discourse— in this particular case, the neutrality of the kinds of linguistic intuitions appealed to by contemporary empirical linguists and philosophical logicians in the Anglo-American world (Hare 1981:11).

This assumption of neutrality is tenable, I would argue, only if we conceptualize the knowing subject as an individualistic, isolated, disembedded entity. If we discount the influence of social factors and social politics in the construction of the knowing subject, then we need not make allowances for the possibilities that there may be biases in the forms of discourse and that these forms could themselves become the subject matter of moral reasoning and dispute. By "biases in the forms of discourse" I mean, for example, that in a society that values dispassionate, abstract argumentation and principled reasoning, those who argue in an emotional, vibrant, physically expressive way or who make appeals from the heart and personal experience are easily discredited and readily excluded from defining the terms of the debate. What I am contending here is that once we abandon the liberal conception of the self—as I have argued Hare must do in order to establish the viability in his model of moral reasoning—we must recognize the possibility that social divisions may infect even the means of discourse and, therefore, may privilege the point of view of the dominant groups within society.

The fact that members of subordinated groups may be disadvantaged in giving voice to their experience, interests, and needs has far-reaching ramifications for moral theory. It means, first, that genuine dialogical interaction does not happen by verbal fiat ("Can we talk?"). Unless the very conditions and constraints that govern dialogical interactions are themselves subject to on-going thematization, critique, and change and until members of subordinated groups are able to represent their experience, interests, and needs in a nondistorted, nonrepressed way, one has, at least from the perspective of the subordinated, not a dialogical determination of the right but a heteronomic[10] or "other-imposed" determination.

Recognizing the possibility that the dominant groups within society may enjoy a privileged relation to the means of discourse means recognizing, then, that for genuine dialogical interaction to occur, the central discursive institutions of society must be capable of giving voice to many different kinds of people. This, in turn, means recognizing that, *pace* Hare, moral autonomy is not the private, inner capacity of individuals to form and express their own opinions about moral questions (Hare 1963:2). Having moral autonomy, rather, is being a member of a group that has sufficient collective control over the sociocultural forms of discourse that one is able to express one's point of view in a nondistorted, nonrepressed way without having it marginalized or discounted.[11]

A more radicalized conception of moral autonomy is called for, then, once we allow for the possibility that social divisions may permeate the means of discourse. We are also required to recognize, I would argue, that meta-ethics is partly social theory. If one major objective of meta-ethics is "to formulate precisely the correct method for justifying normative statements or opinions, and to show that this method is the correct method" (Brandt 1959:8), and if, as I have suggested, the forms of discourse are not socially neutral, then the task of the meta-ethician must include articulating the social conditions and constraints necessary to enable members of subordinated groups to represent their interests and interpretations in a nondistorted, nonmarginalized way. And because meta-ethicians are as socially situated as the rest of us, *their* theoretical activity must also be subject to dialogical constraints, especially given the field's domination by white, middle-class males of European descent. Hence, moral theory involves *critical* social theory, and there cannot be any closure of moral reflexivity. No aspect of moral reasoning should be privileged or shielded from critical scrutiny—whether it be the conditions that ought to govern dialogical interchanges, Hare's rules of moral reasoning, which are arguably androcentric,[12] or the very objectives of meta-ethics.[13]

Recognizing the possibility that there may be biases in the forms of discourse, then, entails acknowledging how radical analytic moral philosophy must become. This essay, obviously, has provided only a limited defense of Hare's moral theory—a defense of its radical future. It is a defense most liberals could do without because it calls for abandoning cherished assumptions. But from a feminist perspective, relinquishing assumptions that are implicated in projects of gender, race, and class domination is de rigueur for anyone claiming commitment to emancipatory goals. In fact, if my argument in this paper is sound, relinquishing assumptions that systematically privilege the point of view of a particular group of people is an essential aspect of moral thinking.

With the recognition that moral theory involves critical social theory and an absence of reflexive closure comes the possibility, I would point out, of reclaiming that which is seen in classic liberal moral theory as hindrances to moral knowing, namely, passion and emotion, subjectivity, the self's contingent existence, partiality, and special connectedness to particular others—all those modalities traditionally associated with "the feminine." In the process of dialogical critical reflection, one *discovers* that our disdaining attitudes toward these modalities are socially produced, not reflections of something "real" and universal about the nature of moral knowing.

In this essay I have tried to encourage the reclamation of modalities historically conceptualized as distinctively "feminine" by deconstructing some fundamental theoretical assumptions of classic liberal moral theory. This approach has the virtue, I hope, of escaping a dualistic confrontation between modalities traditionally conceptualized as "masculine" and modalities traditionally conceptualized as "feminine"—something of utmost importance to feminists because ultimately what most needs reconstruction are not particular qualities and values but the structuring of reality in terms of hierarchial binary oppositions. Besides possessing theoretical value, this deconstructive approach also has practical strategic value: a paradigm shift is more likely effected, or at least assisted, not by trying to make one's opponents "see the light,"[14] but—as Thomas Kuhn has argued—by exposing the problems generated internally by the old paradigm and by exploiting the sense its adherents may have that something has gone wrong with the old paradigm.[15]

NOTES

I would like to thank Susan Bordo for her invaluable comments and suggestions and for her supportive friendship and constant encouragement.

1. This expression is borrowed from the title of Zillah Eisenstein's book, *The Radical Future of Liberal Feminism* (New York: Longman, 1981).
2. Hare regards "overridingness" as another logical property of moral expressions, but I do not include discussion of it because it is not germane to my purposes.
3. Hare's characterization of "identifying with others" or "putting oneself in the shoes of others" as involving a hypothetical thought process reveals his deep commitment to a mind-centered approach to moral reasoning. For a feminist critique of this rationalist bias, see Alison Jaggar's essay in this volume.
4. If empathetic connection were not conceptualized simply as a cognitive process and if the relationship between self and others were construed as fundamentally interdependent, not instrumental and extrinsic, I could imagine cases in which Hare's assumption that it is possible for a person to acquire another person's preferences and desires would not seem so empirically implausible. Mother-child relationships in the modern nuclear family come to mind. But Hare's commitment to a liberal conception of the self precludes this construction (see below.)
5. This expression is borrowed from the title of Thomas Nagel's book, *A View From Nowhere* (New York: Oxford University Press, 1986).
6. See, for example, Bordo 1987; Fee 1983; Harding 1986; Hartsock 1983, 1985; and Smith 1974, 1977, 1979.
7. To explain why objectivity as detachment and noninvolvement is the epistemological stance to which men are predisposed some feminists make recourse to feminist revisions of "object-relations" theory. See, for example, Bordo 1987; Chodorow 1978; Flax 1983; Hartsock 1983, 1985; and Keller 1984. Less psychoanalytically oriented feminists account for the gender specificity of the Cartesian ideal in terms of a post-Marxist theory of labor and its effects upon mental life. See, for example, Rose 1983 and Smith 1974, 1977, 1979.
8. Although Gilligan does not elaborate a theory of gender difference in her book, *A Different Voice,* and although the correlations she draws between gender and epistemological constructions of the self, others, and relationships are historically and ethnocentrically circumscribed, her work does not rest, I would contend, upon essentialist notions of male and female. We can explain the gender correlations she discovers in terms of the effects that particular historical and social factors have had upon mental life.
9. In his work Hare is implicitly committed to a liberal conception of moral autonomy—as the private, inner capacity of individuals to form and express preferences about moral issues. Although I argue in a later section that Hare needs

to radicalize his conception of autonomy, my argument here does not depend upon any particular definition of moral autonomy.

10. This term is borrowed from Kenneth Goodpaster's "Morality and Dialogue" (1975).

11. This understanding of autonomy construes it not so much as an entitlement or something simply given but as an ideal or goal that must be achieved politically through successful coalition-building and a refusal to suppress difference in the interests of forging a collective understanding of the world.

12. With its emphasis upon the division of self and other, impersonality, and the logic of reciprocity, the universalizability criterion embodies a calculative approach to moral decision making that may be characteristic of privileged white males (see Gilligan 1982).

13. The ideas that morality consists in respect for rules, that solving moral problems is a matter of using the proper moral calculus, and that meta-ethics thus consists in identifying precisely the correct method for justifying moral judgments may suppress differences in social life and therefore warrant critical dialogical evaluation.

14. See Donna Wilshire's essay in this volume for a discussion of some of the gender implications of this metaphor.

15. Thomas Kuhn, *The Structure of Scientific Revolutions,* 2d ed. (Chicago: University of Chicago Press, 1970).

REFERENCES

Bordo, Susan R. 1987. *The Flight to Objectivity: Essays on Cartesianism and Culture.* Albany: SUNY Press.

Brandt, Richard B. 1959. *Ethical Theory: The Problems of Normative and Critical Ethics.* Englewood Cliffs, N.J.: Prentice-Hall.

Chodorow, Nancy. 1978. *The Reproduction of Mothering.* Berkeley: University of California Press.

Fee, Elizabeth. 1983. "Women's Nature and Scientific Objectivity." In *Women's Nature: Rationalizations of Inequality,* ed. M. Lowe and R. Hubbard. New York: Pergamon Press.

Flax, Jane. 1983. "Political Philosophy and the Patriarchal Unconscious: A Psychoanalytic Perspective on Epistemology and Metaphysics." In *Discovering Reality: Feminist Perspectives on Epistemology, Metaphysics, Methodology and Philosophy of Science,* ed. S. Harding and M. Hintikka. Dordrecht: Reidel.

———. 1986. "Gender as a Social Problem: In and For Feminist Theory." *American Studies/Amerika Studien,* 193–213.

Gilligan, Carol. 1982. *In a Different Voice: Psychological Theory and Women's Development.* Cambridge, Mass.: Harvard University Press.

Goodpaster, Kenneth E. 1974. "Universal Prescriptivism and/or Utilitarian Methodology." Manuscript.

———. 1975. "Morality and Dialogue." *Southern Journal of Philosophy* 13:55–70.

Harding, Sandra. 1986. *The Science Question in Feminism.* Ithaca, N.Y.: Cornell University Press.

Hare, R. M. 1952. *The Language of Morals.* Oxford: Oxford University Press/Clarendon.

———. 1963. *Freedom and Reason.* Oxford: Oxford University Press/Clarendon.

———. 1981. *Moral Thinking: Its Levels, Method, and Point.* Oxford: Oxford University Press/Clarendon.

Hartsock, Nancy. 1983. "The Feminist Standpoint: Developing the Ground for a Specifically Feminist Historical Materialism." In *Discovering Reality: Feminist Perspectives on Epistemology, Metaphysics, Methodology and Philosophy of Science,* ed. S. Harding and M. Hintikka. Dordrecht: Reidel.

———. 1985. *Money, Sex and Power: Toward a Feminist Historical Materialism.* Boston: Northeastern University Press.

Keller, Evelyn Fox. 1984. *Reflections on Gender and Science.* New Haven, Conn.: Yale University Press.

Kerner, George C. 1966. *The Revolution in Ethical Theory.* New York: Oxford University Press.

Kuhn, Thomas. 1970. *The Structure of Scientific Revolutions.* 2d ed. Chicago: University of Chicago Press.

Moore, G. E. 1903. *Principia Ethica.* Cambridge: Cambridge University Press.

Rose, Hilary. 1983. "Hand, Brain and Heart: A Feminist Epistemology for the Natural Sciences." *Signs: Journal of Women in Culture and Society* 9, no. 1:73–90.

Smith, Dorothy. 1974. "Women's Perspective as a Radical Critique of Sociology." *Sociological Inquiry* 44:7–13.

———. 1977. "Some Implications of a Sociology for

Women." In *Women in a Man-Made World: A Socioeconomic Handbook,* ed. N. Glazer and H. Waehrer. Chicago: Rand-McNally.

———. 1979. "A Sociology For Women." In *Prism of Sex: Essays on the Sociology of Knowledge,* ed. J. Sherman and E. T. Beck. Madison: University of Wisconsin Press.

40. PERVERSIONS OF JUSTICE: A NATIVE-AMERICAN EXAMINATION OF THE DOCTRINE OF U.S. RIGHTS TO OCCUPANCY IN NORTH AMERICA

WARD CHURCHILL

> For the nation, there is an unrequited account of sin and injustice that sooner or later will call for national retribution.
>
> —*George Catlin, 1844*

Recognition of the legal and moral rights by which it occupies whatever land base it calls its own is perhaps the most fundamental issue confronting any nation. Typically, such claims to sovereign and proprietary interest in national

Reprinted from Ward Churchill, *Struggle for the Land* (Common Courage Press, Monroe, ME, 1993) by permission of the author.

territorialities devolve, at least in considerable part, upon supportable contentions that the citizenry is preponderantly composed of persons directly descended from peoples who have dwelt within the geographical area claimed since "time immemorial." The matter becomes infinitely more complex in situations in which the dominant—or dominating—population comprises either the representatives of a foreign power or immigrants ("settlers") who can offer no such assertion of "aboriginal" lineage to justify their presence or ownership of property in the usual sense.

History is replete with instances in which various peoples have advanced philosophical, theological, and juridical arguments concerning their alleged entitlement to the homelands of others, only to have them rebuffed by the community of nations as lacking both moral force and sound legal principle. In such cases, the trend has been that international rejection of "imperial" pretensions has led to the inability of those nations extending such claims to sustain them. Modern illustrations of this tendency include the dissolution of the classic European empires—those of France, the Netherlands, Portugal, and Great Britain, in particular—during the post-World War II period, as well as the resounding defeat of the Axis powers' territorial ambitions during the war itself. Even more recent examples may be found in the breakup of the Soviet (Great Russian) and Yugoslavian (Serbian) states and in the extreme controversy attending maintenance of such settler states as Northern Ireland, Israel, and South Africa.

The purpose of this essay is to examine the basis upon which another contemporary settler state, the United States of America, contends that it possesses legitimate—indeed, inviolate—rights to approximately 2.25 billion acres of territory in North America. Through such scrutiny, the philosophical validity of U.S. legal claims to territorial integrity can be understood and tested against the standards of both logic and morality. This, in turn, is intended to provide a firm foundation from which readers may assess the substance of that image generated by the sweeping pronouncements so frequently offered by official America and its adherents over the years: that this is a country so essentially "peaceful," so uniquely enlightened in its commitments to the rule of law and concept of liberty, that it has inevitably emerged as the natural leader of a global drive to consolidate a "new world order" in which the conquest and occupa-

tion of the territory of any nation by another "cannot and will not stand."

RIGHTS TO TERRITORIAL ACQUISITION IN INTERNATIONAL LAW

From the outset of the "Age of Discovery" precipitated by the Columbian voyages, the European powers, eager to obtain uncontested title to at least some portions of the lands their emissaries were encountering, quickly recognized the need to establish a formal code of juridical standards to legitimate what they acquired. To some extent, this was meant to lend a patina of "civilized"—and therefore, it was imagined, inherently superior—legality to the actions of the European Crowns in their relations with the peoples indigenous to the desired geography. More importantly, however, the system was envisioned as a necessary means of resolving disputes among the Crowns themselves, each of which was vying with the others in a rapacious battle over the prerogative to benefit from wealth accruing through ownership of given regions in the "New World." In order for any such regulatory code to be considered effectively binding by all Old World parties, it was vital that it be sanctioned by the Church.

Hence, the mechanism deployed for this purpose was a theme embodied in a series of Papal bulls begun by Pope Innocent IV during the late-13th-century First Crusade. The bulls were designed to define the proper ("lawful") relationship between Christians and "Infidels" in all such worldly matters as property rights. Beginning in the early 16th century, Spanish jurists in particular did much to develop this theory into what have come to be known as the "Doctrine of Discovery" and an attendant dogma, the "Rights of Conquest." Through the efforts of legal scholars such as Franciscus de Victoria and Matías de Paz, Spanish articulations of Discovery Doctrine, endorsed by the pope, rapidly evolved to hold the following as primary tenets of international law:

1. Outright ownership of land accrued to the Crown represented by a given Christian (European) discoverer only when the land discovered proved to be uninhabited (*territorium res nullius*).

2. Title to inhabited lands discovered by Crown representatives was recognized as belonging inherently to the indigenous people thereby encountered, but rights to acquire land from, and to trade with, the natives of the region accrued exclusively to the discovering Crown vis-à-vis other European powers. In exchange for this right, the discovering power committed itself to proselytizing the Christian gospel among the natives.

3. Acquisition of land title from indigenous peoples could occur only by their consent—by an agreement usually involving purchase—rather than through force of arms, so long as the natives did not arbitrarily decline to trade with Crown representatives, refuse to admit missionaries among them, or inflict gratuitous violence upon citizens of the Crown.

4. In the absence of these last three conditions, utilization of armed force to acquire aboriginally held territory was considered to be unjust and claims to land title accruing therefrom to be correspondingly invalid.

5. Should one or more of the three conditions be present, then it was held that the Crown had a legal right to use whatever force was required to subdue native resistance and impound their property as compensation. Land title gained by prosecution of such "just wars" was considered valid.

Although this legal perspective was hotly debated at the time (it still is, in certain quarters), and saw considerable violation by European colonists, it was generally acknowledged as the standard against which international conduct would be weighed. By the early 17th century, the requirements of Discovery Doctrine had led the European states (England in particular) to adopt a policy of entering into formal treaties—full-fledged international instruments in which the sovereignty of the indigenous parties to such agreements were, by definition, officially recognized as equivalent to that of the respective Crowns—as an expedient to obtaining legally valid land titles from American Indian peoples, first in what is now the State of Virginia and then in areas further north. Treaties concerning trade, professions of peace and friendship, and military alliances were also quite common. Undeniably, there is a certain overweening arrogance embedded in the proposition that Europeans were somehow intrinsically imbued with an authority to unilaterally restrict the range of those to whom Native Americans might sell their property, assuming they wished to sell it at all. Nonetheless, in its recognition that indigenous peoples constituted bona fide nations holding essentially the same rights to land and sovereignty as any other, the legal posture of early European colonialism seems rather advanced and refined in retrospect. In these respects, the Doctrine of Discovery is widely viewed as one of the more important cornerstones of modern international law and diplomacy.

With its adoption of Protestantism, however, Britain had already begun to mark its independence from papal regulation by adding an element of its own to the doctrine. Usually termed the "Norman Yoke," this concept asserted that land rights devolve in large part upon the extent to which the owners demonstrate a willingness and ability to "develop" their territories in accordance with a scriptural obligation to exercise "dominium" over nature. In other words, a person or a people is ultimately entitled to only that quantity of real estate which he/she/they convert from "wilderness" to a "domesticated" state. By this criterion, English settlers were seen as possessing an inherent right to dispossess native people of all land other than that which the latter might be "reasonably expected" to put to such "proper" uses as cultivation. By the same token, this doctrinal innovation automatically placed the British Crown on a legal footing from which it could contest the discovery rights of any European power not adhering to the requirement of "overcoming the wilderness" per se.

This last allowed England to simultaneously "abide by the law" *and* directly confront Catholic France for ascendancy in the Atlantic regions of North America. After a series of "French and Indian Wars" beginning in the late 1600s and lasting nearly a century, the British were victorious, but at a cost more than negating the expected financial benefits to the Crown that had led it to launch its colonial venture in the first place. As one major consequence, King George II, in a move intended to preclude further warfare with indigenous nations, issued the Proclamation of 1763. This royal edict stipulated that all settlement or other forms of land acquisition by British subjects west of a line running along the Allegheny and Appalachian Mountains from Canada to the Spanish colony of Florida would be suspended indefinitely, and perhaps permanently. English expansion on the North American continent was thereby brought to an abrupt halt.

ENTER THE UNITED STATES

The new British policy conflicted sharply with the desires for personal gain evident among a voracious elite that had been growing within England's seaboard colonial population. Most of the colonies held some pretense of title to "western" lands, much of it conveyed by earlier Crown grant, and had planned to use it as a means of bolstering their respective economic positions. Similarly, members of the landed gentry such as George Washington, Thomas Jefferson, John Adams, James Madison, and Anthony Wayne all possessed considerable speculative interests in land parcels on the far side of the 1763 demarcation line. The only way in which these could be converted into profit was for the parcels to be settled and developed. Vociferous contestation and frequent violation of the proclamation, eventually enforced by George III, became quite common. All in all, this dynamic became a powerful precipitating factor in the American Revolution, during which many rank-and-file rebels were convinced to fight against the Crown by promises of western land grants "for services rendered" in the event their revolt was successful.

There was, however, a catch. The United States emerged from its decolonization struggle against Britain—perhaps the most grievous offense that could be perpetrated by any subject people under then-prevailing law—as a pariah, an outlaw state that was shunned as an utterly illegitimate entity by most other countries. Desperate to establish itself as a legitimate nation, and lacking any other viable alternatives with which to demonstrate its aptitude for complying with international legality, the new government was virtually compelled to observe the strictest of protocols in its dealings with Indians. Indeed, what the Continental Congress needed more than anything at the time was for indigenous nations, already recognized as respectable sovereignties via their treaties with the European states, to bestow a comparable recognition upon the fledgling United States by entering into treaties with *it*. The urgency of the matter was compounded by the fact that the Indians maintained military parity with, and in some cases superiority to, the U.S. Army all along the frontier.

As a result, both Articles of Confederation and the subsequent Constitution of the United States contained clauses explicitly and exclusively restricting relations with indigenous nations to the federal government, insofar as the former were recognized as enjoying the same politico-legal status as any other foreign power.

The United States also officially renounced, in the 1789 Northwest Ordinance and elsewhere, any aggressive intent concerning indigenous nations especially with regard to their respective land bases:

> The utmost good faith shall always be observed towards the Indians; their land and property shall never be taken from them without their consent; and in their property, rights, and liberty, they shall never be disturbed . . . but laws founded in justice and humanity shall from time to time be made, for wrongs done to them, and for peace and friendship with them.[1]

This rhetorical stance, reflecting an impeccable observance of international legality, was also incorporated into such instruments of agreement with European states as the United States was able to obtain during its formative years. For instance, in the 1803 Louisiana Purchase from France of much of North America west of the Mississippi, the federal government solemnly pledged itself to protect "the inhabitants of the ceded territory . . . in the free enjoyment of their liberty, property, and the religion they profess."[2] Other phraseology in the purchase agreement makes it clear that federal authorities understood they were acquiring from the French, not the land itself, but France's monopolistic trade rights and prerogative to buy any acreage within the area its indigenous owners wished to sell.

The same understanding certainly pertained to all unceded Indian Country claimed by Britain under Discovery Doctrine east of the Mississippi, after it was quit-claimed by George III in the Treaty of Paris concluding the Revolution. Even if English discovery rights somehow "passed" to the new republic by virtue of this royal action (an extremely dubious premise in itself), there still remained the matter of obtaining native consent to literal U.S. ownership of any area beyond the 1763 proclamation line. Hence, the securing of indigenous agreement to land cessions must be added to the impressive list of diplomatic and military reasons why treaty-making with Indians constituted the main currency of American diplomacy throughout the immediate postrevolutionary period. Moreover, the need to secure valid land title from native people through treaties far outlasted the motivations of diplomatic and military necessity, these having been greatly diminished in importance after U.S. victories over Tecumseh's alliance in 1794 and 1811, over Britain in the War of 1812, and over the Red Stick Confederacy during 1813–1814. The treaties were and remain, in substance, the basic real-estate documents anchoring U.S. claims to land title—and thus to rights of occupancy—in North America.

What was most problematic in this situation for early federal policymakers was the fact that, in gaining diplomatic recognition and land cessions from indigenous nations through treaties, the United States was simultaneously admitting not only that Indians ultimately owned virtually all of the coveted territory but also that they were really under no obligation to part with it. As William Wirt, an early attorney general, put it in 1821: "[Legally speaking,] so long as a tribe exists and remains in possession of its lands, its title and possession are sovereign and exclusive. We treat with them as separate sovereignties, and while an Indian nation continues to exist within its acknowledged limits, we have no more right to enter upon their territory than we have to enter upon the territory of a foreign prince."[3] A few years later, Wirt amplified this point:

> The point, once conceded, that the Indians are independent to the purpose of treating, their independence is to that purpose as absolute as any other nation. Being competent to bind themselves by treaty, they are equally competent to bind the party that treats with them. Such party cannot take benefit of [a] treaty with the Indians, and then deny them the reciprocal benefits of the treaty on the grounds that they are not independent nations to all intents and purposes. . . . Nor can it be conceded that their

independence as a nation is a limited independence. Like all other independent nations, they have the absolute power of war and peace. Like all other independent nations, their territories are inviolate by any other sovereignty.... They are entirely self-governed, self-directed. They treat, or refuse to treat, at their pleasure; and there is no human power that can rightly control them in the exercise of their discretion in this respect.[4]

Such enjoyment of genuine sovereign rights and status by indigenous nations served, during the 20 years following the Revolution (roughly 1790–1810), to considerably retard the assumption of lawful possession of their land grants by revolutionary soldiers, as well as consummation of the plans of the elite caste of prerevolutionary land speculators. Over the next two decades (1810–1830), the issue assumed an ever-increasing policy importance as the matter of native sovereignty came to replace Crown policy in being construed as *the* preeminent barrier to U.S. territorial consolidation east of the Mississippi. Worse, as Chief Justice of the Supreme Court John Marshall pointed out in 1822, any real adherence to the rule of law in regard to native rights might not only block U.S. expansion but—since not all the territory therein had been secured through Crown treaties—cloud title to significant portions of the original 13 states as well. Perhaps predictably, it was perceived in juridical circles that the only means of circumventing this dilemma was through construction of a legal theory—a subterfuge, as it were—by which the more inconvenient implications of international law might be voided even while the republic maintained an appearance of holding to its doctrinal requirements.

EMERGENCE OF THE MARSHALL DOCTRINE

Not unnaturally, the task of forging the required "interpretation" of existing law fell to Marshall,

who was widely considered one of the great legal minds of his time. Whatever his scholarly qualifications, the chief justice can hardly be said to have been a disinterested party, given not only his vociferous ideological advocacy of the rebel cause before and during the Revolution but also the fact that both he and his father were consequent recipients of 10,000-acre grants west of the Appalachians, in what is now the State of West Virginia. His first serious foray into land-rights law thus centered in devising a conceptual basis to secure title for his own and similar grants. In the 1810 *Fletcher* v. *Peck* case, he invoked the Norman Yoke tradition in a manner that far exceeded previous British applications, advancing the patently absurd contention that the areas involved were effectively "vacant" even though very much occupied—and in many instances stoutly defended—by indigenous inhabitants. On this basis, he declared that individual Euro-American deeds within recognized Indian territories might be considered valid whether or not native consent was obtained.

Although *Peck* was obviously useful from the U.S. point of view, resolving as it did a number of short-term difficulties in meeting obligations already incurred by the government vis-à-vis individual citizens, it was in itself a tactical opinion, falling far short of accommodating the country's overall territorial goals and objectives. In the 1823 *Johnson* v. *McIntosh* case, however, Marshall followed up with a more clearly strategic enunciation, reaching for something much closer to the core of what he had in mind. Here he opined that, because discovery rights purportedly constricted native discretion in disposing of property, the sovereignty of discoverers was to that extent inherently superior to that of indigenous nations. From this point of departure, he then proceeded to invert all conventional understandings of Discovery Doctrine, ultimately asserting that native people occupied land within discovered regions at the sufferance of their discoverers rather than the other way around. A preliminary rationalization was thus contrived by which to explain the fact that the United States had already begun depicting its borders as encompassing rather vast portions of unceded Indian country.

Undoubtedly aware that neither *Peck* nor *McIntosh* was likely to withstand the gaze of even minimal international scrutiny, Marshall next moved to bolster the logic undergirding his position. In the two "Cherokee Cases" of the early 1830s, he hammered out the thesis that native nations within North America were "nations like any other" in the sense that they possessed both territories they were capable of ceding and recognizable governmental bodies empowered to cede these areas through treaties. On the other hand, he argued on the basis of the reasoning deployed in *McIntosh,* they were nations of a "peculiar type," both "domestic to" and "dependent upon" the United States, and therefore possessed of a degree of sovereignty intrinsically less than that enjoyed by the United States itself. The essential idea boils down to a presumption that, although native peoples are entitled to exercise some range of autonomy in managing their affairs within their own territories, both the limits of that autonomy and the extent of the territories involved can be "naturally" and unilaterally established by the federal government. At base, this is little more than a judicial description of the classic relationship between colonizer and colonized, but it was put forth in such a way as to seem at first glance to be the exact opposite.

Although it might be contended (and has been, routinely enough) that Marshall's framing of the circumstances pertaining to the Cherokee Nation, already completely surrounded by the territorality of the United States by 1830, bore some genuine relationship to then-prevailing reality, it must be reiterated that he did not confine his observations of the situation to Cherokees, or even to native nations east of the Mississippi. Rather, he purported to articulate the legal status of *all* indigenous nations, including those west of the Mississippi—the Lakota, Cheyenne,

Arapaho, Comanche, Kiowa, Navajo, and Chiricahua Apache, to name but a few—that had not yet encountered the United States in any appreciable way. Self-evidently, these nations could not have been described with the faintest accuracy as domestic to or dependent upon the United States. The clear intent belied by Marshall's formulation was that they be made so in the future. The doctrine completed with elaboration of the Cherokee Cases was thus the pivotal official attempt to rationalize and legitimate a vast campaign of conquest and colonization—absolutely contrary to the customary law of the period—upon which the United States was planning to embark in the years ahead.

A final inversion of accepted international legal norms and definitions stems from this: an outright reversal of what was meant by "just" and "unjust" warfare.[5] Within Marshall's convoluted and falsely premised reasoning, it became arguable that indigenous nations acted unlawfully whenever and wherever they attempted to physically prevent exercise of the U.S. "right" to expropriate their property. Put another way, Indians could be construed as committing "aggression" against the United States at any point when they attempted to resist the invasion of their homelands by American citizens. In this sense the United States could declare itself to be waging a "just"—and therefore lawful—war against native people on virtually any occasion when force of arms was required to realize its territorial ambitions. *Ipso facto,* all efforts of native people to defend themselves against systematic dispossession and subordination could thereby be categorized as "unjust"—and thus unlawful—by the United States.[6]

In sum, the Marshall Doctrine shredded significant elements of the existing Laws of Nations. Given the understandings of these very same legal requirements placed on record by federal judicial officials such as Attorney General Wirt and Marshall himself, not to mention the embodiment of such understandings in the Constitution and formative federal statutes, this cannot be said to have been unintentional or inadvertent. Instead, the chief justice engaged in a calculated exercise in juridical cynicism, quite deliberately confusing and deforming accepted legal principles as an expedient to "justifying" his country's pursuit of a thoroughly illegitimate course of territorial acquisition. Insofar as federal courts and policy-makers elected to adopt his doctrine as the predicate to all subsequent relations with American Indians, it may be said that he not only replicated the initial posture of the United States as an outlaw state but rendered it permanent.

Evolution of the Marshall Doctrine

The Cherokee Cases were followed by a half-century hiatus in important judicial determinations regarding American Indians. On the foundation provided by the Marshall Doctrine, the government felt confident in entering into the great bulk of the at least 371 treaties with indigenous nations by which it professed to have gained the consent of Indians in ceding huge portions of the native land base, assured all the while that, because of its self-anointed position of superior sovereignty, it would be under "no legal obligation" to live up to its end of the various bargains struck. Well before the end of the 19th century, the United States stood in default on virtually every treaty agreement it had made with native people, and there is considerable evidence in many instances that this was intended to be so from the outset. Aside from the fraudulent nature of U.S. participation in the treaty process, there is an ample record that many of the instruments of cession were militarily coerced while the government implemented Marshall's version of "just wars" against Indians. As the U.S. Census Bureau put it in 1894:

> The Indian wars under the United States government have been about 40 in number [most of them occurring after 1835]. They have cost the lives of . . . about 30,000 Indians [at a minimum]. . . . The actual number of killed and wounded Indians must be very much greater than the number given, as they conceal, where possible, their actual loss in battle. . . . Fifty percent additional would be a safe number to add to the numbers given.[7]

The same report noted that some number "very much more" than 8,500 Indians were known to have been killed by government-sanctioned private citizen action—dubbed "individual affairs"—during the course of U.S./Indian warfare.[8] In reality, such citizen action is known to have been primarily responsible for the reduction of the native population of Texas from about 100,000 in 1828 to under 10,000 in 1880.[9] Similarly, in California, an aggregate indigenous population that still numbers approximately 300,000 had been reduced to fewer than 35,000 by 1860, mainly because of "the cruelties and wholesale massacres perpetrated by [American] miners and early settlers."[10] Either of these illustrations offers a death toll several times that officially acknowledged as having accrued through individual affairs within the whole of the 48 contiguous states.

Even while this slaughter was occurring, the government was conducting what it itself frequently described as a "policy of extermination" in its conduct of wars against those indigenous nations that proved "recalcitrant" about giving up their land and liberty. This manifested itself in a lengthy series of massacres of native people—men, women, children, and old people alike—at the hands of U.S. troops. Among the worst were those at Blue River (Nebraska, 1854), Bear River (Idaho, 1863), Sand Creek (Colorado, 1864), Washita River (Oklahoma, 1868), Sappa Creek (Kansas, 1875), Camp Robinson (Nebraska, 1878), and Wounded Knee (South Dakota, 1890). Somewhat different, but comparable, methods of destroying indigenous peoples were evidenced in the forced march of the entire Cherokee Nation along the "Trail of Tears" to Oklahoma during the 1830s (55% attrition)[11] and in the internment of the bulk of the Navajo Nation under abysmal conditions at the Bosque Redondo from 1864 to 1868 (35–50% attrition).[12] Such atrocities against humans were coupled with an equally systematic extermination of an entire animal species, the buffalo or North American bison, as part of a military strategy to starve resistant Indians into submission by "destroying their commissary."

All told, it is probable that more than a quarter-million Indians perished as a direct result of U.S. extermination campaigns directed against them.[13] By the turn of the century, only 237,196 native people were recorded by census as still being alive within the United States,[14] perhaps 2% of the total indigenous population of the U.S. portion of North America at the point of first contact with Europeans.[15] Correlating rather precisely with this genocidal reduction in the number of native inhabitants was an erosion of Indian land holdings to approximately 2.5% of the "lower 48" states.[16] Small wonder that, barely 50 years later, Adolf Hitler would explicitly anchor his concept of *lebensraumpolitik* ("politics of living space") directly upon U.S. practice against American Indians. Meanwhile, even as the 1890 census figures were being tallied, the United States had already moved beyond the "Manifest Destiny" embodied in the conquest phase of its continental expansion and was emphasizing the development of colonial administration over residual indigenous land and lives through the Bureau of Indian Affairs (BIA), a subpart of the War Department that had been reassigned for this purpose to the Department of the Interior.

This was begun as early as 1871, when Congress—having determined that the military capacity of indigenous nations had finally been sufficiently reduced by incessant wars of attrition—elected to consecrate Marshall's description of their "domestic" status by suspending further treaty-making with them. In 1885, the United States moved for the first time to directly extend its internal jurisdiction over reserved

Indian territories through passage of the Major Crimes Act. When this was immediately challenged as a violation of international standards, Supreme Court Justice Samuel F. Miller rendered an opinion that consolidated and extended Marshall's earlier assertion of federal plenary power over native nations, contending that the government held an "incontrovertible right" to exercise authority over Indians as it saw fit and "for their own good." Miller also concluded that Indians lacked any legal recourse in matters of federal interest, their sovereignty being defined as whatever Congress did not remove through specific legislation. This decision opened the door to enactment of more than 5,000 statutes regulating affairs in Indian Country through the present day.

One of the first of these was the General Allotment Act of 1887, "which unilaterally negated Indian control over land tenure patterns within the reservations, forcibly replacing the traditional mode of collective use and occupancy with the Anglo-Saxon system of individual property ownership."[17] The act also imposed for the first time a formal eugenics code—dubbed "blood quantum"—by which American Indian identity would be federally defined on racial grounds rather than by native nations themselves on the basis of group membership/citizenship.[18]

The Allotment Act set forth that each American Indian recognized as such by the federal government would receive an allotment of land according to the following formula: 160 acres for family heads, eighty acres for single persons over eighteen years of age and orphans under eighteen, and forty acres for [non-orphan] children under eighteen. "Mixed blood" Indians received title by fee simple patent; "full bloods" were issued "trust patents," meaning they had no control over their property for a period of twenty-five years. Once each person recognized by the government as belonging to a given Indian nation had received his or her allotment, the "surplus" acreage was "opened" to non-Indian homesteading or conversion into the emerging system of national parks, forests, and grasslands.[19]

Needles to say, there proved to be far fewer Indians identifiable as such under federal eugenics criteria than there were individual parcels available within the reserved land areas of the 1890s. Hence, "not only was the cohesion of indigenous society dramatically disrupted by allotment, and traditional government prerogatives preempted, but it led to the loss of some two-thirds of all the acreage [about 100 million of 150 million acres] still held by native people at the time it was passed."[20] Moreover, the land assigned to individual Indians during the allotment process fell overwhelmingly within arid and semi-arid locales considered to be the least productive in North America; uniformly, the best-watered and otherwise useful portions of the reservations were declared surplus and quickly stripped away. This, of course, greatly reinforced the "dependency" aspect of the Marshall thesis and led U.S. Indian Commissioner Francis Leupp to conclude approvingly that allotment should be considered as "a mighty pulverizing engine for breaking up [the last vestiges of] the tribal mass" that stood as a final barrier to complete Euro-American hegemony on the continent.

As with the Major Crimes Act, native people attempted to utilize their treated standing in federal courts to block the allotment process and corresponding erosion of the reservation land base. In the 1903 *Lonewolf* v. *Hitchcock* case, however, Justice Edward D. White extended the concept of federal plenary power to hold that the government possessed a right to unilaterally abrogate whatever portion of any treaty with Indians it found inconvenient while continuing to consider the remaining terms and provisions binding upon the Indians. In essence, this meant that the United States could point to the treaties as being the instruments that legally validated much of its North American land title while simultaneously avoiding whatever reciprocal obligations it had incurred by way of payment.

White also opined that the government's plenary power over Indians lent it a "trust responsibility" over residual native property such that it might opt to "change the form" of this property—from land, say, to cash or "services"—whenever and however it chose to do so. This final consolidation of the Marshall Doctrine effectively left native people with *no* true national rights under U.S. law while voiding the remaining pittance of conformity to international standards the United States had exhibited with regard to its Indian treaties.

THE OPEN VEINS OF NATIVE AMERICA

A little-discussed aspect of the Allotment Act is that it required each Indian, as a condition of receiving the deed to his or her land parcel, to accept U.S. citizenship. By the early 1920s, when most of the allotment the United States wished to accomplish had been completed, there were still a significant number of native people who still had not been "naturalized," either because they'd been left out of the process for one reason or another or because they'd refused to participate. Consequently, in 1924 the Congress passed a "clean-up bill" entitled the Indian Citizenship Act, which imposed citizenship upon all remaining indigenous people within U.S. borders whether they wished it or not.

> The Indian Citizenship Act greatly confused the circumstances even of many of the blooded and federally certified Indians insofar as it was held to bear legal force, and to carry legal obligations, whether or not any given Indian or group of Indians wished to be U.S. citizens. As for the host of non-certified, mixed-blood people residing in the U.S., their status was finally "clarified"; they had been definitionally absorbed into the American mainstream at the stroke of the congressional pen. And, despite the fact that the act technically left certified Indians occupying the status of citizenship

within their own indigenous nation as well as the U.S. (a "dual form" of citizenship so awkward as to be sublime), the juridical door had been opened by which the weight of Indian obligations would begin to accrue more to the U.S. than to themselves.[21]

All of this—suspension of treaty-making, extension of federal jurisdiction, plenary power and "trust" prerogatives, blood quantum and allotment, and imposition of citizenship—was bound up in a policy officially designated as the compulsory assimilation of American Indians into the dominant (Euro-American) society. Put another way, U.S. Indian policy was carefully (and openly) designed to bring about the disappearance of all recognizable Indian groups, as such. The methods used included the general proscription of native languages and spiritual practices, the systematic and massive transfer of Indian children into non-Indian settings via mandatory attendance at boarding schools remote from their communities, and the deliberate suppression of reservation economic structures. As Indian Commissioner Charles Burke put it at the time, "It is not consistent with the general welfare to promote [American Indian national] characteristics and organization."[22]

The assimilationist policy trajectory culminated during the 1950s with the passage of House Concurrent Resolution 108, otherwise known as the "Termination Act of 1953," a measure through which the United States moved to unilaterally dissolve 109 indigenous nations within its borders. Termination was coupled to the "Relocation Act," a statute passed in 1956 and designed to coerce reservation residents to disperse to various urban centers around the country. As a result of the ensuing programmatic emphasis on creating an American Indian diaspora, by 1990 over half of all U.S. Indians had been severed from their respective land bases and generally acculturated to non-Indian mores. Meanwhile, the enactment of Public Law 280, placing many reservations under the jurisdiction of individual states,

thereby reduced the level of native sovereignty to that held by counties or municipalities. This voided one of the last federal pretenses that Indians retained "certain characteristics of sovereign nations."

The question arises, of course, as to why, given the contours of this aspect of federal policy, the final obliteration of the indigenous nations of North America has not long since occurred. The answer, apparently, resides within something of a supreme irony: unbeknownst to the policymakers who implemented allotment policy against Indians during the late 19th century, much of the ostensibly useless land to which native people were consigned has turned out to be some of the most mineral rich on earth. It is presently estimated that as much as two-thirds of all known U.S. "domestic" uranium reserves lie beneath reservation lands, as well as perhaps a quarter of the readily accessible low-sulphur coal and about a fifth of the oil and natural gas. In addition, the reservations are now known to hold substantial deposits of copper, zinc, iron, nickel, molybdenum, bauxite, zeolites, and gold.

These facts began to surface in the early 1920s. Federal economic planners quickly discerned a distinct advantage in retaining these abundant resources within the framework of governmental trust control, an expedient to awarding extractive leases, mining licenses, and the like to preferred corporate entities in ways that might have proven impossible had the reservations been liquidated altogether. Hence, beginning in 1921, it was determined that selected indigenous nations should be maintained in some semblance of being, and Washington began to experiment with the creating of "tribal governments" intended to administer what was left of Indian Country on behalf of an emerging complex of interlocking federal/corporate interests. In 1934, this resulted in the passage of the Indian Reorganization Act (IRA), a bill that served to supplant virtually every remaining traditional indigenous government in the country, replacing them with federally designed "tribal councils" structured along the lines of corporate boards and empowered primarily to sign off on mineral leases and similar instruments.

The arrangement led to a recapitulation of the Marshall Doctrine's principle of indigenous "quasi-sovereignty" in slightly revised form: now, native nations were cast as always being sovereign enough to legitimate Euro-American mineral exploitation on their reservations but never sovereign enough to prevent it. Predictably, under such circumstances the BIA negotiated mineral leases, duly endorsed by the puppet governments it had installed, "on behalf of" its "Indian wards" that typically paid native people 15% or less of market royalty rates on minerals taken from their lands. The "super-profits" thus generated for major corporations have had a significant positive effect on U.S. economic growth since 1950, a matter amplified by the fact that the BIA also "neglected" to include land restoration and other environmental clean-up clauses into contracts pertaining to reservation land (currently, Indians are always construed as being sovereign enough to waive such things as environmental protection regulations but never sovereign enough to enforce them). One consequence of this trend is that, on reservations where uranium mining has occurred, Indian Country has become so contaminated by radioactive substances that the government has actively considered designating them as "National Sacrifice Areas" unfit for human habitation. At this juncture, planning is also afoot to utilize several reservations as dump sites for high-level nuclear wastes and toxic chemical substances that cannot be otherwise conveniently disposed of.

Further indications of the extent and virulence of the colonial system by which the United States has come to rule Native America are not difficult to find. For instance, dividing the 50-million-odd acres of land still nominally reserved for Indian use and occupancy in the United States by the approximately 1.6 million Indians the government recognized in its 1980 census reveals that native people—on paper, at least—remain the largest landholders on a per capita basis of any population sector on the continent.[23] Given this, in combination with the resources known to lie within their land and the increasingly intensive "development" of these resources over the past 40 years, simple arithmetic strongly suggests that they should also be the wealthiest of all aggregate groups. Instead, according to the federal government's own data, Indians are far and away the poorest in terms of both annual and lifetime per capita income. Correspondingly, we suffer all the standard indices of dire poverty: North America's highest rates of infant mortality and teen suicide and of death from malnutrition, exposure, and plague. Overall, we consistently experience the highest rate of unemployment, lowest level of educational attainment, and one of the highest rates of incarceration of any group. The average life expectancy of a reservation-based American Indian male is currently less than 45 years; that of a reservation-based female, barely over 47.

In Latin America, there is a core axiom that guides understanding of the interactive dynamics between the northern and southern continents of the Western Hemisphere. "Your wealth," Latino analysts point out to their Yanqui counterparts, "is our poverty."[24] Plainly, the structure of the relationship forged by the United States vis-à-vis the indigenous nations of the northern continent itself follows exactly the same pattern of parasitic domination. The economic veins of the prostrate Native North American host have been carefully opened, their content provided lifeblood to the predatory creature that applied the knife. Such are the fruits of John Marshall's doctrine after a century and a half of continuous application to the "real world" context.

INTERNATIONAL SLEIGHT OF HAND

It's not that the United States has ever attempted to mask the face of this reality. Indeed, in the wake of World War II, even as the United States was engaged in setting a "moral example" to all of humanity by assuming a lead role in prosecuting former Nazi leaders for having ventured down much the same road of continental conquest that the United States itself had pioneered, Congress passed what it called the Indian Claims Commission Act. The premise of the bill was that all non-consensual—and therefore illegal—seizures of native property that had transpired during the course of American history had been "errors," sometimes "tragic" ones. As a means, at least figuratively, of separating U.S. historical performance and expansionist philosophy from the more immediate manifestations of the Nazis, the new law established a commission empowered to review the basis of U.S. land title in every quarter of the country and to award retroactive monetary compensation to indigenous nations shown to have been unlawfully deprived of their lands. Tellingly, the commission was authorized to set compensation amounts only on the basis of the estimated per-acre value of illegally taken land *at the time it was taken* (often a century or more before), and was specifically disempowered from restoring land to Indian control, no matter *how* the land was taken or *what* the desires of the impacted native people might be.

Although the life of the commission was originally envisioned as being only ten years, the magnitude of the issues it encountered, and the urgency with which its mission came to be viewed by the Euro-American status quo, caused it to be repeatedly extended. When it was ultimately suspended on September 30, 1978, it sill had 68 cases docketed for review, despite having heard and ostensibly "disposed of" several hundred others over a period of three decades. In the end, although its intent had been the exact opposite, it had accomplished nothing so much as to establish with graphic clarity how little of North America the United States could be said to legally own.

The fact is that about half the land area of the country was purchased by treaty or agreement

at an average price of less than a dollar an acre; another third of a [billion] acres, mainly in the West, were confiscated without confiscation; another two-thirds of a [billion] acres were claimed by the United States without pretense of a unilateral action extinguishing native title.[25]

This summary, of course, says nothing at all about the approximately 44 million acres of land presently being taken from the Indians, Aleuts, and Inuits of the Arctic North under provision of the 1971 Alaska Native Claims Settlement Act, or the several million acres of Hawaii stripped away from the natives of those islands. Similarly, it says nothing of the situation in such U.S. "possessions" as Guam, Puerto Rico, the "U.S." Virgin Islands, "American" Samoa, and the Marshall Islands.

Serious challenges to commission findings have been mounted in U.S. courts, based largely in the cumulative contradictions inherent to federal Indian law. As a consequence, the Supreme Court has been compelled to resort to ever more convoluted and logically untenable argumentation as a means of upholding certain governmental assertions of "legitimate" land title. In its 1980 opinion in the Black Hills Land Claim case, for example, the high court was forced to extend the Marshall Doctrine's indigenous domesticity thesis to a ludicrous extreme, holding that the United States had merely exercised its rightful internal power of "imminent domain" over the territory of the Lakota Nation when it expropriated 90% of the latter's land a century earlier, in direct violation of the 1868 Treaty of Fort Laramie. Similarly, in the Western Shoshone Land Claim case, where the government could show no documentation that it had ever even pretended to assume title to the native land at issue, the Supreme Court let stand the Claims Commission's assignment of an arbitrary date on which a transfer supposedly took place.

During the 1970s, the American Indian Movement (AIM), an organization militantly devoted to the national liberation of Native North America, emerged in the United States.

In part, the group attempted the physical decolonization of the Pine Ridge Reservation in South Dakota (home of the Oglala Lakota people) but was met with a counterinsurgency war waged by federal agencies such as the FBI and U.S. Marshalls Service and by surrogates associated with the reservation's IRA Council. Although unsuccessful in achieving a resumption of indigenous self-determination at Pine Ridge, the tenacity of AIM's struggle (and the ferocity of the government's repression of it) attracted considerable international attention. This led, in 1980, to the establishment of a United Nations Working Group on Indigenous Populations, under auspices of the U.N. Economic and Social Council (UNESCO), an entity mandated to assess the situation of native peoples globally and produce a universal declaration of their rights as a binding element of international law.

Within this arena, the United States, joined by Canada, has consistently sought to defend its relations with indigenous nations by trotting out the Marshall Doctrine's rationalization that the United States has assumed a trust responsibility over, rather than outright colonial domination of, Native North America. Native delegates have countered, correctly, that trust prerogatives, in order to be valid under international law, must be tied to some clearly articulated time interval after which the trustee nations resume independent existence. This has been successfully contrasted to the federal (and Canadian) government's presumption that it enjoys a permanent trust authority over indigenous nations; assumption of permanent plenary authority over another nation's affairs and property is the essential definition of colonialism, it is argued, and is illegal under a number of international covenants.

The United States and Canada have responded with prevarication, contending that their relationship to Native North America cannot be one of colonialism insofar as United Nations Resolution 1541 (XV), the "Blue Water Thesis," specifies that in order to be defined as a colony a nation must be separated from its colo-

nizer by at least 30 miles of open ocean. The representatives of both countries have also done everything in their power to delay or prevent completion of the Universal Declaration of the Rights of Indigenous Peoples, arguing, among other things, that the term "peoples," when applied to native populations, should not carry the force of law implied by its use in such international legal instruments as the Universal Declaration of Human Rights (1948), Covenant on Civil and Political Rights (1978), and the International Convention on Elimination of All Forms of Racial Discrimination (1978). The United States in particular has implied that it will not abide by any declaration of indigenous rights that runs counter to what it perceives as its own interests, a matter that would replicate its posture with regard to the authority of the International Court of Justice (the "World Court")[26] and elements of international law such as the 1948 Convention on Prevention and Punishment of the Crime of Genocide.[27]

Meanwhile, the United States has set out to "resolve things internally" through what may be intended as a capstone extrapolation of the Marshall Doctrine. This strategy has involved a drive to convince Indians to accept the premise that, rather than struggling to regain the self-determining rights to separate sovereign existence embodied in their natural histories and treaty relationships, they should voluntarily merge themselves with the U.S. polity. In this scenario, the IRA administrative apparatus created during the 1930s would assume a position as a "third level of the federal government," finally making indigenous rights within the United States inseparable from those of the citizenry as a whole. This final assimilation of native people into the "American sociopolitical mainstream" would obviously void most (or perhaps all) potential utility for Indian rights that exist or might emerge from international law over the next few years. The option is therefore being seriously pursued at this juncture by a Senate Select Committee on Indians Affairs, chaired by Hawaii Senator Daniel Inouye (who has already done much to undermine the last vestiges of rights held by the native people of his own state).

UNITED STATES OUT OF NORTH AMERICA

During the fall of 1990, President George Bush stepped onto the world stage beating the drums for what he termed a "just war" to roll back the "naked aggression" of Iraq's invasion and occupation of neighboring Kuwait. Claiming to articulate "universal principles of international relations and human decency," Bush stated that such aggression "cannot stand," that "occupied territory must be liberated, legitimate governments must be reinstated, the benefits of their aggression must be denied to aggressive powers."[28] Given the tone and tenor of this Bushian rhetoric—and the undeniable fact that Iraq had a far better claim to Kuwait (its 19th province, separated from the Iraqis by the British as an administrative measure following World War I) than the United States has to virtually any part of North America[29]—one could only wait with baited breath for the American president to call airstrikes in upon his own Capitol as a means of forcing his own government to withdraw from Indian Country. Insofar as he did not, the nature of the "New World Order" [to which] his war in the Persian Gulf harkened tends to speak for itself.

The United States does not now possess, nor has it ever possessed, a legitimate right to occupancy in at least half the territory it claims as its own on this continent. It began its existence as an outlaw state, and, given the nature of its expansion to its present size, it has adamantly remained so through the present moment. In order to make things appear otherwise, its legal scholars and its legislators have persistently and often grotesquely manipulated and deformed accepted and sound legal principles, both internationally and domestically. They have done so in precisely the same fashion, and on the same basis, as the Nazi leaders they stood at the forefront in condemning for Crimes against Humanity at Nuremberg.

In no small part because of its success in consolidating its position on other people's land in North America, the United States may well continue to succeed where the Nazis failed. With the collapse of the Soviet Union, it has emerged as *the* ascendent military power on the planet during the late 20th century. As the sheer margin of its victory over Iraq has revealed, it now possesses the capacity to extend essentially the same sort of relationships it has already imposed upon American Indians to the remainder of the world. And, given the experience it has acquired in Indian Affairs over the years, it is undoubtedly capable of garbing this process of planetary subordination in a legalistic attire symbolizing its deep-seated concern with international freedom and dignity, the sovereignty of other nations, and the human rights of all peoples. At a number of levels, the Marshall Doctrine reckons to become truly globalized in the years ahead.

This is likely to remain the case, unless and until significant numbers of people within the United States as well as without come to recognize the danger, and the philosophical system that underpins it, for what they are. More importantly, any genuine alternative to a consummation of the Bushian vision of world order is predicated upon these same people acting upon their insights, opposing the order implicit to the U.S. status quo both at home and abroad. Ultimately, the dynamic represented by the Marshall Doctrine must be reversed, and the structure it fostered dismantled, within the territorial corpus of the United States itself. In this, nothing can be more central than the restoration of indigenous land and indigenous national rights in the fullest sense of the term. The United States—at least as it has come to be known, and in the sense that it knows itself—must be driven from North America. In its stead resides the possibility, likely the *only* possibility, of a genuinely just and liberatory future for all humanity.

NOTES

1. 1 *Stat.* 50, 1789.
2. Quoted in Lazarus, Edward, *Black Hills, White Justice: The Sioux Nation versus the United States, 1775 to the Present,* Harper Collins, New York, 1991, p. 158.
3. Opinion rendered by the Attorney General (Op. Atty Gen.), April 26, 1821, p. 345.
4. Op. Atty. Gen., 1828, pp. 623–4. For further background, see Berman, Howard, "The Concept of Aboriginal Rights in the Early Legal History of the United States," *Buffalo Law Review,* No. 28, 1998, pp. 637–67. Also see Cohen, Felix. S., "Original Indian Land Title." *Minnesota Law Review,* No. 32, 1947, pp. 28–59.
5. For a comprehensive survey of the meanings of these terms in the international legal vernacular, see Walzer, Michael, *Just and Unjust Wars: A Moral Argument with Historical Illustrations,* Basic Books, New York, 1977.
6. One indicator of the pervasiveness with which this outlook has been implanted is that armed conflicts between the United States and indigenous nations are inevitably described as "Indian Wars" despite the fact that each one was demonstrably initiated by the invasion by American citizens of territory belonging to one or more native peoples. The so-called Indian Wars would thus be accurately depicted as "Settlers' Wars" (or, more appropriately yet, "Wars of Aggression by the United States").
7. U.S. Bureau of the Census, *Report on Indians Taxed and Indians Not Taxed in the United States (except Alaska) at the Eleventh U.S. Census: 1890,* U.S. Government Printing Office, Washington, D.C., 1894, pp. 637–38.
8. Ibid.
9. See Stiffarm and Lane, *op. cit.,* pp. 35–36. The government of first the Republic, and then the State of Texas maintained a bounty on Indian— *any* Indian—scalps until well into the 1870s; see Newcome, W. W., Jr., *The Indians of Texas,* University of Texas Press, Austin, 1961.
10. Mooney, James, "Population," in Frederick W. Dodge (ed.), *Handbook of the Indians North of Mexico, Vol. 2,* Bureau of American Ethnology Bulletin No. 30, Smithsonian Institution, U.S. Government Printing Office, Washington, D.C., 1910, pp. 286–87. Also see Cook, Sherburn F., *The Conflict between the California Indian and White Civilization,* University of California Press, Berkeley, 1976.
11. See Thornton, Russell, "Cherokee Population Losses during the Trail of Tears: A New Perspective and Estimate," *Ethnohistory,* No. 31, 1984, pp. 289–300.
12. See Johansson, S. Ryan, and S. H. Preston, "Tribal Demography: The Navajo and Hopi Populations as Seen through Manuscripts from the 1900 Census," *Social Science History,* No. 3, 1978, p. 26. Also see Salmon, Roberto Mario, "The Disease Complaint at Bosque Redondo (1864–1868)," *The Indian Historian,* No. 9, 1976.
13. Scholarly sources suggest the actual total may have been as high as a half-million. See Thornton, Russell, *American Indian Holocaust and Survival: A Population History since 1492,* University of Oklahoma Press, Norman, 1987, p. 49.
14. This nadir figure is reported in U.S. Bureau of the Census, *Fifteenth Census of the United States, 1930: The Indian Population of the United States and Alaska,* U. S. Government Printing Office, Washington, D.C., 1937. Barely 101,000 Canadian Indians were estimated as surviving in the same year.
15. Estimating native population figures at the point of first contract is, at best, a slippery business. Recent demographic work has, however, produced a broad consensus that the standard anthropological estimates of "about one million north of the Rio Grande" fashioned by James Mooney and Alfred Kroeber, as well as Harold Driver's subsequent upward revision of their calculations to "approximately two million," are *far* too low. The late Henry Dobyns, using more appropriate methodologies than his predecessors, computed a probable aggregate precontact North American Indian population of 18.5 million, about 15 million of them within present U.S. borders (*Their Numbers Become Thinned: Native American Population Dynamics in Eastern North America,* University of Tennessee Press, Knoxville, 1983). A somewhat more conservative successor, the Cherokee demographer Russell Thornton, counters that the figure was more likely about 12.5 million, perhaps 9.5 million of them within the United States (*American Indian Holocaust and Survival, op. cit.*). Splitting the difference between Dobyns and Thornton leaves

one with an approximate 15 million North American population total, about 12.5 million in the United States. Interestingly, no matter which set of the newer estimates one uses, the overall attrition by 1900 is in the upper 90th percentile range.

16. The figure is arrived at by relying upon Royce, Charles C., *Indian Land Cessions in the United States* (2 Vols.), Bureau of American Ethnography, 18th Annual Report, 1896–97, Smithsonian Institution, Washington, D.C., 1899.

17. Ch. 119, 24 *Stat.* 388, now codified as amended at 25 U.S.C. 331 *et seq.*, better known as the "Dawes Act," after its sponsor, Massachusetts Senator Henry Dawes. The quote is from Robbins, Rebecca L., "Self-Determination and Subordination: The Past, Present, and Future of American Indian Governance," in Jaimes, *op. cit.*, p. 93.

18. See Jaimes, M. Annette, "Federal Indian Identification Policy: A Usurpation of Indigenous Sovereignty in North America," in Jaimes, *op. cit.*, pp. 123–38. It is noteworthy that official eugenics codes have been employed by very few states, mostly such unsavory examples as Nazi Germany (against the Jews), South Africa (against "Coloreds"), and Israel (against Palestinian Arabs).

19. Robbins, *op. cit.* Also see McDonnell, Janet A., *The Dispossession of the American Indian, 1887–1934,* Indiana University Press, Bloomington/Indianapolis, 1991.

20. Robbins, *op. cit.* Also see Kicking Bird, Kirk, and Karen Ducheneaux, *One Hundred Million Acres,* Macmillan, New York, 1973.

21. Jaimes, "Federal Indian Identification Policy," *op. cit.*, pp. 127–28.

22. Letter, Charles Burke to William Williamson, September 16, 1921; William Williamson Papers, Box 2, File—Indian Matters, Miscellaneous, I.D. Weeks Library, University of South Dakota, Vermillion. Such articulation of official sensibility was hardly isolated; see Kvasnicka, Robert M., and Herman J. Viola (eds.), *The Commissioners of Indian Affairs, 1824–1977,* University of Nebraska Press, Lincoln, 1979.

23. See U.S. Bureau of the Census, *1980 Census of the Population, Supplementary Reports, Race of the Population by States, 1980,* U.S. Government Printing Office, Washington, D.C., 1981. Also see, U.S. Bureau of the Census, *Ancestry of the Population by State, 1980,* Supp. Rep. PC80-SI-10, U.S. Government Printing Office, Washington, D.C., 1983.

24. The quote is taken from Galeano, Eduardo, *The Open Veins of Latin America: Five Centuries of the Pillage of a Continent,* Monthly Review Press, New York, 1973.

25. Barsh, Russell, "Indian Land Claims Policy in the United States," *North Dakota Law Review,* No. 58, 1982, pp. 1–82.

26. In October 1985, President Ronald Reagan withdrew a 1946 U.S. declaration accepting ICJ jurisdiction in all matters of "international dispute." The withdrawal took effect in April 1986. This was in response to the ICJ determination in *Nicaragua v. United States,* the first substantive case ever brought before it to which the United States was a party. The ICJ ruled the U.S. action of mining Nicaraguan harbors in times of peace to be unlawful. The Reagan administration formally rejected the authority of the ICJ to decide the matter (but removed the mines). It is undoubtedly significant that the Reagan instrument contained a clause accepting continued ICJ jurisdiction over matters pertaining to "international commercial relationships," thus attempting to convert the world court into a mechanism of mere trade arbitration. See *U.S. Terminates Acceptance of ICJ Compulsory Jurisdiction,* Department of State Bulletin No. 86, Washington, D.C., January 1986.

27. The United States declined to ratify the Genocide Convention until 1988, 40 years after it became international law (and after more than 100 other nations had ratified it), and then only with an attached "Sovereignty Package" purporting to subordinate the convention to the U.S. Constitution (thereby seeking to protect certain aspects of genocidal conduct). The U.S. stipulation in this regard is, of course, invalid under Article 27 of the 1969 Vienna Convention on the Law of Treaties and has been protested as such by such countries as Britain, Denmark, and the Netherlands. Further, the Genocide Convention is now customary international law, meaning—according to the United States' own Nuremberg Doctrine—that it is binding upon the United States, whether Congress ratifies its terms or not. For further analysis, see LeBlanc, Lawrence J., *The United States and the Genocide Convention,* Duke University Press, Durham (N.C.)/London, 1991.

28. For the context of this rhetoric, see Chomsky, Noam, "'What We Say Goes': The Middle East in the New World Order," in Cynthia Peters (ed.), *Collateral Damage: The "New World Order" at Home and Abroad.* South End Press, Boston, 1992, pp. 49–92.

29. For further information, see Chomsky, Noam, and Eqbal Ahmed, "The Gulf Crisis: How We Got There," in Greg Bates (ed.), *Mobilizing Democracy: Changing the U.S. Role in the Middle East,* Common Courage Press, Monroe, ME. 1991, pp. 3–24.

RECOMMENDED READINGS

Texts

Barry, Brian. *Justice as Impartiality.* Oxford: Oxford University Press, 1995.

Daniels, N., ed. *Reading Rawls.* Oxford: Basic Blackwell, 1975.

Hare, R. M. "Justice and Equality," in *Justice: Alternative Political Perspectives,* 3rd. Ed. James P. Sterba. Belmont: Wadsworth Publishing Co., 1998.

Hare. R. M. *Sorting Out Ethics.* Oxford University Press, 1997.

Neal, P. "Justice as Fairness: Political or Metaphysical?" *Political Theory* 18:24–50.

Rønnow-Rasmussen, Toni. *Logic, Facts and Representation: An Examination of R. M. Hare's Moral philosophy* Lund: Lund University Press, 1993.

Ryan, A. "John Rawls." In *In Return of Grand Theory in the Human Sciences,* edited by Q. Skinner, 101–119. Cambridge: Cambridge University Press, 1985.

Sandel, M. *Liberalism and the Limits of Justice.* Cambridge, MA: Harvard University Press, 1982.

Sterba, James P. *The Demands of Justice.* Notre Dame: University of Notre Dame Press, 1980.

Feminist Perspective

Brown, Wendy. "Reproductive Freedom and the 'Right to Privacy': A Paradox for Feminists." In *Families, Politics, and Public Policy: A Feminist Dialogue on Women and the State,* edited by Irene Diamond. New York: Longman, 1983.

Pitkin, Hanna. "Justice: On Relating Public and Private." *Political Theory* 9, no. 3 (1981).

Waylen, Georgina. "Women and Neo-Liberalism." In *Feminism and Political Theory,* edited by Judith Evans. London: Sage, 1986.

Multicultural Perspective

Boff, Leonardo and Elizondo, Virgil. *The Voice of the Victims.* Philadelphia: Trinity Press International, 1990.

De Las Casas, Bartolome, *History of the Indies.* New York: Harper & Row, 1971.

PART XI

✌☙

MacIntyre and Nussbaum

INTRODUCTION

Alasdair MacIntyre was born in Glasgow, Scotland, in 1929. He holds degrees from Queen Mary College, Manchester University, and Oxford University. He has taught at Princeton, Oxford, Brandeis, Boston, Vanderbilt and Yale universities, Wellesley College, and the University of Notre Dame, and currently teaches at Duke University. *After Virtue,* his most important book, was published in 1981. Subsequently, he published *Whose Justice? Which Rationality?* in 1988 and *Three Rival Versions of Moral Enquiry* in 1990.

In our selection from *After Virtue,* Alasdair MacIntyre defends a relativistic conception of virtue. MacIntyre begins by distinguishing three different conceptions of virtue. According to one conception of virtue found in Homer, a virtue is a quality that enables an individual to discharge his or her social role. According to another conception found in Aristotle and the New Testament, a virtue is a quality that enables an individual to move toward the achievement of the specifically human telos, whether natural or supernatural. And according to a third conception found in the writings of Benjamin Franklin, among others, a virtue is a quality that has utility in achieving earthly or heavenly success.

After discussing these definitions of virtue, MacIntyre then proposes to define a core concept of virtue in terms of practices. A practice, for MacIntyre, is any coherent and complex form of socially established cooperative human activity through which goods internal to that form of activity are realized in the course of trying to achieve those standards of excellence that are appropriate to and partially definitive of that form of activity, with the result that human powers to achieve excellence, and human conceptions of the ends and goods involved, are systematically extended. As examples of practices, MacIntyre cites arts, sciences, games, and the making and sustaining of family life. MacIntyre then goes on to define virtues in terms of practices: A virtue, such as courage, justice, or honesty, is an acquired human quality, the possession and exercise of which tends to enable us to achieve those goods that are internal to practices and the lack of which prevents us from achieving any such goods. MacIntyre contends that his conception of virtue is compatible with the first and second conceptions of virtue that he earlier distinguished but not with the third conception found in Franklin's works because Franklin's conception is utilitarian and does not favor internal goods over external goods in the way required by MacIntyre's own conception of virtue. According to MacIntyre, if virtue is to be effective in producing internal goods it needs to be exercised without regard to (external) consequences, which is something that MacIntyre thinks a utilitarian account, like Mill's, can never do.

Martha Nussbaum was born in 1947 in New York City. She attended Wellesley College and graduated New York University with a B.A. in 1969. She received a Ph.D. in philosophy from Harvard University in 1975. She taught at Harvard University, Wellesley College, and Brown University. She is currently Professor of Law and Philosophy at the University of Chicago. Nussbaum's major works in ethics are: *The Fragility of Goodness* (1986), *The Therapy of Desire: Theory and Practice in Hellenistic Ethics* (1994), *Poetic Justice* (1996), *Sex and Social Justice* (1998).

In "Non-Relative Virtues: An Aristotelian Approach," Martha Nussbaum, in opposition to MacIntyre, defines Aristotelian virtue as being disposed to choose and respond well in the important spheres of shared human experience. She suggests that these spheres are those of mortality, the body, pleasure and pain, cognitive ability, practical reason, early infant development, affiliation, and humor. With respect to each of these spheres she claims that there are relevant virtues that can be specified in an objective, nonrelativist way.

She then considers three challenges to the possibility of providing such an objective, nonrelativist account. To the challenge as to whether a single practical solution is sought or desirable in each sphere, Nussbaum responds that in many cases, the best we will be able to achieve is a disjunction of solutions, possibly different ones for different contexts, e.g., friendship will be expressed through different customs in different times and places. To the challenge of whether there is a nonrelative, culturally independent way of understanding what are the appropriate spheres of human experience, Nussbaum responds that while there is no completely nonrelative, culturally independent way of understanding these spheres, it will still be possible to show that some understandings are better than others. To the challenge of whether there can be forms of life that do not have all of these spheres, Nussbaum responds that there could be forms of life that do not have private property and hence the virtues that are connected with it, but she is quite skeptical about the possibility of eliminating other spheres of human experience such as those requiring the virtues of courage or justice.

In "Whose Traditions?" Susan Okin objects to what she describes as MacIntyre's uncritical acceptance of certain historical traditions as the basis for the virtuous life that he endorses. For example, MacIntyre does not notice that in the stories he cites as being essential for the moral education of children, girls and women are portrayed disparagingly. According to Okin, while MacIntyre claims to be rejecting the elitism and sexism of those historical traditions that he draws upon, he does little to suggest what a society purged of these defects would actually look like, nor does he adequately take into account how these traditions are viewed by women today.

In "Gender Inequality in China and Cultural Relativism," Xiaorong Li challenges certain romanticized "local cultural" notions of women's well-being in the People's Republic of China and argues that the Aristotelian capacity approach developed by Martha Nussbaum and Amartya Sen presents a useful cross-cultural standard that is still sensitive to cultural traditions.

41. The Nature of Virtues

ALASDAIR MacINTYRE

[It might be suggested] that even within the relatively coherent tradition of thought which I have sketched there are just too many different and incompatible conceptions of a virtue for there to be any real unity to the concept or indeed to the history. Homer, Sophocles, Aristotle, the New Testament, and medieval thinkers differ from each other in too many ways. They offer us different virtues; and they have different and incompatible theories of the virtues. If we were to consider later Western writers on the virtues, the list of differences and incompatibilities would be enlarged still further: and if we extended our enquiry to Japanese, say, or American Indian cultures, the differences would become greater still. It would be all too easy to conclude that there are a number of rival and alternative conceptions of the virtues, but, even within the tradition which I have been delineating, no single core conception.

The case for such a conclusion could not be better constructed than by beginning from a consideration of the very different lists of items which different authors in different times and places have included in their catalogues of virtues. Let me introduce the catalogues of two later Western writers, Benjamin Franklin and Jane Austen.

The first example is that of Homer. At least some of the items in a Homeric list of the *aretai* would clearly not be counted by most of us nowadays as virtues at all, physical strength being the

most obvious example. To this it might be replied that perhaps we ought not to translate the word *aretê* in Homer by our word "virtue," but instead by our word "excellence"; and perhaps, if we were so to translate it, the apparently surprising difference between Homer and ourselves would at first sight have been removed. For we could allow without any kind of oddity that the possession of physical strength is the possession of an excellence. But in fact we would not have removed, but instead would merely have relocated, the difference between Homer and ourselves. For we would now seem to be saying that Homer's concept of an *aretê,* an excellence, is one thing and that our concept of a virtue is quite another since a particular quality can be an excellence in Homer's eyes, but not a virtue in ours and vice versa.

But of course it is not that Homer's list of virtues differs only from our own; it also notably differs from Aristotle's. And Aristotle's of course also differs from our own. For one thing, as I noticed earlier, some Greek virtue-words are not easily translated into English or rather out of Greek. Moreover, consider the importance of friendship as a virtue in Aristotle's list—how different from us! Or the place of *phronêsis*—how different from Homer and from us! The mind receives from Aristotle the kind of tribute which the body receives from Homer. But it is not just the case that the difference between Aristotle and Homer lies in the inclusion of some items and the omission of others in their respective catalogues. It turns out also in the way in which those catalogues are ordered, in which items are ranked as relatively central to human excellence and which marginal.

Moreover the relationship of virtues to the social order has changed. For Homer the paradigm of human excellence is the warrior; for Aristotle it is the Athenian gentleman. Indeed according to Aristotle certain virtues are only available to those of great riches and of high social status; there are virtues which are unavailable to the poor man, even if he is a free man. And those virtues are on Aristotle's view ones central to human life: magnanimity—and once again, any translation of *megalopsuchia* is unsatisfactory—and munificence are not just virtues, but important virtues within the Aristotelian scheme.

At once it is impossible to delay the remark that the most striking contrast with Aristotle's catalogue is to be found neither in Homer's nor in our own, but in the New Testament's. For the New Testament not only praises virtues of which Aristotle knows nothing—faith, hope, and love—and says nothing about virtues such as *phronêsis* which are crucial for Aristotle, but it praises at least one quality as a virtue which Aristotle seems to count as one of the vices relative to magnanimity, namely humility. Moreover since the New Testament quite clearly sees the rich as destined for the pains of Hell, it is clear that the key virtues cannot be available to them; yet they *are* available to slaves. And the New Testament of course differs from both Homer and Aristotle not only in the items included in its catalogue, but once again in its rank ordering of the virtues.

Turn now to compare all three lists of virtues considered so far—the Homeric, the Aristotelian, and the New Testament's—with two much later lists, one which can be compiled from Jane Austen's novels and the other which Benjamin Franklin constructed for himself. Two features stand out in Jane Austen's list. The first is the importance that she allots to the virtue which she calls "constancy," a virtue about which I shall say more in a later chapter [of *After Virtue*]. In some ways constancy plays a role in Jane Austen analogous to that of *phronêsis* in

Aristotle; it is a virtue the possession of which is a prerequisite for the possession of other virtues. The second is the fact that what Aristotle treats as the virtue of agreeableness (a virtue for which he says there is no name) she treats as only the simulacrum of a genuine virtue—the genuine virtue in question is the one she calls amiability. For the man who practices agreeableness does so from considerations of honor and expediency, according to Aristotle; whereas Jane Austen thought it possible and necessary for the possessor of that virtue to have a certain real affection for people as such. (It matters here that Jane Austen is a Christian.) Remember that Aristotle himself had treated military courage as a simulacrum of true courage. Thus we find here yet another type of disagreement over the virtues; namely, one as to which human qualities are genuine virtues and which mere simulacra.

In Benjamin Franklin's list we find almost all the types of difference from at least one of the catalogues we have considered and one more. Franklin includes virtues which are new to our consideration such as cleanliness, silence, and industry; he clearly considers the drive to acquire itself a part of virtue, whereas for most ancient Greeks this is the vice of *pleonexia;* he treats some virtues which earlier ages had considered minor as major, but he also redefines some familiar virtues. In the list of thirteen virtues which Franklin compiled as part of his system of private moral accounting, he elucidates each virtue by citing a maxim obedience to which *is* the virtue in question. In the case of chastity the maxim is "Rarely use venery but for health or offspring—never to dullness, weakness, or the injury of your own or another's peace or reputation." This is clearly not what earlier writers had meant by "chastity."

We have therefore accumulated a startling number of differences and incompatibilities in the five stated and implied accounts of the virtues. So the question which I raised at the outset becomes more urgent. If different writes in different times and places, but all within the history of Western culture, include such different sets and types of items in their lists, what grounds have we for supposing that they do indeed aspire to list items of one and the same kind, that there is any shared concept at all? A second kind of consideration reinforces the presumption of a negative answer to this question. It is not just that each of these five writers lists different and differing kinds of items; it is also that what each of these lists embodies, is the expression of a different theory about what a virtue is.

In the Homeric poems a virtue is a quality the manifestation of which enables someone to do exactly what their well-defined social role requires. The primary role is that of the warrior king and that Homer lists those virtues which he does becomes intelligible at once when we recognize that the key virtues therefore must be those which enable a man to excel in combat and in the games. It follows that we cannot identify the Homeric virtues until we have first identified the key social roles in Homeric society and the requirements of each of them. The concept of *what anyone filling such-and-such a role ought to do* is prior to the concept of a virtue; the latter concept has application only via the former.

On Aristotle's account matters are very different. Even though some virtues are available only to certain types of people, none the less virtues attach not to men as inhabiting social roles, but to man as such. It is the *telos* of man as a species which determines what human qualities are virtues. We need to remember however that although Aristotle treats the acquisition and exercise of the virtues as means to an end, the relationship of means to end is internal and not external. I call a means internal to a given end when the end cannot be adequately characterized independently of a characterization of the means. So it is with the virtues and the *telos* which is the good life for man on Aristotle's account. The exercise of the virtues is itself a crucial component of the good life for man. This distinction between internal and external means to an end is not drawn by Aristotle himself in the

Nicomachean Ethics, as I noticed earlier, but it is an essential distinction to be drawn if we are to understand what Aristotle intended. The distinction *is* drawn explicitly by Aquinas in the course of his defense of St Augustine's definition of a virtue, and it is clear that Aquinas understood that in drawing it he was maintaining an Aristotelian point of view.

The New Testament's account of the virtues, even if it differs as much as it does in content from Aristotle's—Aristotle would certainly not have admired Jesus Christ and he would have been horrified by St Paul—does have the same logical and conceptual structure as Aristotle's account. A virtue is, as with Aristotle, a quality the exercise of which leads to the achievement of the human *telos*. The good for man is of course a supernatural and not only a natural good, but supernature redeems and completes nature. Moreover the relationship of virtues as means to the end which is human incorporation in the divine kingdom of the age to come is internal and not external, just as it is in Aristotle. It is of course this parallelism which allows Aquinas to synthesize Aristotle and the New Testament. A key feature of this parallelism is the way in which the concept of *the good life for man* is prior to the concept of a virtue in just the way in which on the Homeric account the concept of a social role was prior. Once again it is the way in which the former concept is applied which determines how the latter is to be applied. In both cases the concept of a virtue is a secondary concept.

The intent of Jane Austen's theory of the virtues is of another kind. C. S. Lewis has rightly emphasized how profoundly Christian her moral vision is and Gilbert Ryle has equally rightly emphasized her inheritance from Shaftesbury and from Aristotle. In fact her views combine elements from Homer as well, since she is concerned with social roles in a way that neither the New Testament nor Aristotle are. She is therefore important for the way in which she finds it possible to combine what are at first sight disparate theoretical accounts of the virtues. But for the moment any attempt to assess the significance of Jane Austen's synthesis must be delayed. Instead we must notice the quite different style of theory articulated in Benjamin Franklin's account of the virtues.

Franklin's account, like Aristotle's, is teleological; but unlike Aristotle's, it is utilitarian. According to Franklin in his *Autobiography* the virtues are means to an end, but he envisages the means-ends relationship as external rather than internal. The end to which the cultivation of the virtues ministers is happiness, but happiness understood as success, prosperity in Philadelphia and ultimately in heaven. The virtues are to be useful and Franklin's account continuously stresses utility as a criterion in individual cases: "Make no expense but to do good to others or yourself; i.e. waste nothing." "Speak not but what may benefit others or yourself. Avoid trifling conversation" and, as we have already seen, "Rarely use venery but for health or offspring. . . ." When Franklin was in Paris he was horrified by Parisian architecture: "Marble, porcelain, and gilt are squandered without utility."

We thus have at least three very different conceptions of a virtue to confront: a virtue is a quality which enables an individual to discharge his or her social role (Homer); a virtue is a quality which enables an individual to move towards the achievement of the specifically human *telos,* whether natural or supernatural (Aristotle, the New Testament, and Aquinas); a virtue is a quality which has utility in achieving earthly and heavenly success (Franklin). Are we to take these as three different rival accounts of the same thing? Or are they instead accounts of three different things? Perhaps the moral structures in archaic Greece, in fourth-century Greece, and in eighteenth-century Pennsylvania were so different from each other that we should treat them as embodying quite different concepts, whose difference is initially disguised from us by the historical accident of an inherited vocabulary which misleads us by linguistic resemblance long after conceptual identity and similarity

have failed. Our initial question has come back to us with redoubled force.

Yet although I have dwelt upon the prima facie case for holding that the differences and incompatibilities between different accounts at least suggest that there is no single, central, core conception of the virtues which might make a claim for universal allegiance, I ought also to point out that each of the five moral accounts which I have sketched so summarily does embody just such a claim. It is indeed just this feature of those accounts that makes them of more than sociological or antiquarian interest. Every one of these accounts claims not only theoretical, but also an institutional hegemony. For Odysseus the Cyclopes stand condemned because they lack agriculture, an *agora* and *themis.* For Aristotle the barbarians stand condemned because they lack the *polis* and are therefore incapable of politics. For New Testament Christians there is no salvation outside the apostolic church. And we know that Benjamin Franklin found the virtues more at home in Philadelphia than in Paris and that for Jane Austen the touchstone of the virtues is a certain kind of marriage and indeed a certain kind of naval officer (that is, a certain kind of *English* naval officer).

The question can therefore now be posed directly: are we or are we not able to disentangle from these rival and various claims a unitary core concept of the virtues of which we can give a more compelling account than any of the other accounts so far? I am going to argue that we can in fact discover such a core concept and that it turns out to provide the tradition of which I have written the history with its conceptual unity. It will indeed enable us to distinguish in a clear way those beliefs about the virtues which genuinely belong to the tradition from those which do not. Unsurprisingly perhaps it is a complex concept, different parts of which derive from different stages in the development of the tradition. Thus the concept itself in some sense embodies the history of which it is the outcome.

One of the features of the concept of a virtue which has emerged with some clarity from the argument so far is that it always requires for its application the acceptance for some prior account of certain features of social and moral life in terms of which it has to be defined and explained. So in the Homeric account the concept of a virtue is secondary to that of *a social role*, in Aristotle's account it is secondary to that of *the good life for man* conceived as the *telos* of human action, and in Franklin's much later account it is secondary to that of utility. What is it in the account which I am about to give which provides in a similar way the necessary background against which the concept of a virtue has to be made intelligible? It is in answering this question that the complex, historical, multi-layered character of the core concept of virtue becomes clear. For there are no less than three stages in the logical development of the concept which have to be identified in order, if the core conception of a virtue is to be understood, and each of these stages has its own conceptual background. The first stage requires a background account of what I shall call a practice, the second an account of what I have already characterized as the narrative order of a single human life and the third an account a good deal fuller than I have given up to now of what constitutes a moral tradition. Each later stage presupposes the earlier, but not vice versa. Each earlier stage is both modified by and reinterpreted in the light of, but also provides an essential constituent of each later stage. The progress in the development of the concept is closely related to, although it does not recapitulate in any straightforward way, the history of the tradition of which it forms the core.

In the Homeric account of the virtues—and in heroic societies more generally—the exercise of a virtue exhibits qualities which are required for sustaining a social role and for exhibiting excellence in some well-marked area of social practice: to excel is to excel at war or in the games, as Achilles does, in sustaining a household, as Penelope does, in giving counsel in the assembly, as Nestor does, in the telling of a tale, as Homer himself does. When Aristotle speaks of excellence in human activity, he sometimes though not always refers to some well-defined type of human practice: flute-playing, or war, or geometry. I am going to suggest that this notion of a particular type of practice as providing the arena in which the virtues are exhibited and in terms of which they are to receive their primary, if incomplete, definition is crucial to the whole enterprise of identifying a core concept of the virtues. I hasten to add two caveats however.

The first is to point out that my argument will not in any way imply that virtues are *only* exercised in the course of what I am calling practices. The second is to warn that I shall be using the word "practice" in a specially defined way which does not completely agree with current ordinary usage, including my own previous use of that word. What am I going to mean by it?

By a "practice" I am going to mean any coherent and complex form of socially established cooperative human activity through which goods internal to that form of activity are realized in the course of trying to achieve those standards of excellence which are appropriate to, and partially definitive of, that form of activity, with the result that human powers to achieve excellence, and human conceptions of the ends and goods involved, are systematically extended. Tic-tac-toe is not an example of a practice in this sense, nor is throwing a football with skill; but the game of football is, and so is chess. Bricklaying is not a practice; architecture is. Planting turnips is not a practice; farming is. So are the enquiries of physics, chemistry, and biology, and so is the work of the historian, and so are painting and music. In the ancient and medieval worlds the creation and sustaining of human communities—of households, cities, nations—is generally taken to be a practice in the sense in which I have defined it. Thus the range of practices is wide: arts, sciences, games, politics in the Aristotelian sense, the making and sustaining of family life, all fall under the concept. But the question of the precise range of practices is not at this stage of the first importance. Instead let me explain some of the key terms involved in my definition, beginning with the notion of goods internal to a practice.

Consider the example of a highly intelligent seven-year-old child whom I wish to teach to play chess, although the child has no particular desire to learn the game. The child does however have a very strong desire for candy and little chance of obtaining it. I therefore tell the child that if the child will play chess with me once a week I will give the child 50 cents worth of candy; moreover I tell the child that I will always play in such a way that it will be difficult, but not impossible, for the child to win and that, if the child wins, the child will receive an extra 50 cents worth of candy. Thus motivated the child plays and plays to win. Notice however that, so long as it is the candy alone which provides the child with a good reason for playing chess, the child has no reason not to cheat and every reason to cheat, provided he or she can do so successfully. But, so we may hope, there will come a time when the child will find in those goods specific to chess, in the achievement of a certain highly particular kind of analytical skill, strategic imagination, and competitive intensity, a new set of reasons, reasons now not just for winning on a particular occasion, but for trying to excel in whatever way the game of chess demands. Now if the child cheats, he or she will be defeating not me, but himself or herself.

There are thus two kinds of good possibly to be gained by playing chess. On the one hand there are those goods externally and contingently attached to chess-playing and to other practices by the accidents of social circumstance—in the case of the imaginary child candy, in the case of real adults such goods as prestige, status, and money. There are always alternative ways for achieving such goods, and their achievement is never to be had *only* by engaging in some particular kind of practice. On the other hand there are the goods internal to the practice of chess which cannot be had in any way but by playing chess or some other game of that specific kind. We call them internal for two reasons: first, as I have already suggested, because we can only specify them in terms of chess or some other game of that specific kind and by means of examples from such games (otherwise the meagerness of our vocabulary for speaking of such goods forces us into such devices as my own resort to writing of "a certain highly particular kind of"); and secondly because they can only be identified and recognized by the experience of participating in the practice in question. Those who lack the relevant experience are incompetent thereby as judges of internal goods.

This is clearly the case with all the major examples of practices: consider for example—even if briefly and inadequately—the practice of portrait painting as it developed in Western Europe from the late Middle Ages to the eighteenth century. The successful portrait painter is able to achieve many goods which are in the sense just defined external to the practice of portrait painting—fame, wealth, social status, even a measure of power and influence at courts upon occasion. But those external goods are not to be confused with the goods which are internal to the practice. The internal goods are those which result from an extended attempt to show how Wittgenstein's dictum "The human body is the best picture of the human soul" (*Investigations*, p. 178e) might be made to become true by teaching us "to regard ... the picture on our wall as the object itself (the men, landscape and so on) depicted there" (p. 205e) in a quite new way. What is misleading about Wittgenstein's dictum as it stands is its neglect of the truth in George Orwell's thesis "At fifty everyone has the face he deserves." What painters from Giotto to Rembrandt learnt to show was how the face at any age may be revealed as the face that the subject of a portrait deserves.

Originally in medieval paintings of the saints the face was an icon: the question of a resemblance between the depicted face of Christ or St

THE NATURE OF VIRTUES

Peter and the face that Jesus or Peter actually possessed at some particular age did not even arise. The antithesis to this iconography was the relative naturalism of certain fifteenth-century Flemish and German painting. The heavy eyelids, the coifed hair, the lines around the mouth undeniably represent some particular woman, either actual or envisaged. Resemblance has usurped the iconic relationship. But with Rembrandt there is, so to speak, synthesis: the naturalistic portrait is now rendered as an icon, but an icon of a new and hitherto inconceivable kind. Similarly in a very different kind of sequence mythological faces in a certain kind of seventeenth-century French painting become aristocratic faces in the eighteenth century. Within each of these sequences at least two different kinds of good internal to the painting of human faces and bodies are achieved.

There is first of all the excellence of the products, both the excellence in performance by the painters and that of each portrait itself. This excellence—the very verb "excel" suggests it—has to be understood historically. The sequences of development find their point and purpose in a progress towards and beyond a variety of types and modes of excellence. There are of course sequences of decline as well as of progress, and progress is rarely to be understood as straightforwardly linear. But it is in participation in the attempts to sustain progress and to respond creatively to problems that the second kind of good internal to the practices of portrait painting is to be found. For what the artist discovers within the pursuit of excellence in portrait painting—and what is true of portrait painting is true of the practice of the fine arts in general—is the good of a certain kind of life. That life may not constitute the whole of life for someone who is a painter by a very long way or it may at least for a period, Gauguin-like, absorb him or her at the expense of almost everything else. But it is the painter's living out of a greater or lesser part of his or her life *as a painter* that is the second kind of good internal to painting. And judgment

upon these goods requires at the very least the kind of competence that is only to be acquired either as a painter or as someone willing to learn systematically what the portrait painter has to teach.

A practice involves standards of excellence and obedience to rules as well as the achievement of goods. To enter into a practice is to accept the authority of those standards and the inadequacy of my own performance as judged by them. It is to subject my own attitudes, choices, preferences, and tastes to the standards which currently and partially define the practice. Practices of course, as I have just noticed, have a history: games, sciences, and arts all have histories. Thus the standards are not themselves immune from criticism, but none the less we cannot be initiated into a practice without accepting the authority of the best standards realized so far. If, on starting to listen to music, I do not accept my own incapacity to judge correctly, I will never learn to hear, let alone to appreciate, Bartok's last quartets. If, on starting to play baseball, I do not accept that others know better than I when to throw a fast ball and when not, I will never learn to appreciate good pitching let alone to pitch. In the realm of practices the authority of both goods and standards operates in such a way as to rule out all subjectivist and emotivist analyses of judgment. De gustibus *est* disputandum.

We are now in a position to notice an important difference between what I have called internal and what I have called external goods. It is characteristic of what I have called external goods that when achieved they are always some individual's property and possession. Moreover characteristically they are such that the more someone has of them, the less there is for other people. This is sometimes necessarily the case, as with power and fame, and sometimes the case by reason of contingent circumstance as with money. External goods are therefore characteristically objects of competition in which there must be losers as well as winners. Internal goods are indeed the outcome of competition to excel, but it is characteristic of them that their achievement is a good for the whole community who participate in the practice. So when Turner transformed the seascape in painting or W. G. Grace advanced the art of batting in cricket in a quite new way their achievement enriched the whole relevant community.

But what does all or any of this have to do with the concept of the virtues? It turns out that we are now in a position to formulate a first, even if partial and tentative definition of a virtue: *A virtue is an acquired human quality the possession and exercise of which tends to enable us to achieve those goods which are internal to practices and the lack of which effectively prevents us from achieving any such goods.* Later this definition will need amplification and amendment. But as a first approximation to an adequate definition it already illuminates the place of the virtues in human life. For it is not difficult to show for a whole range of key virtues that without them the goods internal to practices are barred to us, but not just barred to us generally, barred in a very particular way.

It belongs to the concept of a practice as I have outlined it—and as we are all familiar with it already in our actual lives, whether we are painters or physicists or quarterbacks or indeed just lovers of good painting or first-rate experiments or a well-thrown pass—that its goods can only be achieved by subordinating ourselves within the practice in our relationship to other practitioners. We have to learn to recognize what is due to whom; we have to be prepared to take whatever self-endangering risks are demanded along the way; and we have to listen carefully to what we are told about our own inadequacies and to reply with the same carefulness for the facts. In other words we have to accept as necessary components of any practice with internal goods and standards of excellence the virtues of justice, courage, and honesty. For not to accept these, to be willing to cheat as our imagined child was willing to cheat in his or her

early days at chess, so far bars us from achieving the standards of excellence or the goods internal to the practice that it renders the practice pointless except as a device for achieving external goods.

We can put the same point in another way. Every practice requires a certain kind of relationship between those who participate in it. Now the virtues are those goods by reference to which, whether we like it or not, we define our relationships to those other people with whom we share the kind of purposes and standards which inform practices. Consider an example of how reference to the virtues has to be made in certain kinds of human relationship.

A, B, C, and D are friends in that sense of friendship which Aristotle takes to be primary: they share in the pursuit of certain goods. In my terms they share in a practice. D dies in obscure circumstances. A discovers how D died and tells the truth about it to B while lying to C. C discovers the lie. What A cannot then intelligibly claim is that he stands in the same relationship of friendship to both B and C. By telling the truth to one and lying to the other he has partially defined a difference in the relationship. Of course it is open to A to explain this difference in a number of ways: perhaps he was trying to spare C pain or perhaps he is simply cheating C. But some difference in the relationship now exists as a result of the lie. For their allegiance to each other in the pursuit of common goods has been put in question.

Just as, so long as we share the standards and purposes characteristic of practices, we define our relationship to each other, whether we acknowledge it or not, by reference to standards of truthfulness and trust, so we define them too by reference to standards of justice and of courage. If A, a professor, gives B and C the grades that their papers deserve, but grades D because he is attracted by D's blue eyes or is repelled by D's dandruff, he has defined his relationship to D differently from his relationship to the other members of the class, whether he wishes it or not. Justice requires that we treat others in respect of merit or desert according to uniform and impersonal standards: to depart from the standards of justice in some particular instance defines our relationship with the relevant person as in some way special or distinctive.

The case with courage is a little different. We hold courage to be a virtue because the care and concern for individuals, communities, and causes which is so crucial to so much in practices requires the existence of such a virtue. If someone says that he cares for some individual, community, or cause, but is unwilling to risk harm or danger on his, her, or its own behalf, he puts in question the genuineness of his care and concern. Courage, the capacity to risk harm or danger to oneself, has its role in human life because of this connection with care and concern. This is not to say that a man cannot genuinely care and also be a coward. It is in part to say that a man who genuinely cares and has not the capacity for risking harm or danger has to define himself, both to himself and to others, as a coward.

I take it then that from the standpoint of those types of relationship without which practices cannot be sustained truthfulness, justice, and courage—and perhaps some others—are genuine excellences, are virtues in the light of which we have to characterize ourselves and others, whatever our private moral standpoint or our society's particular codes may be. For this recognition that we cannot escape the definition of our relationships in terms of such goods is perfectly compatible with the acknowledgment that different societies have and have had different codes of truthfulness, justice, and courage. Lutheran pietists brought up their children to believe that one ought to tell the truth to everybody at all times, whatever the circumstances or consequences, and Kant was one of their children. Traditional Bantu parents brought up their children not to tell the truth to unknown strangers, since they believed that this could render the family vulnerable to witchcraft. In our culture many of us have been brought up not to

tell the truth to elderly great-aunts who invite us to admire their new hats. But each of these codes embodies an acknowledgment of the virtue of truthfulness. So it is also with varying codes of justice and of courage.

Practices then might flourish in societies with very different codes; what they could not do is flourish in societies in which the virtues were not valued, although institutions and technical skills serving unified purposes might well continue to flourish. (I shall have more to say about the contrast between institutions and technical skills mobilized for a unified end, on the one hand, and practices on the other, in a moment.) For the kind of cooperation, the kind of recognition of authority and of achievement, the kind of respect for standards and the kind of risk-taking which are characteristically involved in practices demand for example fairness in judging oneself and others—the kind of fairness absent in my example of the professor, a ruthless truthfulness without which fairness cannot find application—the kind of truthfulness absent in my example of A, B, C, and D—and willingness to trust the judgments of those whose achievement in the practice gives them an authority to judge which presupposes fairness and truthfulness in those judgments, and from time to time the taking of self-endangering and even achievement-endangering risks. It is no part of my thesis that great violinists cannot be vicious or great chess-players mean-spirited. Where the virtues are required, the vices also may flourish. It is just that the vicious and mean-spirited necessarily rely on the virtues of others for the practices in which they engage to flourish and also deny themselves the experience of achieving those internal goods which may reward even not very good chess-players and violinists.

To situate the virtues any further within practices it is necessary now to clarify a little further the nature of a practice by drawing two important contrasts. The discussion so far I hope makes it clear that a practice, in the sense intended, is never just a set of technical skills, even when directed towards some unified purpose and even if the exercise of those skills can on occasion be valued or enjoyed for their own sake. What is distinctive in a practice is in part the way in which conceptions of the relevant goods and ends which the technical skills serve—and every practice does require the exercise of technical skills—are transformed and enriched by these extensions of human powers and by that regard for its own internal goods which are partially definitive of each particular practice or type of practice. Practices never have a goal or goals fixed for all time—painting has no such goal nor has physics—but the goals themselves are transmuted by the history of the activity. It therefore turns out not to be accidental that every practice has its own history and a history which is more and other than that of the improvement of the relevant technical skills. This historical dimension is crucial in relation to the virtues.

To enter into a practice is to enter into a relationship not only with its contemporary practitioners, but also with those who have preceded us in the practice, particularly those whose achievements extended the reach of the practice to its present point. It is thus the achievement, and *a fortiori* the authority, of a tradition which I then confront and from which I have to learn. And for this learning and the relationship to the past which it embodies the virtues of justice, courage, and truthfulness are prerequisite in precisely the same way and for precisely the same reasons as they are in sustaining present relationships within practices.

It is not only of course with sets of technical skills that practices ought to be contrasted. Practices must not be confused with institutions. Chess, physics, and medicine are practices; chess clubs, laboratories, universities, and hospitals are institutions. Institutions are characteristically and necessarily concerned with what I have called external goods. They are involved in acquiring money and other material goods: they are structured in terms of power and status, and they distribute money, power, and status as rewards. Nor could they do otherwise if they are to sustain not only themselves, but also the practices of which they are the bearers. For no practices can survive for any length of time unsustained by institutions. Indeed so intimate is the relationship of practices to institutions—and consequently of the goods external to the goods internal to the practices in question—that institutions and practices characteristically form a single causal order in which the ideals and the creativity of the practice are always vulnerable to the acquisitiveness of the institution, in which the cooperative care for common goods of the practice is always vulnerable to the competitiveness of the institution. In this context the essential function of the virtues is clear. Without them, without justice, courage, and truthfulness, practices could not resist the corrupting power of institutions.

Yet if institutions do have corrupting power, the making and sustaining of forms of human community—and therefore of institutions—itself has all the characteristics of a practice, and moreover of a practice which stands in a peculiarly close relationship to the exercise of the virtues in two important ways. The exercise of the virtues is itself apt to require a highly determinate attitude to social and political issues; and it is always within some particular community with its own specific institutional forms that we learn or fail to learn to exercise the virtues. There is of course a crucial difference between the way in which the relationship between moral character and political community is envisaged from the standpoint of liberal individualist modernity and the way in which that relationship was envisaged from the standpoint of the type of ancient and medieval tradition of the virtues which I have sketched. For liberal individualism a community is simply an arena in which individuals each pursue their own self-chosen conception of the good life, and political institutions exist to provide that degree of order which makes such self-determined activity possible. Government and law are, or ought to be, neutral between rival concepts as of the good life for man, and hence, although it is the task of government to promote law-abidingness, it is on the liberal view no part of the legitimate function of government to inculcate any one moral outlook.

By contrast, on the particular ancient and medieval view which I have sketched political community not only requires the exercise of the virtues for its own sustenance, but it is one of the tasks of parental authority to make children grow up so as to be virtuous adults. The classical statement of this analogy is by Socrates in the *Crito*. It does not of course follow from an acceptance of the Socratic view of political community and political authority that we ought to assign to the modern state the moral function which Socrates assigned to the city and its laws. Indeed the power of the liberal individualist standpoint partly derives from the evident fact that the modern state is indeed totally unfitted to act as moral educator of any community. But the history of how the modern state emerged is of course itself a moral history. If my account of the complex relationship of virtues to practices and to institutions is correct, it follows that we shall be unable to write a true history of practices and institutions unless that history is also one of the virtues and vices. For the ability of a practice to retain its integrity will depend on the way in which the virtues can be and are exercised in sustaining the institutional forms which are the social bearers of the practice. The integrity of a practice causally requires the exercise of the virtues by at least some of the individuals who embody it in their activities: and conversely the corruption of institutions is always in part at least an effect of the vices.

The virtues are of course themselves in turn fostered by certain types of social institution and endangered by others. Thomas Jefferson thought that only in a society of small farmers could the virtues flourish; and Adam Ferguson with a good deal more sophistication saw the institutions of modern commercial society as endangering at least some traditional virtues. It is Ferguson's type of sociology which is the empirical counterpart of the conceptual account of the virtues which I have given, a sociology which aspires to lay bare the empirical, causal connection between virtues, practices, and institutions. For this kind of conceptual account has strong empirical implications; it provides an explanatory scheme which can be tested in particular cases. Moreover my thesis has empirical content in another way; it does entail that without the virtues there could be a recognition only of what I have called external goods and not at all of internal goods in the context of practices. And in any society which recognized only external goods competitiveness would be the dominant and even exclusive feature. We have a brilliant portrait of such a society in Hobbes's account of the state of nature; and Professor Turnbull's report of the fate of the Ik suggests that social reality does in the most horrifying way confirm both my thesis and Hobbes's.

Virtues then stand in a different relationship to external and to internal goods. The possession of the virtues—and not only of their semblance and simulacra—is necessary to achieve the latter; yet the possession of the virtues may perfectly well hinder us in achieving external goods. I need to emphasize at this point that external goods genuinely are goods. Not only are they characteristic objects of human desire, whose allocation is what gives point to the virtues of justice and of generosity, but no one can despise them altogether without a certain hypocrisy. Yet notoriously the cultivation of truthfulness, justice, and courage will often, the world being what it contingently is, bar us from being rich or famous or powerful. Thus although we may hope that we can not only achieve the standards of excellence and the internal goods of certain practices by possessing the virtues *and* become rich, famous, and powerful, the virtues are always a potential stumbling block to this comfortable ambition. We should therefore expect that, if in a particular society the pursuit of external goods were to become dominant, the concept of the virtues might suffer first attrition and then perhaps something near total effacement, although simulacra might abound.

The time has come to ask the question of how far this partial account of a core conception of the virtues—and I need to emphasize that all that I have offered so far is the first stage of such an account—is faithful to the tradition which I delineated. How far, for example, and in what ways is it Aristotelian? It is—happily—not Aristotelian in two ways in which a good deal of the rest of the tradition also dissents from Aristotle. First, although this account of the virtues is teleological, it does not require any allegiance to Aristotle's metaphysical biology. And secondly, just because of the multiplicity of human practices and the consequent multiplicity of goods in the pursuit of which the virtues may be exercised—goods which will often be contingently incompatible and which will therefore make rival claims upon our allegiance—conflict will not spring solely from flaws in individual character. But it was just on these two matters that Aristotle's account of the virtues seemed most vulnerable; hence if it turns out to be the case that this socially teleological account can support Aristotle's general account of the virtues as well as does his own biologically teleological account, these differences from Aristotle himself may well be regarded as strengthening rather than weakening the case for a generally Aristotelian standpoint.

There are at least three ways in which the account that I have given *is* clearly Aristotelian. First it requires for its completion a cogent elaboration of just those distinctions and concepts which Aristotle's account requires: voluntariness, the distinction between the intellectual virtues and the virtues of character, the relationship of both to natural abilities and to the passions and the structure of practical reasoning. On every one of these topics something very like Aristotle's view has to be defended, if my own account is to be plausible.

Secondly my account can accommodate an Aristotelian view of pleasure and enjoyment, whereas it is interestingly irreconcilable with any utilitarian view and more particularly with Franklin's account of the virtues. We can approach these questions by considering how to reply to someone who, having considered my account of the differences between goods internal to and goods external to a practice enquired into which class, if either, does pleasure or enjoyment fall? The answer is, "Some types of pleasure into one, some into the other."

Someone who achieves excellence in a practice, who plays chess or football well or who carries through an enquiry in physics or an experimental mode in painting with success, characteristically enjoys his achievement and his activity in achieving. So does someone who, although not breaking the limit of achievement, plays or thinks or acts in a way that leads towards such a breaking of limit. As Aristotle says, the enjoyment of the activity and the enjoyment of achievement are not the ends at which the agent aims, but the enjoyment supervenes upon the successful activity in such a way that the activity achieved and the activity enjoyed are one and the same state. Hence to aim at the one is to aim at the other; and hence also it is easy to confuse the pursuit of excellence with the pursuit of enjoyment *in this specific sense*. This particular confusion is harmless enough; what is not harmless is the confusion of enjoyment *in this specific sense* with other forms of pleasure.

For certain kinds of pleasure are of course external goods along with prestige, status, power, and money. Not all pleasure is the enjoyment supervening upon achieved activity; some is the pleasure of psychological or physical states independent of all activity. Such states—for example that produced on a normal palate by the closely successive and thereby blended sensations of Colchester oyster, cayenne pepper, and Veuve Cliquot—may be sought as external goods, as external rewards which may be purchased by money or received in virtue of prestige. Hence the pleasures are categorized neatly and appropriately by the classification into internal and external goods.

It is just this classification which can find no place within Franklin's account of the virtues which is framed entirely in terms of external relationships and external goods. Thus although by this stage of the argument it is possible to claim that my account does capture a conception of the virtues which is at the core of the particular ancient and medieval tradition which I have delineated, it is equally clear that there is more than one possible conception of the virtues and that Franklin's standpoint and indeed any utilitarian standpoint is such that to accept it will entail rejecting the tradition and vice versa.

One crucial point of incompatibility was noted long ago by D. H. Lawrence. When Franklin asserts, "Rarely use venery but for health or offspring...," Lawrence replies, "Never *use* venery." It is of the character of a virtue that in order that it be effective in producing the internal goods which are the rewards of the virtues it should be exercised without regard to consequences. For it turns out to be the case that—and this is in part at least one more empirical factual claim—although the virtues are just those qualities which tend to lead to the achievement of a certain class of goods, none the less unless we practice them irrespective of whether in any particular set of contingent circumstances they will produce those goods or not, we cannot possess them at all. We cannot be genuinely courageous or truthful and be so only on occasion. Moreover, as we have seen, cultivation of the virtues always may and often does hinder the achievement of those external goods which are the mark of worldly success. The road to success in Philadelphia and the road to heaven may not coincide after all.

Furthermore we are now able to specify one crucial difficulty for *any* version of utilitarianism—in addition to those which I noticed earlier. Utilitarianism cannot accommodate the distinction between goods internal to and goods external to a practice. Not only is that distinction marked by none of the classical utilitarians—it cannot be found in Bentham's writings nor in those of either of the Mills or of Sidgwick—but internal goods and external goods are not commensurable with each other. Hence the notion of summing goods—and *a fortiori* in the light of what I have said about kinds of pleasure and enjoyment the notion of summing happiness—in terms of one single formula or conception of utility, whether it is Franklin's or Bentham's or Mill's, makes no sense. None the less we ought to note that although *this* distinction is alien to J. S. Mill's thought, it is plausible and in no way patronizing to suppose that something like this is the distinction which he was trying to make in *Utilitarianism* when he distinguished between "higher" and "lower" pleasures. At the most we can say "something like this"; for J. S. Mill's upbringing had given him a limited view of human life and powers, had unfitted him, for example, for appreciating games just because of the way it had fitted him for appreciating philosophy. None the less the notion that the pursuit of excellence in a way that extends human powers is at the heart of human life is instantly recognizable as at home in not only J. S. Mill's political and social thought, but also in his and Mrs Taylor's life. Were I to choose human exemplars of certain of the virtues as I understand them, there would of course be many names to name, those of St Benedict and St Francis of Assisi and St Theresa *and* those of Frederick Engels and Eleanor Marx and Leon Trotsky among them. But that of John Stuart Mill would have to be there as certainly as any other.

Thirdly my account is Aristotelian in that it links evaluation and explanation in a characteristically Aristotelian way. From an Aristotelian standpoint to identify certain actions as manifesting or failing to manifest a virtue or virtues is never only to evaluate; it is also to take the first step towards explaining why those actions rather than some others were performed. Hence for an Aristotelian quite as much as for a Platonist the fate of a city or an individual can be explained by citing the injustice of a tyrant or the courage of its defenders. Indeed without allusion to the place that justice and injustice, courage and cowardice play in human life very little will be genuinely explicable. It follows that many of the explanatory projects of the modern social sciences, a methodological canon of which is the separation of "the facts" from all evaluation, are bound to fail. For the fact that someone was or failed to be courageous or just cannot be recognized as "a fact" by those who accept that methodological canon. The account of the virtues which I have given is completely at one with Aristotle's on this point. But now the question may be raised: your account may be in many respects Aristotelian, but is it not in some respects false? Consider the following important objection.

I have defined the virtues partly in terms of their place in practices. But surely, it may be suggested, some practices—that is, some coherent human activities which answer to the description of what I have called a practice—are evil. So in discussion by some moral philosophers of this type of account of the virtues it has been suggested that torture and sadomasochistic sexual activities might be examples of practices. But how can a disposition be a virtue if it is the kind of disposition which sustains practices and some practices issue in evil? My answer to this objection falls into two parts.

First I want to allow that there *may* be practices—in the sense in which I understand the concept—which simply *are* evil. I am far from convinced that there are, and I do not in fact believe that either torture or sadomasochistic sexuality answer to the description of a practice which my account of the virtues employs. But I do not want to rest my case on this lack of conviction, especially since it is plain that as a matter of contingent fact many types of practice may on particular occasions be productive of evil. For the range of practices includes the arts, the sciences and certain types of intellectual and ath-

letic games. And it is at once obvious that any of these may under certain conditions be a source of evil: the desire to excel and to win can corrupt, a man may be so engrossed by his painting that he neglects his family, what was initially an honorable resort to war can issue in savage cruelty. But what follows from this?

It certainly is not the case that my account entails *either* that we ought to excuse or condone such evils *or* that whatever flows from a virtue is right. I do have to allow that courage sometimes sustains injustice, that loyalty has been known to strengthen a murderous aggressor and that generosity has sometimes weakened the capacity to do good. But to deny this would be to fly in the face of just those empirical facts which I invoked in criticizing Aquinas' account of the unity of the virtues. That the virtues need initially to be defined and explained with reference to the notion of a practice thus in no way entails approval of all practices in all circumstances. That the virtues—as the objection itself presupposed—*are* defined not in terms of good and right practices, but of practices, does not entail or imply that practices as actually carried through at particular times and places do not stand in need of moral criticism. And the resources for such criticism are not lacking. There is in the first place no inconsistency in appealing to the requirements of a virtue to criticize a practice. Justice may be initially defined as a disposition which in its particular way is necessary to sustain practices; it does not follow that in pursuing the requirements of a practice violations of justice are not to be condemned. Moreover, a morality of virtues requires as its counterpart a conception of moral law. Its requirements too have to be met by practices. But, it may be asked, does not all this imply that more needs to be said about the place of practices in some larger moral context? Does not this at least suggest that there is more to the core concept of a virtue than can be spelled out in terms of practices? I have after all emphasized that the scope of any virtue in human life extends beyond the practices in terms of which it is initially defined. What then is the place of the virtues in the larger arenas of human life?

I stressed earlier that any account of the virtues in terms of practices could only be a partial and first account. What is required to complement it? The most notable difference so far between my account and any account that could be called Aristotelian is that although I have in no way restricted the exercise of the virtues to the context of practices, it is in terms of practices that I have located their point and function. Whereas Aristotle locates that point and function in terms of the notion of a type of whole human life which can be called good. And it does seem that the question "What would a human being lack who lacked the virtues?" must be given a kind of answer which goes beyond anything which I have said so far. For such an individual would not merely fail *in a variety of particular ways* in respect of the kind of excellence which can be achieved through participation in practices and in respect of the kind of human relationship required to sustain such excellence. His own life *viewed as a whole* would perhaps be defective; it would not be the kind of life which someone would describe in trying to answer the question, "What is the best kind of life for this kind of man or woman to live?" And that question cannot be answered without at least raising Aristotle's own question, "What is the good life for man?" Consider three ways in which human life informed only by the conception of the virtues sketched so far would be defective.

It would be pervaded, first of all, by *too many* conflicts and *too much* arbitrariness. I argued earlier that it is a merit of an account of the virtues in terms of a multiplicity of goods that it allows for the possibility of tragic conflict in a way in which Aristotle's does not. But it may also produce even in the life of someone who is virtuous and disciplined too many occasions when one allegiance points in one direction, another in another. The claims of one practice may be incompatible with another in such a way that one may find oneself oscillating in an arbitrary way, rather than making rational choices. So it seems to have been with T. E. Lawrence. Commitment to sustaining the kind of community in which the virtues can flourish may be incompatible with the devotion which a particular practice—of the arts, for example—requires. So there may be tensions between the claims of family life and those of the arts—the problem that Gauguin solved or failed to solve by fleeing to Polynesia, or between the claims of politics and those of the arts—the problem that Lenin solved or failed to solve by refusing to listen to Beethoven.

If the life of the virtues is continuously fractured by choices in which one allegiance entails the apparently arbitrary renunciation of another, it may seem that the goods internal to practices do after all derive their authority from our individual choices; for when different goods summon in different and in incompatible directions, "I" have to choose between their rival claims. The modern self with its criterionless choices apparently reappears in the alien context of what was claimed to be an Aristotelian world. This accusation might be rebutted in part by returning to the question of why both goods and virtues do have authority in our lives and repeating what was said earlier in this chapter. But this reply would only be partly successful: the distinctively modern notion of choice would indeed have reappeared, even if with a more limited scope for its exercise than it has usually claimed.

Secondly, without an overriding conception of the *telos* of a whole human life, conceived as a unity, our conception of certain individual virtues has to remain partial and incomplete. Consider two examples. Justice, on an Aristotelian view, is defined in terms of giving each person his or her due or desert. To deserve well is to have contributed in some substantial way to the achievement of those goods, the sharing of which and the common pursuit of which provide foundations for human community. But the goods internal to practices, including the goods internal to the practice of making and sustaining forms of community, need to be ordered and evaluated in some way if we are to assess relative desert. Thus any substantive application of an Aristotelian concept of justice requires an understanding of goods and of the good that goes beyond the multiplicity of goods which inform practices. As with justice, so also with patience. Patience is the virtue of waiting attentively without complaint, but not of waiting thus for anything at all. To treat patience as a virtue presupposes some adequate answer to the question: waiting for what? Within the context of practices a partial, although for many purposes adequate, answer can be given: the patience of a craftsman with refractory material, of a teacher with a slow pupil, of a politician in negotiations, are all species of patience. But what if the material is just too refractory, the pupil too slow, the negotiations too frustrating? Ought we always at a certain point just to give up in the interests of the practice itself? The medieval exponents of the virtue of patience claimed that there are certain types of situation in which the virtue of patience requires that I do not ever give up on some person or task, situations in which, as they would have put it, I am required to embody in my attitude to that person or task something of the patient attitude of God towards his creation. But this could only be so if patience served some overriding good, some *telos* which warranted putting other goods in a subordinate place. Thus it turns out that the content of the virtue of patience depends upon how we order various goods in a hierarchy and *a fortiori* on whether we are able rationally so to order these particular goods.

I have suggested so far that unless there is a *telos* which transcends the limited goods of practices by constituting the good of a whole human life, the good of a human life conceived as a unity, it will *both* be the case that a certain subversive arbitrariness will invade the moral life *and* that we shall be unable to specify the context of certain virtues adequately. These two considerations are reinforced by a third: that there is at least one virtue recognized by the tradition which cannot be specified at all except with reference to the wholeness of a human life—the virtue of integrity or constancy. "Purity of heart," said Kierkegaard, "is to will one thing." This notion of singleness of purpose in a whole life can have no application unless that of a whole life does. . . .

42. Non-Relative Virtues: An Aristotelian Approach

MARTHA NUSSBAUM

All Greeks used to go around armed with swords.

> Thucydides, History of the Peloponnesian War

The customs of former times might be said to be too simple and barbaric. For Greeks used to go around armed with swords; and they used to buy wives from one another, and there are surely other ancient customs that are extremely stupid. (For example, in Cyme there is a law about homicide, that if a man prosecuting a charge can produce a certain number of witnesses from among his own relations, the defendant will automatically be convicted of murder.) In general, all human beings seek not the way of their ancestors, but the good.

> Aristotle, Politics 1268a39ff.

One may also observe in one's travels to distant countries the feelings of recognition and affiliation that link every human being to every other human being.

> Aristotle, Nichomachean Ethics 1155a21–22

I

The virtues are attracting increasing interest in contemporary philosophical debate. From many different sides one hears of a dissatisfaction with ethical theories that are remote from concrete human experience. Whether this remoteness results from the utilitarian's interest in arriving at a universal calculus of satisfactions or from a Kantian concern with universal principles of broad generality, in which the names of particular contexts, histories, and persons do not occur, remoteness is now being seen by an increasing number of moral philosophers as a defect in an approach to ethical questions. In the search for an alternative approach, the concept of virtue is playing a prominent role. So, too, is the work of Aristotle, the greatest defender of an ethical approach based on the concept of virtue. For Aristotle's work seems, appealingly, to combine rigor with concreteness, theoretical power with sensitivity to the actual circumstances of human life and choice in all their multiplicity, variety, and mutability.

But on one central point there is a striking divergence between Aristotle and contemporary virtue theory. To many current defenders of an ethical approach based on the virtues, the return to the virtues is connected with a turn toward relativism—toward, that is, the view that the only appropriate criteria of ethical goodness are local ones, internal to the traditions and practices of each local society or group that asks itself questions about the good. The rejection of general algorithms and abstract rules in favor of an account of the good life based on specific modes

From *Midwest Studies in Philosophy, Volume XIII*, edited by Peter A. French, Theodore E. Uehling, Jr., and Howard K. Wettstein. © 1988 by the University of Notre Dame Press. Used by permission.

of virtuous action is taken, by writers as otherwise diverse as Alasdair MacIntyre, Bernard Williams, and Philippa Foot,[1] to be connected with the abandonment of the project of rationally justifying a single norm of flourishing life for and to all human beings and with a reliance, instead, on norms that are local both in origin and in application.

The positions of all of these writers, where relativism is concerned, are complex; none unequivocally endorses a relativist view. But all connect virtue ethics with a relativist denial that ethics, correctly understood, offers any transcultural norms, justifiable with reference to reasons of universal human validity, with reference to which we may appropriately criticize different local conceptions of the good. And all suggest that the insights we gain by pursuing ethical questions in the Aristotelian virtue-based way lend support to relativism.

For this reason it is easy for those who are interested in supporting the rational criticism of local traditions and in articulating an idea of ethical progress to feel that the ethics of virtue can give them little help. If the position of women, as established by local traditions in many parts of the world, is to be improved, if traditions of slave holding and racial inequality, if religious intolerance, if aggressive and warlike conceptions of manliness, if unequal norms of material distribution are to be criticized in the name of practical reason, this criticizing (one might easily suppose) will have to be done from a Kantian or utilitarian viewpoint, not through the Aristotelian approach.

This is an odd result, where Aristotle is concerned. For it is obvious that he was not only the defender of an ethical theory based on the virtues, but also the defender of a single objective account of the human good, or human flourishing. This account is supposed to be objective in the sense that it is justifiable with reference to reasons that do not derive merely from local traditions and practices, but rather from features of humanness that lie beneath all local traditions and are there

to be seen whether or not they are in fact recognized in local traditions. And one of Aristotle's most obvious concerns is the criticism of existing moral traditions, in his own city and in others, as unjust or repressive, or in other ways incompatible with human flourishing. He uses his account of the virtues as a basis for this criticism of local traditions: prominently, for example, in Book II of the *Politics,* where he frequently argues against existing social forms by pointing to ways in which they neglect or hinder the development of some important human virtue.[2] Aristotle evidently believes that there is no incompatibility between basing an ethical theory on the virtues and defending the singleness and objectivity of the human good. Indeed, he seems to believe that these two aims are mutually supportive.

Now the fact that Aristotle believes something does not make it true. (Though I have sometimes been accused of holding that position!) But it does, on the whole, make that something a plausible *candidate* for the truth, one deserving our most serious scrutiny. In this case, it would be odd indeed if he had connected two elements in ethical thought that are self-evidently incompatible, or in favor of whose connectedness and compatibility there is nothing interesting to be said. The purpose of this paper is to establish that Aristotle does indeed have an interesting way of connecting the virtues with a search for ethical objectivity and with the criticism of existing local norms, a way that deserves our serious consideration as we work on these questions. Having described the general shape of the Aristotelian approach, we can then begin to understand some of the objections that might be brought against such a non-relative account of the virtues, and to imagine how the Aristotelian could respond to those objections.

II

The relativist, looking at different societies, is impressed by the variety and the apparent noncomparability in the lists of virtues she encounters. Examining the different lists, and observing the complex connections between each list and a concrete form of life and a concrete history, she may well feel that any list of virtues must be simply a reflection of local traditions and values, and that, virtues being (unlike Kantian principles or utilitarian algorithms) concrete and closely tied to forms of life, there can in fact be no list of virtues that will serve as normative for all these varied societies. It is not only that the specific forms of behavior recommended in connection with the virtues differ greatly over time and place, it is also that the very areas that are singled out as spheres of virtue, and the manner in which they are individuated from other areas, vary so greatly. For someone who thinks this way, it is easy to feel that Aristotle's own list, despite its pretensions to universality and objectivity, must be similarly restricted, merely a reflection of one particular society's perceptions of salience and ways of distinguishing. At this point, relativist writers are likely to quote Aristotle's description of the "great-souled" person, the *megalopsuchos,* which certainly contains many concrete local features and sounds very much like the portrait of a certain sort of Greek gentleman, in order to show that Aristotle's list is just as culture-bound as any other.[3]

But if we probe further into the way in which Aristotle in fact enumerates and individuates the virtues, we begin to notice things that cast doubt upon the suggestion that he has simply described what is admired in his own society. First of all, we notice that a rather large number of virtues and vices (vices especially) are nameless, and that, among the ones that are not nameless, a good many are given, by Aristotle's own account, names that are somewhat arbitrarily chosen by Aristotle, and do not perfectly fit the behavior he is trying to describe.[4] Of such modes of conduct he writes, "Most of these are nameless, but we must try ... to give them names in order to make our account clear and easy to follow" (*NE* 1108a16-19). This does not sound like

the procedure of someone who is simply studying local traditions and singling out the virtue names that figure most prominently in those traditions.

What *is* going on becomes clearer when we examine the way in which he does, in fact, introduce his list. For he does so, in the *Nicomachean Ethics,*[5] by a device whose very straightforwardness and simplicity has caused it to escape the notice of most writers on this topic. What he does, in each case, is to isolate a sphere of human experience that figures in more or less any human life, and in which more or less any human being will have to make *some* choices rather than others, and act in *some* way rather than some other. The introductory chapter enumerating the virtues and vices begins from an enumeration of these spheres (*NE* 2.7); and each chapter on a virtue in the more detailed account that follows begins with "Concerning *x* ..." or words to this effect, where "*x*" names a sphere of life with which all human beings regularly and more or less necessarily have dealings.[6] Aristotle then asks: What is it to choose and respond well within that sphere? What is it, on the other hand, to choose defectively? The "thin account" of each virtue is that it is whatever it is to be stably disposed to act appropriately in that sphere. There may be, and usually are, various competing specifications of what acting well, in each case, in fact comes to. Aristotle goes on to defend in each case some concrete specifications, producing, at the end, a full or "thick" definition of the virtue.

Here are the most important spheres of experience recognized by Aristotle, along with the names of their corresponding virtues:[7]

Sphere	Virtue
1. Fear of important damages, esp. death	courage
2. Bodily appetites and their pleasures	moderation
3. Distribution of limited resources	justice
4. Management of one's personal property, where others are concerned	generosity

5. Management of personal property, where hospitality is concerned	expansive hospitality
6. Attitudes and actions with respect to one's own worth	greatness of soul
7. Attitude to slights and damages	mildness of temper
8. "Association and living together and the fellowship of words and actions"	
(a) truthfulness in speech	truthfulness
(b) social association of a playful kind	easy grace (contrasted with coarseness, rudeness, insensitivity)
(c) social association more generally	nameless, but a kind of friendliness, (contrasted, with irritability, and grumpiness)
9. Attitude to the good and ill fortune of others	proper judgment (contrasted with enviousness, spitefulness, etc.)
10. Intellectual life	the various intellectual virtues (such as perceptiveness, knowledge, etc.)
11. The planning of one's life and conduct	practical wisdom

There is, of course, much more to be said about this list, its specific members, and the names Aristotle chooses for the virtue in each case, some of which are indeed culture-bound. What I want, however, to insist is the care with which Aristotle articulates his general approach, beginning from a characterization of a sphere of universal experience and choice, and introducing the virtue name as the name (as yet undefined) of whatever it is to choose appropriately in that area of experience. On this approach, it does not seem possible to say, as the relativist wishes to, that a given society does not contain anything that corresponds to a given virtue. Nor does it seem to be an open question, in the case of a particular agent, whether a certain virtue should or should not be included in his or her life—except in the sense that she can always choose to pursue the corresponding deficiency instead. The point is that everyone makes some choices and acts somehow or other in these spheres: if not properly, then improperly. Everyone has *some* atti-

tude and behavior toward her own death; toward her bodily appetites and their management; toward her property and its use; toward the distribution of social goods; toward telling the truth; toward being kindly or not kindly to others; toward cultivating or not cultivating a sense of play and delight; and so on. No matter where one lives one cannot escape these questions, so long as one is living a human life. But then this means that one's behavior falls, willy nilly, within the sphere of the Aristotelian virtue, in each case. If it is not appropriate, it is inappropriate; it cannot be off the map altogether. People will of course disagree about what the appropriate ways of acting and reacting in fact *are*. But in that case, as Aristotle has set things up, they are arguing about the same thing, and advancing competing specifications of the same virtue. The reference of the virtue term in each case is fixed by the sphere of experience—by what we shall from now on call the "grounding experiences." The thin or "nominal definition" of the virtue will be, in each case, that it is whatever it is that being disposed to choose and respond well consists in, in that sphere. The job of ethical theory will be to search for the best further specification corresponding to this nominal definition, and to produce a full definition.

III

We have begun to introduce considerations from the philosophy of language. We can now make the direction of the Aristotelian account clearer by considering his own account of linguistic indicating (referring) and defining, which guides his treatment of both scientific and ethical terms, and of the idea of progress in both areas.[8]

Aristotle's general picture is as follows. We begin with some experiences—not necessarily our own, but those of members of our linguistic community, broadly construed.[9] On the basis of these experiences, a word enters the language of the group, indicating (referring to) whatever it is that is the content of those experiences. Aristotle gives the example of thunder.[10] People hear a noise in the clouds, and they then refer to it, using the word "thunder." At this point, it may be that nobody has any concrete account of the noise or any idea about what it really is. But the experience fixes a subject for further inquiry. From now on, we can refer to thunder, ask "What is thunder?" and advance and assess competing theories. The thin or, we might say, "nominal definition" of thunder is "That noise in the clouds, whatever it is." The competing explanatory theories are rival candidates for correct full or thick definition. So the explanation story citing Zeus' activities in the clouds is a false account of the very same thing of which the best scientific explanation is a true account. There is just one debate here, with a single subject.

So too, Aristotle suggests, with our ethical terms. Heraclitus, long before him, already had the essential idea, saying, "They would not have known the name of justice, if these things did not take place."[11] "These things," our source for the fragment informs us, are experiences of injustice—presumably of harm, deprivation, inequality. These experiences fix the reference of the corresponding virtue word. Aristotle proceeds along similar lines. In the *Politics* he insists that only human beings, and not either animals or gods, will have our basic ethical terms and concepts (such as just and unjust, noble and base, good and bad), because the beasts are unable to form the concepts, and gods lack the experiences of limit and finitude that give a concept such as justice its point.[12] In the *Nicomachean Ethics* enumeration of the virtues, he carries the line of thought further, suggesting that the reference of the virtue terms is fixed by spheres of choice, frequently connected with our finitude and limitation, that we encounter in virtue of shared conditions of human existence.[13] The question about virtue usually arises in areas in which human choice is both nonoptional and somewhat problematic. (Thus, he stresses, there is no

virtue involving the regulation of listening to attractive sounds or seeing pleasing sights.) Each family of virtue and vice or deficiency words attaches to some such sphere. And we can understand progress in ethics, like progress in scientific understanding, to be progress in finding the correct fuller specification of a virtue, isolated by its thin or "nominal" definition. This progress is aided by a perspicuous mapping of the sphere of the grounding experiences. When we understand more precisely what problems human beings encounter in their lives with one another, what circumstances they face in which choice of some sort is required, we will have a way of assessing competing responses to those problems, and we will begin to understand what it might be to act well in the face of them.

Aristotle's ethical and political writings provide many examples of how such progress (or, more generally, such a rational debate) might go. We find argument against Platonic asceticism, as the proper specification of moderation (appropriate choice and response *vis-à-vis* the bodily appetites) and the consequent proneness to anger over slights, that was prevalent in Greek ideals of maleness and in Greek behavior, together with a defense of a more limited and controlled expression of anger, as the proper specification of the virtue that Aristotle calls "mildness of temper." (Here Aristotle evinces some discomfort with the virtue term he has chosen, and he is right to do so, since it certainly loads the dice heavily in favor of his concrete specification and against the traditional one.)[14] And so on for all the virtues.

In an important section of *Politics* II, part of which forms one of the epigraphs to this paper, Aristotle defends the proposition that laws should be revisable and not fixed by pointing to evidence that there is progress toward greater correctness in our ethical conceptions, as also in the arts and sciences. Greeks used to think that courage was a matter of waving swords around; now they have (the *Ethics* informs us) a more inward and a more civic and communally attuned understanding of proper behavior toward the possibility of death. Women used to be regarded as property, bought and sold; now this would be thought barbaric. And in the case of justice as well we have, the *Politics* passage claims, advanced toward a more adequate understanding of what is fair and appropriate. Aristotle gives the example of an existing homicide law that convicts the defendant automatically on the evidence of the prosecutor's relatives (whether they actually witnessed anything or not, apparently). This, Aristotle says, is clearly a stupid and unjust law; and yet it once seemed appropriate—and, to a tradition-bound community, must still be so. To hold tradition fixed is then to prevent ethical progress. What human beings want and seek is not conformity with the past, it is the good. So our systems of law should make it possible for them to progress beyond the past, when they have agreed that a change is good. (They should not, however, make change too easy, since it is no easy matter to see one's way to the good, and tradition is frequently a sounder guide than current fashion.)

In keeping with these ideas, the *Politics* as a whole presents the beliefs of the many different societies it investigates not as unrelated local norms, but as competing answers to questions of justice and courage (and so on) with which all the societies (being human) are concerned, and in response to which they are all trying to find what is good. Aristotle's analysis of the virtues gives him an appropriate framework for these comparisons, which seem perfectly appropriate inquiries into the ways in which different societies have solved common human problems.

In the Aristotelian approach it is obviously of the first importance to distinguish two stages of the inquiry: the initial demarcation of the sphere of choice, of the "grounding experiences" that fix the reference of the virtue term; and the ensuing more concrete inquiry into what appropriate choice, in that sphere, *is*. Aristotle does nor always do this carefully, and the language he has to work with is often not helpful to him. We do not have much difficulty with terms like "moderation" and "justice" and even "courage," which seem vaguely normative but relatively empty, so far, of concrete moral content. As the approach requires, they can serve as extension-fixing labels under which many competing specifications may be investigated. But we have already noticed the problem with "mildness of temper," which seems to rule out by fiat a prominent contender for the appropriate disposition concerning anger. And much the same thing certainly seems to be true of the relativists' favorite target, *megalopsuchia,* which implies in its very name an attitude to one's own worth that is more Greek than universal. (For example, a Christian will feel that the proper attitude to one's own worth requires understanding one's lowness, frailty, and sinfulness. The virtue of humility requires considering oneself *small,* not great.) What we ought to get at this point in the inquiry is a word for the proper behavior toward anger and offense and a word for the proper behavior toward one's worth that are more truly neutral among the competing specifications, referring only to the sphere of experience within which we wish to determine what is appropriate. Then we could regard the competing conceptions as rival accounts of one and the same thing, so that, for example, Christian humility would be a rival specification of the same virtue whose Greek specification is given in Aristotle's account of *megalopsuchia,* namely, the proper way to behave toward the question of one's own worth.

And in fact, oddly enough, if one examines the evolution in the use of this word from Aristotle through the Stoics to the Christian fathers, one can see that this is more or less what happened, as "greatness of soul" became associated, first, with Stoic emphasis on the supremacy of virtue and the worthlessness of externals, including the body, and, through this, with the Christian denial of the body and of the worth of earthly life.[15] So even in this apparently unpromising case, history shows that the Aristotelian approach not only provided the materials for a single debate but actually succeeded in organizing such a debate, across enormous differences of both place and time.

Here, then, is a sketch for an objective human morality based upon the idea of virtuous action—that is, of appropriate functioning in each human sphere. The Aristotelian claim is that, further developed, it will retain virtue morality's immersed attention to actual human experiences, while gaining the ability to criticize local and traditional moralities in the name of a more inclusive account of the circumstances of human life, and of the needs for human functioning that these circumstances call forth.

IV

This proposal will encounter many objections. The concluding sections of this paper will present three of the most serious and will sketch the lines along which the Aristotelian conception might proceed in formulating a reply. To a great extent these objections are not imagined or confronted by Aristotle himself, but his position seems capable of confronting them.

The first objection concerns the relationship between singleness of problem and singleness of solution. Let us grant for the moment that the Aristotelian approach has succeeded in coherently isolating and describing areas of human experience and choice that form, so to speak, the *terrain* of the virtues, and in giving thin definitions of each of the virtues as whatever it is that consists in choosing and responding well within that sphere. Let us suppose that the approach succeeds in doing this in a way that embraces many times and places, bringing disparate cultures together into a single debate about the good human being and the good human life. Different cultural accounts of good choice within the sphere in question in each case are now seen not as untranslatably different forms of life, but as competing answers to a single general question about a set of shared human experiences. Still, it might be argued, what has been achieved is, at best, a single discourse or debate about virtue. It has not been shown that this debate will have, as Aristotle believes, a single answer. Indeed, it has not even been shown that the discourse we have set up will have the form of a *debate* at all, rather than that of a plurality of culturally specific narratives, each giving the thick definition of a virtue that corresponds to the experience and traditions of a particular group. There is an important disanalogy with the case of thunder, on which the Aristotelian so much relies in arguing that our questions will have a single answer. For in that case what is given in experience is the definiendum itself, so that experiences establish a rough extension, to which any good definition must respond. In the case of the virtues, things are more indirect. What is given in experience across groups is only the *ground* of virtuous action, the circumstances of life to which virtuous action is an appropriate response. Even if these grounding experiences are shared, that does not tell us that there will be a shared appropriate response.

In the case of thunder, furthermore, the conflicting theories are clearly put forward as competing candidates for the truth; the behavior of those involved in the discourse suggests that they are indeed, as Aristotle says, searching "not for the way of their ancestors, but for the good." And it seems reasonable in that case for them to do so. It is far less clear, where the virtues are concerned (the objector continues), that a unified practical solution is either sought by the actual participants or a desideratum for them. The Aristotelian proposal makes it possible to conceive of a way in which the virtues might be nonrelative. It does not, by itself, answer the question of relativism.

The second objection goes deeper. For it questions the notion of spheres of shared human experience that lies at the heart of the Aristotelian approach. The approach, says this objector, seems to treat the experiences that ground the virtues as in some way primitive, given, and free from the cultural variation that we find in the plurality of normative conceptions of virtue. Ideas of proper courage may vary, but the fear of death is shared by all human beings. Ideas of moderation may vary, but the experiences of hunger, thirst, and sexual desire are (so the Aristotelian seems to claim) invariant. Normative conceptions introduce an element of cultural interpretation that is not present in the grounding experiences, which are, for that very reason, the Aristotelian's starting point.

But, the objector continues, such assumptions are naive. They will not stand up either to our best account of experience or to a close examination of the ways in which these so-called grounding experiences have in fact been differently constructed by different cultures. In general, first of all, our best accounts of the nature of experience, even perceptual experience, inform us that there is no such thing as an "innocent eye" that receives an uninterpreted "given." Even sense-perception is interpretive, heavily influenced by belief, teaching, language, and in general by social and contextual features. There is a very real sense in which members of different societies do not see the same sun and stars, encounter the same plants and animals, hear the same thunder.

But if this seems to be true of human experience of nature, which was the allegedly unproblematic starting point for Aristotle's account of naming, it is all the more plainly true, the objector claims, in the area of the human good. Here it is only a very naive and historically insensitive moral philosopher who would say that the experience of the fear of death or the experience of bodily appetites is a human constant. Recent anthropological work on the social construction of the emotions,[16] for example, has shown to what extent the experience of fear has learned and culturally variant elements. When we add that the object of the fear in which the Aristotelian takes an interest is death, which has been so variously interpreted and understood by

human beings at different times and in different places, the conclusion that the "grounding experience" is an irreducible plurality of experiences, highly various and in each case deeply infused with cultural interpretation, becomes even more inescapable.

Nor is the case different with the apparently less complicated experience of the bodily appetites. Most philosophers who have written about the appetites have treated hunger, thirst, and sexual desire as human universals, stemming from our shared animal nature. Aristotle himself was already more sophisticated, since he insisted that the object of appetite is "the apparent good" and that appetite is therefore something interpretive and selective, a kind of intentional awareness.[17] But he does not seem to have reflected much about the ways in which historical and cultural differences could shape that awareness. The Hellenistic philosophers who immediately followed him did so reflect, arguing that the experience of sexual desire and of many forms of the desire for food and drink are, at least in part, social constructs, built up over time on the basis of a social teaching about value that is external to start with, but that enters so deeply into the perceptions of the individual that it actually forms and transforms the experience of desire.[18] Let us take two Epicurean examples. People are taught that to be well fed they require luxurious fish and meat, that a simple vegetarian diet is not enough. Over time, the combination of teaching with habit produces an appetite for meat, shaping the individual's perceptions of the objects before him. Again, people are taught that what sexual relations are all about is a romantic union or fusion with an object who is seen as exalted in value, or even as perfect. Over time, this teaching shapes sexual behavior and the experience of desire, so that sexual arousal itself responds to this culturally learned scenario.[19]

This work of social criticism has recently been carried further by Michel Foucault in his *History of Sexuality*.[20] This work has certain gaps as a history of Greek thought on this topic, but it does succeed in establishing that the Greeks saw the problem of the appetites and their management in an extremely different way from the way of twentieth-century Westerners. To summarize two salient conclusions of his complex argument, the Greeks did not single out the sexual appetite for special treatment; they treated it alongside hunger and thirst, as a drive that needed to be mastered and kept within bounds. Their central concern was with self-mastery, and they saw the appetites in the light of this concern. Furthermore, where the sexual appetite is concerned, they did not regard the gender of the partner as particularly important in assessing the moral value of the act. Nor did they identify or treat as morally salient a stable disposition to prefer partners of one sex rather than the other. Instead, they focused on the general issue of activity and passivity, connecting it in complex ways with the issue of self-mastery.

Work like Foucault's—and there is a lot of it in various areas, some of it very good—shows very convincingly that the experience of bodily desire, and of the body itself, has elements that vary with cultural and historical change. The names that people call their desires and themselves as subjects of desire, the fabric of belief and discourse into which they integrate their ideas of desiring, all this influences, it is clear, not only their reflection about desire, but also their experience of desire itself. Thus, for example, it is naive to treat our modern debates about homosexuality as continuations of the very same debate about sexual activity that went on in the Greek world.[21] In a very real sense there was no "homosexual experience" in a culture that did not contain our emphasis on the gender of the object, our emphasis on the subjectivity of inclination and the permanence of appetitive disposition, our particular ways of problematizing certain forms of behavior.

If we suppose that we can get underneath this variety and this constructive power of social discourse in at least one case—namely, with the universal experience of bodily pain as a bad

thing—even here we find subtle arguments against us. For the experience of pain seems to be embedded in a cultural discourse as surely as the closely related experiences of the appetites; and significant variations can be alleged here as well. The Stoics already made this claim against the Aristotelian virtues. In order to establish that bodily pain is not bad by its very nature, but only by cultural tradition, the Stoics had to provide some explanation for the ubiquity of the belief that pain is bad and of the tendency to shun it. This explanation would have to show that the reaction was learned rather than natural, and to explain why, in the light of this fact, it is learned so widely. This they did by pointing to certain features in the very early treatment of infants. As soon as an infant is born, it cries. Adults, assuming that the crying is a response to its pain at the unaccustomed coldness and harshness of the place where it finds itself, hasten to comfort it. This behavior, often repeated, teaches the infant to regard its pain as a bad thing—or, better, teaches it the concept of pain, which includes the notion of badness, and teaches it the forms of life its society shares concerning pain. It is all social teaching, they claim, though this usually escapes our notice because of the early and non-linguistic nature of the teaching.[22]

These and related arguments, the objector concludes, show that the Aristotelian idea that there is a single non-relative discourse about human experiences such as mortality or desire is a naive idea. There is no such bedrock of shared experience, and thus no single sphere of choice within which the virtue is the disposition to choose well. So the Aristotelian project cannot even get off the ground.

Now the Aristotelian confronts a third objector, who attacks from a rather different direction. Like the second, she charges that the Aristotelian has taken for a universal and necessary feature of human life an experience that is contingent on certain non-necessary historical conditions. Like the second, she argues that human experience is much more profoundly shaped by non-necessary social features than the Aristotelian has allowed. But her purpose is not simply, like the second objector's, to point to the great variety of ways in which the "grounding experiences" corresponding to the virtues are actually understood and lived by human beings. It is more radical still. It is to point out that we could imagine a form of human life that does not contain these experiences—or some of them—at all, in any form. Thus the virtue that consists in acting well in that sphere need not be included in an account of the human good. In some cases, the experience may even be a sign of *bad* human life, and the corresponding virtue, therefore, no better than a form of non-ideal adaptation to a bad state of affairs. The really good human life, in such a case, would contain neither the grounding deficiency nor the remedial virtue.

This point is forcefully raised by some of Aristotle's own remarks about the virtue of generosity. One of his points against societies that eliminate private ownership is that they have thereby done away with the opportunity for generous action, which requires having possessions of one's own to give to others.[23] This sort of remark is tailor-made for the objector, who will immediately say that generosity, if it really rests upon the experience of private possession, is a dubious candidate indeed for inclusion in a purportedly non-relative account of the human virtues. If it rests upon a "grounding experience" that is non-necessary and is capable of being evaluated in different ways, and of being either included or eliminated in accordance with that evaluation, then it is not the universal the Aristotelian said it was.

Some objectors of the third kind will stop at this point, or use such observations to support the second objector's relativism. But in another prominent form this argument takes a non-relativist direction. It asks us to assess the "grounding experiences" against an account of human flourishing, produced in some independent manner. If we do so, the objector urges, we will discover that some of the experiences are

remediable deficiencies. The objection to Aristotelian virtue ethics will then be that it limits our social aspirations, getting us to regard as permanent and necessary what we might in fact improve to the benefit of all human life. This is the direction in which the third objection to the virtues was pressed by Karl Marx, its most famous proponent.[24] According to Marx's argument, a number of the leading bourgeois virtues are responses to defective relations of production. Bourgeois justice, generosity, etc. presuppose conditions and structures that are non-ideal and that will be eliminated when communism is achieved. And it is not only the current *specification* of these virtues that will be superseded with the removal of deficiency. It is the virtues themselves. It is in this sense that communism leads human beings beyond ethics.

Thus the Aristotelian is urged to inquire into the basic structures of human life with the daring of a radical political imagination. It is claimed that when she does so she will see that human life contains more possibilities than are dreamed of in her list of virtues.

V

Each of these objections is profound. To answer any one of them adequately would require a treatise. But we can still do something at this point to map out an Aristotelian response to each one, pointing the direction in which a fuller reply might go.

The first objector is right to insist on the distinction between singleness of framework and singleness of answer, and right, again, to stress that in constructing a debate about the virtues based on the demarcation of certain spheres of experience we have not yet answered any of the "What is *x*?" questions that this debate will confront. We have not even said very much about the structure of the debate itself, beyond its beginnings—about how it will both use and criticize traditional beliefs, how it will deal with conflicting beliefs, how it will move critically from the "way of one's ancestors" to the "good"—in short, about whose judgments it will trust. I have addressed some of these issues, again with reference to Aristotle, in two other papers,[25] but much more remains to be done. At this point, however, we can make four observations to indicate how the Aristotelian might deal with some of the objector's concerns here. First, the Aristotelian position that I wish to defend need not insist, in every case, on a single answer to the request for a specification of a virtue. The answer might well turn out to be a disjunction. The process of comparative and critical debate will, I imagine, eliminate numerous contenders—for example, the view of justice that prevailed in Cyme. But what remains might well be a (probably small) plurality of acceptable accounts. These accounts may or may not be capable of being subsumed under a single account of greater generality. Success in the eliminative task will still be no trivial accomplishment. For example, if we should succeed in ruling out conceptions of the proper attitude to one's own human worth that are based on a notion of original sin, this would be moral work of enormous significance, even if we got no further than that in specifying the positive account.

Second, the general answer to a "What is x?" question in any sphere may well be susceptible of several or even of many concrete specifications, in connection with other local practices and local conditions. For example, the normative account where friendship and hospitality are concerned is likely to be extremely general, admitting of many concrete "fillings." Friends in England will have different customs, where regular social visiting is concerned, from friends in ancient Athens. And yet both sets of customs can count as further specifications of a general account of friendship that mentions, for example, the Aristotelian criteria of mutual benefit and well-wishing, mutual enjoyment, mutual awareness, a shared conception of the good, and some form of "living together."[26] Sometimes we may want to

view such concrete accounts as optional alternative specifications, to be chosen by a society on the basis of reasons of ease and convenience. Sometimes, on the other hand, we may want to insist that this account gives the only legitimate specification of the virtue in question for that concrete context; in that case, the concrete account could be viewed as a part of a longer or fuller version of the single normative account. The decision between these two ways of regarding it will depend upon our assessment of its degree of non-arbitrariness for its context (both physical and historical), its relationship to other non-arbitrary features of the moral conception of that context, and so forth.

Third, whether we have one or several general accounts of a virtue, and whether this account or these accounts do or do not admit of more concrete specifications relative to ongoing cultural contexts, the particular choices that the virtuous person, under this conception, makes will always be a matter of being keenly responsive to the local features of his or her concrete context. So in this respect, again, the instructions the Aristotelian gives to the person of virtue do not differ from one part of what a relativist would recommend. The Aristotelian virtues involve a delicate balancing between general rules and the keen awareness of particulars, in which process, as Aristotle stresses, the perception of the particular takes priority. It takes priority in the sense that a good rule is a good summary of wise particular choices and not a court of last resort. Like rules in medicine and in navigation, ethical rules should be held open to modification in the light of new circumstances; and the good agent must therefore cultivate the ability to perceive and correctly describe his or her situation finely and truly, including in this perceptual grasp even those features of the situation that are not covered under the existing rule.

I have written a good deal elsewhere on this idea of the "priority of the particular," exactly what it does and does not imply, in exactly what ways the particular perception is and is not prior to the general rule. Those who want clarification on this central topic will have to turn to those writings.[27]

What I want to stress here is that Aristotelian particularism is fully compatible with Aristotelian objectivity. The fact that a good and virtuous decision is context-sensitive does not imply that it is right only *relative* to, or *inside,* a limited context, any more than the fact that a good navigational judgment is sensitive to particular weather conditions shows that it is correct only in a local or relational sense. It is right absolutely, objectively, from anywhere in the human world, to attend to the particular features of one's context; and the person who so attends and who chooses accordingly is making, according to Aristotle, the humanly correct decision, period. If another situation ever should arise with all the same morally relevant features, including contextual features, the same decision would again be absolutely right.[28]

Thus the virtue-based morality can capture a great deal of what the relativist is after and still lay claim to objectivity. In fact, we might say that the Aristotelian virtues do better than the relativist virtues in explaining what people are actually doing when they scrutinize the features of their context carefully, looking at both the shared and the non-shared features with an eye to what is best. For as Aristotle says, people who do this are usually searching for the good, not just for the way of their ancestors. They are prepared to defend their decisions as good or right, and to think of those who advocate a different course as disagreeing about what is right, not just narrating a different tradition.

Finally, we should point out that the Aristotelian virtues, and the deliberations they guide, unlike some systems of moral rules, remain always open to revision in the light of new circumstances and new evidence. In this way, again, they contain the flexibility to local conditions that the relativist would desire, but, again, without sacrificing objectivity. Sometimes the new circumstances may simply give rise to a new concrete specification of the virtue as previously defined; in some cases it may cause us to change our view about what the virtue itself is. All general accounts are held provisionally, as summaries of correct decisions and as guides to new ones. This flexibility, built into the Aristotelian procedure, will again help the Aristotelian account to answer the questions of the relativist, without relativism.

VI

We must now turn to the second objection. Here, I believe, is the really serious threat to the Aristotelian position. Past writers on virtue, including Aristotle himself, have lacked sensitivity to the ways in which different traditions of discourse, different conceptual schemes, articulate the world, and also to the profound connections between the structure of discourse and the structure of experience itself. Any contemporary defense of the Aristotelian position must display this sensitivity, responding somehow to the data that the relativist historian or anthropologist brings forward.

The Aristotelian should begin, it seems to me, by granting that with respect to any complex matter of deep human importance there is no "innocent eye"—no way of seeing the world that is entirely neutral and free of cultural shaping. The work of philosophers such as Putnam, Goodman, and Davidson[29]—following, one must point out, from the arguments of Kant and, I believe, from those of Aristotle himself[30]—have shown convincingly that even where sense-perception is concerned, the human mind is an active and interpretive instrument and that its interpretations are a function of its history and its concepts, as well as of its innate structure. The Aristotelian should also grant, it seems to me, that the nature of human world-interpretations is holistic and that the criticism of them must, equally well, be holistic. Conceptual schemes, like languages, hang together as whole structures, and we should realize, too, that a change in any single element is likely to have implications for the system as a whole.

But these two facts do not imply, as some relativists in literary theory and in anthropology tend to assume, that all world interpretations are equally valid and altogether non-comparable, that there are no good standards of assessment and "anything goes." The rejection of the idea of ethical truth as correspondence to an altogether uninterpreted reality does not imply that the whole idea of searching for the truth is an old-fashioned error. Certain ways in which people see the world can still be criticized exactly as Aristotle criticized them: as stupid, pernicious, and false. The standards used in such criticisms must come from inside human life. (Frequently they will come from the society in question itself, from its own rationalist and critical traditions.) And the inquirer must attempt, prior to criticism, to develop an inclusive understanding of the conceptual scheme being criticized, seeing what motivates each of its parts and how they hang together. But there is so far no reason to think that the critic will not be able to reject the institution of slavery or the homicide law of Cyme as out of line with the conception of virtue that emerges from reflection on the variety of different ways in which human cultures have had the experiences that ground the virtues.

The "grounding experiences" will not, the Aristotelian should concede, provide precisely a single language—neutral bedrock on which an account of virtue can be straightforwardly and unproblematically based. The description and assessment of the ways in which different cultures have constructed these experiences will become one of the central tasks of Aristotelian philosophical criticism. But the relativist has, so far, shown no reasons why we could not, at the end of the day, say that certain ways of conceptualizing death are more in keeping with the totality of our evidence and with the totality of our wishes for flourishing life than others; that certain ways of experiencing appetitive desire are for similar reasons more promising than others.

Relativists tend, furthermore, to understate the amount of attunement, recognition, and overlap that actually obtains across cultures, particularly in the areas of the grounding experiences. The Aristotelian in developing her conception in a culturally sensitive way, should insist, as Aristotle himself does, upon the evidence of such attunement and recognition. Despite the evident differences in the specific cultural shaping of the grounding experiences, we do recognize the experiences of people in other cultures as similar to our own. We do converse with them about matters of deep importance, understand them, allow ourselves to be moved by them. When we read Sophocles' *Antigone,* we see a good deal that seems strange to us; and we have not read the play well if we do not notice how far its conceptions of death, womanhood, and so on differ from our own. But it is still possible for us to be moved by the drama, to care about its people, to regard their debates as reflections upon virtue that speak to our own experience, and their choices as choices in spheres of conduct in which we too must choose. Again, when one sits down at a table with people from other parts of the world and debates with them concerning hunger or just distribution or in general the quality of human life, one does find, in spite of evident conceptual differences, that it is possible to proceed as if we are all talking about the same human problem; and it is usually only in a context in which one or more of the parties is intellectually committed to a theoretical relativist position that this discourse proves impossible to sustain. This sense of community and overlap seems to be especially strong in the areas that we have called the areas of the grounding experiences. And this, it seems, supports the Aristotelian claim that those experiences can be a good starting point for ethical debate.

Furthermore, it is necessary to stress that hardly any cultural group today is as focused upon its own internal traditions and as isolated from other cultures as the relativist argument presupposes. Cross-cultural communication and debate are ubiquitous facts of contemporary life. Our experience of cultural interaction indicates that in general the inhabitants of different conceptual schemes do tend to view their interaction in the Aristotelian and not the relativist way. A traditional society, confronted with new technologies and sciences, and the conceptions that go with them, does not, in fact, simply fail to understand them or regard them as totally alien incursions upon a hermetically sealed way of life. Instead, it assesses the new item as a possible contributor to flourishing life, making it comprehensible to itself and incorporating elements that promise to solve problems of flourishing. Examples of such assimilation, and the debate that surrounds it,[31] suggest that the parties do, in fact, recognize common problems and that the traditional society is perfectly capable of viewing an external innovation as a device to solve a problem that it shares with the innovating society. The parties do, in fact, search for the good, not the way of their ancestors; only traditionalist anthropologists insist, nostalgically, on the absolute presentation of the ancestral.

And this is so even when cross-cultural discourse reveals a difference at the level of the conceptualization of the grounding experiences. Frequently the effect of work like Foucault's, which reminds us of the non-necessary and non-universal character of one's own ways of seeing in some such area, is precisely to prompt a critical debate in search of the human good. It is difficult, for example, to read Foucault's observations about the history of our sexual ideas without coming to feel that certain ways in which the Western contemporary debate on these matters has been organized, as a result of some combination of Christian morality with nineteenth-century pseudo-science, are especially silly, arbitrary, and limiting, inimical to a human search for flourishing. Foucault's moving account of Greek culture, as he himself insists in a preface,[32]

provides not only a sign that someone once thought differently, but also evidence that it is possible for us to think differently. Foucault announced that the purpose of his book was to "free thought" so that it could think differently, imagining new and more fruitful possibilities. And close analysis of spheres of cultural discourse, which stresses cultural differences in the spheres of the grounding experiences, is being combined, increasingly, in current debates about sexuality and related matters, with the critique of existing social arrangements and attitudes, and with the elaboration of a new norm of human flourishing. There is no reason to think this combination incoherent.[33]

As we pursue these possibilities, the basic spheres of experience identified in the Aristotelian approach will no longer, we have said, be seen as spheres of *uninterpreted* experience. But we have also insisted that there is much family relatedness and much overlap among societies. And certain areas of relatively greater universality can be specified here, on which we should insist as we proceed to areas that are more varied in their cultural expression. Not without a sensitive awareness that we are speaking of something that is experienced differently in different contexts, we can none the less identify certain features of our common humanity, closely related to Aristotle's original list, from which our debate might proceed.

1. *Mortality.* No matter how death is understood, all human beings face it and (after a certain age) know that they face it. This fact shapes every aspect of more or less every human life.

2. *The Body.* Prior to any concrete cultural shaping, we are born with human bodies, whose possibilities and vulnerabilities do not as such belong to one culture rather than any other. Any given human being might have belonged to any culture. The experience of the body is culturally influenced; but the body itself, prior to such experience, provides limits and parameters that ensure a great deal of overlap in what is going to

be experienced, where hunger, thirst, desire, the five senses are concerned. It is all very well to point to the cultural component in these experiences. But when one spends time considering issues of hunger and scarcity, and in general of human misery, such differences appear relatively small and refined, and one cannot fail to acknowledge that "there are no known ethnic differences in human physiology with respect to metabolism of nutrients. Africans and Asians do not burn their dietary calories or use their dietary protein any differently from Europeans and Americans. It follows then that dietary requirements cannot vary widely as between different races."[34] This and similar facts should surely be focal points for debate about appropriate human behavior in this sphere. And by beginning with the body, rather than with the subjective experience of desire, we get, furthermore, an opportunity to criticize the situation of people who are so persistently deprived that their *desire* for good things has actually decreased. This is a further advantage of the Aristotelian approach, when contrasted with approaches to choice that stop with subjective expressions of preference.

3. *Pleasure and pain.* In every culture, there is a conception of pain; and these conceptions, which overlap very largely with one another, can be plausibly seen as grounded in universal and pre-cultural experience. The Stoic story of infant development is highly implausible; the negative response to bodily pain is surely primitive and universal, rather than learned and optional, however much its specific "grammar" may be shaped by later learning.

4. *Cognitive capability.* Aristotle's famous claim that "all human beings by nature reach out for understanding"[35] seems to stand up to the most refined anthropological analysis. It points to an element in our common humanity that is plausibly seen, again, as grounded independently of particular acculturation, however much it is later shaped by acculturation.

5. *Practical reason.* All human beings, whatever their culture, participate (or try to) in the planning and managing of their lives, asking and answering questions about how one should live and act. This capability expresses itself differently in different societies, but a being who altogether lacked it would not be likely to be acknowledged as a human being, in any culture.[36]

6. *Early infant development.* Prior to the greatest part of specific cultural shaping, though perhaps not free from all shaping, are certain areas of human experiences and development that are broadly shared and of great importance for the Aristotelian virtues: experiences of desire, pleasure, loss, one's own finitude, perhaps also of envy, grief, gratitude. One may argue about the merits of one or another psychoanalytical account of infancy. But it seems difficult to deny that the work of Freud on infant desire and of Klein on grief, loss, and other more complex emotional attitudes has identified spheres of human experience that are to a large extent common to all humans, regardless of their particular society. All humans begin as hungry babies, perceiving their own helplessness, their alternating closeness to and distance from those on whom they depend, and so forth. Melanie Klein records a conversation with an anthropologist in which an event that at first looked (to Western eyes) bizarre was interpreted by Klein as the expression of a universal pattern of mourning. The anthropologist accepted her interpretation.[37]

7. *Affiliation.* Aristotle's claim that human beings as such feel a sense of fellowship with other human beings, and that we are by nature social animals, is an empirical claim, but it seems to be a sound one. However varied our specific conceptions of friendship and love are, there is a great point in seeing them as overlapping expressions of the same family of shared human needs and desires.

8. *Humor.* There is nothing more culturally varied than humor, and yet, as Aristotle insists, some space for humor and play seems to be a need of any human life. The human being was

not called the "laughing animal" for nothing; it is certainly one of our salient differences from almost all animals, and (in some form or other) a shared feature, I somewhat boldly assert, of any life that is going to be counted as fully human.

This is just a list of suggestions, closely related to Aristotle's list of common experiences. One could subtract some of these items and/or add others. But it seems plausible to claim that in all these areas we have a basis for further work on the human good. We do not have a bedrock of completely uninterpreted "given" data, but we do have nuclei of experience around which the construction of different societies proceeds. There is no Archimedean point here, and no pure access to unsullied "nature"—even, here, human nature—as it is in and of itself. There is just human life as it is lived. But in life as it is lived, we do find a family of experiences, clustering around certain foci, which can provide reasonable starting points for cross-cultural reflection.

VII

The third objection raises, at bottom, a profound conceptual question: What is it to inquire about the *human* good? What circumstances of existence go to define what it is to live the life of a *human being,* and not some other life? Aristotle likes to point out that an inquiry into the human good cannot, on pain of incoherence, end up describing the good of some other being, say a god, a good, that on account of our circumstances, it is impossible for us to attain (cf. *NE* 1159a10–12, 1166a18–23). Which circumstances then? The virtues are defined relatively to certain problems and limitations, and also to certain endowments. Which ones are sufficiently central that their removal would make us into different beings, and open up a wholly new and different debate about the good? This question is itself part of the ethical debate we propose. For

there is no way to answer it but ask ourselves which elements of our experience seem to us so important that they count, for us, as part of who we are. I discuss Aristotle's attitude to this question elsewhere, and I shall simply summarize here.[38] It seems clear, first of all, that our mortality is an essential feature of our circumstances as human beings. An immortal being would have such a different form of life, and such different values and virtues, that it does not seem to make sense to regard that being as part of the same search for good. Essential, too, will be our dependence upon the world outside of us: some sort of need for food, drink, the help of others. On the side of abilities, we would want to include cognitive functioning and the activity of practical reasoning as elements of any life that we would regard as human. Aristotle argues, plausibly, that we would want to include sociability as well, some sensitivity to the needs of and pleasure in the company of other beings similar to ourselves.

But it seems to me that the Marxian question remains, as a deep question about human forms of life and the search for the human good. For one certainly can imagine forms of human life that do not contain the holding of private property—and, therefore, not those virtues that have to do with its proper management. And this means that it remains an open question whether these virtues ought to be regarded as virtues, and kept upon our list. Marx wished to go much further, arguing that communism would remove the need for justice, courage, and most of the bourgeois virtues. I think we might be skeptical here. Aristotle's general attitude to such transformations of life is to suggest that they usually have a tragic dimension. If we remove one sort of problem—say, by removing private property—we frequently do so by introducing another—say, the absence of a certain sort of freedom of choice, the freedom that makes it possible to do fine and generous actions for others. If things are complex even in the case of generosity, where we can rather easily imagine the transformation that removes the virtue, they are surely far more so in the cases of justice and courage. And we would need a far more detailed description than Marx ever gives us of the form of life under communism, before we would be able even to begin to see whether this form of life has in fact transformed things where these virtues are concerned, and whether it has or has not introduced new problems and limitations in their place.

In general it seems that all forms of life, including the imagined life of a god, contain boundaries and limits.[39] All structures, even that of putative limitlessness, are closed to something, cut off from something—say, in that case, from the specific value and beauty inherent in the struggle against limitation. Thus it does not appear that we will so easily get beyond the virtues. Nor does it seem to be so clearly a good thing for human life that we should.

VIII

The best conclusion to this sketch of an Aristotelian program for virtue ethics was written by Aristotle himself, at the end of his discussion of human nature in *Nicomachean Ethics* I:

> So much for our outline sketch for the good. For it looks as if we have to draw an outline first, and fill it in later. It would seem to be open to anyone to take things further and to articulate the good parts of the sketch. And time is a good discoverer or ally in such things. That's how the sciences have progressed as well: it is open to anyone to supply what is lacking. (*NE* 1098a20–6)

NOTES

This paper was motivated by questions discussed at the WIDER conference on Value and Technology, summer 1986, Helsinki. I would like to thank Steve and Frédérique Marglin for provoking some of these arguments, with hardly any of which they will agree. I also thank Dan Brock for his helpful comments,

and Amartya Sen for many discussions of these issues.

1. A. MacIntyre, *After Virtue* (Notre Dame, IN, 1981); P. Foot, *Virtues and Vices* (Los Angeles, 1978); B. William, *Ethics and the Limits of Philosophy* (Cambridge, MA, 1985) and Tanner Lectures, Harvard, 1983. See also M. Walzer, *Spheres of Justice* (New York, 1983) and Tanner Lectures, Harvard, 1985.

2. For examples of this, see Nussbaum, "Nature, Function, and Capability: Aristotle on Political Distribution," circulated as a WIDER working paper, and in *Oxford Studies in Ancient Philosophy* (1988) and also, in an expanded version, in the Proceedings of the 12th Symposium Aristotelicum.

3. See, for example, Williams, *Ethics and the Limits*, 34–6; Stuart Hampshire, *Morality and Conflict* (Cambridge, MA, 1983), 150ff.

4. For "nameless" virtues and vices, see *NE* 1107b1–2, 1107b8, 1107b30–1, 1108a17, 1119a10–11, 1126b20, 1127a12, 1127a14; for recognition of the unsatisfactoriness of names given, see 1107b8, 1108a5–6, 1108a20ff. The two categories are largely overlapping, on account of the general principles enunciated at 1108a16–19, that where there is no name a name should be given, unsatisfactory or not.

5. It should be noted that this emphasis on spheres of experience is not present in the *Eudemian Ethics*, which begins with a list of virtues and vices. This seems to me a sign that that treatise expresses a more primitive stage of Aristotle's thought on the virtues—whether earlier or not.

6. For statements with *peri,* connecting virtues with spheres of life, see 1115a6–7, 1117a29–30, 1117b25, 27, 1119b23, 1122a19, 1122b34, 1125b26, 1126b13; and *NE* 2.7 throughout. See also the related usages at 1126b11, 1127b32.

7. My list here inserts justice in a place of prominence. (In the *NE* it is treated separately, after all the other virtues, and the introductory list defers it for that later examination.) I have also added at the end of the list categories corresponding to the various intellectual virtues discussed in *NE* 6, and also to *phronesis* or practical wisdom, discussed in 6 as well. Otherwise the order and wording of my list closely follows 2.7, which gives the program for the more detailed analyses of 3.5–4.

8. For a longer account of this, with references to the literature and to related philosophical discussions, see Nussbaum, *The Fragility of Goodness* (Cambridge, MA, 1986), ch. 8.

9. Aristotle does not worry about questions of translation in articulating this idea; for some worries about this, and an Aristotelian response, see below sections IV and VI.

10. *Posterior Analytics,* 2.8, 93a21ff.; see *Fragility,* ch. 4, 8.

11. Heraclitus, fragment DK B23; see Nussbaum, "*Psuche* in Heraclitus, II," *Phronesis* 17 (1972): 153–70.

12. See *Politics* 1.2. 1253al–18; that discussion does not deny the virtues to gods explicitly, but this denial is explicit at *NE* 1145a25–7 and 1178b10ff.

13. Aristotle does not make the connection with his account of language explicit, but his project is one of defining the virtues, and we would expect him to keep his general view of defining in mind in this context. A similar idea about the virtues, and experience of a certain sort as a possible basis for a non-relative account, is developed, without reference to Aristotle, in a review of P. Foot's *Virtues and Vices* by N. Sturgeon, *Journal of Philosophy,* 81 (1984), pp. 326–33.

14. 1108a5, where Aristotle says that the virtues and the corresponding person are "pretty much nameless," and says "Let us call . . ." when he introduces the names. See also 1125b29, 1126a3–4.

15. See John Procope, *Magnanimity* (1987); also R.-A. Gauthier, *Magnanimité* (Paris, 1951).

16. See, for example, *The Social Construction of the Emotions,* edited by Rom Harré (Oxford, 1986).

17. See Nussbaum, *Aristotle's De Motu Animalium* (Princeton, NJ, 1976), notes on ch. 6, and *Fragility,* ch. 9.

18. A detailed study of the treatment of these ideas in the three major Hellenistic schools was presented in Nussbaum, *The Therapy of Desire: Theory and Practice in Hellenistic Ethics,* The Martin Classical Lectures 1986, and forthcoming.

19. The relevant texts are discussed in Nussbaum, *The Therapy,* chs 4–6. See also Nussbaum, "Therapeutic Arguments: Epicurus and Aristotle," in *The Norms of Nature,* edited by M. Schofield and G. Striker (Cambridge, 1986), pp. 314–74.

20. M. Foucault, *Histoire de la sexualité,* vols 2 and 3 (Paris, 1984).

21. See the papers by D. Halperin and J. Winkler in *Before Sexuality,* edited by D. Halperin, J. Winkler, and F. Zeitlin, forthcoming (Princeton).

22. The evidence for this part of the Stoic view is discussed in Nussbaum, *The Therapy.*

23. *Politics* 1263b11ff.

24. For a discussion of the relevant passages, see S. Lukes, *Marxism and Morality* (Oxford, 1987). For an acute discussion of these issues I am indebted to an exchange between Alan Ryan and Stephen Lukes at the Oxford Philosophical Society, March 1987.

25. *Fragility,* ch. 8, and "Internal Criticism and Indian Rationalist Traditions," the latter co-authored with Amartya Sen, in *Relativism,* edited by M. Krausz (Notre Dame, IN, 1988) and a WIDER Working Paper.

26. See *Fragility,* ch. 12.

27. *Fragility,* ch. 10, "The Discernment of Perception," *Proceedings of the Boston Area Colloquium in Ancient Philosophy,* 1 (1985), pp. 151–201; "Finely Aware and Richly Responsible: Moral Awareness and the Moral Task of Literature," *Journal of Philosophy,* 82 (1985), pp. 516–29, reprinted in expanded form in *Philosophy and the Question of Literature,* edited by A. Cascardi (Baltimore, 1987).

28. I believe, however, that some morally relevant features, in the Aristotelian view, may be features that are not, even in principle, replicable in another context. See "The Discernment," and *Fragility,* ch. 10.

29. See H. Putnam, *Reason, Truth, and History* (Cambridge, 1981); *The Many Faces of Realism,* The Carus Lectures, forthcoming; and *Meaning and the Moral Sciences* (London, 1979); N. Goodman, *Languages of Art* (Indianapolis, 1968) and *Ways of World-Making* (Indianapolis, 1978); D. Davidson, *Inquiries into Truth and Interpretation* (Oxford, 1984).

30. On his debt to Kant, see Putnam, *The Many Faces,* on Aristotle's "internal realism," see Nussbaum, *Fragility,* ch. 8.

31. C. Abeysekera, paper presented at Value and Technology Conference, WIDER 1986.

32. Foucault, *Histoire,* vol. 2, preface.

33. This paragraph expands remarks made in a commentary on papers by D. Halperin and J. Winkler at the conference on "Homosexuality in History and Culture" at Brown University, February 1987. The combination of historically sensitive analysis with cultural criticism was force-

fully developed at the same conference in Henry Abelove's "Is Gay History Possible?" (forthcoming).

34. C. Gopalan, "Undernutrition: Measurement and Implications," paper prepared for the WIDER Conference on Poverty, Undernutrition, and Living Standards, Helsinki, 27–31 July 1987, and forthcoming in the volume of Proceedings, edited by S. Osmani.

35. *Metaphysics* 1.1.

36. See Nussbaum, "Nature, Function, and Capability," where this Aristotelian view is compared with Marx's views on human functioning.

37. M. Klein, in Postscript to "Our Adult World and its Roots in Infancy," in *Envy, Gratitude and Other Works 1946–1963* (London, 1984), pp. 247–63.

38. "Aristotle on Human Nature and the Foundations of Ethics," forthcoming in a volume of essays on the work of Bernard Williams, edited by R. Harrison and J. Altham (Cambridge). This paper will be a WIDER Working Paper.

39. See *Fragility,* ch. 11.

43. WHOSE TRADITIONS?

❧❧

SUSAN OKIN

In his 1981 book, *After Virtue,* MacIntyre aims to show that we must turn to what he calls "the classical tradition" of ethics, revolving around the concept of the virtues, if we are to be rescued from what he regards as the incoherence of modern moral language and practice. In contrast with liberal theories that value "the capacity to detach oneself from any particular standpoint or point of view,"[1] what characterizes the ethics of tradition, centered on Aristotle, is its thorough rootedness in the context of a particular social order. Specific social roles are the most fundamental assumptions on which the traditions build, and their ethics center on the virtues that are necessary for the performance of these roles.

More recently, in his 1988 book, *Whose Justice? Which Rationality?* MacIntyre promises to address that crucial question left unanswered in his earlier defense of a tradition-based morality of the virtues. He will, he says, supply "an account of what rationality is, in the light of which rival and incompatible evaluations of the arguments of *After Virtue* could be adequately accounted for."[2] After a lengthy exposition of the history of three ethical traditions he finds, after a few sentences of argument, that Thomas Aquinas's synthesis of the Aristotelian and the Augustinian Christian traditions best exemplifies rationality and justice. As he admits, he has arrived, at the end of the book, at the starting point for his own moral theorizing. Presumably another book will follow.

In spite of its unfinished nature, MacIntyre's work has become an influential defense of tradition-based thinking about social justice. It is treated, in some circles at least, as a worthy critique of contemporary liberalism. Most of those who discuss it seem far more interested in its methodology than in its political implications. Few reviewers or critics have confronted the pervasive elitism of MacIntyre's defense of tradition as a basis for justice, and its equally pervasive sexism has scarcely been mentioned.[3] In fact, one moral philosopher has suggested that MacIntyre be recognized as an "honorary woman," because of the contextuality of his ethics.[4] I shall offer here a much-needed critique, showing how a primarily feminist analysis can serve to uncover a more general and basic problem of this way of thinking—its incapacity to deal critically with the fact and the effects of domination.

MacIntyre's language in both *After Virtue* and *Whose Justice?* is a clear case of false gender neutrality. He writes of "men and women," or "he or she," in contexts where to do so is patently absurd. He uses these terms, for example, when discussing the quest of classical Athenian citizens for riches, power and prestige, although in fact Athenian women were not citizens with access to any of these things. Occasionally, where the use of gender-neutral terms might seem so absurd as to strike even the most insensitive reader, MacIntyre reverts to the use of *men, boys,* and *he.*[5] Sometimes in his discussions of Aristotle's conception of the *polis,* MacIntyre so closely intertwines references to "the good man" or "he" with references to "the virtuous person," "the human individual," or "he or she" that one is left with the impression that it is his conscious intention to make the reader forget about the exclusionary nature of Aristotle's views about who could lead "the good life for a human being."[6] MacIntyre uses these terms to discuss Aristotle's question, "What is the good life for man?" in spite of the fact that Aristotle's answer to this question was a life that he thought women (as well as slaves and manual workers) were necessarily excluded from, and one that depended in large part on the performance by these excluded people of subordinate functions.[7] Again, in the context of the Adam and Eve story and Augus-

tine's conception of the will, MacIntyre persistently employs gender-neutral language, even though Christian (especially Catholic) theology has assigned to Eve the primary blame for the fall from grace. The same thing happens all through his discussion of Aquinas's theory, even though he notes in passing that "in the household and family structures of which he knew everyone else acted as the agent of the male head of household."[8]

This use of gender-neutral language in the discussion of traditions and societies in which sex difference was a central and determining feature that justified the subordination of women continues throughout MacIntyre's recent work. It is particularly striking in a passage in which he presents human life as a narrative, in which each character's role is largely predetermined. Given this, he says, unless children are educated into the virtues through being told the stories of their moral tradition, they will be left "unscripted, anxious stutterers in their actions as in their words." And what stories are these? Stories "about wicked stepmothers, lost children, good but misguided kings, wolves that suckle twin boys, youngest sons who receive no inheritance but must make their own way in the world and eldest sons who waste their inheritance on riotous living and go into exile to live with the swine." These are the stories that teach children "the cast of characters ... in the drama into which they have been born and what the ways of the world are."[9] Despite his use of the gender-neutral word *children,* MacIntyre fails entirely to notice that the vast preponderance of the cast is male, and that the only explicitly female characters mentioned are a wicked stepmother and a suckling wolf. Faced with this choice of roles—human but wicked, nurturing but bestialized—surely girls are more likely to be rendered "unscripted, anxious stutterers" by being *subjected* to than by being deprived of such stories. For these stories, as well as many others in "our" mythology, are themselves basic building blocks of male domination. . . .

MacIntyre presents, most of the time, a benign portrait of the three traditions he prefers to liberalism, and of the societies in which they were embedded. This starts with the Homeric world view, which he evaluates differently from many who have studied it. According to him, the wars fought by the Homeric heroes were to protect and bring prosperity to their households and local communities, whose members therefore all benefited from their warrior elites' virtues of physical strength, courage, intelligence, and prosperity. He is only momentarily puzzled by the paradox raised by this rather one-sided interpretation of Homer—that in order to achieve contentment and prosperity both for themselves and for those left at home, the heroes "pursue a course whose characteristic end is death."[10] Other interpretations of Homer, in which the hero's own success and immortal fame are recognized as the driving forces, do not raise any such paradoxes.[11] Though MacIntyre emphasizes the connection of role and status with privileges and duties, his benign interpretation de-emphasizes both the social hierarchy of heroic societies and the heavy sanctions that reinforced it.[12] Those who stayed at home, and their points of view, are virtually ignored.

This is particularly noticeable the few times that MacIntyre mentions Homeric women. "Andromache and Hector, Penelope and Odysseus are friends (*philos*)," MacIntyre asserts, "as much as are Achilles and Patroclus," but he does not point out here that this indicates no necessary similarity between the two relationships, since to call someone a friend in the Homeric context could simply indicate kinship.[13] He acknowledges that women's virtues were different from men's, consisting primarily in their physical attractions and their fidelity. But he does not confront the fact that women's virtues were defined in relation to men, whereas men's virtues were not defined in relation to women. Neither does he see that this entails no possibility of equality, or friendship based on equality, between the sexes. Mortal women appear most

often in Homer as causes of conflict between men or armies, or as part of the booty. For a clearer picture than MacIntyre provides, we must turn to M. I. Finley, who writes:

> There is no mistaking the fact that Homer fully reveals what remained true for the whole of antiquity, that women were held to be naturally inferior and therefore limited in their function to the production of offspring and the performance of household duties, and that the meaningful social relationships and the strong personal attachments were sought and found among men.[14]

As for the rest of the social hierarchy, MacIntyre does not mention the free members of the non-elite classes, who could not possess the virtues no matter what they did. When he writes that "the word *aretê* . . . is in the Homeric poems used for excellence of any kind," the *reader* must provide the caution "except excellence in any activity not valued by the male elite." It is not until his later chapter on classical Greek society, wishing to make it appear more egalitarian, that MacIntyre makes explicit the fact that "virtue" and "honor" in Homer are the virtue of and the honor due to a warrior king.[15] Slaves, MacIntyre admits, were not much better off than the dead, but he defines them as "outside the heroic community." Having defined the community so as to exclude its slaves, he claims that the Homeric virtues were those qualities that protected and furthered the interests of the community as a whole.

Even with slaves excluded, this interpretation of heroic Greece as a communitarian culture with a tradition of shared values is not convincing. What evidence is there that the warrior kings fought their wars and cultivated their virtues primarily for the sake of the community and its households, rather than that the household was viewed largely as the economic and reproductive base for wars fought primarily to bring glory, wealth, and immortal fame to the heroes? If Odysseus's success as a warrior was for the sake of his household and community, why did he spend ten years on the journey home from a nine-year-long war? Was the Trojan War itself really embarked on for the sake of the warriors' households and kinship groups, or was it rather an essentially masculine war of revenge for the honor of a king, who had been slighted by his wife's defection? MacIntyre neither asks nor answers such questions. But other commentators, such as M. I. Finley, A. W. H. Adkins, and Nancy Hartsock, freely acknowledge that the Homeric epics depict a society in which most people were perceived as existing for the sake of the male elite, and in which what are presented as "the virtues" were reserved for these few.

The core problem with MacIntyre's account of Homeric society lies in his accounts of all the societies in which his traditions flourished. It is his failure to ask: "By what ethical standard can its entire social structure be defended?" At one point he comes close to asking this vital question, when he compares the evaluative rules and terms of the *Iliad* to the rules of a game, such as chess. This analogy, he admits, is dangerous as well as illuminating, because games are played for a number of purposes. Surely the implication is that these purposes must themselves be subject to ethical scrutiny, which would seem especially called for when the "game" requires a social structure of hierarchy and domination. Having raised the problem, however, MacIntyre immediately dismisses it:

> There is nothing to be made of the question: for what purpose do the characters in the *Iliad* observe the rules that they observe and honour the precepts which they honour? It is rather the case that it is only within their framework of rules and precepts that they are able to frame purposes at all.

For MacIntyre, this very feature of the heroic ethic makes it vastly preferable to the stance of "some modern moral philosophers" who value "the capacity to detach oneself from any particular standpoint or point of view, to step backwards, as it were, and view and judge that stand-

point or point of view from the outside. In heroic society there is no 'outside' except that of the stranger."[16]

It is important to recognize that MacIntyre's cavalier dismissal of the importance of objectivity in ethics is clearly linked to the fact that he assumes that if "we" were members of heroic society, we would be *heroes.* Asking "what relevance can [the heroic virtues] possess for us?" since "nobody now can be a Hector or a Gisli," he gives no thought to the far greater probability, if one were transported back, of being not a hero but, though not a stranger, an outsider to his or her culture's highest virtues—a slave, an ordinary male member of the underclass, or (more probably still) a woman. This is why he can be so dismissive of what he calls the "outside" point of view, which takes into account the viewpoint of those excluded from the dominant group. But it seriously damages his reliance on the Homeric ethic and, as we shall see, on the other traditional ethics on which he depends for his theory of justice. If it is the case, as MacIntyre claims, that "heroic society is still inescapably a part of us all,"[17] then we must confront the fact that its ethic reflected not "shared values" but the dominance of a male warrior elite. Given this, it is especially urgent that we evaluate both the society and its ethic from the points of view of *all* its members.

This is equally the case with classical Greek society. It is particularly important with Aristotle's ethics, central to the tradition that MacIntyre thinks can rescue us from the mires into which, he alleges, contemporary moral philosophy has led. He concludes in *After Virtue* that "the Aristotelian tradition can be restated in a way that restores intelligibility and rationality to our moral and social attitudes and commitments."[18] And in *Whose Justice?* he takes the equally strong stand that "the importance of other subsequent moral and political philosophies will turn on whether they do or do not impugn, vindicate, or correct and supplement Aristotle's answers to Plato's questions."[19] Here again, MacIntyre does not confront the pivotal fact that "the good life" not only excludes but *depends* upon the exclusion of the great majority of people, including all women.

What does MacIntyre find so compelling about the Aristotelian ethic? First, that it rejects the false distinction between fact and value, and equates the good with the realization of man's essential nature. It presupposes "some account of the essence of man as a rational animal and above all some account of the human *telos*." To act in accordance with its virtues enables us "to realise our true nature and to reach our true end. To defy them will be to be frustrated and incomplete, to fail to achieve that good of rational happiness which it is peculiarly ours as a species to pursue." MacIntyre indicts the Enlightenment for, among other things, rejecting any such teleological view of human nature. Second, he values the Aristotelian tradition's functional concept of a man, rooted in particular forms of social life: "according to that tradition to be a man is to fill a set of roles each of which has its own point and purpose: member of a family, citizen, soldier, philosopher, servant of God." Again, it was the Enlightenment's error to reject this concept, instead considering it a form of liberation to conceive of man "as an individual prior to and apart from all roles."[20]

As in his discussion of the heroic ethic, here too MacIntyre de-emphasizes the centrality of sexism and elitism in the tradition whose modern relevance he hopes to establish. And in neither book does MacIntyre confront what he as a modern Aristotelian must confront—the far-ranging *implications* of the inherent sexism and elitism of the Aristotelian ethic.[21] On the one hand, aided by falsely gender-neutral language, he writes much of the time as if when Aristotle used the term *anthropos* ("human being") he really did mean it inclusively.[22] He also says that the scope of justice in the post-Homeric city-state necessarily was "the whole life of the community of a *polis*," and that it and the other virtues were aimed at securing "not merely the goods of this or that form of activity, but also the overall good of the *polis*." "The soundness of a particular practical argument, framed in terms of the goods of excellence," he claims, "is independent of its force for any particular person."[23] The impression left by these phrases, and reinforced by the use of gender-neutral language, is that all were at least eligible to participate in such a life and such a good. How else might the soundness of an argument be "independent of its force for any particular person," regardless of whether that person was man or woman, slave or free, manual worker or leisured man?

But of course this impression is false. And so, some of the time, MacIntyre writes in direct contradiction to it. He acknowledges that the ordering of goods in the *polis* was hierarchical, as when he explains that some goods were "valued only for their own sake" and others "only . . . valued as means to some further good," or when he says that in Aristotle's universe "each level of the hierarchy provides the matter in and through which the forms of the next higher level actualize and perfect themselves."[24] It is, we might add, this hierarchy of things and persons, and the goods they produce, that makes Aristotle describe farmers, craftsmen, and day laborers as "necessary conditions" for but not "integral parts" of the best city-state.[25] In *After Virtue*, MacIntyre briefly mentions the fact that many categories of people were excluded from what Aristotle calls "the good life for man." He writes:

> What is likely to affront us—and rightly—is Aristotle's writing off of non-Greeks, barbarians and slaves, as not merely not possessing political relationships, but as incapable of them. . . . [C]raftsmen and tradesmen constitute an inferior class, even if they are not slaves. Hence the peculiar excellences of the exercise of craft skill and manual labour are invisible from the standpoint of Aristotle's catalogue of the virtues.[26]

He completely omits the fact that, in addition to these groups of men, *all* women were excluded by Aristotle from "the good life." In *Whose Justice?*, noting feminist critique of Aristotle, he does briefly discuss the issue, but his response is totally unsatisfactory, even within the context of his own theory.

MacIntyre points out that Aristotle's merito-cratic theory of political justice "unfortunately" depends on his belief that farmers, artisans, merchants, and women cannot exercise the virtues "necessary for participation in the active life of the best kind of *polis*."[27] But he does not explain how a modern Aristotelian might overcome this rather large problem. In fact, although the Aris-totelian tradition, as presented by MacIntyre, is supposedly aimed at the human good, only those whose productive, reproductive, and daily ser-vice needs are fully taken care of by others, and who are therefore free to engage in the highest goods—political activity and intellectual life—are regarded as fully human. This would seem to be a philosophy in need of some considerable adaptation, if it is to be relevant in the late twen-tieth century! Sometimes MacIntyre seems to be aware of the seriousness of the problem, as when he says: "It is crucial to the structure of Aristo-tle's extended argument that the virtues are unavailable to slaves or to barbarians and so therefore is the good for man." But just a few pages later, giving no reasons, he refers to Aris-totle's "indefensible defence of slavery" as a part of his theory "whose rejection need not carry any large implications for our attitudes to his overall theory."[28] It is by no means clear why this should be so, especially since Aristotle's conceptions of the human *telos* and the good life present serious problems not only for slaves but for the vast majority of people.

In *Whose Justice?* MacIntyre tries to rectify the "mistake" that Aristotle made in excluding women from citizenship. He does not explain how this exclusion is connected with the claims made in Aristotle's biological writings that women are "a deformity, though one which occurs in the ordinary course of nature," and that their very existence is due only to the need for men to be reproduced sexually, so that their (superior) form can be kept separate from their (inferior) matter.[29] Moreover, his response to the problem of the specifically feminist challenge to Aristotle and the Aristotelian legacy is quite inadequate. Arguing that women *can* be in-cluded, "without denying [Aristotle's] central claims about the best kind of *polis*," he suggests that it would require their occupational and social roles to be restructured in a way that was inconceivable to Aristotle, but was "envisaged . . . by Plato."[30]

MacIntyre's appeal to Plato presents several serious problems. First, Plato's radical proposals about women were made only for those in the ruling elite of an ideal society that both he and Aristotle thought was impracticable in the real world. Second, Plato's restructuring of the roles of the guardian women in the *Republic* was intrinsically connected with his abolition of the private family.[31] His guardian men and women are "mated" for eugenic breeding purposes, and are not allowed to be attached to their own chil-dren, or even to know who they are. This is why Aristotle, having considered it, explicitly re-jected Plato's argument about women.[32] Clearly, given Catholic teachings about marriage and sexuality, MacIntyre the Thomist is even less in a position to adopt Plato's abolition of the family as a solution to Aristotle's "mistake" about women. The third problem is that, both in the chapters concerning Aristotle and throughout the rest of the book, MacIntyre clearly *assumes* the continuance of the nuclear family, thereby totally undermining his appeal to Plato's solution.[33]

The last problem with MacIntyre's solution, which is also a problem with his dismissal of Aristotle's defense of slavery, is that it takes no account of the extent to which Aristotle's entire conception of what constitutes "the good life" *depends* on the exclusion from it of the great majority of people. As MacIntyre makes clear, the "supreme good" for a human being, accord-ing to Aristotle, consists in the combination of virtuous moral and political activity with con-templative enquiry.[34] And though his tone is dif-ferent in the case of the exclusion of manual workers than in the case of women and slaves, Aristotle makes it clear that all those who participate in the performance of those necessary but inferior functions such as domestic management, child rearing, and the production of daily necessities cannot live this life of excellence. The kind of redistribution of tasks that MacIntyre suggests as a solution to the problem of the exclusion of women and laborers is simply not acceptable within an Aristotelian framework. For it would result in a citizenry that, because partly occupied with domestic and other manual work, would not be able (as the free and leisured citizens Aristotle envisages would be) to focus entirely on politics and intellectual activity—his "highest life for a human being." Not only his conception of this highest life but his conception of the type of rationality that is required in order to participate in it depend on the performance of all the other functions of life—its "necessary conditions"—by persons who do *not* share in this rationality nor in the virtues required of citizens.

MacIntyre says that he rejects Aristotle's metaphysical biology. But he does not adequately address the problem that then faces him, as an Aristotelian who rejects the belief that not only the nonhuman natural world but also the vast majority of human beings are naturally intended to be the providers of productive and reproductive services for the few. A modern Aristotelian must confront the issue of how "the good life for man" is to be redefined once it is assumed that the differences established by social hierarchies of dominance and submission are *not* natural, and are ethically indefensible. Once "the good life" is really understood to mean the good *human* life, it must be seen to encompass vast aspects of life that are not considered even a part of the subject matter of an ethics that still rests on sexist and elitist assumptions. It must, in the absence of slaves and largely dehumanized workers, discuss how the products and services necessary for human life can be provided in the context of the good life. Likewise, with women not functionally defined by

their biology, the raising of children to the point where, and in a way that, they will be able to lead good lives becomes itself necessarily a part of discussion of the good life.

While MacIntyre does not ignore the family, he lists "the making and sustaining of family life" among practices such as playing games and following intellectual pursuits.[35] But this blurs the difference between essential and elective practices and neglects two important facts. First, if it were not for the childbearing, nurturance, and socialization that have taken place within the family, there would be no people to live the good life. Second, throughout recorded history, the institution and practices of the family have been so structured as to render it virtually impossible for women, who have primarily performed these essential human functions, to participate in what men have defined as "the good life for man." MacIntyre's works ignore children and their rearing. Strikingly, not one of those persons whom he lists as exemplars of the virtues was a participating parent.[36] Despite his insistence that we think in terms of a complete human life—"a concept of a self whose unity resides in the unity of a narrative which links birth to life to death as narrative beginning to middle to end"[37]—his moral subjects, like those of most ethical theories, are apparently born directly into adulthood. And so, in spite of his usage of "men and women" and "he and she," MacIntyre—like the traditions he celebrates—ignores a great deal of what most women since Homeric times have contributed to the human good: the bearing of children and the raising of them to the point where they have the qualities required of human moral subjects, capable of choosing their own mode of the good life, and living it.

MacIntyre's eventual conclusion in *Whose Justice?* is that Thomas Aquinas's synthesis of Aristotle with Augustinian Christianity offers the best, the most defensible account of justice and practical rationality. Thomism is presented as a version of Aristotelianism that can be applied outside the context of the Greek city-state.[38] The works of Augustine and Aquinas have had immense influence on the development of the Christian tradition, not least on its attitudes toward women and their subordinate roles in church and society. But throughout his discussions of Augustine and Aquinas, aided again by his use of falsely gender-neutral language, MacIntyre ignores the problems that are raised for a potential twentieth-century adherent to these traditions by what they have to say about the nature of women and about just relations between the sexes. In his praise for Aquinas's capacity to synthesize Aristotle's philosophy with Christian theology, he ignores the fact that on these issues, the synthesis compounds the sexism and the misogyny of both.

Theologians and political theorists have paid considerable attention to Augustine's and Aquinas's dispositions of women in recent years, but MacIntyre ignores their work.[39] Augustine's more complex and nuanced conclusions about women's place are well captured in Genevieve Lloyd's phrase "spiritual equality and natural subordination."[40] Perhaps in part because he regarded his mother as an ideal Christian, in part because of the influence of Plato, and in part because of his emphasis on the more egalitarian version of the creation myth, Augustine believed that men and women were equal in soul and in their capacity to share in the divine life: "not only men but also women might contemplate the eternal reasons of things."[41] However, he also said that, viewed alone, in her quality as man's "help-meet," woman is not, as man alone is, in the image of God; and he referred allegorically to man as higher reason and to woman as lower reason or sensuality. Because of her bodily difference from man and her association with carnality, passion, and therefore sin, as symbolized by Eve's role in the Fall, Augustine saw woman as properly and naturally subordinated to man. In the City of God, woman and man are equal, but in the City of Man woman is man's subject and properly restricted to the domestic sphere or, even better, to celibacy. That these are not mere archaic myths that can safely be ignored was confirmed in 1988, when Pope John Paul II reaffirmed these limitations on women, justifying them, as did Augustine, by the sin of Eve.[42]

In the works of Thomas Aquinas, in which MacIntyre sees the best account of justice and practical rationality to be found in any tradition, the Christian association of women with sin is synthesized with Aristotle's teleological biology. Aquinas places far more emphasis than Augustine on the City of Man—the world of politics and the family. Here his reliance on Aristotle is clear, most centrally in his notions that a woman is "a misbegotten male," intended only for the work of reproduction, defective in her reason, and therefore "naturally subject to man, because in man the discretion of reason predominates."[43] As Arlene Saxonhouse sums up his views:

> In Thomas' thought, the body and the soul are not separated, as they are in Augustine's. . . . Since the rational soul is proportionate to the body, the misbegotten body of the female has a soul that is proportionate to it and, therefore, inferior. Thomas concludes that she must be subordinate to the male for her own interest, since, as Aristotle had taught, the inferior must accept the rule of the superior. Like her children, woman benefits when she performs the role in marriage to which her lower capacities are suited.[44]

Apart from one brief mention of Aquinas's assumption that households were male-headed, MacIntyre simply ignores all this. He continually employs gender-neutral language in his discussions of Augustine and Aquinas, just as in those about Homer and Aristotle. Moreover, he contrasts the inclusiveness of the thought of these Christian thinkers with the limitations and exclusions imposed by his historical context on Aristotle's conceptions of justice and practical rationality.[45]

It is by now obvious that many of "our" traditions, and certainly those evaluated most highly by MacIntyre, are so permeated by the patriarchal power structure within which they evolved as to require nothing less than radical and intensive challenge if they are to meet truly humanist conceptions of the virtues. When MacIntyre begins to try to evaluate the rationality of traditions, he says: "The test for truth in the present, therefore, is always to summon up as many questions and as many objections of the greatest strength possible; what can be justifiably claimed as true is what has sufficiently withstood such dialectical questioning and framing of objections."[46] But he reaches his own conclusions about the superiority of the Thomistic synthesis without even subjecting it to what is one of the most crucial tests of it in his time—the challenge of whether this tradition can include women as full human beings.[47]

MacIntyre says that "the initial answer" to questions about practical rationality and justice (questions about "What ought I to do?"), in the light of the claims of the various traditions, "will depend upon who you are and how you understand yourself." Let us, then, imagine a young woman in the United States today taking up MacIntyre's invitation. Let us see whether she will find among his preferred traditions one in which her life will become intelligible and whether, by engaging in conversation with his traditions, she will be helped to become aware of her "incoherence" and to provide an account of it. Let us imagine, at first, that the woman is young, able-bodied, white, heterosexual, married, and that the income of her household is average. Raised in a fairly traditional family, she has nonetheless, like many of her peers, come to have expectations of leading a life that involves both motherhood and wage work. She is contented with her family and other personal relations, but frustrated by the boredom, dead-endedness, and low pay of her wage work, which she stays with because its hours and demands are compatible with the responsibilities she perceives are hers as a wife and mother. She worries that taking up a more demanding though more interesting occupation might strain her marriage and shortchange her children. How will engaging in conversation with the Aristotelian-

Christian traditions that MacIntyre prefers to liberalism help her?

To start with, these traditions have no comprehension of her need to be both family member and wage worker. Engaging in conversation with Aristotle will first tell her that her sex is "a deformity in nature," which exists only for the purpose of procreating the male sex, the original and true form of the human being. Engaging in conversation with MacIntyre on Aristotle's exclusion of women from all but domestic life will raise the possibility of Plato's solution: abolish the family. But this woman loves and cherishes her family life and does not relish the idea of living in communal barracks, mating when and with whom she is told to, and not knowing who her children are. And, even if she did, none of the other traditions that MacIntyre suggests she engage in conversation with would tolerate such an idea for an instant. For one thing, they regard sexual activity outside of lifelong marriage as a serious sin. Turning to Augustine, she may be comforted by his conviction that she is the spiritual equal to man, but his equally firm conviction that her physical sexuality makes her necessarily man's inferior is unlikely to help her provide an account of her "incoherence." It seems more likely to exacerbate it. Turning to Thomism—the tradition MacIntyre finds the best embodiment of rationality because of its ability to accommodate Augustinian insights with Aristotelian theorizing—she will encounter the problems of Aristotle and the problems of Augustinian Christianity compounded. For Aquinas synthesizes the Aristotelian view that women are a deformity in nature with the Christian view that women's sexuality is to blame for men's sinful lust. In this tradition, she will find serious consideration being given to questions such as whether women were included in the original Creation and whether, in order to be resurrected, they must be reborn as men. Aquinas is hardly likely to provide the calm coherence for this woman's life that MacIntyre finds in him. And the woman I have imagined presents the *easiest* female test of these traditions, being among the most advantaged of women. If she were poor, black, lesbian, old, disabled, a single parent, or some combination of these, she would surely be even less likely to find herself and her situation rendered more coherent by turning to MacIntyre's traditions.

MacIntyre says that traditions are also to be tested by whether they help persons to answer the real, difficult moral questions they may have to face. Our hypothetical woman's questions may include whether to have an abortion if she accidentally becomes pregnant just as she is completing many years of dedicated and joyful primary parenting and wants to become involved in a fulfilling job; whether to divorce her husband if he has an affair and neglects his family, even though she knows that she and the children are likely to be economically devastated as well as to be faced with the psychological and social stress of divorce; whether to run for office in order to contribute to the solution of political problems about which she has strong convictions, though she knows her children will have less of her time and attention than they are used to. How will MacIntyre's preferred traditions help her, given that with few exceptions the theories that constitute them are unwilling even to grant her the status of full humanity? She is unlikely to conclude from her attempt to engage in conversation with MacIntyre's traditions that she is incoherent, or to find her thinking about justice and practical rationality enhanced. She may indeed conclude, without looking much further into them, that there is something fundamentally incoherent about the traditions themselves and that she will have to look elsewhere for answers to questions about justice and rationality.

FEMINISM AS A TRADITION

In spite of MacIntyre's persistent use of gender-neutral language, it is clear that most women, as well as men who have any kind of feminist consciousness, will not find in any of his traditions a rational basis for moral and political action. Where, then, do we stand? Are we outside all traditions and therefore, in MacIntyre's view at least, "in a state of moral and intellectual destitution"? Can one be anything *but* an outsider to a tradition that excludes one, and some of the things one values most, from what it regards as the best in human life? Can we find, in the history of feminist thought and action, another tradition, that derives much from the liberal tradition MacIntyre distorts and rejects, and that gives an account of rationality and justice superior to that provided by any other? As we saw, he gives conflicting accounts of what a tradition *is*. At times he describes it as a defining context, stressing the authoritative nature of its "texts;" at times he talks of a tradition as "living," as a "not-yet-completed narrative," as an argument about the goods that constitute the tradition.[48]

Feminism is clearly not a tradition in the former sense. Most feminists do not have authoritative texts. We do not assume that we *must* refer back to any particular canons, as medieval scholastics did when citing Aristotle. Feminist theorists disagree with one another on many counts, arguing with both predecessors and contemporaries on all but the most basic issue—our conviction that women are human beings in no way inferior to men, who warrant equal consideration with men in any political or moral theory.

Feminism *is* clearly a tradition, though, in the second sense, that of being a living argument. From Astell, Wollstonecraft, and de Gouges to Thompson, Mill, and Taylor, from Stanton and Anthony to Gilman and Shaw, from Woolf and de Beauvoir to Firestone, Friedan, Oakley, Mitchell, Chodorow, Pateman, and all the other great feminist thinkers of the last two decades, there has been much disagreement about the causes and the nature of the oppression of women, and the solutions to it. But all have agreed that any tradition that does not address these questions, especially if it *cannot* address them because its most fundamental assumptions about what is "the human good" do not even enable these questions to become visible, can no longer be regarded as just or rational.

Of the traditions MacIntyre discusses, only the liberalism he so decisively rejects contains the possibility of encompassing the answers to feminist questions. This is not to say that, as it stands, the liberal tradition has been free of neglect of and rationalizations for women's oppression—far from it.[49] But, as many feminist theorists recognize, a number of the basic tenets of liberalism—including the replacement of the belief in natural hierarchy by a belief in the fundamental equality of human beings, and the placing of individual freedoms before any unified construction of "the good"—have been basic tenets in the development of feminism, too. Though by no means all contemporary feminists are liberals, virtually all acknowledge the vast debts of feminism to liberalism. They know that without the liberal tradition, feminism would have had a much more difficult time emerging.

NOTES

1. MacIntyre, *After Virtue,* p. 119.
2. MacIntyre, *Whose Justice?* p. ix.
3. A number of critics, however, have pointed out the lack of political engagement and of consideration of "hard cases" in the works of MacIntyre and other communitarians. See, for example, Amy Gutmann, "Communitarian Critics of Liberalism," *Philosophy and Public Affairs* 14, no. 3 (1985); H. N. Hirsch, "The Threnody of Liberalism: Constitutional Liberty and the Renewal of Community," *Political Theory* 14, no. 3 (1986); Will Kymlicka, "Liberalism and Communitarianism," *Canadian Journal of Philosophy* 18, no. 2 (1988); John R. Wallach, "Liberals, Communitarians, and the Tasks of Political Theory," *Political Theory* 15, no. 4 (1987). Gutmann and Kymlicka both briefly raise the problem of gender, as does Thomas Nagel in his review of *Whose Justice?*, "Agreeing in Principle," *Times Literary Supplement,* July 8, 1988.
4. Baier, "What Do Women Want?" p. 54.
5. MacIntyre, *Whose Justice? Which Rationality?* for example, pp. 25 and 54, when he is discussing

education in Athens, which was of course restricted to boys, and the first half of p. 45; see also pp. 32–39, passim.
6. See, for example, ibid., pp. 108–9.
7. MacIntyre, *After Virtue,* p. 187.
8. MacIntyre, *Whose Justice?* pp. 157, p. 179. Cf. chap. 11, passim.
9. MacIntyre, *After Virtue,* p. 201.
10. MacIntyre, *After Virtue,* pp. 115–16, 119, 120.
11. For example, A. W. H. Adkins, *Merit and Responsibility: A Study in Greek Values* (Oxford: Oxford University Press, 1960); M. I. Finley, *The World of Odysseus* (New York: Viking, 1978); Nancy C. M. Hartsock, *Money, Sex, and Power* (New York: Longman, 1983), chap. 8.
12. This is somewhat less the case in *Whose Justice?* See p. 14, but cf. p. 20, where he downplays conflicts of interests in the hierarchy.
13. MacIntyre, *After Virtue,* p. 116. Cf. *Whose Justice?* p. 42.
14. Finley, *The World of Odysseus,* p. 128.
15. MacIntyre, *After Virtue,* pp. 115, 124.
16. Ibid., pp. 118, 119.
17. Ibid., pp. 119, 122.
18. Ibid., p. 241 (restated in *Whose Justice?* p. ix); see also p. 111.
19. MacIntyre, *Whose Justice?* p. 85.
20. MacIntyre, *After Virtue,* pp. 50, 56; see also p. 58.
21. Feminist analyses and critiques of Aristotle, which MacIntyre virtually ignores even in *Whose Justice?* include Jean Bethke Elshtain, *Public Man, Private Woman: Women in Social and Political Thought* (Princeton: Princeton University Press, 1981), chap. 1; Lynda Lange, "Woman Is Not a Rational Animal: On Aristotle's Biology of Reproduction," in *Discovering Reality: Feminist Perspectives on Epistemology, Metaphysics, Methodology, and Philosophy of Science,* ed. Sandra Harding and Merrill B. Hintikka (Dordrecht, Holland: Reidel, 1983); Susan Moller Okin, *Women in Western Political Thought* (Princeton: Princeton University Press, 1979), chap. 4; Arlene W. Saxonhouse, *Women in the History of Political Thought: Ancient Greece to Machiavelli* (New York: Praeger, 1985); Elizabeth V. Spelman, "Aristotle and the Politicization of the Soul," in *Discovering Reality.*
22. He asserts, for example, that "what constitutes the good for man is a complete human life lived at its best," and that "on Aristotle's account . . .

[e]ven though some virtues are available only to certain types of people, none the less virtues attach not to men as inhabiting social roles, but to man as such" (*After Virtue*, pp. 140, 172).

23. MacIntyre, *Whose Justice?* pp. 44–45. Numerous similarly inclusive statements occur in chaps. 6–8, which are specifically about Aristotle.

24. Ibid., pp. 34, 101.

25. Aristotle, *The Politics*, 1328a–29a.

26. MacIntyre, *After Virtue*, p. 149; see also p. 170.

27. MacIntyre, *Whose Justice?* pp. 104–5. See also p. 121, where he notes again how what Aristotle says about justice is "deformed by his beliefs about women and about the nature of slaves."

28. MacIntyre, *After Virtue*, pp. 148–49, 152.

29. Aristotle, *The Generation of Animals*, 4, 767b, 775a. On this connection, see Lange, "Woman Is Not a Rational Animal"; Okin, *Women in Western Political Thought* (pp. 81–84 and notes). MacIntyre says that Aristotle's ethics "presupposes his metaphysical biology" but that he rejects this metaphysical biology, "as we must" (*After Virtue*, p. 152; see also p. 139). However, he does not provide the alternative teleological account that he says is needed.

30. MacIntyre, *Whose Justice?* p. 105.

31. This is confirmed by the fact that in *The Laws*, when Plato reinstates the private family, he reassigns women to their domestic role, even though he reiterates his beliefs about the undeveloped potential of women. See Okin, *Women in Western Political Thought*, chap. 3.

32. Plato, *The Republic*, book 5; Aristotle, *The Politics*, 1261a–1264b.

33. MacIntyre, *Whose Justice?* See, for example, p. 126, where he cites Aristotle on the importance of participating in the management of a household for a person's having "a good of his own"; pp. 194–95, where in the context of discussing Aquinas he refers, as a "fundamental *inclinatio*," to its "being good for human beings to live together commodiously in families." Other brief passages in which the continuance of the private family is clearly taken for granted appear on pp. 202, 227, 263, 273, 307, and 397.

34. Ibid., pp. 142–43.

35. MacIntyre, *After Virtue*, p. 175.

36. Ibid., p. 185.

37. Ibid., p. 191.

38. MacIntyre, *Whose Justice?* p. 10. He says that it "escapes the limitations of the *polis*."

39. For example, Kari Elizabeth Børreson, *Subordination and Equivalence: The Nature and Role of Women in Augustine and Thomas Aquinas* (Washington, D.C.: University Press of America, 1981; originally published Oslo: Universitetsforlaget, 1967); Maryanne Cline Horowitz, "The Image of God in Man—Is Woman Included?" *Harvard Theological Review* 72, no. 3–4 (July-October 1979); Genevieve Lloyd, *The Man of Reason: "Male" and "Female" in Western Philosophy* (Minneapolis: University of Minnesota Press, 1984), chap. 2; Martha Lee Osborne, *Woman in Western Thought* (New York: Random House, 1978), part 2; Saxonhouse, *Women in the History of Political Thought*, chap. 6.

40. Lloyd, *The Man of Reason*, p. 28.

41. Augustine, *Confessions*, 9.8; *De trinitate*, 12.7.12.

42. Pope John Paul II, "On the Dignity of Women," as quoted in the *New York Times*, October 1, 1988, pp. A1 and 6.

43. Aquinas, *Summa Theologica*, part 1, question 92, quoted from the translation in Osborne, *Women in Western Thought*, p. 69.

44. Saxonhouse, *Women in the History of Political Thought*, p. 147.

45. MacIntyre, *Whose Justice?* pp. 162–63, 181, 339. The middle passage reads, "As on Aristotle's view the law stands to the citizen in the best kind of *polis*, so on Aquinas' view the natural law stands to every human being in the *civitas Dei*." What he does not mention is that while the natural law, according to Aquinas, *applies* to every human being, it legitimizes the subjection of women to men.

46. Ibid., p. 358.

47. Another undeniable "test" the twentieth century presents Aquinas with, which MacIntyre also ignores, is the discovery of nuclear fission. The challenge here is whether the "just war" tradition can respond to the moral dilemmas of nuclear deterrence and the threat of human annihilation. See Susan Moller Okin, "Taking the Bishops Seriously," *World Politics* 36, no. 4 (1984).

48. Cf. *Whose Justice?* pp. 354, 383 with *After Virtue*, p. 207.

49. See, for example, Carole Pateman, *The Sexual Contract* (Stanford: Stanford University Press, 1988).

44. Gender Inequality in China and Cultural Relativism

❦

XIAORONG LI

INTRODUCTION

This paper questions the romanticized 'local cultural' notions of women's well-being and their adverse impact on women's struggle for equality as, for instance, in the People's Republic of China (PRC). It argues, on the basis of one case study, that the non-relativist notion developed in the 'capability approach' provides a promising alternative in addressing the problems raised originally by relativists.

Specifically, I will contend that the notions of gender relations and women's well-being that have been touted by some women activists, either as official spokespersons of governmental ideology or independent feminists, have limited and misguided women's cause for equality. Such misconceptions, as this paper tries to establish, have contributed to the failure to liberate women. In particular, I will examine the conceptions of women's quality of life as expressed by political ideology, traditional norms, and women's own perceptions.

Alongside these lessons I draw, I will explore an alternative notion—a Kantian-Aristotelian notion, as embodied in Nussbaum and Sen's 'capability approach' toward the value of gender equality. Such a notion provides a more plausible foundation for evaluating the well-being of women (as well as men). The 'capability approach' presents a cross-cultural notion of

Reprinted from *Women, Culture and Development* by permission of Oxford University Press.

being human and the human good that is at the same time sensitive to cultural traditions. Thus, it embraces the hope of overcoming the pitfalls of cultural insensitivity while avoiding the mere projection of local preferences.

[1]

In this section, I will make a case against the claim by relativists that, because of differing cultural conceptions of women, family, and society, it is insensitive, if not imperialist, to criticize Chinese women's apparent lack of gender equality.[1] I make my case by demonstrating that uncritical and unreflective local traditional cultural notions of women's well-being have been detrimental to women's struggle for a better quality of life in China.

Gender inequality in the PRC is not so much ignored as misunderstood. The PRC government has, since the early years of its rule, paid much attention, in its ideology and policy-making, to women's subordinate status. The revolution helped to raise the status of women. Legislation like the Marriage Law of the 1950s not only outlawed the most extreme forms of female subordination and repression, such as prostitution, concubinage, sale of women, and child brides, but also gave women the opportunity to make their own marital decisions. Women were no longer restricted to the home—they joined the agricultural and industrial work forces. Education, which was denied to women in traditional China, has become more accessible. And the arena of politics is no longer exclusively male.

However, gender disparity has persisted and has even increased in recent years. After the Marriage Law gave women the right to choose husbands, the traditional business of selling women for marriage is coming back. In 1990 alone, 18,692 cases were investigated by the authorities.[2] While women are said to have equal opportunity to work, many have to take lower-paid and less challenging jobs.[3] While women are said to have an equal say in politics, leadership positions are dominated by men, or given to women simply as window-dressing.[4] The nation's education system has given first priority to males, and illiterates and school dropouts have been mainly female.

Women in China have thus failed to 'hold up half the sky', as Chairman Mao promised they would do if they simply embraced a communist 'new China'. The failure cannot simply be attributed to governmental negligence and policy shortcomings. Its roots extend to conceptional manipulation and illusions in the areas where the following questions are relevant: 'What is women's well-being?' and 'How is well-being measured?'

One version of relativism, the 'local tradition' relativism[5] argues that notions of women's well-being (or, human good in general) should be drawn from local culture. It rejects universal notions because such notions would be culturally insensitive, neglecting historical and cultural differences.

Different cultural traditions and communities, it is said, diverge in their understanding of human values as well as women's status and roles in society. In this view, any attempt to produce a cross-cultural notion of human well-being is bound to enshrine certain understandings of the human good and to dismiss others.

This version of relativism is based on the fear that dominant social prejudices would be imposed on women by a dominant group's (stronger foreign culture, majority social members, or popular consensus) understanding of human value. Because societies are often patriarchally structured and controlled by dominant groups, cultural relativists do have a point for suspicion: the dominant understandings of human good will be likely to put females at a disadvantage.[6] This concern suggests some of the difficulties that attend any project of building a non-relativist norm of women's well-being.

But the same difficulty besets cultural relativism itself. Who should speak for 'the local tradition' in the absence of any universal normative evaluation? Should it be the local government (the state), the traditional philosophical or religious doctrines, or women's own perceptions of their interest? As the Chinese case makes clear, voices from these 'local' structures, without critical reflection, turn out to represent the patriarchal *status quo* and put females at a disadvantage.

Consider, for example, three Chinese conceptions of women's well-being that are perfectly 'local cultural'. One is the Communist Party-state's political ideology that drove the official campaigns for gender equality since the 1950s. Secondly, the ideas expressed in dominant traditional philosophy and religion, such as Confucianism and Taoism, which shaped the Chinese mentality and rituals of daily life, have also functioned as a voice of 'local culture'. Finally, the voice most frequently referred to by the relativist is that of Chinese women, expressing their desired roles in society. We shall see whether and how these three expressions reflect dominant male understandings of the role of women.

1   THE OFFICIAL VOICE

The official ideology in China has worked against the idea of women's freedom to choose and a respect for them as individuals, equal to men in dignity. It has treated gender equality as instrumental to political solidarity, and women as instruments for enhancing the national GNP. The increased role of women in workplaces outside the home is praised by the governmental All-China Women's Federation (ACWF) for its 'contribution to the building of socialist material and spiritual civilization'.[7] When the ACWF shows concern over insufficient educational training for women, it worries that 'if this situation is not remedied, the country's socialist modernization drive will be impeded'.[8] Similarly, rural women's status is studied only 'for the purpose of getting rid of this cancer [the illiteracy of rural women] in Chinese society as a burden on China's modernization'.[9] Recently, the ACWF's local divisions in Guangzhou and Shanghai have set up cosmetic surgery businesses in the accelerated national quest for profit. This has the effect of a symbolic call by authorities for women to beautify themselves in order to enhance men's strive for business profit or managerial excellence. At the same time, women are being systematically rejected for executive positions and find themselves before a growing pool of jobs in bars and hotel lobbies; working as waitresses, accompanying ladies, and prostitutes.

During the 45 years of communist rule, only when women's inferior treatment conflicted with the objectives of political campaigns did the issue of gender inequality become a policy concern. Thus, campaigns for women seemingly took place only in connection with political movements such as the Great Leap Forward movement of 1957–9, the rural 'responsibility system' reform since 1978 and the 'one-child' family planning project. Accordingly, gender equality has been largely reduced to 'labour equality' and pursued in the name of the national interest.

The recent drive for profit proceeds in the absence of equal opportunity for women to take high-skilled and highly paid positions. Profit-minded companies refuse to hire female graduates from universities because their parenting responsibilities may impede business.

The 'equality campaigns' indoctrinated women to view their roles in society in a particular way rather than helping them to cultivate their capability to reflect on and challenge the traditional patriarch *status quo*. The party line has always dominated the definition of 'women's liberation'. During the Great Leap Forward movement, 'liberation' meant enabling women to perform heavy manual labour in the field—'what men can do, women can do also'. In the Great Cultural Revolution, 'liberation' meant that women should become no different from men, even wearing men's clothing and behaving in a 'unisex' manner. During the current economic reforms, official publications argue that the 'responsibility system'[10] and labour efficiency considerations justify women's return to the kitchen, resuming the role of 'a virtuous wife and good mother'. The 'new Chinese woman' is told by the authorities that she could attain 'equality' with men by turning herself into a 'man'. Male character traits are presented as the common humanity that woman, as man's equal, is to live up to. Woman's 'equal' entitlement to humanity means her entitlement to 'man-ness'. The underlying assumption is that women are degenerate exemplars of humanity (man-ness). As in other societies, such a judgement of inferiority is often used, as Nussbaum observes, 'to justify and stabilize oppression'.[11]

The Chinese woman is told that she is 'liberated', but she is discouraged from and punished for thinking independently on gender issues. Lacking opportunities for critical thinking and information, she must adhere to rigid instructions on how to be the 'equal' of men. State persecution of critical thinkers has stifled critical thinking by women (as well as by men) and helped to reinforce biases against women despite the government's vow to eradicate them.

The ideology that motivates the state-sponsored 'women's equality' campaigns has mixed instrumentalist and utilitarian ideas. These campaigns have aimed at certain utilities defined by the state's political interest, either increasing the GNP or mobilizing massive support for the party. They have made the need for gender equality *contingent* on the government's political objectives. Such an instrumental notion, however, has proved to be no guarantee of equal treatment for women. This is because, first, all tolerated campaigns and activities, including the women's movement, have to adhere to official party doctrines ('the four cardinal principles',[12] for example), which are antithetical to freedom of thought and expression, among other civil liberties. Thus, any official campaign to improve the treatment of women will not tolerate criticism of the established party line.

Secondly, the official campaigns for gender equality are defective because they are based only on the instrumental value of women's social status. Efforts to reverse the inferior social status of women will fail if women's equality and freedom of choice are not valued for their own sake. The Chinese Communist Party's repeated purges of liberal ideas since the 1950s, such as the anti-rightist movement and the Cultural Revolution, have excluded any sincere promotion of such values.

The voice of the party-state, which turns out to be the voice of the dominant male, has not only misrepresented women's real interest in equality, but has also contributed to the failure of the official 'equality campaigns'. If the party-state ideology, which controls public media and the educational system, is taken to be the voice of the 'local community', then, as the above analysis shows, it could be very detrimental to women's struggle against subordination.

2 PATRIARCHAL TRADITIONS OF CHINESE THOUGHT

I have shown that the party-state ideology does not represent the 'local community' voice for Chinese women. Do the dominant philosophy and religion better represent that voice? Have they been able to offset the prejudices against women and express their real interest? There are reasons to take these thoughts as the voice of Chinese cultural tradition because they still strongly influence people's decisions in daily life, especially social attitude towards women. According

to a report on the second National Symposium on Women, family (not individual human beings) is still widely regarded as the cell of society responsible for the functions of reproduction, production, consumption, providing for the old, and nursing the young. And women are regarded as the nucleus around which family responsibilities are conceived.[13]

The core of traditional thought, however, has perpetuated, through philosophy, religion, and aesthetics, a subordination of women. Confucianism, a moral philosophy dating to 400 BC, morally evaluates a person according to his or her adherence to social roles prescribed by ancient rituals that were designed for collective achievement. The goodness of a man is determined by how well he plays his set of social roles as son, husband, father, and/or public official (servant). Accordingly, a woman is judged by her performance as daughter, wife, and mother. These roles carry very specific moral codes passed on from generations' worth of ritual practice: one virtue of the wife is 'obedience' to her husband, who in return is to provide for her and protect her. The virtue of a child is filial piety to the parents, whose virtue is, in return, love and fairness. Confucian philosophers argue that when different roles are performed in accordance with traditional rituals, society as a whole will be harmonious, with each assuming his/her role and all carrying out the mandate of heaven.

The roles assigned to women, however, were inferior since they involved only domestic and thus less important activities. This inferiority was clear to Confucius, who once said, 'Women and small men are the only burdensome people'.[14] That is to say that women do not belong to the Confucian moral category. Women are not only accorded less respect, but also, their inferior roles are said to be part of, and necessary for, the natural (heavenly) harmonious order. There is no room for women's own voice. Their mission and destiny in life (a conception of their good) has been predetermined by a male-dominated society and the theorists who justify the *status quo* social hierarchy. The long-dominant Confucian moral tradition, repeatedly enforced by rulers through laws and social customs over many generations, has been largely responsible for preventing women from identifying themselves as equally worthy human beings.

Over time, the social enforcement of Confucianism distorted its valuable points to suit political expediency. Chinese society, during its long history of male domination, carried to the extreme the Confucian view of women as subordinate to men, and failed to substantialize the equally important Confucian idea of loving, caring, responsible, and just male roles. The statute that 'Wives should be obedient to their husbands' every wish' was first stressed in the Western and Eastern Han Dynasties (206 BC–AD 220). The social institution for the absolute repression of women was completed in the Song Dynasty (906–1279). Its key moral code was the 'three obediences and four virtues'. These were: obedience to the father before marriage, to the husband after marriage, and to the son after the husband's death; and the virtues of loyalty, proper speech, modest demeanour, and diligent work. Central to this tradition were the ideas that 'men should be respectable and women humble', and that 'the lack of learning in woman is a virtue'.

Consequently, the Confucian ideals of family, society, and women's role have not significantly changed over the past 2,500 years. For example, women in today's China continue to be evaluated first and foremost by their traditionally primary roles as wives and mothers, and are expected to make sacrifices for the family. A traditionally female virtue, the idea of 'sharing', still functions as a norm for female performance of their social roles: women as wives 'share' their husbands' career achievement, fame, and success, by playing the roles of housekeepers and raising children while taking lower paid and less challenging jobs. Women are told to be satisfied by such a 'sharing'. A variant of this norm is expressed in the phrase, 'behind-the-scene great-

ness': women's greatness stands behind their husbands' achievements, fame, and success; each successful man has a virtuous woman supporting him. In both views, the virtue of female excellence is couched in the context of family unit. Female moral values are defined in terms of men's success.

The defect of this form of Confucianism is its collective moral evaluation, which does not embody the concept of individual worth of female social members, and respects a female only for her performance of the traditionally predetermined social roles. One may point out that, in the same way, male Chinese have also been restricted by their traditional roles and prevented from developing their complete human capabilities, such as the capability to love and care for their spouse and family before and above their country, or to achieve excellence in housework. However, the rigid traditional hierarchy works mainly to the disadvantage of women. In the traditional family, a woman had no inheritance rights as a result of being perceived as not fully human; she was merely an instrument for housework and reproduction; she remained at home and was subjected to restrictive and humiliating rituals, enslaved by the father, brother(s), and husband.

Buddhism, an imported religion, is perhaps another main source of the view of women as inferior. Briefly stated, the traditional contempt for women in China is linked to the Buddhist ascetic teaching that women are the source of all evils on earth because female sexuality causes men to commit crimes. Thus, women are condemned for distracting Buddhist monks from reaching 'the other shore'—Faramita. Buddha advised his disciples, 'Women are the vicious enemy of a wise man.' One doctrine of the Buddhist Mahayana (Great Vehicle), called 'nine meditations to extinguish sex desires', was adopted in order to condition monks to see rotten corpses when they looked at beautiful women. Buddhism became well-adapted and widely accepted in Chinese society for reasons that cannot be discussed here. It is clear, though, that its success strengthened the social prejudice against women.

Taoism, the rival teaching to Confucianism, may have been the only major philosophical school that worships femininity. In the Taoist bible *Dao De Jing,* Lao Tzu, the founder, built his cosmology (the 'natural' order) and ethics—the philosophy of Yin and Yang—on female virtues and characteristics traditionally attributed to women, such as gentleness, softness, humbleness, tolerance, obedience, and women's function to give birth and take 'lower positions', etc. Lao Tzu wrote:

> The Tao is an empty vessel; it is used, but
>   never filled.
> Oh, unfathomable source of ten thousand
>   things!
> Blunt the sharpness,
> Untangle the knot,
> Soften the glare,
> Merge with dust . . .[15]

The philosophy of Lao Tzu uses conventional female images to interpret conflicts and interactions and the cycle in nature and human life. He suggests a technique to survive natural calamities.

> The valley spirit never dies;
> It is the women, primal mother.
> Her gateway is the root of heaven and earth.
> It is like a veil barely seen.
> Use it; it will never fail.[16]

However, Lao Tzu's Taoism hardly embodies a fair conception of femininity. Some of the female images, such as 'obedience' and 'humbleness', regarded as 'natural' by Lao Tzu, are products of certain social divisions of labour and perpetuated by social prejudices. Thus, despite his favourable view of women, Lao Tzu takes for granted the dominant social perspective of his time and views women from the conventional position of a dominant male. Unfortunately, the legacy of Lao Tzu, perhaps contrary to his intention, serves to reaffirm socially constructed gender difference as the 'natural order', providing a philosophical justification for the unjust practice.

Moreover, since his philosophy aims at revealing the skills to survive, to prevail, and to win, his praising of 'female' (Yin) virtues is a mere stratagem. Women are valued by him, but only because of their usefulness for other ends. This instrumentalist evaluation of women's status explains why Taoism did not spur the development of significant feminist philosophies, for it failed to generate a real respect for women for their own worth as equal human beings.

This unfortunately over-simplified survey of major Chinese conceptions of women and their status in family and society provides only preliminary and limited insights about their defects as a 'local traditional' voice for women. These conceptions, as I have tried to demonstrate, played a harmful role in women's struggle for equality by perpetuating the subordinating social *status quo* as 'natural' social order.

3 FALSE SELF-CONSCIOUSNESS

Who, then, should be the voice of the Chinese 'local traditional' view on female virtues or women's well-being? What about women themselves who are raised and live in the Chinese cultural context? Talking about women's own opinions, we have to be cautious. It is not always true that the victims of an unjust treatment have a clear sense of what is just. For example, according to a research from the Chinese Academy of Social Sciences, the lack of protection of women's equality is often due to the lack of demands by women themselves to exercise their rights. They tend to rely on the state and society for assigned benefits and care.[17] Does this mean that they are not equal human beings since they lack the demands for equality? Subordinated groups have often absorbed their oppression so well that they are unaware of their own equal worth. Only the subordinated group's critically reflected opinions of social norms would represent its long-term real interest. An implementation or restoration of justice should make reference to such reflected views. Chinese women have not yet come to terms with such critical thinking and conscious rejection of their own subordination due to their deprivation. They are raised and conditioned to perceive the *status quo* social order as 'natural'. For example, at the peak of women's awakening in the 1980s, some activists felt the future of women lay in reinforcing traditional female virtues. They claimed that they were in favour of the moral model of 'a virtuous wife and good mother'. Some activists claimed the rediscovery of traditional roles with a sense of liberation:

> ... women should establish their credit. They need a more complete education than men—to cultivate refinement ... develop poise ...—so that they can become the mistresses of society ... When people see women, including their own wives, being polite, well-behaved, and well-dressed, they will say, this is such a civilized society, and those are such respectable women.[18]

This tendency to return to the past looking for female virtues and women's proper role in society is revealing about the formation of illusion ('false-consciousness'). First, women are still so captivated by their longstanding indoctrination by the patriarchal society. Growing up in the shadow of the Chinese sexist morality, women have, deposited within them, a 'psychological complex': the inferior mentality. They feel comfortable with the idea that women are not expected to do the same thing as men; they often resort to passive acceptance when confronted with problems. This mentality leads them to set low standards for themselves, to be easily satisfied and to be intimidated by difficulties. Their ideal in life is often to find a husband who is emotionally stronger and economically better off.[19] The way '(political) power abandons

women and women distance themselves from power' is also a symptom of this 'inferior complex'. Due to social discouragement, Chinese women tend to be passive about politics and regard it as a dirty game played by men. This attitude provides evidence that women have not transcended male domination and have taken it so much for granted that they even inflict repression on themselves.[20]

Secondly, they have not had much opportunity to be exposed to, nor allowed to, hold alternative ideas of female role. In the absence of alternative conceptions, they could only react against, from an older traditional point of view, the alienated tough heroine model idolized by the communist revolutionaries—someone who is intellectually and almost physically equal to men, and lacking entirely in feminist sensitivity and uniqueness. Such a repressive model was perpetuated through a series of Cultural Revolution model operas, ballet, movies, and stories in the late 1960s and 1970s, in which the heroines wore men's clothing, marched like men, and did battle with or against men. As the crazy years of the Cultural Revolution passed, so did the pressure women felt to become the same as the dominant males. And they are left with the traditional models.

Thirdly, I speculate that Chinese women will also have to learn how to appreciate an opportunity to reflect on their culturally immersed aspirations. It is not enough to overcome a false consciousness. In addition to fighting to remove countless socially imposed and self-imposed hurdles, they face the task of learning how to live as reflective, choosing, and equal human beings. Some successful women, for example, can't help feeling a loss even after they have found ways to realize their talents and potential capabilities. One female secretary at a provincial Party Committee said she felt a need to 'apologize' to her family. 'Along with my success in career, there appears in my heart the uneasiness—the increasing sense of guilt towards my child.'[21] This indicates an unavoidable hesitation women experience when they are confronted with the choice between tradition and modernity. But to become men's equal at the workplace and in politics, women have to go beyond the humble image that was conventionally assigned to them. As Ye Changzheng, a member of the Chengdu Municipal Political Consultative Committee, realizes when she comments on the lack of women participants in politics, they should become politically active in order 'to cultivate Chinese women's independent personality, give up the feeling of petty and low in their sub-consciousness, break the pattern of strong men and weak women, shift their focus of social role from husbands and children to their career success.'[22]

It may seem clear in the case of China, that women's unreflective opinion, as a 'local traditional' voice, has helped to perpetuate dominant establishment. A movement among women themselves to struggle against their own inferior mentality has to be the first step towards equality.

The above survey of three possible voices of the Chinese 'local tradition' lend evidence to the defect of 'local cultural' relativist approach. While the relativist legitimately fears that a cross-cultural conception of women's well-being would reinforce some dominant groups' view, the restriction to local communal tradition does not seem to help avoiding the perceived danger.

[2]

In the place of the misleading 'local cultural' notions, as those shown in the above cases, I will, in an unfortunately brief section, adapt an alternative notion to the Chinese context, suggesting how it may provide sensible guidelines in measuring the quality of women's life in China. This is the notion that has been eloquently developed in Nussbaum's and Sen's 'capability approach'.[23] Their notion is Kantian because it stresses the value of respect and freedom of choice based on practical reasoning and critical reflections;[24] and it is Aristotelian because it is based on a notion of human flourishing. I will probe how this

approach can encounter the 'local tradition' relativist's charges. Especially, I am interested in the question how the 'universal traits' of general human well-being, which the 'capability conception' claims to capture, apply to our case and how it responds to the Chinese experiences.

Nussbaum[25] argues that a cross-cultural assessment of women's well-being is feasible by applying a 'thick vague conception of the good'. She claims that this conception defines the 'shape of the human form of life' and a good human life, which 'abstract[s] from traditional gender distinctions as morally irrelevant'.[26] Starting from the intuitive idea of a human being who is 'capable and needy',[27] she argues that a life, if it is constituted by certain traits, is characteristically *human,* no matter within what culture it is lived. These traits include the fact of mortality (a fear of and an aversion to death); the bodily needs for food and drink, shelter, sex, and mobility; the capacity for pleasure and pain; the cognitive capabilities; early childhood development; practical reason; affiliation and concern for other human beings; relatedness to other species and to nature; humour and play; and separateness.[28]

Now, for Nussbaum, what human beings are, empirically speaking, regardless of their nationality, colour, gender, and religion, has an evaluative claim in a most general way on what human life *should* be lived. Hence, 'this list of capabilities is a . . . minimal conception of the good.'[29] In other words, it serves as a criterion to judge whether a creature is a human being and whether the creature's life is lived as a human life in any cultural contexts, be it Chinese, Indian, or European, for it captures 'the characteristic activities of the human being: what does the human being do, characteristically, *as such,* and not, say, as the member of a particular local community.'[30] This list hence sanctions women's entitlement to general humanity and provides a measurement of female well-being, transcending the views from local political ideology, traditional norms, or women's own opinions. To contest this point, we can run the sort of thought-experiment Nussbaum proposed: take away certain properties such as being Chinese, or being female, and we still have a human being in front of us. But take away properties on her list, especially the capability of practical reasoning to plan the future, to choose and to respond and love other humans, we no longer have a human life at all.[31]

Though these traits depict a minimal human life, they do not characterize a *good* human life. For Nussbaum, there is a higher threshold below which a life is not considered good. Nussbaum describes a *good human life* as a life in which one is able to live to the end of a complete human life as far as is possible; to have good health; to be adequately nourished; to have adequate shelter; having opportunities for sexual satisfaction; being able to move around; to avoid pain and have pleasure; to have adequate education, enabling one to use five senses and the cognitive capabilities; to care and love others; to be able to form a conception of the good and to engage in critical reflection; to affiliate, having the capability for justice and friendship; to live with concern for and in relation to animals, plants, and nature; to be able to laugh and play; to live one's own life and nobody else's, in one's own surroundings and context.[32]

In differentiating a minimal *human* life from a *good* human life, Nussbaum has introduced two thresholds, the first is 'a threshold of capability to function beneath which a life will be so impoverished that it will not be human at all', and beneath the second, 'those characteristic functions are available in such a reduced way that, though we may judge the form of life a human one, we will not think it a good human life'.[33] Accordingly, a society may have provided the conditions for a *human* life, in the minimal sense, but not the conditions for a *good* human life.

It is significant to note that the first threshold, an evaluative criterion of societies or forms of life for being *human,* would fail authoritarian societies, including religious fundamentalist or communist societies. Authoritarian societies systematically deprive the conditions for certain basic capabilities to function, such as the capability to engage in practical reasoning, the need for separateness and strong separateness. And clearly, in Nussbaum's view, an impoverished society in which the state makes an escape from hunger and homelessness impossible is not a *human society.*

Nussbaum emphasizes that a life has to have *all and every* traits at the first threshold in order to be human. Accordingly, a *human* society has to create and maintain conditions that make such a human life possible. No one trait is prioritized over others. At the second threshold, the basic capabilities collectively, rather than any one or a few of them, define a *good* human life: 'a life that lacks any one of these, no matter what else it has, will fall short of a good human life'.[34] These human goods are many and each is 'distinct in quality' and of 'central importance'.[35] A trade-off of some capacities for others does not make a human life *good.*

> All are of central importance and all are distinct in quality. This limits the trade-offs that it will be reasonable to make, and thus limits the applicability of quantitative cost-benefit analysis.[36]

Consequently, a society that fails to provide all the conditions for a good human life is not a good society. Nussbaum would thus reject the apologetic claim that suppressing the exercise of the capabilities of practical reason and of affiliation (required for the exercise of political/civil liberties), for instance, is justified by the achievement of the capability to have good health, adequate nutrition and shelter and so on (normally referred to as social/economic rights). Variable capabilities are 'incommensurable' for 'we cannot satisfy the need for one of them by giving a larger amount of another one'.[37]

Nussbaum's thresholds are therefore highly idealistic, judging societies against a standard that would fail many contemporary societies in a test of their being human and being good. Since each condition on Nussbaum's first list is viewed as necessary, and together as sufficient for something (a creature or a society) being counted as human, her first level threshold implies that many societies do not qualify as being human, including, for example, the famine-rampaged and severely impoverished countries, as well as authoritarian societies, such as China, where the state punishes individualism and invades the most intimate personal space. We may all agree that life in these societies is less humane. But we would hesitate to view them as non-human societies. In the same way, we would hesitate to view a blind person (lacking the capability to perceive by sight) as not human, as Crocker points out.[38] Nor would we regard the Chinese woman, who has been raised in a way as to lose her capability for critical thinking, as not human. As Crocker proposed, for a weaker and more plausible interpretation, we may read Nussbaum's 'threshold' not as necessary and sufficient conditions but a more or less minimum for what counts as human.[39]

Note that Nussbaum's rejection of trade-offs does not imply that Chinese women, in our concern here, should choose to cultivate excellences, say, in both caring for family and flourishing in professional careers. The 'capability approach' does not require the actual exercise by each citizens of all the capabilities. Rather, it emphasizes that a good life should have the possibility (opportunity) to exercise them. Chinese women may choose to flourish in housework or child-nursing, as some have expressed such a preference. Nussbaum's theory advocates the provision of conditions for them to achieve excellence elsewhere as well, for example, in politics and higher education, if they choose to do so.

A problem might appear to lie in the possible conflict between various goods on the list. These capabilities may not be able to function simultaneously. As we have discussed early, Chinese women share the trauma facing all mothers of our time if they decide to achieve both fulfilling work and loving child-care, two intrinsically valuable human functionings. In this situation, we seem to run into a dead-end if no ranking or trade-off is permissible. Nussbaum's reply to this challenge is to point to current and remediable institutional arrangements that have forced those women who pursue both goods into unnecessary tragic conflicts. She hopes that by acting to change the social world in which we live, we can have these goods all at once.[40] Justice for women is in this way closely tied to a just society. Even under just social institutions, however, Nussbaum concedes that, given the circumstances of life, we may have to live with a tragic value-conflict.[41]

Though treating all goods as essential, Nussbaum does attribute 'a special role' to two of the capabilities, *practical reason* and *affiliation,* considering them as 'architectonic, holding the whole enterprise together and making it human'.[42] Other things equal, these two distinguish human beings from other creatures. 'What is distinctive, and distinctively valuable to us, about the human way of doing all this is that each and every one of these functions is, first of all, planned and organized by practical reason and, second, done with and to others.'[43] Here, the development of the capability to evaluate, choose, plan, and execute plans of life or conception of the good, and the capability to live to and with others, are said to need 'special attention' because 'none of the others will be truly human without them'.[44]

It is important to point out that this recognition of 'practical reason' as an essential character of a good human life is the key to distinguishing Nussbaum's 'capability approach' from the 'local tradition' cultural relativism. Recall that this version of relativism emerges, partially, from a fear for the danger to impose ruling ideology upon the disadvantaged female in a society tormented by gender discrimination. As I have shown, the cultural relativism's rejection of any universal or cross-cultural conception, and its proposal to assess women's conditions by 'local traditional' norms, have not been able to avoid this danger in the case of China. Instead, such an approach has contributed to, as the Chinese case demonstrates, perpetuating the *status quo*.

The capability to conduct practical reasoning, which is restricted by the Chinese political ideology as well as the Confucian moral doctrines, would provide Chinese women with the power to reflect and criticize the pervasive social norms. Their having not been portrayed as capable of practical reasoning does not imply that they cannot achieve the capability for practical reasoning. What philosophers or ethicists conceive as social norms may not correspond to, nor reflect, what people really are or have in common, especially when philosophers themselves disagree on what the norms are. As Nussbaum observes, with regard to the dispute as to whether the capability of practical reasoning is essential, 'the very act of entering a disagreement seems to be an acknowledgement of the importance of the component',[45] as long as the disagreement is based on reasonable argumentation.

In any case, traditional philosophy and cultural norms may not be the only (nor indisputable) place to search for answers to the questions as to whether Chinese women are capable of practical reasoning or whether the capability to engage in independent reflection is foreign to them. The answer should, among other things, come from ongoing free and open debates, participated not just by men.

Studies show encouraging signs. Women activists in China are beginning to develop a critical attitude toward the dominant traditional notions of women's roles. Some have been able to rise above the illusion, rejecting the precommunist model on the basis that it cannot give a fair presentation of the aspirations of contemporary women.[46] One critic sees the traditional model as detrimental to women's independence: 'Woman is not the moon. She must rely on herself to shine . . . Hopefully each person can find her own path in life and develop her own brilliance.'[47] Luo

Ping, an associate professor at the Department of Philosophy, Wuhan University, criticizes the idea of sharing husbands' fame, viewing it as an example of the feudal saying 'If a husband makes a fortune, his wife is honored' ('fugui girong').[48]

Already in 1984, Wang Youqin, a vocal student then at Beijing University, boldly suggested that women have to take the first step toward their liberation. '"Spiritual footbinding" has deformed our soul . . . It is not high mountains and wide rivers that hinder our footsteps, but rather our own spirit.'[49] She was one of the first to raise the issue of women's internalized sense of inferiority and refer to women as victims of their own preconception. It has been proposed that:

> the official propaganda on equality should not promote the model of 'virtuous wife and good mother', who prioritize family duties, nor advocate female strongman who 'shoulder both burdens' [of family and career]. What should be promoted is equality in social values, family obligations, and rights, thus to wake up women's consciousness of their status as human beings.[50]

Some critics have also expressed doubts about the view that the participation of women in work is needed for a socialist modernization. In a report on the second National Symposium on Women's Studies, some speakers were quoted saying:

> To acquire genuine equality, it is far from adequate for women merely to participate in social labor and strive for political and economic emancipation; they must fight for the awakening of their self-consciousness, a complete establishment of their values, and a thorough liberation of their personality.[51]

The increasing awareness demonstrates that the capability to engage in critical thinking is not alien to Chinese women and they are able to cultivate and exercise it. The commonly held picture of obedient Chinese women, as I have shown, is rather a reflection of the dominant male viewpoint, reinforced by the actual lack of freedom of choice (for male members too) under the communist rule.

While agreeing with Nussbaum that an evaluative list of what are 'deepest and most essential in human life need presuppose no external metaphysical foundation',[52] I find her description of the 'internalist account' sometimes puzzling. For example, she writes at one place that the list of properties of human beings can be obtained by 'looking at ourselves, asking what we really think about ourselves and what holds our history'.[53] I suspect that, as the Chinese experience may have taught us, in this more or less closed society with a history of Confucian practices and authoritarian rule, a quite different list of human life essentials could have been sorted out by taking an 'internal' look at its history and at what it is all about being Chinese. The question is 'who is the "we"'. As my analysis shows, a deeply rooted traditional perspective is very persistent on projecting its demands on a list of life essentials if selected in this way.

However, Nussbaum clearly states elsewhere that a notion of what human beings are should be arrived at through a critical reflection of what we are and we aspire to be, taking into consideration of all available relevant information,[54] especially when she singles out 'practical reason' as a more fundamental property of a *good* human life. A notion of what human beings are and should be, in Nussbaum's words, relies on: 'the exchange of reasons and arguments by human beings within history, in which, for reasons that are historical and human . . . we hold some things to be good and others bad, some arguments to be sound and others not sound'.[55]

The 'capability approach', in any case, does not propose to muzzle or ignore local voices, such as the three voices about women's well-being in the case of China. Rather, it wishes to retain plurality through 'plural specification' and 'local specification' of the components of human life in specific and historically rich cultures. Nussbaum's 'vague and universal form' is meant to provide 'sufficient overlap to sustain a working conversation' between different plural specifications.[56] This approach, after all, would retain 'rich and full formation' of a conception of women's well-being, to be gathered from the voices, in our case, of Chinese women and those affected, who live their life in the Chinese cultural environment. It would criticize the Chinese tradition only when this tradition (as it does) prevents women from functioning in a fully human way.

Finally, how does the 'capability approach' deal with the legitimate fear by 'local tradition' relativists that a universal conception of the human would perpetuate the established practices and norms? To conclude, I will use Nussbaum's reply[57] to this question as a suggestive motion for the development of a conception of women's well-being. Her suggestions coincide with the conclusions that could be derived from my early analysis of the Chinese case.

Her first suggestion is to consider the experiences and sense of important functions from females as well as males. This will result in new perspectives on the conception of human (and women's) good that had not emerged as so important when only males were reflecting. This step will offset the institutionalized projection of male preferences in local culture. The goodness of excellence in professional careers, for example, which has been excluded from the list of Confucian female virtues (their 'obedience to father, brother, and husband', for instance), may become important now, and has indeed been so regarded as the recent female reflections have shown. Secondly, Nussbaum warns that, 'one must not assume that the statements of people who have long been subordinated are reliable indicators of what is truly essential'.[58] The result of long-term subordination is evident in the case of China. What we need to do to avoid misleading by unreflective and uncritical self-expressions, Nussbaum suggests, is to provide education, raising consciousness, making sure that women have 'adequate information' about alternative ways of life, and 'real freedom to form a conception of the good without fear'.[59] To cultivate the critical reflective capability and to gain, above all, the freedom to do so, are two tasks that Chinese women have to strive to achieve. And they are beginning to recognize the importance of these tasks, as I remarked early. Thirdly, concurring with the implication of my discussion about the unreflective Chinese local traditional voices, Nussbaum advises that we must 'be skeptical of the accounts we find in local traditions'. The study on the case in China substantiates her concern that the traditional accounts often tell us characteristics of the lives of women that derive from male desires to have power over them, for example. Women are said to be less reasonable or less rational and can only take the submissive and obedient roles.

Taking caution in these areas, the 'capability approach' aspires to deal with problems raised by 'local tradition' relativism, advancing a conception of women's well-being that attends fully to the rich culture and tradition of local communities, while opening up for cross-cultural scrutiny. Such a scrutiny gives it a universal perspective and embodies the hope to divulge 'false consciousness'.

NOTES

1. See E. Marks and I. de Courtivronk (eds.), *New French Feminism: An Anthology* (New York: Schocken Books, 1981), 137–40 (in which this seems to be the view).
2. Sheryl WuDunn, 'Feudal China's Evil Revived: Wives for Sale', *New York Times,* 3 August (1991). The pressure to produce male offspring has led to a startling increase in female infanticide. Newly released data from China's 1990 census support the suspicion that 5% of all infant girls are unaccounted for and infanticide is said to be largely responsible. See Nicholas Kristof, 'A Mystery From China's Census: Where Have Young Girls Gone?' *New York Times,* 17 June (1991).
3. In 1988, women accounted for only 36.5% of China's total number of scientific and technological personnel, 37% of the teaching staff, and 48% of the accounting and statistical staff. See 'Accomplishments of 8 Million Female Cadres.' *People's Daily,* 8 March (1988), 1.
4. In 1988, the Politburo of the CCP Central Committee had no woman full member or alternate member. There were 12 vice-ministers among the more than 200 in total. There were only 10 women provincial governors or vice-governors, compared to about 50 men at this level. See FBIS, 'CCP Official Says Policy on Women Unchanged.' OW121006, *Beijing, Xinhua,* 12 January (1988).

   According to a survey of women cadres by the All-China Woman's Federation in 1987, some women complained that their applications for the Party membership were not accepted because the Party had to have nonparty member/women as representatives. The same survey also revealed that outstanding women are often passed over for men who are merely 'fairly competent.' See *Women's Work (funu gongzhuo),* 4 (1987), 6–9.

   Further criticism has been levelled at the 'quota' system used to protect women's promotion. This system was said to shield incompetent women cadres and give women positions without real power. This system thus manipulates women in order to propagate the 'equality' ideology.
5. Nussbaum has given it this name. 'Local tradition relativism' is different from metaphysical relativism, which suspects that there is any determinate way the world exists apart from the interpretive workings of the cognitive faculties of living beings. See Nussbaum, 'Human Capabilities, Female Human Beings', in this volume.
6. Ibid.
7. Shen Zhi, 'Development of Women's Studies—The Chinese Way', *Trends in Academic Circles,* 25 December (1984), 42. This article summarizes proceedings at the First National Symposium on Theoretical Studies on Women.
8. Ibid.
9. From a report by Zhang Hua, a lecturer in sociology from Beijing University, at the Beijing Information Exchange Meeting, March 1991.
10. Under the 'responsibility system', each rural family is assigned a piece of the collectively owned land and the family collects the products

after paying a portion to the state. This system was part of the 1978 rural reform package.

11. Nussbaum, 'Human Capabilities, Female Human Beings', in this volume.

12. The principles of insisting the party's absolute leadership, proletarian dictatorship, socialism, and Marxism—Maoism.

13. Zhu Qing, 'Summary of the Second National Symposium on Women's Studies', *Trends in Academic Circles,* January (1987).

14. *Analects (Lun Yu),* by Confucius, 17: 23.

15. Lao Tzu, *Dao De Jing,* ch. 4.

16. Ibid., ch. 6.

17. See proceedings of the third National Symposium on Women in 1990.

18. Tang Min, 'Women's Training Must Be Improved', *Fujian Youth* (July 1985), 19.

19. Zhang Xiping, 'Cultivation of New Women', *Youth Studies,* 9 (September 1985).

20. Zhou Yi and Wang Jian, 'The Puzzle Why Women Avoid Political Power', *Chinese Women* (March 1991).

21. 'The Other Side of Female Success', from a Chinese women's magazine (December 1988).

22. Ye Changzheng, 'Sharing Power, Transcending Power', *Chinese Women* (March 1991).

23. See Martha Nussbaum, 'Nature, Function, and Capability: Aristotle on Political Distribution', *Oxford Studies in Ancient Philosophy,* suppl. vol. (1988); *Love's Knowledge: Essays on Philosophy and Literature* (Oxford: NY: Oxford University Press, 1990); and other articles referred in the footnotes of this paper. Also, see Nussbaum and Sen (eds.), *The Quality of Life* (Oxford: Clarendon Press, 1993); Sen, 'Equality of What?', in Sterling McMurrin (ed.), *Tanner Lectures on Human Values,* vol. I (Salt Lake City, Utah: University of Utah Press, 1980); *Resources, Values and Development* (Oxford: Blackwell, and Cambridge, Mass.: Harvard University Press, 1984); *Commodities and Capabilities* (Amsterdam: North-Holland, 1985); 'Well-being, Agency and Freedom: The Dewey Lectures, 1984', *Journal of Philosophy,* 82; 'The Concept of Development', in Hollis Chenery and Srinivasan (eds.), *Handbook of Development Economics,* vol. 1 (Amsterdam: North-Holland, 1988); 'Gender Inequality and Theories of Justice', in this volume.

24. The Kantianism in Nussbaum's conception has not been adequately appreciated, though she declares that 'my approach agrees with the Kant-

ian approach far more than it disagrees, disagreeing primarily in wishing to attend more centrally to need, limitation, and vulnerability in defining the being for whom justice is being sought.' 'Human Capabilities, Female Human Beings', in this volume.

25. I have to focus on Nussbaum's view in order not to get into a discussion of the differences between her view and that of Sen's.

26. Nussbaum, 'Human Capabilities, Female Human Beings'.

27. Ibid.

28. Ibid.

29. Nussbaum, 'Aristotelian Social Democracy', in R. Bruce Douglass, Gerald R. Mara, and Henry Richardson (eds.), *Liberalism and the Good* (New York and London: Routledge, 1990), 224.

30. Nussbaum, 'Human Capabilities, Female Human Beings'.

31. Ibid.

32. Ibid.

33. Ibid.

34. Nussbaum, 'Human Capabilities, Female Human Beings'.

35. Nussbaum, 'Human Functioning and Social Justice: In Defense of Aristotelian Essentialism', *Political Theory* (forthcoming).

36. Nussbaum, 'Human Capabilities, Female Human Beings'.

37. Nussbaum, 'Human Functioning and Social Justice'.

38. David Crocker, 'Functioning and Capability: The Foundations of Sen's and Nussbaum's Development Ethics, Part 2: The Capability Ethic', paper presented at the WIDER conference, August 1991.

39. Ibid.

40. Nussbaum, 'Aristotelian Social Democracy', 212.

41. Ibid.

42. Nussbaum, 'Human Capabilities'.

43. Nussbaum, 'Human Capabilities'.

44. Ibid.

45. Ibid.

46. Zhu Qing, 'Summary of the Second National Symposium on Women's Studies', *Trends in Academic Circle* (January 1987).

47. Ting Lan, 'Woman Is Not the Moon', *Women's World* (June 1985), I.

48. See Luo Ping's presentation at the Symposium on Chinese Women's Social Participation and Development, March 1990, Zhengzhou, China.

49. Wang Youqin, 'Let Us Have A New Concept of Womanhood', *Chinese Women* (March 1984), 1. Ms. Wang is now an editor for the *Woman— Human* journal and a visiting scholar at Stanford University.
50. 'About the Issues of Women's Political Participation', From the Editor, *Chinese Women* (1991).
51. *Trends in Academic Circles* (January 1978).
52. Nussbaum, 'Human Capabilities'.
53. Nussbaum, 'Human Capabilities'.
54. For a constructive discussion of a critically reflected conception of the good, see John Rawls, *A Theory of Justice* (1971), ch. 7, esp. s. 64, 416–24.
55. Nussbaum, 'Human Capabilities'.
56. Ibid.
57. Ibid.
58. Ibid.
59. Ibid.

RECOMMENDED READINGS

Texts

Bell, Daniel. *Communitarianism and its Critics*. Oxford: Clarendon Press, 1993.

Buchanan, A. "Assessing Communitarian Critique of Liberalism." *Ethics* 99 (1989):852–882.

Kymlika, W. *Liberalism, Community and Culture*. Oxford: Oxford University Press, 1989.

Larmore, C. *Patterns of Moral Complexity*. Cambridge: Cambridge University Press, 1987.

MacIntyre, A. *Whose Justice, Which Rationality?* London: University of Notre Dame Press, 1989.

Nussbaum, Martha Craven. *Cultivating Humanity*. Cambridge, MA: Harvard University Press, 1997.

Nussbaum, Martha. *Sex and Social Justice*. New York: Oxford University Press, 1999.

Raz, J. "Liberalism, Autonomy and the Politics of Neutral Concern." *Midwest Studies in Philosophy* 7 (1982):89–120.

———. *The Morality of Freedom*. Oxford: Oxford University Press, 1986.

Sandel, M. *Liberalism and the Limits of Justice*. Cambridge: Cambridge University Press, 1982.

Walzer, M. "The Communitarian Critique of Liberalism." *Political Theory* 18, no. 1 (1990):6–23.

Feminist Perspective

Friedman, Marilyn. *What are friends for?: Feminist perspectives on personal relationships and moral theory*. Ithaca: Cornell University Press, 1993.

Young, Iris. *Justice and the Politics of Difference*. Princeton: Princeton University Press, 1990.

Multicultural Perspective

Mohanty, Chrandra, Ann Russo, and Loures Torres. *Third World Women and the Politics of Feminism*. Bloomington: Indiana University Press, 1991.

Nussbaum, Martha and Jonathan Glover. *Women, Culture and Development*. New York: Oxford University Press, 1995.

PART XII

❦

GEWIRTH AND KORSGAARD

INTRODUCTION

Alan Gewirth was born in 1912 in Union City, New Jersey. He joined the University of Chicago philosophy department in 1947, and was named Edward Carson Waller Distinguished Service Professor of Philosophy in 1975, the same year that he served as President of the American Philosophical Association. Gewirth published *Reason and Morality* in 1978, *Human Rights: Essays on Justification and Application* in 1982, and *Community of Rights* in 1996.

In our selection from "The Justificatory Argument for Human Rights," Alan Gewirth proposes a justification for morality. The central premises of Gewirth's argument can be summarized as follows:

1. All agents regard their purposes as good according to whatever criteria are involved in their actions to fulfill them.

2. Therefore, all agents must affirm a right to the freedom and well-being necessary to achieve their purposes.

3. All agents must affirm such a right on the basis of simply being prospective, purposive agents.

4. Hence, all agents must affirm that every prospective, purposive agent has a right to freedom and well-being.

Gewirth claims that the universalized right affirmed in the conclusion of his argument is a *moral* right and that every agent has to endorse that right under pain of self-contradiction.

Many of Gewirth's critics have focused on the inference from (1) to (2), contending that rational agents need not endorse *moral* rights to freedom and well-being simply because they accept (1).[1] In response, Gewirth has claimed that, as he interprets the argument, rational agents in accepting (2) do not commit themselves to moral rights, but only to prudential rights. According to Gewirth, moral rights appear only in the argument in step (4) through the application of the principle of universalizability.

To many, the notion of prudential rights is a strange notion, and Gewirth has attempted to elucidate the concept by pointing out that the grounds for the prudential right claim in (b) are simply the prudential purposes of the agent, not the prudential purposes or interests of other persons to whom the right claim is directed. I take this to mean that in endorsing (b), agents are not assuming that other people have any reasons in terms of their prudential or moral purposes that would lead them to respect the right claims they, the agents, are making. Notice that in this respect Gewirth's notion of prudential rights is strikingly different from the standard understanding of moral rights, because the grounds for moral rights are usually thought to include not only reasons or purposes the agent has but also reasons or purposes others have or should have as well. For example, if I say that I have a moral right based on a contractual agreement to lecture at a particular university, I imply not only that I have moral or prudential reasons for exercising this right, but also that others have moral or prudential reasons for permitting me to do so. I point this out simply to indicate the special way that Gewirth is using the notion of rights in step (2) of his argument. Once one understands how Gewirth is using the notion of rights, there appears to be no problem with his inference from (1) to (2).

Now one might think that the problematic inference in Gewirth's argument is the inference from (3) to (4). This is because, as Gewirth contends, the notion of rights that an agent endorses in (4) is moral, not prudential, as it is in (2) and also in (3). According to Gewirth, it is by the process of universalizing that the prudential right claim in (3) is transformed into a moral right claim in (4). But why does Gewirth think that this inference is valid? What Gewirth says to justify the inference is the following:

> Now the resulting generalization is a moral judgment, because it requires the agent to take favorable account of the interests of persons other than or in addition to himself. The agent logically must here recognize that other persons have the same rights he claims for himself because they fulfill the same justifying condition on which he has based his own right claim.[2]

Here again, a number of Gewirth's critics have not found this justification compelling, but although they have questioned this inference in Gewirth's argument, none of them has attempted to show exactly what would follow from the application of the principle of universalizability to step (3) of the argument.[3] This failure to justify an alternative inference may be what has kept Gewirth and his critics from reaching agreement concerning this important step of his argument. In "The Justification for Morality and the Behavior of Women," I consider this possibility and try to determine what actually does follow from Gewirth's argument.

Christine Korsgaard was born in Chicago in 1951. She received her B.A. from the University of Illinois in 1974 and her Ph.D. from Harvard University in 1981. She taught at Yale University and the University of California at Santa Barbara before coming to the University of Chicago in 1983. Korsgaard remained at the University of Chicago as a colleague of Alan Gewirth until she was appointed professor of philosophy at Harvard University in 1991. She published *Standpoint of Practical Reason* in 1990, *Creating the Kingdom of Ends* in 1996, and *Sources of Normativity* also in 1996.

In our selection from *Sources of Normativity,* Korsgaard argues that the necessity of acting in the light of reflection makes us authorities over ourselves. And insofar as we have authority over ourselves, Korsgaard argues, we can make laws for ourselves, and those laws will be normative. Nevertheless, Korsgaard allows that we can make different kinds of laws for ourselves. If we favor the law of acting on the desire of the moment, then we will treat each desire as it arises as irresistible, and we will be like wantons. If the law we favor ranges over just our own the interests, then we will be egoists. Only if the law we favor ranges over every rational being, as in the Kantian Kingdom of Ends, will we be moral. Korsgaard argues that the laws we give ourselves must be public in the same way as the rules of language are public. According to Korsgaard, this publicity requirement eliminates the possibility of egoism because egoism is possible only if reasons could be private, which they are not. Korsgaard argues that morality also includes obligations to animals because they also communicate with us, for instance by telling us when we are causing them pain.

In "The Justification of Morality and the Behavior of Women," I consider Gewirth's and Korsgaard's attempts to justify morality, and, unfortunately, why they fail. I then offer my own justification for morality, which draws significantly on the behavior of women.

In "Harmony with Nature and Indigenous African Culture" Moshoeshoe II argues that a study of other cultures and ways of living in harmony with nature could offer the West the seeds of a new relationship with nature. He argues that much can be learned from comparing the dominant model of development—that of the industrial, market society—with those traditional models that sustained the indigenous cultures of Africa over thousands of years. While Korsgaard seeks to provide a Kantian foundation for obligations to animals, Moshoeshoe II shows that within indigenous African culture there is a deep respect for the natural environment.

NOTES

1. See, for example, the articles by R. M. Hare, D. D. Raphael, Kai Nielson and W. D. Hudson in *Gewirth's Ethical Rationalism* edited by Edward Regis (Chicago, 1984).
2. *Ibid.* p. 210.
3. *Ibid.* See, for example, the articles by R. M. Hare and Jesse Kalin.

45. THE JUSTIFICATORY ARGUMENT FOR HUMAN RIGHTS

❦

ALAN GEWIRTH

I now wish to present my own answer to the justificatory or epistemological question of human rights. It will be recalled that the Justifying Basis or Ground of human rights must be a normative moral principle that serves to prove or establish that every person morally ought to have the necessary goods of action as something to which he or she is entitled. The epistemological question, hence, comes down to whether such a moral principle can be rationally justified.

It is important to note that not all moral principles will serve for this purpose. Utilitarian, organicist, and elitist moral principles either do not justify any moral rights at all, or justify them only as ancillary to and contingent upon various collective goals,[1] or do make rights primary but not as equally distributed among all humans. Hence, it will be necessary to show how the moral principle that justifies equal human rights is superior, in point of rational cogency, to these other kinds of moral principles.

Now, there are well-known difficulties in the attempt to provide a rational justification of any moral principle. Obviously, given some high-level moral principle, we can morally justify some specific moral rule or particular moral judgment or action by showing how its rightness follows from the principle. But how can we justify the basic principle itself? Here, by definition, there is no higher or more general moral princi-

ple to be appealed to as an independent variable. Is it the case, then, that justification comes to a stop here? This would mean that we cannot rationally adjudicate between *conflicting* moral principles and ways of life and society, such as those epitomized, for example, by Kant's categorical imperative, Bentham's utilitarianism, Kierkegaard's theological primacy, Stirner's egoism, Nietzsche's exaltation of the superman, Spencer's doctrine of the survival of the fittest, and so on.

THE PROBLEM OF THE INDEPENDENT VARIABLE

One of the central problems here is that of the independent variable. Principles serve as independent variables for justifying lower-level rules and judgments; but what is the independent variable for justifying principles themselves? Another way to bring out this problem in relation to morality is to contrast particular empirical statements and particular moral judgments. Consider, on the one hand, such a statement as "Mrs Jones *is* having an abortion," and, on the other hand, "Mrs Jones *ought* to have an abortion." We know, at least in principle, how to go about checking the truth of the first statement, namely, by referring to certain empirical facts that serve as the independent variables for the statement to be checked against. But how do we go about checking the truth of the second statement, that Mrs Jones *ought* to have an abortion? Indeed, what would it *mean* for the second state-

---

Reprinted from "The Justificatory Argument for Human Rights" by permission of the author and Blackwell Publishers.

ment to be true? What is the independent variable for *it* to be checked against? For the first statement to be true means that it corresponds to certain empirical facts. But with regard to a judgment like "Mrs Jones *ought* to have an abortion," what facts would *it* have to correspond to in order to be true? Is there any moral *'ought'* in the world, in the way in which the factual *'is'* is in the world, serving as the independent variable for testing or confirming the relevent statements? If not, then is the moral judgment in no sense either true or false?

The problem we have reached, then, is whether there is any non-question-begging answer to the problem of the independent variable in morality. I now want to suggest that there is. To see this, we must recall that all moral precepts, regardless of their greatly varying contents, are concerned with how persons ought to *act* toward one another. Think, for example, of the Golden Rule: "Do unto others as you would have them do unto you." Think also of Kant's categorical imperative: "*Act* in such a way that the maxim of your action can be a universal law." Similarly, Bentham tells us to *act* so as to maximize utility; Nietzsche tells us to *act* in accord with the ideals of the superman; Marx tells us to *act* in accord with the interests of the proletariat; Kierkegaard tells us to *act* as God commands, and so forth.

The independent variable of all morality, then, is human *action*. This independent variable cuts across the distinctions between secular and religious moralities, between egalitarian and elitist moralities, between deontological and teleological moralities, and so forth.

But how does this independent variable of action help us to resolve the difficulties of moral justification? Surely we can't take the various rival moral principles and justify one of them as against the others simply by checking it against the fact of human action. Moreover, since if action is to be genuinely the non-question-begging independent variable of morality, it must fit *all* moral principles, how does action enable us to justify *one* moral principle *as against* its rivals?

The answer to these questions is given by the fact that action has what I have called a *normative structure,* in that, logically implicit in action, there are certain evaluative and deontic judgments, certain judgments about goods and rights made by agents; and when these judgments are subjected to certain morally neutral rational requirements, they entail a certain supreme moral principle. Hence, if any agent denies the principle, he can be shown to have contradicted himself, so that his denial, and the actions stemming from it, cannot be rationally justifiable. Thus, together with action, the most basic kind of reason, deductive rationality, also serves as an independent variable for the justification of the supreme principle of morality.

WHY ACTION GIVES THE PRINCIPLE A RATIONALLY NECESSARY ACCEPTABILITY

It is important to note that because the principle is grounded in the generic features of action, it has a certain kind of *material necessity*. It will be recalled that some of the justificatory arguments for rights examined above failed because they did not satisfy the condition that they be acceptable to all rational persons as a matter of rational necessity. For example, why must any rational person accept Rawls's starting point in the "veil of ignorance?" Why, for that matter, is it rationally necessary for any rational person to accept the Golden Rule or any other moral principle that has hitherto been propounded?

The condition of rationally necessary acceptability is fulfilled, however, when the independent variable of the argument is placed in the generic features of action. For this involves that, simply by virtue of being an agent, one logically must accept the argument and its conclusion that all persons equally have certain moral rights. Now, being an actual or prospective agent is not an optional or variable condition for any person, except in the sense that he may choose to commit suicide or, perhaps, to sell himself into

THE JUSTIFICATORY ARGUMENT FOR HUMAN RIGHTS 491

slavery; and even then the steps he intentionally takes toward these goals involve agency on his part. Hence, if there are moral rights and duties that logically accrue to every person simply by virtue of being an actual or prospective agent, the argument that traces this logical sequence will necessarily be rationally acceptable to every agent: he will have to accept the argument on pain of self-contradiction.

There is a sense in which this grounding of the moral principle in action involves a foundationalist conception of justification. For, as we shall see, the argument begins with a statement attributable to any agent, that he performs some purposive action. This statement is based on the agent's direct awareness of what he is doing, and it leads, in a unilinear sequence, to his statement that he and all other agents have certain rights and correlative duties. I need not be concerned, in the present context, with further epistemological issues about the certainty or trustworthiness of the rational agent's direct awareness or about any presumed "data" on which this awareness might be based. . . .

My argument, in contrast, begins not from variable moral judgments but from statements that must be accepted by every agent because they derive from the generic features of purposive action. Hence, my argument is not "foundationalist" in the sense that it begins from *moral* or *evaluative* statements that are taken to be self-justifying or self-evident. The present argument is one in which statements about actions, and not statements about values or duties, are taken as the basic starting point. And these statements entail, in a non-circular sense, certain judgments about the existence of human rights.

THE ARGUMENT FOR EQUAL HUMAN RIGHTS

I shall, now, give a brief outline of the rational line of argument that goes from action, through its normative structure, to the supreme principle of morality, and thence to equal human rights.

In my book, *Reason and Morality,*[2] I have presented a full statement of the argument, so that for present purposes I shall stress only certain main points.

To begin with, we must note certain salient characteristics of action. In ordinary as well as scientific language, the word "action" is used in many different senses: we talk, for example, about physical action at a distance, about the action of the liver, and so forth. But the meaning of "action" that is relevant here is that which is the common object of all moral and other practical precepts, such as the examples I gave before. Moral and other practical precepts, as we have seen, tell persons to *act* in many different ways. But amid these differences, the precepts all assume that the persons addressed by them can control their behavior by their unforced choice with a view to achieving whatever the precepts require. All actions as envisaged by moral and other practical precepts, then, have two *generic features*. One is *voluntariness* or *freedom,* in that the agents control or can control their behavior by their unforced choice while having knowledge of relevant circumstances. The other generic feature is *purposiveness* or *intentionality,* in that the agents aim to attain some end or goal which constitutes their reason for acting; this goal may consist either in the action itself or in something to be achieved by the action.

Now, let us take any agent A, defined as an actual or prospective performer of actions in the sense just indicated. When he performs an action, he can be described as saying or thinking:

(1) I do X for end or purpose E.

Since E is something he unforcedly chooses to attain, he thinks E has sufficient value to merit his moving from quiescence to action in order to attain it. Hence, from his standpoint, (1) entails

(2) "E is good."

Note that (2) is here presented in quotation marks, as something said or thought by the agent A. The kind of goodness he here attributes to E need not be moral goodness; its criterion varies with whatever purpose the agent may have in doing *X*. But what it shows already is that, in the context of action, the "Fact–Value gap" is already bridged, for by the very *fact* of engaging in action, every agent must implicitly accept for himself a certain *value*-judgment about the value or goodness of the purposes for which he acts.

Now, in order to act for *E*, which he regards as good, the agent *A* must have the proximate necessary conditions of action. These conditions are closely related to the generic features of action that I mentioned before. You will recall that these generic features are voluntariness or freedom and purposiveness or intentionality. But when purposiveness is extended to the general conditions required for success in achieving one's purposes, it becomes a more extensive condition which I shall call *well-being*. Viewed from the standpoint of action, then, well-being consists in having the various substantive conditions and abilities, ranging from life and physical integrity to self-esteem and education, that are required if a person is to act either at all or with general chances of success in achieving the purposes for which he acts. So freedom and well-being are the necessary conditions of action and of successful action in general. Hence, from the agent's standpoint, from (2) "*E* is good" there follows

    (3) My freedom and well-being are necessary goods.

This may also be put as

    (4) I must have freedom and well-being,

where this "must" is a practical-prescriptive requirement, expressed by the agent, as to his having the necessary conditions of his action.

Now from (4) there follows

    (5) I have rights to freedom and well-being.

To show that (5) follows from (4), let us suppose that the agent were to deny (5). In that case, because of the correlativity of rights and strict "oughts," he would also have to deny

    (6) All other persons ought at least to refrain from removing or interfering with my freedom and well-being.

By denying (6), he must accept

    (7) It is not the case that all other persons ought at least to refrain from removing or interfering with my freedom and well-being.

By accepting (7), he must also accept

    (8) Other persons may (i.e. It is permissible that other persons) remove or interfere with my freedom and well-being.

And by accepting (8), he must accept

    (9) I may not (i.e. It is permissible that I not) have freedom and well-being.

But (9) contradicts (4), which said "I must have freedom and well-being." Since every agent must accept (4), he must reject (9). And since (9) follows from the denial of (5), "I have rights to freedom and well-being," every agent must also reject that denial. Hence, every agent logically must accept (5) "I have rights to freedom and well-being."

What I have shown so far, then, is that the concept of a right, as a justified claim or entitlement, is logically involved in all action as a concept that signifies for every agent his claim and requirement that he have, and at least not be prevented from having, the necessary conditions that enable him to act in pursuit of his purposes. I shall sometimes refer to these rights as *generic rights,* since they are rights that the generic features of action and of successful action characterize one's behavior.

It must be noted, however, that, so far, the criterion of these rights that every agent must claim for himself is only prudential, not moral, in that the criterion consists for each agent in his own needs of agency in pursuit of his own purposes. Even though the right-claim is addressed to all other persons as a correlative "ought"-judgment, still its justifying criterion for each agent consists in the necessary conditions of his own action.

To see how this prudential right-claim also becomes a moral right, we must go through some further steps. Now, the sufficient as well as the necessary reason or justifying condition for which every agent must hold that he has rights to freedom and well-being is that he is a prospective purposive agent. Hence, he must accept

(10) I have rights to freedom and well-being because I am a prospective purposive agent,

where this "because" signifies a sufficient as well as a necessary justifying condition.

Suppose some agent were to reject (10), and were to insist, instead, that the only reason he has the generic rights is that he has some more restrictive characteristic R. Examples of R would include: being an American, being a professor, being an *Übermensch,* being male, being a capitalist or a proletarian, being white, being named "Wordsworth Donisthorpe," and so forth. Thus, the agent would be saying

(11) I have rights to freedom and well-being *only* because I am R,

where "R" is something more restrictive than being a prospective purposive agent.

Such an agent, however, would contradict himself. For he would then be in the position of saying that if he did *not* have R, he would *not* have the generic rights, so that he would have to accept

(12) I do not have rights to freedom and well-being.

But we saw before that, as an agent, he *must* hold that he has rights to freedom and well-being. Hence, he must drop his view that R alone is the sufficient justifying condition of his having the generic rights, so that he must accept that simply being a prospective purposive agent is a sufficient as well as a necessary justifying condition of his having rights to freedom and well-being. Hence, he must accept (10).

Now by virtue of accepting (10), the agent must also accept

(13) All prospective purposive agents have rights to freedom and well-being.

(13) follows from (10) because of the principle of universalization. If some predicate P belongs to some subject S because that subject has some general quality Q (where this "because" signifies a sufficient reason), then that predicate logically must belong to every subject that has Q. Hence, since the predicate of having the generic rights belongs to the original agent because he is a prospective purposive agent, he logically must admit that every purposive agent has the generic rights.

At this point the rights become moral ones, and not only prudential, on that meaning of "moral" where it has both the formal component of setting forth practical requirements that are categorically obligatory, and the material component that those requirements involve taking favorable account of the interests of persons other than or in addition to the agent or the speaker. When the original agent now says that *all* prospective purposive agents have rights to freedom and well-being, he is logically committed to respecting and hence taking favorable account of the interests of all other persons with regard to their also having the necessary goods or conditions of action.

Since all other persons are actual or potential recipients of his action, every agent is logically committed to accepting

(14) I ought to act in accord with the generic rights of my recipients as well as of myself.

This requirement can also be expressed as the general moral principle:

(15) Act in accord with the generic rights of your recipients as well as of yourself.

I shall call this the Principle of Generic Consistency (*PGC*), since it combines the formal consideration of consistency with the material consideration of the generic features and rights of action. As we have seen, every agent, on pain of contradiction and hence of irrationality, must accept this principle as governing all his interpersonal actions.

This, then, completes my argument for equal human rights. Its central point can be summarized in two main parts. In the first part (steps 1 to 9), I have argued that every agent logically must hold or accept that he has rights to freedom and well-being as the necessary conditions of his action, as conditions that he *must* have; for if he denies that he has these rights, then he must accept that other persons may remove or interfere with his freedom and well-being, so that he *may not* have them; but this would contradict his belief that he *must* have them. In the second part (steps 10 to 14), I have argued that the agent logically must accept that all other prospective purposive agents have the same rights to freedom and well-being as he claims for himself.

Since all humans are actual, prospective, or potential agents, the rights in question belong equally to all humans. Thus, the argument fulfills the specifications for human rights that I mentioned at the outset: that both the Subjects and the Respondents of the rights are all humans equally, that the Objects of the rights are the necessary goods of human action, and that the Justifying Basis of the rights is a valid moral principle.

NOTES

1. I have tried to show this elsewhere with regard to utilitarianism. See Alan Gewirth, "Can Utilitarianism Justify Any Moral Rights?" in *Nomos XXIV: Ethics, Economics, and the Law,* ed. J. Roland Pennock and John W. Chapman (New York: New York University Press, 1982), pp. 158–78.
2. Alan Gewirth, *Reason and Morality* (Chicago: University of Chicago Press, 1978), chs 1–3.

46. THE SOURCES OF NORMATIVITY

CHRISTINE KORSGAARD

LECTURE III: THE AUTHORITY OF REFLECTION

Introduction

Over the course of the last two lectures I have sketched the way in which the normative question took shape in the debates of modern moral philosophy. Voluntarism tries to explain normativity in what is in some sense the most natural way: we are subject to laws, including the laws of morality, because we are subject to lawgivers. But when we ask why we should be subject to those lawgivers, an infinite regress threatens. Realism tries to block that regress by postulating the existence of entities—objective values, reasons, or obligations—whose intrinsic normativity forbids further questioning. But why should we

Reprinted from *The Tanner Lectures on Human Values*. Vol. 15 by permission of the University of Utah Press and the Trustees of the Tanner Lectures on Human Values.

believe in these entities? In the end, it seems we will be prepared to assert that such entities exist only because—and only if—we are already confident that the claims of morality are justified.

The reflective endorsement theorist tries a new tack. Morality is grounded in human nature. Obligations and values are projections of our own moral sentiments and dispositions. To say that these sentiments and dispositions are justified is not to say that they track the truth, but rather to say that they are good. We are the better for having them, for they perfect our social nature and promote our self-interest.

But the normative question is one that arises in the heat of action. So it is not just our dispositions, but rather the particular motives and impulses that spring from them, that must seem to us to be normative. It is this line of thought that presses us toward Kant. Kant, like the realist, thinks we must show that particular actions are right and particular ends are good. Each impulse as it offers itself to the will must pass a kind of test for normativity before we can adopt it as a reason for action. But the test that it must pass is not the test of knowledge or truth. For Kant, like Hume and Williams, thinks that morality is grounded in human nature and that moral properties are projections of human dispositions. So the test is one of reflective endorsement.

In what follows I will lay out the elements of a theory of normativity. This theory derives its main inspiration from Kant, but with some modifications that I have come to think are needed. What I say will necessarily be sketchy, and sketchily argued. My attention here will be focused on four points: first, that autonomy is the source of obligation, and in particular of our ability to obligate ourselves; second, that we have *moral* obligations, by which I mean obligations to humanity as such; third, that since we can obligate ourselves, we can also be obligated by other people; and fourth, that we have obligations to other living things. I will have little to say about the content of any of these obligations. And it will be no part of my argument to suggest either that all obligations are moral or that obli-

gations can never conflict. My aim is to show you where obligation comes from. Exactly which obligations we have and how to negotiate among them is a topic for another day.

The Problem

The human mind is self-conscious. Some philosophers have supposed that this means that our minds are internally luminous, that their contents are completely accessible to us, that we always can be certain what we are thinking and feeling and wanting, and so that introspection yields certain knowledge of the self. Like Kant, and many philosophers nowadays, I do not think that this is true. Our knowledge of our own mental states and activities is no more certain than anything else.

But the human mind *is* self-conscious in the sense that it is essentially reflective. I'm not talking about being *thoughtful,* which of course is an individual property, but about the structure of our minds that makes thoughtfulness possible. A lower animal's attention is fixed on the world. Its perceptions are its beliefs and its desires are its will. It is engaged in conscious activities, but it is not conscious *of* them. That is, they are not the objects of its attention. But we human animals turn our attention on to our perceptions and desires themselves, and we are conscious *of* them. That is why we can think *about* them.

And this sets us a problem no other animal has. It is the problem of the normative. For our capacity to turn our attention onto our own mental activities is also a capacity to distance ourselves from them and to call them into question. I perceive, and I find myself with a powerful impulse to believe. But I back up and bring that impulse into view and then I have a certain distance. Now the impulse doesn't dominate me and now I have a problem. Shall I believe? Is this perception really a *reason* to believe? I desire and I find myself with a powerful impulse to act. But I back up and bring that impulse into view and then I have a certain distance. Now the impulse doesn't dominate me and now I have a problem.

Shall I act? Is this desire really a *reason* to act? The reflective mind cannot settle for perception and desire, not just as such. It needs a *reason*. Otherwise, at least as long as it reflects, it cannot commit itself or go forward.

If the problem springs from reflection then the solution must do so as well. If the problem is that our perceptions and desires might not withstand reflective scrutiny, then the solution is that they might. We need reasons because our impulses must be able to withstand reflective scrutiny. We have reasons if they do. The normative word "reason" refers to a kind of reflective success. If "good" and "right" are also taken to be intrinsically normative words then they too must refer to reflective success. And they do. Think of what they mean when we use them as *exclamations:* "Good!" "Right!" There they mean: I'm satisfied, I'm happy, I'm committed, you've convinced me, let's go. They mean the work of reflection is done.

"Reason" then means reflective success. So if I decide that my desire is a reason to act, I must decide that on reflection I endorse that desire. And here we find the problem. For how do I decide that? Is the claim that I look at the desire and see that it is intrinsically normative or that its object is? Then all of the arguments against realism await us. Does the desire or its object inherit its normativity from something else? Then we must ask what makes that other thing normative, what makes it the source of a reason. And now of course the usual regress threatens. So what brings reflection to an end?

Kant described this same problem in terms of freedom. It is because of the reflective structure of the mind that we must act, as he puts it, under the idea of freedom. He says, "We cannot conceive of a reason which consciously responds to a bidding from the outside with respect to its judgments."[1] If the bidding from outside is desire, then his point is that the reflective mind must endorse the desire before it can act on it— it must say to itself that the desire is a reason. We must, as he puts it, *make it our maxim* to act on the desire. And this is something we must do of our own free will.

Kant defines a free will as a rational causality that is effective without being determined by any alien cause. Anything outside of the will counts as an alien cause, including the desires and inclinations of the person. The free will must be entirely self-determining. Yet, because the will is a causality, it must act according to some law or other. Kant says, "Since the concept of a causality entails that of laws . . . it follows that freedom is by no means lawless. . . ."[2] Alternatively, we may say that since the will is practical reason, it cannot be conceived as acting and choosing for no reason. Since reasons are derived from principles, the free will must have a principle. But because the will is free, no law or principle can be imposed on it from outside. Kant concludes that the will must be autonomous: that is, it must have its *own* law or principle. And here again we arrive at the problem. For where is this law to come from? If it is imposed on the will from outside then the will is not free. So the will must adopt the law for itself. But until the will has a law or principle, there is nothing from which it can derive a reason. So how can it have any reason for adopting one law rather than another?

Well, here is Kant's answer. The categorical imperative tells us to act only on a maxim that we could will to be a law. And *this,* according to Kant, *is* the law of a free will. To see why, we need only compare the problem faced by the free will with the content of the categorical imperative. The problem faced by the free will is this: the will must have a law, but because the will is free, it must be its own law. And nothing determines what that law must be. *All that it has to be is a law.* Now consider the content of the categorical imperative. The categorical imperative simply tells us to choose a law. Its only constraint on our choice is that it have the form of a law. And nothing determines what that law must be. *All that it has to be is a law.*

Therefore the categorical imperative is the law of a free will. It does not impose any external constraint on the free will's activities, but simply arises from the nature of the will. It describes what a free will must do in order to be what it is. It must choose a maxim it can regard as a law.[3]

Now I'm going to make a distinction that Kant doesn't make. I am going to call the law of acting only on maxims you can will to be laws "the categorical imperative." And I am going to distinguish it from what I will call "the moral law." The moral law, in the Kantian system, is the law of what Kant calls the Kingdom of Ends, the republic of all rational beings. The moral law tells us to act only on maxims that all rational beings could agree to act on together in a workable cooperative system. Now the Kantian argument that I have just described establishes that *the categorical imperative* is the law of a free will. But it does not establish that *the moral law* is the law of a free will. Any law is universal, but the argument doesn't settle the question of the *domain* over which the law of the free will must range. And there are various possibilities here. If the law is the law of acting on the desire of the moment, then the agent will treat each desire as it arises as a reason, and her conduct will be that of a wanton.[4] If the law ranges over the interests of an agent's whole life, then the agent will be some sort of egoist. It is only if the law ranges over every rational being that the resulting law will be the moral law, the law of the Kingdom of Ends.

Because of this, it has sometimes been claimed that the categorical imperative is an empty formalism. And this in turn has been conflated with another claim, that the moral law is an empty formalism. Now that second claim is false.[5] But it is true that the argument that shows that we are bound by the categorical imperative does not show that we are bound by the moral law. For that we need another step. The agent must think of *herself* as a Citizen of the Kingdom of Ends.

The Solution

Those who think that the human mind is internally luminous and transparent to itself think that the term "self-consciousness" is appropriate because what we get in human consciousness is a direct encounter with the self. Those who think that the human mind has a reflective structure use the term too, but for a different reason. The reflective structure of the mind is a source of "self-consciousness" because it forces us to have a *conception* of ourselves. As Kant argues, this is a fact about what it is *like* to be reflectively conscious and it does not prove the existence of a metaphysical self. From a third person point of view, outside of the deliberative standpoint, it may look as if what happens when someone makes a choice is that the strongest of his conflicting desires wins. But that isn't the way it is *for you* when you deliberate. When you deliberate, it is as if there were something over and above all of your desires, something that is *you,* and that *chooses* which desire to act on. This means that the principle or law by which you determine your actions is one that you regard as being expressive of *yourself.* To identify with such a principle or law is to be, in St. Paul's famous phrase, a law to yourself.[6]

An agent might think of herself as a Citizen in the Kingdom of Ends. Or she might think of herself as a member of a family or an ethnic group or a nation. She might think of herself as the steward of her own interests, and then she will be an egoist. Or she might think of herself as the slave of her passions, and then she will be a wanton. And how she thinks of herself will determine whether it is the law of the Kingdom of Ends, or the law of some smaller group, or the law of the egoist, or the law of the wanton that is the law that she is to herself.

The conception of one's identity in question here is not a theoretical one, a view about what as a matter of inescapable scientific fact you are. It is better understood as a description under which you value yourself, a description under which you find your life to be worth living and your actions to be worth undertaking. So I will call this a conception of your practical identity. Practical identity is a complex matter and for the average person there will be a jumble of such conceptions. You are a human being, a woman or a man, an adherent of a certain religion, a member of an ethnic group, someone's friend, and so on. And all of these identities give rise to reasons and obligations. Your reasons express your identity, your nature; your obligations spring from what that identity forbids.

Our ordinary ways of talking about obligation reflect this connection to identity. A century ago a European could admonish another to civilized behavior by telling him to act like a Christian. It is still true in many quarters that courage is urged on males by the injunction "Be a man!" Duties more obviously connected with social roles are of course enforced in this way. "A psychiatrist doesn't violate the confidence of her patients." No "ought" is needed here because the normativity is built right into the role. But it isn't only in the case of social roles that the idea of obligation invokes the conception of practical identity. Consider the astonishing but familiar "I couldn't live with myself if I did that." Clearly there are two selves here, me and the one I must live with and so must not fail. Or consider the protest against obligation ignored: "Just who do you think you are?"

The connection is also present in the concept of integrity. Etymologically, integrity is oneness, integration is what makes something one. To be a thing, one thing, a unity, an entity; to be anything at all: in the metaphysical sense, that is what it means to have integrity. But we use the term for someone who lives up to his own standards. And that is because we think that living up to them is what makes him one, and so what makes him a person at all.

It is the conceptions of ourselves that are most important to us that give rise to unconditional obligations. For to violate them is to lose your integrity and so your identity, and no longer to be who you are. That is, it is no longer to be able to think of yourself under the description under which you value yourself and find your life worth living and your actions worth undertaking. That is to be for all practical purposes dead

or worse than dead. When an action cannot be performed without loss of some fundamental part of one's identity, and an agent would rather be dead, then the obligation not to do it is unconditional and complete. If reasons arise from reflective endorsement, then obligation arises from reflective *rejection*.

But the question how exactly an agent *should* conceive her practical identity, the question which law she should be to herself, is not settled by the arguments I have given. So moral obligation is not yet on the table. To that extent the argument is formal, and in one sense empty.

But in another sense it is not empty at all. What we have established is this. The reflective structure of human consciousness requires that you identify yourself with some law or principle that will govern your choices. It requires you to be a law to yourself. And that is the source of normativity. So the argument shows just what Kant said that it did: that our autonomy is the source of obligation.

It will help to put the point in Joseph Butler's terms, in terms of the distinction between power and authority. We do not always do what upon reflection we would do or even what upon reflection we have already decided to do. Reflection does not have irresistible power over us. But when we do reflect we cannot but think that we ought to do what on reflection we conclude we have reason to do. And when we don't do that we punish ourselves, by guilt and regret and repentance and remorse. We might say that the acting self concedes to the thinking self its right to government. And the thinking self, in turn, tries to govern as well as it can. So the reflective structure of human consciousness establishes a relation here, a relation that we have to ourselves. And it is a relation not of mere power but rather of *authority*. And *that* is the authority that is the source of obligation.

Notice that this means that voluntarism is true after all. The source of obligation is a legislator, one whose authority is beyond question and does not need to be established. But there is only one such authority and it is the authority of your own mind and will.[7] So Pufendorf and Hobbes were right. It is not the bare fact that it would be a good idea to perform a certain action that obligates us to perform it. It is the fact that we *command ourselves* to do what we find it would be a good idea to do.

One more step is necessary. The acting self concedes to the thinking self its right to govern. But the thinking self in turn must try to govern well. It is its job to make what is in any case a good idea into law. How do we know what is a good idea or what should be a law? Kant proposes that we can tell whether our maxims should be laws by attending not to their matter but to their form.

To understand this idea, we need to return to its origins, which are in Aristotle. According to Aristotle, a thing is composed of a form and a matter. The matter is the material, the parts, from which it is made. The form of a thing is its functional arrangement. That is, it is the arrangement of the matter or of the parts that enables the thing to serve its purpose, to do whatever it does. For example, the purpose of a house is to be a shelter, so the form of a house is the way the arrangement of the parts—the walls and the roof—enables it to serve as a shelter. "Join the walls at the corner, put the roof on top, and that's how we keep the weather out." That is the form of a house.[8]

Next consider the maxim of an action. Since every human action is done for an end, a maxim has two parts, the act and the end. The form of the maxim is the arrangement of its parts. Take, for instance, Plato's famous example of the three maxims.[9]

1. I will keep my weapon, because I want it for myself.

2. I will refuse to return your weapon, because I want it for myself.

3. I will refuse to return your weapon, because you have gone mad and may hurt someone.

Maxims 1 and 3 are good; maxim 2 is bad. What makes them so? Not the actions, for maxims 2 and 3 have the same actions; not the purposes, for maxims 1 and 2 have the same purposes. The goodness does not rest in the parts; but rather in the way the parts are combined and related; so the goodness does not rest in the matter, but rather in the form of the maxim. But form is not merely the arrangement of the parts; it is the *functional* arrangement—the arrangement that enables the thing to do what it does. If the walls are joined and roof placed on top *so that* the building can keep the weather out, then the building has the form of a house. So: if the action and the purpose are related to one another *so that* the maxim can be willed as a law, then the maxim is good.

Notice what this establishes. A good maxim is good in virtue of its internal structure. Its internal structure, its form, makes it fit to be willed as a law. A good maxim is therefore an *intrinsically normative entity*. So realism is true after all, and Nagel, in particular, was right. When an impulse presents itself to us, as a kind of candidate for being a reason, we look to see whether it really is a reason, whether its claim to normativity is true.

But this isn't an exercise of intuition or a discovery about what is out there in the world. The test for determining whether an impulse is a reason is whether *we* can will the maxim of acting on that impulse as law. So the test is a test of endorsement.

This completes the first part of my argument, so let me sum up what I've said. What I have shown so far is why there is such a thing as obligation. The reflective structure of human consciousness forces us to act for reasons. At the same time, and relatedly, it forces us to have a conception of our own identity, a conception that identifies us with the source of our reasons. In this way, it makes us laws to ourselves. When an impulse presents itself to us we ask whether it could be a reason. We answer that question by seeing whether the maxim of acting on it can be willed as a law by a being with the identity in question. If it can be willed as a law, it is a reason, for it has an intrinsically normative structure. If it cannot be willed as a law, we must reject it, and in that case we get obligation.

A moment ago I said that realism is true after all. But that could be misleading. That we obligate ourselves is simply a fact about human nature. But whether a maxim can serve as a law still depends upon the way that we think of our identities. So there is still an element of relativism in the system. In order to establish that there are moral obligations we will need another step.

Moral Obligation

There is another way to make the points I have been making, and in approaching the problem of relativism it will be helpful to employ it. We can take as our model the way Rawls employs the concept/conception distinction in *A Theory of Justice*. There, the *concept* of justice refers to a problem, the problem of how the benefits of social cooperation are to be distributed. A *conception* of justice is a principle that is proposed as a solution to that problem.[10]

In the same way, the most general normative concepts, the right and the good, are names for problems—for the normative problems that spring from our reflective nature. "Good" names the problem of what we are to strive for, aim for, and care about in our lives. "Right" names the more specific problem of what we are to do. The "thinness" of these terms, to use Bernard Williams's language, comes from the fact that they are only concepts, names for whatever it is that solves the problems in question.

How do we get from concepts to conceptions? What mediates is a conception of practical identity. In Rawls's argument, we move from concept to conception by taking up the standpoint of the pure citizen and asking what principles such a citizen would have reason to adopt. In Kant's argument, we move from concept to conception by taking up the standpoint of a Citizen in the Kingdom of Ends and asking what principles that citizen would have reason to adopt.

Because they are normative, thick ethical concepts stand to thin ones as conceptions to concepts. They represent solutions, or at least reasons that will be weighed in arriving at solutions, to the problems that are set by reflection. And that means that they embody a view about what is right or good. If this is right, then Williams is wrong to say that reflection is not inherent in, or already implied by, thick ethical concepts. As normative concepts, they are essentially reflective.

Furthermore, our thin ethical concepts, although not necessarily our thick ones, will be shared with those alien scientific investigators. For the fact that they are scientific investigators means that they have asked themselves what they ought to believe and that they have decided that the question is worth pursuing. And that in turn means that they are rational and social beings, who face normative problems like our own and sometimes solve them. The exact shape of their problems may be different from ours, and so they may have different conceptions. But if we can see their conceptions as solutions to the normative problems that *they* face, there will even be a kind of convergence.

But this does not eliminate the element of relativism that Williams has sought to preserve. The mediation between concepts and conceptions comes by way of practical identity. And human identity has been differently constituted in different social worlds. Sin, dishonor, and moral wrongness all represent conceptions of what one cannot do without being diminished or disfigured, without loss of identity, and therefore conceptions of what one must not do. But they belong to different worlds in which human beings thought of themselves and of what made them themselves in very different ways. Where sin is the conception, my identity is my soul and it exists in the eyes of my God. Where dishonor is the conception, my identity is my reputation, my position in some small and knowable social world. The conception of *moral* wrongness as we now understand it belongs to the world *we* live in, the one brought about by the Enlightenment, where one's identity is one's relation to humanity itself. Hume said at the height of the Enlightenment that to be virtuous is to think of yourself as a member of the "party of humankind, against vice or disorder, its common enemy."[11] And that is now true. But we coherently can grant that it was not always so.

But this is not to say that there is nothing to be said in favor of the Enlightenment conception. This sort of relativism has its limits, and they come from two different but related lines of thought.

We have already seen one of them set forward by Bernard Williams. We could, with the resources of a knowledge of human nature, rank different sets of values according to their tendency to promote human flourishing. If values are associated with ways of thinking of what we most fundamentally are, then the point will be that some ways of conceiving one's identity are healthier and better for us than others.

But it is also important to remember that no argument can preserve any form of relativism without on another level eradicating it. This is one of the main faults with one well-known criticism of liberalism, that the conception of the person that is employed in its arguments is an "empty self."[12] It is urged by communitarians that people need to conceive themselves as members of smaller communities, essentially tied to particular others and traditions. This is an argument about how human beings need to constitute our practical identities, and if it is successful what it establishes is a *universal* fact, namely that our practical identities must be constituted in part by particular ties and commitments. And the communitarian who has reflected and reached this conclusion now has a conception of his own identity that is universal: he is an animal that needs to live in community.

And there is a further implication of this that is important. Once the communitarian sees himself this way, his particular ties and commitments will remain normative for him only if this more fundamental conception of his identity is one that he can see as normative as well. A further stretch of reflection requires a further stretch of endorsement. So he must endorse this new view of his identity. He is an animal that needs to live in community, and he now takes *this* to be a normative identity. He treats it as a source of reasons, for he argues that it matters that he gets what he needs. And this further stretch of endorsement is exactly what occurs. Someone who is moved to urge the value of *having* particular ties and commitments has discovered that part of their normativity comes from the fact that human beings need to have them. He urges that our lives are meaningless without them. That is not a reason that *springs from* one of his own particular ties and commitments. It is a plea on behalf of all human beings. And that means that he is no longer immersed in a normative world of particular ties and commitments. Philosophical reflection does not leave everything just where it was.

This is just a fancy new model of an argument that first appeared in a much simpler form, Kant's argument for his Formula of Humanity. The form of relativism with which Kant began was the most elementary one we encounter—the relativity of value to human desires and interests. He started from the fact that when we make a choice we must regard its object as good. His point is the one I have been making—that being human we must endorse our impulses before we can act on them. Kant asked what it is that makes these objects good, and, rejecting one form of realism, he decided that the goodness was not in the objects themselves. Were it not for our desires and inclinations, we would not find their objects good. Kant saw that we take things to be important because they are important to us—and he concluded that we must therefore take ourselves to be important. In this way, the value of humanity itself is implicit in every human choice.[13] If normative skepticism is to be avoided—if there is any such thing as a reason for action—then humanity as the source of all reasons and values must be valued for its own sake.[14]

The point I want to make now is the same. In this lecture I have offered an account of the source of normativity. I have argued that a human being is an animal who needs a practical conception of her own identity, a conception of who she is that is normative for her. Otherwise she could have no reasons to act, and since she is reflective she needs reasons to act. But you are a human being and so if you believe my argument you can now see that *this* is your identity. You are an animal of the sort I have just described. And that is not merely a contingent conception of your identity, which you have constructed or chosen for yourself or could conceivably reject. It is simply the truth. Now that you see that your need to have a normative conception of yourself comes from the sort of animal you are, you can ask whether it really matters whether animals of this kind conform to their normative practical identities. Does it really matter what human beings do? And here you have no option but to say yes. Since you are human you *must* take something to be normative, that is, some conception of practical identity must be normative for you. If you had no normative conception of your identity, you could have no reasons for action, and because your consciousness is reflective, you could then not act at all. Since you cannot act without reasons and your humanity is the source of your reasons, you must endorse your own humanity if you are to act at all.

It follows from this argument that human beings are valuable. Enlightenment morality is true.

Obligating One Another

So far I have argued that the reflective structure of human consciousness gives us legislative authority over ourselves. That is why we are able to obligate ourselves. And just now I argued that once we understand how all of this works, we must concede that our humanity is an end in itself, that human nature as the source of our values is itself a value. This, I should add, is what gives rise to *moral* obligation.

You might suppose that I am claiming that this settles the question of our obligations to others. Since I regard my humanity as a source of value, I must in the name of consistency regard your humanity that way as well. So I must value the things that you value. Or, to put it another way, since I think my humanity is what makes my desires into normative reasons, I must suppose that the humanity of others makes their desires into normative reasons as well.

This is a familiar form of argument. Versions of it appear in Thomas Nagel's book *The Possibility of Altruism,* and in Alan Gewirth's book *Reason and Morality.* And the criticism of this form of argument is always the same. Consistency can force me to grant that your humanity is normative for you just as mine is normative for me. It can force me to acknowledge that your desires have the status of reasons for you, in exactly the same way that mine do for me. But it does not force me to share in your reasons or make *your* humanity normative for me.[15] It could still be true that I have my reasons and you have yours, and indeed that they leave us eternally at odds.[16] Human beings might be egoistic, not in the sense of being concerned only about themselves, but in the sense defined by Nagel in *The Possibility of Altruism.* The egoist thinks that reasons are a kind of private property. We each act on our own private reasons, and we need some special reason, like friendship or contract, for taking the reasons of others into account.

In one sense this objection is correct. Consistency is not what forces us to share our reasons. And even if these arguments did work, they would work in the wrong way. They would show that I have an obligation *to myself* to treat you in ways that respect the value that I place on you. But they would not show that I have obligations *to you.* So we need something more.

As we have seen, I can obligate myself because I am conscious of myself. So if you are going to obligate me I must be conscious of you. You must be able to intrude on my reflections—you must be able to get under my skin. People suppose that practical reasons are private because they suppose that reflection is a private activity. And they suppose that, in turn, because they believe in the privacy of consciousness. So what we need at this point is some help from Wittgenstein.

Consider the private language argument. As Wittgenstein defines it, a private language would be a language that referred to something essentially private and incommunicable, say for instance a sensation that is yours alone, and cannot be described in any other way than by a name that you give to it. You can't even call it a tickle or an itch, for then it would be communicable. So you just call it 'S.' And whenever you experience it, you say to yourself, "That was S."[17]

Wittgenstein argues that there couldn't be any such language. One way to understand his argument goes like this: Meaning is relational because it is a *normative* notion: to say that X means Y is to say that one ought to take X for Y; and this requires two, a legislator to lay it down that one ought to take X for Y and a citizen to obey. And the relation between these two is not merely causal because the citizen can disobey: there must be a possibility of misunderstanding or mistake. Since it is a relation in which one gives a law to another, it takes two to make a meaning. So you cannot peer inwardly at an essentially private and incommunicable sensation and say, "That is what I mean by S" and so in that way mean something. For if that is what you mean by S, then when you call something S it must be *that,* and if you call something else S you must be wrong. But if what you call S is just that sensation that makes you feel like saying "S," and it cannot be identified in any other way, then you cannot be wrong.[18] The idea of a private language is inconsistent with the normativity of meaning.

If we read Wittgenstein that way, there is an obvious similarity between the kind of norma-tivity that he thinks characterizes language and the kind of normativity that I have been attributing to practical reasons. We could make a parallel argument against private reasons: Reasons are relational because reason is a normative notion: to say that R is a reason for A is to say that one should do A because of R; and this requires two, a legislator to lay it down and a citizen to obey. And the relation between them is not just causal because the citizen can disobey: there must be a possibility of irrationality—or wrong-doing. Since it is a relation in which one gives a law to another, it takes two to make a reason. And here the two are the two elements of reflective consciousness, the thinking self and the active self: what I have been talking about all along is how you can make laws and reasons for your self.[19]

There are two important points here. The first point is that the mistake involved in thinking that a meaning is a mental entity is exactly like that involved in thinking that a reason or a value is a mental entity. To talk about reasons and meanings is not to talk about entities, but to talk in a shorthand way about relations we have with ourselves and one another. The normative demands of meaning and reason are not demands that are made on us by objects, but are demands that we make on ourselves and each other.

The second point concerns privacy. The private language argument does not show that I could not have my own personal language. It shows that I could not have a language that is in principle incommunicable to anybody else. When I make a language, I make its meanings normative for me. As Wittgenstein puts it, I *undertake* to use words in certain ways.[20] And however I go about binding myself to those meanings, it must be possible for me to bind another in exactly the same way.

If I say to you, "Picture a yellow spot!" you will. What exactly is happening? Are you simply cooperating with me? No, because at least without a certain active resistance you will not be able to help it. Is it a causal connection then? No, or at least not merely that, for if you picture a *pink* spot you will be mistaken, wrong. Causal connections cannot be wrong. What kind of necessity is this, both normative and compulsive? It is *obligation*.

Philosophers have been concerned for a long time about how we understand the meanings of words, but we have not paid enough attention to the fact that it is so hard not to. It is nearly impossible to hear the words of a language you know as mere noise. And this has implications for the supposed privacy of human consciousness. For it means that I can always intrude myself into your consciousness. All I have to do is talk to you in the words of a language you know, and in this way I can force you to think. The space of linguistic consciousness is essentially public, like a town square. You might happen to be alone in yours, but I can get in anytime. Wittgenstein says, "Think in this connection how singular is the use of a person's name to *call* him."[21]

If I call out your name, I make you stop in your tracks. (If you love me, I make you come running.) Now you cannot proceed as you did before. Oh, you can proceed, all right, but not just as you did before. For now if you walk on, you will be ignoring me and slighting me. It will probably be difficult for you, and you will have to muster a certain active resistance, a sense of rebellion. But why should you have to rebel against me? It is because I am a law to you. By calling out your name, I have obligated you. I have given you a reason to stop.[22]

Of course you might not stop. You have reasons of your own, and you might decide, rightly or wrongly, that they outweigh the one I have given you. But that I have given you a reason is clear from the fact that, in ordinary circumstances, you will feel like giving me one back. "Sorry, I must run, I'm late for an appointment." We all know that reasons must be met with reasons, and that is why we are always exchanging them.

We do not seem to need a reason to take the reasons of others into account. We seem to need

a reason not to. Certainly we do things because others want us to, ask us to, tell us to, all the time. We give each other the time and directions, open doors and step aside, warn each other of imminent perils large and small. We respond with the alacrity of obedient soldiers to telephones and door-bells and cries for help. You could say that it is because we want to be cooperative, but that is like saying that you understand my words because you want to be cooperative. It ignores the same essential point, which is that it is so hard not to.

Now the egoist may reply that this does not establish that other people's reasons are reasons for me. He'll say that I am merely describing a deep psychological fact—that human beings are very susceptible to one another's pressure. We tend to cave in to the demands of others. But nothing I have said so far shows that we have to treat the demands of others as *reasons*. It is at this point that Thomas Nagel's argument, from *The Possibility of Altruism,* comes into its own.

Suppose that we are strangers and that you are tormenting me, and suppose that I call upon you to *stop*. I say, "How would you like it if someone did that to you?" Now you cannot proceed as you did before. Oh, you can proceed all right, but not just as you did before. For I have obligated you to stop.

How does the obligation come about? Just the way that Nagel says that it does. I invite you to consider how you would like it if someone did that to you. You realize that you would not merely dislike it, you would resent it. You would think that the other has a reason to stop—more, that he has an obligation to stop. And that obligation would spring from your own objection to what he does to you. You make yourself an end for others; you make yourself a law to them. But if you are a law to others insofar as you are just a person, just *someone,* then others are also laws to you.[23] By making you think these thoughts, I force you to acknowledge the value of *my* humanity, and I obligate you to act in a way that respects it.

As Nagel observes, the argument does not go through if you fail to see yourself, to identify yourself, as just someone, a person, one person among others who are equally real.[24] The argument invites you to change places with the other, and you cannot do this if you fail to see what you and the other have in common. Suppose you could say, "Someone doing that to *me,* why that would be terrible! But then I am *me,* after all." Then the argument would fail of its effect; it would not find a foothold in you. But the argument never really fails in *that* way.

For it to fail in that way, I would have to hear your words as mere noise, not as intelligible speech. And it is impossible to hear the words of a language you know as mere noise. In hearing your words as *words,* I acknowledge that you are *someone.* In acknowledging that I can hear them, I acknowledge that I am *someone.* If I listen to the argument at all, I have already admitted that each of us is *someone.*

Consider an exchange of reasons. A student comes to your office door and says, "I need to talk to you. Are you free now?" You say, "No, I've got to finish this letter right now and then I've got to go home. Could you possibly come around tomorrow, say about three?" And your student says, "Yes, that will be fine. I'll see you tomorrow at three then."

What is happening here? On my view, the two of you are reasoning together, to arrive at a decision, a single shared decision, about what to do. And I take that to be the natural view. But if egoism is true, and reasons cannot be shared, then that is not what is happening. Instead, each of you backs into the privacy of his practical consciousness, reviews his own reasons, comes up with a decision, and then reemerges to announce the result to the other. And the process stops when the results happen to coincide, and the agents know it, because of the announcements they have made to each other.

Now consider an exchange of ideas, rather than an exchange of practical reasons. Here we do not find these two possibilities. If meanings could not be shared, there would be no point in announcing the results of one's private thinking to anybody else. If they can be shared, then it is in principle possible to think the issues through together, and that is what people do when they talk. But if we have to grant that meanings can be shared, why not grant that practical reasons can be shared too?

The egoist may reply that I am leaving out an option. The student/teacher relation is a personal one. People who enter into particular personal relationships have special reasons to take each other's reasons into account. So the exchange I've just described takes place against a background agreement that the parties involved will take each other's reasons into account. The egoist is someone who only acts on his own reasons, not someone who has no concern for others. So you and your student reason together because you have tacitly agreed to, but this does not show that this is what usually happens.

But the objection reemerges within this framework. How are we to understand this personal relationship? If reasons are still private then it goes like this: each of you has a private reason to take the reasons of the other into account. A personal relationship is an interest in one another's interests.[25] This doesn't change the shape of the deliberation—you still back into your private deliberative spaces and then reemerge to announce the results. This only shows why you think there's a point in the exercise at all, why you hope to reach a convergence. But if you are really reasoning together, if you have joined your wills to arrive at a single decision— well, then that can happen, can't it? And why shouldn't it be what usually happens? Why shouldn't language force us to reason practically together, in just the same way that it forces us to think together?

I believe that the myth of egoism will die with the myth of the privacy of consciousness. Now you may object that the way in which I have argued against the privacy of consciousness—by arguing that we can think and reason together—

has nothing to do with what philosophers mean when they discuss that privacy. What they mean by privacy is that you don't always know what someone else is thinking or feeling. The way in which you have access to the contents of another person's mind—through words and expressions and other such forms of evidence—doesn't allow you to look around in it freely, and make sure that you know what's there and what's not.

But that's not an issue about privacy. If you accept the thesis that consciousness is reflective rather than internally luminous, then you must admit that you don't have access to your *own* mind in *that* way. So that doesn't mark a difference between the kind of relationship you have to yourself and the kind that you have to other people. All we've got here is a matter of degree. You know some people better than others; if you're honest and lucky, you know yourself pretty well.

Human beings are social animals in a deep way. It is not just that we go in for friendship or prefer to live in swarms or packs. The space of linguistic consciousness—the space in which meanings and reasons exist—is a space that we occupy together.

The Origin of Value and the Value of Life

Pain is an objection. Interestingly, it is an objection to several of the views that I have discussed here. First, for many, pain is the biggest stumbling block to accepting Wittgenstein's views about our mental lives. It seems to them that pain is a sensation and that it is in the mind and therefore that what it is to be in pain is to have a sensation in your mind. And it seems to them that there could be a pain that was private in just the sense that Wittgenstein denied. Second, for many, pain is the biggest temptation to some form of naturalistic realism about normativity. One can have doubts about pleasure, for there are pleasures we deplore, but pain seems obviously to be a normative fact. And, third, if that is so, pain is an objection to Kantian ethics, or to any ethics that makes the value of humanity the foundation of value. For the other animals suffer pain, and if pain is intrinsically normative, then it matters that they do. Animals just as such should have moral standing.

The first two objections are related. Wittgenstein's argument against a private language deploys one of the standard objections against any form of normative naturalism—that you cannot be wrong. Hobbes said you could only be obligated by the law if the sovereign is able to punish you. But if you break the law and get away with it, then the sovereign was not after all able to punish you and so you were not wrong. Hume says that your reason is your strongest desire. But if you always act from your strongest desire, then you always do what you have reason to do, and you cannot be wrong. Wittgenstein says that if a word just refers to the very sensation that makes you feel like saying that word, then you cannot be wrong.

But both the opponent of Wittgenstein and the normative realist point to pain, and more generally to sensation, as a case where it seems to be no objection to say that we cannot be wrong. In fact it creates a foundation. The utilitarian claims that pleasure and pain are facts that are also values, a place where the natural and the normative are one, and so where ethics can find a foundation in the world. And this is exactly analogous to the epistemological claim that our sensations are the place where the natural and the normative are one, and so where knowledge can find a foundation in the world. Sensations are seen to be intrinsically normative entities, about which we cannot be wrong.

But can't we? "I cannot be wrong about whether I am seeing red." If you mean that the object before you is red, you can certainly be wrong "No, I mean that I am having a red sensation." And what is that? It is the sensation that makes you feel like saying that a thing is red. You are not describing a condition that explains what you are inclined to say. You are simply announcing what you are inclined to say. In the same way, someone who says he is in pain is not describing a condition that gives him a reason to change his condition. He is announcing that he has a *very* strong impulse to change his condition.

Now that way of putting it, inspired by Wittgenstein, has a problem. People have thought that Wittgenstein was making a point about *language,* to the effect that when people talk about their own inner states and sensations they must be using language expressively, as if "I am in pain" could only be a cry of pain, and you could not simply be reporting your condition. Of course you can report your condition; once you've mastered the language, you can do anything that you like. His point is rather about mental activities, and whether a way of talking leaves anything for them to *be.* If "I see something red" *means* "I am having a red sensation" then one can never perceive; one can only announce the results of a perception that has already taken place. For what is this "having"? Did the little person in your mind perceive the red sensation? Wittgenstein is attacking a certain picture of what it is like to be conscious, which reduces all mental activity to the contemplation of sensations and ideas. And the language of "having" supports this picture. Does "I am in pain" mean "I am having a horrible sensation"? What here is the form of the "having"? Are you contemplating it? What would be so horrible about that?

But surely, you will reply, a *physical* pain is not just an impulse to change your condition. It *is* a sensation of a certain character. Now I am not denying that when we are in pain part of what is going on is that we are having sensations of a certain character. I am however denying that the painfulness of pain consists entirely in the character of those sensations. The painfulness of pain consists in the fact that these are sensations that we are inclined to fight. You may want to ask: why are we inclined to fight them if they are not horrible in themselves? Well, in some cases we are biologically wired this way; pain could not do its biological job if we were not inclined to

fight it. When nature equipped us with pain she was giving us a way of taking care of ourselves, not a *reason* to take care of ourselves. Why do you thrash? Is it as if you were trying to hurl your body away from itself? Why do you say "as if"? Pain really is less horrible if you can curb your inclination to fight it. This is why it helps, in dealing with pain, to take a tranquilizer or to lie down. Ask yourself how, if the painfulness of pain rested just in the character of the sensations, it could help to lie down? The sensations do not change. Pain wouldn't hurt if you could just relax and enjoy it.

If the painfulness of pain rested in the character of the sensations rather than in our tendency to revolt against them, our belief that physical pain has something in common with grief, rage, and disappointment would be inexplicable. For that matter, what physical pains have in common with each other would be inexplicable, for the sensations are of many different kinds. What do nausea, migraine, menstrual cramps, pinpricks, and pinches have in common that makes us call them all pains? What emotional pains have in common with physical ones is that in these cases too we are in the grip of an overwhelming urge to do battle, not now against our sensations, but against the world. Stoics and Buddhists are right in thinking that we could put an end to pain if we could just stop fighting. The person who cared only for his own virtue, if there could *be* such a person, would be happy on the rack.[26] They are wrong if they conclude that we should therefore stop fighting. Many pains are worth having; one may even say that they are true. Pain is not the condition that is a reason to change your condition, the condition in which the natural and the normative are one. It is our *perception* that we have a reason to change our condition.[27] Pain itself is not a reason at all.

But pain is the perception of a reason. Since animals have pain, and until now I have seemed to suggest that only human beings have reasons, this will take a moment to explain.

The best account of what an animal is comes

from Aristotle. We have already seen that Aristotle thought that the form of a thing is the organization or arrangement of its parts that allows it to be what it is, to do what it does, to do its job. Now Aristotle thought that a *living* thing is a thing with a special kind of form. A living thing is so designed as to maintain and reproduce itself. It has what we might call a self-maintaining form. So it is its own end; its job is just to keep on being what it is. Its business in life is to preserve its own *identity*. And its organs and activities are arranged to that end.[28]

If a living thing is an animal, if it is conscious, then part of the way it preserves its own identity is through its sensations. And this is where pain comes in. When something is a threat to its physical existence, or would be if it went on long enough, the animal perceives that fact and revolts against it. The animal is moved to take action to fix what is wrong. Suppose for instance that the animal needs nourishment. It perceives that by getting hungry. It finds this unpleasant and is moved to get something to eat. Don't be confused here: it is not that the pain is an unpleasant sensation that gives the animal a reason to eat. The animal has a reason to eat, which is that it will die if it does not. It does not know that it has that reason, but it does perceive it. The sensation in question is the sensation of hunger, not of pain. But an animal is designed to perceive and revolt against threats to the preservation of its identity, such as hunger. When it does that, it is in pain.

Now consider this comparison. A human being is an animal whose nature it is to construct a practical identity that is normative for her. She is a law to herself. When some way of acting is a threat to her practical identity and reflection reveals that fact, the person finds that she must reject that way of acting, and act in another way. In that case, she is obligated.

A living thing is an entity whose nature it is to preserve and maintain its physical identity. It is a law to itself. When something it is doing is a threat to that identity and perception reveals that fact, the animal finds that it must reject what it is

doing and do something else instead. In that case, it is in pain.

Obligation is the reflective rejection of a threat to your identity. Pain is the *unreflective* rejection of a threat to your identity. So pain is the *perception* of a reason, and that is why it seems normative.

To say that life is a value is almost a tautology. Since a living thing is a thing for which the preservation of identity is imperative, life is a form of morality. Or to put the point less strangely and in a way that has been made more familiar to us by Aristotle, morality is just the form that *human life* takes.

From here the argument proceeds as it did in the case of other people. I won't spell out the details here. Roughly it will look like this: I first point out to you that your animal nature is a fundamental form of identity on which your human identity depends. A further stretch of reflection requires a further stretch of endorsement. If you don't value your animal nature, you can value nothing. So you must endorse its value. Perhaps that by itself doesn't show us that we have obligations to the other animals, since the value could still be private. To show us that we have obligations, animals must have a way of impressing their value upon us, the way we impress our value on each other when we ask, "How would you like it if someone did that to you?" They must be able to intrude into our consciousness and make us think.

But that isn't a problem, is it? The cries of an animal are no more mere noise than the words of a person. An animal's cries express pain, and they mean that there is a reason to change its condition. Another animal can obligate you in exactly the same way another person can. It is a way of being *someone* that you share. So of course we have obligations to animals.

Conclusion

I hope by now it is clear that all of the accounts of normativity that I have discussed in these lectures are true.

Voluntarists like Pufendorf and Hobbes held that normativity must spring from the commands of a legislator. A good legislator commands us to do only what it is in any case a good idea to do, but the bare fact that an action is a good idea cannot make it a requirement. For that, it must be made law by someone in a position to command us.

As we saw, that view is true. What it describes is the relation in which we stand to ourselves. The fact that we must act in the light of reflection gives us a double nature. The thinking self has the power to command the acting self, and it is only its command that can make action obligatory. A good thinking self commands the acting self only to do what is good, but the acting self must in any case do what it says.

Realists like Nagel think that reasons are intrinsically normative entities and that what we should do when a desire presents itself is to look at it more objectively, to see whether it is such an entity. This view is also true. What it describes is the activity of the thinking self as it assesses the impulses that present themselves to us, the legislative proposals of our nature.

Reflection has the power to compel obedience and to punish us for disobedience. It in turn is bound to govern us by laws that are good. Together these facts yield the conclusion that the relation of the thinking self to the acting self is the relation of legitimate authority. That is to say, the necessity of acting in the light of reflection makes us authorities over ourselves. And insofar as we have authority over ourselves, we can make laws for ourselves, and those laws will be normative. So Kant's view is also true. Autonomy is the source of obligation.

Once we see this, we can see that the reflective endorsement theory is true on another level as well. In the end, nothing can be normative unless we endorse our own nature, unless we place a value upon ourselves. Reflection reveals to us that the normativity of our values springs from the fact that we are animals of a certain kind, autonomous moral animals. That is, in the Aristotelian sense, our human form. If we do not place a value on being such animals, then nothing will be normative at all.

That means realism is true on another level too. To see this, recall once again John Mackie's famous "argument from queerness." According to Mackie, it is fantastic to think that the world contains objective values or intrinsically normative entities. For in order to do what values do, they would have to be entities of a very strange sort, utterly unlike anything else in the universe. The way that we know them would have to be different from the way that we know ordinary facts. Knowledge of them, Mackie says, would have to provide the knower with both a direction and a motive. For when you met an objective value, according to Mackie, it would have to be—and I'm nearly quoting now—able both to tell you what to do and to make you do it. And nothing is like that.

But Mackie is wrong and realism is right. Of course there are entities that meet these criteria. It's true that they are queer sorts of entities and that knowing them isn't like anything else. But that doesn't mean that they don't exist. John Mackie must have been alone in his room with the Scientific World View when he wrote those words. For it is the most familiar fact of human life that the world contains entities that can tell us what to do and make us do it. They are people, and the other animals.[29]

NOTES

1. Kant, *Foundations of the Metaphysics of Morals,* p. 448; in Lewis White Beck's translation (Indianapolis: Bobbs-Merrill, 1959), p. 66.
2. Ibid., p. 446; in Beck's translation, p. 65.
3. This is a reading of the argument Kant gives in ibid., pp. 446–48; in Beck's translation, pp. 64–67; and in *The Critique of Practical Reason* under the heading "Problem II," p. 29; in Beck's translation (Indianapolis, Bobbs-Merrill, 1955), pp. 28–29. It is explained in greater detail in my "Morality as Freedom," in *Kant's Practical Philosophy Reconsidered,* ed. Y. Yovel (Dordrecht, Netherlands: Kluwer Academic Publishers, 1989).
4. I have a reason for saying that her behavior will

be that of a wanton rather than simply saying that she will be a wanton. Harry Frankfurt, from whom I am borrowing the term, defines a wanton as someone who has no second-order volitions. An animal, whose desire is its will, is a wanton. I am arguing here that a person cannot be like that, because of the reflective structure of human consciousness. A person must act on a reason, and so the person who acts like a wanton must be treating the desire of the moment as a reason. That commits her to the principle that the desire of the moment is a reason, and her commitment to that principle counts as a second-order volition. See H. Frankfurt, "Freedom of the Will and the Concept of a Person," *Journal of Philosophy* 68 (1971): 5–20, esp. the discussion on pp. 16–19. The affinity of my account with Frankfurt's will be evident.

5. Bradley and others understood Hegel's famous objection this way, and if it is taken this way it is a mistake. I argue for this in my paper "Kant's Formula of Universal Law," *Pacific Philosophical Quarterly* 66 (1985): 24–47. In that paper, however, I do not distinguish the categorical imperative from the moral law, and my arguments there actually only show that the moral law has content.

6. Romans II:14.

7. This remark needs a qualification, which springs from the fact that we can unite our wills with the wills of others. In Kant's theory, this happens when we are citizens who together form a general will or when we make friends or get married. In those cases it is sometimes the united will that has authority over our conduct. For further discussion, see my "Creating the Kingdom of Ends: Reciprocity and Responsibility in Personal Relations," *Philosophical Perspectives* 6 (1992): 305–32.

8. These views are found throughout Aristotle's writings, but centrally discussed in books VII-IX of the *Metaphysics* and in *On the Soul*.

9. Plato, *Republic,* I, 331c., p. 580.

10. Rawls, *A Theory of Justice,* (Cambridge, Mass.: Harvard University Press, 1971), p. 5.

11. Hume, *Enquiry concerning the Principles of Morals,* in *Enquiries concerning Human Understanding and concerning the Principles of Morals,* ed. L. A. Selby-Bigge, 3d ed. (Oxford: Clarendon, 1975), p. 275.

12. See, e.g., Michael Sandel, *Liberalism and the Limits of Justice.*

13. Kant, *Foundations of the Metaphysics of Morals,* pp. 427–28; in Beck's translation, pp. 45–47. I am here summarizing the interpretation of this argument I give in "Kant's Formula of Humanity," *Kantstudien* 77 (1986): 183–202.

14. This implies that you must accept the laws that arise from this more fundamental view of your identity, the laws of morality. But it does not imply that the less fundamental laws no longer exist or that the more fundamental ones always trump them. The view I have as I have spelled it out so far leaves room for conflict. Some account of how such conflicts might be negotiated is desirable, but I do not mean to be giving or implying any such account here.

15. See, e.g., Williams's criticism of Gewirth in chap. 4 of *Ethics and the Limits of Philosophy* (Cambridge, Mass.: Harvard University Press, 1985).

16. In contemporary jargon, the objection is that the reasons the argument reveals are "agent-relative" rather than "agent-neutral."

17. See Wittgenstein, *Philosophical Investigations,* trans. G. E. M. Anscombe (London: Macmillan, 1953), secs. 243 ff., pp. 88 ff.

18. See especially ibid., sec. 258, p. 92: "But 'I impress it on myself' can only mean: this process brings it about that I remember the connection *right* in the future. But in the present case I have no criterion of correctness. One would like to say: whatever is going to seem right to me is right. And that only means that here we cannot talk about 'right.'"

19. It may look as if there is a disanalogy here. The private language argument shows that you cannot mean a certain sensation by '*S*' just now and never again, because then you could not be wrong. The remark I just made makes it look as if you could have a reason just now and never again—the thinking self could bind the acting self to act a certain way just now. Actually, however, I do not think that is a possibility, since the acting self cannot coherently be taken to exist just at a particular moment. See my "Personal Identity and the Unity of Agency: A Kantian Response to Parfit," *Philosophy and Public Affairs* 18 (1989): 113–14.

20. Wittgenstein, *Philosophical Investigations,* sec. 262, p. 93.

21. Ibid., sec. 27, p. 13.

22. More strictly speaking, the needs and demands of others present us with what Kant calls "incentives," just as our own inclinations do. Incentives

come up for automatic consideration as candidates for being reasons. I thank Ulrike Heuer for prompting me to be clearer on this point.

23. See Nagel, *The Possibility of Altruism* (Princeton: Princeton University Press, 1978), pp. 82–84.

24. Ibid., chap. 9.

25. And that's not what a personal relationship is. See note 7 above.

26. Of course there could not be such a person, or at least, he could not *have* the virtues that were the only things he cared about. To have the virtues is in part to care about certain external things.

27. When you feel pity for someone, why does it strike you as a reason to help him? Why don't you just take a tranquilizer? Hucheson says, "If our sole Intention, in Compassion or Pity, was the Removal of our Pain, we should run away, shut our Eyes, divert our Thoughts from the miserable Object, to avoid the Pain of Compassion, which we seldom do . . ." (this passage is not in Raphael; one may find it in L. A. Selby-Bigge, *British Moralists* (Indianapolis: Bobbs-Merrill, 1964), p. 93). The point is reiterated by Nagel: "Sympathy is not, in general, just a feeling of discomfort produced by the recognition of distress in others, which in turn motivates one to relieve their distress. Rather, it is the pained awareness of their distress as *something to be relieved*" (*The Possibility of Altruism*, p. 80n). Wittgenstein says, "How am I filled with pity *for this man?* How does it come out what the object of my pity is? (Pity, one may say, is a form of conviction that someone else is in pain)" (*Philosophical Investigations*, sec. 287, p. 98). Pity is painful because it is the perception of *another's* pain, and so the perception that there is a reason to change *his* condition.

28. This account of the nature of an animal is based primarily on *On the Soul,* bk. II.

29. I would like to thank Charlotte Brown, Peter Hylton, Arthur Kuflik, Andrews Reath, Amélie Rorty, Thomas Scanlon, Jay Schleusener, and my commentators on the occasion of the lectures, Gerald Cohen, Raymond Geuss, Thomas Nagel, and Bernard Williams, for comments on earlier versions of these lectures. A longer version of the lectures, together with commentary by Cohen, Geuss, Nagel, and Williams, is forthcoming from Cambridge University Press.

47. The Justification of Morality and the Behavior of Women

꽃

James P. Sterba

Reprinted from "The Justification of Morality and the Behavior of Women" by permission of the author.

To defend morality, it would be helpful to show morality is grounded in rationality. This requires not simply showing that morality is rationally permissible, because that would imply that egoism and immorality were rationally permissible as well. Rather, what needs to be shown is that morality is rationally required, thus excluding egoism and immorality as rationally permissible.[1] Unfortunately, the goal of showing that morality is rationally required has been abandoned by most contemporary philosophers, who seem content to show that morality is simply rationally permissible.[2] No doubt most contemporary philosophers would like to have an argument showing that morality is rationally required, but given the history of past failures to provide a convincing argument of this sort, most of them have simply given up hope of defending morality in this way.[3] In this paper, I propose to provide just such a defense of a morality. I will begin in Section I by considering the attempts by Alan Gewirth and Christine Korsgaard to defend morality as rationally required and, unfortunately, why these attempts fail. In Section II, I will offer my own defense of morality as rationally required which draws significantly on the behavior of women. In Section III, I will consider some objections that can be raised against it.

I. GEWIRTH'S AND KORSGAARD'S ATTEMPTS TO JUSTIFY MORALITY

The central premises of Alan Gewirth's argument for morality can be summarized as follows:

1. All agents regard their purposes as good according to whatever criteria are involved in their actions to fulfill them.

2. Therefore, all agents must affirm a right to the freedom and well-being necessary to achieve their purposes.

3. All agents must affirm such a right on the basis of simply being prospective, purposive agents.

4. Hence, all agents must affirm that every prospective, purposive agent has a right to freedom and well-being.[4]

Gewirth claims that the universalized right affirmed in the conclusion of his argument is a moral right, that is, a right that is action-guiding for the rightholder and for others as well, a right that implies at least that others ought not to interfere with the exercise of that right. Such rights are symmetrically action-guiding because they are action-guiding both for the rightholder and for others as well.

Nevertheless, the success of Gewirth's argument depends on the impossibility of interpreting the universalized right in his conclusion as anything other than a moral right. Unfortunately for Gewirth's argument, another interpretation is possible. According to this interpretation, a universalized right can be deduced from the premises of his argument, but it is a prudential right, not a moral right. This interpretation is plausible because Gewirth maintains that the right referred to in premise (3) is prudential,[5] and the universalization of a prudential right can be understood to be a prudential right, albeit a universal one.[6]

Now what distinguishes a prudential right from a moral right is that a prudential right is action-guiding for the rightholder only and not for others, and so it does not imply that others ought not to interfere with the exercise of that right. Such rights are asymmetrically action-guiding because they are action-guiding only for the rightholder and not for others. Prudential rights are also analogous to the "oughts" found in most ordinary cases of competitive games—cases that we otherwise would have thought conform to the requirements of practical reason. For example, in football a defensive player may think that the opposing team's quarterback ought to pass on a third down with five yards to go, while not wanting the quarterback to do so and indeed hoping to foil any such attempt the quarterback makes. Or, to adapt an example of Jesse Kalin's, if you and I are playing chess, at a certain point in the game I may judge that you ought to move your bishop and put my king in check, but this judgment is not action-guiding for me. What I in fact should do is sit quietly and hope that you do not move as you ought. If you fail to make the appropriate move and, later in the game, I judge that I ought to put your king in check, that judgment, by contrast, would be action-guiding for me. So prudential rights are asymmetrically action-guiding in just the same way as these "oughts" of competitive games are asymmetrically action-guiding.

Given that the universal right to freedom and well-being in the conclusion of Gewirth's argument can thus plausibly be interpreted to be a prudential right, Gewirth's justification of morality cannot succeed, because it depends on the impossibility of interpreting the universal right in the conclusion of his argument as anything other than a moral right.

Turning to Christine Korsgaard's attempt to justify morality, Korsgaard begins by arguing that the necessity of acting in the light of reflection makes us authorities over ourselves.[7] And insofar as we have authority over ourselves, Korsgaard argues, we can make laws for ourselves, and those laws will be normative. Nevertheless, Korsgaard allows that we can make different kinds of laws for ourselves. If we favor the law of acting on the desire of the moment, then we will treat each desire as it arises as irresistible and we will be like wantons. If the law we favor ranges over just our own interests, then we will be like egoists. Only if the law we favor ranges over the interests of every rational being will we be moral. Accordingly, Korsgaard thinks that we can conceive of ourselves as being either wantons, egoists, or rational beings, and each of these different conceptions of our practical identity will be normative for us. Thus, in order to show that we should conceive of ourselves as rational beings, as in Kant's Kingdom of Ends, and that the laws we give ourselves should be moral laws, Korsgaard argues that the laws we give ourselves must be public just as the rules of language are public. According to Korsgaard, this requirement eliminates the possibility of really conceiving of ourselves as egoists given that the laws and reasons that egoists give themselves would have to be private. Since laws and interests can no more be private than words can be private, Korsgaard argues, egoism is actually no more possible than private languages are possible.

Korsgaard may be right that any normative ideal must be public, that is, communicable to others, just as languages are public. Even so, egoism may be able to satisfy this requirement of publicity. If we consider the egoistic ideal in the form of universal ethical egoism according to which everyone ought to do what best serves his or her overall self-interest, we find numerous attempts in the history of philosophy from Plato to the present at defending the consistency and reasonableness of this ideal. So there really is no question that philosophers have discussed the egoistic ideal and communicated with each other about it. Moreover, in practice, egoists would also communicate their reasons or interests to others who have overlapping or compatible reasons or interests so as to secure for themselves the benefits of coordination and joint action.

But what about those occasions when the reasons or interests of egoists conflict with the reasons or interests of others? Surely then egoists will not want to communicate their reasons or interests to those with whom they are in conflict in order not to lose out. So it is just here that egoists will want their reasons and interests to be private. In this respect, egoists do differ sharply from those who are committed to morality. Those committed to morality frequently want to communicate their reasons and interests to those with whom they are in conflict in the hope that a mutually acceptable resolution of the conflict can be achieved. So we can agree with Korsgaard that egoistic reasons and interests have a private dimension to them that moral reasons and interests lack. Nevertheless, even when egoists are striving to keep their reasons and interests private, their reasons and interests are still public in the sense that they are communicable to others. In such cases, their reasons and interests can be found out even when they are striving to hide them.

In this respect, egoistic reasons and interests are analogous to the reasons and interests found in most ordinary cases of competitive games. For example, players in football are usually trying to conceal the particular reasons and interests they have for being in certain formations, just as players in chess are usually trying to disguise the particular reasons and interests they have for making certain moves. Nevertheless, in both cases, the players can be found out, and frequently they are found out. Sometimes players will communicate their true reasons and interests by making a false move, as when an offensive lineman in football inadvertently signals a running play by the way he lines up to block. What this shows is that egoism can meet the publicity requirements of language by being communicable to others even though it cannot meet the stronger publicity requirement of morality of usually wanting its recommendations to be communicable to others.[8]

Yet Korsgaard wants to show that we cannot escape having a moral identity.[9] She wants to show that we cannot fail to identify ourselves as just someone, a person, one person among others who are equally real. So she asks us to consider a situation where she is being tormenting by a stranger. She asks her tormentor, "How would you like it if someone did that to you?" Her tormentor, whom we can presume believes herself to be an egoist, responds, "Someone doing that to *me,* why that would be terrible! But then I am *me* after all." According to Korsgaard, this response is not intelligible speech because in this situation her tormentor cannot fail to see Korsgaard as another person like herself equally real.

Now suppose we grant that Korsgaard is right that each of us must think of himself or herself as one person among others who are equally real. Would it still be possible then for one of us—a would-be egoist—to intelligibly say what Korsgaard's hypothetical tormentor said to her?

Clearly, to be an egoist is to have an overriding concern for one's own interests. Yet to be a consistent egoist one would also have to acknowledge that given that one's interests are overriding for oneself, the interests of every other person must be similarly overriding for each one of them. This would lead the consistent egoist to endorse universal ethical egoism according to which everyone ought to do what

best serves his or her own interests. For the egoist, the "oughts" here, like Gewirth's notion of prudential right, are asymmetrically action-guiding, that is, they require each person to do what best serves his or her own interests, but they do not require anyone to do what best serves the interests of anyone else unless that also happens to best serve his or her own interests. Like Gewirth's notion of a prudential right, the egoist's "oughts" are also analogous to the oughts found in most ordinary cases of competitive games. For example, in baseball a catcher may think that the runner on second ought to try to steal third, while not wanting runner to do so and indeed hoping to throw the runner out if he or she tries to do so. Or, in a cross country race, I might know that a competitor ought to charge "Cardiac Hill" if he is going to have any chance of beating me in a 5K race, while still hoping that he just takes the hill at his regular pace, mistakenly thinking that he can later make up the distance between us by outsprinting me in the last leg of the race. So the egoist's "oughts" are asymmetrically action-guiding in just the same way as the "oughts" of competitive games are asymmetrically action-guiding.

So when Korsgaard's tormentor says, "Someone doing that to *me,* why that would be terrible! But then I am *me* after all." She is speaking about her overriding concern for her own interests. She is not denying that Korsgaard is another person; she is just saying that from her egoistic point of view, her interest in tormenting Korsgaard is totally overriding. Moreover, egoists can actually be helpful to others, or at least not hinder them in situations where their interests are not at stake. Egoism does not require that you always disregard or go against the interest of others, it only requires that you do so when it would best serve your own interests. Egoists can recognize the reality of other persons and sometimes serve their interests without also granting them either equal rights or moral standing.

In addition, although Korsgaard in her example draws her tormentor into a public discussion of her views, egoists tend to avoid such discussions. In public, egoists usually defend morality as strongly as anyone, because it is when other people are moral that egoists usually benefit most from being egoists. And they usually benefit most when they are not known to be egoists but are thought to be moral. So egoists generally try to cover their self-interested tracks, so to speak, and do everything in their power to foster morality in others. But while egoists are reluctant to speak their views in public, Korsgaard's tormentor is not speaking "mere noise" to her. She is simply telling Korsgaard that from her perspective her own interests are the only ones that count in this context. Obviously, this is not a very consoling message for someone who is being tormented, but it is an intelligible message nonetheless especially when we imagine analogous exchanges in the context of competitive games. Thus, imagine a quarterback saying to an defensive lineman who has just sacked him three times, "How would you like it if someone did that to you?" To which the lineman responded, "Someone doing that to *me,* why that would be terrible! But then I am a *defensive lineman* playing against you after all." So unable to show that egoism cannot meet the publicity requirement of language or that egoists can be reduced to talking "mere noise," Korsgaard fails to provide the justification for morality over egoism that she was seeking.[10]

II. THE JUSTIFICATION OF MORALITY AND THE BEHAVIOR OF WOMEN

Throughout the history of philosophy, most defenses of morality have, like Gewirth's and Korsgaard's, focused on egoism.[11] The strategy of these attempts to defend morality has been to begin with the egoistic or self-interested reasons a person has and then to try to show that these reasons either entail morality (Kant, Gewirth) or are compatible with it (Hobbes), or alternatively,

that egoism is impossible or incoherent (G. E. Moore and Korsgaard). But the focus has always been on egoism or egoistic or self-interested reasons. In defense of this general approach, it might be argued that from observing ourselves and others, we find that egoistic or self-interested reasons are better motivators than are altruistic reasons, as evidenced by the fact that there seem to be more egoistically inclined people in the world than there are altruistically-inclined people.

But is there really this difference in motivational capacity? Do human beings really have a greater capacity for self-interested behavior than for moral or altruistic behavior? If we focus for a change on the behavior of women, I think we are likely to observe considerably more altruism than egoism among women, particularly with respect to the care of their families.[12] Of course, if we look to men, given the prevailing patriarchal social structures, we may tend to find more egoism than altruism.[13] But most likely any differences that exist between men and women in this regard, irrespective of whether we consider them to be good or bad, are primarily due to the dominant patterns of socialization—nurture rather than nature.[14] In any case, it is beyond dispute that we humans are capable of both self-interested and altruistic behavior, and given that we have these capabilities, both of these capabilities should be taken into account, as I propose to do, in fashioning a justification of morality.[15] As I will show, it is because philosophers in the past, who were virtually all men—women, for the most part, being excluded from doing philosophy until recent times—failed to take into account the behavior of women and focus on altruism as well as egoism that they were unable to come up with an adequate justification for morality.[16]

Let us begin by imagining that each of us is capable of entertaining and acting upon both self-interested and moral reasons and that the question we are seeking to answer is what sorts of reasons for action it would be rational for us to accept.[17] This question is not about what sorts of reasons we should publicly affirm, as people will sometimes publicly affirm reasons quite different from those upon which they are prepared to act. Rather it is a question about what reasons it would be rational for us to accept at the deepest level—in our heart of hearts.

Of course, there are people who are incapable of acting upon moral reasons. For such people, there is no question about their being required to act morally or altruistically. Yet the interesting philosophical question is not about such people but about people, like ourselves, who are capable of acting self-interestedly or morally and are seeking a rational justification for following a particular course of action.

In trying to determine how we should act, we would like to be able to construct a *good* argument favoring morality over egoism, and given that good arguments are non-question-begging, we would like to construct an argument that does not beg the question against egoism.[18] The question at issue here is what reasons each of us should take as supreme, and this question would be begged against egoism if we propose to answer it simply by assuming from the start that moral reasons are the reasons that each of us should take as supreme. But the question would be begged against morality as well if we proposed to answer the question simply by assuming from the start that self-interested reasons are the reasons that each of us should take as supreme. This means, of course, that we cannot answer the question of what reasons we should take as supreme simply by assuming the general principle of egoism:

Each person ought to do what best serves his or her overall self-interest.

We can no more argue for egoism simply by denying the relevance of moral reasons to rational choice than we can argue for pure altruism simply by denying the relevance of self-interested reasons to rational choice and assuming the following principle of pure altruism:

Each person ought to do what best serves the overall interest of others.[19]

Consequently, in order not to beg the question against either egoism or altruism, we have no other alternative but to grant the prima facie relevance of both self-interested and moral reasons to rational choice and then try to determine which reasons we would be rationally required to act upon, all things considered.[20]

Our situation is that we find ourselves with some capacity to move along a spectrum from egoism to pure altruism, with someone like Mother Teresa of Calcutta representing the paradigm of pure altruism and someone like Thrasymachus of Plato's *Republic* representing the paradigm of egoism. Obviously, our ability to move along this spectrum will depend on our starting point, the strength of our habits, and the social circumstances under which we happen to be living. But at the outset, it is reasonable to abstract from these individual variations and simply focus on the general capacity virtually all of us have to act on both self-interested and moral reasons. From this, we should conclude that both sorts of reasons are relevant to rational choice and then ask the question which reasons should have priority. Later, with this question answered, we can take into account individual differences and the effects of socialization to adjust our expectations and requirements for particular individuals and groups. Initially, however, all we need to recognize is the relevance of both self-interested and altruistic reasons to rational choice.

In this regard, two kinds of cases must be considered. First are cases in which there is a conflict between the relevant self-interested and moral reasons.[21] Second are cases in which there is no such conflict. Now it seems obvious that where there is no conflict and both reasons are conclusive reasons of their kind, both reasons should be acted upon. In such contexts, we should do what is favored by both morality and self-interest.

Consider the following example. Suppose you accepted a job marketing a baby formula in underdeveloped countries where the formula was improperly used, leading to increased infant mortality.[22] Imagine that you could just as well have accepted an equally attractive and rewarding job marketing a similar formula in developed countries where the misuse does not occur, so that a rational weighing of the relevant self-interested reasons alone would not have favored your acceptance of one of these jobs over the other.[23] At the same time, there were obviously moral reasons that condemned your acceptance of the first job—reasons that you presumably are or were able to acquire. Moreover, by assumption in this case, the moral reasons did not clash with the relevant self-interested reasons; they simply made a recommendation where the relevant self-interested reasons were silent. Consequently, a rational weighing of all the relevant reasons in this case could not but favor acting in accord with the relevant moral reasons.[24]

Yet it might be objected that in cases of this sort there frequently will be other reasons significantly opposed to the relevant moral reasons—reasons that you are or were able to acquire. Such reasons will be either *malevolent* reasons seeking to bring about the suffering and death of other human beings, *benevolent* reasons concerned to promote nonhuman welfare even at the expense of human welfare, or *aesthetic* reasons concerned to preserve and promote objects of aesthetic value even if those objects will not be appreciated by any living being. But assuming that such malevolent reasons are ultimately rooted in some conception of what is good for oneself or others, these reasons would have already been taken into account, and by assumption outweighed by the other relevant reasons in this case.[25] And although benevolent reasons concerned to promote nonhuman welfare would have to be taken into account, such reasons are not directly relevant to justifying morality over egoism.[26] Finally, although aesthetic reasons concerned to preserve and promote aesthetic objects, even if those objects will not be appreciated by any living being, might theoretically weigh against human interests, for all practical purposes, the value of such aesthetic objects will tend to correlate with the value of the aesthetic experiences such objects provide to humans.[27]

Consequently, even with the presence of these other kinds of reasons, your acceptance of the first job can still be seen to be contrary to the relevant reasons in this case.

Needless to say, defenders of egoism cannot but be disconcerted by this result since it shows that actions that accord with egoism are contrary to reason, at least when there are two equally good ways of pursuing one's self-interest, only one of which does not conflict with the basic requirements of morality. Notice also that in cases where there are two equally good ways of fulfilling the basic requirements of morality, only one of which does not conflict with what is in a person's overall self-interest, it is not at all disconcerting for defenders of morality to admit that we are rationally required to choose the way that does not conflict with what is in our overall self-interest. Nevertheless, exposing this defect in egoism for cases where moral reasons and self-interested reasons do not conflict would be but a small victory for defenders of morality if it were not also possible to show that in cases where such reasons do conflict, moral reasons would have priority over self-interested reasons.

Now when we rationally assess the relevant reasons in such cases of conflict, it is best to cast the conflict not as one between self-interested reasons and moral reasons, but as one between self-interested and altruistic reasons.[28] Viewed in this way, three solutions are possible. First, we could say that self-interested reasons always have priority over conflicting altruistic reasons. Second, we could say just the opposite, that altruistic reasons always have priority over conflicting self-interested reasons. Third, we could say that some kind of compromise is rationally required. In this compromise, sometimes self-interested reasons would have priority over altruistic ones, and sometimes altruistic reasons would have priority over self-interested ones.

Once the conflict is described in this manner, the third solution can be seen to be the one that is rationally required. This is because the first and second solutions give exclusive priority to one class of relevant reasons over the other, and only a completely question-begging justification can be given for such an exclusive priority. Only by employing the third solution, and sometimes giving priority to self-interested reasons and sometimes giving priority to altruistic reasons, can we avoid a completely question-begging resolution.

Consider the following example. Suppose you are in the waste disposal business and you have decided to dispose to toxic wastes in a manner that is cost-efficient for you but predictably causes significant harm to future generations. Imagine that there are alternative methods available for disposing of the waste that are only slightly less cost-efficient and will not cause any significant harm to future generations.[29] In this case, you are to weigh your self-interested reasons favoring the most cost-efficient disposal of the toxic wastes against the relevant altruistic reasons favoring the avoidance of significant harm to future generations. If we suppose that the projected loss of benefit to yourself was ever so slight and the projected harm to future generations ever so great, then a nonarbitrary compromise between the relevant self-interested and altruistic reasons would have to favor the altruistic reasons in this case. Hence, as judged by a non-question-begging standard of rationality, your method of waste disposal is contrary to the relevant reasons.

Notice also that this standard of rationality will not support just any compromise between the relevant self-interested and altruistic reasons. The compromise must be a nonarbitrary one, for otherwise it would beg the question with respect to the opposing egoistic and altruistic views. Such a compromise would have to respect the rankings of self-interested and altruistic reasons imposed by the egoistic and altruistic views, respectively. Since for each individual there is a separate ranking of that individual's relevant self-interested and altruistic reasons, we can represent these rankings from the most important reasons to the least important reasons as follows:

Individual A		Individual B	
Self-Interested Reasons	Altruistic Reasons	Self-Interested Reasons	Altruistic Reasons
1	1	1	1
2	2	2	2
3	3	3	3
.	.	.	.
.	.	.	.
.	.	.	.
N	N	N	N

Accordingly, any nonarbitrary compromise among such reasons in seeking not to beg the question against egoism or altruism will have to give priority to those reasons that rank highest in each category. Failure to give priority to the highest-ranking altruistic or self-interested reasons would, other things being equal, be contrary to reason.

Of course, there will be cases in which the only way to avoid being required to do what is contrary to your highest-ranking reasons is by requiring someone else to do what is contrary to her highest-ranking reasons. Some of these cases will be "lifeboat cases." But although such cases are surely difficult to resolve (maybe only a chance mechanism can offer a reasonable resolution), they do not reflect the typical conflict between the relevant self-interested and altruistic reasons that we are or were able to acquire. Typically, one or the other of the conflicting reasons will rank significantly higher on its respective scale, thus permitting a clear resolution.[30]

Now it is important to see how morality can be viewed as just such a nonarbitrary compromise between self-interested and altruistic reasons. First, a certain amount of self-regard is morally required, or at least morally acceptable. Where this is the case, high-ranking self-interested reasons have priority over low-ranking altruistic reasons. Second, morality obviously places limits on the extent to which people should pursue their own self-interest. Where this is the case, high-ranking altruistic reasons have priority over low-ranking self-interested reasons. In this way, morality can be seen to be a nonarbitrary compromise between self-interested and altruistic reasons, and the "moral reasons" that constitute that compromise can be seen as having a priority over the self-interested or altruistic reasons that conflict with them.[31]

Now it might be objected that although the egoistic and the altruistic views are admittedly question-begging, the compromise view is equally so and hence is in no way preferable to the other views. In response, I deny that the compromise view is equally question-begging when compared with the egoistic and altruistic views, but I concede that the view is to a lesser degree question-begging nonetheless, for a completely non-question-begging view starts with assumptions that are acceptable to all sides of a dispute. However, the assumption of the compromise view that high-ranking altruistic reasons have priority over conflicting low-ranking self-interested reasons is not acceptable from an egoistic perspective. Nor is the compromise view's assumption that high-ranking self-interested reasons have priority over conflicting low-ranking altruistic reasons acceptable from an altruistic perspective. Relevantly, what altruism assumes is that:

1. All high-ranking altruistic reasons have priority over conflicting lower-ranking self-interested reasons.

2. All low-ranking altruistic reasons have priority over conflicting higher-ranking self-interested reasons.

By contrast, what egoism assumes is that:

1'. All high-ranking self-interested reasons have priority over conflicting lower-ranking altruistic reasons.

2'. All low-ranking self-interested reasons have priority over conflicting higher-ranking altruistic reasons.

And what the compromise view assumes is (1) and (1'). So part of what the compromise view assumes about the priority of reasons, i.e., (1) is not acceptable from an egoistic perspective, and another part, i.e., (1') is not acceptable from an altruistic perspective; hence, to that extent, the compromise view does beg the question against each view. Nevertheless, since the whole of what egoism assumes about the priority of reasons, that is, (1) and (2) are unacceptable from an altruistic perspective and the whole of what altruism assumes about the priority of reasons, that is, (1') and (2') are unacceptable from an egoistic perspective, each of these views begs the question against the other to a far greater extent than the compromise view does against either of them. Of course, it would be preferable to have an alternative that did not beg the question at all, but with respect to specifying the priority of self-interested and altruistic reasons, no such alternative exists. Consequently, on the basis of making the fewest question-begging assumptions given that it shares important common ground with both the egoistic and the altruistic perspectives, the compromise view is the only nonarbitrary resolution of the conflict between egoism and altruism.

Notice, too, that this defense of morality succeeds not only against the view that egoism is rationally preferable to morality but also against the view that egoism is only rationally on a par with morality. The "weaker view" does not claim that we all ought to be egoists. Rather, it claims that there is just as good reason for us to be egoists as there is for us to be pure altruists or anything in between. Kai Nielson summarizes this view:

> We have not been able to show that reason requires the moral point of view or that all really rational persons not be individual egoists. Reason doesn't decide here.[32]

Yet because the above defense of morality shows morality to be the only nonarbitrary resolution of the conflict between self-interested and altruistic reasons, it is not the case that there is just as good reason for us to endorse morality as there is for us to endorse egoism or altruism. Thus, the above defense of morality succeeds against the weaker as well as against the stronger interpretation of egoism.

It might be objected that this defense of morality could be undercut if in the debate over egoism, altruism, and morality we simply give up any attempt to show that any one of these views is rationally preferable to the others. But we cannot rationally do this. For we are engaged in this debate as people who can act self-interestedly, can act altruistically, and can act morally; and we are trying to discover which of these ways of acting is rationally justified. To resolve this question rationally, we must be committed to finding out whether one of these views is more rationally defensible than the others. So as far as I can tell, there is no escaping the conclusion that morality is more rationally defensible than either egoism and altruism.

Unfortunately, this approach to defending morality has been generally neglected by previous moral theorists. The reason is that such theorists have tended to cast the basic conflict with egoism as a conflict between morality and self-interest. For example, according to Kurt Baier,

> The very *raison d'etre* of a morality is to yield reasons which overrule the reasons of self-interest in those cases when everyone's following self-interest would be harmful to everyone.[33]

Viewed in this light, it did not seem possible for the defender of morality to support a compromise view, for how could such a defender say that, when morality and self-interest conflict, morality should sometimes be sacrificed to self-interest? But though previous theorists understood correctly that moral reasons could not be compromised in favor of self-interested ones, they failed to recognize that this is because moral reasons are already the result of a nonarbitrary compromise between self-interested and altruistic reasons. Thus, unable to see how morality can be represented as a compromise solution, previous theorists have generally failed to recognize this approach to defending morality.

In setting out this defense of morality, I assumed that we humans have the capacity to move along a spectrum from egoism to pure altruism. I granted that our ability to move along this spectrum will depend on our starting point, the strength of our habits, and the social circumstances under which we happen to be living. But I argued that, at the outset, it is reasonable to abstract from these individual variations and simply focus on the general capacity virtually all of us have to act on both self-interested and moral reasons. Now, however, that I have argued that both self-interested and altruistic reasons are relevant to rational choice and are assigned priorities in cases of conflict, it is appropriate to return to the question of how individual differences and the effects of socialization should adjust our expectations and requirements for particular individuals and groups.

Here two kinds of cases seem particularly relevant. In one case, certain people by nature lack, to some degree, the capacity to act on high-ranking altruistic reasons when they conflict with low-ranking self-interested reasons. In the other case, certain people, due to socialization, lack to some degree the capacity to act on high-ranking altruistic reasons when they conflict with low-ranking self-interested reasons. Obviously, people who have the capacity for altruism will have to try to work around and, if necessary, protect themselves from those who, to varying degrees, lack this capacity. In cases in which those who lack this capacity are themselves at least partially responsible for this lack, blame and censure are also appropriate.[34] Nevertheless, as long as the greater majority of people have by nature and/or by nurture the capacity to act on high-ranking altruistic reasons when they conflict with low-ranking self-interested reasons, it should be possible to set up a social order that corresponds with the requirements of morality. Moreover, once we take into account the behavior of *both* men and women, there is good reason to think that the greater majority of humankind do have this capacity for altruism.[35]

III.   OBJECTIONS

Let's call my defense of morality "Morality as Compromise."[36] I now want to deal with three specific objections that have been raised against it. These objections come from Jeffrey Reiman and Eric Mack.[37]

In responding to an earlier version of Morality as Compromise, Jeffrey Reiman questions whether my argument suffices to show that altruistic reasons should be regarded as prima facie relevant to rational choice. Reiman claims that to regard them as prima facie relevant, it is not enough to show that a person does not have any non-question-begging grounds for *rejecting* altruistic reasons. Before regarding them as relevant, Reiman thinks that a person who already regards self-interested reasons as obviously relevant must be given a non-question-begging reason for *accepting* altruistic reasons as prima facie relevant. Presumably, Reiman also thinks that a person who already regards altruistic reasons as obviously relevant must be given a non-question-begging reason for *accepting* self-interested reasons as well.

But why is it reasonable to demand non-question-begging grounds for accepting reasons to which I am not already committed when I don't require non-question-begging grounds for continuing to accept the reasons to which I am already committed? Why is it reasonable to demand a higher standard of acceptability of reasons that I might come to accept than I demand of reasons I have already accepted?

The situation is even worse, because by allowing ourselves to retain our old reasons on lesser grounds than we require of ourselves for accepting new reasons, we may effectively block the acquisition of new reasons that are better grounded than our old reasons simply because these new reasons happen to conflict with our old ones. Clearly a more reasonable strategy

would be to evaluate both new and old reasons by the same standard. If we were to proceed in this fashion, then both self-interested and altruistic reasons would have to be regarded as prima facie relevant since we lack a non-question-begging reason to reject reasons of either kind.

It is also the case that we all find ourselves somewhere on the spectrum between egoism and altruism with some capacity and opportunity to move toward one or the other, and with a strong interest in resolving the question of how we should act in this regard in a reasonable manner. Reiman goes on to suggest that regarding both self-interested and altruistic reasons as prima facie relevant on these grounds would be analogous to naturalists and supernaturalists splitting the difference between their views and counting supernatural reasons as valid half the time. But as I understand the debate between naturalism and supernaturalism, many naturalists claim to have non-question-begging reasons for rejecting supernaturalism, and some supernaturalists claim to have non-question-begging grounds for rejecting naturalism. So this example does not parallel the case of egoism and altruism as I envision it.

But suppose there were equally good reasons for naturalism as for supernaturalism, would we be rationally required to act on naturalism half the time and supernaturalism the other half of the time, as Reiman suggests? In this case, a far more reasonable resolution would be to continue to lead the life of a naturalist or a supernaturalist at the practical level while periodically reevaluating the relevant reasons with the hope of some day resolving this issue. This interim solution is preferable because there is no way to compromise the issue between naturalism and supernaturalism that would respect the most important elements of each view. That is why the conflict between naturalism and supernaturalism differs from the conflict between egoism and altruism because in the latter case there is a way to compromise the issue between the two views that respects the most important elements of each, namely, by favoring high-ranking self-interested reasons over low-ranking altruistic reasons and favoring high-ranking altruistic reasons over low-ranking self-interested reasons.

This illustrates how the requirement of non-question-beggingness favors different solutions in different contexts. Thus, in contexts where action can be deferred, it favors deferring action until compelling reasons favoring one course of action can be found—for example, putting off your choice of a vacation spot until you have good reasons for going to a particular place. However, in contexts where action cannot be deferred, either it is or it is not possible to combine the best parts of the existing alternatives into a single course of action. If it is not possible to combine the best parts of the existing alternatives, as in the case of naturalism and supernaturalism, the requirement of non-question-beggingness favors arbitrarily choosing between them, while periodically reexamining the situation to determine whether compelling reasons can be found to favor one alternative over the others. If it is possible to combine existing alternatives, however, as in the case of egoism and altruism, the requirement of non-question-beggingness favors this course of action. It is on this account that I argue that Morality as Compromise is rationally preferable to either egoism or altruism.[38]

Eric Mack has raised a different objection to Morality as Compromise.[39] He questions whether a nonarbitrary weighing of all the relevant self-interested and altruistic reasons would lead to the kind of resolutions that I favor. He gives the example of a rich woman in severe conflict with a poor man, having the following self-interested and altruistic reasons:

Altruistic Reasons

1. not to kill the poor man
2. not to exploit the poor man

3. not to prevent the poor man from appropriating her surplus

Self-Interested Reasons

1. to retain control of her body
2. to retain control of her possessions crucial for meeting basic needs
3. to retain control of her possessions

4. to retain her surplus

Given these rankings, Mack claims that the rich woman's third place altruistic reason would triumph over her fourth place self-interested reason. But suppose that we alter the list of altruistic reasons to include two other reasons as follows:

Altruistic Reasons

1. not to kill the poor man
2. not to exploit the poor man
3. not to maim the poor man
4. not to deceive the poor man
5. not to prevent the poor man from appropriating her surplus

Given these rankings, Mack claims that the rich woman's fifth-place altruistic reason would no longer triumph over her fourth-place self-interested reason. Mack contends that this shows that this whole procedure for ranking reasons is arbitrary, and so cannot be used to support morality over egoism in the way I propose.

Actually, I agree with Mack that *his procedure* for determining the ranking of self-interested and altruistic reasons is arbitrary. The arbitrariness is evident in the fact that Mack's lists of self-interested and altruistic reasons are not of the same sort: His list of self-interested reasons is more generic whereas his lists of altruistic reasons are more specific. No wonder then that Mack derives from these lists results everyone would want to reject. But this does not show that no nonarbitrary ranking is possible.

For example, suppose we make both lists generic, as follows:

Altruistic Reasons

1. to meet the basic needs of others
2. to meet the nonbasic needs of others

Self-Interested Reasons

1. to meet one's basic needs
2. to meet one's nonbasic needs

Here there is no problem in determining that a nonarbitrary weighing of these prima facie relevant reasons would require us to rank the first-place self-interested reason over the second-place altruistic reason, other things being equal, and rank the first-place altruistic reason over the second-place self-interested reason, other things being equal.

Of course, there will be problems in determining which particular needs are basic or nonbasic; obviously, some needs are near the borderline. But just as obviously many needs can be seen to belong to one class or the other, thereby enabling us nonarbitrarily to resolve conflicts between self-interested and altruistic reasons in the way I propose in Morality as Compromise.

The last specific objection that I wish to consider is one that was raised by Jeffrey Reiman.[40] The objection is that a justification of morality like my own does not succeed even in its own terms, that is, it does not succeed in justifying morality. According to Reiman, avoiding inconsistency (as in Gewirth's justification) or avoiding question-beggingness (as in mine) are only logical requirements, whereas the offense of being immoral is something more than a logical offense. Reiman claims that a justification of morality like my own only succeeds in showing that the egoist or immoralist is guilty of a logical mistake, and that is not enough. Reiman asks us to imagine a murderer who says, "Yes, I've been inconsistent (or begged the question) but that is *all* I've done." Reiman claims that morality requires something more, it requires that we recognize the reality of other people, and immorality denies that reality.[41]

But notice that if Reiman's view of morality were sound, egoists and immoralists, by denying the reality of other people, would be solipsists, but clearly they are not.[42] Nevertheless, there is something to Reiman's objection. Putting a defense of morality in terms of a non-question-begging compromise between relevant self-interested and altruistic reasons for action can obscure the fact that what is at stake is the prohibition of the infliction of basic harm on others for the sake of nonbasic benefit to oneself, given that the infliction of such harm is what egoism would require. Thus, what needs to be made clear is that the failure to be moral involves both a logical and a material mistake. The logical

mistake is that of begging the question or acting contrary to reason. The material mistake is the infliction of basic harm for the sake of nonbasic benefit. Both of these mistakes characterize any failure to be moral, and they mutually entail each other.[43] They are simply two different aspects of the same act.

In this paper, I have argued that a commitment to morality is not only rationally permissible but also rationally required. Morality is rationally required, I claim, as a compromise that favors high-ranking self-interested reasons over low-ranking altruistic reasons and high-ranking altruistic reasons over low-ranking self-interested reasons. Of course, exactly how this compromise is to be worked out is a matter of considerable debate. Utilitarians favor one sort of a resolution, contractarians another, and libertarians yet another. My own view is that this debate can be adequately resolved at the practical level by showing how theoretically different views led to the same practical requirements. For example, I have argued that libertarian, contractarian, and socialist views, when properly interpreted, all lead to the same practical requirements. Yet however this debate is resolved, what I have argued here is that Morality as Compromise is rationally preferable to either egoism or pure altruism when judged from a non-question-begging standpoint, and that this defense of morality becomes available once we take into account the behavior of women and focus on altruism as well as egoism in fashioning a justification of morality.

NOTES

1. While egoism is an ethical perspective because it provides norms about how one should behave, it is not a moral perspective because it never requires a person to sacrifice her overall interest for the sake of others.
2. Again John Rawls is typical here. See his *A Theory of Justice* (Cambridge: Harvard University Press, 1971) p. 136.

3. *Ibid.*

4. Alan Gewirth, *Reason and Morality* (Chicago: University of Chicago Press, 1978) Chapters 1 and 2, "The Rationality of Reasonableness," *Synthese* Vol. 57 (1983), pp. 225–247, "From the Prudential to the Moral," *Ethics* Vol. 95 (1985) pp. 302–4, "Why There Are Human Rights," *Social Theory and Practice* Vol. 11 (1985) pp. 235–248, "Ethics and the Pain of Contradiction," *Philosophical Forum* Vol. 23 (1992) pp. 259–277.

5. For Gewirth's claim that the right in premises (3) is prudential, see "Replies to My Critics" in *Gewirth's Ethical Rationalism* edited by Edward Regis (Chicago: University of Chicago Press, 1984), pp. 205–212.

6. No doubt some will find Gewirth's notion of a "prudential right" to be something of an oxymoron, but in his account the notion is clearly defined to be the equivalent of a prudential as opposed to a moral ought. So if it would help, barring a little awkwardness, it is possible to restate Gewirth's argument, as well as my response, by simply replacing every occurrence of "right" with one of "ought.".

7. Christine Korsgaard, "The Sources of Normativity," in *The Tanner Lectures on Human Values,* Vol. 15, edited by Grethe B. Peterson (Salt Lake City: University of Utah Press, 1994), pp. 19–113 especially Lecture 3 as reprinted in this volume; *The Sources of Normativity*. (Cambridge: Cambridge University Press, 1996) especially Lectures 3 and 4.

8. Meeting the stronger publicity requirement of morality would render the practice of egoism self-defeating in just the same way that it would render the practice of many competitive games self-defeating. But this fact could only count against the practice of egoism if it also counted against the practice of competitive games, which it does not.

9. *The Tanner Lectures on Human Values,* Lecture 3, pp. 93ff; *The Sources of Normativity,* Lecture 4 pp. 132ff

10. There may be a way, however, to bring Christine Korsgaard's work in line with the defense of morality I am proposing the in next section. At the very end of her responses to her critics in *The Sources of Normativity,* Korsgaard remarks that perhaps the most essential rule of reflection is "that we should never stop reflecting until we have reached a satisfactory answer, one that admits of no further questioning." p. 258 If we interpret this rule as requiring a non-question-begging starting point, and thus taking into account the behavior of women and focusing on altruism as well as egoism, then, it may be possible see Korsgaard's work and my own as pointing toward a common justification of morality.

11. Korsgaard claimed (in personal correspondence) that her defense of morality is *not* focused on egoism. But this seems to be true only in the sense that she thinks she can easily dismiss egoism with her "impossibility" argument, which, however, I have just argued cannot be done.

12. Nell Nodding, *Caring: A Feminine Approach to Ethics and Moral Education* (Berkeley: University of California Press, 1984); Joyce Trebilcot, ed. *Mothering* (Totowa: Rowman and Littlefield, 1983); Susan Brownmiller, *Femininity* (New York: Ballantine Books, 1984).

13. James Doyle, *The Male Experience* (Dubuque: W. C. Brown & Co., 1983); Marie Richmond-Abbot, ed. *Masculine and Feminine* Second Edition (New York: Random House, 1991).

14. Victor Seidler, *Rediscovering Masculinity* (New York: Routledge, 1989); Larry May and Robert Strikwerda, *Rethinking Masculinity* (Lanham: Rowman and Littlefield, 1992).

15. This is not to deny that we usually have greater knowledge and certainty about what is in our own self-interest than about what is in the interest of others, and that this difference in our knowledge and certainty can have a practical effect on what good we should do in particular contexts. It is just that the debate between egoism and morality gets started at the theoretical level where no assumption is made about this difference in our knowledge and certainty, since we can, and frequently do, have adequate knowledge and certainty about both what is in our own self-interest and what is in the interest of others.

16. Even in recent times, Christine Korsgaard is one of a very few women philosophers who have written on the justification of morality.

17. "Ought" presupposes "can" here. So unless people have the capacity to entertain and follow both self-interested and moral reasons for acting, it does not make any sense to ask whether they ought or ought not to do so. Moreover, moral reasons here are understood necessarily to include (some) altruistic reasons but not necessarily to exclude (all) self-interested reasons. So

the question of whether it would be rational for us to follow self-interested reasons rather than moral reasons should be understood as the question of whether it would be rational for us to follow self-interested reasons exclusively rather than some appropriate set of self-interested reasons and altruistic reasons that constitutes the class of moral reasons.

18. Of course, we don't need to seek to construct a good argument in support of all of our views, but our view about whether morality or egoism has priority is an important enough question to call for the support of a good argument.

19. I understand the pure altruist to be the mirror image of the pure egoist. Whereas the pure egoist thinks that the interests of others count for them but not for herself except instrumentally, the pure altruist thinks that the her own interests count for others but not for herself except instrumentally.

20. Self-interested reasons favor both relational and nonrelational goods for the self, while altruistic reasons favor both relational and nonrelational goods for others.

21. Not all the reasons that people are or were able to acquire are *relevant* to an assessment of the reasonableness of their conduct. First, reasons that are evokable only from some logically possible set of opportunities are simply not relevant; the reasons must be evokable from the opportunities people actually possessed. Second, reasons that radically different people could have acquired are also not relevant. Instead, relevant reasons are those which people could have acquired without radical changes in their developing identities. Third, some reasons are not important enough to be relevant to a reasonable assessment of conduct. For example, a reason that I am able to acquire which would lead me to promote my own interests or that of a friend just slightly more than I am presently doing is hardly relevant to an assessment of the reasonableness of my conduct. Surely, I could not be judged as unreasonable for failing to acquire such a reason. Rather, relevant reasons are those which would lead one to avoid a *significant harm* to oneself (or others) or to secure a *significant benefit* to oneself (or others) at an acceptable cost to oneself (or others).

It is also worth noting that a given individual may not actually reflect on all the reasons that are relevant to deciding what she should do. In fact,

one could do so only if one had already acquired all the relevant reasons. Nevertheless, reasonable conduct is ideally determined by a rational weighing of all the reasons that are relevant to deciding what one should do so that failing to accord with a rational weighing of all such reasons is to act contrary to reason.

22. For a discussion of the causal links involved here, see *Marketing and Promotion of Infant Formula in Developing Countries*. Hearing before the Subcommittee of International Economic Policy and Trade of the Committee on Foreign Affairs, U.S. House of Representatives, 1980. See also Maggie McComas et al. *The Dilemma of Third World Nutrition* (1983).

23. Assume that both jobs have the same beneficial effects on the interests of others.

24. I am assuming that acting contrary to reason is a significant failing with respect to the requirements of reason, and that there are many ways of not acting in (perfect) accord with reason that do not constitute acting contrary to reason.

25. To deal with pure sadists (if any exist) for whom malevolent reasons or the reasons on which such reasons are grounded would not have been outweighed by other self-interested reasons, we might introduce an additional argument to show that pure sadists should team up with pure masochists (if any exist)!

26. Of course, such reasons will have to be taken into account at some point in a conception of justice for here and now, but the method of integrating such reasons will simply parallel the method already used for integrating self-interested and altruistic reasons. In *Justice for Here and Now* Chapter 6, I will consider how such reasons to promote nonhuman welfare should be integrated into a conception of justice for here and now. It is not clear how there could be any other kind of reasons that would be relevant to rational choice, but if there were such they would have to relate to some other kind of good that we could plausibly be maintained to pursue.

27. In G. E. Moore's thought experiment of whether a beautiful world should be preferred to an ugly world if no one were to have had experience of either, Moore's preference for the beautiful world was based on the assumption that humans would not be affected one way or the other by the choice. See G. E. Moore, *Principia Ethica* (Cambridge: Cambridge University Press, 1966), pp.

83–85. Moreover, although there are many aesthetic objects that we restrict our experience of in order to better preserve them, even in such cases it still seems that the value of such objects correlates with the value of the aesthetic experiences that such objects have produced in the past or could produce in the future for beings like ourselves.

28. This is because, as I shall argue, morality itself already represents a compromise between egoism and altruism. So to ask that moral reasons be weighed against self-interested reasons is, in effect, to count self-interested reasons twice—once in the compromise between egoism and altruism and then again when moral reasons are weighed against self-interested reasons. But to count self-interested reasons twice is clearly objectionable.

29. Assume that all these methods of waste disposal have roughly the same amount of beneficial effects on the interests of others.

30. It is important to point out here that this defense of morality presupposes that we can establish a conception of the good, at least to the degree that we can determine high- and low-ranking self-interested and altruistic reasons for each agent.

31. It is worth pointing out here an important difference between these self-interested and altruistic reasons that constitute moral reasons. It is that the self-interested reasons render the pursuit of self-interest permissible, whereas the altruistic reasons require the pursuit of altruism. This is because it is always possible to sacrifice oneself more than morality demands and thus act supererogatorily. Yet even here there are limits and one can sacrifice oneself too much, as presumably the pure altruist does, and consequently be morally blameworthy for doing so.

32. Kai Nielson, "Why Should I be Moral? Revisited," *American Philosophical Quarterly* Vol. 21 (1984) p. 90.

33. Kurt Baier, *The Moral Point of View,* Abridged edition (New York: Random House, 1965) p. 150.

34. The justification for blaming and censuring such persons is not based on any possibility for reforming them because we were assuming that they were incapable of reform. Rather the justification is based on what the persons in question deserve because of their past behavior and on whatever usefulness blaming and censuring them would have in deterring others.

35. What it is rational for those who lack even the minimal capacity for altruism to do is a question that I will not take up here.

36. For a more detailed defense, see Chapter 2 of my book *Justice for Here and Now* (Cambridge University Press, 1998).

37. Jeffrey Reiman, "What Ought "'Ought' Implies 'Can'" Imply? Comments on James Sterba's *How To Make People Just," Journal of Social Philosophy,* Special Issue Vol. 22 (1991), pp. 73–80; Eric Mack, "Libertarianism Untamed," *Journal of Social Philosophy,* Special Issue Vol. (1991), pp. 64–72. See also Jeffrey Reiman, *Justice and Modern Moral Philosophy* (New Haven: Yale University Press. 1990) pp. 97–112.

38. There is also the additional reason discussed earlier that egoism fails to meet its burden of proof.

39. Mack, "Libertarianism Untamed."

40. Reiman, "What Ought "'Ought' Implies 'Can'" Imply? Comments on James Sterba's *How To Make People Just,"* pp. 73–80. This objection was actually directed against Alan Gewirth's defense of morality, but in private correspondence, Reiman has directed it against my own view as well.

41. *Ibid.* pp. 112–129.

42. In private correspondence, Reiman claims that, as he understands the denial of the reality of other people, it does not require solipsism but only the failure to "recognize the first-person reality of other people." (August 2, 1995) But even given this interpretation, it still seems that Reiman is making too strong a claim about the egoist. For example, the egoist does not have to deny that other human beings are in pain, as would seemingly be the case if she failed to "recognize the first-person reality of other people." See also my discussion of Korsgaard's work.

43. The logical mistake of begging the question entails, in this context, preferring low-ranking self-interested reasons over high-ranking altruistic reasons or low-ranking altruistic reasons over high-ranking self-interested reasons, which, in turn, entails the material mistake of inflicting basic harm for the sake of nonbasic benefit. Likewise, the material mistake of inflicting basic harm for the sake of nonbasic benefit entails preferring low-ranking self-interested reasons over high-ranking altruistic reasons which, in turn, entails the logical mistake of begging the question.

48. Harmony with Nature and Indigenous African Culture

❧

MOSHOESHOE II

Today Africans, like all the Earth's children, are born into a world with polluted air and water, into a world whose irreplaceable natural resources are rapidly disappearing.

They are born into a continent where many thousands die from starvation in a world where food is plentiful; a continent that, until recent times, was able to feed itself and produce surpluses, and where abject poverty was unknown; a continent where oppressive regimes, propped up by international finance institutions and local greedy elites, often deny basic human rights to their own people.

They are born into a world where technological advance now has the capacity to produce food for all and to provide each human being with the basic ability to seek and fulfill his or her own culturally defined well-being while preserving the natural environment.

Knowledge has been used to seek domination over nature, not to maintain the ecological balance, and to bolster an arms race that has used up vast quantities of the world's resources and many of the skills so urgently needed to meet the very basic needs of millions of the world's citizens.

Most of our global crises—war, pollution, overpopulation, overconsumption, hunger, and oppression—are symptoms of a single cultural

evolution that is often referred to as "civilization." This is not to say that this culture—the Western evolutionist culture—has not shown brilliant success or offered much that is of value for the good of the rest of the world. But equally, careful study of other cultures, their forms of spirituality and ways of living in harmony with nature, could offer the West the seeds of a new relationship with nature, replacing the aggressive search for domination of nature and matter.

In the search for solutions to today's rapidly increasing and interconnected global threats to the survival of all forms of life on our planet, much can be learned from comparing the dominant model of development—that of the industrial market society—with those traditional models that sustained the indigenous cultures of Africa, Asia, and Latin America. As little as two hundred years ago, indigenous cultures, having evolved and successfully adapted to change over thousands of years, still occupied most of the world. But in these last two centuries, the culture of the industrial market society has become a global process, attempting—whether by seduction or coercion—to destroy all other existing cultural forms. In so doing, it has also created its own contradictions, giving humanity the power to extinguish not only itself but also many of the world's other species.

Outstripping human capacity to adapt in such a short space of time, the Western model of development, with its apparently inbuilt need to ensure access to and control of the world's resources, has drastically depleted these resources in a process of overconsumption. In

From *Story Earth: Native Voices on the Environment,* compiled by Inter Press Service, © 1993. Published by Mercury House, San Francisco, CA, and reprinted by permission.

Africa, as in the rest of the so-called Third World, the result has been ever-increasing levels of domination and dependence, socioeconomic decline, and a tragic loss of cultural identity. Once an integral part of African culture, life and survival skills—such as the ability to feed people, to provide a secure and stable community-based life, and to meet basic physical and emotional needs in a balanced relationship with the natural environment—have dwindled. These skills had been practiced over thousands of years, with no need for overconsumption, elaborate technology, centralized state structures, or the domination of the short-term material profit motive over nature.

The loss of such a way of life, and with it, of cultural identity, lies at the root of African underdevelopment and of the current African crisis—political instability, social and economic decline, poor governance, extensive corruption of power and privilege, and much else.

When a people lose their identity, they also lose their capacity for self-development, self-reliance, and self-determination. Society begins to disintegrate, and self-respect is replaced by alienation. Such is the experience of African culture in the face of colonization and neocolonialism. Having exploited and almost exhausted Africa's natural resources for over five hundred years, the West is only now awakening to the realities of the crisis in Africa. It has become more and more difficult for Africa's farmers to escape from, or to ignore, the agricultural and environmental dictates imposed on them by governments and their experts. But any intervention in the African environment is a much more serious undertaking for a subsistence economy than for Western society, whose industrial base acts as a safety net.

For the African farmer, conservation is a vital political and socioeconomic issue, a matter of survival. The management and ownership of land provide both livelihood and shelter. For indigenous African people, land has a mix of cultural and social meanings, in addition to its role as habitat and as a source of resources for production activities. In some African societies, land is related to lineage groupings, where boundary limits can be extended until an entire group is included in one single area, depending on the availability of unclaimed and unoccupied land, as is the case of the Tiv people of Nigeria.

There are also cases in which land is linked to social organization through a series of rallying points marked in a distinctive manner, as with the Tonga people of Zambia, who use what they called "rain shrines." Other people, like the Kikuyu of Kenya, had—and still have to some extent—a notion of territorial boundaries that could lead to the development of lineage estates or to units controlled by their management committees. In some parts of Africa, land was considered a national and social asset to be enjoyed by all with equal rights and obligations.

The central point is that land has always played a significant role in the indigenous culture of African people, and in their power systems and ideologies. It has always been a significant political and social issue, and it provided the basis for indigenous civilization, the molding of people's attitudes and behavior.

The environmental and agricultural dictates of Western solutions have seldom been instituted with the consent of, or in consultation with, local farmers and communities whose lives have been so vitally affected. "Experts" have shown a total disregard and ignorance of the African's long-established and successful methods to ensure their survival and well-being while safeguarding the soil, plants, and animals on which they have always depended for survival. Such "experts" have also failed to understand either the social or the ecological base of the cultural practices on which they seek to impose their externally derived solutions, constructed in an entirely different socioeconomic and ecological context. The result is that many of their agricultural strategies and environmental "solutions" have proved disastrous for the people, wildlife, and natural environment of Africa.

Indigenous cultures may not be able to replace modern political and socioeconomic analyses of world realities, but they can provide creative and innovative power to complement and correct current international thinking.

Environmental problems have always existed in all cultures and will continue to exist wherever there is an imbalance between the human population and its resource base. But today's environmental crisis is different in scale, being a global problem that has been caused by cultural forces unknown before the imposition of the modern industrial market society and its particular development model.

Before the arrival of slavery and colonization, African culture had its own structures of knowledge, values, religious beliefs, and social systems that ensured the protection of the natural environment. Africa was on course for progressive evolution, however differently the goals of that progress were defined from the progress of the Western development model.

African traditional belief regarded all natural resources as sacred and held in common and in trust both for those living and those yet to be born. In my own local culture of Lesotho, all land belongs to the nation—to the people as a collective whole. It is held in trust by the chieftainship system, whose member chiefs are responsible for its protection. Every citizen is entitled to a share of the land—for building a home, for pasture, for cultivation. These rights accrue on marriage, but single people are also entitled to land to build a home, independent of their parents' rights. In this way, the needs of the whole community are met—community good reigns supreme.

Traditionally, at the end of any growing season, all land was opened up to communal grazing, and the stalks of cereal crops had to be left in the ground for such grazing. No land was fenced. Other natural resources, such as trees, grasses, and reeds, were also communally owned. The woods were open only on certain days for the people to collect dead wood. Only the community could give permission for cutting other wood needed for building houses, and this permission had to be sought from the chief as the community's representative.

Traditionally, all local decision making is on a consensus basis, however long that process may take. Conflicts between individuals and offences against property are subject to community court procedures. The good of both parties is taken into consideration, in a search for solutions acceptable to all.

Within the priority of the good of the community, the dominant institution is the household—the extended family, comprising not only husband, wife, and children, but also brothers, sisters, parents, grandparents, and all other relatives, however remotely connected—in which individual duties to other members of the family are clearly defined.

The core household within the extended family is the basic production unit, creating its own economic system of satisfying material needs—the base of traditional African adaptive success. This mode of production is based on a division of labor, in which each member has a defined role, permitting the performance of all the technological functions involved in satisfying the needs of a family.

Wealth is traditionally measured in terms of the number of cattle owned. There is no limit to wealth, providing it does not challenge the stability and social cohesion of the community. If it does, the community reacts. The test would be whether an individual's accumulation led to undue envy, conflict, or fragmentation. Any community action would be seen as in the interests of its stability and coherence, and therefore legitimate.

Kinship also brings obligations on the wealthier to look after the needs of those who are less fortunate because of sickness, old age, lack of resources, or any other reason. Elderly people are respected because one day they will become the ancestors of the family.

Before the birth of the postcolonial African

state, the preservation of equality was of central importance. The concept of social class as such was unknown. Status was a matter of age, sex, and personal qualities. Authority vested in chieftainship did not allow for personal aggrandizement. In African culture, the community could not shed its collective moral responsibility for the actions of the individual, and this in turn bound the individual to the religious and moral norms of the community.

In contrast, the Western idea of community is restricted to those living at any given time, without much sense of continuity between the past, the present, and the future.

In African traditional culture, there was a sacred bond between the individual, his community, his land, and the environment—the traditional source of African livelihood, of African culture, and of African thought. Such a bond engendered a collective moral responsibility for the present and the future. This sacred bond is only one aspect of African religion, which underpins all African thought and action and which is expressed in an ongoing and unending process of divine creativity—not only through nature but through each human being. In such a continuum, the individual is seen as a replica of the external universe, which is why it makes sense for each being to always seek harmony with the physical laws of the natural environment.

In this respect, Christianity and Islam have not been absorbed in total, but have been Africanized. Indigenous African religion has always believed in one god whose many aspects are reflected in the many aspects of nature. God is both within and without creation, present in all things as one all-pervading life force. It is not animism, as it is so often described, but a kind of pantheism where nature is seen as an essential part of a system of vital forces, which exist in equilibrium and which continually nourish nature.

In the traditional African world view, therefore, there exists an analogy between the behavior of matter and that of human society. The world is seen as a duality of matter and spirit, both in the person and in the natural environment—the spiritual being manifested through the physical. In short, two dimensions of the same divine creation.

In traditional African communities, everyone participated in all cultural activities and decisions and in this way achieved personal fulfillment. Poverty and alienation did not exist. The indigenous cultures of Africa developed their own science of social engineering, which aimed to satisfy, to reconcile, to harmonize, and to adjust all overlapping, and often conflicting, claims and demands in order to give stability to a society, clan, or other grouping. The ultimate objectives were to enhance social well-being, to promote economic growth for members of society, and to give pride of place to the individual's moral nature amidst the process of social change.

There was a conscious effort to improve living conditions—by creating new wealth and spreading existing wealth among all classes of society—so that the scourges of deprivation, marginalization, and poverty that endanger equality and cohesion would always be kept to a minimum. Indigenous traditional culture aimed to ensure that the physical surroundings—land, water, trees, grass, and other forms of vegetation—were conserved and developed to help all members equitably, protecting the poorer members. Indigenous culture was committed to social justice, social management, and the popular participation of all members, which in turn produced a fundamental cultural ethic of mutual assistance and cooperation.

In Africa, this culture fully understood what the environment was all about—a natural habitat in which the human being lives and interacts and on which it depends for survival. It was recognized that harmony between the human being and the environment is an essential requirement for any sustainable livelihood and development and that the overall balance and well-being of both the human being and the environment are vital. Within this world view, the human condition became a challenge, because the emphasis was placed on the dependence of human beings on the quality, protection, and conservation of the natural physical surroundings. This dependence constituted an essential link between the human being and the environment, and individual members of a community were called on to consider and decide upon actions for the protection and conservation of the surroundings.

Since the African concept of community covered not only those living at any particular time but also the dead (ancestors) and those yet to be born—in a process of community continuity that was seen as part of divine creation—African traditional culture had a fundamentally ecological nature, recognizing the equality of the needs of present and future generations.

Such a traditional concept required Africans to live in harmony with nature and so avoid any disturbance of the delicate balance between satisfying the needs of all equitably and conserving and protecting the resource base of the natural environment. Traditional communities knew immediately if their patterns of demand were creating any environmental damage. The traditional African economy operated on the principle that each person had an inalienable right to basic need fulfillment—food, shelter, clothing, education, and health care, as well as emotional and spiritual satisfaction.

This imperative took priority over profit making. Any attempt by one person to exceed certain limits of personal acquisition was seen as a threat to the stability of the community and discouraged by community disapproval. Isolation from community norms, and therefore from the community itself, was seen as emotionally and physically intolerable, devastating. Thus, when it came to the environment and protecting the needs of those yet to be born, the threat of community sanctions worked to put a brake on the destruction of too many trees.

With the introduction of external development strategies devised in the name of some external self-interest, alien monocultures were imposed on traditional communities and their modes of production, further impoverishing already fragile soils. Pressure was exerted on governments to enforce capital intensive technological cultivation of agricultural products for export, at the direct expense of production for local food needs, thus contributing to the present levels of malnutrition in Africa.

For example, the irrigation systems brought to the Sahel have caused a drastic change in the level of the water table and an increase in salinity. Instead of reversing desertification, such measures have only served to increase it. Large-scale project dams have put large areas under water, increasing waterborne diseases and reducing soil fertility.

The recommended use of expensive fertilizers and chemicals has increased the costs of food production and made many thousands of African farmers redundant, while increasing crop disease. Forests have also been uprooted in the name of increasing exports according to the needs of the Western markets, with catastrophic implications for Africa's ecological balance.

The strategies of Western development not only ignored African indigenous knowledge and expertise, but saw African culture merely as an obstruction to its goals, a barrier that had to be removed. This tragic failure to recognize the strength, the capacity of resistance, the durability, and the creative force of African culture is one of the main reasons for the abject failure of these externally derived strategies and structures. If African culture had been seen as the real and only creative base for change, the story might have been very different.

Instead, African culture faced no alternative but to surrender its capacity for self-reliance, self-sufficiency, and sustainable levels of consumption, a capacity that had existed before colonization. Such a surrender has opened the door to inequality, class divisions and conflicts, social and political instability, economic decline, and all the human deprivation that goes with the loss of African cultural identity.

Crude, repressive, and ruthless dictatorships have been consistently supported externally and so have reigned—in exchange for their compliance with the interests of the patron powers. Indeed, many of the African elites must share responsibility for this tragic sequence of events. Africans must not underestimate the degree of complicity of their ruling elites in acting to marginalize and sometimes even to repress their own African culture—for their own narrow power and privilege interests. In such a situation, those African leaders who wished to preserve their people's indigenous cultural paths to self-reliance and to socioeconomic progress through alternative development strategies found themselves isolated and under external threat.

By making it almost impossible for Africans to live outside the neocolonial system, Western development strategies—from colonization to the present day—have divorced Africans from their traditional ways of living in harmony with their natural environment. The collapse of the traditional system of local community control over its own destiny was what marked the beginning of Africa's current crisis of socioeconomic, cultural, and political decline. However, African resistance to acculturation from outside has always been there, and very many Africans have continued to live according to their traditional cultural values, proving how durable African culture will always be.

The Western economic model, seen as the panacea for world economic development, has stressed the relationship between human beings and material possessions—on the basis of competition—in stark contrast to the African emphasis on a socioeconomic order that regulates more equitable and harmonious relationships among people and between people and their natural environment. Modern Western political economy is based on the concept of the human being as *homo economicus,* someone who puts cost-profit analysis before anything else. Such a concept is alien to African thought.

The present African tragedy is, in my view,

profoundly cultural and spiritual, rather than merely economic or technical. The attempt to destroy the African cultural base of daily living is at the heart of Africa's seeming inability to attain socioeconomic progress. It is not that Africans wish to return to the past as it was, but that Africans now know that they must have recourse to the past as an essential base for the future and for change, so that African culture may become the force for reconstructing African identity. Africa can then seek a cultural revolution that will enable and empower those changes necessary to meet Africa's own defined needs, within the world's realities.

Recognition of the African right to be different need not put an end to all forms of Western development. Africans can make constructive use of Western rationalism and expertise—just as long as they do not feel that their African identity is threatened or undermined in the process. Africans want to reacquire the right to decide for themselves what constitutes the "good life." The heart of the indigenous African culture's concept of self-reliance, all that constitutes their cultural identity, must become the basis for sustainable and ecologically sound African socioeconomic progress.

This is an environmental issue, in so far as self-reliance once again focuses economic activities on local needs and the careful sustainable use of local resources. Collective self-reliance has the ability to enable local autonomy, national self-determination, and self-development. But self-reliance itself depends on the existence of a nation's recourse to its own indigenous culture as its foundation, because it is the wisdom, skill, religion, and knowledge of the people that underpins their self-confidence in their own ability and in their own creativity.

Self-reliance is therefore an act of emancipation from all harmful forms of dependence-a fundamental factor in cultural identity and in the liberation of the African mind. Self-reliance erases excessive compartmentalism of the economic, political, social, and cultural spheres, uniting them into one culturally derived, sustainable, and locally understood means of progress.

Although Western-style economics and politics have acted to ignore the vital role of culture, a self-reliant culture must not ignore politics and economics. Africa does not deny the help and expertise of the West, but it wants to see this given on a more equitable basis of genuine partnership, in an alliance with the progressive forces of the North—a coming together in a joint effort to deal with the common problems of humanity, whose causes and manifestations cut across all borders and cultures, but which require the recognition that all peoples have the right to be different.

There is increasing evidence that many people in our world are recognizing this need for an alternative world order based on new concepts of what constitutes sustainable development for our common future and on a new mutual respect for the right to be different.

RECOMMENDED READINGS

Texts

Boylan, Michael. *Gewirth: Critical Essays on Action, Rationality and Community.* Lanham, MD: Rowman and Littlefield, 1999.
Ginsborg, Hanna. "Korsgaard on Choosing Nonmoral Ends," *Ethics* 1998: 5–21.
Guyer, Paul. "The Value of Reason and the Value of Freedom," *Ethics* 1998: 22–35.
Korsgaard, Christine, with G. A. Cohen, Raymond Geuss, Thomas Nagel, and Bernard William. *The Sources of Normativity.* New York: Cambridge University Press, 1996.
Regis, Edward. *Gewirth's Ethical Rationalism : Critical Essays with a Reply by Alan Gewirth.* Chicago: University of Chicago Press, 1984.
Schneewind, J. B. "Korsgaard and the Unconditional in Morality," *Ethics* 1998: 36–48.

Feminist Perspective

Held, Virginia. *Feminist morality: transforming culture, society, and politics.* Chicago: University of Chicago Press, 1993.
Lloyd, Genevieve. *The Man of Reason: "Male" and "Female" in Western Philosophy,* 2nd ed. Minneapolis: University of Minnesota Press, 1993.

Multicultural Perspective

Callicott, Baird. *Earth's Insights.* Berkeley: University of California Press, 1994.
Story Earth. Compiled by Inter Press Service. San Francisco: Mercury House, 1993.

PART XIII

༜༜

Martin Luther King Jr. and Carol Gilligan

INTRODUCTION

Martin Luther King Jr. was born in 1929 in Atlanta, Georgia. His mother was a schoolteacher before her marriage, and her father, Adam Daniel Williams, was pastor of the Ebenezer Baptist Church. When Williams died in 1931, Martin's father succeeded him as pastor of the church. In 1948, he graduated from Morehouse College, the alma mater of his father and grandfather. King attended the racially integrated Crozer Theological Seminary in Chester, Pennsylvania. In 1951, he obtained his B.D. and received the J. Lewis Crozer Fellowship for graduate study, which he decided to use at Boston University. While at Crozer, he took courses in philosophy at the University of Pennsylvania, and while at Boston University, he took courses in philosophy at Harvard University. He was awarded a Ph.D. in systematic theology in 1955. While he was still working on his dissertation, he accepted the post as pastor of the Dexter Avenue Baptist Church in Montgomery, Alabama, taking up residence in the city in 1954.

In 1955, Rosa Parks refused to give up her seat on a bus to a white person and was arrested. Her arrest led to a citywide boycott of buses organized by the Montgomery Improvement Association, of which King had become the president. During the course of the boycott, which lasted 382 days, King was arrested for driving thirty miles an hour in a twenty-five mile-an-hour zone, and his home was firebombed. In November of 1956, the U.S. Supreme Court declared unconstitutional Alabama's laws requiring segregation on buses, and a month later blacks and whites for the first time rode Montgomery buses on an unsegregated basis. From this victory, King emerged as a national hero of the civil rights movement. Black leaders from ten Southern states met in Ebenezer Baptist Church in 1957 to form what came to be called the Southern Christian Leadership Conference, and King was elected its first president. In 1963, he was arrested for defying a court order banning demonstrations in Birmingham. During his confinement he wrote "Letter from a Birmingham Jail." Tensions eased when black and white leaders negotiated a phased program of desegregation.

In 1963, King organized what until then was the largest civil rights demonstration in the history of the United States in Washington D.C. The highlight of the event was King's "I Have a Dream" speech. In the summer of 1964, Congress passed its ground-breaking Civil Rights Act, and later that year King received the Nobel Peace Prize. He also published his *Why We Can't Wait* in 1964. In Memphis, Tennessee in 1968, King was assassinated while supporting sanitation workers in their strike against the city.

In "Letter from a Birmingham Jail," King replies to white religious leaders of Birmingham—Catholic, Protestant, and Jewish—who criticized him for his "unwise and untimely actions." King responds to their criticism point by point. He argues that his Southern Christian Leadership Conference had been invited to Birmingham by a local affiliate, that negotiations had been tried, that they had waited a considerable time before calling for a demonstration, that although they had broken laws (such as parading without a permit), those laws were supporting injustice, and, moreover, their willingness to accept the penalty for such violations shows their ultimate respect for the law. King also blamed white moderates and white churches for contributing to racial injustice by their failure to take action against it.

In "I Have a Dream," King draws on the Bible, the U.S. Constitution, and the national anthem to inspire us to believe that America will yet live up to its promise of equality and freedom for all.

Carol Gilligan was born in New York City in 1936. Her father was a lawyer and her mother a teacher. She attended Swarthmore College, graduating in 1958. She earned an M.A. degree from Radcliffe College in 1960 and a Ph.D. in clinical psychology from Harvard University in 1964. In her dissertation, she demonstrated that young children who had been read stories about robber barons were more likely to cheat at games than children who had been read stories about honorable people. After receiving her degree, she worked as a dancer with an interracial modern dance company in Cleveland and became active in the peace and civil rights movements. In 1968, she returned to Harvard as a part-time psychology lecturer. She was promoted to assistant professor in 1971 and to associate professor in 1978. In 1986, she accepted a tenured professorship in the Graduate School of Education at Harvard. In 1983, she published *In A Different Voice: Psychological Theory and Women's Development,* in which she argued against the prevailing view that women's moral development tended to lag behind that of men. According to Gilligan, men and women do tend to make different moral judgments, but there is no basis for claiming the moral judgments of the men are better than the moral judgments of the women. All we can justifiably say is that they are different. *In A Different Voice* has been translated into nine languages and has sold more than 600,000 copies. In 1996, Gilligan was named by *Time* as one of the 25 most influential people in America. The magazine called *In A Different Voice* a book that changed "the rules of psychology." Gilligan is married to a psychiatrist, and they have three grown sons.

In "Moral Orientation and Moral Development," Carol Gilligan contrasts a caring perspective with a justice perspective. Using these perspectives as classificatory tools, Gilligan reports that 69 percent of her sample raised considerations of both justice and care, while 67 percent focused their attention on one set of concerns (with focus defined as 75 percent or more of the considerations raised pertaining either to justice or to care). It is significant that, with one exception, all of the men who focused, focused on justice. The women divided, with roughly one-third focusing on care and one-third on justice.

The conclusion that Gilligan want to draws from this research is that the caring perspective is an equally valid moral perspective, which has been disregarded in moral theory and psychological research because of male bias. To evaluate Gilligan's conclusion, we first need to elucidate the contrast between the two perspectives. If women and men differ with regard to the perspectives on which they tend to focus, it must be possible to distinguish clearly between the two perspectives. Otherwise bias could enter into the researcher's classification of people's reasons as belonging to one or the other perspective.

Consider Gilligan's example of two teenagers who disagree with their parents over religious views. On the one hand, the individual who is said to have a justice perspective asserts, "I have a right to my religious views," and then referring to his parents adds, "I respect their views." On the other hand, the individual who is said to have a caring perspective asserts, "I understand their fears of my religious ideas," and then adds, "but they really ought to listen to me and try to understand my beliefs." How distinct are these reasons? Couldn't a person's right to her religious views go beyond a negative right of noninterference and entail that family members at least listen to and try to understand one's beliefs? Likewise, couldn't understanding the fears one's parents have of one's different religious ideas be part of showing respect for their views? At one point, Gilligan characterizes the justice perspective by the injunction "not to act unfairly toward others" and the caring perspective by the injunction "do not turn away from someone in need." But these two injunctions are inextricably linked in some conceptions of justice. For example, in a welfare liberal conception of justice, to treat people fairly is to respond to their needs.

Sometimes Gilligan seem to think that a justice perspective is distinct from a caring perspective, because her understanding of a justice perspective is more restrictive than the previous characterizations would indicate. Thus, Gilligan sometimes describes the justice perspective as simply requiring a right of noninterference and a corresponding duty of others not to interfere. Similarly, the editors of a recent collection of essays inspired by Gilligan's work contend that in a justice perspective, "People are surely entitled to noninterference; they may not be entitled to aid." But this is to identify a justice perspective with a libertarian view that purports to reject rights to welfare and equal opportunity. Assuming this identification, we do find a contrast between a justice perspective and a caring perspective. But not only does this characterization of a justice perspective misrepresent the libertarian view which, when correctly interpreted, can be shown to require rights to welfare and equal opportunity,[1] it also fails to countenance our other conceptions of justice, like a welfare liberal conception of justice, which clearly go beyond a right to noninterference.

Now if we can't distinguish in theory between a justice perspective and a caring perspective, it is going to be impossible for researchers to use this distinction in practice to characterize people as focusing on one or the other perspective. Of course, people will tend to use the language of rights with the frequencies Gilligan observes, but we will have to look behind this usage to see what people are claiming when they use or don't use this language. If there is no viable theoretical distinction between a justice perspective and a caring perspective, people frequently will be found to express care and concern for the needs of others by using the language of rights. We are going to have to look behind the words people are using to discover when they are, in fact, showing insensitivity to the needs of others. When we can determine that, we will also be in a position to determine whether such insensitivity is more characteristic of men than women. For example, one might argue, as I do in Selection 47, that we are likely to observe more altruism than egoism among women, particularly with respect to the care of their families.

NOTES

1. See my *Justice for Here and Now* (New York: Cambridge University Press, 1998) Chapter 3.

49. LETTER FROM BIRMINGHAM CITY JAIL

MARTIN LUTHER KING JR.

My dear Fellow Clergymen,

While confined here in the Birmingham City Jail, I came across your recent statement calling our present activities "unwise and untimely." Seldom, if ever, do I pause to answer criticism of my work and ideas. If I sought to answer all of the criticisms that cross my desk, my secretaries would be engaged in little else in the course of the day, and I would have no time for constructive work. But since I feel that you are men of genuine goodwill and your criticisms are sincerely set forth, I would like to answer your statement in what I hope will be patient and reasonable terms.

I think I should give the reason for my being in Birmingham, since you have been influenced by the argument of "outsiders coming in." I have the honor of serving as president of the Southern Christian Leadership Conference, an organization operating in every Southern state, with headquarters in Atlanta, Georgia. We have some eighty-five affiliate organizations all across the South—one being the Alabama Christian Movement for Human Rights. Whenever necessary and possible we share staff, educational and financial resources with our affiliates. Several months ago our local affiliate here in Birmingham invited us to be on call to engage in a nonviolent direct action program if such were deemed necessary. We readily consented and when the hour came we lived up to our promises. So I am

here, along with several members of my staff, because we were invited here. I am here because I have basic organizational ties here.

Beyond this, I am in Birmingham because injustice is here. Just as the eighth century prophets left their little villages and carried their "thus saith the Lord" far beyond the boundaries of their home towns; and just as the Apostle Paul left his little village of Tarsus and carried the gospel of Jesus Christ to practically every hamlet and city of the Graeco-Roman world, I too am compelled to carry the gospel of freedom beyond my particular home town. Like Paul, I must constantly respond to the Macedonian call for aid.

Moreover, I am cognizant of the interrelatedness of all communities and states. I cannot sit idly by in Atlanta and not be concerned about what happens in Birmingham. *Injustice anywhere is a threat to justice everywhere.* We are caught in an inescapable network of mutuality, tied in a single garment of destiny. Whatever affects one directly affects all indirectly. Never again can we afford to live with the narrow, provincial "outside agitator" idea. Anyone who lives inside the United States can never be considered an outsider anywhere in this country.

You deplore the demonstrations that are presently taking place in Birmingham. But I am sorry that your statement did not express a similar concern for the conditions that brought the demonstrations into being. I am sure that each of you would want to go beyond the superficial social analyst who looks merely at effects, and does not grapple with underlying causes. I would not hesitate to say that it is unfortunate that so-called demonstrations are taking place in Birmingham at this time, but I would say in more emphatic terms that it is even more unfortunate that the white power structure of this city left the Negro community with no other alternative.

In any nonviolent campaign there are four basic steps: 1) Collection of the facts to determine whether injustices are alive. 2) Negotiation. 3) Self-purification and 4) Direct Action. We have gone through all of these steps in Birmingham. There can be no gainsaying of the fact that racial injustice engulfs this community.

Birmingham is probably the most thoroughly segregated city in the United States. Its ugly record of police brutality is known in every section of this country. Its injust treatment of Negroes in the courts is a notorious reality. There have been more unsolved bombings of Negro homes and churches in Birmingham than any city in this nation. These are the hard, brutal and unbelievable facts. On the basis of these conditions Negro leaders sought to negotiate with the city fathers. But the political leaders consistently refused to engage in good faith negotiation.

Then came the opportunity last September to talk with some of the leaders of the economic community. In these negotiating sessions certain promises were made by the merchants-such as the promise to remove the humiliating racial signs from the stores. On the basis of these promises Rev. Shuttlesworth and the leaders of the Alabama Christian Movement for Human Rights agreed to call a moratorium on any type of demonstrations. As the weeks and months unfolded we realized that we were the victims of a broken promise. The signs remained. Like so many experiences of the past we were confronted with blasted hopes, and the dark shadow of a deep disappointment settled upon us. So we had no alternative except that of preparing for direct action, whereby we would present our very bodies as a means of laying our case before the conscience of the local and national community. We were not unmindful of the difficulties involved. So we decided to go through a process of self-purification. We started having workshops on nonviolence and repeatedly asked ourselves the questions, "Are you able to accept blows without retaliating?" "Are you able to endure the ordeals of jail?" We decided to set our direct action program around the Easter season, realizing that with the exception of Christmas, this was the largest shopping period of the year. Knowing that a strong economic withdrawal program would be the by-product of direct action, we felt that this was the best time to bring pressure on the merchants for the needed changes. Then it occurred to us that the March election was ahead and so we speedily decided to postpone action until after election day. When we discovered that Mr. Connor was in the run-off, we decided again to postpone action so that the demonstrations could not be used to cloud the issues. At this time we agreed to begin our nonviolent witness the day after the run-off.

This reveals that we did not move irresponsibly into direct action. We too wanted to see Mr. Connor defeated; so we went through postponement after postponement to aid in this community need. After this we felt that direct action could be delayed no longer.

You may well ask, "Why direct action? Why sit-ins, marches, etc.? Isn't negotiation a better path?" You are exactly right in your call for negotiation. Indeed, this is the purpose of direct action. Nonviolent direct action seeks to create such a crisis and establish such creative tension that a community that has constantly refused to negotiate is forced to confront the issue. It seeks so to dramatize the issue that it can no longer be ignored. I just referred to the creation of tension as a part of the work of the nonviolent resister. This may sound rather shocking. But I must confess that I am not afraid of the word tension. I have earnestly worked and preached against violent tension, but there is a type of constructive nonviolent tension that is necessary for growth. Just as Socrates felt that it was necessary to create a tension in the mind so that individuals could rise from the bondage of myths and half-truths to the unfettered realm of creative analysis and objective appraisal, we must see the need of having nonviolent gadflies to create the kind of tension in society that will help men to rise from the dark depths of prejudice and racism to the majestic heights of understanding and brotherhood. So the purpose of the direct action is to create a situation so crisis-packed that it will inevitably open the door to negotiation. We, therefore, concur with you in your call for negotiation. Too long has our beloved Southland been bogged down in the tragic attempt to live in monologue rather than dialogue.

One of the basic points in your statement is that our acts are untimely. Some have asked, "Why didn't you give the new administration time to act?" The only answer that I can give to this inquiry is that the new administration must be prodded about as much as the outgoing one before it acts. We will be sadly mistaken if we feel that the election of Mr. Boutwell will bring the millennium to Birmingham. While Mr. Boutwell is much more articulate and gentle than Mr. Connor, they are both segregationists, dedicated to the task of maintaining the status quo. The hope I see in Mr. Boutwell is that he will be reasonable enough to see the futility of massive resistance to desegregation. But he will not see this without pressure from the devotees of civil rights. My friends, I must say to you that we have not made a single gain in civil rights without determined legal and nonviolent pressure. History is the long and tragic story of the fact that privileged groups seldom give up their privileges voluntarily. Individuals may see the moral light and voluntarily give up their unjust posture; but as Reinhold Niebuhr has reminded us, groups are more immoral than individuals.

We know through painful experience that freedom is never voluntarily given by the oppressor; it must be demanded by the oppressed. Frankly, I have never yet engaged in a direct action movement that was "well timed," according to the timetable of those who have not suffered unduly from the disease of segregation.

For years now I have heard the words "Wait!" It rings in the ear of every Negro with a piercing familiarity. This "Wait" has almost always meant "Never." It has been a tranquilizing thalidomide, relieving the emotional stress for a moment, only to give birth to an ill-formed infant of frustration. We must come to see with the distinguished jurist of yesterday that "justice too long delayed is justice denied." We have waited for more than three hundred and forty years for our constitutional and God-given rights. The nations of Asia and Africa are moving with jet-like speed toward the goal of political independence, and we still creep at horse and buggy pace toward the gaining of a cup of coffee at a lunch counter. I guess it is easy for those who have never felt the stinging darts of segregation to say, "Wait." But when you have seen vicious mobs lynch your mothers and fathers at will and drown your sisters and brothers at whim; when you have seen hate-filled policemen curse, kick, brutalize and even kill your black brothers and sisters with impunity; when you see the vast majority of your twenty million Negro brothers smothering in an air-tight cage of poverty in the midst of an affluent society; when you suddenly find your tongue twisted and your speech stammering as you seek to explain to your six-year-old daughter why she can't go to the public amusement park that has just been advertised on television, and see tears welling up in her little eyes when she is told that Funtown is closed to colored children, and see the depressing clouds of inferiority begin to form in her little mental sky, and see her begin to distort her little personality by unconsciously developing a bitterness toward white people; when you have to concoct an answer for a five-year-old son asking in agonizing pathos: "Daddy, why do white people treat colored people so mean?"; when you take a cross country drive and find it necessary to sleep night after night in the uncomfortable corners of your automobile because no motel will accept you; when you are humiliated day in and day out by nagging signs reading "white" and "colored";

when your first name becomes "nigger" and your middle name becomes "boy" (however old you are) and your last name becomes "John," and when your wife and mother are never given the respected title "Mrs."; when you are harried by day and haunted at night by the fact that you are a Negro, living constantly at tip-toe stance never quite knowing what to expect next, and plagued with inner fears and outer resentments; when you are forever fighting a degenerating sense of "nobodiness"; then you will understand why we find it difficult to wait. There comes a time when the cup of endurance runs over, and men are no longer willing to be plunged into an abyss of injustice where they experience the blackness of corroding despair. I hope, sirs, you can understand our legitimate and unavoidable impatience.

You express a great deal of anxiety over our willingness to break laws. This is certainly a legitimate concern. Since we so diligently urge people to obey the Supreme Court's decision of 1954 outlawing segregation in the public schools, it is rather strange and paradoxical to find us consciously breaking laws. One may well ask, "How can you advocate breaking some laws and obeying others?" The answer is found in the fact that there are two types of laws: There are *just* and there are *unjust* laws. I would agree with Saint Augustine that "An unjust law is no law at all."

Now what is the difference between the two? How does one determine when a law is just or unjust? A just law is a man-made code that squares with the moral law or the law of God. An unjust law is a code that is out of harmony with the moral law. To put it in the terms of Saint Thomas Aquinas, an unjust law is a human law that is not rooted in eternal and natural law. Any law that uplifts human personality is just. Any law that degrades human personality is unjust. All segregation statutes are unjust because segregation distorts the soul and damages the personality. It gives the segregator a false sense of superiority, and the segregated a false sense of inferiority. To use the words of Martin Buber, the great Jewish philosopher, segregation substitutes an "I-it" relationship for the "I-thou" relationship, and ends up relegating persons to the status of things. So segregation is not only politically, economically and sociologically unsound, but it is morally wrong and sinful. Paul Tillich has said that sin is separation. Isn't segregation an existential expression of man's tragic separation, an expression of his awful estrangement, his terrible sinfulness? So I can urge men to disobey segregation ordinances because they are morally wrong.

Let us turn to a more concrete example of just and unjust laws. An unjust law is a code that a majority inflicts on a minority that is not binding on itself. This is difference made legal. On the other hand a just law is a code that a majority compels a minority to follow that it is willing to follow itself. This is sameness made legal.

Let me give another explanation. An unjust law is a code inflicted upon a minority which that minority had no part in enacting or creating because they did not have the unhampered right to vote. Who can say that the legislature of Alabama which set up the segregation laws was democratically elected? Throughout the state of Alabama all types of conniving methods are used to prevent Negroes from becoming registered voters and there are some counties without a single Negro registered to vote despite the fact that the Negro constitutes a majority of the population. Can any law set up in such a state be considered democratically structured?

These are just a few examples of unjust and just laws. There are some instances when a law is just on its face and unjust in its application. For instance, I was arrested Friday on a charge of parading without a permit. Now there is nothing wrong with an ordinance which requires a permit for a parade, but when the ordinance is used to preserve segregation and to deny citizens the First Amendment privilege of peaceful assembly and peaceful protest, then it becomes unjust.

I hope you can see the distinction I am trying to point out. In no sense do I advocate evading or defying the law as the rabid segregationist would do. This would lead to anarchy. One who breaks an unjust law must do it *openly, lovingly* (not hatefully as the white mothers did in New Orleans when they were seen on television screaming "nigger, nigger, nigger"), and with a willingness to accept the penalty. I submit that an individual who breaks a law that conscience tells him is unjust, and willingly accepts the penalty by staying in jail to arouse the conscience of the community over its injustice, is in reality expressing the very highest respect for law.

Of course, there is nothing new about this kind of civil disobedience. It was seen sublimely in the refusal of Shadrach, Meshach and Abednego to obey the laws of Nebuchadnezzar because a higher moral law was involved. It was practiced superbly by the early Christians who were willing to face hungry lions and the excruciating pain of chopping blocks, before submitting to certain unjust laws of the Roman empire. To a degree academic freedom is a reality today because Socrates practiced civil disobedience.

We can never forget that everything Hitler did in Germany was "legal" and everything the Hungarian freedom fighters did in Hungary was "illegal." It was "illegal" to aid and comfort a Jew in Hitler's Germany. But I am sure that if I had lived in Germany during that time I would have aided and comforted my Jewish brothers even though it was illegal. If I lived in a Communist country today where certain principles dear to the Christian faith are suppressed, I believe I would openly advocate disobeying these anti-religious laws. I must make two honest confessions to you, my Christian and Jewish brothers. First, I must confess that over the last few years I have been gravely disappointed with the white moderate. I have almost reached the regrettable conclusion that the Negro's great stumbling block in the stride toward freedom is not the White Citizen's Council-er or the Ku Klux Klanner, but the white moderate who is more devoted to "order" than to justice; who prefers a negative peace which is the absence of tension to a positive peace which is the presence of justice; who constantly says, "I agree with you in the goal you seek, but I can't agree with your methods of direct action"; who paternalistically feels that he can set the timetable for another man's freedom; who lives by the myth of time and who constantly advises the Negro to wait until a "more convenient season." Shallow understanding from people of goodwill is more frustrating than absolute misunderstanding from people of ill will. Lukewarm acceptance is much more bewildering than outright rejection.

I had hoped that the white moderate would understand that law and order exist for the purpose of establishing justice, and that when they fail to do this they become dangerously structured dams that block the flow of social progress. I had hoped that the white moderate would understand that the present tension of the South is merely a necessary phase of the transition from an obnoxious negative peace, where the Negro passively accepted his unjust plight, to a substance-filled positive peace, where all men will respect the dignity and worth of human personality. Actually, we who engage in nonviolent direct action are not the creators of tension. We merely bring to the surface the hidden tension that is already alive. We bring it out in the open where it can be seen and dealt with. Like a boil that can never be cured as long as it is covered up but must be opened with all its pus-flowing ugliness to the natural medicines of air and light, injustice must likewise be exposed, with all of the tension its exposing creates, to the light of human conscience and the air of national opinion before it can be cured.

In your statement you asserted that our actions, even though peaceful, must be condemned because they precipitate violence. But can this assertion be logically made? Isn't this like condemning the robbed man because his possession of money precipitated the evil act of robbery? Isn't this like condemning Socrates

544   MARTIN LUTHER KING JR. AND CAROL GILLIGAN

because his unswerving commitment to truth and his philosophical delvings precipitated the misguided popular mind to make him drink the hemlock? Isn't this like condemning Jesus because His unique God-Consciousness and never-ceasing devotion to His will precipitated the evil act of crucifixion? We must come to see, as federal courts have consistently affirmed, that it is immoral to urge an individual to withdraw his efforts to gain his basic constitutional rights because the quest precipitates violence. Society must protect the robbed and punish the robber.

I had also hoped that the white moderate would reject the myth of time. I received a letter this morning from a white brother in Texas which said: "All Christians know that the colored people will receive equal rights eventually, but it is possible that you are in too great of a religious hurry. It has taken Christianity almost 2000 years to accomplish what it has. The teachings of Christ take time to come to earth." All that is said here grows out of a tragic misconception of time. It is the strangely irrational notion that there is something in the very flow of time that will inevitably cure all ills. Actually time is neutral. It can be used either destructively or constructively. I am coming to feel that the people of ill will have used time much more effectively than the people of goodwill. We will have to repent in this generation not merely for the vitriolic words and actions of the bad people, but for the appalling silence of the good people. We must come to see that human progress never rolls in on wheels of inevitability. It comes through the tireless efforts and persistent work of men willing to be co-workers with God, and without this hard work time itself becomes an ally of the forces of social stagnation. We must use time creatively, and forever realize that the time is always ripe to do right. Now is the time to make real the promise of democracy, and transform our pending national elegy into a creative psalm of brotherhood. Now is the time to lift our national policy from the quicksand of racial injustice to the solid rock of human dignity.

You spoke of our activity in Birmingham as extreme. At first I was rather disappointed that fellow clergymen would see my nonviolent efforts as those of the extremist. I started thinking about the fact that I stand in the middle of two opposing forces in the Negro community. One is a force of complacency made up of Negroes who, as a result of long years of oppression, have been so completely drained of self-respect and a sense of "somebodiness" that they have adjusted to segregation, and, of a few Negroes in the middle class who, because of a degree of academic and economic security, and because at points they profit by segregation, have unconsciously become insensitive to the problems of the masses. The other force is one of bitterness and hatred, and comes perilously close to advocating violence. It is expressed in the various black nationalist groups that are springing up over the nation, the largest and best known being Elijah Muhammad's Muslim movement. This movement is nourished by the contemporary frustration over the continued existence of racial discrimination. It is made up of people who have lost faith in America, who have absolutely repudiated Christianity, and who have concluded that the white man is an incurable "devil." I have tried to stand between these two forces, saying that we need not follow the "donothingism" of the complacent or the hatred and despair of the black nationalist. There is the more excellent way of love and nonviolent protest. I'm grateful to God that, through the Negro church, the dimension of nonviolence entered our struggle. If this philosophy had not emerged, I am convinced that by now many streets of the South would be flowing with floods of blood. And I am further convinced that if our white brothers dismiss as "rabble rousers" and "outside agitators" those of us who are working through the channels of nonviolent direct action and refuse to support our nonviolent efforts, millions of Negroes, out of frustration and despair, will seek solace and security in black nationalist ideologies, a development that will lead inevitably to a frightening racial nightmare.

Oppressed people cannot remain oppressed

forever. The urge for freedom will eventually come. This is what happened to the American Negro. Something within has reminded him of his birthright of freedom; something without has reminded him that he can gain it. Consciously and unconsciously, he has been swept in by what the Germans call the *Zeitgeist,* and with his black brothers of Africa, and his brown and yellow brothers of Asia, South America and the Caribbean, he is moving with a sense of cosmic urgency toward the promised land of racial justice. Recognizing this vital urge that has engulfed the Negro community, one should readily understand public demonstrations. The Negro has many pent-up resentments and latent frustrations. He has to get them out. So let him march sometime; let him have his prayer pilgrimages to the city hall; understand why he must have sit-ins and freedom rides. If his repressed emotions do not come out in these nonviolent ways, they will come out in ominous expressions of violence. This is not a threat; it is a fact of history. So I have not said to my people "get rid of your discontent." But I have tried to say that this normal and healthy discontent can be channelized through the creative outlet of nonviolent direct action. Now this approach is being dismissed as extremist. I must admit that I was initially disappointed in being so categorized.

But as I continued to think about the matter I gradually gained a bit of satisfaction from being considered an extremist. Was not Jesus an extremist in love—"Love your enemies, bless them that curse you, pray for them that despitefully use you." Was not Amos an extremist for justice—"Let justice roll down like waters and righteousness like a mighty stream." Was not Paul an extremist for the gospel of Jesus Christ—"I bear in my body the marks of the Lord Jesus." Was not Martin Luther an extremist—"Here I stand; I can do none other so help me God." Was not John Bunyan an extremist—"I will stay in jail to the end of my days before I make a butchery of my conscience." Was not Abraham Lincoln an extremist—"This nation cannot survive half slave and half free." Was not

Thomas Jefferson an extremist—"We hold these truths to be self-evident, that all men are created equal." So the question is not whether we will be extremist but what kind of extremist will we be. Will we be extremists for hate or will we be extremists for love? Will we be extremists for the preservation of injustice—or will we be extremists for the cause of justice? In that dramatic scene on Calvary's hill, three men were crucified. We must not forget that all three were crucified for the same crime—the crime of extremism. Two were extremists for immorality, and thusly fell below their environment. The other, Jesus Christ, was an extremist for love, truth and goodness, and thereby rose above his environment. So, after all, maybe the South, the nation and the world are in dire need of creative extremists.

I had hoped that the white moderate would see this. Maybe I was too optimistic. Maybe I expected too much. I guess I should have realized that few members of a race that has oppressed another race can understand or appreciate the deep groans and passionate yearnings of those that have been oppressed and still fewer have the vision to see that injustice must be rooted out by strong, persistent and determined action. I am thankful, however, that some of our white brothers have grasped the meaning of this social revolution and committed themselves to it. They are still all too small in quantity, but they are big in quality. Some like Ralph McGill, Lillian Smith, Harry Golden and James Dabbs have written about our struggle in eloquent, prophetic and understanding terms. Others have marched with us down nameless streets of the South. They have languished in filthy roach-infested jails, suffering the abuse and brutality of angry policemen who see them as "dirty nigger lovers." They, unlike so many of their moderate brothers and sisters, have recognized the urgency of the moment and sensed the need for powerful "action" antidotes to combat the disease of segregation.

Let me rush on to mention my other disappointment. I have been so greatly disappointed with the white church and its leadership. Of course, there are some notable exceptions. I am not unmindful of the fact that each of you has taken some significant stands on this issue. I commend you, Rev. Stallings, for your Christian stand on this past Sunday, in welcoming Negroes to your worship service on a non-segregated basis. I commend the Catholic leaders of this state for integrating Springhill College several years ago.

But despite these notable exceptions I must honestly reiterate that I have been disappointed with the church. I do not say that as one of the negative critics who can always find something wrong with the church. I say it as a minister of the gospel, who loves the church; who was nurtured in its bosom; who has been sustained by its spiritual blessings and who will remain true to it as long as the cord of life shall lengthen.

I had the strange feeling when I was suddenly catapulted into the leadership of the bus protest in Montgomery several years ago that we would have the support of the white church. I felt that the white ministers, priests and rabbis of the South would be some of our strongest allies. Instead, some have been outright opponents, refusing to understand the freedom movement and misrepresenting its leaders; all too many others have been more cautious than courageous and have remained silent behind the anesthetizing security of the stained-glass windows.

In spite of my shattered dreams of the past, I came to Birmingham with the hope that the white religious leadership of this community would see the justice of our cause, and with deep moral concern, serve as the channel through which our just grievances would get to the power structure. I had hoped that each of you would understand. But again I have been disappointed. I have heard numerous religious leaders of the South call upon their worshippers to comply with a desegregation decision because it is the *law,* but I have longed to hear white ministers say, "Follow this decree because integration is morally *right* and the Negro is

your brother." In the midst of blatant injustices inflicted upon the Negro, I have watched white churches stand on the sideline and merely mouth pious irrelevancies and sanctimonious trivialities. In the midst of a mighty struggle to rid our nation of racial and economic injustice, I have heard so many ministers say, "Those are social issues with which the gospel has no real concern," and I have watched so many churches commit themselves to a completely other-worldly religion which made a strange distinction between body and soul, the sacred and the secular.

So here we are moving toward the exit of the twentieth century with a religious community largely adjusted to the status quo, standing as a tail-light behind other community agencies rather than a headlight leading men to higher levels of justice.

I have traveled the length and breadth of Alabama, Mississippi and all the other southern states. On sweltering summer days and crisp autumn mornings I have looked at her beautiful churches with their lofty spires pointing heavenward. I have beheld the impressive outlay of her massive religious education buildings. Over and over again I have found myself asking: "What kind of people worship here? Who is their God? Where were their voices when the lips of Governor Barnett dripped with words of interposition and nullification? Where were they when Governor Wallace gave the clarion call for defiance and hatred? Where were their voices of support when tired, bruised and weary Negro men and women decided to rise from the dark dungeons of complacency to the bright hills of creative protest?"

Yes, these questions are still in my mind. In deep disappointment, I have wept over the laxity of the church. But be assured that my tears have been tears of love. There can be no deep disappointment where there is not deep love. Yes, I love the church; I love her sacred walls. How could I do otherwise? I am in the rather unique position of being the son, the grandson and the great-grandson of preachers. Yes, I see the church as the body of Christ. But, oh! How we have blemished and scarred that body through social neglect and fear of being nonconformists.

There was a time when the church was very powerful. It was during that period when the early Christians rejoiced when they were deemed worthy to suffer for what they believed. In those days the church was not merely a thermometer that recorded the ideas and principles of popular opinion; it was a thermostat that transformed the mores of society. Wherever the early Christians entered a town the power structure got disturbed and immediately sought to convict them for being "disturbers of the peace" and "outside agitators." But they went on with the conviction that they were "a colony of heaven," and had to obey God rather than man. They were small in number but big in commitment. They were too God-intoxicated to be "astronomically intimidated." They brought an end to such ancient evils as infanticide and gladiatorial contest.

Things are different now. The contemporary church is often a weak, ineffectual voice with an uncertain sound. It is so often the arch supporter of the status quo. Far from being disturbed by the presence of the church, the power structure of the average community is consoled by the church's silent and often vocal sanction of things as they are.

But the judgment of God is upon the church as never before. If the church of today does not recapture the sacrificial spirit of the early church, it will lose its authentic ring, forfeit the loyalty of millions, and be dismissed as an irrelevant social club with no meaning for the twentieth century. I am meeting young people every day whose disappointment with the church has risen to outright disgust.

Maybe again, I have been too optimistic. Is organized religion too inextricably bound to the status quo to save our nation and the world? Maybe I must turn my faith to the inner spiritual church, the church within the church, as the true

ecclesia and the hope of the world. But again I am thankful to God that some noble souls from the ranks of organized religion have broken loose from the paralyzing chains of conformity and joined us as active partners in the struggle for freedom. They have left their secure congregations and walked the streets of Albany, Georgia, with us. They have gone through the highways of the South on tortuous rides for freedom. Yes, they have gone to jail with us. Some have been kicked out of their churches, and lost support of their bishops and fellow ministers. But they have gone with the faith that right defeated is stronger than evil triumphant. These men have been the leaven in the lump of the race. Their witness has been the spiritual salt that has preserved the true meaning of the Gospel in these troubled times. They have carved a tunnel of hope through the dark mountain of disappointment.

I hope the church as a whole will meet the challenge of this decisive hour. But even if the church does not come to the aid of justice, I have no despair about the future. I have no fear about the outcome of our struggle in Birmingham, even if our motives are presently misunderstood. We will reach the goal of freedom in Birmingham and all over the nation, because the goal of America is freedom. Abused and scorned though we may be, our destiny is tied up with the destiny of America. Before the pilgrims landed at Plymouth we were here. Before the pen of Jefferson etched across the pages of history the majestic words of the Declaration of Independence, we were here. For more than two centuries our foreparents labored in this country without wages; they made cotton king; and they built the homes of their masters in the midst of brutal injustice and shameful humiliation—and yet out of a bottomless vitality they continued to thrive and develop. If the inexpressible cruelties of slavery could not stop us, the opposition we now face will surely fail. We will win our freedom because the sacred heritage of our nation and the eternal will of God are embodied in our echoing demands.

I must close now. But before closing I am impelled to mention one other point in your statement that troubled me profoundly. You warmly commended the Birmingham police force for keeping "order" and "preventing violence." I don't believe you would have so warmly commended the police force if you had seen its angry violent dogs literally biting six unarmed, nonviolent Negroes. I don't believe you would so quickly commend the policemen if you would observe their ugly and inhuman treatment of Negroes here in the city jail; if you would watch them push and curse old Negro women and young Negro girls; if you would see them slap and kick old Negro men and young boys; if you will observe them, as they did on two occasions, refuse to give us food because we wanted to sing our grace together. I'm sorry that I can't join you in your praise for the police department.

It is true that they have been rather disciplined in their public handling of the demonstrators. In this sense they have been rather publicly "nonviolent." But for what purpose? To preserve the evil system of segregation. Over the last few years I have consistently preached that nonviolence demands that the means we use must be as pure as the ends we seek. So I have tried to make it clear that it is wrong to use immoral means to attain moral ends. But now I must affirm that it is just as wrong, or even more so, to use moral means to preserve immoral ends. Maybe Mr. Connor and his policemen have been rather publicly nonviolent, as Chief Pritchett was in Albany, Georgia, but they have used the moral means of nonviolence to maintain the immoral end of flagrant racial injustice. T. S. Eliot has said that there is no greater treason than to do the right deed for the wrong reason.

I wish you had commended the Negro sitinners and demonstrators of Birmingham for their subline courage, their willingness of suffer and their amazing discipline in the midst of the most inhuman provocation. One day the South will recognize its real heroes. They will be the James Merediths, courageously and with a majestic sense of purpose facing jeering and hostile mobs and the agonizing loneliness that characterizes the life of the pioneer. They will be old, oppressed, battered Negro women, symbolized in a seventy-two year old woman of Montgomery, Alabama, who rose up with a sense of dignity and with her people decided not to ride the segregated buses, and responded to one who inquired about her tiredness with ungrammatical profundity: "My feet is tired, but my soul is rested." They will be the young high school and college students, young ministers of the Gospel and a host of their elders courageously and nonviolently sitting-in at lunch counters and willingly going to jail for conscience's sake. One day the South will know that when these disinherited children of God sat down at lunch counters they were in reality standing up for the best in the American dream and the most sacred values in our Judeo-Christian heritage, and thusly, carrying our whole nation back to those great wells of democracy which were dug deep by the founding fathers in the formulation of the Constitution and the Declaration of Independence.

Never before have I written a letter this long (or should I say a book?). I'm afraid that it is much too long to take your precious time. I can assure you that it would have been much shorter if I had been writing from a comfortable desk, but what else is there to do when you are alone for days in the dull monotony of a narrow jail cell other than write long letters, think strange thoughts, and pray long prayers?

If I have said anything in this letter that is an overstatement of the truth and is indicative of an unreasonable impatience, I beg you to forgive me. If I have said anything in this letter that is an understatement of the truth and is indicative of my having a patience that makes me patient with anything less than brotherhood, I beg God to forgive me.

I hope this letter finds you strong in the faith. I also hope that circumstances will soon make it possible for me to meet each of you, not as an integrationist or a civil-rights leader, but as a fellow clergyman and a Christian brother. Let us all hope that the dark clouds of racial prejudice will soon pass away and the deep fog of misunderstanding will be lifted from our fear-drenched communities and in some not too distant tomorrow the radiant stars of love and brotherhood will shine over our great nation with all of their scintillating beauty.

Yours for the cause of Peace and Brotherhood,

Martin Luther King, Jr.

50. I Have a Dream

MARTIN LUTHER KING JR.

I am happy to join with you today in what will go down in history as the greatest demonstration for freedom in the history of our nation.

Fivescore years ago, a great American, in whose symbolic shadow we stand today, signed the Emancipation Proclamation. This momentous decree came as a great beacon light of hope to millions of Negro slaves who had been seared in the flames of withering injustice. It came as a joyous daybreak to end the long night of their captivity.

But one hundred years later, the Negro still is not free; one hundred years later, the life of the Negro is still sadly crippled by the manacles of segregation and the chains of discrimination; one hundred years later, the Negro lives on a lonely island of poverty in the midst of a vast ocean of material prosperity; one hundred years later, the Negro is still languished in the corners of American society and finds himself in exile in his own land.

Reprinted from "I Have a Dream" *Congressional Record*, Vol. 109, September 3, 1963.

So we've come here today to dramatize a shameful condition. In a sense we've come to our nation's capital to cash a check. When the architects of our republic wrote the magnificent words of the Constitution and the Declaration of Independence, they were signing a promissory note to which every American was to fall heir. This note was the promise that all men, yes, black men as well as white men, would be guaranteed the unalienable rights of life, liberty, and the pursuit of happiness.

It is obvious today that America has defaulted on this promissory note in so far as her citizens of color are concerned. Instead of honoring this sacred obligation, America has given the Negro people a bad check; a check which has come back marked "insufficient funds." We refuse to believe that there are insufficient funds in the great vaults of opportunity of this nation. And so we've come to cash this check, a check that will give us upon demand the riches of freedom and the security of justice.

We have also come to this hallowed spot to remind America of the fierce urgency of now. This is no time to engage in the luxury of cool-

ing off or to take the tranquilizing drug of grad-
ualism. Now is the time to make real the promises of democracy; now is the time to rise from
the dark and desolate valley of segregation to the
sunlit path of racial justice; now is the time to lift
our nation from the quicksands of racial injustice to the solid rock of brotherhood; now is the
time to make justice a reality for all God's children. It would be fatal for the nation to overlook
the urgency of the moment. This sweltering
summer of the Negro's legitimate discontent
will not pass until there is an invigorating
autumn of freedom and equality.

Nineteen sixty-three is not an end, but a
beginning. And those who hope that the Negro
needed to blow off steam and will now be content, will have a rude awakening if the nation
returns to business as usual.

There will be neither rest nor tranquility in
America until the Negro is granted his citizenship rights. The whirlwinds of revolt will continue to shake the foundations of our nation
until the bright day of justice emerges.

But there is something that I must say to my
people who stand on the warm threshold which
leads into the palace of justice. In the process of
gaining our rightful place we must not be guilty
of wrongful deeds.

Let us not seek to satisfy our thirst for freedom by drinking from the cup of bitterness and
hatred. We must forever conduct our struggle
on the high plane of dignity and discipline. We
must not allow our creative protest to degenerate
into physical violence. Again and again we must
rise to the majestic heights of meeting physical
force with soul force.

The marvelous new militancy which has
engulfed the Negro community must not lead us
to a distrust of all white people, for many of our
white brothers, as evidenced by their presence
here today, have come to realize that their destiny is tied up with our destiny and they have
come to realize that their freedom is inextricably
bound to our freedom. This offense we share
mounted to storm the battlements of injustice

must be carried forth by a biracial army. We cannot walk alone.

And as we walk, we must make the pledge
that we shall always march ahead. We cannot
turn back. There are those who are asking the
devotees of civil rights, "When will you be satisfied?" We can never be satisfied as long as the
Negro is the victim of the unspeakable horrors
of police brutality.

We can never be satisfied as long as our bodies, heavy with fatigue of travel, cannot gain
lodging in the motels of the highways and the
hotels of the cities. We cannot be satisfied as long
as the Negro's basic mobility is from a smaller
ghetto to a larger one.

We can never be satisfied as long as our children are stripped of their selfhood and robbed of
their dignity by signs stating "for whites only."
We cannot be satisfied as long as a Negro in Mississippi cannot vote and a Negro in New York
believes he has nothing for which to vote. No, we
are not satisfied, and we will not be satisfied until
justice rolls down like waters and righteousness
like a mighty stream.

I am not unmindful that some of you have
come here out of excessive trials and tribulation.
Some of you have come fresh from narrow jail
cells. Some of you have come from areas where
your quest for freedom left you battered by the
storms of persecution and staggered by the
winds of police brutality. You have been the vet-
erans of creative suffering. Continue to work
with the faith that unearned suffering is
redemptive.

Go back to Mississippi; go back to Alabama;
go back to South Carolina; go back to Georgia; go
back to Louisiana; go back to the slums and ghet-
tos of the northern cities, knowing that somehow
this situation can, and will be changed. Let us not
wallow in the valley of despair.

So I say to you, my friends, that even though
we must face the difficulties of today and tomorrow, I still have a dream. It is a dream deeply
rooted in the American dream that one day this
nation will rise up and live out the true meaning

of its creed—we hold these truths to be self-evident, that all men are created equal.

I have a dream that one day on the red hills of Georgia, sons of former slaves and sons of former slave-owners will be able to sit down together at the table of brotherhood.

I have a dream that one day, even the state of Mississippi, a state sweltering with the heat of injustice, sweltering with the heat of oppression, will be transformed into an oasis of freedom and justice.

I have a dream my four little children will one day live in a nation where they will not be judged by the color of their skin but by content of their character. I have a dream today!

I have a dream that one day, down in Alabama, with its vicious racists, with its governor having his lips dripping with the words of interposition and nullification, that one day, right there in Alabama, little black boys and black girls will be able to join hands with little white boys and white girls as sisters and brothers. I have a dream today!

I have a dream that one day every valley shall be exalted, every hill and mountain shall be made low, the rough places shall be made plain, and the crooked places shall be made straight and the glory of the Lord will be revealed and all flesh shall see it together.

This is our hope. This is the faith that I go back to the South with.

With this faith we will be able to hear out of the mountain of despair a stone of hope. With this faith we will be able to transform the jangling discords of our nation into a beautiful symphony of brotherhood.

With this faith we will be able to work together, to pray together, to struggle together, to go to jail together, to stand up for freedom together, knowing that we will be free one day. This will be the day when all of God's children will be able to sing with new meaning—"my country 'tis of thee; sweet land of liberty; of thee I sing; land where my fathers died, land of the pilgrim's pride; from every mountain side, let freedom ring"—and if America is to be a great nation, this must become true.

So let freedom ring from the prodigious hill-tops of New Hampshire.

Let freedom ring from the mighty mountains of New York.

Let freedom ring from the heightening Alleghenies of Pennsylvania.

Let freedom ring from the snow-capped Rockies of Colorado.

Let freedom ring from the curvaceous slopes of California.

But not only that.

Let freedom ring from Stone Mountain of Georgia.

Let freedom ring from Lookout Mountain of Tennessee.

Let freedom ring from every hill and molehill of Mississippi, from every mountainside, let freedom ring.

And when we allow freedom to ring, when we let it ring from every village and hamlet, from every state and city, we will be able to speed up that day when all of God's children—black men and white men, Jews and Gentiles, Catholics and Protestants—will be able to join hands and to sing in the words of the old Negro spiritual, "Free at last, free at last; thank God Almighty, we are free at last."

51. Moral Orientation and Moral Development

꒰꒱

CAROL GILLIGAN

When one looks at an ambiguous figure like the drawing that can be seen as a young or old woman, or the image of the vase and the faces, one initially sees it in only one way. Yet even after seeing it in both ways, one way often seems more compelling. This phenomenon reflects the laws of perceptual organization that favor certain modes of visual grouping. But it also suggests a tendency to view reality as unequivocal and thus to argue that there is one right or better way of seeing.

The experiments of the Gestalt psychologists on perceptual organization provide a series of demonstrations that the same proximal pattern can be organized in different ways so that, for example, the same figure can be seen as a square or a diamond, depending on its orientation in relation to a surrounding frame. Subsequent studies show that the context influencing which of two possible organizations will be chosen may depend not only on the features of the array presented but also on the perceiver's past experience or expectation. Thus, a bird-watcher and a rabbit-keeper are likely to see the duck-rabbit figure in different ways; yet this difference does not imply that one way is better or a higher form of perceptual organization. It does, however, call attention to the fact that the rabbit-keeper, perceiving the rabbit, may not see the ambiguity of the figure until someone points out that it can also be seen as a duck.

This paper presents a similar phenomenon with respect to moral judgment, describing two moral perspectives that organize thinking in different ways. The analogy to ambiguous figure perception arises from the observation that although people are aware of both perspectives, they tend to adopt one or the other in defining and resolving moral conflict. Since moral judgments organize thinking about choice in difficult situations, the adoption of a single perspective may facilitate clarity of decision. But the wish for clarity may also imply a compelling human need for resolution or closure, especially in the face of decisions that give rise to discomfort or unease. Thus, the search for clarity in seeing may blend with a search for justification, encouraging the position that there is one right or better way to think about moral problems. This question, which has been the subject of intense theological and philosophical debate, becomes of interest to the psychologist not only because of its psychological dimensions—the tendency to focus on one perspective and the wish for justification—but also because one moral perspective currently dominates psychological thinking and is embedded in the most widely used measure for assessing the maturity of moral reasoning.

In describing an alternative standpoint, I will reconstruct the account of moral development around two moral perspectives, grounded in different dimensions of relationship that give rise to moral concern. The justice perspective, often equated with moral reasoning, is recast as one way of seeing moral problems and a care per-

Reprinted from *Women and Moral Theory* by permission of the Rowman and Littlefield.

spective is brought forward as an alternate vision or frame. The distinction between justice and care as alternative perspectives or moral orientations is based empirically on the observation that a shift in the focus of attention from concerns about justice to concerns about care changes the definition of what constitutes a moral problem, and leads the same situation to be seen in different ways. Theoretically, the distinction between justice and care cuts across the familiar divisions between thinking and feeling, egoism and altruism, theoretical and practical reasoning. It calls attention to the fact that all human relationships, public and private, can be characterized *both* in terms of equality and in terms of attachment, and that both inequality and detachment constitute grounds for moral concern. Since everyone is vulnerable both to oppression and to abandonment, two moral visions—one of justice and one of care—recur in human experience. The moral injunctions, not to act unfairly toward others, and not to turn away from someone in need, capture these different concerns.

The conception of the moral domain as comprised of at least two moral orientations raises new questions about observed differences in moral judgment and the disagreements to which they give rise. Key to this revision is the distinction between differences in developmental stage (more or less adequate positions within a single orientation) and differences in orientation (alternative perspectives or frameworks). The findings reported in this paper of an association between moral orientation and gender speak directly to the continuing controversy over sex differences in moral reasoning. In doing so, however, they also offer an empirical explanation for why previous thinking about moral development has been organized largely within the justice framework.

My research on moral orientation derives from an observation made in the course of studying the relationship between moral judgment and action. Two studies, one of college students describing their experiences of moral con-

flict and choice, and one of pregnant women who were considering abortion, shifted the focus of attention from the ways people reason about hypothetical dilemmas to the ways people construct moral conflicts and choices in their lives. This change in approach made it possible to see what experiences people define in moral terms, and to explore the relationship between the understanding of moral problems and the reasoning strategies used and the actions taken in attempting to resolve them. In this context, I observed that women, especially when speaking about their own experiences of moral conflict and choice, often define moral problems in a way that eludes the categories of moral theory and is at odds with the assumptions that shape psychological thinking about morality and about the self.[1] This discovery, that a different voice often guides the moral judgments and the actions of women, called attention to a major design problem in previous moral judgment research: namely, the use of all-male samples as the empirical basis for theory construction.

The selection of an all-male sample as the basis for generalizations that are applied to both males and females is logically inconsistent. As a research strategy, the decision to begin with a single-sex sample is inherently problematic, since the categories of analysis will tend to be defined on the basis of the initial data gathered and subsequent studies will tend to be restricted to these categories. Piaget's work on the moral judgment of the child illustrates these problems since he defined the evolution of children's consciousness and practice of rules on the basis of his study of boys playing marbles, and then undertook a study of girls to assess the generality of his findings. Observing a series of differences both in the structure of girls' games and "in the actual mentality of little girls," he deemed these differences not of interest because "it was not this contrast which we proposed to study." Girls, Piaget found, "rather complicated our interrogatory in relation to what we know about boys," since the changes in their conception of rules, although following the same sequence observed in boys, did not stand in the same relation to social experience. Nevertheless, he concluded that "in spite of these differences in the structure of the game and apparently in the players' mentality, we find the same process at work as in the evolution of the game of marbles."[2]

Thus, girls were of interest insofar as they were similar to boys and confirmed the generality of Piaget's findings. The differences noted, which included a greater tolerance, a greater tendency toward innovation in solving conflicts, a greater willingness to make exceptions to rules, and a lesser concern with legal elaboration, were not seen as germane to "the psychology of rules," and therefore were regarded as insignificant for the study of children's moral judgment. Given the confusion that currently surrounds the discussion of sex differences in moral judgment, it is important to emphasize that the differences observed by Piaget did not pertain to girls' understanding of rules *per se* or to the development of the idea of justice in their thinking, but rather to the way girls structured their games and their approach to conflict resolution—that is, to their use rather than their understanding of the logic of rules and justice.

Kohlberg, in his research on moral development, did not encounter these problems since he equated moral development with the development of justice reasoning and initially used an all-male sample as the basis for theory and test construction. In response to his critics, Kohlberg has recently modified his claims, renaming his test a measure of "justice reasoning" rather than of "moral maturity" and acknowledging the presence of a care perspective in people's moral thinking.[3] But the widespread use of Kohlberg's measure as a measure of moral development together with his own continuing tendency to equate justice reasoning with moral judgment leaves the problem of orientation differences unsolved. More specifically, Kohlberg's efforts to assimilate thinking about care to the six-stage developmental sequence he derived and refined

by analyzing changes in justice reasoning (relying centrally on his all-male longitudinal sample), underscores the continuing importance of the points raised in this paper concerning (1) the distinction between differences in developmental stage within a single orientation and differences in orientation, and (2) the fact that the moral thinking of girls and women was not examined in establishing either the meaning or the measurement of moral judgment within contemporary psychology.

An analysis of the language and logic of men's and women's moral reasoning about a range of hypothetical and real dilemmas underlies the distinction elaborated in this paper between a justice and a care perspective. The empirical association of care reasoning with women suggests that discrepancies observed between moral theory and the moral judgments of girls and women may reflect a shift in perspective, a change in moral orientation. Like the figure-ground shift in ambiguous figure perception, justice and care as moral perspectives are not opposites or mirror-images of one another, with justice uncaring and care unjust. Instead, these perspectives denote different ways of organizing the basic elements of moral judgment: self, others, and the relationship between them. With the shift in perspective from justice to care, the organizing dimension of relationship changes from inequality/equality to attachment/detachment, reorganizing thoughts, feelings, and language so that words connoting relationship like "dependence" or "responsibility" or even moral terms such as "fairness" and "care" take on different meanings. To organize relationships in terms of attachment rather than in terms of equality changes the way human connection is imagined, so that the images or metaphors of relationship shift from hierarchy or balance to network or web. In addition, each organizing framework leads to a different way of imagining the self as a moral agent.

From a justice perspective, the self as moral agent stands as the figure against a ground of social relationships, judging the conflicting claims of self and others against a standard of equality or equal respect (the Categorical Imperative, the Golden Rule). From a care perspective, the relationship becomes the figure, defining self and others. Within the context of relationship, the self as a moral agent perceives and responds to the perception of need. The shift in moral perspective is manifest by a change in the moral question from "What is just?" to "How to respond?"

For example, adolescents asked to described a moral dilemma often speak about peer or family pressure in which case the moral question becomes how to maintain moral principles or standards and resist the influence of one's parents or friends. "I have a right to my religious opinions," one teenager explains, referring to a religious difference with his parents. Yet, he adds, "I respect their views." The same dilemma, however, is also construed by adolescents as a problem of attachment, in which case the moral question becomes: how to respond both to oneself and to one's friends or one's parents, how to maintain or strengthen connection in the face of differences in belief. "I understand their fear of my new religious ideas," one teenager explains, referring to her religious disagreement with her parents, "but they really ought to listen to me and try to understand my beliefs."

One can see these two statements as two versions of essentially the same thing. Both teenagers present self-justifying arguments about religious disagreement; both address the claims of self and of others in a way that honors both. Yet each frames the problem in different terms, and the use of moral language points to different concerns. The first speaker casts the problem in terms of individual rights that must be respected within the relationship. In other words, the figure of the considering is the self looking on the disagreeing selves in relationship, and the aim is to get the other selves to acknowledge the right to disagree. In the case of the second speaker, figure and ground shift. The rela-

tionship becomes the figure of the considering, and relationships are seen to require listening and efforts at understanding differences in belief. Rather than the right to disagree, the speaker focuses on caring to hear and to be heard. Attention shifts from the grounds for agreement (rights and respect) to the grounds for understanding (listening and speaking, hearing and being heard). This shift is marked by a change in moral language from the stating of separate claims to rights and respect ("I have a right . . . I respect their views.") to the activities of relationship—the injunction to listen and try to understand ("I understand . . . they ought to listen . . . and try to understand."). The metaphor of moral voice itself carries the terms of the care perspective and reveals how the language chosen for moral theory is not orientation neutral.

The language of the public abortion debate, for example, reveals a justice perspective. Whether the abortion dilemma is cast as a conflict of rights or in terms of respect for human life, the claims of the fetus and of the pregnant woman are balanced or placed in opposition. The morality of abortion decisions thus construed hinges on the scholastic or metaphysical question as to whether the fetus is a life or a person, and whether its claims take precedence over those of the pregnant woman. Framed as a problem of care, the dilemma posed by abortion shifts. The connection between the fetus and the pregnant woman becomes the focus of attention and the question becomes whether it is responsible or irresponsible, caring or careless, to extend or to end this connection. In this construction, the abortion dilemma arises because there is no way not to act, and no way of acting that does not alter the connection between self and others. To ask what actions constitute care or are more caring directs attention to the parameters of connection and the costs of detachment, which become subjects of moral concern.

Finally, two medical students, each reporting a decision not to turn in someone who has violated the school rules against drinking, cast their decision in different terms. One student constructs the decision as an act of mercy, a decision to override justice in light of the fact that the violator has shown "the proper degrees of contrition." In addition, this student raises the question as to whether or not the alcohol policy is just, i.e., whether the school has the right to prohibit drinking. The other student explains the decision not to turn in a proctor who was drinking on the basis that turning him in is not a good way to respond to this problem, since it would dissolve the relationship between them and thus cut off an avenue for help. In addition, this student raises the question as to whether the proctor sees his drinking as a problem.

This example points to an important distinction, between care as understood or construed within a justice framework and care as a framework or a perspective on moral decision. Within a justice construction, care becomes the mercy that tempers justice; or connotes the special obligations or supererogatory duties that arise in personal relationships; or signifies altruism freely chosen—a decision to modulate the strict demands of justice by considering equity or showing forgiveness; or characterizes a choice to sacrifice the claims of the self. All of these interpretations of care leave the basic assumptions of a justice framework intact: the division between the self and others, the logic of reciprocity or equal respect.

As a moral perspective, care is less well elaborated, and there is no ready vocabulary in moral theory to describe its terms. As a framework for moral decision, care is grounded in the assumption that self and other are interdependent, an assumption reflected in a view of action as responsive and, therefore, as arising in relationship rather than the view of action as emanating from within the self and, therefore, "self governed." Seen as responsive, the self is by definition connected to others, responding to perceptions, interpreting events, and governed by the organizing tendencies of human interaction and human language. Within this framework, detachment, whether from self or from others, is

morally problematic, since it breeds moral blindness or indifference—a failure to discern or respond to need. The question of what responses constitute care and what responses lead to hurt draws attention to the fact that one's own terms may differ from those of others. Justice in this context becomes understood as respect for people in their own terms.

The medical student's decision not to turn in the proctor for drinking reflects a judgment that turning him in is not the best way to respond to the drinking problem, itself seen as a sign of detachment or lack of concern. Caring for the proctor thus raises the question of what actions are most likely to ameliorate this problem, a decision that leads to the question of what are the proctor's terms.

The shift in organizing perspective here is marked by the fact that the first student does not consider the terms of the other as potentially different but instead assumes one set of terms. Thus the student alone becomes the arbiter of what is *the* proper degree of contrition. The second student, in turn, does not attend to the question of whether the alcohol policy itself is just or fair. Thus each student discusses an aspect of the problem that the other does not mention.

These examples are intended to illustrate two cross-cutting perspectives that do not negate one another but focus attention on different dimensions of the situation, creating a sense of ambiguity around the question of what is the problem to be solved. Systematic research on moral orientation as a dimension of moral judgment and action initially addressed three questions: (1) Do people articulate concerns about justice and concerns about care in discussing a moral dilemma? (2) Do people tend to focus their attention on one set of concerns and minimally represent the other? and (3) Is there an association between moral orientation and gender? Evidence from studies that included a common set of questions about actual experiences of moral conflict and matched samples of males and females provides affirmative answers to all three questions.

When asked to describe a moral conflict they

had faced, 55 out of 80 (69 percent) educationally advantaged North American adolescents and adults raised considerations of both justice and care. Two-thirds (54 out of 80) however, focused their attention on one set of concerns, with focus defined as 75 percent or more of the considerations raised pertaining either to justice or to care. Thus the person who presented, say, two care considerations in discussing a moral conflict was more likely to give a third, fourth, and fifth than to balance care and justice concerns—a finding consonant with the assumption that justice and care constitute organizing frameworks for moral decision. The men and the women involved in this study (high school students, college students, medical students, and adult professionals) were equally likely to demonstrate the focus phenomenon (two-thirds of both sexes fell into the outlying focus categories). There were, however, sex differences in the direction of focus. With one exception, all of the men who focused, focused on justice. The women divided, with roughly one third focusing on justice and one third on care.[4]

These findings clarify the different voice phenomenon and its implications for moral theory and for women. First, it is notable that if women were eliminated from the research sample, care focus in moral reasoning would virtually disappear. Although care focus was by no means characteristic of all women, it was almost exclusively a female phenomenon in this sample of educationally advantaged North Americans. Second, the fact that the women were advantaged means that the focus on care cannot readily be attributed to educational deficit or occupational disadvantage—the explanation Kohlberg and others have given for findings of lower levels of justice reasoning in women.[5] Instead, the focus on care in women's moral reasoning draws attention to the limitations of a justice-focused moral theory and highlights the presence of care concerns in the moral thinking of both women and men. In this light, the Care/Justice group composed of one third of the women and one third of the men becomes of particular interest, pointing to the need for further research that attends to the way people organize justice and care in relation to one another—whether, for example, people alternate perspectives, like seeing the rabbit and the duck in the rabbit-duck figure, or integrate the two perspectives in a way that resolves or sustains ambiguity.

Third, if the moral domain is comprised of at least two moral orientations, the focus phenomenon suggests that people have a tendency to lose sight of one moral perspective in arriving at moral decision—a liability equally shared by both sexes. The present findings further suggest that men and women tend to lose sight of different perspectives. The most striking result is the virtual absence of care-focus reasoning among the men. Since the men raised concerns about care in discussing moral conflicts and thus presented care concerns as morally relevant, a question is why they did not elaborate these concerns to a greater extent.

In summary, it becomes clear why attention to women's moral thinking led to the identification of a different voice and raised questions about the place of justice and care within a comprehensive moral theory. It also is clear how the selection of an all-male sample for research on moral judgment fosters an equation of morality with justice, providing little data discrepant with this view. In the present study, data discrepant with a justice-focused moral theory comes from a third of the women. Previously, such women were seen as having a problem understanding "morality." Yet these women may also be seen as exposing the problem in a justice-focused moral theory. This may explain the decision of researchers to exclude girls and women at the initial stage of moral judgment research. If one begins with the premise that "all morality consists in respect for rules,"[6] or "virtue is one and its name is justice,"[7] then women are likely to appear problematic within moral theory. If one begins with women's moral judgments, the problem becomes how to construct a theory that encompasses care as a focus of moral attention rather than as a subsidiary moral concern.

The implications of moral orientation for moral theory and for research on moral development are extended by a study designed and conducted by Kay Johnston.[8] Johnston set out to explore the relationship between moral orientation and problem-solving strategies, creating a standard method using fables for assessing spontaneous moral orientation and orientation preference. She asked 60 eleven- and fifteen-year-olds to state and to solve the moral problem posed by the fable. Then she asked: "Is there another way to solve this problem?" Most of the children initially constructed the fable problems either in terms of justice or in terms of care; either they stood back from the situation and appealed to a rule or principle for adjudicating the conflicting claims or they entered the situation in an effort to discover or create a way of responding to all of the needs. About half of the children, slightly more fifteen- than eleven-year-olds, spontaneously switched moral orientation when asked whether there was another way to solve the problem. Others did so following an interviewer's cue as to the form such a switch might take. Finally, the children were asked which of the solutions they described was the best solution. Most of the children answered the question and explained why one way was preferable.

Johnston found gender differences parallel to those previously reported, with boys more often spontaneously using and preferring justice solutions and girls more often spontaneously using and preferring care solutions. In addition, she found differences between the two fables she used, confirming Langdale's finding that moral orientation is associated both with the gender of the reasoner and with the dilemma considered.[9] Finally, the fact that children, at least by the age of eleven, are able to shift moral orientation and can explain the logic of two moral perspectives, each associated with a different problem-solving strategy, heightens the analogy to ambiguous figure perception and further supports the conception of justice and care as organizing frameworks for moral decision.

The demonstration that children know both orientations and can frame and solve moral problems in at least two different ways means that the choice of moral standpoint is an element of moral decision. The role of the self in moral judgment thus includes the choice of moral standpoint, and this decision, whether implicit or explicit, may become linked with self-respect and self-definition. Especially in adolescence when choice becomes more self-conscious and self-reflective, moral standpoint may become entwined with identity and self-esteem. Johnston's finding that spontaneous moral orientation and preferred orientation are not always the same raises a number of questions as to why and under what conditions a person may adopt a problem-solving strategy that he or she sees as not the best way to solve the problem.

The way people chose to frame or solve a moral problem is clearly not the only way in which they can think about the problem, and is not necessarily the way they deem preferable. Moral judgments thus do not reveal *the* structure of moral thinking, since there are at least two ways in which people can structure moral problems. Johnston's demonstration of orientation-switch poses a serious challenge to the methods that have been used in moral judgment and moral development research, introducing a major interpretive caution. The fact that boys and girls at eleven and fifteen understand and distinguish the logics of justice and care reasoning directs attention to the origins and the development of both ways of thinking. In addition, the tendency for boys and girls to use and prefer different orientations when solving the same problem raises a number of questions about the relationship between these orientations and the factors influencing their representation. The different patterns of orientation use and preference, as well as the different conceptions of justice and of care implied or elaborated in the fable judgments, suggest that moral development cannot be mapped along a single linear stage sequence.

One way of explaining these findings, suggested by Johnston, joins Vygotsky's theory of cognitive development with Chodorow's analysis of sex differences in early childhood experiences of relationship.[10] Vygotsky posits that all of the higher cognitive functions originate as actual relations between individuals. Justice and care as moral ideas and as reasoning strategies thus would originate as relationships with others—an idea consonant with the derivation of justice and care reasoning from experiences of inequality and attachment in early childhood. All children are born into a situation of inequality in that they are less capable than the adults and older children around them and, in this sense, more helpless and less powerful. In addition, no child survives in the absence of some kind of adult attachment—or care, and through this experience of relationship children discover the responsiveness of human connection including their ability to move and affect one another.

Through the experience of inequality, of being in the less powerful position, children learn what it means to depend on the authority and the good will of others. As a result, they tend to strive for equality of greater power, and for freedom. Through the experience of attachment, children discover the ways in which people are able to care for and to hurt one another. The child's vulnerability to oppression and to abandonment thus can be seen to lay the groundwork for the moral visions of justice and care, conceived as ideals of human relationship and defining the ways in which people "should" act toward one another.

Chodorow's work then provides a way of explaining why care concerns tend to be minimally represented by men and why such concerns are less frequently elaborated in moral theory. Chodorow joins the dynamics of gender identity formation (the identification of oneself as male or female) to an analysis of early childhood relationships and examines the effects of maternal child care on the inner structuring of self in relation to others. Further, she differentiates a positional sense of self from a personal sense of self, contrasting a self defined in terms of role or position from a self known through the experience of connection. Her point is that maternal child care fosters the continuation of a relational sense of self in girls, since female gender identity is consonant with feeling connected with one's mother. For boys, gender identity is in tension with mother-child connection, unless that connection is structured in terms of sexual opposition (e.g., as an Oedipal drama). Thus, although boys experience responsiveness or care in relationships, knowledge of care or the need for care, when associated with mothers, poses a threat to masculine identity.[11]

Chodorow's work is limited by her reliance on object relations theory and problematic on that count. Object relations theory ties the formation of the self to the experience of separation, joining separation with individuation and thus counterposing the experience of self to the experience of connection with others. This is the line that Chodorow traces in explicating male development. Within this framework, girls' connections with their mothers can only be seen as problematic. Connection with others or the capacity to feel and think *with* others is, by definition, in tension with self-development when self-development or individuation is linked to separation. Thus, object-relations theory sustains a series of oppositions that have been central in Western thought and moral theory, including the opposition between thought and feelings, self and relationship, reason and compassion, justice and love. Object relations theory also continues the conventional division of psychological labor between women and men. Since the idea of a self, experienced in the context of attachment with others, is theoretically impossible, mothers, described as objects, are viewed as selfless, without a self. This view is essentially problematic for women, divorcing the activity of mothering from desire, knowledge, and agency, and implying that insofar as a mother experiences herself as a subject rather than as an object (a mirror reflecting her child), she is "self-ish" and not a good mother. Winnicott's phrase "good-enough mother" represents an effort to temper this judgment.

Thus, psychologists and philosophers, aligning the self and morality with separation and autonomy—the ability to be self-governing—have associated care with self-sacrifice, or with feelings—a view at odds with the current position that care represents a way of knowing and a coherent moral perspective. This position, however, is well represented in literature written by women. For example the short story "A Jury of Her Peers," written by Susan Glaspell in 1917, a time when women ordinarily did not serve on juries, contrasts two ways of knowing that underlie two ways of interpreting and solving a crime.[12] The story centers on a murder; Minnie Foster is suspected of killing her husband.

A neighbor woman and the sheriff's wife accompany the sheriff and the prosecutor to the house of the accused woman. The men, representing the law, seek evidence that will convince a jury to convict the suspect. The women, collecting things to bring Minnie Foster in jail, enter in this way into the lives lived in the house. Taking in rather than taking apart, they begin to assemble observations and impressions, connecting them to past experience and observations until suddenly they compose a familiar pattern, like the log-cabin pattern they recognize in the quilt Minnie Foster was making. "Why do we *know*—what we know this minute?" one woman asks the other, but she also offers the following explanation:

> We live close together, and we live far apart. We all go through the same things—it's all just a different kind of the same thing! If it weren't—why do you and I *understand*.[13]

The activity of quilt-making—collecting odd scraps and piecing them together until they form a pattern—becomes the metaphor for this way of knowing. Discovering a strangled canary buried under pieces of quilting, the women make a series of connections that lead them to understand what happened.

The logic that says you don't kill a man because he has killed a bird, the judgment that finds these acts wildly incommensurate, is counterposed to the logic that sees both events as part of a larger pattern—a pattern of detachment and abandonment that led finally to the strangling. "I *wish* I'd come over here once in a while," Mrs. Hale, the neighbor, exclaims. "That was a crime! Who's going to punish that?" Mrs. Peters, the sheriff's wife, recalls that when she was a girl and a boy killed her cat, "If they hadn't held me back I would have—" and realizes that there had been no one to restrain Minnie Foster. John Foster was known as "a good man . . . He didn't drink, and he kept his word as well as most, I guess, and paid his debts." But he also was "a hard man," Mrs. Hale explains, "like a raw wind that gets to the bone."

Seeing detachment as the crime with murder as its ultimate extension, implicating themselves and also seeing the connection between their own and Minnie Foster's actions, the women solve the crime by attachment—by joining together, like the "knotting" that joins pieces of a quilt. In the decision to remove rather than to reveal the evidence, they separate themselves from a legal system in which they have no voice but also no way of voicing what they have come to understand. In choosing to connect themselves with one another and with Minnie, they separate themselves from the law that would use their understanding and their knowledge as grounds for further separation and killing.

In a law school class where a film-version of this story was shown, the students were divided in their assessment of the moral problem and in their evaluation of the various characters and actions. Some focused on the murder, the strangling of the husband. Some focused on the evidence of abandonment or indifference to others. Responses to a questionnaire showed a bi-modal distribution, indicating two ways of viewing the film. These different perspectives led to different ways of evaluating both the act of murder and the women's decision to remove the evidence. Responses to the film were not aligned with the sex of the viewer in an absolute way, thus dispelling any implication of biological determinism or of a stark division between the way women and men know or judge events. The knowledge gained inductively by the women in the film, however, was also gained more readily by women watching the film, who came in this way to see a logic in the women's actions and to articulate a rationale for their silence.

The analogy to ambiguous figure perception is useful here in several ways. First, it suggests that people can see a situation in more than one way, and even alternate ways of seeing, combining them without reducing them—like designating the rabbit-duck figure both duck and rabbit. Second, the analogy argues against the tendency to construe justice and care as opposites or mirror-images and also against the implication that these two perspectives are readily integrated or fused. The ambiguous figure directs attention to the way in which a change in perspective can reorganize perception and change understanding, without implying an underlying reality or pure form. What makes seeing both moral perspectives so difficult is precisely that the orientations are not opposites nor mirror images or better and worse representations of a single moral truth. The terms of one perspective do not contain the terms of the other. Instead, a shift in orientation denotes a restructuring of moral perception, changing the meaning of moral language and thus the definition of moral conflict and moral action. For example, detachment is considered the hallmark of mature moral thinking within a justice perspective, signifying the ability to judge dispassionately, to weigh evidence in an even-handed manner, balancing the claims of others and self. From a care perspective, detachment is *the* moral problem.

"I could've come," retorted Mrs. Hale ..."I wish I had come over to see Minnie Foster sometimes. I can see now ... If there had been

years and years of—nothing, then a bird to sing to you, it would be awful—still—after the bird was still. ... I know what stillness is."

The difference between agreement and understanding captures the different logics of justice and care reasoning, one seeking grounds for agreement, one seeking grounds for understanding, one assuming separation and thus the need for some external structure of connection, one assuming connection and thus the potential for understanding. These assumptions run deep, generating and reflecting different views of human nature and the human condition. They also point to different vulnerabilities and different sources of error. The potential error in justice reasoning lies in its latent egocentrism, the tendency to confuse one's perspective with an objective standpoint or truth, the temptation to define others in one's own terms by putting oneself in their place. The potential error in care reasoning lies in the tendency to forget that one has terms, creating a tendency to enter into another's perspective and to see oneself as "selfless" by defining oneself in other's terms. These two types of error underlie two common equations that signify distortions or deformations of justice and care: the equation of human with male, unjust in its omission of women; and the equation of care with self-sacrifice, uncaring in its failure to represent the activity and the agency of care.

The equation of human with male was assumed in the Platonic and in the Enlightenment tradition as well as by psychologists who saw all-male samples as "representative" of human experience. The equation of care with self-sacrifice is in some ways more complex. The premise of self-interest assumes a conflict of interest between self and other manifest in the opposition of egoism and altruism. Together, the equations of male with human and of care with self-sacrifice form a circle that has had a powerful hold on moral philosophy and psychology. The conjunction of women and moral theory thus challenges the traditional definition of

562 MARTIN LUTHER KING JR. AND CAROL GILLIGAN

human and calls for a reconsideration of what is meant by both justice and care.

To trace moral development along two distinct although intersecting dimensions of relationship suggests the possibility of different permutations of justice and care reasoning, different ways these two moral perspectives can be understood and represented in relation to one another. For example, one perspective may overshadow or eclipse the other, so that one is brightly illuminated while the other is dimly remembered, familiar but for the most part forgotten. The way in which one story about relationship obscures another was evident in high-school girls' definitions of dependence. These definitions highlighted two meanings—one arising from the opposition between dependence and independence, and one from the opposition of dependence to isolation ("No woman," one student observed, "is an island.") As the word "dependence" connotes the experience of relationship, this shift in the implied opposite of dependence indicates how the valence of relationship changes, when connection with others is experienced as an impediment to autonomy or independence, and when it is experienced as a source of comfort and pleasure, and a protection against isolation. This essential ambivalence of human connection provides a powerful emotional grounding for two moral perspectives, and also may indicate what is at stake in the effort to reduce morality to a single perspective.

It is easy to understand the ascendance of justice reasoning and of justice-focused moral theories in a society where care is associated with personal vulnerability in the form of economic disadvantage. But another way of thinking about the ascendance of justice reasoning and also about sex differences in moral development is suggested in the novel *Masks,* written by Fumiko Enchi, a Japanese woman.[14] The subject is spirit possession, and the novel dramatizes what it means to be possessed by the spirits of others. Writing about the Rokujo lady in the *Tales of Genji,* Enchi's central character notes that:

Her soul alternates uncertainly between lyricism and spirit possession, making no philosophical distinction between the self alone and in relation to others, and is unable to achieve the solace of a religious indifference.[15]

The option of transcendance, of a religious indifference or a philosophical detachment, may be less available to women because women are more likely to be possessed by the spirits and the stories of others. The strength of women's moral perceptions lies in the refusal of detachment and depersonalization, and insistence on making connections that can lead to seeing the person killed in war or living in poverty as someone's son or father or brother or sister, or mother, or daughter, or friend. But the liability of women's development is also underscored by Enchi's novel in that women, possessed by the spirits of others, also are more likely to be caught in a chain of false attachments. If women are at the present time the custodians of a story about human attachment and interdependence, not only within the family but also in the world at large, then questions arise as to how this story can be kept alive and how moral theory can sustain this story. In this sense, the relationship between women and moral theory itself becomes one of interdependence.

By rendering a care perspective more coherent and making its terms explicit, moral theory may facilitate women's ability to speak about their experiences and perceptions and may foster the ability of others to listen and to understand. At the same time, the evidence of care focus in women's moral thinking suggests that the study of women's development may provide a natural history of moral development in which care is ascendant, revealing the ways in which creating and sustaining responsive connection with others becomes or remains a central moral concern. The promise in joining women and moral theory lies in the fact that human survival, in the late twentieth century, may depend less on formal agreement than on human connection.

NOTES

1. Gilligan, C. (1977). "In a Different Voice: Women's Conceptions of Self and of Morality." *Harvard Educational Review* 47 (1982):481–517; *In a Different Voice: Psychological Theory and Women's Development.* Cambridge, Mass.: Harvard University Press.

2. Piaget, J. (1965). *The Moral Judgment of the Child.* New York, N.Y.: The Free Press Paperback Edition, pp. 76–84.

3. Kohlberg, L. (1984). *The Psychology of Moral Development.* San Francisco, Calif.: Harper & Row, Publishers, Inc.

4. Gilligan, C. and J. Attanucci. (1986). *Two Moral Orientations.* Harvard University, unpublished manuscript.

5. See Kohlberg, L. *op. cit.,* also Walker, L. (1984). "Sex Differences in the Development of Moral Reasoning: A Critical Review of the Literature." *Child Development* 55 (3):677–91.

6. Piaget, R., *op. cit.*

7. Kohlberg, L., *op. cit.*

8. Johnston, K. (1985). *Two Moral Orientations— Two Problem-solving Strategies: Adolescents Solutions to Dilemmas in Fables.* Harvard University, unpublished doctoral dissertation.

9. Langdale, C. (1983). *Moral Orientation and Moral Development: The Analysis of Care and Justice Reasoning Across Different Dilemmas in Females and Males from Childhood through Adulthood.* Harvard University, unpublished doctoral dissertation.

10. Johnston, K., *op. cit.;* Vygotsky, L. (1978). *Mind in Society.* Cambridge, Mass.: Harvard University Press; Chodorow, N. (1974). "Family Structure and Feminine Personality" in *Women, Culture and Society,* L. M. Rosaldo and L. Lamphere, eds., Stanford, Calif.: Stanford University Press; see also Chodorow, N. (1978). *The Reproduction of Mothering: Psychoanalysis and the Sociology of Gender,* Berkeley, Calif.: University of California Press.

11. Chodorow, N., *op. cit.*

12. Glaspell, S. (1927). *A Jury of Her Peers,* London: E. Benn.

13. *Ibid.*

14. Fumiko, E. (1983). *Masks.* New York: Random House.

15. *Ibid.* p. 54.

RECOMMENDED READINGS

Texts

Colaiaco, James A. *Martin Luther King, Jr.: Apostle of Militant Nonviolence.* New York: St. Martin's Press, 1988.

Franklin, Robert Michael. *Liberating Visions: Human Fulfillment and Social Justice in African-American Thought.* Minneapolis, MN: Fortress Press, 1990.

Gilligan, Carol, Nora Lyons, and Trudy Hanmer, eds. *Making Connections.* Cambridge: Harvard University Press, 1990.

Hekman, Susan J. *Moral Voices, Moral Selves: Carol Gilligan and Feminist Moral Theory.* University Park, PA: Pennsylvania State University Press, 1995.

Kittay, Eva. *Women and Moral Theory.* Totowa: Rowman and Littlefield, 1987.

Walton, Hanes. *The Political Philosophy of Martin Luther King, Jr.* Westport, CT: Greenwood Pub. Corp., 1971.

Zepp, Ira G. *The Social Vision of Martin Luther King, Jr.* Brooklyn, NY: Carlson Pub., 1989.

Concluding Feminist and
Multicultural Postscript

Let us reflect back on the selections in this anthology and ask what have we learned from putting classical Western texts in ethics in feminist and multicultural perspectives.

Feminist Perspectives

What Plato's work shows, of course, is that even in classical times the idea of equality for women was there to be considered, even though, as Julia Annas argues, it is quite wrong to think of Plato as a feminist because he was neither interested in ending women's subordination to men nor in establishing equality between the sexes. Rather, he was interested in benefiting the state by securing the best people for his guardian class. Unfortunately, as Eve Browning Cole shows, Aristotle's deficiencies in this regard are even greater. Aristotle should have recognized that based on his own theory, the inability to have one's deliberations carry authority into action, which he took to be characteristic of women, is actually a failure of education that is correctable by providing women with an adequate education. This is, of course, just what Musonius Rufus, "the Roman Socrates," recognized when he argued for equality of education between men and women.

Augustine and Aquinas also shared a particularly deficient view of women. Augustine, along with many other Church Fathers, had argued that man alone reflects the divine image and that woman stands in her relationship to man as body to soul. Aquinas, following Aristotle, regarded woman as a misbegotten man, claiming that a woman is a helpmate to man

only with respect to procreation and the care of children, but, for all other things, men are better served by other men. Nevertheless, according to Augustine and Aquinas, there was one way that woman could escape the subordination and inferiority to which she is ordained by her sex. It was by choosing to follow the virginal life in a religious order. This life involved renouncing what it was to be a woman and virtually assuming the nature of a man. Unfortunately, even in religious orders, women were still not the equal of men because they were not allowed to enter the priesthood.

In her own time, Christine de Pizan opposed this dominant view of women, arguing that it was based on the radically different opportunities offered to men and women. In our own time, Rosemary Radford Ruether and Eleanor McLaughlin have argued for a new Christian anthropology characterized by a positive role for human sexuality, a true equality between the sexes, and a recognition of the extent to which sexual differences are conventional.

In contrast to previous ethical theories, Hume's moral theory, Annette Baier argues, shares a number of features with the caring ethics perspective developed by contemporary feminists like Carol Gilligan. Baier also contends that many of the apparently sexist comments that Hume made about women are simply meant to be descriptive of actual inequalities between men and women, not inequalities that Hume necessarily endorsed.

In accord with his times, Immanuel Kant held that there is a basic and pervasive difference between the sexes. Kant thought that beauty is a woman's most dominant feature, just as man's is to be noble or sublime. According to Kant, woman's understanding is also different from man's—it is a fine understanding as opposed to the deep or profound understanding of a man. And woman's virtue is a beautiful virtue as opposed to the noble virtue of a man. Kant claims that though a woman may succeed in rigorous study, this takes away from the excellence peculiar to her sex. Hence, disciplines, such as geometry, geography, philosophy, astronomy, history, and physics are not for her. A woman is not to reason but to feel. Since a woman tends to be resistant to restraint, incapable of principles, and motivated by pleasure, virtue is best instilled in her by using examples rather than universal principles and by making what is good pleasing to her. In marriage, Kant thought, husband and wife are like a single moral person, guided by the understanding of the husband and the taste of the wife. Sadly, Kant offers little by way of a defense of these views, and in his exchange of letters with Maria von Herbert, he shows how difficult it is for him to appreciate fully the different circumstances in which women find themselves in society.

Marking a significant break with much of previous ethical theory, John Stuart Mill in the *Subjection of Women* and Harriet Taylor in the *Enfranchisement of Women* offer what are now regarded as classic defenses of the equality of women. Mill argued that society must remove the legal restrictions that deny women the same opportunities that are enjoyed by men in society. Unfortunately, he did not consider whether because of past discrimination against women, it may be necessary to do more than simply remove legal restrictions to provide women with the same opportunities that men enjoy. Thus, he doesn't consider whether positive assistance may also be required. Mill also does not see any need to compensate women for the work they do in the home, whereas Taylor contends that it would be preferable "if women both earned and had a right to possess, a part of the income of the family." Taylor also speaks out more strongly in

favor of married women having a life and career of their own. In these respects, Taylor is clearly more in accord with present-day feminism than is Mill. Nevertheless, as Maria Morales points out, Mill did hold that human happiness required perfect equality, and so he opposed the unequal gender roles in society as being harmful to both men and women.

Friedrich Nietzsche is well known for his many negative remarks about women, but it is interesting to note that there was a time when he wrote more favorably about them. This was when he thought that a young woman, Lou Solomé, might be his disciple and carry on his work. Kathryn Pyne Addelson also argues that Nietzsche's own idea of a moral revolution applies straightforwardly to the women's revolution of the nineteenth century, although Nietzsche himself failed to recognize this.

Obviously, a very interesting issue between Jean-Paul Sartre and Simone de Beauvoir is the extent to which Sartre borrowed from and was influenced by de Beauvoir's work, and why it is that we are just becoming aware of the extent to which this was the case. A pioneer in the feminist movement, in *The Second Sex* de Beauvoir seeks to answer the question: What is a woman? The answer she gives is that woman is the Other, man is the One. Men are active, transcendent, able to transform their environment; women are passive and immanent, that is, existing within themselves, with little capacity to affect the outside world. Men are the "subjects" of their own lives; women are the "objects," the acted upon. However, de Beauvoir argues that this state of affairs is not an immutable state of nature, but rather is socially constructed and can be changed. De Beauvoir goes on to explain why women have been defined as the Other, and what has to be done if they are to escape from the sphere hitherto assigned to them and aspire to full membership in the human race.

Elizabeth Spelman criticizes de Beauvoir for conflating "woman" with a small group of women—namely, white, middle-class women in

Western countries. While this would be a serious mistake, one that contemporary feminists have become particularly sensitized to avoid, it is not clear that de Beauvoir actually does make this mistake in *The Second Sex*.

Continuing the feminist critique, Lynne Arnault argues that R. M. Hare's own ethical theory must allow for the possibility that social divisions may be so embedded in the structure of things that it can be very difficult to put oneself in the situation of others who are quite different from us. In particular, Arnault suggests, it could be especially difficult for men to understand the position of women in society.

Furthering the critique of contemporary ethical theory, Susan Okin objects to what she describes as Alasdair MacIntyre's uncritical acceptance of certain historical traditions as the basis for the virtuous life that he endorses. For example, MacIntyre does not notice that in the stories he cites as being essential for the moral education of children, girls and women are portrayed disparagingly. According to Okin, while MacIntyre claims to be rejecting the elitism and sexism of those historical traditions that he draws upon, he does little to suggest what a society purged of these defects would actually look like, nor does he adequately take into account how these traditions are viewed by women today.

In my own contribution to the feminist critique, I object to the defenses of morality offered by Alan Gewirth and Christine Korsgaard for their focus on egoism. I argue that if we focus, for a change, on the behavior of women, we are likely to observe considerably more altruism than egoism among women, particularly with respect to the care of their families. Of course, if we look to men, given the prevailing patriarchal social structures, we may tend to find more egoism than altruism. But most likely any differences that exist between men and women in this regard, irrespective of whether we consider them to be good or bad, are primarily due to the dominant patterns of socialization—nurture rather than nature. In any case, it is beyond dispute that we humans are capable of both self-interested and altruistic behavior, and given that we have these capabilities, both of these capabilities should be taken into account, as I do, in fashioning my own justification of morality. I argue that it is because philosophers in the past, who were virtually all men—women, for the most part, being excluded from doing philosophy until recent times—failed to take into account the behavior of women and failed to focus on altruism as well as egoism that they were unable to come up with an adequate justification for morality.

Finally, Carol Gilligan, in her influential work *In A Different Voice,* argues against the prevailing view that women's moral development tended to lag behind that of men. According to Gilligan, men and women do tend to make different moral judgments, but there is no basis for claiming the moral judgments of the men are better than the moral judgments of the women. All we can justifiably say is that they are different.

Gilligan contrasts a caring perspective with a justice perspective. According to Gilligan, these two perspectives are analogous to the alternative ways we tend to organize ambiguous perceptual patterns, for example, seeing a figure first as a square then as a diamond depending on its relationship to the surrounding frame. More specifically, Gilligan claims:

> From a justice perspective, the self as moral agent stands as the figure against a ground of social relationships, judging the conflicting claims of self and others against a standard of equality or equal respect (the Categorical Imperative, the Golden Rule). From a care perspective, the relationship becomes the figure, defining self and others. Within the context of relationship, the self as a moral agent perceives and responds to the perception of need. The shift in moral perspective is manifest by a change in the moral question from "What is just?" to "How to respond?"

Using these perspectives as classificatory tools, Gilligan reports that 69 percent of her sample raised considerations of both justice and care while 67 percent focused their attention on one set of concerns (with focus defined as 75 percent or more of the considerations raised pertaining either to justice or to care.) Significantly, with one exception, all of the men who focused, focused on justice. The women were divided, with roughly one-third focusing on care and one-third on justice.

The conclusion that Gilligan wants to draw from this research is that the caring perspective is an equally valid moral perspective that has tended to be disregarded in moral theory and psychological research alike because of male bias. To determine whether this conclusion is justified, however, we would need to get clearer about the contrast between the two perspectives. If women and men differ with regard to the perspectives on which they tend to focus, it must be possible to distinguish clearly between the two perspectives. Otherwise bias could enter into the reseacher's classification of people's reasons as belonging to one or the other perspective.

Now, if we can't distinguish in theory between a justice perspective and a caring perspective, it is going to be impossible for researchers to use this distinction in practice to characterize people as focusing on one or the other perspective. Of course, people will tend to use the language of rights with the frequencies Gilligan observes, but we will have to look behind this usage to see what people are claiming when they use or don't use this language. If there is no viable theoretical distinction between a justice perspective and a caring perspective, people frequently will be found to express care and concern for the needs of others by using the language of rights. We are going to have to look behind the words people are using to discover when they are, in fact, showing insensitivity to the needs of others. When we can determine that, we will be in a position also to determine whether such insensitivity is more characteristic

of men than women. For example, one might argue, as I do, that we are likely to observe more altruism than egoism among women, particularly with respect to the care of their families.

MULTICULTURAL PERSPECTIVES

Turning to the multicultural perspectives represented in this anthology, we can see that Confucius advocates a virtue ethics that is similar in certain respects yet different in other respects from the virtue ethics advocated by Plato and Aristotle. For Plato, the just individual is modeled on the just state, but for Confucius, the state should be thought of as the family writ large. Confucius also advocates meritocracy, various forms of which were incorporated into Chinese society. One also finds in Confucius negative versions of the Golden Rule: "What you do not want done to yourself, do not do to others."

Chuang Tzu's *The Book of Chuang Tzu* sought to provide an alternative to Confucianism. A central idea of the book is the need to free oneself from the baggage of conventional values to follow the way (Tao) of nature. In this respect, *The Book of Chuang Tzu* contrasts sharply with Aristotle's work, given that Aristotle was seeking, for the most part, to articulate and provide a justification for the conventional values of his time. Yet rather than challenging the neo-Aristotelian capacity approach recently developed by Martha Nussbaum and Amartya Sen, Xiaorong Li argues that it presents a useful cross-cultural standard that is still sensitive to cultural traditions.

Noting that a more egalitarian interpretation of the relationship between men and women would surely have been easier to come by if the central Judeo-Christian religious texts had themselves portrayed the Godhead in feminine as well as masculine terms, Jorge Valadez points out that that is exactly how the Aztecs conceived of their supreme deity Ometeotl. Valadez also points out that the Mayans saw themselves as not

CONCLUDING FEMINIST AND MULTICULTURAL POSTSCRIPT

standing against nature but rather as an integral part of it, which led them to be more respective of nature than Eurocentric societies have been.

Like Aquinas, yet writing before him, Maimonides sought to reconcile reason, particularly as reflected in the work of Aristotle, with faith, but in Maimonides's case, it is Judaism, not Christianity, that is to be reconciled with reason. Maimonides claims that it is possible to reconcile all 613 commandments of the Jewish Law with reason, on the grounds that they all serve the general welfare. However, most people today would have difficulty believing that putting a stubborn and rebellious son to death or renouncing sexual intercourse would serve the general welfare or in any other way be a requirement of reason.

Contrasting with some of the requirements of the Jewish Law that Maimonides sought to defend, the Ewe Proverbs convey the universality of moral experience. Thus, those who think that all morality is relative and contextual need to explain why these proverbs seem to have such universal moral authority.

Like Kant's view, the *Bhagavad Gita* emphasizes the importance of acting from duty and not from inclination. The text argues that if one is to achieve identity with the unchanging ultimate reality (Brahman), then, one must do one's duty without attachment, without desires, without inclinations.

While the *Bhagavad Gita* expresses a view that is in some ways similar to the view of Kant, the similarities of Mo Tzu's *Universal Love,* to Mill's utilitarianism are even more striking. In Moism, as in utilitarianism, actions are evaluated in terms of their overall consequences. Mo Tzu argues that the best overall consequences are achieved through the practice of universal, mutual love. There are also obvious similarities between Moism and the later Christian doctrine of universal love.

Friedrich Nietzsche was one of the few philosophers in the history of Western philosophy who was directly influenced by non-Western sources. Nietzsche viewed Indian philosophy as the only major parallel to Western philosophy, and he tried to use what he knew of Indian thought to undermine traditional Western categories.

Eagle Man, an Oglala Sioux, defends a situated freedom that is different from that defended by most Western philosophers. According to Eagle Man, we are to respect individual freedom provided that it does not threaten the tribe, or the people, or Mother Earth. Eagle Man introduces a concern for Mother Earth because, he says, we are all related. We all come from this Mother Earth and we will all return to her. Accordingly, we should use no more resources than we need, and we should be sharing and generous with other living beings, including nonhuman living beings.

Ward Churchill offers another American Indian perspective that also challenges Western ethics. He argues that the United States does not now possess, nor has it ever possessed, a legitimate right to occupancy in at least half the territory it claims as its own on this continent. What we need to ask ourselves is whether Western ethical theories, like Rawls's or Hare's theory, would support Churchill's contention. If they do support Churchill's contention, what would this show, if anything, about the validity of Western ethical theories?

In sympathy with the view that Western ethics could learn much from non-Western perspectives, Moshoeshoe II argues that much can be learned from comparing the dominant model of development—that of the industrial market society—with those traditional models that sustained the indigenous cultures of Africa over thousands of years. He shows that within indigenous African culture there is a deep respect for the natural environment.

Martin Luther King Jr.'s life and writings challenged the dominant racial ethics of his time. In "Letter from a Birmingham Jail," he replied to white religious leaders of Birmingham—Catholic, Protestant, and Jewish—who criticized him for his "unwise and untimely actions."

King responded that his Southern Christian Leadership Conference had been invited to Birmingham by a local affiliate, that negotiations had been tried, that they had waited a considerable time before calling for a demonstration, that although they had broken laws (such as parading without a permit), those laws were supporting injustice, and, moreover, their willingness to accept the penalty for such violations, shows their ultimate respect for the law. King also blamed white moderates and white churches for contributing to racial injustice by their failure to take action against it. In "I Have a Dream," King draws on the Bible, the U.S. Constitution, and the National Anthem to inspire us to believe that America will yet live up to its promise of equality and freedom for all.

CONCLUSION

So what, in general, have we learned from putting some of the classical Western texts in ethics in feminist and multicultural perspectives? I think we have learned that we have to see things from perspectives other than our own, particularly from less dominant, less well-represented perspectives. But this can be quite difficult to do. It is particularly difficult for men to put themselves in the position of women and see the world from their perspectives, and it is particularly difficult for those in Western culture to see the world from the perspective of those in non-Western cultures. But a defensible ethics requires that we take all the relevant perspectives into account, and this surely includes the perspectives of women as well as men and the perspectives of those in non-Western cultures as well as those in Western culture. Without taking all these perspectives into account, we cannot have a defensible ethics.

Clearly, there is the need to take women's perspectives into account adequately when fashioning ethical theories. Given that virtually all past ethical theories have been developed by men—women for the most part being excluded from doing philosophy—it is not at all surprising that these theories have failed to adequately take women's perspectives into account. Nor is it surprising that philosophers, like Aristotle, Aquinas, Kant, or Nietzsche, given the low opinion they had of women, have failed to adequately take women's perspectives into account. Surely, their theories need to be significantly supplemented or radically refurbished to include women's perspectives, if they are to become defensible.

This need to take women's perspectives into account in fashioning an ethical theory has manifested itself in a number of ways. One is the emergence of an interest in developing a caring ethics sparked by the work of Carol Gilligan and others. Caring ethics are clearly an attempt to bring to bear how women see the world in the fashioning of an ethical theory. Another manifestation of this need to take women's perspectives into account is the emphasis that contemporary feminists have placed on emotion as well as reason in fashioning an ethical theory. Since men have been traditionally associated with reason and women with emotion, it would seem that if an ethical theory is to include women's perspectives, it must be more attuned with our emotional nature. A third manifestation of this need to take women's perspectives into account is the emphasis that contemporary feminists have placed on the structuring of family life and other so-called areas of private life in constructing an ethical theory. Susan Okin, for example, has argued for the importance of justice to family life. I have argued that in a just family structure all children, irrespective of their sex, must be given the same type of upbringing consistent with their native capabilities, and that normally mothers and fathers must also have the same opportunities for education and employment consistent with their native capabilities. Other feminists have been working on incorporating accounts of sexual and spousal abuse so as to fashion an ethical theory that is adequate to the needs of both women and men. Obviously, there is much more work of this sort that must be done if we are to have a defensible ethics.

Similarly, much work has to be done with respect to fashioning an ethical theory that adequately includes the perspective of those in non-Western cultures. In the first place, those of us in Western culture generally have an inflated view about the achievements of our culture with respect to ethical theory. Thus, we are generally ignorant of how the work of philosophers in non-Western cultures either compares favorably with, is on a par with, or predates work of Western philosophers. For example, prior to reading this anthology, many of you probably did not know that the work of Confucius compares favorably or at least is on a par with the work of Plato and Aristotle, or that the work of Mo Tzu on utilitarian theory predates that of John Stuart Mill by 2,400 years! Secondly, there are many ways in which work in Western ethics is challenged by work in non-Western ethics. For example, the work of American Indians, such as Ward Churchill, or the life and work of Dr. King make us aware of the long reach of past injustices into our lives and the necessity for us to do something about them. Likewise, the work of many indigenous peoples from Central America to India to Africa challenges how we think about ourselves in relationship to other living things in the environments in which we live. Indeed, many of us in Western culture have not adequately faced the question of who is to count

morally in ways that those in non-Western cultures have. We need to consider whether we have legitimate grounds for failing to constrain our own interests for the sake of nonhuman nature. We tend to think of ourselves as radically separate from and superior to nonhuman nature, so as to justify our domination over it. Accordingly, we need to reflect on whether there is any compelling ground for thinking that we are superior to nonhuman nature in ways that would justify this domination. It may be that we need to learn from non-Western cultures that the intrinsic value of nonhuman species places a significant constraint on how we pursue our own interests. If we adopt this view, we will have to modify significantly our understanding of basic human rights so as to rule out our unquestioned domination of nonhuman nature.

Until quite recently, we have been hindered from reaching a defensible ethics by the failure of ethical theorists to take the perspectives of women into account adequately and by the failure of those in Western culture to take into account adequately the perspectives of those in non-Western cultures. But a new era is dawning, and many, like yourselves, are struggling to incorporate these new perspectives in the fashioning of an ethical theory. This is a very important period in the history of ethical theory. For the first time, we now have the resources available to fashion a truly defensible ethical theory. Maybe you will be able to contribute to this endeavor.